T0215598

jQuery 2 Recipes

A Problem-Solution Approach

Arun K. Pande

Apress®

jQuery 2 Recipes: A Problem-Solution Approach

Copyright © 2014 by Arun K. Pande

This work is subject to copyright. All rights are reserved by the Publisher, whether the whole or part of the material is concerned, specifically the rights of translation, reprinting, reuse of illustrations, recitation, broadcasting, reproduction on microfilms or in any other physical way, and transmission or information storage and retrieval, electronic adaptation, computer software, or by similar or dissimilar methodology now known or hereafter developed. Exempted from this legal reservation are brief excerpts in connection with reviews or scholarly analysis or material supplied specifically for the purpose of being entered and executed on a computer system, for exclusive use by the purchaser of the work. Duplication of this publication or parts thereof is permitted only under the provisions of the Copyright Law of the Publisher's location, in its current version, and permission for use must always be obtained from Springer. Permissions for use may be obtained through RightsLink at the Copyright Clearance Center. Violations are liable to prosecution under the respective Copyright Law.

ISBN-13 (pbk): 978-1-4302-6433-0

ISBN-13 (electronic): 978-1-4302-6434-7

Trademarked names, logos, and images may appear in this book. Rather than use a trademark symbol with every occurrence of a trademarked name, logo, or image we use the names, logos, and images only in an editorial fashion and to the benefit of the trademark owner, with no intention of infringement of the trademark.

The use in this publication of trade names, trademarks, service marks, and similar terms, even if they are not identified as such, is not to be taken as an expression of opinion as to whether or not they are subject to proprietary rights.

While the advice and information in this book are believed to be true and accurate at the date of publication, neither the authors nor the editors nor the publisher can accept any legal responsibility for any errors or omissions that may be made. The publisher makes no warranty, express or implied, with respect to the material contained herein.

Publisher: Heinz Weinheimer
Lead Editor: James DeWolf
Technical Reviewer: Todd Meister
Editorial Board: Steve Anglin, Mark Beckner, Ewan Buckingham, Gary Cornell, Louise Corrigan, Jim DeWolf, Jonathan Gennick, Robert Hutchinson, Michelle Lowman, James Markham, Matthew Moodie, Jeff Olson, Jeffrey Pepper, Douglas Pundick, Ben Renow-Clarke, Dominic Shakeshaft, Gwenan Spearing, Matt Wade, Steve Weiss
Coordinating Editor: Kevin Walter
Copy Editor: Kezia Endsley
Compositor: SPi Global
Indexer: SPi Global
Artist: SPi Global
Cover Designer: Anna Ishchenko

Distributed to the book trade worldwide by Springer Science+Business Media New York, 233 Spring Street, 6th Floor, New York, NY 10013. Phone 1-800-SPRINGER, fax (201) 348-4505, e-mail orders-ny@springer-sbm.com, or visit www.springeronline.com. Apress Media, LLC is a California LLC and the sole member (owner) is Springer Science + Business Media Finance Inc (SSBM Finance Inc). SSBM Finance Inc is a Delaware corporation.

For information on translations, please e-mail rights@apress.com, or visit www.apress.com.

Apress and friends of ED books may be purchased in bulk for academic, corporate, or promotional use. eBook versions and licenses are also available for most titles. For more information, reference our Special Bulk Sales–eBook Licensing web page at www.apress.com/bulk-sales.

Any source code or other supplementary materials referenced by the author in this text is available to readers at www.apress.com. For detailed information about how to locate your book's source code, go to www.apress.com/source-code/.

This book is dedicated to my mother, Neelam Pande (1941 – 2012).

Contents at a Glance

Contents

About the Author

Arun Pande is working as the lead architect with the leading financial institution in Chicago. He has been working with financial industries for the past 25 years in various technology roles. During this period his major responsibilities included analysis, design and development of the desktop applications, web applications and mobile applications using various technologies and frameworks on Windows and UNIX platforms. He also taught an Object Oriented Analysis and Design course at one of the leading universities. He graduated with a Masters of Computer Applications (MCA) degree from Birla Institute of Technology, India.

About the Technical Reviewer

Todd Meister has been working in the IT industry for over twenty years. He's been a Technical Editor on over 75 titles ranging from SQL Server to the .NET Framework. Besides technical editing titles he is the Assistant Vice President/Chief Enterprise Architect at Ball State University in Muncie, Indiana. He lives in central Indiana with his wife, Kimberly, and their five canny children.

Acknowledgments

I thank my family, especially my wife, Veena, and my daughters, Vinnie and Ria, for their love, understanding and encouragement, due to which I was able to finish this book. I would also like to thank all the team members at Apress for working on this book with their full dedication. In particular, I am grateful to the Development Editor, Kate Blackham, who provided feedback and corrections to maintain consistency and accuracy throughout the book. I am thankful to James DeWolf and Kevin Walter for coordinating the editorial process and for keeping publication of this book on schedule. I sincerely thank the technical reviewer, Todd Meister, for validating the accuracy of the technical concepts and the source code and for providing helpful suggestions. Special thanks to the copyeditor, Kezia Endsley, for the excellent proofreading and for making this book conform to the editorial style.

—Arun K. Pande

CHAPTER 1

■ ■ ■

Introduction

1-1. About jQuery 2.0

jQuery is a multi-browser, lightweight, and extensible open source JavaScript library that can be used to simplify client-side and client-to-server communication scripting. It simplifies coding by replacing many lines of JavaScript code with fewer lines by using jQuery built-in methods. Some of the main features of jQuery include:

- Dynamic HTML creation and manipulation
- HTML events handling
- Effects and animations
- Client to server communication

In addition to core jQuery, this book also covers jQuery UI and jQueryMobile, which are built on the core.

As of writing of this book, the latest version of jQuery is 2.1.0. This version has the same API as the previous version 1.x, but it isn't supported on older browsers like Internet Explorer 8 and older. The main reason for this release is to eliminate the code required to support older browsers. This has made smaller jQuery files possible and hence produced an improvement in performance. If your user base is still using Internet Explorer 8 or older, you should use the latest version of the jQuery 1.x series.

jQuery can be downloaded from `http://jquery.com/download/`.

jQuery 2 is compatible with jQuery 1.9. All features of jQuery 1.9 have been included in jQuery 2.

1-2. Migration Plan

If you are using a version older than jQuery 1.9, upgrade it to jQuery 1.9+ first by using the jQuery migration plug-in. As of the writing of this book, the latest version of the jQuery 1 series is 1.10.2 and latest version of the jQuery 2 series is 2.1.0.

You can use migration plug-in by replacing your current reference to jQuery library by the following:

```
<script src="http://code.jquery.com/jquery-1.10.2.js"></script>
<script src="http://code.jquery.com/jquery-migrate-1.2.1.js"></script>
```

If you want to use a local copy of the jQuery and the jQuery migration plug-in, download it from the following locations:

jQuery 1.10.2 (Development version): `http://code.jquery.com/jquery-1.10.2.js`

jQuery Migrate 1.2.1: `http://code.jquery.com/jquery-migrate-1.2.1.js`

Use the following path to use them (assuming you have saved the downloaded files under the `scripts` folder under your website's root folder).

```
<script src="scripts/jquery-1.10.2.js"></script>
<script src="scripts/jquery-migrate-1.2.1.js"></script>
```

This migration tool will help you identify features/APIs that are deprecated in older versions of jQuery and removed in jQuery 1.9+. The development version of the migration plug-in will display a warning in the broswer's console. Be sure to use browsers that support console interface. The browser console is an interface where developers and users can view information like network requests, JavaScript code, CSS, warnings, errors, and messages logged by JavaScript. Newer versions of Internet Explorer, Firefox, Chrome, Safari, and Opera have built-in consoles. Refer to Appendix B to learn about how to open the web console in different browsers.

1-3. Objects–Basic Concept

Objects are the key to understanding object-oriented technology. Each object has a state (attributes or properties) and a behavior (methods). In object-oriented terms, objects don't have to be seen or touched. Some examples of objects are cars, bank accounts, and rectangles. A car has attributes (or properties), such as the manufacturer, model, category, color, and so on, and it has methods, such as start the car, stop the car, put it in park, apply the hand brake, and so on. A bank account has attributes, such as account holder's name, account number, account type, current balance. It has methods such as withdraw money, deposit money, transfer money, and so on. A rectangle has attributes such as length and width and has methods such as determine its area, parameter, and so on.

A *class* is a general specification from which individual objects are created (instantiated).

Table 1-1 displays examples of classes and objects.

Table 1-1. *Examples of classes and objects*

Class	Object	
Class Name: Car	Object Name: `myCar`	
Attributes	**Attributes**	**Value**
Manufacturer	Manufacturer	Lexus
Model	Model	ES 350
Category	Category	Sedan
Color	Color	White
	Object Name: `rentalCar`	
	Attributes	**Value**
	Manufacturer	Chverlot
	Model	Impala
	Category	Sedan
	Color	Blue
Class Name: Account	Object Name: `customer1Account`	
Attributes	**Attributes**	**Value**
AccountHolderName	AccountHolderName	John Smith
AccountNumber	AccountNumber	7823712924
AccountType	AccountType	Checking
CurrentBalance	CurrentBalance	$1,560.78
	Object Name: `customer2Account`	
	Attributes	**Value**
	AccountHolderName	Jane Smith
	AccountNumber	89127312
	AccountType	Saving
	CurrentBalance	$14,590.80

1-4. Introduction to JavaScript

JavaScript is an object-oriented scripting language that is commonly used to create interactive effects and to dynamically create web page content. JavaScript language is case sensitive. JavaScript code is executed within the web browser, on the client side. It is used to retrieve and manipulate web page data objects (DOM) for interactivity and dynamic creation of presentation.

JavaScript code can be included on the same page as the HTML code or in a separate file, which is then included in the HTML file.

The following is the syntax for the internal JavaScript code:

```
<script>
// JavaScript Code
</script>
```

The following is the syntax for including external JavaScript code:

```
<script src="myJavaScript.js"></script>
```

Note: In myJavaScript.js, the <script> and </script> tags are not needed.

1-4-1. Data Types

JavaScript has dynamic types. The DataType of the variable is based on its value. Same variables can be used as different types. If no value is assigned to the variable, the default value of null is assigned.

- **Strings** – Used to hold texts and are declared as follows:

  Syntax: var <variableName> = "<value>";

  Example: var firstName = "John";

- **Numbers** – Used to hold numbers (integers and decimals):

  Syntax: var <variableName> = "<value>";

  Example: var monthlySalary = 5450;

- **Booleans** – Used to hold two values—true or false. Booleans are used to check for certain conditions:

  Syntax: var <variableName> = "<value>";

  Example: var isContractor = true;

- **Arrays** – Used to hold one or more than one value. They can be of the same data type of different types:

  Syntax: var <variableName> = new Array();

  Example: Arrays can be declared and set using any of the following three methods:

  ```
  var departments = new Array();
       departments[0]= "Sales";
       departments[1]= "Marketing";
       departments[2]= "Technology";

       var departments = new Array("Sales", "Marketing", "Technology");
       var departments = ["Sales", "Marketing", "Technology"];
  ```

It is not necessary that all the elements of an array are of the same data type.
The following is the syntax to access elements in an array –

```
arrayName[indexNumber];
```

where, *indexNumber* is the element number in the array and it is 0 based.
For example, document.write(departments[2]) displays "Technology".

- **Objects** – A variable can be defined as a built-in object (like Date, Image, Array, and String) or as a custom (user-defined) object.

    Syntax: `var <variableName> = new ObjectName();`

    Examples:

    - `var syst emDate = new Date(); // for current date`
    - `// parameters- yr_num, mo_num, day_num`

        `// optional - hr_num, min_num, sec_num, ms_num`

        `var dateOfBirth - new Date(1972, 11, 30);`
    - `// parameter - dateString`

        `var joiningDate = new Date("10/10/2004");`
    - `var logoImage = new Image("images/logo.jpg");`
    - `var firstName = new String("John");`
    - `var employee = {firstName: "John", lastName: "Smith", monthlySalary: 5450};`

An example of an array of objects:

```
var employees = new Array(
        {firstName:"John", lastName:"Smith", monthlySalary:5000},
        {firstName:"Jane", lastName:"Smith", monthlySalary:5450});
```

To access the *firstName* of the *employee* object, you can use `employee.firstName`.

1-4-2. Commonly Used JavaScript Objects and Events

When a DOM element is created using a tag in HTML code, a JavaScript object is created. This object's attributes can be accessed (get) and set using JavaScript code. Alternatively, JavaScript can be used to create DOM elements. Listing 1-1 demonstrates an example of creating DOM elements.

Listing 1-1. DOM elements creation

```
<!DOCTYPE html>
<html lang=en>
<head>
    <title>HTML5 Anchor</title>
    <meta charset=utf-8>
</head>
<body>
    <a id="newsLink" href="http://msnbc.com">News</a>
</body>
</html>
```

When the code in the listing 1-1 is executed in a browser and the user clicks on the News link, a page will be displayed from msnbc.com. Due to the line `<a id="newsLink" href="http://msnbc.com">MSNBCNews</a>`, a JavaScript object called Anchor is created that can be referenced and manipulated using the JavaScript code. Listing 1-2 demonstrates an example to access and set a DOM element.

Listing 1-2. Access and manipulate a DOM element

```html
<!DOCTYPE html>
<html lang=en>
<head>
<title>HTML5 Anchor</title>
<meta charset=utf-8>
<script>
    function changeNewsLink() {
        var objAnchor = document.getElementById("newsLink");
                    alert(objAnchor.href);
                    objAnchor.href = "http://cnn.com";
    }
</script>
</head>
<body onload="changeNewsLink();">
    <a id="newsLink" href="http://msnbc.com">News</a>
</body>
</html>
```

Here's a detailed explanation of this code:

- `onload="changeNewsLink();"`

  calls the JavaScript function `changeNewsLink` when all the elements in the body of the HTML page are loaded (i.e., the DOM elements are created). It is advisable to call functions that access DOM elements using this method.

- `var objAnchor = document.getElementById("newsLink");`

  looks for an element with the ID as `newsLink` and then reference that element by using the JavaScript variable `objAnchor`.

- `alert(objAnchor.href);`

  displays the current `href` value of the Anchor object.

- `objAnchor.href = "http://cnn.com";`

  changes the `href` attribute of the Anchor object to `http://cnn.com`. Now, when the user clicks the News link on the web page, a page from `cnn.com` will be displayed instead.

The following is the list of commonly used JavaScript statements:

- `for.` This is used to create a loop to iterate through a list of elements or perform repetitive operations for a range of values.

  Syntax:

  `for (var i=initialValue; condition while true; incrementOrDecrementTheCount)`

Listing 1-3 demonstrates an example to use *for* statement to display multiplication table of number 4.

Listing 1-3. Using for statement to display multiplication table

```
<!DOCTYPE html>
<html lang=en>
<head>
<title>Multiplication Table</title>
<meta charset=utf-8>
<script>
    for (var i=1; i <= 10; i++) {
        document.write(4 + " x " + i + " = " + (4*i) +"<br>");
    }
</script>
</head>
<body>
</body>
</html>
```

Listing 1-4 demonstrates an example to use for statement to iterate through an array to objects and display FirstName.

Listing 1-4. Using for statement to iterate through an array

```
<!DOCTYPE html>
<html lang=en>
<head>
<title>Iterate Through Objects</title>
<meta charset=utf-8>
<script>
var employees = new Array(
    {"FirstName":"John", "LastName":"Smith", "MonthlySalary": 5000},
    {"FirstName":"Jane", "LastName":"Smith", "MonthlySalary":5450});

    for (var i=0; i < employees.length; i++) {
        document.write(employees[i].FirstName +"<br>");
    }
</script>
</head>
<body>
</body>
</html>
```

In the above code, the short form of this line

```
for (var i=0; i < employees.length; i++)
```

can be written as

```
for (var i in employees)
```

- if ... else ... This is used to execute lines of code (logic) when certain conditions are true and execute different logic when conditions are not true.

Syntax:

```
if (condition is true) {
// JavaScript Code
} else {
// JavaScript Code
}
```

Listing 1-5 demonstrates an example to display the names and bonuses for employees by using a 5% bonus for employees with a salary of $5,000 or less and a 3% bonus for others.

Listing 1-5. Using if else statement

```
<!DOCTYPE html>
<html lang=en>
<head>
    <title>Iterate Through Objects</title>
    <meta charset=utf-8>
    <script>
        var employees = new Array(
{"FirstName":"John", "LastName":"Smith", "MonthlySalary": 5000},
{"FirstName":"Jane", "LastName":"Smith", "MonthlySalary":5450});

    for (var i in employees) {
        var bonusPercentage;
        if (employees[i].MonthlySalary <= 5000) {
            bonusPercentage = 0.05;
        } else {
            bonusPercentage = 0.03;
        }
        document.write(employees[i].FirstName + " " +
            (employees[i].MonthlySalary*bonusPercentage) + "<br>");
    }
    </script>
</head>

<body>
</body>
</html>
```

- *continue* statement is used to go to the next iteration of the loop without performing subsequent statements in the loop block.

- *break* statement is used to break the loop to exit out of the loop.

The following is a list of commonly used JavaScript objects:

- Anchor

- Array

- Boolean

- Button

- Checkbox

- Date

- Document

- Form

- Image

- String

- Window

- Location

The table 1-2 lists the commonly used DOM events that occur when users perform an action. For example, when a user clicks a button on a web page, the onclick() event is triggered. If there is any function associated with the onclick event for the button, that function is executed as well.

Table 1-2. *Commonly used DOM events*

Event Type	Event Name	Description
Mouse Event	onclick	When the user clicks on an element.
Mouse Event	ondblclick	When the user clicks on an element.
Form Event	onblur	When the user clicks some other form element or tab on the form element.
Form Event	onchange	When a value of a form element is changed.
Form Event	onfocus	When a form element gets focus.
Form Event	onsubmit	When a form is submitted, that is, when a submit button is clicked in the form.
Body Event	onload	After a page is loaded and all DOM elements are created.

Developers can specify which JavaScript statement or function to call when an event occurs. Listing 1-6 demonstrates an example to display a message when user clicks the button.

Listing 1-6. Event handling

```
<!DOCTYPE html>
<html lang=en>
<head>
<title>Events</title>
<meta charset=utf-8>
<script>
    function displayName() {
      alert(frmRegister.txtName.value);
    }
</script>
</head>
<body>
<form id="frmRegister">
```

```
Name: <input type="text" name="txtName"><br>
    <input type="button" value="Register" onclick="displayName();"><br>
</form>
</body>
</html>
```

When the user clicks the Register button, the `onclick` event occurs, which calls the `displayName()` JavaScript function. The `displayName` function gets the value entered in the textbox, which is `txtName`, and displays it as a popup message.

1-5. About XML

XML (eXtensible Markup Language) is designed to carry and store data. It is a representation of data in a structured and pre-defined format.

```
Syntax: <xmlTag attributeName="attributeValue">
            elementValue
        </xmlTag>
```

`elementValue` can be a literal value or another XML node.

An XML tag name doesn't have any space in it. It can have zero or more attribute names and `attributeValue` pairs. It can have only one value. It can be nested. The start and end of a data element are represented by `openingTag` and `closingTag`, respectively. Refer to Listing 1-7 for XML representation of employee information.

Listing 1-7. XML representation of employee information

```
<Employees>
    <Employee>
        <Name>John Doe</Name>
        <Department>Sales</Department>
        <DateOfJoining>09/12/2001</DateOfJoining>
        <Salary>75000</Salary>
    </Employe>
    <Employee>
        <Name>Jane Doe</Name>
        <Department>Technology</Department>
        <DateOfJoining>09/12/1998</DateOfJoining>
        <Salary>85000</Salary>
    </Employe>
</Employees>
```

Data elements enclosed in `<>` are called tags. Each tag `<tagName>` has a closing tag, which is specified as `</tagName>`. For example, the `<Employee>`'s closing tag is `</Employee>`.

1-6. About JSON

JSON (JavaScript Object Notation) is a lightweight data-interchange format. A JSON object is represented as `{"objectName":objectValue}`. An array is represented as `[object,object,...]`.

For example, `Employees` information can be represented as `{"Employees":[]}` where `Employee` is an object and `Employees` is an array of `Employee` objects. This example has two object types: `Employees` and `Employee`.

In JavaScript, the JSON string can be converted to a JavaScript object and each element can be accessed using the code segment specified in Listing 1-8.

Listing 1-8. JSON representation of employee information

```
<script>
   var jsonString = '{"Employees":[{"Name":"John", "Department":"Sales"},
      {"Name":"Jane", "Department":"Technology"}]}';
   var jsonObj = jQuery.parseJSON(jsonString);
   var employeesObj = jsonObj.Employees;
   for (var i=0; i<employeesObj.length; i++) {
      var employeeObj = employeesObj[i];
      var employeeName = employeeObj.Name;
      alert(i + ": " + employeeName);
   }
</script>
```

1-7. Introduction to Web Services

Web services are application components that can be used by other applications over HTTP or HTTPS. In a typical application (desktop and web applications), their functional components are defined in the same source code or in the same package or externally packaged software (like DLL and JAR) located on the same machine. In the case of web services, the functions provider and consumer are usually on separate servers. The web service provider and consumers don't have to be written using same language and be running on the same type of operating system. This is one of the main advantages of using web services—it operates under heterogeneous environments.

Here's an example of a web service specification:

> Web Service – WeatherService
>
> Function / Operation – `getCurrentTemperature()`
>
> Input: Zip Code
>
> Result: Temperature in Celsius

Figure 1-1 dispays web service request and response between the consumer and the provider.

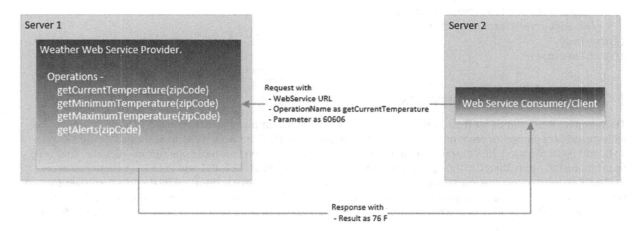

Figure 1-1. *Web Service request and response*

1-7-1. SOAP Web Services

The acronym SOAP stands for Simple Object Access Protocol. It is an XML-based protocol used to consume web services. A protocol is a contract between the provider and consumer for the specification of the format of requests and responses between them. Details of services (the operations) provided by the web services are defined (by the provider) and accessed (by the users) using the Web Services Description Language (WSDL), which is in XML format. WSDL has following four main sections—`message`, `portType`, `binding`, and `service`.

Developers don't need to code each element of the SOAP message. There are many libraries, utilities, and plug-ins available that can take an object and build the SOAP message request. Upon receiving the response, they can parse the SOAP message and build the object, which can then be used in the program. Listing 1-9 shows an example of a SOAP message request.

Listing 1-9. SOAP message request

```
<?xml version="1.0"?>
<soap:Envelope xmlns:soap="http://www.w3.org/2003/05/soap-envelope">
<soap:Header>
</soap:Header>
<soap:Body>
    <m:GetCurrentTemperatureRequest xmlns:m="http://www.myWeather.org/weather">
      <m:ZipCode>60606</m:ZipCode>
    </m: GetCurrentTemperatureRequest>
</soap:Body>
</soap:Envelope>
```

Listing 1-10 shows an example of a SOAP message response.

Listing 1-10. SOAP message response

```
<?xml version="1.0"?>
<soap:Envelope xmlns:soap="http://www.w3.org/2003/05/soap-envelope">
<soap:Header>
</soap:Header>
<soap:Body>
    <m:GetCurrentTemperatureResponse xmlns:m="http://www.myWeather.org/weather">
      <m:ZipCode>60606</m:ZipCode>
      <m:CurrentTemperature>76 F</m:CurrentTemperature>
    </m: GetCurrentTemperatureResponse>
</soap:Body>
</soap:Envelope>
```

1-7-2. RESTful Web Services

The acronym REST stands for Representational State Transfer. It is a simpler alternative to SOAP and is gaining widespread acceptance for creating web services. It transfers XML, JSON, or both (refer to Sections 1-5 and 1-6 for XML and JSON formats). REST establishes a one-to-one mapping between four basic operations—`Create`, `Retrieve`, `Update`, and `Delete` (called CRUD) operations and HTTP methods—`POST`, `GET`, `PUT` and `DELETE`. A client can access the REST resource using the unique URI and a representation of the resource is returned by the REST web service. Unlike SOAP, REST doesn't contain a messaging layer. SOAP uses the Web Services Description Language (WSDL) to define the web services interface, whereas REST uses the Web Application Description Language (WADL) to define the web services interface.

Consider the same example from SOAP to invoke a REST service:

```
http://www.myWeather.com/weather/CurrentTemperature/60606
```

This is not the request body—it's just the URL. This URL is sent to the server using a simpler GET request, and the HTTP reply is the raw result data in XML or JSON. Unlike with SOAP, the response is not embedded inside anything.

Here's an example of a response in JSON format:

```
{"ZipCode":"60606", "Temerature":"76 F"}
```

1-8. About jQuery UI

jQuery UI is collection of commonly used user interface widgets that responds to user initiated events and provides prebuilt themes and easily maintainable custom themes. It is built on top of the jQuery JavaScript library.

jQueryUI can be downloaded from `http://jqueryui.com/download/`. Refer to the listing 1-11 to see how to use the widgets available in the jQuery UI library.

Listing 1-11. Using the jQuery UI datepicker widget

```
<!DOCTYPE html>
<html>
<head>
    <link rel="stylesheet" href="http://code.jquery.com/ui/1.11.1/themes/start/jquery-ui.min.css"/>
    <script src="http://code.jquery.com/jquery-2.1.0.min.js"></script>
    <script src="http://code.jquery.com/ui/1.11.1/jquery-ui.min.js"></script>
    <script>
        $(document).ready(function(){
            $("#datepicker").datepicker();
          });
    </script>
</head>
<body>
    Date: <input type="text" id="datepicker" />
</body>
</html>
```

Figure 1-2 displays jQuery UI datepicker widget which is created by the above code.

Figure 1-2. *Datepicker widget*

The jQuery UI is built on the jQuery JavaScript library. In order to use it, you need to download jQuery in addition to jQuery UI and include the jQuery JavaScript file before including the jQuery UI JavaScript file. Table 1-3 lists commonly used jQuery UI Widgets.

Table 1-3. *Commonly used jQuery UI Widgets*

UI Widget	Display As
Accordion	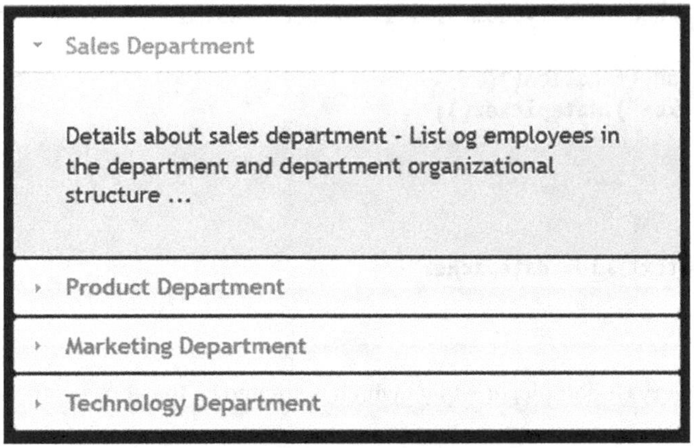
Autocomplete	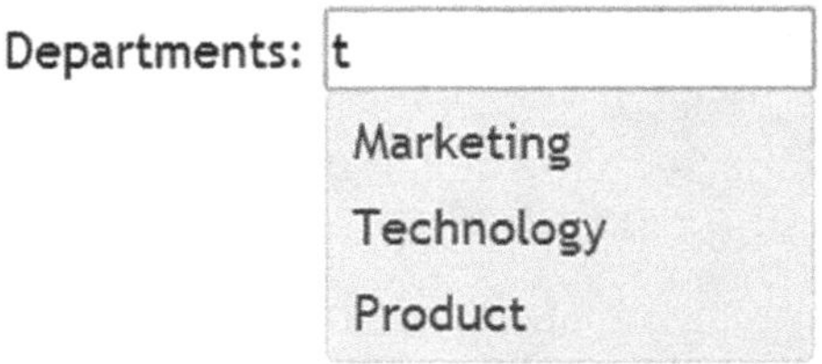

(*continued*)

Table 1-3. (*continued*)

UI Widget	Display As
Button	Simple button: Icons: Checkboxes: Radio buttons: Toolbar:
Datepicker	
Dialog	

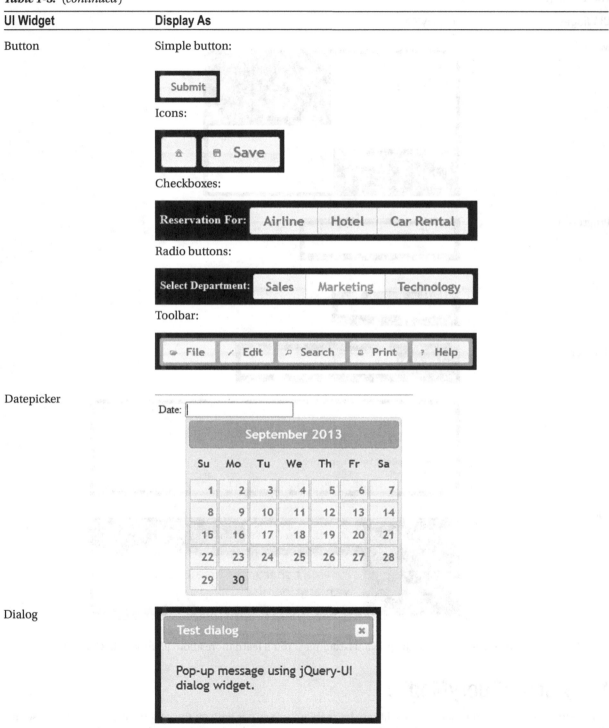

(*continued*)

Table 1-3. (*continued*)

UI Widget	Display As
Menu	
Progress bar	
Slider	
Spinner	
Tabs	
Tooltip	

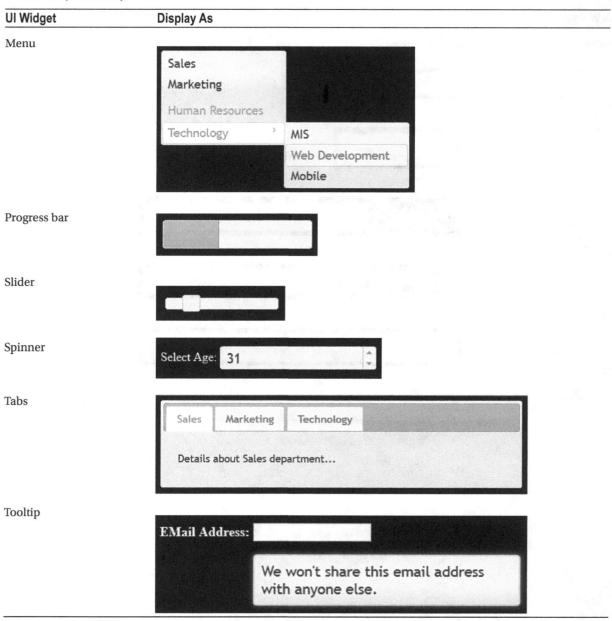

The ui-lightness theme is in for the previous examples. You'll learn more about jQuery UI in Chapter 10.

1-9. About jQueryMobile

jQueryMobile is a JavaScript user interface library for mobile devices. It is built on the jQuery and jQuery UI JavaScript libraries. It supports responsive design, which means the user interface is adjusted depending on target platform (such as desktop browsers, smartphones, and tablets).

jQueryMobile is built on HTML5, CSS3, and the jQuery JavaScript library. In order to use it, you need to download jQuery in addition to jQueryMobile and include the jQuery .js file before including the jQueryMobile .js file.

The jQueryMobile JavaScript library can be downloaded from `http://jquerymobile.com/download/`. You'll learn more about jQueryMobile in Chapter 11.

1-10. Introduction to jqWidgets

jqWidgets is a JavaScript user interface library for developing websites and applications on mobile devices. It is built on HTML5, CSS3, JavaScript, and the jQuery libraries. jQuery UI provides basic widgets, whereas jqWidgets provides advanced user interface components such as jqxGrid, jqxChart, jqxTree, and so on.

jQueryMobile is built on HTML5, CSS3, and the jQuery JavaScript library. In order to use it, you need to download jQuery in addition to jQueryMobile and include the jQuery .js file before including the jQueryMobile js file.

The jqWidgets library can be downloaded from `http://www.jqwidgets.com/download/`.

In order to use jqWidgets, include jQuery JavaScript and the respective jqwidgets JavaScript file in the HTML file. The table 1-4 lists commonly used widgets.

Table 1-4. *Commonly used jqWidgets*

Widget	Display As
jqxInput	Enter a Country
jqxNumberInput	Number ___,___,__0.00 Percentage __0.00% Currency $__,___,__0.00
jqxCalendar	February 2012

Table 1-4. (*continued*)

Widget	Display As
jqxTree	
jqxMenu	

(*continued*)

Table 1-4. (*continued*)

Widget	Display As
jqxGrid	

First Name	Last Name	Product	In Stock	Quantity	Price
Andrew	Bjorn	Peppermint Mocha Twist	☐	8	$4.00
Nancy	Burke	Cappuccino	☑	11	$5.00
Yoshi	Davolio	Caffe Espresso	☑	10	$3.00
Nancy	Winkler	Espresso Truffle	☐	9	$1.75
Yoshi	Peterson	Espresso con Panna	☑	5	$3.25
Shelley	Murphy	White Chocolate Mocha	☐	2	$3.60
Andrew	Fuller	White Chocolate Mocha	☐	5	$3.60
Shelley	Ohno	Black Tea	☑	5	$2.25
Elio	Nagase	Espresso con Panna	☑	8	$3.25
Nancy	Davolio	Caffe Latte	☑	10	$4.50
Andrew	Rossi	Espresso Truffle	☐	3	$1.75
Guylene	Davolio	Caffe Espresso	☑	5	$3.00
Yoshi	Saylor	Caffe Americano	☐	5	$2.50
		Count:200 Cappuccino Items:12	In Stock:95 Not In Stock:105	Min: 1 Max: 11	Sum:$624.10 Avg:$3.12

More details about jqWidget's widgets are specified in Chapter 12.

1-12. About Eclipse IDE

Eclipse is an open source integrated development environment (IDE) that provides features like folder structure creation, suggestions, auto-complete, and the ability to check code in and out from commonly used source control repositories like Subversion. Eclipse installation is optional. In place of Eclipse, you can use any text editor or other IDE tools like Microsoft Visual Studio.

To download Eclipse, go to http://www.eclipse.org/downloads/. Figure 1-3 displays the latest version of eclipse available at the time of writing of this book.

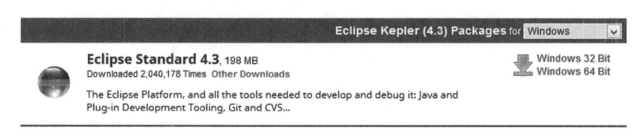

Figure 1-3. *Eclipse version*

Check the appropriate Windows 32-Bit or Windows 64-Bit link, depending on your Windows operating system. Figure 1-4 displays the page when "Windows 64 Bit" link is clicked.

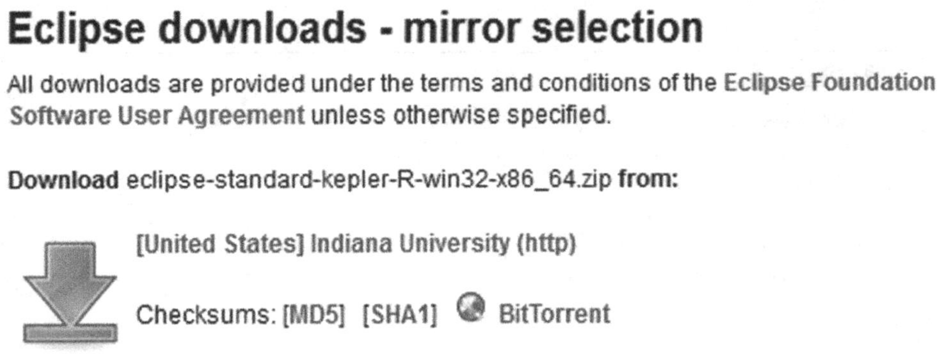

Eclipse downloads - mirror selection

All downloads are provided under the terms and conditions of the Eclipse Foundation
Software User Agreement unless otherwise specified.

Download eclipse-standard-kepler-R-win32-x86_64.zip **from:**

[United States] Indiana University (http)

Checksums: [MD5] [SHA1] ● BitTorrent

Figure 1-4. *Eclipse 64 Bit downloadable file*

Click on the down arrow to download and save the file. Extract the folders and files from the downloaded file
called `eclipse-standard-kepler-R-win32-x86_64.zip` using Winzip or any other compression/decompression
utility. Save the extracted files and folders under `c:\eclipse` or any other folder you prefer. You can run eclipse by
double clicking eclipse.exe.

Summary

This chapter was a high-level overview of technologies used to develop static and dynamic web and mobile
applications. It introduced JavaScript, jQuery, jQueryUI, jqWidgets, and jQueryMobile, which are used to create
a rich user interface. It also covered web services (SOAP and RESTful), XML, and JSON, which are used to transfer
information between tiers within the same infrastructure or within infrastructures spread across the globe. The
following chapters will use these technologies to understand how different sub-components of an application are
designed, built, and implemented.

CHAPTER 2

■ ■ ■

jQuery Fundamentals

This chapter covers the fundamentals of the jQuery library, including the following topics:

- How to access jQuery library functionalities
- Using conditional statements
- Looping
- The structure of the Document Object Model (DOM)
- Commonly used objects in the jQuery library
- jQuery functions
- Method chaining

2-1. Setting Up jQuery

As with any other JavaScript library, if you want to access functionalities of the jQuery library, you need to include the jQuery JavaScript file. There are two ways to include the jQuery JavaScript library in an HTML file:

- **Using a local file**—The jQuery library can be downloaded from http://jquery.com/download/. At the time of this writing, the latest version of jQuery was 2.1.0. Download the compressed (production) version of the library if you don't intend to modify or debug the jQuery JavaScript code. Otherwise, you can download the uncompressed (development) version.

  If your user base is still using Internet Explorer 8 or older, download the latest version of jQuery 1.x. You should download the latest version of jQuery 2.x if your user base is using Internet Explorer 9 (or newer) or any other new version of browsers such as Firefox, Google Chrome, and Apple Safari.

- **Using the Content Delivery Network (CDN)**—CDN is a distributed network of servers that hosts open source libraries like jQuery. When a request is made in a browser to access the jQuery library, CDN identifies the closest server and provides the jQuery JavaScript file to the browser.

The advantages of using CDN include:

- If another application has already used the CDN to locate the jQuery JavaScript file, the chances are the file is in the browser's cache. If it is in the cache, that copy of the library will be used; otherwise it will be downloaded from the closest server.
- Has a faster download since the closest server is used to deliver the file.

The only problem with using CDN is that if an Internet connection is not available, the web page won't work. This is an issue for developers who sometimes want to develop and test their sites offline.

Setting Up the Development Environment

Before you start a new project, you need to set up the development environment folder structure so that files with a similar purpose are in the same folder and are easy to find. For example, all JavaScript library files should be in the `scripts` folder, all images should be in the `images` folder, and all CSS files and image files used in the CSS should be in the `styles` folder. To set up your development environment, create a new folder (called for example, `jQueryLearn`) where you want to keep all your HTML (.htm and .html) files and folders that contain JavaScript (.js) files, CSS (.css) files, and image (.jpg, .png, .bmp, and so on) files.

The structure of your development environment should follow this:

- jQueryLearn/
  - Images/*.png, *.gif, *.jpg, etc.
  - Scripts/*.js
  - Styles/*.css
  - Styles/images/*.png, *.gif, *.jpg, etc.
  - *.htm

Copy the downloaded jQuery compressed file called `jquery-2.1.0.min.js` in the `scripts/` folder.

Create a template HTML file in the `jQueryLearn` folder. You can use this `template.htm` file to create other HTML files. Listing 2-1 displays the content of the `template.htm` file.

Listing 2-1. Including jQuery library in the HTML page (the template.htm file)

```
<!doctype html>
<html lang="en">
   <head>
      <meta charset="utf-8">
      <script src="scripts/jquery-2.1.0.min.js"></script>
   </head>
   <body>
   </body>
</html>
```

Replace `jquery-2.1.0.min.js` with the jQuery library version you have downloaded and are planning to use. If you are planning to step through the jQuery library code during debugging, you should use an uncompressed development version of jQuery library.

If instead of using a local downloaded jQuery file, you want to use the CDN, include one of the following lines in your code:

```
<script src="http://ajax.googleapis.com/ajax/libs/jquery/2.1.0/jquery.min.js">
</script>
<script src="http://code.jquery.com/jquery-2.1.0.min.js">
</script>
```

2-2. Using Conditional Statements

There are two types of conditional statements—if...else and switch. The if...else statement is used if the value of the variable is checked only a few times. If the value of the same variable is checked many times and a different set of statements is executed, a switch statement is used. These conditional statements are not specific to the jQuery library, they are native to the JavaScript.

if...else Statements

Conditional statements tests whether a certain condition is true. If the condition is true, all the statements between the curly braces immediately after the if statement are executed. If the condition is false, all the statements between the curly braces immediately after the else statement are executed. If there is only one statement you want to execute when the condition is true or false, you don't need to specify the braces but it is preferable to use braces all the time.

In JavaScript and jQuery, the basic syntax for conditional statements is as follows:

```
if (condition) {
  // code segment if condition is true
} else {
  // code segment if condition is false
}
```

Listing 2-2 demonstrates the use of the if...else statement.

Listing 2-2. Using the if...else statement

```
<!DOCTYPE html>
<html lang="en">
   <head>
      <meta charset="utf-8">
      <script>
         function submitForm() {
          var firstName = document.getElementById("txtFirstName");

             if (firstName.value == "") {
                alert("Please enter First Name before submitting");
                return false;
             } else {
                // Perform some action
                alert("Form is successfully submitted");
                return true;
             }
         }
      </script>
   </head>
   <body>
      <form>
         First Name: <input id="txtFirstName" type="text"><br><br>
         <input type="button" value="Submit" onClick="submitForm()">
      </form>
   </body>
</html>
```

Figure 2-1 displays the page created by Listing 2-2 when viewed in a browser.

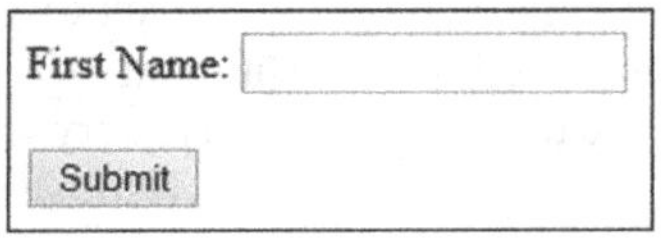

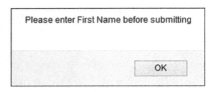

First Name: [   ]

Submit

Figure 2-1. *Using a conditional statement*

This code is binding the submitForm() function to the button's click event. When a user clicks the button, submitForm() function is executed. In the submitForm() function, you are first getting the input element with the ID txtFirstName using the getElementById() method and then checking its value property. If value is blank, "Please enter First Name before submitting" is displayed; otherwise "Form is successfully submitted" is displayed. Figures 2-2 and 2-3 show the pop-up messages that are displayed depending on the value entered for First Name.

Please enter First Name before submitting

OK

Figure 2-2. *The message displayed when First Name is left blank*

Form is successfully submitted

OK

Figure 2-3. *The message displayed when value is entered for First Name*

if ... if else ... else Statements

If the logic is more complex and you have to check multiple conditions, you can use the following syntax:

```
if (condition1) {
    // code segment if condition1 is true
} else if (condition2) {
    // code segment if condition2 is true
} else {
    // code segment if condition1 is not true and
    // condition2 is not true
}
```

Listing 2-3 demonstrates the use of an if...else if...else statement.

Listing 2-3. Using multiple conditional statements

```
<!DOCTYPE html>
<html lang="en">
<head>
    <meta charset="utf-8">

    <script>
        function getDepartmentName() {
            var departmentID = document.getElementById("departmentID").value;
          var departmentName = "";

        if (departmentID == "") {
                    alert("Please enter Department ID");
        } else if (departmentID == "S")  {
                    departmentName = "Sales";
        } else if (departmentID == "M")  {
                    departmentName = "Marketing";
        } else if (departmentID == "T")  {
                    departmentName = "Technology";
        } else if (departmentID == "C")  {
                    departmentName = "Customer Support";
        } else {
                    departmentName = "Unknown";
        }
        document.getElementById("departmentName").innerHTML = departmentName;
        }
    </script>
</head>
<body>
        Department ID [S, M, T, C]:<input id="departmentID" type="text">
        <label id="departmentName"></label>
        <br>
        <input type="button" value="Get Department Name" onClick="getDepartmentName();">
</body>
</html>
```

Figure 2-4 displays the page when viewed in a browser.

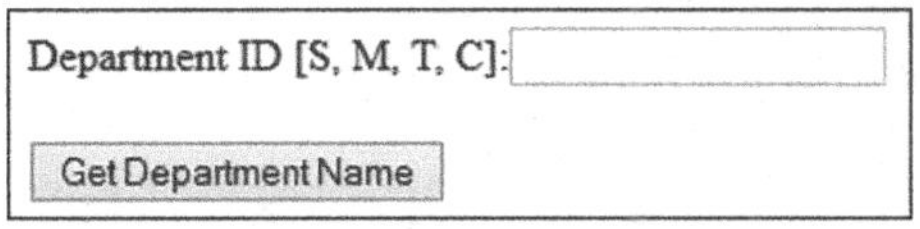

Figure 2-4. *Using multiple conditional statements*

This code binds the getDepartmentName() function to the button's click event. When a user clicks the button, the getDepartmentName() function is executed. In the getDepartmentName() function, you first get the input element with the ID departmentID using the getElementById() method and then check its value property. If value is blank, "Please enter Department ID" is displayed; otherwise, based on the value entered for the Department ID, departmentName is set. Its value is then used to set the innerHTML property of the label tag with an ID of departmentName. Figures 2-5 and 2-6 show the pop-up messages depending on the value entered for the Department ID.

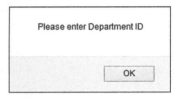

Figure 2-5. *The message displayed when the Department ID is left blank*

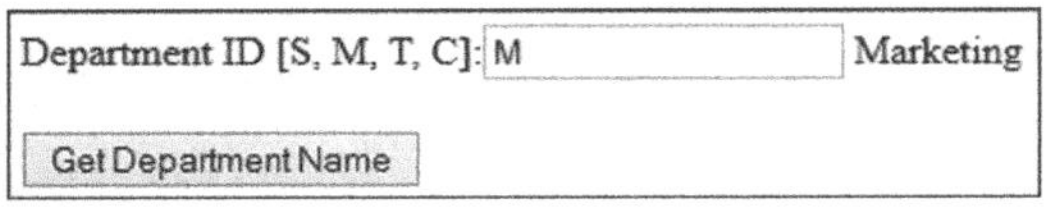

Department ID [S, M, T, C]: M   Marketing

Get Department Name

Figure 2-6. *The Department Name is displayed when a valid value is entered for the Department ID*

switch Statements

In place of multiple if...else statements, you can use the switch statement. In the case of the switch statement, the value of the expression is compared with the value of each case statement and if it matches, the following block of statements is executed until a break statement is encountered. If none of the case statements is true, the block of statements in the default statement will be executed. The switch statement is used in place of an if...else statement to make the code more organized and readable.

The syntax for a switch statement is:

```
switch(n) {
  case 1:
    // code segment if n == 1
    break;
  case 2:
    // code segment if n == 2
    break;
  default:
    // code segment if none of the above case statements is true
}
```

Listing 2-4 demonstrates the use of a switch statement.

Listing 2-4. Using the switch statement

```html
<!DOCTYPE html>
<html lang="en">
<head>
    <meta charset="utf-8">
    <script>
        function getDepartmentName() {
            var departmentID = document.getElementById("departmentID").value;
            var departmentName = "";

        switch (departmentID) {
                        case "": alert("Please enter Department ID");
                                    break;
                        case "S": departmentName = "Sales";
                                        break;
                        case "M": departmentName = "Marketing";
                                            break;
                        case "T": departmentName = "Technology";
                                        break;
                        case "C": departmentName = "Customer Support";
                                        break;
                        default:  departmentName = "Unknown";
                    }
        document.getElementById("departmentName").innerHTML = departmentName;
        }
    </script>
</head>
<body>
        Department ID [S, M, T, C]:<input id="departmentID" type="text">
        <label id="departmentName"></label>
        <br>
        <input type="button" value="Get Department Name" onClick="getDepartmentName();">
</body>
</html>
```

2-3. Looping

Loops are used when the same statements need to be executed for a range of values (each time with a different value from the range) or for each element in an array or in the collection of objects. A loop statement is also used when the same statements are executed until a condition becomes true. The two commonly used looping statements are for and while. These looping statements are not specific to the jQuery library; they are native to JavaScript.

for Loops

The for loop executes the same code segment for each element from a collection or for a number of times until a condition becomes true.

In JavaScript and jQuery, the syntax for using the for loop is as follows:

```
for (var i=initialValue; i <= finalValue; i++) {
    // code logic
}
```

Listing 2-5 demonstrates the use of a for loop.

Listing 2-5. Using a for loop to display all the elements in an array

```
<!DOCTYPE html>
<html lang="en">
<head>
    <meta charset="utf-8">
    <script>
        var departments = [
                "Sales",
                "Marketing",
                "Technology",
                "Customer Support"
        ];
                for (var i=0; i<departments.length; i++) {
                    document.write(departments[i] + "<br>");
                }
    </script>
</head>
<body>
</body>
</html>
```

Figure 2-7 displays the page when viewed in a browser.

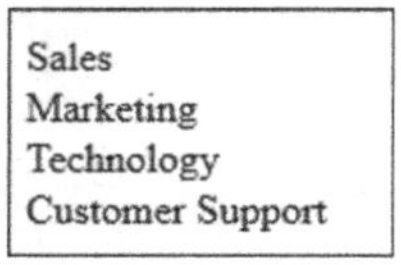

Sales
Marketing
Technology
Customer Support

Figure 2-7. *Using a for loop*

This code creates an array called departments with a list of department names. Since the index in an array is 0-based, the loop starts with position number i as 0 and then displays the department name stored at the 0th position in the array. The for loop repeats the execution of the same code segment until it reaches the end of the array. With each iteration, the position number is incremented by 1 by using the i++ statement.

while Loops

The while loop is used to execute the same code segment as long as a condition is true.

The syntax for the while loop is:

```
while (condition) {
    // code segment if condition is true
}
```

Listing 2-6 demonstrates the use of a while loop.

Listing 2-6. Using a while loop to display all the elements in an array

```
<!DOCTYPE html>
<html lang="en">
<head>
   <meta charset="utf-8">
   <script>
     var departments = [
          "Sales",
          "Marketing",
          "Technology",
          "Customer Support"
     ];
     var i=0;
        while (i < departments.length) {
                document.write(departments[i] + "<br>");
                i++;
              }
   </script>
</head>
<body>
</body>
</html>
```

Figure 2-8 displays the page when viewed in a browser.

```
Sales
Marketing
Technology
Customer Support
```

Figure 2-8. *Using a while loop*

This code creates an array called departments with a list of department names. Since the index in an array is 0-based, it starts the loop with position number i as 0 and then displays the department name stored at the 0th position in the array. The while loop repeats the execution of the same code segment until it reaches the end of the array. With each iteration, the position number is incremented by 1 by using the i++ statement. In the while loop, the same logic is implemented as in the for loop in Listing 2-5. The difference is in the way the looping counter (i.e., the i variable) is initialized and incremented. In the while loop, the looping counter is initialized before the while statement and it is incremented inside the while loop.

For both the for and while loops, the following statements can be used inside the looping logic:

– The break statement breaks out of the loop without executing the code segment of the remainder of the items in the iteration. This is used when a particular condition is true and no further processing inside the loop is needed.

– The continue statement skips the current iteration and continues with the next iteration. This is used when the current element in the loop doesn't need to be processed.

2-4. Understanding the Document Object Model (DOM)

When a browser loads a web page, it creates a document object model (DOM) of the page within its memory. Using this object model, you can programmatically access, update, and restructure all the HTML elements in the web page. The DOM interface gives access to HTML elements' attributes, properties, content, styles, and events.

The DOM Structure

The DOM is represented by a tree structure with the document as the root node and all other elements in the document as descendant nodes. Each node in the tree structure is an HTMLElement object with its associated attributes, properties, styles (CSS), and events.

For example, a button:

```
<input id="btnSubmit" type="button" value="Submit">
```

is represented as an object node in the DOM with the tagName property of INPUT, an id attribute with the value "btnSubmit", a type attribute with the value "button," and a value attribute with the value "Submit".

Listing 2-7 demonstrates the concept of the DOM structure.

Listing 2-7. Code to demonstrate the DOM structure

```
<!DOCTYPE html>
<html lang="en">
    <head>
        <meta charset="utf-8">
        <title>Title Text</title>

        <style>
            .btn {
                background-color: lightblue;
                color: blue
            }
        </style>
        <script>
            alert("JavaScript Code Placeholder...");
        </script>
    </head>
    <body>
        <H1>Sample HTML Page</H1>
        <p>Employee Information:</p>
        Department
        <ul>
          <li>Marketing</li>
          <li>Sales</li>
         </ul>
        <form id="frmRegistration">
            <label id="lblFirstName">First Name:</label>
            <input id="txtFirstName" />
            <button id="btnSubmit" class="btn">Submit</button>
        </form>
```

```
    <table id="tblEmployee">
        <tr>
            <td>Employee Name</td>
            <td>Department Name</td>
        </tr>
        <tr>
            <td>John Smith</td>
            <td>Technology</td>
        </tr>
    </table>
  </body>
</html>
```

Figure 2-9 represents the DOM tree of the previous code.

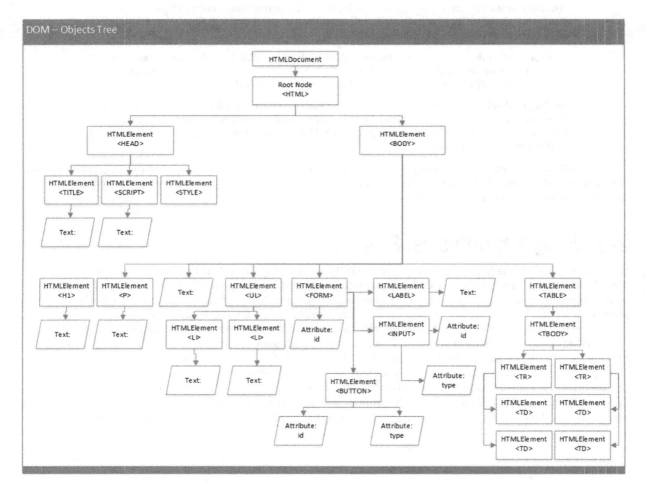

Figure 2-9. *DOM objects tree*

jQuery methods can manage the DOM and its elements by:

- Changing HTML elements, including their properties, attributes, and styles

- Removing existing HTML elements

- Adding new HTML elements

- Binding event handlers to HTML elements

- Restructuring the DOM

2-5. Navigating the DOM

The DOM hierarchy is represented as a tree structure. In this structure, starting from any node, you can get:

- **Ancestor nodes** by traversing upward until you reach the root node. For example, in Figure 2-9, for the HTMLElement (<INPUT>) node, the ancestors are HTMLElement (<FORM>), HTMLElement (<BODY>), and HTMLElement (<HTML>).

- **Descendent nodes** by traversing downward through all possible branches until you reach leaf nodes. For example, for the HTMLElement (<TABLE>), the descendents are HTMLElement (<TBODY>), two HTMLElements (<TR>), and four HTMLElements (<TD>).

- **Sibling nodes** by traversing to the parent node and then traversing down one level. For example, for the HTMLElement (<BUTTON>), the sibling nodes are HTMLElement ("<LABEL>") and HTMLElement ("<INPUT>"). This concept is helpful for applying the same action to all elements within the same container.

The DOM native methods and jQuery methods provide mechanisms to traverse the DOM tree to get the ancestor, descendent, and sibling nodes, and to perform actions on those nodes if needed. You will read about node(s) selection and manipulation in the next chapter.

2-6. Using Attributes vs. Properties

When a web page is loaded, the browser parses the HTML code and, for each HTML tag, a corresponding HTMLElement object is created in the DOM. Like any other object, this object has properties and methods. Some of the properties are attributes, class names, child nodes, IDs, inner HTML, tag names, and so on. In addition to a predefined set of properties, a property corresponding to each attribute of the HTML tag is also created.

For an HTML tag, each of its attributes and values are saved in the attributes properties of the HTMLElement object (DOM node) as a collection of key/value pairs and each attribute-value pair is also saved as a property of the HTMLElement. For example, for the HTML tag <input id="txtName" type="text" value="Default Value">, its corresponding HTMLElement in DOM will have ID, type, and value properties and also an attributes property with key/value pairs as {id: "txtName" type: "text", value: "Default Value"}. When a user changes the value, the current value is reflected in the value of the property and in the value of the attribute. Table 2-1 is the partial representation of the HTMLElement object that's created by the HTML tag <input id="txtName" type="text" value="Default Value">.

Table 2-1. *Partial Representation of the HTML Element Object*

Property Name	Property Value	
tagName	input	
id	txtName	
type	text	
value	defaultValue	
attributes	**Attribute Name**	**Attribute Value**
	id	txtName
	type	text
	value	Default Value

Listing 2-8 demonstrates the difference between attributes and properties.

Listing 2-8. Code to demonstrate the difference between attributes and properties

```
<!DOCTYPE html>
<html lang="en">
<head>
   <meta charset="utf-8">
   <script>
      function displayValues() {
         var name = document.getElementById("txtName");
         alert("Attribute value of 'value': " +
            name.attributes["value"].value + "\n" +
            "Property value of 'value': " + name.value);
      }
   </script>
</head>
<body>
   Name: <input id="txtName" type="text" value="Default Value" ><br><br>
   <input id="btnDisplay" type="button" value="Display Attributes and Properties"
   onClick="displayValues();">
</body>
</html>
```

Figure 2-10 displays the page when viewed in a browser.

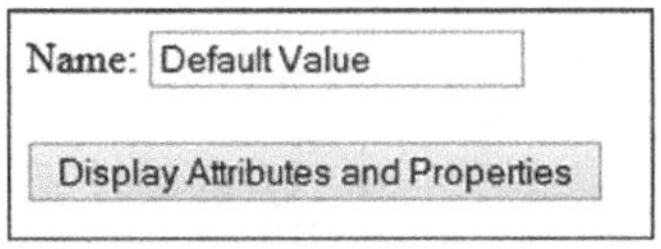

Figure 2-10. *Attributes vs. properties*

This code binds the displayValues() function to the button's click event. When a user clicks the button, the displayValues() function is executed. In the displayValues() function, you get the input element with the ID of txtName using the getElementById() method and then display its value of the value attribute and value property. Figure 2-11 shows the pop-up message when the value of the field Name: is not changed and the Display Attributes and Properties button is clicked. Initially, the attribute and property value are the same.

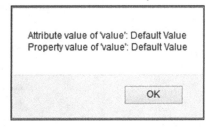

Figure 2-11. *The initial attribute and property values*

Notice that the attribute and property value of value is the same. Now change Name: to something else (for example, to John Smith) and click the button again. Figure 2-12 shows the pop-up message when the value of the Name: field is changed and the Display Attributes and Properties button is clicked.

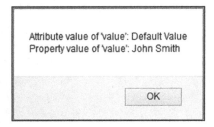

Figure 2-12. *Attribute and property value after a value is entered in the Name: field*

The value of the value property has changed to John Smith, but the attribute value remains unaffected.

2-7. Commonly Used Objects in jQuery

The jQuery library is based on JavaScript and hence supports all JavaScript data types (string, number, Boolean, array, and object), which are covered in Chapter 1. The following are the other commonly used objects used in jQuery:

- Map object
- HTMLElement object
- jQuery object

Map Object

The map object contains key/value pairs. The syntax for declaring a map object is:

```
var variableName = { key1: value1, key1: value1, ... };
```

The key and value entries can be either primitive types or objects.
For example, to declare a map object, you'd use this code:

```
var employeeMap = {
            "Name": "John Smith",
            "Department": "Technology",
            "Salary":50000,
            "Joining Date": new Date("01/05/2010")
};
```

To display a key's value in the map object, you'd use this code:

```
alert(employeeMap.Name);
```

To display all the key/value pairs in the map object, you'd use this code:

```
for (var k in employeeMap){
   alert("Key: " + k + " Value:" + employeeMap[k]);
}
```

HTML Element

In this book, I use HTMLElement as a generic term for all the types of elements in the DOM tree—it can refer to HTMLFormElement (for <form>), HTMLDivElement (for <div>), HTMLParagraphElement (for <p>), HTMLInputElement (for <input>), and so on.

Each HTMLElement in the DOM has properties like any other JavaScript object. One of the important properties is attributes, which contains an element's attributeName and attributeValue pairs. HTML elements have methods like appendChild(), getAttribute(), and getElementByTagName().

Listing 2-9 demonstrates how an HTML element from the DOM can be referenced and how to use its property and execute its method.

Listing 2-9. Code to demonstrate how to access to an HTMLElement's property and method

```
<!doctype html>
<html lang="en">
   <head>
      <meta charset="utf-8">
      <script>
         function getFirstName() {
            var htmlElement = document.getElementById("txtFirstName");
                        alert("Value: " + htmlElement.value);
                        alert("Type: " + htmlElement.getAttribute("type"));
         }
      </script>
   </head>
```

```
    <body>
        First Name: <input id="txtFirstName" type="text"><br>
        <input type="button" value="Get First Name & Type" onClick="getFirstName()">
    </body>
</html>
```

Figure 2-13 displays the page when viewed in a browser.

First Name:
Get First Name & Type

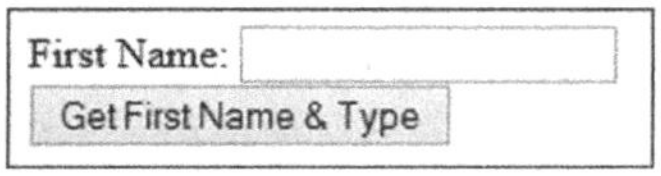

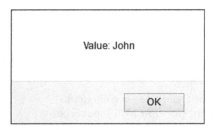

Figure 2-13. *An HTML element's property and method*

The `var htmlElement = document.getElementById("txtFirstName");` line gets the `HTMLElement` from the DOM that has an ID of `txtFirstName`. Once you have the `HTMLElement`, you can get and set its properties and attributes and execute DOM methods on it. This example is getting its property `value` by using `htmlElement.value` and getting its attribute `type` by executing the `getAttribute()` method.

Figures 2-14 and 2-15 show the pop-up messages that appear when any name (for example, John) is entered and the Get First Name & Type button is clicked.

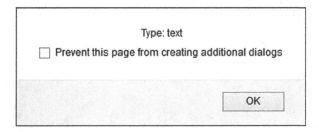

Value: John
OK

Figure 2-14. *An HTML element and its value property*

Type: text
Prevent this page from creating additional dialogs
OK

Figure 2-15. *An HTML element and its type attribute*

The screen and messages in the previous figures are from Firefox browser; you might see slightly different format depending on the browser you are using.

jQuery Objects

When creating new HTML elements or selecting existing ones, jQuery returns a jQuery object that's a collection of HTML elements. A jQuery object wraps these HTML elements and native DOM methods to make them work across different browsers and to implement consistent behavior. A jQuery object enables you to achieve tasks easily and with less code compared to using native DOM method calls. jQuery objects are not dynamic in the sense that their HTMLElements collection won't grow or shrink based on addition or removal of elements in the HTML document.

Chapters 3, 4, 5, and 6 cover how jQuery objects are created and explain the methods you can use to act on HTML elements within the jQuery object.

2-8. Using the jQuery Function

You can access the jQuery library's properties and methods using the jQuery function. One of the most commonly used methods is ready(), which accepts a function parameter and binds it to the document's ready event.

The syntax is as follows:

```
jQuery(document).ready(function () {
    // Code segment to execute when document is ready
    // (i.e., when DOM is completely created)
});
```

In place of jQuery, you can use its shorthand $. Using $, you can rewrite the previous code as:

```
$(document).ready(function () {
    // Code segment to execute when document is ready
    // (i.e., when DOM is completely created)
});
```

The previous code can also be written as:

```
$(function () {
    // Code segment to execute when document is ready
    // (i.e., when DOM is completely created)
});
```

which has the same effect as the original code.

If you are using some other JavaScript library that also uses $ as shorthand, in order to prevent a conflict between the JavaScript libraries, you should instead set your own shorthand (for example, jq) for the jQuery library by using the following code:

```
var jq = jQuery.noConflict();
```

jQuery Function Arguments

The following is the list of jQuery function's ($) arguments and their purposes:

- $(function)—A code segment in the specified function is executed when the DOM is ready. The following is the syntax to define the DOM-ready function:

    ```
    $(function() { ... });
    ```

When you specify a function and its code, you are just defining the function and logic in it. It won't be executed until the document-ready event is triggered. If you use a function name in its place, that function is executed immediately when the browser interprets the line, without waiting for the DOM to be ready.

- `$("selector")`—Selects HTML elements that match the specified `selector` and returns a jQuery object.

- `$(HTMLElement)`—Returns a jQuery object with the specified `HTMLElement` in it.

- `$(HTMLElement[])`—Returns a jQuery object with the HTML elements specified in the `HTMLElement[]` array.

- `$("HTMLString")`—Creates new HTML elements from the specified `HTMLString`.

Chapters 3, 4, 5, and 6 cover these function arguments in detail. Here I am simply providing very basic examples to familiarize you with the concepts.

The jQuery Function with the Function as an Argument

Using the jQuery function ($) with the function as an argument is the most used feature in the jQuery. If the code is accessing or manipulating DOM elements, then that code must be defined inside this function. The body of the function will be executed only when all the DOM elements are created and are ready to be used. Listing 2-10 demonstrates the use of the jQuery function with the `function` as an argument.

Listing 2-10. jQuery function with the function as an argument

```
<!DOCTYPE html>
<html lang="en">
<head>
    <meta charset="utf-8">
    <script src="scripts/jquery-2.1.0.min.js"></script>
    <script>
            $(function() {
                    alert("DOM is ready. Now, we can perform actions on HTML Elements in this page.");
            });
    </script>
</head>

<body>
</body>
</html>
```

This jQuery code is binding `function() {...}` to the document ready event. After the DOM is ready, this function will be executed. Such functions, which are bound to events, are also called event handlers. Figure 2-16 show the pop-up message after the DOM is ready.

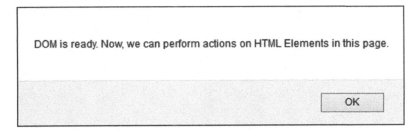

Figure 2-16. *Message displayed after the DOM is ready*

The jQuery Function with the Selector as an Argument

Using a jQuery function with the selector as an argument enables you to select DOM elements that match the `selector`, so that selected elements' values can be accessed and/or manipulated by using jQuery object's methods. Listing 2-11 demonstrates the use of the jQuery function with the `selector` as an argument.

Listing 2-11. jQuery function with the selector as an argument

```html
<!DOCTYPE html>
<html lang="en">
<head>
    <meta charset="utf-8">
    <script src="scripts/jquery-2.1.0.min.js"></script>
    <script>
            $(function() {
                $("img").mouseover(function () {
                    $(this).css("opacity", "0.3");
                });
                $("img").mouseout(function () {
                    $(this).css("opacity", "1.0");
                });
            });
    </script>
</head>
<body>
    <img src="images/panda.png">
</body>
</html>
```

Figure 2-17 displays the page when viewed in a browser.

Figure 2-17. *Image with the default opacity of 1*

This code has an image tag. Inside the DOM-ready function, this image is selected by the jQuery selector, `$("img")`, and then a function is bound to its `mouseover` event. When the mouse moves over the image, the `mouseover` event is triggered and this function is executed, which changes the opacity of the image to 0.3. Opacity can range from 0 to 1. The higher the number, the sharper the image will be. Another function is bound to the `mouseout` event, and it changes the opacity to its default value of 1. Figure 2-18 displays the image with opacity of 0.3 when the mouse cursor moves over the image.

Figure 2-18. *Opacity changes to 0.3 when mouse cursor moves over the image*

The jQuery Function with the HTMLElement as an Argument

Using a jQuery function with the HTML element as an argument enables you to put an HTML element into a jQuery object so that the jQuery object's methods can be executed on the HTML element, in order to access or manipulate its value. Listing 2-12 demonstrates the use of the jQuery function with the `HTMLElement` as an argument.

Listing 2-12. jQuery function with the HTMLElement as an argument

```
<!DOCTYPE html>
<html lang="en">
<head>
    <meta charset="utf-8">
    <script src="scripts/jquery-2.1.0.min.js"></script>
```

```
<script>
  $(function() {
                    var currentDateTime = document.getElementById("currentDatetime");
                    $(currentDateTime).prop("innerHTML", new Date());
  });
  </script>
</head>
<body>
  <div id="currentDatetime"></div>
</body>
</html>
```

Figure 2-19 displays the page when viewed in a browser.

Wed Mar 12 2014 14:39:43 GMT-0500 (Central Standard Time)

Figure 2-19. *Current system datetime set to an HTMLElement*

In this code, a div tag is created with the currentDateTime ID. When the DOM is ready, the document-ready function is executed, which gets the HTMLElement from the DOM using the statement $("#currentDatetime").first(). The same HTML element can be selected by using the native DOM method called document.getElementById ("currentDatetime"). In the $(currentDateTime) statement, the HTMLElement currentDateTime is passed to the jQuery function ($) as an argument. The jQuery object is returned due to this statement. On this jQuery object, the prop() method is executed to set its innerHTML property with the current system date and time.

The jQuery Function with the HTMLString as an Argument

Using a jQuery function with the HTML string as an argument enables you to convert an HTML string into a jQuery object so that the jQuery object's methods can be applied to the HTML elements in the jQuery object or it can be appended to an existing element. Listing 2-13 demonstrates the use of the jQuery function with the HTMLString as an argument.

Listing 2-13. The jQuery function with the HTMLString as an argument

```
<!DOCTYPE html>
<html lang="en">
<head>
  <meta charset="utf-8">
  <script src="scripts/jquery-2.1.0.min.js"></script>
  <script>
    $(function() {
        var newDepartment = $("<li>Implementation</li>")
        $("#listDepartments").append(newDepartment);
    });
    </script>
</head>
<body>
  Departments:
  <ul id="listDepartments">
    <li>Sales</li>
    <li>Marketing</li>
```

41

```
        <li>Technology</li>
        <li>Customer Support</li>
    </ul>
</body>
</html>
```

Figure 2-20 displays the page when viewed in a browser.

```
Departments:

    • Sales
    • Marketing
    • Technology
    • Customer Support
    • Implementation
```

Figure 2-20. *Adding a new department to the list at runtime*

In this code when an HTMLString called "<li>Implementation</li>" is passed to the jQuery function ($), an HTMLElement is created. This new <li> element (newDepartment) can be appended to an existing list of departments by executing the method append() on the, $("#listDepartments") jQuery object. listDepartments is the ID of the <ul> tag. Due to the statement $("#listDepartments").append(newDepartment), a new department ("Implementation") is added to the list of existing departments at runtime.

2-9. jQuery Methods Chaining

jQuery code is concise due to the availability of various shorthand notations, execution of the same method on multiple elements within the same jQuery object with one method call, and because of the *chaining* concept. Most of the jQuery methods you'll execute on jQuery objects will return another jQuery object. That means that more jQuery methods can be executed on the return value of the previous call in a single statement.

Listing 2-14 demonstrates the use of method chaining.

Listing 2-14. Method chaining

```
<!DOCTYPE html>
<html lang="en">
<head>
    <meta charset="utf-8">
    <script src="scripts/jquery-2.1.0.min.js"></script>
    <script>
                $(function() {
                        $("ul").css("color", "blue").css("text-decoration",
                                "underline").append("<li>Implementation</li>").css("color", "green");
                });
    </script>
</head>
<body>
    Departments:
    <ul id="listDepartments">
      <li>Sales</li>
      <li>Marketing</li>
```

```
    <li>Technology</li>
    <li>Customer Support</li>
  </ul>
</body>
</html>
```

Figure 2-21 displays the page when viewed in a browser.

Departments:

- Sales
- Marketing
- Technology
- Customer Support
- Implementation

Figure 2-21. *Method chaining*

This code uses the ul selector to get a jQuery object containing the <ul> HTML element. Once you have the jQuery object, you can execute methods such as css(), append(), and so on, on it. These methods will manipulate the HTML element contained in the object. The css() method sets the CSS property and the append() method adds new element(s) to the existing HTML element as its children.

In the statement:

```
$("ul").css("color", "blue").css("text-decoration", "underline").append("<li>Implementation</li>").
css("color", "green")
```

- $("ul") gets the <ul> HTML element from the DOM.

- css("color", "blue") changes the CSS color property of HTML element <ul> to blue.

- css("text-decoration", "underline") changes the CSS text-decoration property of the HTML element <ul> to underline.

- append("<li>Implementation</li>") appends a new child (item) to the HTML element <ul>.

- css("color", "green") changes the CSS color property of the HTML element <ul> to green.

All of this is done in one single statement.

In the code example, I set the CSS color property twice to demonstrate that when chaining, method execution is performed from left to right.

Summary

This chapter covered how to reference the jQuery library file, the typical folder structure of a web application, and conditional and loop statements. It also covered the most important aspect of the jQuery library—the DOM. You looked into the details of its structure and how to navigate through it. You also read about the difference between attributes and properties. Other important fundamental topics covered in this chapter are commonly used objects in jQuery and different forms for jQuery functions. The following chapters will develop real-life application functionalities based on the fundamentals you learned in this chapter.

jQuery Selectors

This chapter covers jQuery selectors, which are used to get (or select) HTML elements based on their ID, tag name, class name, types, attributes, attributes values, and other criteria. The set of selected elements can be fine-tuned further by using selector extensions or jQuery methods and the set can be expanded by using certain jQuery methods. Once you have a desired set of elements, you can access and manipulate their attributes values, properties, and style.

In this chapter and next two chapters, you will work on recipes that show you how you can use jQuery to select HTML elements directly or indirectly (by traversing through the node tree) at runtime in order to:

- Access their style, properties, and attributes
- Manipulate their style, properties, and attributes

Some points to note before you start working on the recipes in this chapter:

- For the document-ready event, the $(function() {...}) shorthand notation is used throughout this book. It is same as $(document).ready(function() {...}). In this chapter, I have used the jQuery css() method to highlight items that are selected by the jQuery selector. You can perform any valid actions on the selected elements. Chapters 4, 5 and 6 covers commonly used actions.

- If you need to put nested quotes (" and ') in any code, you can use any of the following methods:

```
" value1 = 'value2' "
' value1 = "value2" '
" value1 = \"value2\" "
" value1 = \"value2\" "
```

- All of these are valid forms; it is just a matter of preference.
- While displaying a page in the web console window with jQuery code in it, you see an error such as "ReferenceError: $ is not defined", the jQuery library is not included or it is referenced with the wrong path or URL.

Before you start looking into methods used for selectors and DOM traversing, refer to Appendix B for the list of browsers I used for testing and for details about how to invoke the web console to identify script syntax errors and runtime errors.

3-1. Examples

In order to illustrate various concepts of the jQuery library, this chapter uses the following simple applications: human resources, a publishing house, and a photo album.

3-1-1. Human Resources Example

For the human resources application, department and employee entities and their attributes will be displayed and managed in the example code. The following tables contain human resources-related entities, their attributes, and sample data. Table 3-1 has the department's attributes and Table 3-2 includes the sample data for departments.

Table 3-1. *Department's Attributes*

Attributes
DepartmentCode
DepartmentName

Table 3-2. *Department's Sample Data*

Department Code	Department Name
D001	Marketing
D002	Sales
D003	Technology

Table 3-3 contains the employee's attributes and Table 3-4 contains sample data for the employees.

Table 3-3. *Employee's Attributes*

Attributes
EmployeeID
EmployeeName
EmployeeTitle
EmployeeJoiningDate
EmployeeSalary
EmployeeDepartmentCode
ManagerEmployeeID

Table 3-4. *Employee Sample Data*

ID	Name	Title	Joining Date	Salary	Dept. Code	Manager ID
E001	Jane Smith	Marketing Manager	03/12/2008	$95,000	D001	
E003	Brian Adam	Sales Rep.	04/14/2009	$72,000	D002	E001

3-1-2. Publishing House Example

For the publishing house application, the book entity and its attributes will be displayed and managed in the example code. The following tables contain publishing house-related entities, the attributes, and the sample data. Table 3-5 contains the book's attributes and Table 3-6 contains sample data for the books.

Table 3-5. *Book's Attributes*

Attributes
BookID
BookCategory
BookTitle

Table 3-6. *Book Sample Data*

ID	Category	Title
B001	.NET	Windows Phone Recipes
B002	.NET	Visual C# 2010 Recipes
B003	.NET	UML Applied
B004	.NET	Sharepoint 2010 Designer Guide

This information is sufficient to use in this chapter's examples. You'll add more entities and attributes as you progress through other chapters.

3-1-3. Photo Album Example

For the photo album application, album and photo entities and their attributes will be displayed and managed in the example code. The following tables contain photo album-related entities, their attributes, and the sample data. Table 3-7 contains the album attributes and Table 3-8 contains the sample data for the albums.

Table 3-7. *Album Attributes*

Attributes
AlbumID
AlbumName

Table 3-8. *Album Sample Data*

ID	Name
AL01	Animals
AL02	Birds
AL03	Sea Animals
AL04	Insects

Table 3-9 contains photo attributes and Table 3-10 contains the sample data for the photos.

Table 3-9. *Photo Attributes*

Attributes
PhotoID
AlbumID
PhotoFileName
PhotoImage

Table 3-10. *Photo Sample Data*

Photo ID	Album ID	Filename	Image	Photo ID	Album ID	Filename	Image
P001	AL01	images/cat.png		P011	AL03	images/ butterfly1.jpg	
P002	AL01	images/dog.png		P012	AL03	images/ butterfly2.jpg	

3-2. Selecting the HTML Element by its ID

Problem

You want to know how to select the HTML element by using its ID.

Solution

The following jQuery selector syntax selects the HTML element with the specified ID:

$("#*id***")**

id is the value of the HTML element's attribute "id" and the return value is a jQuery object.

For example, for <input type="button" id="btnTestIt" value="Test It">, id is btnTestIt and its selector is specified as "#btnTestIt". Listing 3-1 demonstrates the use of jQuery selector to select the HTML element by its ID.

Listing 3-1. jQuery selector to select element by id

```
<!DOCTYPE html>
<html lang="en">
   <head>
       <meta charset="utf-8">
       <script src="scripts/jquery-2.1.0.min.js"></script>

       <style>
           ol {
               width:350px;
               }
       </style>
        <script>
             $(function(){
                   $("#btnTestIt").click(function () {
                          $("#WEB-02").css("background-color", "yellow");
                   });
             });
        </script>
   </head>
   <body>
       <ol>
           <li id=".NET-01">Windows Phone Recipes</li>
           <li id=".NET-02">Visual C# 2010 Recipes</li>
           <li id=".NET-03">UML Applied</li>
           <li id=".NET-04">Sharepoint 2010 Designer Guide</li>
           <li id=".NET-05">Pro WPF in C# 2010</li>
           <li id="WEB-01">Zend Enterprise PHP Patterns</li>
           <li id="WEB-02">Web Designer's Reference</li>
           <li id="WEB-03">Practical Ajax Projects with Java</li>
           <li id="WEB-04">The Definitive Guide to HTML5 WebSocket</li>
           <li id="WEB-05">The Essential Guide to HTML5 and CSS3</li>
       </ol>
       <input id="btnTestIt" type="button" value="Test It">
   </body>
</html>
```

How It Works

In the code, book titles are listed using <ol> and <li> HTML tags. If you want to select a single node and then perform an action on it, use the "#id" selector.

After the DOM is ready (i.e., all HTML elements are created and loaded in the browser memory), the following code is executed as a result of the document-ready event handler.

```
$("#btnTestIt").click(function () {
       $("#WEB-02").css("background-color", "yellow");
});
```

This code selects the input button with id as btnTestIt and binds a function (the event handler) to its click event. When the user clicks this button, the following code is executed.

```
$("#WEB-02").css("background-color", "yellow");
```

$("#WEB-02") selects the HTML element <li id="WEB-02">Web Designer's Reference</li> and returns the jQuery object. The css() method is executed on all the HTML elements in the returned jQuery object. The first parameter of the css() method is the style's property name and the second parameter is the value that you want to use to set this property. css("background-color", "yellow") changes the background color of the selected element to yellow. css() and other DOM manipulation methods are covered in the Chapter 6. Figure 3-1 displays the page when it is viewed in a browser.

1. Windows Phone Recipes
2. Visual C# 2010 Recipes
3. UML Applied
4. Sharepoint 2010 Designer Guide
5. Pro WPF in C# 2010
6. Zend Enterprise PHP Patterns
7. Web Designer's Reference
8. Practical Ajax Projects with Java
9. The Definitive Guide to HTML5 WebSocket
10. The Essential Guide to HTML5 and CSS3

Test It

Figure 3-1. *Initial page display*

When you press the Test It button, the button's click event handler changes the background color of the selected element to yellow. Figure 3-2 displays the effect of clicking the Test It button.

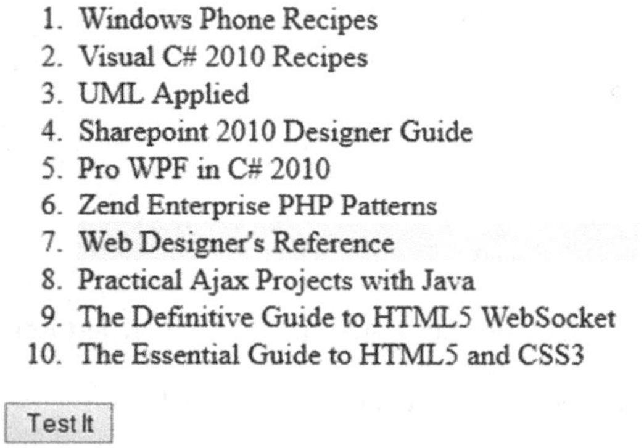

1. Windows Phone Recipes
2. Visual C# 2010 Recipes
3. UML Applied
4. Sharepoint 2010 Designer Guide
5. Pro WPF in C# 2010
6. Zend Enterprise PHP Patterns
7. Web Designer's Reference
8. Practical Ajax Projects with Java
9. The Definitive Guide to HTML5 WebSocket
10. The Essential Guide to HTML5 and CSS3

Test It

Figure 3-2. *Highlighted item when the Test It button is clicked*

3-3. Selecting All the HTML Elements on a Page

Problem

You want to know how to select all the HTML elements on a page.

Solution

The following jQuery selector syntax selects all the HTML elements on a page:

$("*")

The return value is a jQuery object. Listing 3-2 demonstrates the use of jQuery selector to select all the HTML elements on the page.

Listing 3-2. jQuery selector to select all elements

```
<!DOCTYPE html>
<html lang="en">
   <head>
      <meta charset="utf-8">
      <script src="scripts/jquery-2.1.0.min.js"></script>
      <style>
        ol {
             width:350px;
             }
      </style>
      <script>
        $(function(){
                      $("#btnTestIt").click(function () {
                           $("*").css("background-color", "yellow");
                                                                   });
                      });
      </script>
   </head>
   <body>
      <ol>
         <li id=".NET 01">Windows Phone Recipes</li>
         <li id=".NET 02">Visual C# 2010 Recipes</li>
         <li id=".NET 03">UML Applied</li>
         <li id=".NET 04">Sharepoint 2010 Designer Guide</li>
         <li id=".NET 05">Pro WPF in C# 2010</li>
         <li id="WEB 01">Zend Enterprise PHP Patterns</li>
         <li id="WEB 02">Web Designer's Reference</li>
         <li id="WEB 03">Practical Ajax Projects with Java</li>
         <li id="WEB 04">The Definitive Guide to HTML5 WebSocket</li>
         <li id="WEB 05">The Essential Guide to HTML5 and CSS3</li>
      </ol>
      <input id="btnTestIt" type="button" value="Test It">
   </body>
</html>
```

How It Works

In this code, I have listed book titles using the HTML tag `<li>` surrounded by ancestors nodes—`<ol>`, `<body>`, and `<html>`. The page also contains other nodes—`<head>`, `<script>`, and `<input>`. If you want to select all the nodes (i.e., all the HTML elements and text content), you use the "*" selector.

After the DOM is ready, the following code is executed as a result of the document-ready event:

```
$("#btnTestIt").click(function () {
   $("*").css("background-color", "yellow");
});
```

This code selects the input button with id as `btnTestIt` and binds a function (the event handler) to its click event. When the user clicks this button, the following code is executed.

```
$("*").css("background-color", "yellow");
```

`$("*")` selects all the HTML elements and text on the page and returns the jQuery object. Refer to Recipe 3-2 for the `css()` method explanation. For the initial page display, refer to Figure 3-1.

When you press the Test It button, the click event is triggered and its event handler is executed. The button's click handler changes the background color of all selected elements to yellow. Figure 3-3 displays the effect of clicking the Test It button.

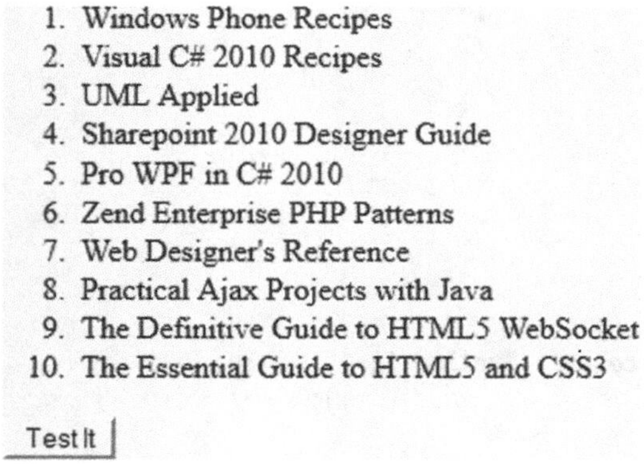

1. Windows Phone Recipes
2. Visual C# 2010 Recipes
3. UML Applied
4. Sharepoint 2010 Designer Guide
5. Pro WPF in C# 2010
6. Zend Enterprise PHP Patterns
7. Web Designer's Reference
8. Practical Ajax Projects with Java
9. The Definitive Guide to HTML5 WebSocket
10. The Essential Guide to HTML5 and CSS3

Test It

Figure 3-3. *Highlighted items when the Test It button is clicked*

3-4. Selecting an HTML Element by ID to Highlight All Child Nodes

Problem

You want to know how to change the CSS properties of all child nodes of an HTML element.

Solution

The following jQuery selector syntax selects the HTML element with the specified ID:

$("#*id*")

where `id` is the value of the HTML element's attribute ID and the return value is a jQuery object.

When the CSS property of a parent node is changed, it becomes effective for all child nodes too (unless the child node specifically overrides that property), due to the cascading nature. Listing 3-3 demonstrates the use of jQuery selector to change the CSS property of all the child nodes of a selected HTML element.

Listing 3-3. jQuery selector highlights all child nodes of the selected element

```html
<!DOCTYPE html>
<html lang="en">
    <head>
        <meta charset="utf-8">
        <script src="scripts/jquery-2.1.0.min.js"></script>
        <script>
                $(function() {
                                $("#btnSubmit").click( function() {
                        $("#listDepartments").css("background-color", "yellow");
                        });
                });
        </script>
    </head>
    <body>
        Departments:
            <ul id="listDepartments">
                <li>Marketing</li>
                <li>Sales</li>
                <li>Technology</li>
                <li>Customer Support</li>
            </ul>
            <input id="btnSubmit" type="button" value="Submit">
    </body>
</html>
```

How It Works

In the code, department names are listed. If you want to select a single node to perform an action on it and/or on its child nodes, you use "#id" selector.

After the DOM is ready, the following code is executed as a result of the document-ready event handler.

```
$("#btnSubmit").click( function() {
        $("#listDepartments").css("background-color", "yellow");
});
```

This code selects the input button with id as btnSubmit and binds a function (the event handler) to its click event. When the user clicks this button, the following code is executed.

```
$("#listDepartments").css("background-color", "yellow");
```

$("#listDepartments") selects the HTML element <ul id="listDepartments"> and returns the jQuery object. Refer to Recipe 3-2 for the css() method explanation. Since the background colors of the child nodes (<li>) are not specified, all <li> elements will inherit the background color from its parent node (<ul>). Figure 3-4 displays the page when it is viewed in a browser.

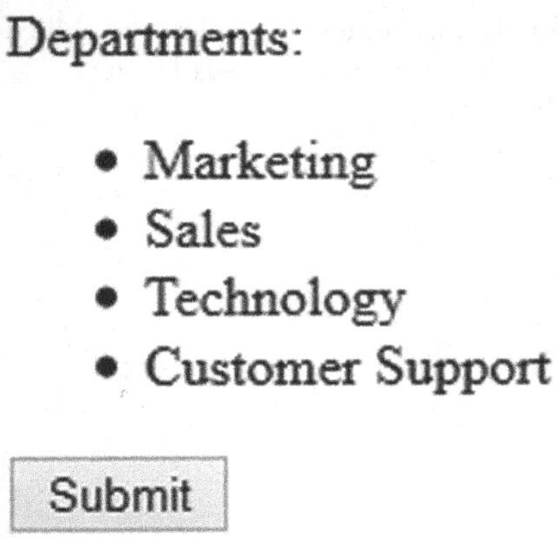

Departments:

- Marketing
- Sales
- Technology
- Customer Support

Submit

Figure 3-4. *Initial page display*

When you press the Submit button, the button's click event handler changes the background color of the selected element and its child nodes to `lightyellow`. Figure 3-5 displays the effect of clicking the Submit button.

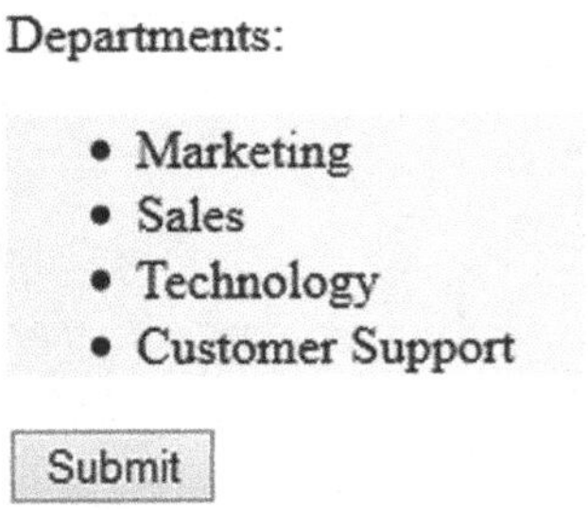

Departments:

- Marketing
- Sales
- Technology
- Customer Support

Submit

Figure 3-5. *Highlighted items when the Submit button is clicked*

3-5. Selecting HTML Elements by Tag Name
Problem
You want to know how to select all HTML elements by their HTML tag names.

Solution
The following jQuery selector syntax selects all HTML elements with the specified `htmlElementTagName`:

`$("htmlElementTagName")`

where `htmlElementTagName` is the tag name of the HTML element and the return value is a jQuery object.

For example, for <IMG SRC=" images/penguin1.png">, IMG is the tag name and its selector is specified as "IMG". Listing 3-4 demonstrates the use of jQuery selector to select an HTML element by its tag name.

Listing 3-4. jQuery selector to select all elements with the specified tag name

```html
<!DOCTYPE html>
<html lang="en">
    <head>
        <meta charset="utf-8">
        <script src="scripts/jquery-2.1.0.min.js"></script>
        <script>
                $(function() {
                            $("#btnReduceOpacity").click( function() {
                                    $("img").css("opacity", "0.3");
                            });

                            $("#btnReset").click( function() {
                                    $("img").css("opacity", "1.0");
                            });
                });
        </script>
    </head>
    <body>
        <div id="livingBeings">
            <div id="animals">
                <img src="images/Cat.png"/>
                <img src="images/Dog.png"/>
                <img src="images/Elephant.png"/>
                <img src="images/Hippopotamus.png"/>
                <img src="images/Panda.png"/>
            </div>
            <div id="birds">
                <img src="images/Bird1.png"/>
                <img src="images/Bird2.png"/>
                <img src="images/Owl.png"/>
                <img src="images/Penguin1.png"/>
                <img src="images/Penguin2.png"/>
            </div>
            <div id="insects">
                <img src="images/Butterfly1.png"/>
                <img src="images/Butterfly2.png"/>
                <img src="images/Butterfly3.png"/>
                <img src="images/Grasshopper.png"/>
                <img src="images/LadyBug.png"/>
            </div>
            <div id="seaAnimals">
                <img src="images/Fish2.png"/>
                <img src="images/Dolphin.png"/>
                <img src="images/Fish1.png"/>
```

```
            <img src="images/JellyFish.png"/>
            <img src="images/WireShark.png"/>
        </div>
    </div>
    <input id="btnReduceOpacity" type="button" value="Reduce Opacity">
    <input id="btnReset" type="button" value="Reset">
  </body>
</html>
```

How It Works

In this code, various photos are displayed using the <IMG> tag. If you want to select all images (i.e., all HTML elements with tag name as IMG), you use the "htmlElementTagName" selector.

After the DOM is ready (i.e., all HTML elements are created and loaded in the browser memory), the following code is executed as a result of the document-ready event handler.

```
$("#btnReduceOpacity").click( function() {
     $("img").css("opacity", "0.3");
 });

$("#btnReset").click( function() {
     $("img").css("opacity", "1.0");
});
```

This code selects the input button with id as btnReduceOpacity and binds a function (the event handler) to its click event. When the user clicks this button, the following code is executed.

```
$("img").css("opacity", "0.3");
```

$("img") selects all the HTML elements with the tag name <IMG> and returns the jQuery object. The css() method is executed on all the HTML elements in the returned jQuery object. Refer to Recipe 3-2 for the css() method explanation. css("opacity", "0.3") changes the opacity of all selected elements (i.e., all images) to 0.3. When the Reset button is clicked, the opacity reverts to its default value of 1.0. Opacity ranges from 0.0 (fully transparent) to 1.0 (full opaque). Figure 3-6 displays the page when it is viewed in a browser.

Figure 3-6. *Initial page display with images opacity set to 1.0*

When you press the Reduce Opacity button, the button's click event handler changes the opacity of all selected elements to 0.3. Figure 3-7 displays the effect of clicking the Reduce Opacity button.

Reduce Opacity   Reset

Figure 3-7. *Reduced opacity when the Reduce Opacity button is clicked*

3-6. Selecting HTML Elements by Tag Name to Highlight a Focused Field

Problem

You want to know how to highlight a focused field by using the tagName selector.

Solution

The following jQuery selector syntax selects all the HTML elements with the specified htmlElementTagName:

$("*htmlElementTagName***")**

where htmlElementTagName is the tag name of the HTML element and the return value is a jQuery object. Listing 3-5 demonstrates the use of the jQuery tagName selector to highlight a field that's in focus.

Listing 3-5. Using the jQuery tagName selector to highlight a focused field

```
<!DOCTYPE html>
<html lang="en">
   <head>
      <meta charset="utf-8">
      <script src="scripts/jquery-2.1.0.min.js"></script>
      <style>
         label {
                   float:left;
                   display:block;
                   width: 75px;
                   font-weight: bold;
                 }
      </style>
      <script>
            $(function () {
                    $("input").focus(function () {
                            $(this).css("background-color", "yellow");
                    });

                    $("input").blur(function () {
                            $(this).css("background-color", "white");
                    });
            });
      </script>
   </head>
   <body>
      <label>Name:</label> <input id="txtName" type="text" size="30"><br>
      <label>Address:</label> <input id="txtAddress" type="text" size="50"><br>
      <label>City:</label> <input id="txtCity" type="text" size="35"><br>
      <label>State:</label> <input id="txtState" type="text" size="2"><br>
      <label>Zip Code:</label> <input id="txtZipCode" type="text" size="5"><br>
   </body>
</html>
```

How It Works

In this code, a typical form is created to accept data entry from the user. If you want to highlight the current data-entry field when the user moves from field to field, you can use the htmlElementTagName selector.

After the DOM is ready (i.e., all HTML elements are created and loaded in the browser memory), the following code is executed as a result of the document-ready event handler.

```
$("input").focus(function () {
        $(this).css("background-color", "yellow");
});

$("input").blur(function () {
        $(this).css("background-color", "white");
});
```

This code selects all HTML elements with tag name "input" and binds event handlers to the focus and blur events. The first event handler, which is attached to the focus event, is triggered when an input HTML element gets the focus. The second event handler, which is attached to the blur event, is triggered when it loses the focus.

On the input focus event, the following code is executed.

```
$(this).css("background-color", "yellow");
```

$(this) selects the HTML element that triggered the event and returns the jQuery object. The css() method is executed on all the HTML elements in the returned jQuery object. Refer to Recipe 3-2 for the css() method explanation.

On the input blur event, the following code is executed.

```
$(this).css("background-color", "white");
```

This reverts the background color to the default value of "white". Figure 3-8 displays the page when it is viewed in a browser.

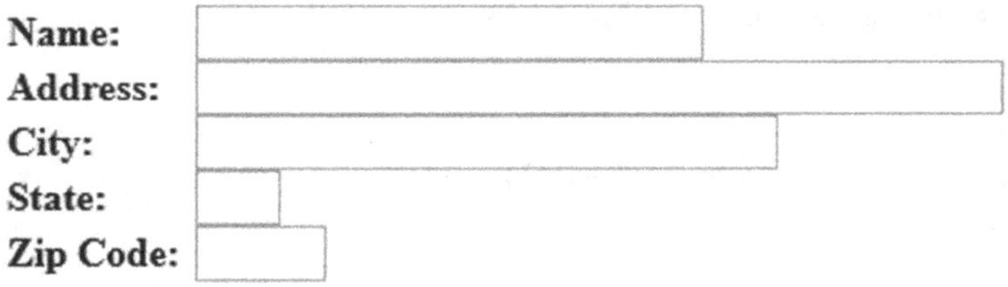

Figure 3-8. *Initial page display*

When the user tabs through the data-entry fields, the currently focused field is highlighted. Figure 3-9 displays a highlighted field that has the focus.

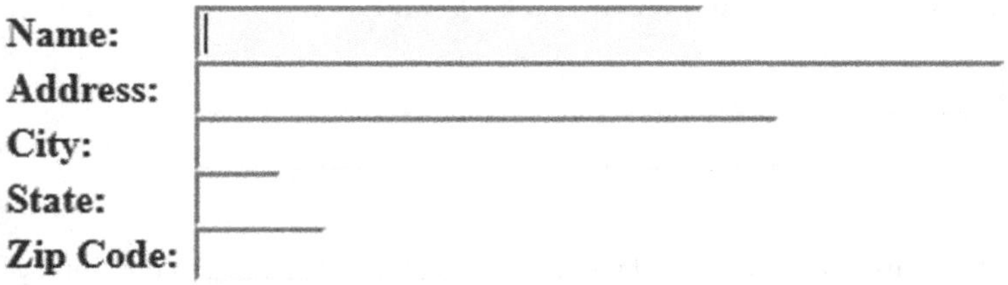

Figure 3-9. *Highlighted input field when it has the focus*

3-7. Selecting HTML Elements by Class Name
Problem

You want to select all the HTML elements that match a specified class name.

Solution

The following jQuery selector syntax selects all the HTML elements with the specified className:

$(".className**")**

where className is one of the CSS class names of the HTML element and the return value is a jQuery object. For example, for `<input type="text" id="txtName" class="dataEntry mandatoryField">`, dataEntry and mandatoryField are CSS classes of this input form field. Listing 3-6 demonstrates the use of jQuery selector to select all the HTML elements that match the specified class name.

Listing 3-6. jQuery selector selects all the HTML elements that match the specified class name

```
<!DOCTYPE html>
<html lang="en">
    <head>
        <meta charset="utf-8">
        <script src="scripts/jquery-2.1.0.min.js"></script>
        <style>
            .headerRow {
                            font-family: Verdana;
                            font-weight: bold
                        }

            .evenRow {
                            font-family: Verdana;
                            font-style: normal;
                        }

            .oddRow {
                            font-family: Verdana;
                            font-style: italic
                        }
        </style>
        <script>
            $(function() {
                    $("#btnTestIt").click(function () {
                            $(".evenRow").css("background-color", "lightyellow");
                            $(".oddRow").css("background-color", "lightblue");
                    });
            });
        </script>
    </head>
    <body>
        <table style="border:0px" id="tblEmployee">
            <tr class="headerRow">
                <td>Employee Name</td><td>Department</td><td>Salary</td>
            </tr>
            <tr class="oddRow">
                <td>Jane Smith</td><td>Marketing</td><td>$95,000</td>
            </tr>
            <tr class="evenRow">
                <td>John Smith</td><td>Technology</td><td>$90,000</td>
            </tr>
```

```
        <tr class="oddRow">
            <td>Brian Adam</td><td>Sales</td><td>$72,000</td>
        </tr>
        <tr class="evenRow">
            <td>Mary Jones</td><td>Support</td><td>$60,000</td>
        </tr>
        <tr class="oddRow">
            <td>Michael Jefferson</td><td>Technology</td><td>$85,000</td>
        </tr>
    </table>
    <input id="btnTestIt" type="button" value="Test It">
  </body>
</html>
```

How It Works

In this code, the employees' details—employee name, department, and salary—are listed in a tabular format. If you want to select all the HTML elements with a specific class name, use the `.className` selector.

After the DOM is ready (i.e., all HTML elements are created and loaded in the browser memory), the following code is executed as a result of the document-ready event handler.

```
$("#btnTestIt").click(function () {
    $(".evenRow").css("background-color", "lightyellow");
    $(".oddRow").css("background-color", "lightblue");
});
```

This code selects the input button with id as btnTestIt and binds a function (the event handler) to its click event. When the user clicks this button, the following code is executed.

```
$(".evenRow").css("background-color", "lightyellow");
$(".oddRow").css("background-color", "lightblue");
```

`$(".evenRow")` selects all the HTML elements with class evenRow and returns the jQuery object. The `css()` method is executed on all the HTML elements in the returned jQuery object. Refer to Recipe 3-2 for the `css()` method explanation. Similarly, for all HTML elements with the class name as oddRow, the `background-color` is changed to lightblue. Figure 3-10 displays the page when it is viewed in a browser.

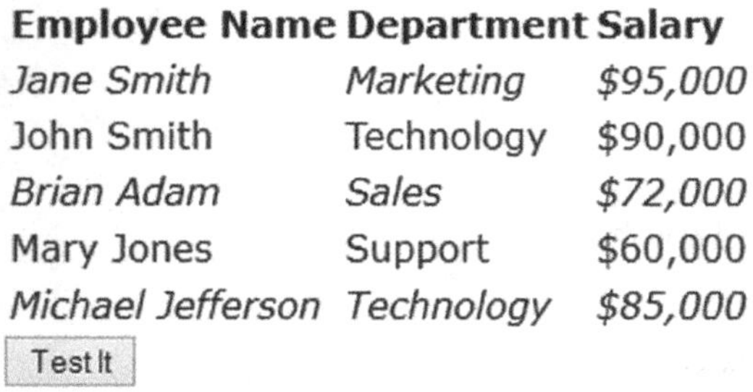

Employee Name	Department	Salary
Jane Smith	Marketing	$95,000
John Smith	Technology	$90,000
Brian Adam	Sales	$72,000
Mary Jones	Support	$60,000
Michael Jefferson	Technology	$85,000

Test It

Figure 3-10. *Initial page display*

When you press the Test It button, the button's click event handler changes the background color of the selected elements. Elements with an evenRow class name change to lightyellow and the elements with the class oddRow change to lightblue. Figure 3-11 displays the effect of clicking the Test It button.

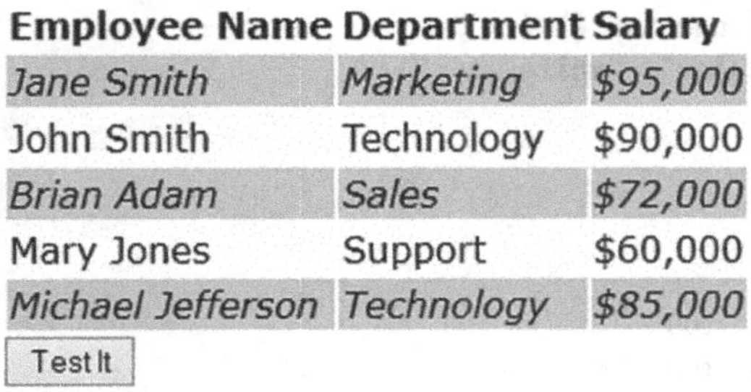

Employee Name	Department	Salary
Jane Smith	Marketing	$95,000
John Smith	Technology	$90,000
Brian Adam	Sales	$72,000
Mary Jones	Support	$60,000
Michael Jefferson	Technology	$85,000

Test It

Figure 3-11. *Even and odd numbered rows are highlighted with different background colors*

3-8. Selecting HTML Elements that Match Any of the Specified Multiple Selectors

Problem

You want to know how to get a single set of selected elements using multiple selection criteria (selectors).

Solution

The following jQuery selector syntax selects the HTML element with the specified ID:

```
$("selector1, selector2, ...")
```

The return value is a jQuery object. Listing 3-7 demonstrates the use of multiple jQuery selectors to get a combined set of selected elements matching any of the specified selectors.

Listing 3-7. Selecting elements that match any of the specified selectors

```
<!DOCTYPE html>
<html lang="en">
   <head>
      <meta charset="utf-8">
      <script src="scripts/jquery-2.1.0.min.js"></script>
      <style>
         label {
                  float:left;
                  display:block;
                  width: 100px;
                  font-weight: bold;
                }
      </style>
      <script>
```

```
        $(function () {
                $("input, select, textarea" ).focus(function () {
                        $(this).css("background-color", "yellow");
                });

                $("input, select, textarea").blur(function () {
                        $(this).css("background-color", "white");
                });
        });
    </script>
  </head>
  <body>
    <label>Name:</label> <input id="txtName" type="text"><br>
    <label>Address:</label> <input id="txtAddress" type="text"><br>
    <label>State:</label>
        <select><option>IL</option><option>NY</option></select><br>
    <label>Comments:</label><textarea></textarea><br><br>
  </body>
</html>
```

How It Works

In this code, the form data-entry screen is created so users can enter their names, addresses, state, and any comments. These form elements use the following HTML tags—input, select, and textarea. If you want to perform the same action on elements with these different HTML tags, you use the multiple selector syntax.

After the DOM is ready (i.e., all HTML elements are created and loaded in the browser memory), the following code is executed as a result of the document-ready event handler.

```
$("input, select, textarea" ).focus(function () {
    $(this).css("background-color", "yellow");
});

$("input, select, textarea").blur(function () {
    $(this).css("background-color", "white");
});
```

This code selects all HTML elements with tag name of input, select, or textarea and binds two event handlers to them—the first one is triggered when a selected HTML element gets the focus and the second event handler is triggered when it loses the focus.

On the input focus event, the following code is executed.

```
$(this).css("background-color", "yellow");
```

$(this) selects the HTML element that triggered the event and returns the jQuery object. The css() method is executed on all the HTML elements in the returned jQuery object. Refer to Recipe 3-2 for the css() method explanation.

On the selected element's blur event, the following code is executed.

```
$(this).css("background-color", "white");
```

This reverts background-color to the default value of "white". Figure 3-12 displays the page when it is viewed in a browser.

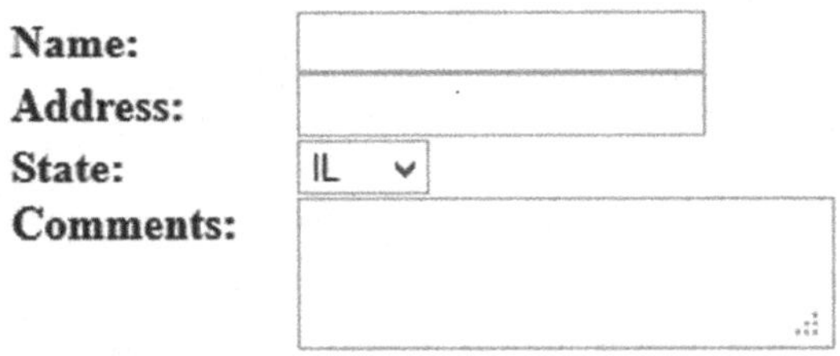

Figure 3-12. *Initial page display*

When the user tabs through data-entry fields, the currently focused field is highlighted. Figure 3-13 displays the highlighted field when the Comments data-entry field has the focus.

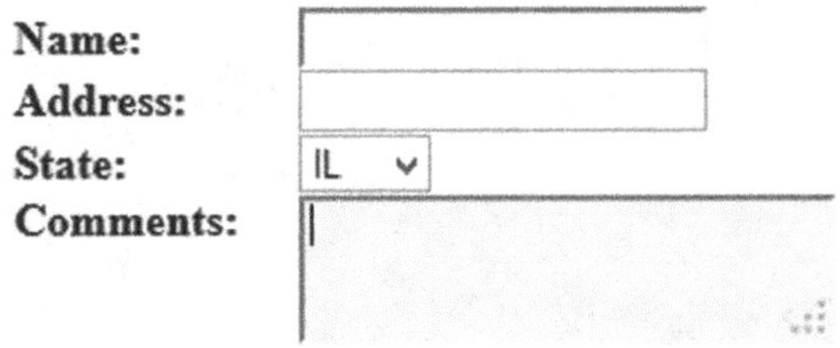

Figure 3-13. *Highlighted input, select, or textarea field when it gets focus*

3-9. Selecting HTML Elements with an Attribute's Value Starting with a Specified Value Followed by a Hyphen

Problem

You want to perform some action on a group of HTML elements for which one of the attributes has the same value or has a value that starts with same specified value followed by hyphen (-).

Solution

The following jQuery selector syntax selects the HTML element with the prefix of the attributeName's value that matches the specified attributeValue:

$("[*attributeName*** |= '***attributeValue***']")**

For example, for <input id="txtName-First" type="text">, the attribute name is id, the prefix of the attribute value is textName, and its selector can be specified as "[id |= 'txtName']". Listing 3-8 demonstrates the use of a jQuery attribute selector that matches the prefix of the attribute value with the specified value in the selector.

Listing 3-8. Attribute value contains the specified selector as a prefix

```html
<!DOCTYPE html>
<html lang="en">
    <head>
        <meta charset="utf-8">
        <script src="scripts/jquery-2.1.0.min.js"></script>
        <style>
            ol {
                width:350px;
                }
        </style>
        <script>
                $(function(){
                        $("#btnTestIt").click(function () {
                            $("[id |= 'WEB']").css("background-color", "yellow");
                        });
                });
        </script>
    </head>
    <body>
        <ol>
            <li id=".NET-01">Windows Phone Recipes</li>
            <li id=".NET-02">Visual C# 2010 Recipes</li>
            <li id=".NET-03">UML Applied</li>
            <li id=".NET-04">Sharepoint 2010 Designer Guide</li>
            <li id=".NET-05">Pro WPF in C# 2010</li>
            <li id="WEB-01">Zend Enterprise PHP Patterns</li>
            <li id="WEB-02">Web Designer's Reference</li>
            <li id="WEB-03">Practical Ajax Projects with Java</li>
            <li id="WEB-04">The Definitive Guide to HTML5 WebSocket</li>
            <li id="WEB-05">The Essential Guide to HTML5 and CSS3</li>
        </ol>
        <input id="btnTestIt" type="button" value="Test It">
    </body>
</html>
```

How It Works

In this code, book titles are listed under two categories—.NET and WEB—and the category is specified as a prefix of the value of the id attribute. If you want to select all the book titles with the same category, you use "[attributeName |= 'attributeValue']" selector.

After the DOM is ready (i.e., all HTML elements are created and loaded in the browser memory), the following code is executed as a result of the document-ready event handler.

```javascript
$("#btnTestIt").click(function () {
    $("[id |= 'WEB']").css("background-color", "yellow");
});
```

This code selects the input button with `id` as `btnTestIt` and binds a function (the event handler) to its click event. When the user clicks this button, the following code is executed.

```
$("[id |= 'WEB']").css("background-color", "yellow");
```

`$("[id |= 'WEB']")` selects all the HTML elements that have an attribute `id` that matches `WEB` or that start with `WEB` followed by a hyphen (`-`). It then returns the jQuery object. The `css()` method is executed on all the HTML elements in the returned jQuery object. Refer to Recipe 3-2 for the `css()` method explanation. For the initial page display, refer to Figure 3-1.

When you press the Test It button, the button's click event handler changes the background color of all the selected elements to yellow. Figure 3-14 displays the effect of clicking the Test It button.

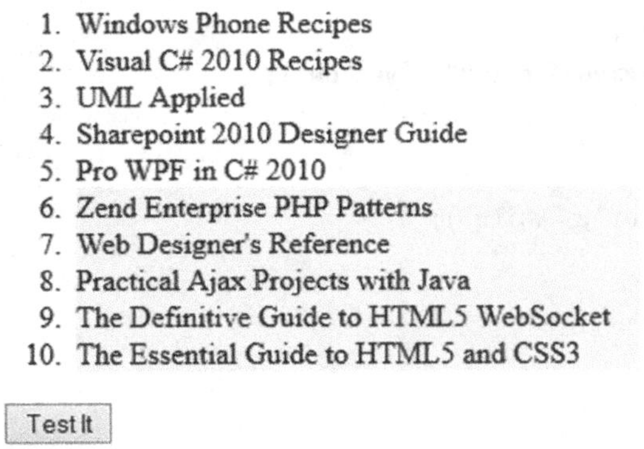

1. Windows Phone Recipes
2. Visual C# 2010 Recipes
3. UML Applied
4. Sharepoint 2010 Designer Guide
5. Pro WPF in C# 2010
6. Zend Enterprise PHP Patterns
7. Web Designer's Reference
8. Practical Ajax Projects with Java
9. The Definitive Guide to HTML5 WebSocket
10. The Essential Guide to HTML5 and CSS3

Test It

Figure 3-14. *Highlighted items when the Test It button is clicked*

3-10. Selecting HTML Elements with the Attribute's Value Containing a Specified Value as a Word (Separated by Spaces)

Problem

You want to perform some action on a group of HTML elements for which a word (delimited by space) in the attribute value matches the value specified in the selector.

Solution

The following jQuery selector syntax selects the HTML element having a word in its `attributeName`'s value that matches the specified `attributeValue`:

$("[*attributeName*** ~= '***attributeValue***']")**

For example, for `<input id="First Name" type="text">`, the attribute name is id, the words in the attribute value are `First` and `Name`, and its selector can be specified as `"[ id ~= 'First' ]"` or `"[ id ~= 'Name' ]"`. Listing 3-9 demonstrates the use of jQuery attribute selector that matches a word of the attribute value with the specified value in the selector.

Listing 3-9. Attribute value contains specified selector as a word

```html
<!DOCTYPE html>
<html lang="en">
    <head>
        <meta charset="utf-8">
        <script src="scripts/jquery-2.1.0.min.js"></script>
        <style>
            ol {
                width:350px;
            }
        </style>
        <script>
            $(function(){
                $("#btnTestIt").click(function () {
                    $("[id ~= '01']").css("background-color", "yellow");
                });

                $("#btnReset").click(function () {
                    $("li").css("background-color", "white");
                });
            });
        </script>
    </head>
    <body>
        <ol>
            <li id=".NET 01">Windows Phone Recipes</li>
            <li id=".NET 02">Visual C# 2010 Recipes</li>
            <li id=".NET 03">UML Applied</li>
            <li id=".NET 04">Sharepoint 2010 Designer Guide</li>
            <li id=".NET 05">Pro WPF in C# 2010</li>
            <li id="WEB 01">Zend Enterprise PHP Patterns</li>
            <li id="WEB 02">Web Designer's Reference</li>
            <li id="WEB 03">Practical Ajax Projects with Java</li>
            <li id="WEB 04">The Definitive Guide to HTML5 WebSocket</li>
            <li id="WEB 05">The Essential Guide to HTML5 and CSS3</li>
        </ol>
        <input id="btnTestIt" type="button" value="Test It">
        <input id="btnReset" type="reset" value="Reset">
    </body>
</html>
```

How It Works

In this code, the book titles are listed under two categories—.NET and WEB—and the category is specified as prefix of the value of the id attribute. Likewise, the book's item number is specified with the following numeric value. If you want to select the first book title from each category (.NET or WEB), use the "[attributeName ~= 'attributeValue']" selector.

After the DOM is ready (i.e., all HTML elements are created and loaded in the browser memory), the following code is executed as a result of the document-ready event handler.

```
$("#btnTestIt").click(function () {
    $("[id ~= '01']").css("background-color", "yellow");
});
```

This code selects the input button with id as btnTestIt and binds a function (the event handler) to its click event. When the user clicks this button, the following code is executed.

```
$("[id ~= '01']").css("background-color", "yellow");
```

$("[id ~= '01']") selects all the HTML elements with a value in the attribute id of 01 and returns the jQuery object. The css() method is executed on all the HTML elements in the returned jQuery object. Refer to Recipe 3-2 for the css() method explanation. For the initial page display, refer to Figure 3-1.

When you press the Test It button, the button's click event handler changes the background color of all the selected elements to yellow. Figure 3-15 displays the effect of clicking the Test It button.

1. Windows Phone Recipes
2. Visual C# 2010 Recipes
3. UML Applied
4. Sharepoint 2010 Designer Guide
5. Pro WPF in C# 2010
6. Zend Enterprise PHP Patterns
7. Web Designer's Reference
8. Practical Ajax Projects with Java
9. The Definitive Guide to HTML5 WebSocket
10. The Essential Guide to HTML5 and CSS3

Figure 3-15. *Highlighted items when the Test It button is clicked*

3-11. Selecting HTML Elements that Have a Specified Attribute Regardless of its Value

Problem

You want to perform some action on a group of HTML elements with the same attribute name regardless of the attribute's value.

Solution

The following jQuery selector syntax selects the HTML element with the specified attributeName:

$("[*attributeName*]")

where attributeName is the attribute name of the HTML element and the return value is a jQuery object. For example, for <input id="First Name" type="text">, the attribute names are id and type and its selector can be specified as [id] or [type]. Listing 3-10 demonstrates the use of the jQuery selector to select the HTML element by its attribute name.

Listing 3-10. Selector to select all elements with the specified attribute name

```html
<!DOCTYPE html>
<html lang="en">
    <head>
        <meta charset="utf-8">
        <script src="scripts/jquery-2.1.0.min.js"></script>
        <style>
            ol {
                width:350px;
                }
        </style>
        <script>
                $(function(){
                        $("#btnTestIt").click(function () {
                                $("[href]").css("background-color", "yellow");
                            });
                    });
        </script>
    </head>
    <body>
        <ol>
            <li id=".NET 01"><a href="Ch03-Listing 3-11-Windows Phone Recipes.htm">
                                    Windows Phone Recipes</a></li>
            <li id=".NET 02">Visual C# 2010 Recipes</li>
            <li id=".NET 03">UML Applied</li>
            <li id=".NET 04">Sharepoint 2010 Designer Guide</li>
            <li id=".NET 05">Pro WPF in C# 2010</li>
            <li id="WEB 01">Zend Enterprise PHP Patterns</li>
            <li id="WEB 02">Web Designer's Reference</li>
            <li id="WEB 03">Practical Ajax Projects with Java</li>
            <li id="WEB 04">The Definitive Guide to HTML5 WebSocket</li>
            <li id="WEB 05">The Essential Guide to HTML5 and CSS3</li>
        </ol>
        <input id="btnTestIt" type="button" value="Test It">
    </body>
</html>
```

How It Works

In this code, the book titles are listed with the hyperlink on the first book title. If you want to select all the items that have an <a> tag and a hyperlink attribute with them, use the "[attributeName]" selector.

After the DOM is ready (i.e., all HTML elements are created and loaded in the browser memory), the following code is executed as a result of the document-ready event handler.

```javascript
$("#btnTestIt").click(function () {
    $("[href]").css("background-color", "yellow");
});
```

This code selects the input button with id as btnTestIt and binds a function (the event handler) to its click event. When a user clicks this button, the following code is executed.

```
$("[href]").css("background-color", "yellow");
```

$("[href]") selects the HTML element `<a href="Chapter03-Listing3.11-windowsPhoneRecipes.htm">` and returns the jQuery object. The css() method is executed on the HTML element in the returned jQuery object. Refer to Recipe 3-2 for the css() method explanation. Figure 3-16 displays the page when it is viewed in a browser.

1. Windows Phone Recipes
2. Visual C# 2010 Recipes
3. UML Applied
4. Sharepoint 2010 Designer Guide
5. Pro WPF in C# 2010
6. Zend Enterprise PHP Patterns
7. Web Designer's Reference
8. Practical Ajax Projects with Java
9. The Definitive Guide to HTML5 WebSocket
10. The Essential Guide to HTML5 and CSS3

Test It

Figure 3-16. *Initial page display*

When you press the Test It button, the button's click event handler changes the background color of the selected element to yellow. Figure 3-17 displays the effect of clicking the Test It button.

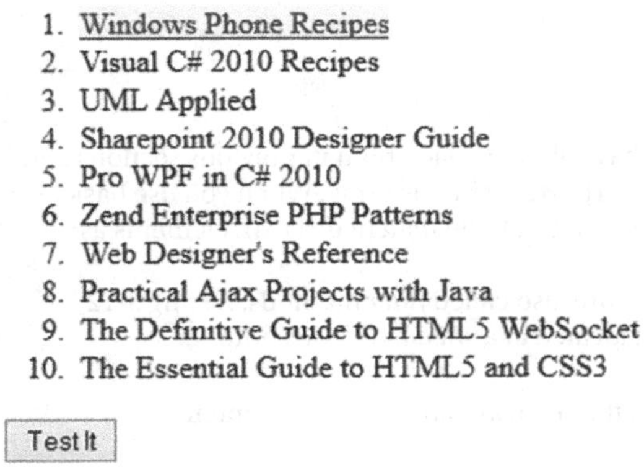

1. Windows Phone Recipes
2. Visual C# 2010 Recipes
3. UML Applied
4. Sharepoint 2010 Designer Guide
5. Pro WPF in C# 2010
6. Zend Enterprise PHP Patterns
7. Web Designer's Reference
8. Practical Ajax Projects with Java
9. The Definitive Guide to HTML5 WebSocket
10. The Essential Guide to HTML5 and CSS3

Test It

Figure 3-17. *Highlighted item when the Test It button is clicked*

Listing 3-11 provides the code for the HTML file that is displayed when the "Windows Phone Recipes" link is clicked.

Listing 3-11. Contents of the file Ch03-Listing 3-11-Windows Phone Recipes.htm

```
<!DOCTYPE html>
<html lang="en">
  <head>
    <meta charset="utf-8">
  </head>
  <body>
```

71

```
            <strong>Category:</strong>.NET<br>
            <strong>Book ID:</strong> B001<br>
            <strong>Title:</strong>Windows Phone Recipes<br>
        </body>
</html>
```

Figure 3-18 displays the page when the book title/hyperlink "Windows Phone Recipes" is clicked.

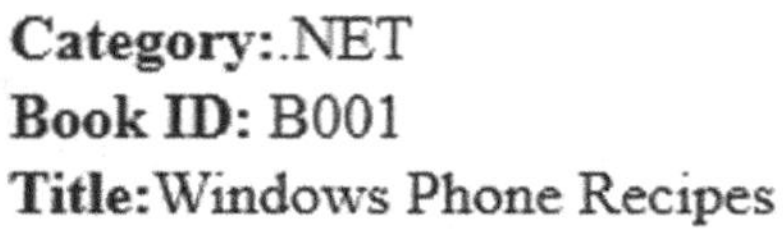

Category:.NET
Book ID: B001
Title: Windows Phone Recipes

Figure 3-18. *Displays the book's details*

3-12. Selecting the nth Item from the Selected HTML Elements
Problem
You want to select a particular HTML element from an already selected set of HTML elements.

Solution
The following jQuery selector syntax selects an HTML element at a specific index number from the set of already selected (matched) HTML elements.

$(selector**).eq(**indexNumber**)**

where `selector` is any of the basic selector types, most of which you have already read about in previous sections and `indexNumber` is the zero-based index number of the desired item in the HTML elements array. When you use basic selector types, it returns a jQuery object. The returned jQuery object contains all the matched HTML elements as an array.

Such methods, which narrow down the selected HTML elements, are also called *filter* methods. Listing 3-12 demonstrates the use of the eq() method to select an HTML element located at a specified index number.

Listing 3-12. Using the eq() method to select a specific element from the set of already selected elements

```
<!DOCTYPE html>
<html lang="en">
    <head>
        <meta charset="utf-8">
        <script src="scripts/jquery-2.1.0.min.js"></script>
        <style>
            h4 {
                    color:green;
                    text-decoration: underline;
            }
            table {
                    border:3px double green;
            }
```

```
        .listDepartments {
                                    width: 300px;
                                    border: 3px double green;
                                    background-color: lightyellow;

        }
    </style>
    <script>
            $(function(){
                    $("#btnTestIt").click(function () {
                                    $("tr").eq(0).css("background-color", "lightgray");
                    });
            });
    </script>
</head>
<body>
    <table id="tblEmployee">
        <tr>
            <td>Employee Name</td><td>Department Name</td><td>Salary</td>
        </tr>
        <tr>
            <td>Jane Smith</td><td>Marketing</td><td>$95,000</td>
        </tr>
        <tr>
            <td>John Smith</td><td>Technology</td><td>$90,000</td>
        </tr>
        <tr>
            <td>Brian Adam</td><td>Sales</td><td>$72,000</td>
        </tr>
        <tr>
            <td>Mary Jones</td><td>Support</td><td>$60,000</td>
        </tr>
        <tr>
            <td>Michael Jefferson</td><td>Technology</td><td>$85,000</td>
        </tr>
    </table><br>
    <input id="btnTestIt" type="button" value="Test It">
</body>
</html>
```

How It Works

In this code, the employee details—employee name, department name, and salary—are listed in a tabular form using the <table>, <tr>, and <td> HTML tags. If you want to select the first record and perform an action on it, you must first select all the records using $("tr") and use the eq(0) method to select the first record out of these selected records.

After the DOM is ready (i.e., all HTML elements are created and loaded in the browser memory), the following code is executed as a result of the document-ready event handler.

```
$("#btnTestIt").click(function () {
   $("tr").eq(0).css("background-color", "lightgray");
});
```

This code selects the input button with id as btnTestIt and binds a function (the event handler) to its click event. When a user clicks this button, the following code is executed.

```
$("tr").eq(0).css("background-color", "lightgray");
```

The above code statement can also be written as

```
$("tr:eq(0)").css("background-color", "lightgray");
```

or as

```
$("tr:first").css("background-color", "lightgray");
```

$("tr") selects all the HTML elements with tag name "tr" and returns the jQuery object. .eq(0) selects the HTML element at the index number 0 out of these selected HTML elements in the returned jQuery object and returns another jQuery object. The css() method is executed on the selected HTML element in the returned jQuery object. css("background-color", "lightgray") changes the background color of the selected element to light gray. Figure 3-19 displays the page when it is viewed in a browser.

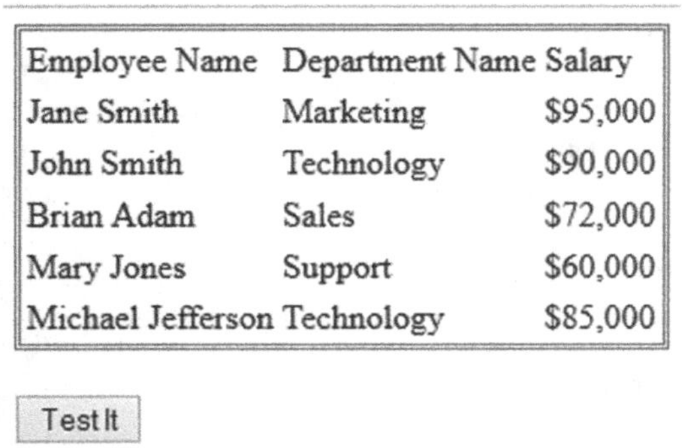

Employee Name	Department Name	Salary
Jane Smith	Marketing	$95,000
John Smith	Technology	$90,000
Brian Adam	Sales	$72,000
Mary Jones	Support	$60,000
Michael Jefferson	Technology	$85,000

Test It

Figure 3-19. *Initial page display*

When you press the Test It button, the button's click event handler changes the background color of the selected element to yellow. Figure 3-20 displays the effect of clicking the Test It button.

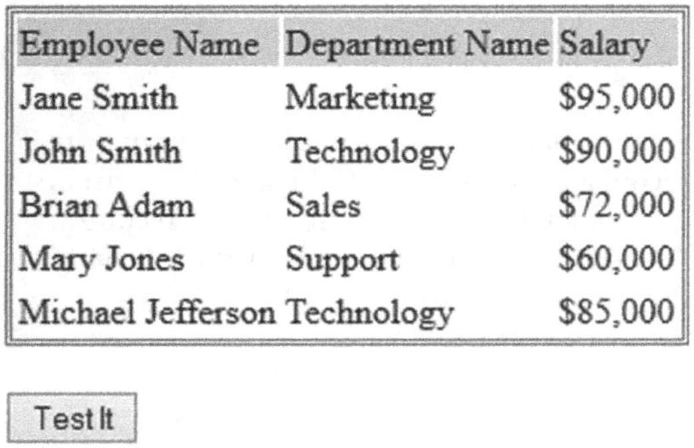

Employee Name	Department Name	Salary
Jane Smith	Marketing	$95,000
John Smith	Technology	$90,000
Brian Adam	Sales	$72,000
Mary Jones	Support	$60,000
Michael Jefferson	Technology	$85,000

Test It

Figure 3-20. *Table header with a light gray background*

3-13. Selecting Even and Odd Numbered Items from the Matched HTML Elements

Problem

You want to select even or odd numbered HTML elements from the matched set of HTML elements.

Solution

The following jQuery selector syntax selects even or odd numbered HTML elements from the set of already selected (matched) HTML elements.

$(selector**:even)**
$(selector**:odd)**

where selector is any of the basic selector types. You can use selector extensions like :even and :odd to narrow down the matched HTML elements. Listing 3-13 demonstrates the use of the :even and :odd selector extensions to select the HTML element located at the even and odd numbered locations, respectively. In the array of HTML elements, location number is zero-based.

Listing 3-13. Selects even and odd numbered elements

```
<!DOCTYPE html>
<html lang="en">
    <head>
        <meta charset="utf-8">
        <script src="scripts/jquery-2.1.0.min.js"></script>
        <style>
          .headerRow {
                            font-family: Verdana;
                            font-weight: bold;
                            background-color: lightgray;
                    }
            .row {
                  font-family: Verdana;
                  font-style: normal;
                  }
        </style>
        <script>
              $(function() {
                    $(".row:even").css("background-color", "lightblue");
                    $(".row:odd").css("background-color", "lightyellow");
              });
        </script>
    </head>
    <body>
        <table style="border:0px" id="tblEmployee">
            <tr class="headerRow">
                <td>Employee Name</td><td>Department</td><td>Salary</td>
            </tr>
            <tr class="row">
```

```
            <td>Jane Smith</td><td>Marketing</td><td>$95,000</td>
        </tr>
        <tr class="row">
            <td>John Smith</td><td>Technology</td><td>$90,000</td>
        </tr>
        <tr class="row">
            <td>Brian Adam</td><td>Sales</td><td>$72,000</td>
        </tr>
        <tr class="row">
            <td>Mary Jones</td><td>Support</td><td>$60,000</td>
        </tr>
        <tr class="row">
            <td>Michael Jefferson</td><td>Technology</td><td>$85,000</td>
        </tr>
    </table>
  </body>
</html>
```

How It Works

In this code, the employee details—Employee Name, Department Name, and Salary—are listed in a tabular form using the `<table>`, `<tr>`, and `<td>` HTML tags. Other than the first record (the header record), all the other records (`<tr>`) have the **"row"** CSS class. If you want to select the even numbered or odd numbered rows, excluding the header record, you first select all the records using $(".row") selector and then use the :even and :odd extensions to select the even and odd numbered elements from these matched records.

After the DOM is ready (i.e., all HTML elements are created and loaded in the browser memory), the following code is executed as a result of the document-ready event handler.

```
$(".row:even").css("background-color", "lightblue");
$(".row:odd").css("background-color", "lightyellow");
```

$(".row") selects all the HTML elements with the class name **"row"** and then $(".row:even") narrows down the matched elements to select only the even numbered elements and returns a jQuery object. The css() method is executed on the selected HTML element in the returned jQuery object. css("background-color", "lightblue") changes the background color of the selected elements (the even numbered ones) to light blue. Similarly, the odd numbered selected elements' background color changes to light yellow. Figure 3-21 displays the page when it is viewed in a browser.

Employee Name	Department	Salary
Jane Smith	Marketing	$95,000
John Smith	Technology	$90,000
Brian Adam	Sales	$72,000
Mary Jones	Support	$60,000
Michael Jefferson	Technology	$85,000

Figure 3-21. *Even and odd numbered elements with different background colors*

3-14. Selecting All Elements up to nth Element from the Matched HTML Elements

Problem

You want to select all the elements up to the *n*th element from the matched set of HTML elements.

Solution

The following jQuery selector syntax selects all HTML elements up to *n*th element from the set of already selected (matched) HTML elements.

$(selector**:lt(**indexNumber**))**

where selector is any of the basic selector types. You can use selector extensions like :lt and :gt to narrow down the matched HTML elements. Listing 3-14 demonstrates the use of the :lt selector extension to select HTML elements located at the location less than the specified index number. In the array of HTML elements, location number is zero-based.

Listing 3-14. Selects elements with an index number that's less than the specified index number

```
<!DOCTYPE html>
<html lang="en">
    <head>
        <meta charset="utf-8">
        <script src="scripts/jquery-2.1.0.min.js"></script>
        <style>
          ol {
                width:350px;
              }
        </style>
        <script>
                $(function(){
                        $("#btnTestIt").click(function () {
                                        $("li:lt(5)").css("background-color", "yellow");
                        });
                });
        </script>
    </head>
    <body>
        <ol>
            <li id=".NET 01">Windows Phone Recipes</li>
            <li id=".NET 02">Visual C# 2010 Recipes</li>
            <li id=".NET 03">UML Applied</li>
            <li id=".NET 04">Sharepoint 2010 Designer Guide</li>
            <li id=".NET 05">Pro WPF in C# 2010</li>
            <li id="WEB 01">Zend Enterprise PHP Patterns</li>
            <li id="WEB 02">Web Designer's Reference</li>
            <li id="WEB 03">Practical Ajax Projects with Java</li>
            <li id="WEB 04">The Definitive Guide to HTML5 WebSocket</li>
            <li id="WEB 05">The Essential Guide to HTML5 and CSS3</li>
```

```
    </ol>
    <input id="btnTestIt" type="button" value="Test It">
  </body>
</html>
```

How It Works

In this code, the book titles are listed using the <ol> and <li> HTML tags. if you want to select all the book titles that have an index number that's less than 5, you first select all the records using the $("li") tagName selector and then use the :lt(5) extension to select the elements with an index number that's less than 5 from the matched records. If you want to select elements greater than a specific index number, you can use the :gt(indexNumber) selector extension.

After the DOM is ready (i.e., all HTML elements are created and loaded in the browser memory), the following code is executed as a result of the document-ready event handler.

```
$("#btnTestIt").click(function () {
    $("li:lt(5)").css("background-color", "yellow");
});
```

This code selects the input button with id as btnTestIt and binds a function (the event handler) to its click event. When the user clicks this button, the following code is executed.

```
$("li:lt(5)").css("background-color", "yellow");
```

$("li") selects all the HTML elements with the tag name "li", and then $("li:lt(5)") narrows down the matched elements to select only those elements with an index number less than 5 and returns a jQuery object. The css() method is executed on all of the selected HTML elements in the returned jQuery object. css("background-color", "yellow") changes the background color of the selected elements to yellow. For the initial page display, refer to Figure 3-1.

When you press the Test It button, the button's click event handler changes the background color of the selected element to yellow. Figure 3-22 displays the effect of clicking the Test It button.

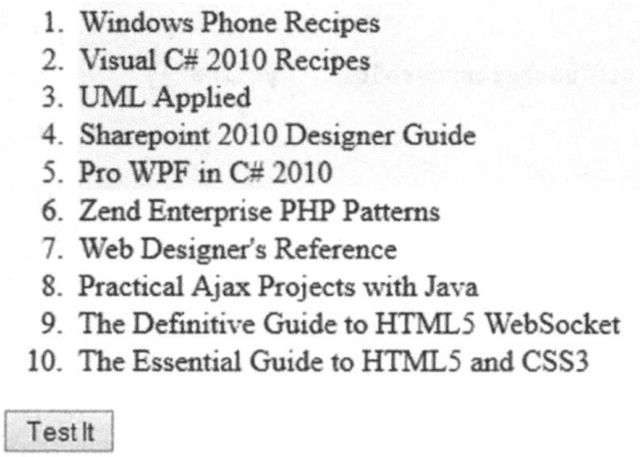

1. Windows Phone Recipes
2. Visual C# 2010 Recipes
3. UML Applied
4. Sharepoint 2010 Designer Guide
5. Pro WPF in C# 2010
6. Zend Enterprise PHP Patterns
7. Web Designer's Reference
8. Practical Ajax Projects with Java
9. The Definitive Guide to HTML5 WebSocket
10. The Essential Guide to HTML5 and CSS3

Test It

Figure 3-22. *Highlighted items when the Test It button is clicked*

3-15. Selecting All Header HTML Elements

Problem

You want to select all the header elements (h1, h2, and so on) on the page.

Solution

The following jQuery selector syntax selects all the header elements.

$(":_header_**")**

Since no basic selector is used, the default selector "*" will be used. This statement is the same as $("*:header"). Listing 3-15 demonstrates the use of the header selector extension to select all header HTML elements on the page.

Listing 3-15. Selects all header elements

```
<!DOCTYPE html>
<html lang="en">
    <head>
        <meta charset="utf-8">
        <script src="scripts/jquery-2.1.0.min.js"></script>
        <script>
                $(function () {
                        $("#btnTestIt").click( function () {
                                        $(":header").css("background-color", "yellow");
                                });
                    });
        </script>
    </head>
    <body>
        <h1>Acme Incorporation</h1>
        <h2>Corporate Office</h2>
        <h3>Departments List</h3>
        <input id="btnTestIt" type="button" value="Test It">
    </body>
</html>
```

How It Works

In this code, the headers are displayed using the <h1>, <h2>, and <h3> HTML tags. If you want to select all the header elements and perform an action on them, use the :header extension.

After the DOM is ready (i.e., all HTML elements are created and loaded in the browser memory), the following code is executed as a result of the document-ready event handler.

```
$("#btnTestIt").click(function () {
    $(":header").css("background-color", "yellow");
});
```

This code selects the input button with `id` as `btnTestIt` and binds a function (the event handler) to its click event. When the user clicks this button, the following code is executed.

```
$(":header").css("background-color", "yellow");
```

`$(":header")` selects all the header HTML elements and returns a jQuery object. The `css()` method is executed on all the selected HTML elements in the returned jQuery object. `css("background-color", "yellow")` changes the background color of the selected elements to yellow. Figure 3-23 displays the page when it is viewed in a browser and the Test It button is clicked.

Acme Incorporation

Corporate Office

Departments List

[Test It]

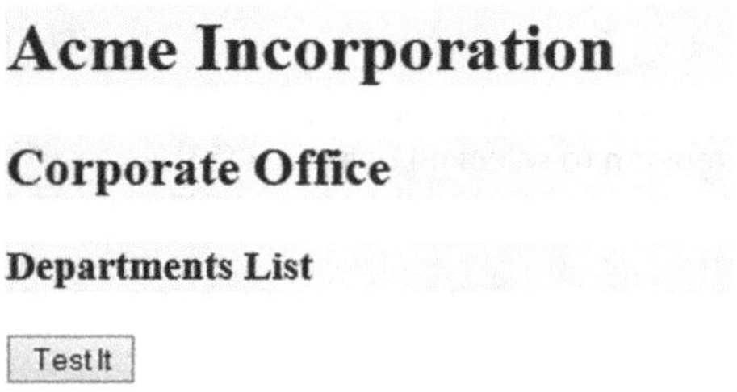

Figure 3-23. *Highlighted item when the Test It button is clicked*

3-16. Selecting the First and/or Last Element from the Selected HTML Elements
Problem

You want to select the first or last element from the selected HTML elements in order to perform some action on it.

Solution

The following jQuery selector syntax selects the first or last HTML element from the set of already selected (matched) HTML elements.

```
$("selector").first()
$("selector").last()
```

where *selector* is any of the basic selector types. When you use basic selector types, it returns a jQuery object. The returned jQuery object contains all the matched HTML elements as an array on which you can use filter methods to narrow down the selection. Listing 3-16 demonstrates the use of the `first()` and `last()` methods to select the HTML element located at the first and last locations of the array.

Listing 3-16. Selects first and last elements from the matched elements

```
<!DOCTYPE html>
<html lang="en">
    <head>
        <meta charset="utf-8">
        <script src="scripts/jquery-2.1.0.min.js"></script>
        <style>
```

```
        table {
                border:3px double green;
              }
    </style>
    <script>
          $(function(){
                $("#btnTestIt").click(function () {
                                    $("tr").first().css("background-color", "lightgray");
                                    $("tr").last().css("background-color", "lightgray");
                            });
            });
    </script>
  </head>
  <body>
    <table id="tblEmployee">
        <tr>
            <td>Employee Name</td><td>Department Name</td><td>Salary</td>
        </tr>
        <tr>
            <td>Jane Smith</td><td>Marketing</td><td>$95,000</td>
        </tr>
        <tr>
            <td>John Smith</td><td>Technology</td><td>$90,000</td>
        </tr>
        <tr>
            <td>Brian Adam</td><td>Sales</td><td>$72,000</td>
        </tr>
        <tr>
            <td>Mary Jones</td><td>Support</td><td>$60,000</td>
        </tr>
        <tr>
            <td>Michael Jefferson</td><td>Technology</td><td>$85,000</td>
        </tr>
        <tr>
            <td colspan="2">Total Salary:</td><td>$373,000</td>
        </tr>
    </table><br>
    <input id="btnTestIt" type="button" value="Test It">
</body>
</html>
```

How It Works

In this code, the employee details—employee names, department names, and salary—are listed in a tabular form using the <table>, <tr>, and <td> HTML tags. If you want to select the first and last record and perform an action on them, first select all the records using $("tr") and then use the first() and last() methods to select the first and last records from these selected records.

After the DOM is ready (i.e., all HTML elements are created and loaded in the browser memory), the following code is executed as a result of the document-ready event handler.

```
$("#btnTestIt").click(function () {
    $("tr").first().css("background-color", "lightgray");
    $("tr").last().css("background-color", "lightgray");
});
```

This code selects the input button with id as btnTestIt and binds a function (the event handler) to its click event. When the user clicks this button, the following code is executed.

```
$("tr").first().css("background-color", "lightgray");
$("tr").last().css("background-color", "lightgray");
```

$("tr") selects all the HTML elements with tag name "tr" and returns the jQuery object. .first() selects the HTML element at the first location of the selected HTML elements array in the returned jQuery object and returns another jQuery object. The css() method is executed on the selected HTML element in the returned jQuery object. css("background-color", "lightgray") changes the background color of the selected element to light gray. Similarly, .last() selects the HTML element at the last location of the selected HTML elements' array. Figure 3-24 displays the page when it is viewed in a browser.

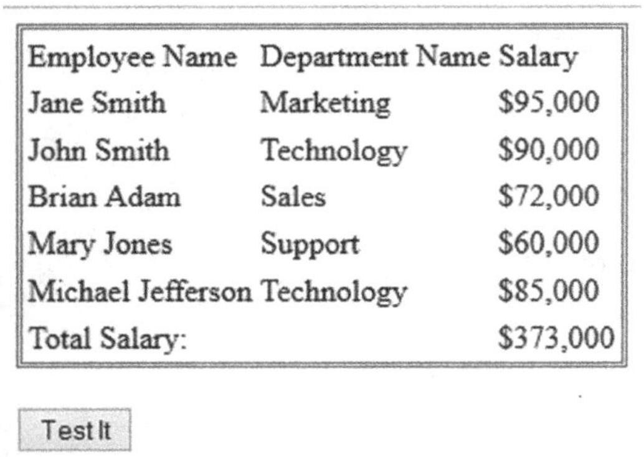

Employee Name	Department Name	Salary
Jane Smith	Marketing	$95,000
John Smith	Technology	$90,000
Brian Adam	Sales	$72,000
Mary Jones	Support	$60,000
Michael Jefferson	Technology	$85,000
Total Salary:		$373,000

Test It

Figure 3-24. *Initial page display*

When you press the Test It button, the button's click event handler changes the background color of the selected element to light gray. Figure 3-25 displays the effect of clicking the Test It button.

Employee Name	Department Name	Salary
Jane Smith	Marketing	$95,000
John Smith	Technology	$90,000
Brian Adam	Sales	$72,000
Mary Jones	Support	$60,000
Michael Jefferson	Technology	$85,000
Total Salary:		$373,000

Test It

Figure 3-25. *Header and footer with gray background*

3-17. Excluding Some Elements from the Matched HTML Elements

Problem

You want to exclude some elements from the matched HTML elements so that the intended action is not performed on them.

Solution

The following jQuery selector syntax excludes HTML elements from the set of already selected (matched) HTML elements.

```
$("selector:not(excludeSelector) ")
```

where *selector* and *excludeSelector* are any of the basic selector types. You can use selector extension like :not to narrow down the matched HTML elements. Listing 3-17 demonstrates the use of the :not selector extension to exclude the HTML element matched by excludeSelector.

Listing 3-17. Select all input elements except for buttons

```
<!DOCTYPE html>
<html lang="en">
    <head>
        <meta charset="utf-8">
        <script src="scripts/jquery-2.1.0.min.js"></script>
        <style>
            label {
                float:left;
                display:block;
                width: 80px;
                font-weight: bold;
            }
        </style>
```

```
<script>
        $(function () {
                $("input:not([type='button']), select, textarea" ).focus(function () {
                                $(this).css("background-color", "yellow");
                });
                $("input:not([type='button']), select, textarea").blur(function () {
                                $(this).css("background-color", "white");
                });
        });
</script>
</head>
<body>
    <label>Name:</label> <input id="txtName" type="text"><br>
    <label>Address:</label> <input id="txtAddress" type="text"><br>
    <label>State:</label>
    <select><option>IL</option><option>NY</option></select><br>
    <label>Comments:</label> <textarea></textarea><br><br>
    <input id="btnSubmit" type="button" value="Submit">
    <input id="btnReset" type="button" value="Reset">
</body>
</html>
```

How It Works

In this code, a basic data-entry form is created using the <input>, <select>, and <textarea> HTML tags. If you want to select all the input HTML elements except for the button type, first select all the input HTML elements using using the $("input") selector and then use the :not() extension to exclude [type='button'] from the matched records.

After the DOM is ready (i.e., all HTML elements are created and loaded in the browser memory), the following code is executed as a result of the document-ready event handler.

```
$("input:not([type='button']), select, textarea" ).focus(function () {
    $(this).css("background-color", "yellow");
});
$("input:not([type='button']), select, textarea").blur(function () {
    $(this).css("background-color", "white");
});
```

$("input:not([type='button']), select, textarea") selects all the HTML elements with tag names as input (except where the type is button), select, and textarea and returns a jQuery object. .focus() and .blur() bind the event handler to all the selected elements, which is executed when these elements get focus or lose focus, respectively. $(this) represents the element that triggered the event. If any of the selected elements gets the focus, the css() method is executed. It changes the background color to yellow. If any of the selected elements lose the focus, the css() method is executed and it changes the background color to white. Figure 3-26 displays the page when it is viewed in a browser.

Name:
Address:
State:
IL
Comments:
Submit
Reset

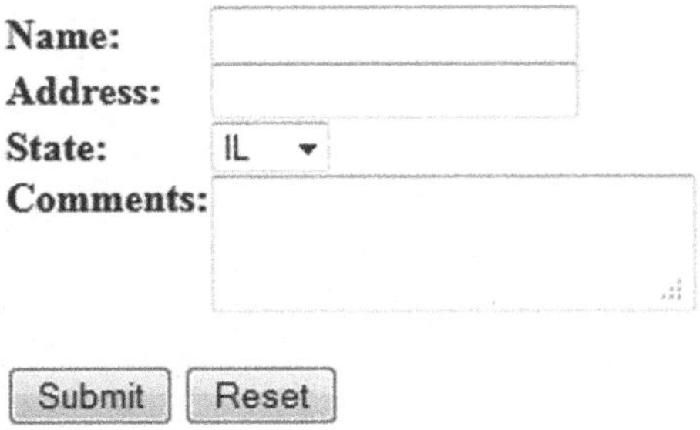

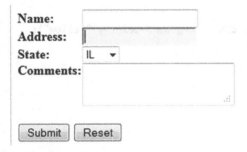

Figure 3-26. *Initial page display*

Figure 3-27 displays the change in background color upon entering and leaving the form field.

Name:
Address:
State:
IL
Comments:
Submit
Reset

Figure 3-27. *Change in a field's background color on getting focus*

3-18. Selecting the First or *n*th Child Node of the Matched HTML Element's Parent

Problem

You want to perform an action on a specific child node of the matched HTML element's parent.

Solution

The following jQuery selector syntax selects the first or *n*th element from the set of already selected (matched) HTML elements.

```
$("selector:first-child")
$("selector:nth-child(indexNumber)")
```

where `selector` is any of the basic selector types. You can use selector extensions like `:first-child` and `3:nth-child(indexNumber)` to select another set of elements based on already matched HTML elements. Listing 3-18 demonstrates the use of the `:first-child` and `:nth-child` selector extensions to select an HTML element located at the first location or at the *n*th location of the child nodes of the matched HTML element's parent.

Listing 3-18. Selector extension to select first or nth child

```html
<!DOCTYPE html>
<html lang="en">
    <head>
        <meta charset="utf-8">
        <script src="scripts/jquery-2.1.0.min.js"></script>
        <style>
            ul {
                width:150px;
                }
        </style>
        <script>
                $(function () {
                        $("#btnFirstChild").click(function () {
                                        $("li:first-child").css("background-color", "yellow");
                        });
                        $("#btnNthChild").click(function () {
                                        $("li:nth-child(3)").css("background-color", "yellow");
                        });
                });
        </script>
    </head>
    <body>
        <ul>
            <li>Item 1</li>
            <li>Item 2</li>
            <li>item 3</li>
            <li>item 4</li>
        </ul>
        <ul>
            <li>Item A</li>
            <li>Item B</li>
            <li>Item C</li>
            <li>Item D</li>
        </ul>
        <input id="btnFirstChild" type="button" value="First Child"><br><br>
        <input id="btnNthChild" type="button" value="3rd Child">
    </body>
</html>
```

How It Works

In this code, two lists of items are created using the <ul> and <li> HTML tags. If you want to select the nth child of the <ul> tag, first select all the items using the $("li") selector and then use the :first-child or the :nth-child (indexNumber) extensions to select the first or nth child of the parent of the matched HTML elements.

After the DOM is ready (i.e., all HTML elements are created and loaded in the browser memory), the following code is executed as a result of the document-ready event handler.

```
$("#btnFirstChild").click(function () {
    $("li:first-child").css("background-color", "yellow");
});
$("#btnNthChild").click(function () {
    $("li:nth-child(3)").css("background-color", "yellow");
});
```

This code selects the input button with id as btnFirstChild and binds a function (the event handler) to its click event. When the user clicks this button, the following code is executed.

```
$("li:first-child").css("background-color", "yellow");
```

$("li") selects all the HTML elements with the tag name "li", and then $("li:first-child") selects the first child of the parent of matched elements and returns a jQuery object. Since there are two parents of all the <li> elements, two child nodes (one from each parent) will be selected. The css() method is executed on all the selected HTML elements in the returned jQuery object. css("background-color", "yellow") changes the background color of the selected elements to yellow. Similarly, when the 3rd Child button is clicked, the $("#btnNthChild").click() event handler is executed and the nth child node's background color changes to yellow. Figure 3-28 displays the page when it is viewed in a browser.

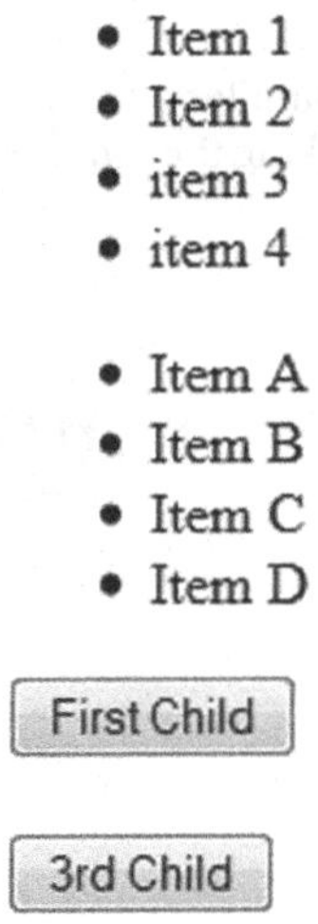

- Item 1
- Item 2
- item 3
- item 4

- Item A
- Item B
- Item C
- Item D

First Child

3rd Child

Figure 3-28. *Initial page display*

When you press the First Child button, the button's click event handler changes the background color of the first child element to yellow. Figure 3-29 displays the effect of clicking the First Child button.

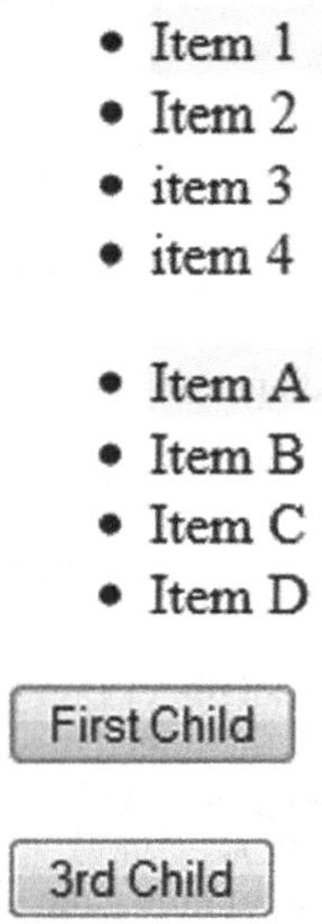

- Item 1
- Item 2
- item 3
- item 4

- Item A
- Item B
- Item C
- Item D

[First Child]

[3rd Child]

Figure 3-29. *Highlighted items when the First Child button is clicked*

After you refresh the page in the browser and press the 3rd Child button, that button's click event handler changes the background color of the third child element to yellow. Figure 3-30 displays the effect of clicking the 3rd Child button.

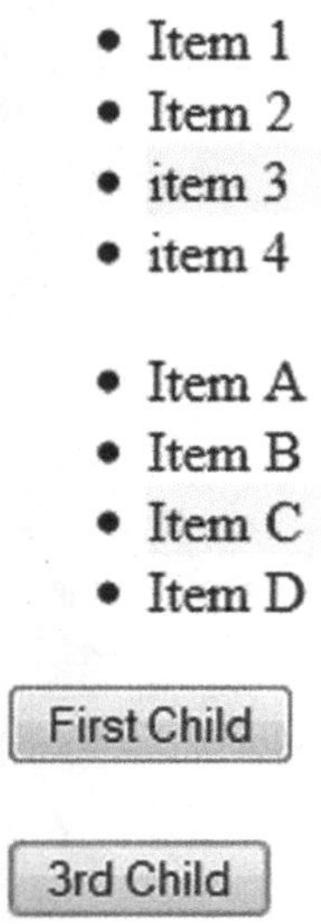

- Item 1
- Item 2
- item 3
- item 4

- Item A
- Item B
- Item C
- Item D

[First Child]

[3rd Child]

Figure 3-30. *Highlighted items when the 3rd Child button is clicked*

3-19. Selecting All Elements that Contain the Specified Text
Problem

You want to select elements that contain the specified text.

Solution

The following jQuery selector syntax selects the first or *n*th element from the set of already selected (matched) HTML elements.

$("*selector***:contains(***searchText***)")**

where selector is any of the basic selector types. You can use selector extensions like :contains to filter out only those elements with text content that contains specified searchText. Listing 3-19 demonstrates the use of the :contains selector extension.

Listing 3-19. jQuery selector extension to select elements with specified text

```html
<!DOCTYPE html>
<html lang="en">
    <head>
        <meta charset="utf-8">
        <script src="scripts/jquery-2.1.0.min.js"></script>
        <script>
            $(function() {
                $("#btnTestIt").click(function() {
                    var searchText = $("#txtSearch").val();
                    $("td:contains('" + searchText + "')").css("background-color", "yellow");
                });
                $("#btnReset").click(function () {
                    $("td").css("background-color", "white");
                });
            });
        </script>
    </head>
    <body>
        <table>
            <tr><td>John Smith</td><td>Marketing</td></tr>
            <tr><td>Jane Smith</td><td>Sales</td></tr>
            <tr><td>Mike Jordon</td><td>Technology</td></tr>
            <tr><td>Mary Jones</td><td>Customer Support</td></tr>
        </table><p>
        Search: <input id="txtSearch" type="text">
        <input id="btnTestIt" type="button" value="Test It">
        <input id="btnReset" type="reset" value="Reset">
    </body>
</html>
```

How It Works

In this code, the employee details—employee name and department name—are listed in a tabular form using the <table>, <tr>, and <td> HTML tags. If you want to select elements containing specific text, first select all the elements using the $("td") selector and then use the :contains(searchText) extension.

After the DOM is ready (i.e., all HTML elements are created and loaded in the browser memory), the following code is executed as a result of the document-ready event handler.

```
$("#btnTestIt").click(function() {
    var searchText = $("#txtSearch").val();
    $("td:contains('" + searchText + "')").css("background-color", "yellow");
});
```

This code selects the input button with id as btnTestIt and binds a function (the event handler) to its click event. When the user clicks this button, the following code is executed.

```
var searchText = $("#txtSearch").val();
    $("td:contains('" + searchText + "')").css("background-color", "yellow");
```

$("#txtSearch") selects the HTML element with id txtSearch. .val() gets the value the user entered. You'll use this value to search the text contents.

$("td") selects all the HTML elements with the tag name "td", and then $("td:contains('" + searchText + "')") selects the "td" elements that have the text that contains the searchText and returns a jQuery object. The css() method is executed on all the selected HTML elements in the returned jQuery object. css ("background-color", "yellow") changes the background color of the selected elements to yellow. Figure 3-31 displays the page when it is viewed in a browser. 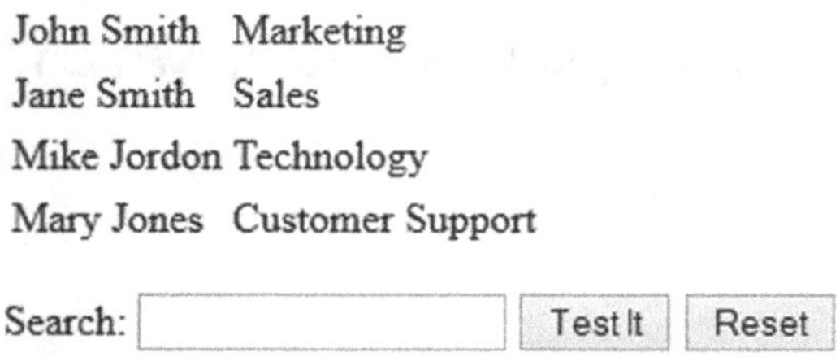

John Smith	Marketing
Jane Smith	Sales
Mike Jordon	Technology
Mary Jones	Customer Support

Search: [   ] [Test It] [Reset]

Figure 3-31. *Initial page display*

When you enter the search criteria in the Search text box (for example, Smith) and press the Test It button, the button's click event handler highlights the elements whose text content contains the search text. Figure 3-32 shows the result of a text search. 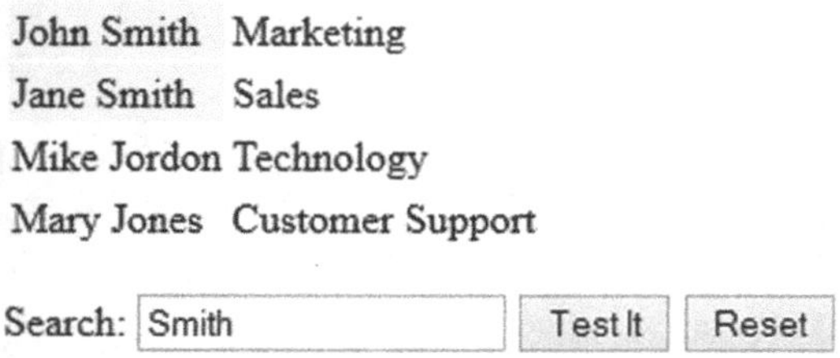

John Smith	Marketing
Jane Smith	Sales
Mike Jordon	Technology
Mary Jones	Customer Support

Search: [Smith   ] [Test It] [Reset]

Figure 3-32. *Elements containing "Smith" are highlighted*

3-20. Selecting Elements that Have No Child Nodes (Including Text)

Problem

You want to perform some action on a group of HTML elements that don't have any child nodes or text content, (i.e., elements that are empty).

Solution

The following jQuery selector syntax selects empty HTML elements from the set of already selected (matched) HTML elements.

$("selector**:empty")**

where selector is any of the basic selector types. You can use selector extensions like :empty to narrow down the matched HTML elements. Listing 3-20 demonstrates the use of the :empty selector extension to select an empty HTML element.

Listing 3-20. Select empty HTML elements

```html
<!DOCTYPE html>
<html lang="en">
   <head>
      <meta charset="utf-8">
      <script src="scripts/jquery-2.1.0.min.js"></script>
      <script>
            $(function() {
                  $("#btnTestIt").click(function() {
                                    $("td:empty").css("background-color", "yellow")
                  });
            });
      </script>
   </head>
   <body>
      <table>
         <tr><td>John Smith</td><td>Marketing</td></tr>
         <tr><td>Jane Smith</td><td></td></tr>
         <tr><td>Mike Jordon</td><td>Technology</td></tr>
         <tr><td>Mary Jones</td><td>Marketing</td></tr>
      </table><p>
      <input id="btnTestIt" type="button" value="Test It">
   </body>
</html>
```

How It Works

In this code, the employee details—employee name and department name—are listed in a tabular form using the <table>, <tr>, and <td> HTML tags. If you want to select empty cells, first select all the cells using the $("td") selector and then use the :empty extension to select the empty elements from these matched cells. This extension can also be used to check if there is an empty form field.

After the DOM is ready (i.e., all HTML elements are created and loaded in the browser memory), the following code is executed as a result of the document-ready event handler.

```
$("#btnTestIt").click(function() {
    $("td:empty").css("background-color", "yellow")
});
```

This code selects the input button with id as btnTestIt and binds a function (event handler) to its click event. When a user clicks this button, the following code is executed.

```
$("td:empty").css("background-color", "yellow")
```

$("td") selects all the HTML elements with the tag name "td", and then $("td:empty") narrows down the matched elements to select only empty elements and returns a jQuery object. The css() method is executed on the selected HTML element in the returned jQuery object. css("background-color", "yellow") changes the background color of the selected elements to yellow. Figure 3-33 displays the page when it is viewed in a browser.

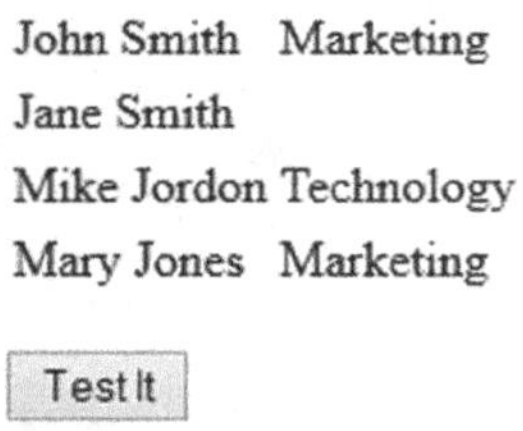

John Smith   Marketing
Jane Smith
Mike Jordon Technology
Mary Jones   Marketing

Test It

Figure 3-33. *Initial page display*

On pressing the Test It button, the button's click event handler changes the background color of the selected element to yellow. Figure 3-34 displays the effect of clicking the Test It button.

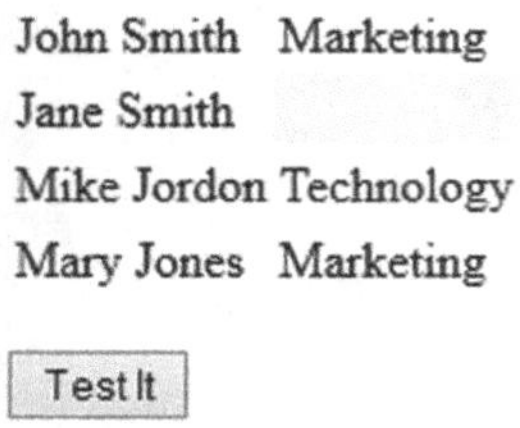

John Smith   Marketing
Jane Smith
Mike Jordon Technology
Mary Jones   Marketing

Test It

Figure 3-34. *Empty items are highlighted when the Test It button is clicked*

3-21. Selecting Elements that Have at Least One Child Node Matching the Specified Selector

Problem

You want to perform some action on a group of HTML elements that have at least one child node matching the specified selector.

Solution

The following jQuery selector syntax selects only those elements that have child nodes matching the specified selector from the set of already selected (matched) HTML elements.

$("*selector*:has(*childSelector*)")

where `selector` and `childSeletor` are any of the basic selector types. You can use selector extensions like :has to narrow down the matched HTML elements. Listing 3-21 demonstrates the use of the :has selector extension to select an HTML element that has a child matching a specified selector.

Listing 3-21. Select HTML elements with child nodes that match another selector

```
<!DOCTYPE html>
<html lang="en">
    <head>
        <meta charset="utf-8">
        <script src="scripts/jquery-2.1.0.min.js"></script>
        <style>
            div {
                width: 150px;
            }
        </style>
        <script>
                $(function(){
                        $("#btnTestIt").click(function () {
                                        $("div:has(p, li)").css("background-color", "yellow");
                        });
                });
        </script>
    </head>
    <body>
        <div><p>Test Message</p><b> Have a nice day! </b></div><br>
        <div>Test 2</div>
        <div><ul><li>Test 3</li></ul></div>
        <input id="btnTestIt" type="button" value="Test It">
    </body>
</html>
```

How It Works

In this code, some text contents are embedded within various HTML tags—<div>, <p>, and <li>. If you want to select only specific <div> elements that match a specified selector, first select all the DIV elements using the $("div") selector and then use the :has extension and specify the child selector.

After the DOM is ready (i.e., all HTML elements are created and loaded in the browser memory), the following code is executed as a result of the document-ready event handler.

```
$("#btnTestIt").click(function () {
    $("div:has(p, li)").css("background-color", "yellow");
});
```

This code selects the input button with id as btnTestIt and binds a function (the event handler) to its click event. When the user clicks this button, the following code is executed.

```
$("div:has(p, li)").css("background-color", "yellow");
```

$("div") selects all the HTML elements with the tag name "div", and then $("div:has(p, li)") narrows down the matched elements to select only those elements that have child nodes with the tag name "p" or "li" and returns a jQuery object. The css() method is executed on the selected HTML element in the returned jQuery object. css("background-color", "yellow") changes the background color of the selected elements to yellow. Figure 3-35 displays the page when it is viewed in a browser.

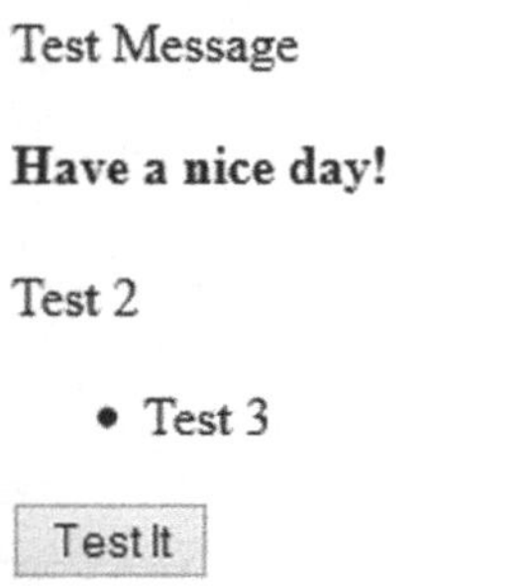

Test Message

Have a nice day!

Test 2

- Test 3

| Test It |

Figure 3-35. *Initial page display*

When you press the Test It button, the button's click event handler changes the background color of the selected element to yellow. Figure 3-36 displays the effect of clicking the Test It button.

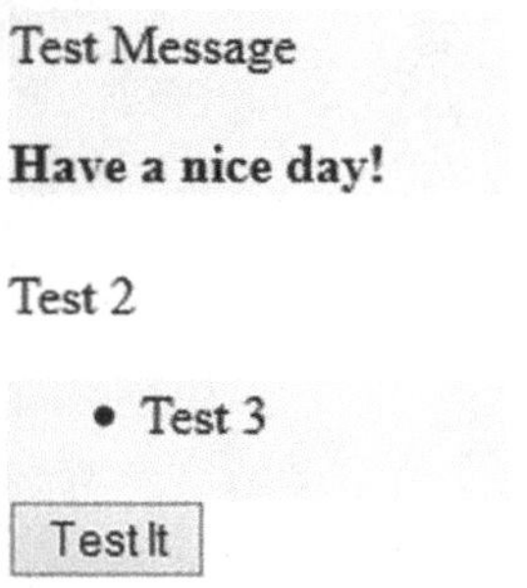

Test Message

Have a nice day!

Test 2

- Test 3

| Test It |

Figure 3-36. *Selected <DIV> items are highlighted when the Test It button is clicked*

3-22. Selecting Form Elements Based on Their Type and Attributes

Problem

You want to perform some action on a group of HTML elements based on their attribute or on the value of their type attribute.

Solution

The following jQuery selectors syntax are used to select form elements based on their type (such as password, radio, checkbox, and so on) or their attribute (such as checked, selected, disabled, enabled, and so on). Table 3-11 lists the selector extension to use depending on which form HTML elements you want to select. Listing 3-22 demonstrates some of the form element selectors.

Table 3-11. *Form Elements and Selector Extensions*

To Select HTML Elements	Use Selector Extension
With tag name—input, select, textarea, and button	$(":input")
With type—text	$(":text")
With type—password	$(":password")
With type—radio	$(":radio")
With type—checkbox	$(":checkbox")
With tag name button or input type—button	$(":button")
With type—submit	$(":submit")
With type—reset	$(":reset")
With type—file	$(":file")
With type—image	$(":image")
Which are checked	$(":checked")
Which are selected	$(":selected")
Which are disabled	$(":disabled")
Which are enabled	$(":enabled")

Listing 3-22. Select form elements based on their type or attribute

```
<!DOCTYPE html>
<html lang="en">
    <head>
    <meta charset="utf-8">
    <script src="scripts/jquery-2.1.0.min.js"></script>
    <style>
```

```
        label {
                float:left;
                display:block;
                width: 100px;
                font-weight: bold;
        }
    </style>
    <script>
                $(function () {
                        $("[id ^= 'btn']").click( function () {
                                var selector = $(this).val();
                                $(selector).css("background-color", "yellow");
                        });
                         $("#buttonReset").click( function () {
                                $("*").css("background-color", "white");
                        });
                });
    </script>
    </head>
    <body>
        <form>
            <label>User Name: </label> <input type="text"><br>
            <label>Password: </label> <input type="password"><br>
            <label>Gender: </label>
            <input type="radio" name="gender" checked>Male
            <input type="radio" name="gender">Female
            <br>
            <label>Hobbies: </label>
            <input type="checkbox" name="hobbies" checked>Music
            <input type="radio" name="hobbies">Travel
            <input type="radio" name="hobbies" disabled>Gardening
            <br><br>
            <input type="file">
            <br><br><br><br>
            <input id="btnButton" type="button" value=":button">
            <input id="btnEnabled" type="button" value=":enabled">
            <input id="btnFile" type="button" value=":file">
            <input id="btnFocus" type="button" value=":focus">
            <input id="btnInput" type="button" value=":input">
            <input id="btnPassword" type="button" value=":password">
            <input id="btnReset" type="button" value=":reset">
            <input id="btnSubmit" type="button" value=":submit">
            <input id="btnText" type="button" value=":text">
            <br><br>
            <button type="submit" id="buttonSubmit">Submit</button>
            <button type="reset" id="buttonReset">Reset</button>
        </form>
    </body>
</html>
```

How It Works

In this code, various form elements are created using the input and button HTML tags. For demonstration purposes, I used the value of the buttons to determine which selector to use.

After the DOM is ready (i.e., all HTML elements are created and loaded in the browser memory), the following code is executed as a result of the document-ready event handler.

```
$("[id ^= 'btn']").click( function () {
    var selector = $(this).val();
    $(selector).css("background-color", "yellow");
});
```

$("[id ^= 'btn']").click() binds the click event handler to all the HTML elements whose id starts with the value btn. The ^= operator can be read as "starts with." The selector $("[attributeName ^= 'startingPartialValue']") selects all the elements whose *attributeName*'s value starts with the specified startingPartialValue. When a button is clicked, the following code is executed.

```
var selector = $(this).val();
$(selector).css("background-color", "yellow");
```

For example, if a button with an Id of "btnInput" is clicked, the selector variable gets the value :input and $(selector) selects all the HTML elements with the tag names—input, select, textarea, and button. It then returns a jQuery object. The css() method is executed on the selected HTML element in the returned jQuery object. css("background-color", "yellow") changes the background color of the selected elements to yellow. Figure 3-37 displays the page when it is viewed in a browser.

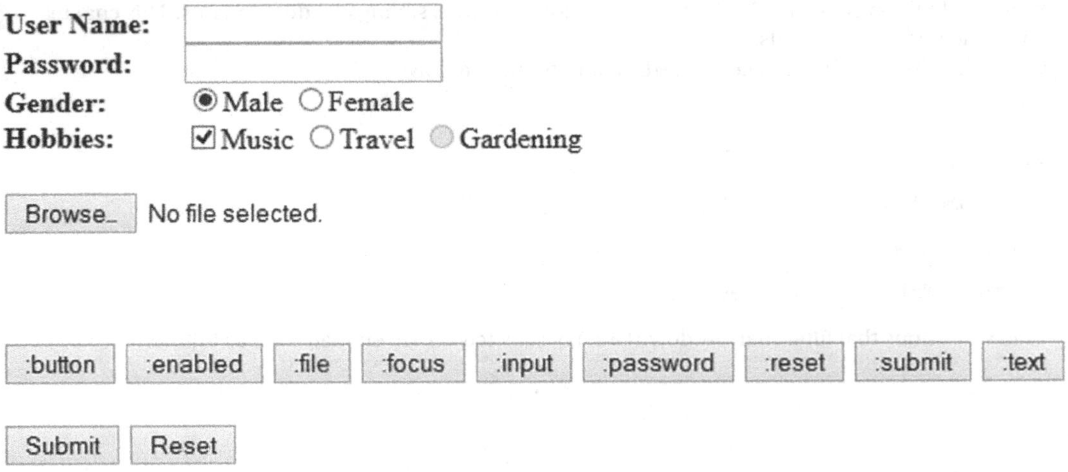

User Name:
Password:
Gender: ⦿ Male ○ Female
Hobbies: ☑ Music ○ Travel ◉ Gardening

Browse_ No file selected.

| :button | :enabled | :file | :focus | :input | :password | :reset | :submit | :text |

Submit Reset

Figure 3-37. *Initial page display*

When you press the :input button, the button's click event handler changes the background color of all the selected elements to yellow. Figure 3-38 displays the effect of clicking the :input button.

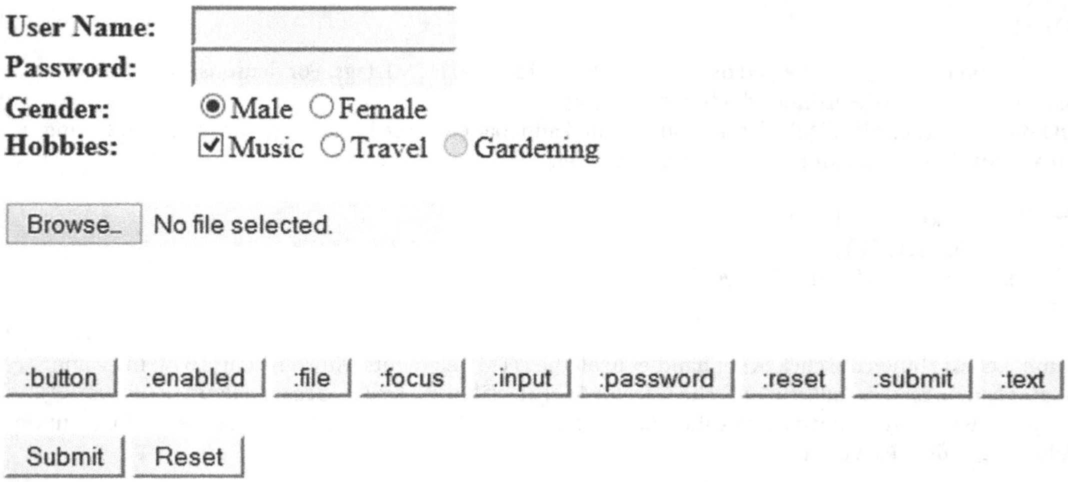

User Name:

Password:

Gender: ● Male ○ Female

Hobbies: ☑ Music ○ Travel ○ Gardening

Browse… No file selected.

| :button | :enabled | :file | :focus | :input | :password | :reset | :submit | :text |

Submit   Reset

Figure 3-38. Input elements are highlighted when the :input button is clicked

Summary

This chapter covered jQuery selectors and selector extensions. To access the attributes, properties, text content, and HTML content of HTML elements or to change the value of their attributes and properties, you first need to select them—either directly by using `id`, `className`, `attributeName`, `attributeValue`, and so on or indirectly by first selecting a node and then traversing the DOM tree looking for ancestors, siblings, or descendants. This chapter covered the following selectors and methods.

Commonly used selectors that directly select HTML elements are as follows:

- `$("#id")`
- `$("tagName")`
- `$(".className")`
- `$("[attributeName]")`
- `$("[attributeName = 'attributeValue']")`

Commonly used extensions that filter (narrow down) a set of selected HTML elements are as follows:

- `:even`
- `:odd`
- `:lt(indexNumber)`
- `:gt(indexNumber)`
- `:not(selector)`
- `:has(selector)`

The `css()` method was used extensively in this chapter and it's covered in detail in Chapter 6.

jQuery Selectors Filtering and Expansion

This chapter covers jQuery selectors filtering (narrowing) and expansion. jQuery selector filtering is used to narrow down the set of selected elements and the expansion method is used to add more elements to the set of selected elements. Programming logic can be used to include, exclude, or replace selected elements in the set. Once you have the desired set of elements, you can access and manipulate their attributes values, properties, and style.

This chapter includes recipes that show you how to fine-tune sets of selected elements using filtering and expansion in order to:

- Access their style, properties, and attributes
- Manipulate their style, properties, and attributes

4-1. Narrowing the Set of Selected Elements by Using Selector/jQuery Object Filter

Problem

You want to narrow down the set of selected elements by selecting only specific elements.

Solution

The following jQuery selector syntax selects the HTML elements from the set of already selected HTML elements, which match the specified selector.

$(selector**).filter(**filterSelector**)**

Listing 4-1 provides an example to demonstrate the use of the filter() method to select specific HTML elements from the set of selected elements.

Listing 4-1. Using filter( ) to select specific elements

```html
<!DOCTYPE html>
<html lang="en">
<head>
    <meta charset="utf-8">
    <script src="scripts/jquery-2.1.0.min.js"></script>
    <style>
        table {
        border:3px double green;
        }
        .tblHdr {
            background-color: lightgray;
        }
        .newRecord {
            background-color: lightyellow;
        }
        .listDepartments {
            width: 200px;
        }
    </style>
    <script>
        $(function(){
            $("#btnTestIt").click(function () {
                $("tr").filter(".newRecord").css("background-color", "lightblue");
            });
        });
    </script>
</head>
<body>
    <strong>Employees:</strong>
    <table id="listEmployees">
        <tr class="tblHdr">
        <td>Employee Name</td><td>Department Name</td><td>Salary</td>
        </tr>
        <tr>
            <td>Jane Smith</td><td>Marketing</td><td>$95,000</td>
        </tr>
        <tr class="newRecord">
            <td>John Smith</td><td>Technology</td><td>$76,000</td>
        </tr>
        <tr>
            <td>Brian Adam</td><td>Sales</td><td>$72,000</td>
        </tr>
        <tr>
            <td>Mary Jones</td><td>Customer Support</td><td>$60,000</td>
        </tr>
        <tr>
        <td>Michael Jefferson</td><td>Technology</td><td>$85,000</td>
        </tr>
    </table><br>
```

```
    <strong>Departments:</strong>
        <ul class="listDepartments">
            <li>Marketing</li>
            <li>Sales</li>
            <li class="newRecord">Technology</li>
            <li>Customer Support</li>
        </ul><br>
        <input id="btnTestIt" type="button" value="Test It">
</body>
</html>
```

How It Works

In this code, the employee details—employee name, department name, and salary—are listed in tabular form using the <table>, <tr>, and <td> HTML tags and the departments' names are listed using the <ul> and <li> HTML tags. In both lists, there is one record with the class newRecord. If you want to select newRecord from the table only to perform an action on it, you first select all the records using $("tr") and then use filter(".newRecord").

When the user clicks the Test It button, the following code is executed:

```
$("tr").filter(".newRecord").css("background-color", "lightblue");
```

$("tr") selects all HTML elements with tag name "tr" and returns the jQuery object. .filter(".newRecord") selects the HTML element with the class name newRecord from the selected HTML elements array in the returned jQuery object and returns another jQuery object. Refer to Recipe 3-2 for an explanation of the css() method.

When you press the Test It button, the button's click event handler changes the background color of the selected element to light blue. Figure 4-1 displays the effect of clicking the Test It button. 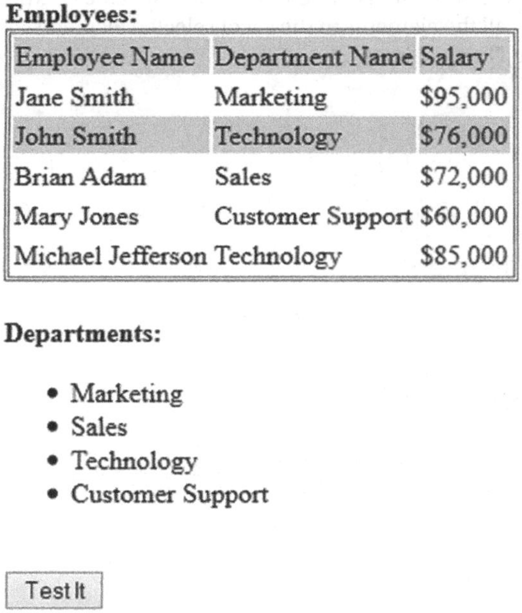

Employees:

Employee Name	Department Name	Salary
Jane Smith	Marketing	$95,000
John Smith	Technology	$76,000
Brian Adam	Sales	$72,000
Mary Jones	Customer Support	$60,000
Michael Jefferson	Technology	$85,000

Departments:

- Marketing
- Sales
- Technology
- Customer Support

Test It

Figure 4-1. *Record with newRecord class with light blue background*

There are two other ways to filter elements:

1. Use the `filter()` method with the argument: selector:

   ```
   $("tr").filter(".newRecord");
   ```

2. Use the `filter()` method with the argument: jQuery object:

   ```
   var newRecords = $(".newRecord");;
   $("tr").filter(newRecords);
   ```

4-2. Narrowing the Set of Selected Elements by Using the Filter Function

Problem

You want to narrow down the set of selected elements by selecting specific elements based on the return value of a function.

Solution

The following jQuery selector syntax selects HTML elements from the set of already selected HTML elements, from which the `filter` function returns `true`.

`$(selector).filter( function() { ... });`

Listing 4-2 demonstrates the use of the `filter()` method with the argument as a function to select specific HTML elements from the set of selected elements. The function iterates over all the elements in the set of selected elements and if it returns `true`, the current element is included in the resultant jQuery object.

Listing 4-2. Using filter(function( )) to select specific elements

```
<!DOCTYPE html>
<html lang="en">
<head>
  <meta charset="utf-8">
  <script src="scripts/jquery-2.1.0.min.js"></script>
  <style>
    table {
      border:3px double green;
    }
    .tblHdr {
      background-color: lightgray;
    }
  </style>
```

```
    <script>
      $(function(){
        $("#btnTestIt").click(function () {
          $("tr").filter(function() {
                                return ($(this).children().eq(1).text() == "Technology");
                }).css("background-color", "lightblue");
        });
      });
    </script>
</head>
<body>
    <strong>Employees:</strong>
    <table id="listEmployees">
      <tr class="tblHdr">
        <td>Employee Name</td><td>Department Name</td><td>Salary</td>
      </tr>
      <tr>
        <td>Jane Smith</td><td>Marketing</td><td>$95,000</td>
      </tr>
      <tr>
        <td>John Smith</td><td>Technology</td><td>$90,000</td>
      </tr>
      <tr>
        <td>Brian Adam</td><td>Sales</td><td>$72,000</td>
      </tr>
      <tr>
        <td>Mary Jones</td><td>Customer Support</td><td>$60,000</td>
      </tr>
      <tr>
        <td>Michael Jefferson</td><td>Technology</td><td>$85,000</td>
      </tr>
    </table><br>
    <input id="btnTestIt" type="button" value="Test It">
</body>
</html>
```

How It Works

In this code, the employee details—employee name, department name, and salary—are listed in tabular form using the <table>, <tr>, and <td> HTML tags and the departments' names are listed using the <ul> and <li> HTML tags. In both lists, there is one record with the class newRecord. If you want to select newRecord from the table only to perform an action on it, you first select all the records using $("tr") and then use filter(".newRecord").

When the user clicks the Test It button, the following code is executed:

```
$("tr").filter(function() {
   return ($(this).children().eq(1).text() == "Technology");
   }). css("background-color", "lightblue");
```

$("tr") selects all the HTML elements with tag name "tr" and returns the jQuery object. .filter(function()) iterates over each element of the selected HTML elements in the returned jQuery object. If the function returns true for the current element, that element is included in resultant jQuery object. At the end of the iteration, the resultant jQuery object is returned. In this case, $(this) is the current element, so $(this).children() returns all the children (i.e., TD elements), $(this).children().eq(1) returns the second TD element, and $(this).children().eq(1). text() returns the text content of the second TD element, which is the department name. This function returns true if the department name is "Technology". Refer to Recipe 3-2 for information on the css() method. The children() method is discussed in the next chapter.

When you press the Test It button, the button's click event handler changes the background color of the selected element to light blue. Figure 4-2 displays the effect of clicking the Test It button.

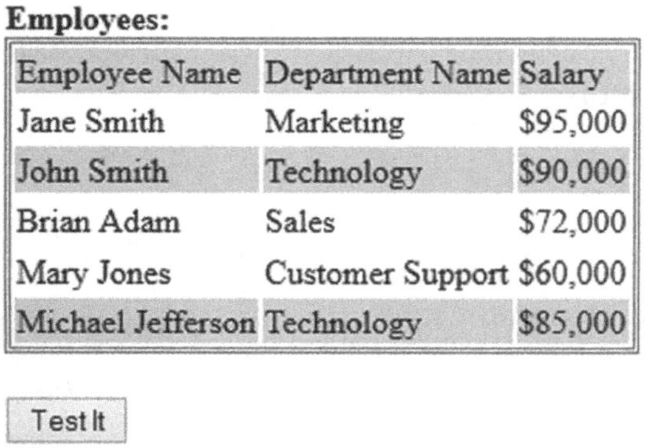

Employees:

Employee Name	Department Name	Salary
Jane Smith	Marketing	$95,000
John Smith	Technology	$90,000
Brian Adam	Sales	$72,000
Mary Jones	Customer Support	$60,000
Michael Jefferson	Technology	$85,000

Test It

Figure 4-2. *Records from the Technology department have a light blue background*

4-3. Narrowing the Set of Selected Elements by Checking Their Descendant Nodes' Attributes

Problem

You want to narrow down the set of selected elements by selecting only those elements that have descendants that match the specified selector.

Solution

The following jQuery syntax selects only those HTML elements from the set of already selected HTML elements that have descendants matching the specified selector.

$(selector**).has(**descendantSelector**)**

Listing 4-3 demonstrates the use of the has() method to select specific HTML elements when their descendant matches the specified selector.

Listing 4-3. Using has( ) to select specific elements

```
<!DOCTYPE html>
<html lang="en">
<head>
    <meta charset="utf-8">
    <script src="scripts/jquery-2.1.0.min.js"></script>
    <style>
        .tableWithNewRecord {
            border:3px double green;
        }
        .tblHdr {
            background-color: lightgray;
        }
        .listDepartments {
            width: 200px;
        }
        .newRecord {
            background-color: lightyellow;
        }
    </style>
    <script>
        $(function(){
            $("#btnTestIt").click(function () {
                $("table").has(".newRecord").addClass("tableWithNewRecord");
            });
        });
    </script>
</head>
<body>
    <strong>Employees:</strong>
    <table id="listEmployees">
        <tr class="tblHdr">
            <td>Employee Name</td><td>Department Name</td><td>Salary</td>
        </tr>
        <tr>
            <td>Jane Smith</td><td>Marketing</td><td>$95,000</td>
        </tr>
        <tr class="newRecord">
            <td>John Smith</td><td>Technology</td><td>$90,000</td>
        </tr>
        <tr>
            <td>Brian Adam</td><td>Sales</td><td>$72,000</td>
        </tr>
        <tr>
            <td>Mary Jones</td><td>Customer Support</td><td>$60,000</td>
        </tr>
```

```
        <tr>
            <td>Michael Jefferson</td><td>Technology</td><td>$85,000</td>
        </tr>
    </table><br><br>
    <strong>Departments:</strong>
    <table id="listDepartments">
        <tr class="tblHdr">
            <td>Department Code</td><td>Department Name</td></tr>
        <tr><td>D01</td><td>Marketing</td></tr>
        <tr><td>D02</td><td>Sales</td></tr>
        <tr><td>D03</td><td>Technology</td></tr>
        <tr><td>D04</td><td>Customer Support</td></tr>
    </table><br>
    <input id="btnTestIt" type="button" value="Test It">
</body>
</html>
```

How It Works

In this code, the employee details—employee name, department name, salary, and the departments names—are listed in tabular form using the <table>, <tr>, and <td> HTML tags. In the employee list, there is one record with the class newRecord. If you want to select a table that has decendent(s) (<TR> or <TD>) with the class name newRecord, you first select all the table elements using $("table") and then use the descendant filter as has(".newRecord").

When the user clicks Test It button, the following code is executed:

```
$("table").has(".newRecord").addClass("tableWithNewRecord");
```

$("table") selects all the HTML elements with tag name "table" and returns a jQuery object. .has(". newRecord") selects HTML elements with a descendent's class name newRecord from the selected HTML elements and returns another jQuery object. The addClass("tableWithNewRecord") method is executed on the selected HTML element in the returned jQuery object. addClass("tableWithNewRecord") adds the CSS class to the selected elements.

When you press the Test It button, the button's click event handler adds a new class (tableWithNewRecord) to the employee table. Figure 4-3 displays the effect of clicking the Test It button.

Employees:

Employee Name	Department Name	Salary
Jane Smith	Marketing	$95,000
John Smith	Technology	$90,000
Brian Adam	Sales	$72,000
Mary Jones	Customer Support	$60,000
Michael Jefferson	Technology	$85,000

Departments:

Department Code	Department Name
D01	Marketing
D02	Sales
D03	Technology
D04	Customer Support

Test It

Figure 4-3. *Table with descendent(s) having newRecord class*

4-4. Narrowing the Set of Selected Elements by Excluding Elements Using Selectors
Problem

You want to narrow down the set of selected elements by excluding some elements specified by the exclusion selector.

Solution

The following jQuery selector syntax selects the HTML elements from the set of already selected HTML elements that are not matching specified selector.

$(*selector***).not(***exclusionSelector***)**

The not() method's functionality is the reverse of the filter() functionality, where filter allows elements to go through based on the specified selector, not blocks certain elements that match the specified selector. Listing 4-4 provides an example to demonstrate the use of the not() method to exclude specific HTML elements from the set of selected elements.

Listing 4-4. Using not( ) to exclude specific elements

```
<!DOCTYPE html>
<html lang="en">
<head>
    <meta charset="utf-8">
    <script src="scripts/jquery-2.1.0.min.js"></script>
    <style>
        table {
            border:3px double green;
        }
        .tblHdr {
            background-color: lightgray;
        }
        .newRecord {
            background-color: lightyellow;
        }
        .listDepartments {
            width: 200px;
        }
    </style>
    <script>
        $(function(){
            $("#btnTestIt").click(function () {
                $("tr").not(".newRecord").css("background-color", "lightblue");
            });
        });
    </script>
</head>
<body>
    <strong>Employees:</strong>
    <table id="listEmployees">
        <tr class="tblHdr">
            <td>Employee Name</td><td>Department Name</td><td>Salary</td>
        </tr>
        <tr>
            <td>Jane Smith</td><td>Marketing</td><td>$95,000</td>
        </tr>
        <tr class="newRecord">
            <td>John Smith</td><td>Technology</td><td>$90,000</td>
        </tr>
        <tr>
            <td>Brian Adam</td><td>Sales</td><td>$72,000</td>
        </tr>
        <tr>
            <td>Mary Jones</td><td>Customer Support</td><td>$60,000</td>
        </tr>
        <tr>
            <td>Michael Jefferson</td><td>Technology</td><td>$85,000</td>
        </tr>
    </table><br>
```

```
    <strong>Departments:</strong>
    <ul class="listDepartments">
       <li>Marketing</li>
       <li>Sales</li>
       <li class="newRecord">Technology</li>
       <li>Customer Support</li>
    </ul><br>
    <input id="btnTestIt" type="button" value="Test It">
</body>
</html>
```

How It Works

In this code, the employee details—employee name, department name, and salary—are listed in tabular form using the `<table>`, `<tr>`, and `<td>` HTML tags and the departments' names are listed using the `<ul>` and `<li>` HTML tags. In both lists, there is one record with the class `newRecord`. If you want to select non-`newRecord` records from the table only to perform an action on them, you first select all the records using `$("tr")` and then use `filter(".newRecord")`.

When the user clicks the Test It button, the following code is executed:

```
$("tr").not(".newRecord").css("background-color", "lightblue");
```

`$("tr")` selects all the HTML elements with tag name `"tr"` and returns a jQuery object. `.not(".newRecord")` selects all the HTML elements except the element with the class name of `"newRecord"` from the selected HTML elements and returns another jQuery object. Refer to Recipe 3-2 for an explanation of the `css()` method.

When you press the Test It button, the button's click event handler changes the background color of the selected elements to light blue. Figure 4-4 displays the effect of clicking the Test It button. 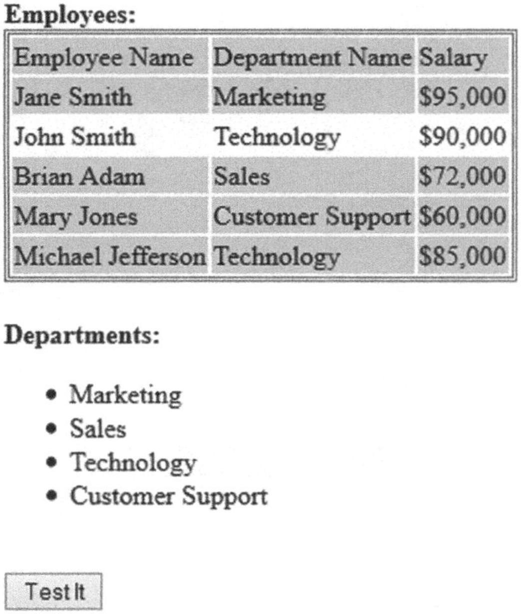

Employees:

Employee Name	Department Name	Salary
Jane Smith	Marketing	$95,000
John Smith	Technology	$90,000
Brian Adam	Sales	$72,000
Mary Jones	Customer Support	$60,000
Michael Jefferson	Technology	$85,000

Departments:

- Marketing
- Sales
- Technology
- Customer Support

Test It

Figure 4-4. *All records except the record with the newRecord class are highlighted with a light blue background*

Here are two other ways to filter elements using the not() method:

1. Using the not() method with the argument: selector:

    ```
    $("tr").not(".newRecord");
    ```

2. Using the not() method with the argument: jQuery object:

    ```
    var newRecords = $(".newRecord");
    $("tr").not(newRecords);
    ```

4-5. Narrowing Down the Set of Selected Elements by Excluding Elements Using a Function

Problem

You want to narrow down the set of selected elements by excluding some elements identified by a function.

Solution

The following jQuery selector syntax selects the HTML elements from the set of already selected HTML elements that do not match elements for which a function has returned true.

$(*selector*).not(function () {...})

Listing 4-5 provides an example to demonstrate the use of the not() method, with a function as an argument, to exclude specific HTML elements from the set of selected elements.

Listing 4-5. Using not(function()) to exclude specific elements

```
<!DOCTYPE html>
<html lang="en">
<head>
   <meta charset="utf-8">
   <script src="scripts/jquery-2.1.0.min.js"></script>
   <style>
      table {
         border:3px double green;
      }
      .tblHdr {
         background-color: lightgray;
      }
      .listDepartments {
         width: 200px;
      }
   </style>
```

```
    <script>
      $(function(){
        $("#btnTestIt").click(function () {
          $("tr:gt(0)").not(function(index) {
                          return ($(this).children().eq(1).text() == "Technology");
                      }).css("background-color", "lightblue");
        });
      });
    </script>
</head>
<body>
    <strong>Employees:</strong>
    <table id="listEmployees">
        <tr class="tblHdr">
            <td>Employee Name</td><td>Department Name</td><td>Salary</td>
        </tr>
        <tr>
            <td>Jane Smith</td><td>Marketing</td><td>$95,000</td>
        </tr>
        <tr>
            <td>John Smith</td><td>Technology</td><td>$76,000</td>
        </tr>
        <tr>
            <td>Brian Adam</td><td>Sales</td><td>$72,000</td>
        </tr>
        <tr>
            <td>Mary Jones</td><td>Customer Support</td><td>$60,000</td>
        </tr>
        <tr>
            <td>Michael Jefferson</td><td>Technology</td><td>$85,000</td>
        </tr>
    </table><br>
    <input id="btnTestIt" type="button" value="Test It">
</body>
</html>
```

How It Works

In this code, the employee details—employee name, department name, and salary—are listed in tabular form using the <table>, <tr>, and <td> HTML tags. If you want to select all the records except for the header record and records with department name as "Technology" and perform an action on the selected items, you first select all records except for header record using $("tr:gt(0)") and then use not(function() { ... }). The function will return true if current record has the department name of "Technology".

When the user clicks the Test It button, the following code is executed:

```
$("tr:gt(0)").not(function(index) {
    return ($(this).children().eq(1).text() == "Technology");
}).css("background-color", "lightblue");
```

$("tr:gt(0)") selects all the HTML elements with tag name "tr" with index number > 0 and returns a jQuery object. The .not(function()) iterates over each element of the selected HTML elements in the returned jQuery object. If the function returns true for the current element, that element is excluded in resultant jQuery object and after the end of the iteration, the resultant jQuery object is returned. In this case, $(this) is the current element, $(this).children() returns all the children (i.e., TD elements), $(this).children().eq(1) returns the second TD element, and $(this).children().eq(1).text() returns the text content of the second TD element, which is the department name. This function returns true if the department name is "Technology" and hence is excluded. Refer to Recipe 3-2 for an explanation of the css() method. The children() method is discussed in the next chapter.

When you press the Test It button, the button's click event handler changes the background color of all the selected elements to light blue. Figure 4-5 displays the effect of clicking the Test It button.

Employees:

Employee Name	Department Name	Salary
Jane Smith	Marketing	$95,000
John Smith	Technology	$76,000
Brian Adam	Sales	$72,000
Mary Jones	Customer Support	$60,000
Michael Jefferson	Technology	$85,000

Test It

Figure 4-5. *Records are highlighted if the department name is not Technology*

4-6. Narrowing Down the Set of Selected Elements by Selecting a Range of Elements by Index

Problem

You want to narrow down the set of selected elements by selecting elements within a range of indexes.

Solution

The following jQuery selector syntax selects HTML elements from the set of already selected HTML elements with an index number within a specified index range.

$(selector**).slice(**startIndexNumber, endIndexNumber**)**

HTML elements are selected with an index number greater than or equal to startIndexNumber and less than endIndexNumber. endIndexNumber is optional, if it is not specified all the elements starting with startIndexNumber until the end of the array will be selected. Listing 4-6 provides an example to demonstrate the use of the slice() method to select a range of HTML elements based on their index number. The index number is zero-based.

Listing 4-6. Using slice( ) to select a range of elements

```html
<!DOCTYPE html>
<html lang="en">
<head>
    <meta charset="utf-8">
    <script src="scripts/jquery-2.1.0.min.js"></script>
    <style>
        table {
            border:3px double green;
        }
        .tblHdr {
            background-color: lightgray;
        }
        .listDepartments {
            width: 200px;
        }
    </style>
    <script>
        $(function(){
            $("#btnTestIt").click(function () {
                $("tr").slice(2,4).css("background-color", "lightblue");
                            $("li").slice(1).css("background-color", "lightblue");
            });
        });
    </script>
</head>
<body>
    <strong>Employees:</strong>
    <table id="listEmployees">
        <tr class="tblHdr">
            <td>Employee Name</td><td>Department Name</td><td>Salary</td>
        </tr>
        <tr>
            <td>Jane Smith</td><td>Marketing</td><td>$80,000</td>
        </tr>
        <tr>
            <td>John Smith</td><td>Technology</td><td>$76,000</td>
        </tr>
        <tr>
            <td>Brian Adam</td><td>Sales</td><td>$72,000</td>
        </tr>
        <tr>
            <td>Mary Jones</td><td>Customer Support</td><td>$60,000</td>
        </tr>
        <tr>
            <td>Michael Jefferson</td><td>Technology</td><td>$85,000</td>
        </tr>
    </table><br>
    <strong>Departments:</strong>
    <ul class="listDepartments">
        <li>Marketing</li>
        <li>Sales</li>
```

```
        <li>Technology</li>
        <li>Customer Support</li>
    </ul><br>
    <input id="btnTestIt" type="button" value="Test It">
</body>
</html>
```

How It Works

In this code, the employee details—employee name, department name, and salary—are listed in tabular form using the <table>, <tr>, and <td> HTML tags and the departments' names are listed using the <ul> and <li> HTML tags. In both lists, there is one record with the class newRecord. If you want to select newRecord from the table only to perform an action on it, you first select all records using $("tr") and then use filter(".newRecord").

When the user clicks the Test It button, the following code is executed:

```
$("tr").slice(2,4).css("background-color", "lightblue");
$("li").slice(1).css("background-color", "lightblue");
```

$("tr") selects all HTML elements with tag name "tr" and returns the jQuery object. .slice(2, 4) selects HTML elements with index numbers 2 and 3 from the selected HTML elements and returns another jQuery object. The css() method is executed on the selected HTML element in the returned jQuery object. css("background-color", "lightblue") changes the background color of the selected element to light blue.

$("li") selects all the HTML elements with tag name "li" and returns a jQuery object. .slice(1) selects HTML elements starting with index number 1 until the end from the selected HTML elements and returns another jQuery object. Refer to Recipe 3-2 for an explanation of the css() method.

When you press the Test It button, the button's click event handler changes the background color of the selected elements to light blue. Figure 4-6 displays the effect of clicking the Test It button. 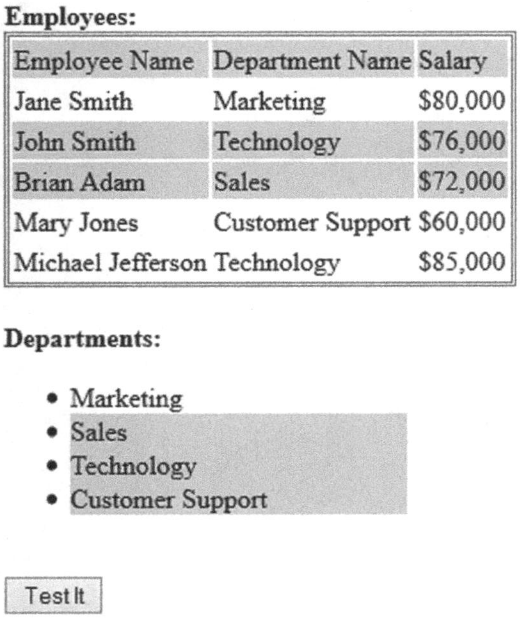

Employees:

Employee Name	Department Name	Salary
Jane Smith	Marketing	$80,000
John Smith	Technology	$76,000
Brian Adam	Sales	$72,000
Mary Jones	Customer Support	$60,000
Michael Jefferson	Technology	$85,000

Departments:

- Marketing
- Sales
- Technology
- Customer Support

Test It

Figure 4-6. *Selecting records using the slice() method*

4-7. Adding More Elements to the Set of Selected Elements

Problem

You want to add more HTML elements to a set of selected elements.

Solution

The following jQuery syntax adds more elements to the set of selected elements:

$(selector1**).add(**selector2**)**

Listing 4-7 provides an example to demonstrate the use of the add() method.

Listing 4-7. Adding more elements to already selected ones

```
<!DOCTYPE html>
<html lang="en">
<head>
    <meta charset="utf-8">
    <script src="scripts/jquery-2.1.0.min.js"></script>
    <style>
        table {
            border:3px double green;
        }
        .tblHdr {
            background-color: lightgray;
        }
        .listDepartments {
            width: 200px;
        }
    </style>
    <script>
        $(function(){
            $("#btnTestIt").click(function () {
                $("tr:gt(0)").add("li").css("background-color", "lightblue");
            });
        });
    </script>
</head>
<body>
    <strong>Employees:</strong>
    <table id="listEmployees">
        <tr class="tblHdr">
            <td>Employee Name</td><td>Department Name</td><td>Salary</td>
        </tr>
        <tr>
            <td>Jane Smith</td><td>Marketing</td><td>$95,000</td>
        </tr>
        <tr>
            <td>John Smith</td><td>Technology</td><td>$90,000</td>
        </tr>
```

```
    <tr>
        <td>Brian Adam</td><td>Sales</td><td>$72,000</td>
    </tr>
    <tr>
        <td>Mary Jones</td><td>Customer Support</td><td>$60,000</td>
    </tr>
    <tr>
        <td>Michael Jefferson</td><td>Technology</td><td>$85,000</td>
    </tr>
</table><br>
<strong>Departments:</strong>
<ul class="listDepartments">
    <li>Marketing</li>
    <li>Sales</li>
    <li>Technology</li>
    <li>Customer Support</li>
</ul><br>
<input id="btnTestIt" type="button" value="Test It">
</body>
</html>
```

How It Works

In this code, the employee details—employee name, department name, and salary—are listed in tabular form using the <table>, <tr>, and <td> HTML tags and the departments list is displayed using the <ul> and <li> tags. If you want to select table records except for the header record and then add the departments list, begin by selecting the table records using $("tr:gt(0) ") and then use the add("li") method to add elements to previously selected ones.

When the user clicks the Test It button, the following code is executed:

```
$("tr:gt(0)").add("li").css("background-color", "lightblue");
```

$("tr:gt(0)") selects all the HTML elements with the tag name "tr" whose index is greater than 0 and returns a jQuery object. .add("li") selects HTML elements with the tag name "li" and adds them to the previously selected records. It returns a resultant jQuery object with the combined set of elements. Refer to Recipe 3-2 for an explanation of the css() method.

When you press the Test It button, the button's click event handler changes the background color of the selected elements to light blue. Figure 4-7 displays the effect of clicking the Test It button.

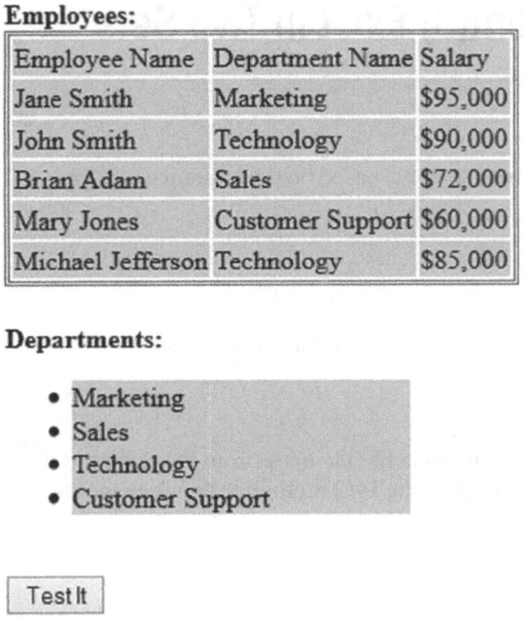

Employees:

Employee Name	Department Name	Salary
Jane Smith	Marketing	$95,000
John Smith	Technology	$90,000
Brian Adam	Sales	$72,000
Mary Jones	Customer Support	$60,000
Michael Jefferson	Technology	$85,000

Departments:

- Marketing
- Sales
- Technology
- Customer Support

Test It

Figure 4-7. *Selected elements with a light blue background*

Here are three additional ways to add elements:

1. Using the add() method with the argument: selector:

   ```
   $("tr:gt(0)").add("li");
   ```

2. Using the add() method with the argument: HTMLElements:

   ```
   var liElements = document.getElementsByTagName("li");
   $("tr:gt(0)").add(liElements);
   ```

3. Using the add() method with the argument: jQuery object:

   ```
   var jqObj = $("li");
   $("tr:gt(0)").add(jqObj);
   ```

4-8. Checking if Common HTML Element(S) Exist in Two Sets of Selected HTML Elements

Problem

You want to perform an action on elements from a set of selected HTML elements based on the existence of at least one element in another set of selected HTML elements.

Solution

The following jQuery syntax determines if element(s) from one set of HTML elements exist in another set.

$(selector1**).is(**selector2**)**

This method returns a Boolean. If at least one element from *selector1* matches elements from selector2, it returns true; otherwise, false is returned. Listing 4-8 demonstrates the use of the is() method to check elements in two sets.

Listing 4-8. Using is( ) to check elements from two sets

```
<!DOCTYPE html>
<html lang="en">
<head>
    <meta charset="utf-8">
    <script src="scripts/jquery-2.1.0.min.js"></script>
    <style>
        .tableWithNewRecord {
            border:3px double green;
        }
        .tblHdr {
            background-color: lightgray;
        }
        .listDepartments {
            width: 200px;
        }
        .newRecord {
            background-color: lightyellow;
        }
    </style>
    <script>
        $(function(){
            $("#btnTestIt").click(function () {
                if ($("tr").is(".newRecord")) {
                    $("#message").prop("innerHTML", "<strong>There is a new record in the
                    table.</strong>");
                }
            });
        });
    </script>
</head>
```

```
<body>
    <strong>Employees:</strong>
    <table id="listEmployees">
        <tr class="tblHdr">
            <td>Employee Name</td><td>Department Name</td><td>Salary</td>
        </tr>
        <tr>
            <td>Jane Smith</td><td>Marketing</td><td>$95,000</td>
        </tr>
        <tr class="newRecord">
            <td>John Smith</td><td>Technology</td><td>$90,000</td>
        </tr>
        <tr>
            <td>Brian Adam</td><td>Sales</td><td>$72,000</td>
        </tr>
        <tr>
            <td>Mary Jones</td><td>Customer Support</td><td>$60,000</td>
        </tr>
        <tr>
            <td>Michael Jefferson</td><td>Technology</td><td>$85,000</td>
        </tr>
    </table><br><br><br>
    <input id="btnTestIt" type="button" value="Test It"><br><br>
    <div id="message"></div>
</body>
</html>
```

How It Works

In this code, the employee details—employee name, department name, and salary—are listed in tabular form using the <table>, <tr>, and <td> HTML tags. If you want to check if any of the "tr" elements have a "newRecord" class, you first select all the records using $("tr") and then use is(".newRecord") to check the condition.

When the Test It button is clicked, the following code is executed:

```
if ($("tr").is(".newRecord")) {
    $("#message").prop("innerHTML", "<strong>There is a new record in the table.</strong>");
}
```

$("tr") selects all the HTML elements with the tag name "tr" and returns a jQuery object. .is(".newRecord") checks if any of the HTML elements exist in the set of elements with class name newRecord. In this case, true is returned. $("#message").prop("innerHTML", "There is a new record in the table.") gets the <div> with id #message and sets its innerHTML property with the message.

When you press the Test It button, the button's click event handler displays the message. Figure 4-8 displays the message when the Test It button is clicked.

119

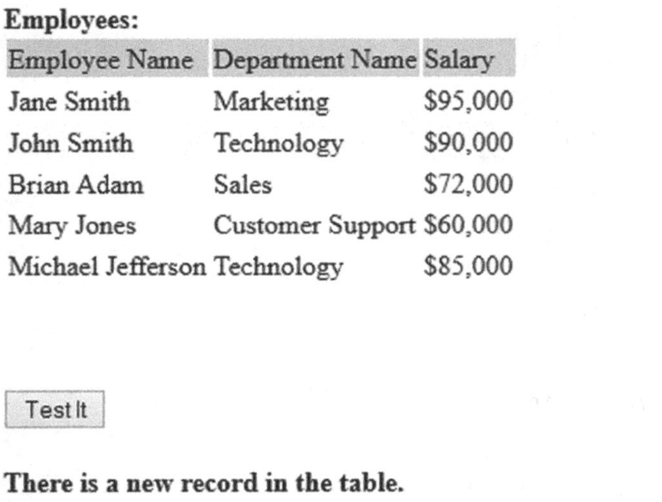

Employees:

Employee Name	Department Name	Salary
Jane Smith	Marketing	$95,000
John Smith	Technology	$90,000
Brian Adam	Sales	$72,000
Mary Jones	Customer Support	$60,000
Michael Jefferson	Technology	$85,000

Test It

There is a new record in the table.

Figure 4-8. *Message displayed when the is( ) method returns true*

4-9. Iterating Over Each HTML Element in the jQuery Object to Perform an Action

Problem

You want to perform a different action on each element from a group of HTML elements.

Solution

So far this chapter has discussed how HTML elements can be selected using various basic jQuery selectors and selector extensions and has performed the same action on all of the selected elements. This section covers how different actions can be performed on each of the selected elements based on some logic.

The following jQuery syntax selects each element individually from the set of selected HTML elements.

```
$("selector").each(function (currentIndexNumber, currentElement) {
    // Code segment to process each element
});
```

These are the arguments of the inline function():

- currentElement is the HTML element that's being processed in this iteration. It is from the array of HTML elements in the jQuery object, which is returned by $("selector").

- currentIndexNumber is the index number of the current HTML element being processed.

Inside the function, the current element can be accessed using $(this) or $(*currentElement*). Listing 4-9 demonstrates the use of the each() method, which iterates over each element from the set of selected elements.

Listing 4-9. Iterate over each element in the set of selected elements

```
<!DOCTYPE html>
<html lang="en">
<head>
    <meta charset="utf-8">
    <script src="scripts/jquery-2.1.0.min.js"></script>
    <style>
        table {
            border:3px double green;
        }
    </style>
    <script>
        $(function(){
            $("#btnTestIt").click(function () {
                $("tr").each(function (index, htmlElement){
                    var bgColor = "";
                    if (index == 0) {
                        bgColor = "lightgray";
                    } else if (index % 2 == 0) {
                        bgColor = "lightyellow";
                    } else {
                        bgColor = "lightblue";
                    }
                    $(this).css("background-color", bgColor);
                });
            });
        });
    </script>
</head>
<body>
    <table id="tblEmployee">
        <tr>
            <td>Employee Name</td><td>Department Name</td><td>Salary</td>
        </tr>
        <tr>
            <td>Jane Smith</td><td>Marketing</td><td>$95,000</td>
        </tr>
        <tr>
            <td>John Smith</td><td>Technology</td><td>$90,000</td>
        </tr>
        <tr>
            <td>Brian Adam</td><td>Sales</td><td>$72,000</td>
        </tr>
        <tr>
            <td>Mary Jones</td><td>Support</td><td>$60,000</td>
        </tr>
```

```
    <tr>
        <td>Michael Jefferson</td><td>Technology</td><td>$85,000</td>
    </tr>
  </table><br>
  <input id="btnTestIt" type="button" value="Test It">
</body>
</html>
```

How It Works

In this code, the employee details—employee name, department name, and salary—are listed in tabular form using the <table>, <tr>, and <td> HTML tags. Other than the first record (the header record), all the other records (<tr>) use the row CSS class. If you want to select even numbered and odd numbered rows, excluding the header record, you first select all the records using the $(".row") selector and then use the :even and :odd extensions to select the even and odd numbered elements from these matched records.

When the user clicks the Test It button, the following code is executed:

```
$("tr").each(function (index, htmlElement){
    var bgColor = "";
    if (index == 0) {
       bgColor = "lightgray";
    } else if (index % 2 == 0) {
       bgColor = "lightyellow";
    } else {
       bgColor = "lightblue";
    }
    $(this).css("background-color", bgColor);
});
```

$("tr") selects all the HTML elements with the tag name "tr" and returns a jQuery object. .each() iterates through each element in the set of selected HTML elements in the returned jQuery object. The argument of the each() method is an inline function() that has access to the current HTML element being processed and its index number. Based on the index number, code logic decides the value of background color. If it is the first element (index: 0), i.e. header, the background color variable is set as light gray. If the index number is an even number, the background color is set as light yellow. Otherwise, the background color is set to light blue. $(this) is the current HTML element being processed. css("background-color", bgcolor) changes the background color of the currently selected element to the value of bgcolor.

When you press the Test It button, the button's click event handler changes the background color of selected elements. Figure 4-9 displays the effect of clicking the Test It button.

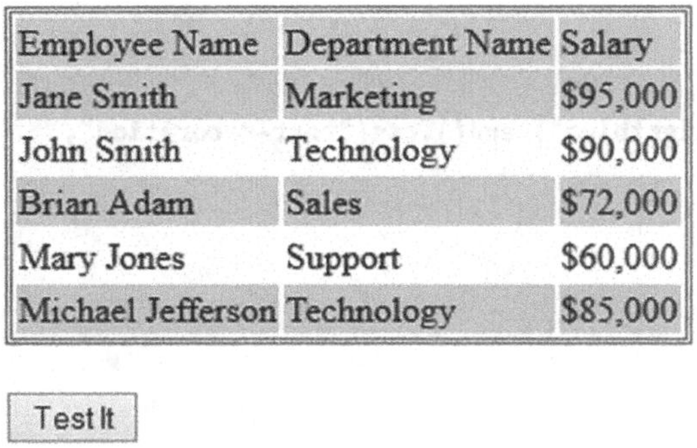

Employee Name	Department Name	Salary
Jane Smith	Marketing	$95,000
John Smith	Technology	$90,000
Brian Adam	Sales	$72,000
Mary Jones	Support	$60,000
Michael Jefferson	Technology	$85,000

Test It

Figure 4-9. *Change in background color when Test It button is clicked*

4-10. Reverting to the Most Recent Expansion or Narrowing a Set of Selected Elements

Problem

You want to revert (undo) the effect of an expansion or narrow a set of selected elements.

Solution

The following examples of jQuery syntax are used to undo the most recent change and revert to a set of selected elements.

$(*selector***).add(***additonalSelector***).***manipulationMethod***().end()**
$(*selector***).filter(***filterSelector***).***manipulationMethod***().end()**

Listing 4-10 demonstrates the use of the end() method to revert to the effect of the add() method.

Listing 4-10. Using end() method to revert to the effect of add()

```
<!DOCTYPE html>
<html lang="en">
<head>
   <meta charset="utf-8">
   <script src="scripts/jquery-2.1.0.min.js"></script>
   <style>
      table {
         border:3px double green;
      }
      .tblHdr {
         background-color: lightgray;
      }
      .listDepartments {
         width: 200px;
      }
   </style>
```

```
<script>
  $(function(){
    $("#btnTestIt").click(function () {
      $("tr:gt(0)").add("li").css("background-color", "lightblue").end().css("text-decoration",
      "underline");
    });
  });
</script>
</head>
<body>
  <strong>Employees:</strong>
  <table id="listEmployees">
    <tr class="tblHdr">
      <td>Employee Name</td><td>Department Name</td><td>Salary</td>
    </tr>
    <tr>
      <td>Jane Smith</td><td>Marketing</td><td>$95,000</td>
    </tr>
    <tr>
      <td>John Smith</td><td>Technology</td><td>$90,000</td>
    </tr>
    <tr>
      <td>Brian Adam</td><td>Sales</td><td>$72,000</td>
    </tr>
    <tr>
      <td>Mary Jones</td><td>Customer Support</td><td>$60,000</td>
    </tr>
    <tr>
      <td>Michael Jefferson</td><td>Technology</td><td>$85,000</td>
    </tr>
  </table><br>
  <strong>Departments:</strong>
  <ul class="listDepartments">
    <li>Marketing</li>
    <li>Sales</li>
    <li>Technology</li>
    <li>Customer Support</li>
  </ul><br>
  <input id="btnTestIt" type="button" value="Test It">
</body>
</html>
```

How It Works

In this code, the employee details—employee name, department name, and salary—are listed in tabular form using the <table>, <tr>, and <td> HTML tags. When the Test It button is clicked, the following code is executed:

```
$("tr:gt(0)").add("li").css("background-color",
  "lightblue").end().css("text-decoration", "underline");
```

`$("tr:gt(0)")` selects all the HTML elements with the tag name "tr", where the index number is greater than 0 and returns the jQuery object. All the records from the table are selected except for the first one.

`.add("li")` adds all the HTML elements with the tag name "li" to the previous set of selected records.

`css("background-color", "lightblue")` changes the background color of the selected elements to light blue.

`end()` reverts to the most recent expansion or narrowing of elements. In this case, the addition of HTML elements with the tag name "li" is reverted.

`css("text-decoration", "underline")` changes the text decoration of the current set of elements to underline.

When you press the Test It button, the button's click event handler changes the background color of all the "tr" elements (except for the header) and "li" elements to light blue and underlines the "tr" elements only. Figure 4-10 displays the change in the background color and text decoration.

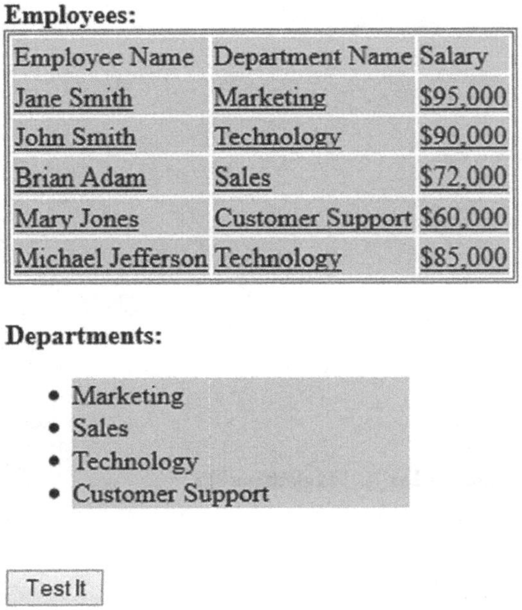

Employees:

Employee Name	Department Name	Salary
Jane Smith	Marketing	$95,000
John Smith	Technology	$90,000
Brian Adam	Sales	$72,000
Mary Jones	Customer Support	$60,000
Michael Jefferson	Technology	$85,000

Departments:

- Marketing
- Sales
- Technology
- Customer Support

Test It

Figure 4-10. *Selected elements are highlighted with light blue background and table records are underlined*

4-11. Adding the Previous Set of Elements to the Current Set
Problem

You want to add the previous set of selected elements to the current set.

Solution

The following example of jQuery syntax adds the previous set of selected elements to the current set of selected elements.

`$(selector1).selectionMethod().addBack(selector2)`

selector2 is optional. If it is specified, elements from previous selection are matched against this selector before adding them back to the composite selection. Listing 4-11 demonstrates the use of the addBack( ) method to merge the previous and current selections.

Listing 4-11. Using addBack( ) method to merge the previous and current selections

```html
<!DOCTYPE html>
<html lang="en">
<head>
    <meta charset="utf-8">
    <script src="scripts/jquery-2.1.0.min.js"></script>
    <style>
        table {
            border:3px double green;
        }
        .tblHdr {
            background-color: lightgray;
        }
        .newRecord {
            background-color: lightyellow;
        }
        .listDepartments {
            width: 200px;
        }
    </style>
    <script>
        $(function(){
            $("#btnTestIt").click(function () {
                $(".newRecord").nextAll().addBack().css("background-color", "lightblue");
            });
        });
    </script>
</head>
<body>
    <strong>Employees:</strong>
    <table class="listEmployees">
        <tr class="tblHdr">
            <td>Employee Name</td><td>Department Name</td><td>Salary</td>
        </tr>
        <tr>
            <td>Jane Smith</td><td>Marketing</td><td>$95,000</td>
        </tr>
        <tr class="newRecord">
            <td>John Smith</td><td>Technology</td><td>$90,000</td>
        </tr>
        <tr>
            <td>Brian Adam</td><td>Sales</td><td>$72,000</td>
        </tr>
```

```
      <tr>
         <td>Mary Jones</td><td>Customer Support</td><td>$60,000</td>
      </tr>
      <tr>
         <td>Michael Jefferson</td><td>Technology</td><td>$85,000</td>
      </tr>
   </table><br>
   <input id="btnTestIt" type="button" value="Test It">
</body>
</html>
```

How It Works

In this code, the employee details—employee name, department name, and salary—are listed in tabular form using the <table>, <tr>, and <td> HTML tags. When the Test It button is clicked, the following code is executed:

```
$(".newRecord").nextAll().addBack().css("background-color", "lightblue");
```

$(".newRecord") selects all the HTML elements with the class name newRecord and returns a jQuery object. The <tr class="newRecord"> element is selected.

.nextAll("") selects all the following sibling HTML elements of the selected element, which is all the "tr" elements following the "tr" element but not including it.

.addBack() adds the previous selection (tr with the class name newRecord) to the set of currently selected elements.

css("background-color", "lightblue") changes the background color of the selected elements to light blue.

When you press the Test It button, the button's click event handler changes the background color of the "tr" element with the class name newRecord, as well as all of its siblings, to light blue. Figure 4-11 displays the background color of the selected elements. 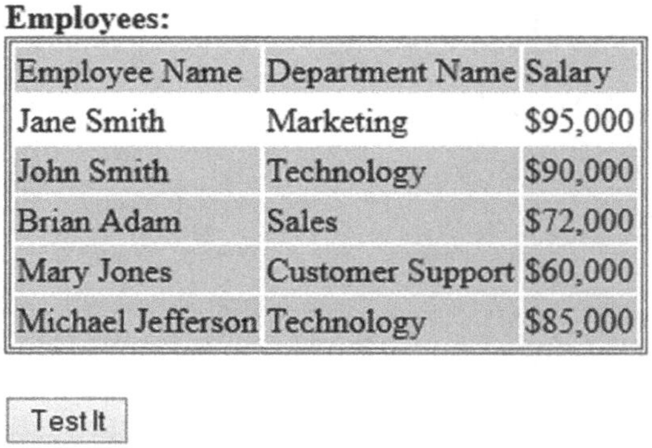

Employees:

Employee Name	Department Name	Salary
Jane Smith	Marketing	$95,000
John Smith	Technology	$90,000
Brian Adam	Sales	$72,000
Mary Jones	Customer Support	$60,000
Michael Jefferson	Technology	$85,000

Test It

Figure 4-11. *Selected elements are highlighted with light blue*

4-12. Creating a New jQuery Object from an Existing jQuery Object Using a Function

Problem

You want to create a new jQuery object based on each element of a set of selected elements using a function. The new jQuery object can contain the same element as the current one, a different element based on the attribute or property of current element, or no element at all.

Solution

The following example of jQuery syntax creates a new jQuery object from an existing one using the return value of the function.

$(*selector*).map(function() { ... return(*element*) })

It returns the jQuery object. Each element from the set of selected elements is mapped to some other (or the same) element. If you don't want to add an element for the current selected element, return null. Listing 4-12 demonstrates the use of the jQuery method map() to create a new jQuery object using mapped elements.

Listing 4-12. Using the map() method and function to create a new jQuery object

```
<!DOCTYPE html>
<html lang="en">
<head>
   <meta charset="utf-8">
   <script src="scripts/jquery-2.1.0.min.js"></script>
   <style>
      table {
         border:3px double green;
      }
      .highlight {
         background-color: yellow;
      }
   </style>
   <script>
      $(function(){
         $("#btnTestIt").click(function () {
            var jqObj = $("tr:gt(0)").map(function() {
               return $(this).children().first().text();
            })
            var employeesName = jqObj.get().join(", ");
            $("#message").prop("innerHTML", "<strong>Employees List: "+ employeesName +
"</strong>");
         });
      });
   </script>
</head>
```

```
<body>
    <table id="tblEmployee">
        <tr>
            <td>Employee Name</td><td>Department Name</td><td>Salary</td>
        </tr>
        <tr>
            <td>Jane Smith</td><td>Marketing</td><td>$95,C00</td>
        </tr>
        <tr>
            <td>John Smith</td><td>Technology</td><td>$90,000</td>
        </tr>
        <tr>
            <td>Brian Adam</td><td>Sales</td><td>$72,000</td>
        </tr>
        <tr>
            <td>Mary Jones</td><td>Support</td><td>$60,000</td>
        </tr>
        <tr>
            <td>Michael Jefferson</td><td>Technology</td><td>$85,000</td>
        </tr>
    </table><br>
    <input id="btnTestIt" type="button" value="Test It"><br><br>
    <div id="message" class="highlight"></div>
</body>
</html>
```

How It Works

In this code, the employee details—employee name, department name, and salary—are listed in tabular form using the <table>, <tr>, and <td> HTML tags. When the Test It button is clicked, the following code is executed:

```
var jqObj = $("tr:gt(0)").map(function() {
    return $(this).children().first().text();
})
    var employeesName = jqObj.get().join(", ");
    $("#message").prop("innerHTML", "<strong>Employees List: "+ employeesName + "</strong>");
```

$("tr:gt(0)") selects all the HTML elements with the tag name "tr" except for the first record and returns the jQuery object.

.map() iterates through each element from the set of selected elements and processes them in the function.

return $(this).children().first().text() returns the text content of the first child element (td) of each selected "tr" element, which is the employee name.

A new jQuery object (jqObj) is created that contains elements as a result of the return value of the function.

jqObj.get() gets all the HTML elements from the jQuery object as an array.

.join(", ") joins all elements from the array, delimits them with commas (,) and returns a string that contains a comma-delimited list of all the employees' names.

$("#message").prop("innerHTML", "Employees List: "+ employeesName + "") sets the innerHTML of the element with id set to "message", which is a div tag with the list of employees' names.

When you press the Test It button, the button's click event handler gets the employees list and displays it. Figure 4-12 displays the employees list.

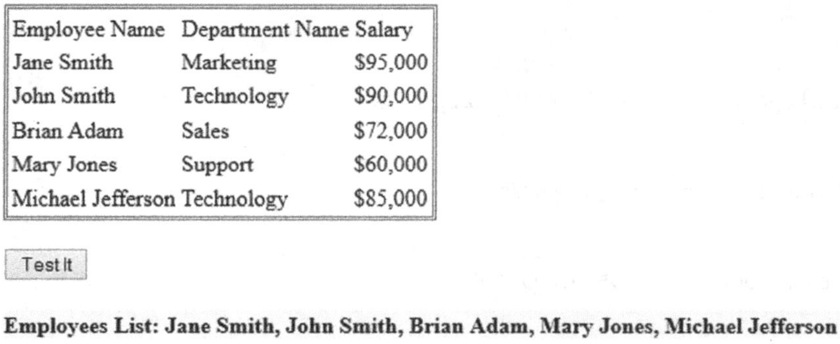

Employee Name	Department Name	Salary
Jane Smith	Marketing	$95,000
John Smith	Technology	$90,000
Brian Adam	Sales	$72,000
Mary Jones	Support	$60,000
Michael Jefferson	Technology	$85,000

Test It

Employees List: Jane Smith, John Smith, Brian Adam, Mary Jones, Michael Jefferson

Figure 4-12. *Employees names are selected and displayed*

Summary

This chapter covered jQuery selectors filtering and expansion methods. To access the attributes, properties, text content, and HTML content of HTML elements or to change the value of their attributes and properties, you first need to select them by using id, className, attributeName, attributeValue, and so on. Then if needed, you fine-tune the set of selected elements by using the filtering and expansion methods. This chapter covered the following filtering and expansion methods:

- Commonly used methods to filter (narrow down) the set of selected HTML elements are:

    - eq(indexNumber)

    - first()

    - last()

    - filter(selector)

    - not(selector)

    - slice(startIndex, endIndex)

- The method to expand the set of selected HTML elements is add()

- Other methods you saw in this chapter, all of which are covered in detail in Chapter 6, are:

    - get()

    - text()

    - css()

CHAPTER 5

DOM Traversing

This chapter covers jQuery methods for DOM traversing. Chapter 3 explained how to use jQuery selectors to get (or select) HTML elements based on their ID, tag name, class name, types, attributes, attribute values, and other criteria. Chapters 3 and 4 covered how a set of selected elements can be further fine-tuned using selector extensions, filtering methods, and expansion methods. DOM traversing methods can be used to select ancestors, descendants, and siblings of selected elements. Once you have the desired set of elements, you can access and manipulate their attributes (including values), properties, and styles.

This chapter's recipes show how jQuery methods can be used to select HTML elements by traversing through the node tree at runtime in order to:

- Access their styles, properties, and attributes

- Manipulate their styles, properties, and attributes

Refer to Chapter 2 for a review of the DOM tree structure, nodes, ancestors, siblings, and descendants.

5-1. Getting the Child Nodes of Each Selected Element
Problem

You want to get the children of each element from the set of selected elements.

Solution

The following jQuery syntax selects the child nodes of each selected HTML element.

$(_selector_**).children(**_childSelector_**)**

childSelector is optional. If it is specified, only the children that match childSelector are selected. Listing 5-1 demonstrates the use of the children() method to get child elements of each element from the set of selected elements.

Listing 5-1. Using the children() method to select children elements

```
<!DOCTYPE html>
<html lang="en">
<head>
    <meta charset="utf-8">
    <script src="scripts/jquery-2.1.0.min.js"></script>
```

```
    <style>
        .list {
            border:3px double green;
            width:350px;
        }
        .newRecord {
            background-color: lightyellow;
        }
        .tblHdr {
            background-color: lightgray;
        }
        .listDepartments {
            width: 200px;
        }
    </style>
    <script>
        $(function(){
            $("#btnTestIt").click(function () {
                        $(".newRecord").children().each(function () {
                                            alert($(this).text());
                        });
            });
        });
    </script>
</head>
<body>
    <strong>Employees:</strong>
    <table class="list">
        <tr class="tblHdr">
            <td>Employee Name</td><td>Department Name</td><td>Salary</td>
        </tr>
        <tr>
            <td>Jane Smith</td><td>Marketing</td><td>$95,000</td>
        </tr>
        <tr class="newRecord">
            <td>John Smith</td><td>Technology</td><td>$90,000</td>
        </tr>
        <tr>
            <td>Brian Adam</td><td>Sales</td><td>$72,000</td>
        </tr>
        <tr>
            <td>Mary Jones</td><td>Customer Support</td><td>$60,000</td>
        </tr>
        <tr>
            <td>Michael Jefferson</td><td>Technology</td><td>$85,000</td>
        </tr>
    </table><br>
     <input id="btnTestIt" type="button" value="Test It">
</body>
</html>
```

How It Works

In this code, the employee details—employee name, department name, and salary—are listed in tabular form using the <table>, <tr>, and <td> HTML tags. In the tabular list, there is one record with the class newRecord. When the Test It button is clicked, the following code is executed:

```
$(".newRecord").children().each(function () {
   alert($(this).text());
});
```

$(".newRecord") selects all HTML elements with the class name newRecord and returns a jQuery object. The following element is selected:

- <tr class="newRecord">

.children() selects all children elements of each of the selected HTML elements. The following children elements are selected:

- <td>John Smith</td>

- <td>Technology</td>

- <td>$90,000</td>

each() iterates over all of the selected elements and alert() displays each selected element's content, as follows:

- John Smith

- Technology

- $90,000

Figure 5-1 displays the page when it is viewed in a browser. 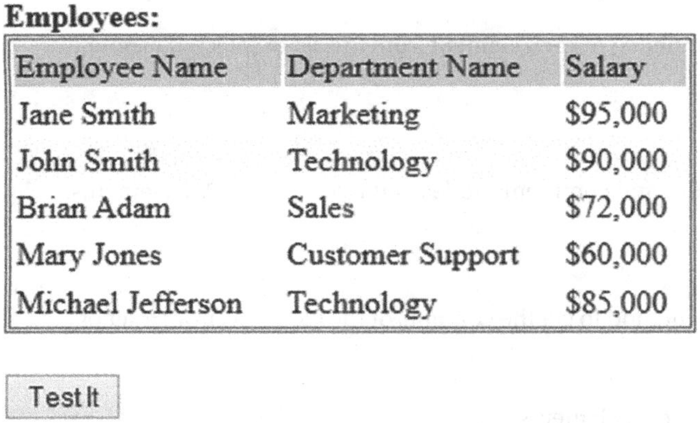

Employees:

Employee Name	Department Name	Salary
Jane Smith	Marketing	$95,000
John Smith	Technology	$90,000
Brian Adam	Sales	$72,000
Mary Jones	Customer Support	$60,000
Michael Jefferson	Technology	$85,000

Test It

Figure 5-1. *Initial page display*

When you press the Test It button, the button's click event handler displays the text content of each child element. Figure 5-2 displays the pop-up messages.

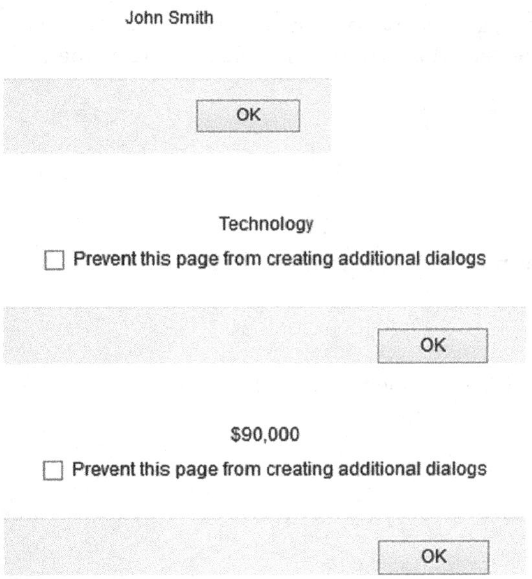

John Smith

OK

Technology

☐ Prevent this page from creating additional dialogs

OK

$90,000

☐ Prevent this page from creating additional dialogs

OK

Figure 5-2. *Text content of selected children elements*

5-2. Getting the Children Nodes of All Selected Elements, Including Text and Comments Nodes

Problem

You want to get the children (including any text and comments) of each element from the set of selected elements.

Solution

The following jQuery syntax selects the content (child, text, and comment) nodes of the selected HTML elements.

$(*selector*).contents()

Listing 5-2 demonstrates the use of the contents() method to get the contents of the elements from a set of selected elements.

Listing 5-2. Using the contents() method to select all contents elements

```
<!DOCTYPE html>
<html lang="en">
<head>
    <meta charset="utf-8">
    <script src="scripts/jquery-2.1.0.min.js"></script>
```

```
<style>
  .list {
    border:3px double green;
    width:350px;
  }
  .tblHdr {
    background-color: lightgray;
  }
  .listDepartments {
    width: 200px;
  }
</style>
<script>
  $(function(){
        $("#btnTestIt").click(function () {
                              $(".list").contents().each(function() {
                                  alert($(this).text());
                              });
        });
  });
</script>
</head>
<body>
  <div class="list">
            Departments:
      <ul>
        <li>Marketing</li>
        <li>Sales</li>
        <li>Technology</li>
        <li>Customer Support</li>
      </ul>
  </div><br>
  <input id="btnTestIt" type="button" value="Test It">
</body>
</html>
```

How It Works

In this code, the departments' names are listed using the `<ul>` and `<li>` HTML tags. The departments' text and `<ul>` are embedded in the `<div>` tag, which uses the "list" CSS class. When the Test It button is clicked, the following code is executed:

```
$(".list").contents().each(function() {
   alert($(this).text());
});
```

`$(".list")` selects all HTML elements with the class name "list" and returns a jQuery object. Only the `<div>` element is selected.

`.contents()` selects all the contents elements of each of the selected HTML elements. The following three content elements are selected:

Departments: literal string

```
<li>Marketing</li>
<li>Sales</li>
<li>Technology</li>
<li>Customer Support</li>
```

Empty string: a newline character and space between `</ul>` and `</div>` tags

`each()` iterates over all of the selected elements and `alert()` displays each selected element's text content. Figure 5-3 displays the page when it is viewed in a browser.

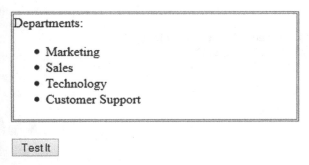

Figure 5-3. *Initial page display*

When you press the Test It button, the button's click event handler displays the text content of each child element. Figure 5-4 displays the pop-up messages.

Figure 5-4. *Text content of selected content elements*

5-3. Getting the Descendant Nodes of All Selected Elements Filtered by a Specified Selector, jQuery Object, or HTML Element

Problem

You want to get all the descendants of each element from the set of selected elements filtered by a selector.

Solution

The following jQuery syntax selects the descendant nodes of each selected HTML element that is filtered by the specified descendantSelector as an argument.

$(selector**).find(**descendantSelector**)**

Listing 5-3 demonstrates the use of the find() method to get the descendant elements of each element from the set.

Listing 5-3. Using the find() method to select any descendant elements

```
<!DOCTYPE html>
<html lang="en">
<head>
    <meta charset="utf-8">
    <script src="scripts/jquery-2.1.0.min.js"></script>
    <style>
        .list {
            border:3px double green;
            width:350px;
        }
        .newRecord {
            font-weight: bold;
        }
        .tblHdr {
            background-color: lightgray;
        }
        .listDepartments {
            width: 200px;
        }
    </style>
    <script>
        $(function(){
            $("#btnTestIt").click(function () {
                            $("table, ul").find(".newRecord").css("background-color", "lightblue");
                        });
        });
    </script>
</head>
```

```
<body>
    <strong>Employees:</strong>
    <table class="list">
        <tr class="tblHdr">
            <td>Employee Name</td><td>Department Name</td><td>Salary</td>
        </tr>
        <tr>
            <td>Jane Smith</td><td>Marketing</td><td>$95,000</td>
        </tr>
        <tr class="newRecord">
            <td>John Smith</td><td>Technology</td><td>$90,000</td>
        </tr>
        <tr>
            <td>Brian Adam</td><td>Sales</td><td>$72,000</td>
        </tr>
        <tr>
            <td>Mary Jones</td><td>Customer Support</td><td>$60,000</td>
        </tr>
        <tr>
            <td>Michael Jefferson</td><td>Technology</td><td>$85,000</td>
        </tr>
    </table><br>
    <strong>Departments:</strong>
    <div>
        <ul class="list">
            <li>Marketing</li>
            <li>Sales</li>
            <li class="newRecord">Technology</li>
            <li>Customer Support</li>
        </ul>
    </div><br>
    <input id="btnTestIt" type="button" value="Test It">
</body>
</html>
```

How It Works

In this code, the employee details—employee name, department name, and salary—are listed in tabular form using the <table>, <tr>, and <td> HTML tags and the departments' names are listed using the <ul> and <li> HTML tags. In both lists, there is one record with the class newRecord. When the Test It button is clicked, following code is executed:

```
$("#btnTestIt").click(function () {
  $("table, ul").find(".newRecord").css("background-color", "lightblue");
});
```

$("table, ul") selects all HTML elements with the "table" or "ul" tag name and returns a jQuery object. The following two elements are selected:

- <table class="list">

- <ul class="list">

`.find(".newRecord")` selects all descendant elements that have the `newRecord` class from the selected HTML elements. The following children elements are selected:

- `<tr class="newRecord">`

- `<li class="newRecord">`

`.css("background-color", "lightblue")` sets the background color of the selected elements to light blue. Figure 5-5 displays the page when it is viewed in a browser.

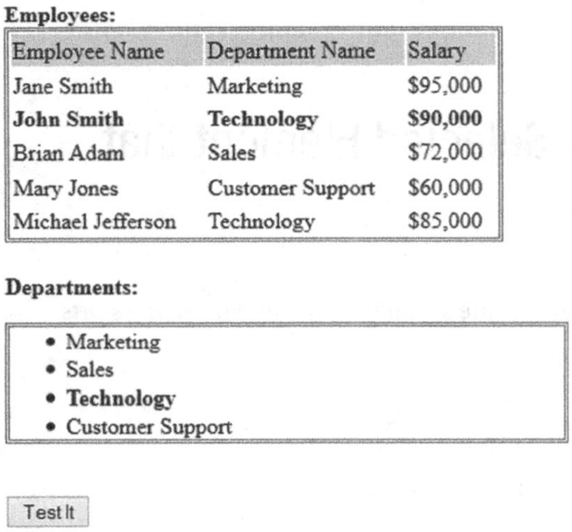

Employees:

Employee Name	Department Name	Salary
Jane Smith	Marketing	$95,000
John Smith	**Technology**	**$90,000**
Brian Adam	Sales	$72,000
Mary Jones	Customer Support	$60,000
Michael Jefferson	Technology	$85,000

Departments:

- Marketing
- Sales
- **Technology**
- Customer Support

[Test It]

Figure 5-5. *Initial page display*

When you press the Test It button, the button's click event handler highlights the records with the `newRecord` class name. Figure 5-6 displays the descendants that are selected by matching the specified selector.

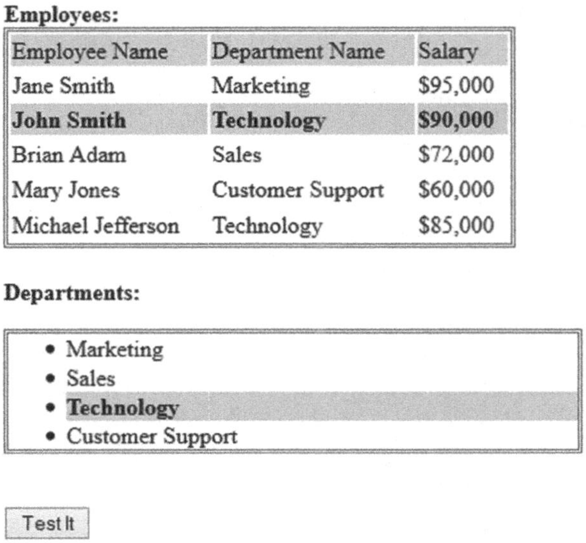

Employees:

Employee Name	Department Name	Salary
Jane Smith	Marketing	$95,000
John Smith	**Technology**	**$90,000**
Brian Adam	Sales	$72,000
Mary Jones	Customer Support	$60,000
Michael Jefferson	Technology	$85,000

Departments:

- Marketing
- Sales
- **Technology**
- Customer Support

[Test It]

Figure 5-6. *Descendant elements that have the newRecord CSS class are highlighted*

Here are two other ways to use the find() method with different argument types:

1. Using the find() method with the argument: jQuery object:

```
var jqObj = $(".newRecord");
$("table, ul").find(jqObj) ...
```

2. Using the find() method with the argument: HTML elements:

```
var nestedUL = document.getElementsByTagName("ul");
$("ul").find(nestedUL) ...
```

5-4. Getting the First Ancestor of Each Selected Element that Matches the Specified Selector

Problem

You want to find the closest ancestor of the selected elements that matches the specified selector. Traversing starts with the element itself.

Solution

The following jQuery syntax selects the closest ancestor of each selected HTML element.

$(selector**).closest(**ancestorSelector**)**

Listing 5-4 demonstrates the use of the closest() method to get the closest ancestor element from the set.

Listing 5-4. Using the closest() method to select the closest ancestor element

```
<!DOCTYPE html>
<html lang="en">
<head>
    <meta charset="utf-8">
    <script src="scripts/jquery-2.1.0.min.js"></script>
    <style>
        .list {
            border:3px double green;
            width:350px;
        }
        .newRecord {
            background-color: lightyellow;
        }
    </style>
</head>
```

```
    <script>
       $(function(){
          $("#btnTestIt").click(function () {
                        $(".newRecord").closest(".list").each(function () {
                                        alert($(this).prop("tagName"));
                        });
          });
       });
    </script>
</head>
<body>
    <strong>Departments:</strong>
    <div class="list">
       <ul>
          <li>Marketing</li>
          <li>Sales</li>
          <li class="newRecord">Technology</li>
          <li>Customer Support</li>
       </ul>
    </div><br>
    <input id="btnTestIt" type="button" value="Test It">
</body>
</html>
```

How It Works

In this code, the departments' names are listed using the <ul> and <li> HTML tags. One of the "li" elements has the newRecord CSS class. When the Test It button is clicked, the following code is executed:

```
$(".newRecord").closest(".list").each(function () {
   alert($(this).prop("tagName"));
});
```

$(".newRecord") selects all HTML elements with the class name newRecord and returns a jQuery object. The following element is selected:

```
<li class="newRecord">Technology</li>
```

.closest(".list") selects the closest ancestor that matches the class "list", including itself. The following ancestor element is selected:

```
<div class="list">
```

each() iterates over all of the selected elements and alert() displays each selected element's tag name, which is:

DIV

Here is the other way to use the closest() method with a different argument type:

1. Using the closest() method with the argument: jQuery object:

```
var jqObj = $(".list ");
$(".newRecord").closest(jqObj) ...
```

Figure 5-7 displays the page when it is viewed in a browser.

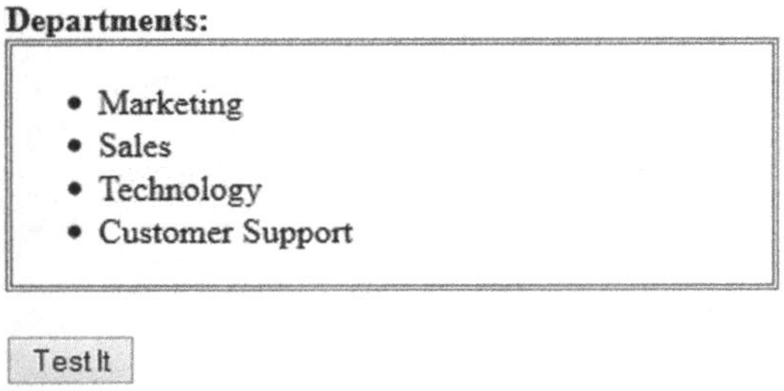

Departments:

- Marketing
- Sales
- Technology
- Customer Support

Test It

Figure 5-7. *Initial page display*

When you press the Test It button, the button's click event handler displays the tag name of each selected element. Figure 5-8 displays the closest ancestor element that matches the specified selector.

DIV

OK

Figure 5-8. *Ancestor element's tag name that has the list CSS class*

5-5. Getting the Parent of Each Selected Element
Problem

You want to get the parent of each element from the selected set.

Solution

The following jQuery syntax selects the parent node of each selected HTML element.

$(*selector*)**.parent(***parentSelector***)**

parentSelector is optional. If it is specified, only the parents that match parentSelector are selected. Listing 5-5 demonstrates the use of the parent() method to get the parent elements from the set of selected elements.

Listing 5-5. Using the parent() method to select the parent elements

```html
<!DOCTYPE html>
<html lang="en">
<head>
    <meta charset="utf-8">
    <script src="scripts/jquery-2.1.0.min.js"></script>
    <style>
        table {
            border:3px double green;
        }
    </style>
    <script>
        $(function(){
            $("#btnTestIt").click(function () {
                $("td").each(function (index, htmlElement){
                                    var cellValue =$(this).text();
                                    // if Department is Technology, do something
                                    if (cellValue == "Technology") {
                                        $(this).parent().css("background-color", "yellow");
                                    }
                });
            });
        });
    </script>
</head>
<body>
    <table id="tblEmployee">
        <tr>
            <td>Employee Name</td><td>Department Name</td><td>Salary</td>
        </tr>
        <tr>
            <td>Jane Smith</td><td>Marketing</td><td>$95,000</td>
        </tr>
        <tr>
            <td>John Smith</td><td>Technology</td><td>$90,000</td>
        </tr>
        <tr>
            <td>Brian Adam</td><td>Sales</td><td>$72,000</td>
        </tr>
        <tr>
            <td>Mary Jones</td><td>Support</td><td>$60,000</td>
        </tr>
        <tr>
            <td>Michael Jefferson</td><td>Technology</td><td>$85,000</td>
        </tr>
    </table><br>
    <input id="btnTestIt" type="button" value="Test It">
</body>
</html>
```

How It Works

In this code, the employee details—employee name, department name, and salary—are listed in tabular form using the <table>, <tr>, and <td> HTML tags. When the Test It button is clicked, the following code is executed:

```
$("td").each(function (index, htmlElement){
    var cellValue = $(this).text();
    // if Department is Technology, do something
    if (cellValue == "Technology") {
            $(this).parent().css("background-color", "yellow");
    }
});
```

$("td") selects all HTML elements with the tag name "td" and returns a jQuery object.

.each() iterates through all the selected elements in the returned jQuery object, with the current index and htmlElement arguments.

$(this).text() gets the text content of each td element. If the text content (i.e., cell value) is equal to "Technology", $(this).parent().css("background-color", "yellow") is executed. $(this).parent() gets the parent of the td element that has a value of Technology, i.e., the "tr" element is selected. css("background-color", "yellow") changes the background color of the parent element (tr) to yellow. Figure 5-9 displays the page when it is viewed in a browser.

Employee Name	Department Name	Salary
Jane Smith	Marketing	$95,000
John Smith	Technology	$90,000
Brian Adam	Sales	$72,000
Mary Jones	Support	$60,000
Michael Jefferson	Technology	$85,000

Test It

Figure 5-9. *Initial page display*

When you press the Test It button, the button's click event handler highlights the parent element if the selected element's text value is Technology. Figure 5-10 displays highlighted parent record.

Employee Name	Department Name	Salary
Jane Smith	Marketing	$95,000
John Smith	Technology	$90,000
Brian Adam	Sales	$72,000
Mary Jones	Support	$60,000
Michael Jefferson	Technology	$85,000

Test It

Figure 5-10. *Highlighted parent records whose cell value is Technology*

5-6. Getting the Ancestors of Each Selected Element

Problem

You want to get the ancestors of each element from the selected set.

Solution

The following jQuery syntax selects the ancestor nodes of each selected HTML element.

$$\$(selector).\textbf{parents}(ancestorSelector)$$

ancestorSelector is optional. If it is specified, only the ancestors that match ancestorSelector are selected. Listing 5-6 demonstrates the use of the parents() method to get the ancestor elements of each element from the set.

Listing 5-6. Using the parents() method to select the ancestors' elements

```
<!DOCTYPE html>
<html lang="en">
<head>
    <meta charset="utf-8">
    <script src="scripts/jquery-2.1.0.min.js"></script>

    <style>
      .list {
        border:3px double green;
        width:250px;
      }
       .newRecord {
          background-color: lightyellow;
       }
    </style>
    <script>
      $(function(){
        $("#btnTestIt").click(function () {
          $(".newRecord").parents().each(function () {
                                    alert($(this).prop("tagName"));
                      });
        });
      });
    </script>
</head>
<body>
    <strong>Departments:</strong>
    <div>
      <ul class="list">
        <li>Marketing</li>
        <li>Sales</li>
```

```
        <li class="newRecord">Technology</li>
        <li>Customer Support</li>
      </ul>
  </div><br>
  <input id="btnTestIt" type="button" value="Test It">
</body>
</html>
```

How It Works

In this code, the departments' names are listed using the `<ul>` and `<li>` HTML tags. When the Test It button is clicked, the following code is executed:

```
$(".newRecord").parents().each(function () {
    alert($(this).prop("tagName"));
});
```

$(".newRecords") selects all HTML elements with the newRecords class name and returns a jQuery object. The following element is selected:

```
<li class="newRecord">
```

.parents() gets all the ancestors of each element. The following ancestor elements are selected:

```
<UL>, <DIV>, <BODY>, <HTML>
```

.each() iterates through each element of the selected elements.

$(this).prop("tagName") gets the value of the property tagName of the currently processed element. The tagName is displayed as a pop-up message. Figure 5-11 displays the page when it is viewed in a browser.

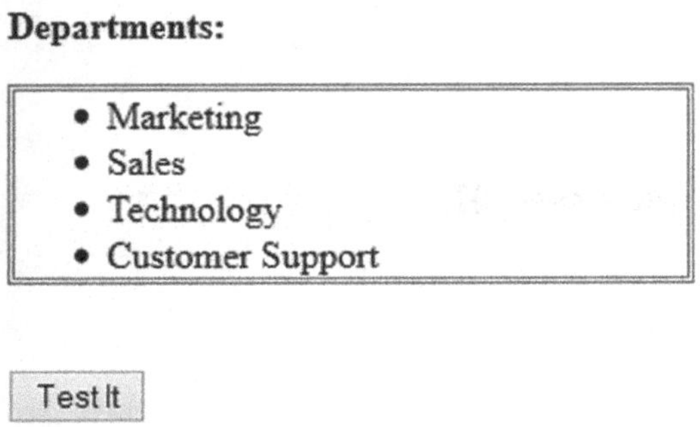

Departments:

- Marketing
- Sales
- Technology
- Customer Support

Test It

Figure 5-11. Initial page display

When you press the Test It button, the button's click event handler displays the tagName of all the ancestors of the element that has a class with the name newRecord. Figure 5-12 displays the ancestors' tag names as a pop-up message.

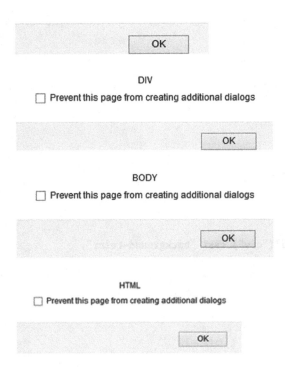

UL

OK

DIV

☐ Prevent this page from creating additional dialogs

OK

BODY

☐ Prevent this page from creating additional dialogs

OK

HTML

☐ Prevent this page from creating additional dialogs

OK

Figure 5-12. *Ancestors' tag names*

5-7. Getting the Ancestors of Each Selected Element Until a Node Is Reached

Problem

You want to get all the ancestors of each selected element until a node is reached that matches the specified selector.

Solution

The following jQuery syntax selects the ancestors of each selected HTML element until an ancestor is reached that matches the specified ancestorSelector.

$(selector**).parentUntil(**ancestorSelector**)**

Listing 5-7 demonstrates the use of the parentUntil() method to get all the ancestor elements until the ancestor node is reached that matches the ancestorSelector. The ancestor node that matches the specified ancestorSelector is not selected.

Listing 5-7. Using the parentUntil() method to select ancestor elements up to a specific ancestor.

```html
<!DOCTYPE html>
<html lang="en">
<head>
    <meta charset="utf-8">
    <script src="scripts/jquery-2.1.0.min.js"></script>
    <style>
        .oldRecord {
            font-style: italic;
        }
        .listDepartments {
            width: 200px;
        }
    </style>
    <script>
        $(function(){
            $("#btnTestIt").click(function () {
                    $( ".oldRecord" ).parentsUntil("div").css( "background-color",
                    "lightblue" );
                });
        });
    </script>
</head>
<body>
    <strong>Departments:</strong>
    <div>
        <ul class="listDepartments">
            <li>Marketing</li>
            <li>Sales</li>
            <li style="position: relative">Technology
                <ul>
                    <li>Hardware Technology</li>
                    <li class="oldRecord">Software Technology</li>
                </ul>
            </li>
            <li>Customer Support</li>
        </ul>
    </div><br>
    <input id="btnTestIt" type="button" value="Test It">
</body>
</html>
```

How It Works

In this code, the departments' names are listed using the <ul> and <li> HTML tags. There is one <li> item with the oldRecord class. When the Test It button is clicked, the following code is executed:

```javascript
$(".oldRecord").parentsUntil("div").css( "background-color","lightblue" );
```

`$(".oldRecord")` selects all the HTML elements with the `oldRecord` class name and returns a jQuery object. The following element is selected:

`<li class="oldRecord">`

`.parentsUntil("div")` selects the ancestors of the selected elements until an ancestor with a `div` tag name is found. The following ancestor elements are selected:

`<ul>` and `<ul>`

`css( "background-color", "lightblue")` changes the background color of the selected elements to light blue. Figure 5-13 displays the page when it is viewed in a browser.

Departments:

- Marketing
- Sales
- Technology
  - Hardware Technology
  - *Software Technology*
- Customer Support

Test It

Figure 5-13. *Initial page display*

When you press the Test It button, the button's click event handler changes the background color of the ancestors of the element having the `oldRecord` class name to light blue. Figure 5-14 displays the change in background color.

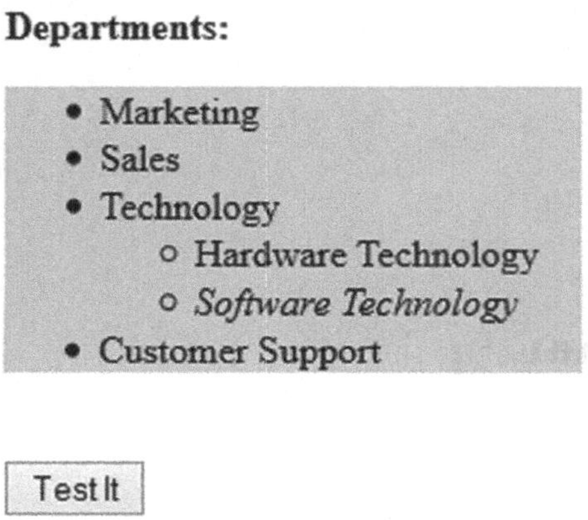

Departments:

- Marketing
- Sales
- Technology
  - Hardware Technology
  - *Software Technology*
- Customer Support

Test It

Figure 5-14. *Change in ancestor elements background color*

5-8. Getting the Immediately Preceding Sibling of Each Element of the Selected Elements

Problem

You want to get the preceding sibling of each element from the selected set.

Solution

The following jQuery syntax selects the immediately preceding sibling of each selected HTML element.

$(selector**).prev(**siblingSelector**)**

siblingSelector is optional. If it is specified, only the siblings that match siblingSelector are selected. Listing 5-8 demonstrates the use of the prev() method to get the preceding sibling element from the set.

Listing 5-8. Using the prev() method to select the preceding sibling elements

```
<!DOCTYPE html>
<html lang="en">
<head>
   <meta charset="utf-8">
   <script src="scripts/jquery-2.1.0.min.js"></script>
   <style>
      table {
         border:3px double green;
      }
      .tblHdr {
         background-color: lightgray;
      }
       .newRecord {
          background-color: lightyellow;
       }
      .listDepartments {
         width: 200px;.
      }
   </style>
   <script>
      $(function(){
         $("#btnTestIt").click(function () {
            $(".newRecord").prev().css("background-color", "lightblue");
         });
      });
   </script>
</head>
<body>
   <strong>Employees:</strong>
   <table id="listEmployees">
      <tr class="tblHdr">
         <td>Employee Name</td><td>Department Name</td><td>Salary</td>
      </tr>
```

```
        <tr>
           <td>Jane Smith</td><td>Marketing</td><td>$95,000</td>
        </tr>
        <tr class="newRecord">
           <td>John Smith</td><td>Technology</td><td>$90,000</td>
        </tr>
        <tr>
           <td>Brian Adam</td><td>Sales</td><td>$72,000</td>
        </tr>
        <tr>
           <td>Mary Jones</td><td>Customer Support</td><td>$60,000</td>
        </tr>
        <tr>
           <td>Michael Jefferson</td><td>Technology</td><td>$85,000</td>
        </tr>
     </table><br>
     <strong>Departments:</strong>
     <ul class="listDepartments">
        <li>Marketing</li>.
        <li>Sales</li>
        <li class="newRecord">Technology</li>
        <li>Customer Support</li>
     </ul><br>
     <input id="btnTestIt" type="button" value="Test It">
</body>
</html>
```

How It Works

In this code, the employee details—employee name, department name, and salary—are listed in tabular form using the <table>, <tr>, and <td> HTML tags and the departments' names are listed using the <ul> and <li> HTML tags. In both lists, there is one record with the class newRecord. When the Test It button is clicked, the following code is executed:

```
$(".newRecord").prev().css("background-color", "lightblue");
```

$(".newRecord") selects all HTML elements with the class name newRecord and returns a jQuery object. The following two elements are selected:.

- <tr class="newRecord">
- <li class="newRecord">Technology</li>

.prev() selects the immediately preceding sibling of each of the selected HTML elements. The following sibling elements are selected:

- <tr><td>Jane Smith</td><td>Marketing</td><td>$95,000</td></tr>
- <li>Sales</li>

css("background-color", "lightblue") changes the background color of the selected elements to light blue. Figure 5-15 displays the page when it is viewed in a browser.

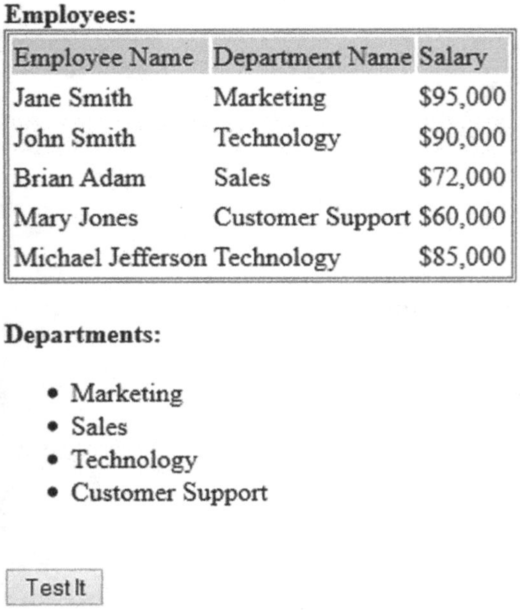

Employees:

Employee Name	Department Name	Salary
Jane Smith	Marketing	$95,000
John Smith	Technology	$90,000
Brian Adam	Sales	$72,000
Mary Jones	Customer Support	$60,000
Michael Jefferson	Technology	$85,000

Departments:

- Marketing
- Sales
- Technology
- Customer Support

Test It

Figure 5-15. Initial page display

When you press the Test It button, the button's click event handler changes the background color of the preceding sibling of each originally selected element. Figure 5-16 displays the change in the background color.

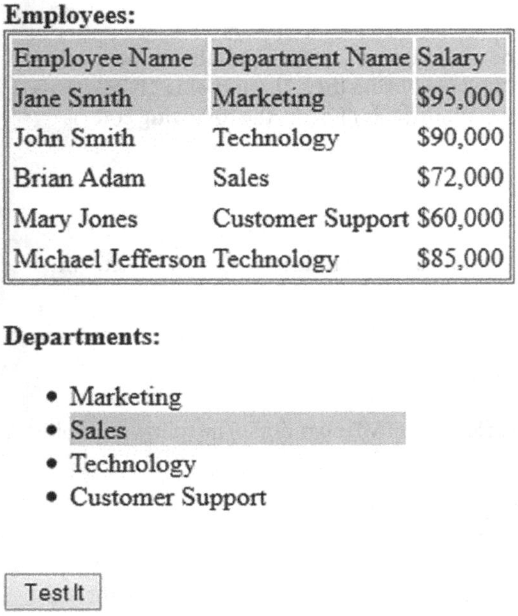

Employees:

Employee Name	Department Name	Salary
Jane Smith	Marketing	$95,000
John Smith	Technology	$90,000
Brian Adam	Sales	$72,000
Mary Jones	Customer Support	$60,000
Michael Jefferson	Technology	$85,000

Departments:

- Marketing
- Sales
- Technology
- Customer Support

Test It

Figure 5-16. Preceding sibling elements are highlighted with a light blue background color

The syntax for similar methods, which can be used to get siblings, is as follows:

The $(selector).prevAll() method can be used to get all the preceding siblings of each element from the selected elements.

The $(selector).prevUntil(siblingSelector) method can be used to get all the preceding siblings of each element from the selected elements until a sibling matching the siblingSelector is found. All the preceding siblings up to (but not including) the sibling element that match the specified siblingSelector are selected.

5-9. Getting the Immediately Following Sibling of Each Element from the Set

Problem

You want to get the immediately following sibling of each element from the set.

Solution

The following jQuery syntax selects the immediately following sibling of each selected HTML element.

$(*selector*)**.next(***siblingSelector***)**

siblingSelector is optional. If it is specified, only the siblings that match siblingSelector are selected. Listing 5-9 demonstrates the use of the next() method to get the following sibling element of each element from the set of selected elements.

Listing 5-9. Using the next() method to select the preceding sibling element

```
<!DOCTYPE html>
<html lang="en">
<head>
    <meta charset="utf-8">
    <script src="scripts/jquery-2.1.0.min.js"></script>
    <style>
        table {
            border:3px double green;
        }
        .tblHdr {
            background-color: lightgray;
        }
        .newRecord {
            background-color: lightyellow;
        }
        .listDepartments {
            width: 200px;
        }
    </style>
```

```
    <script>
        $(function(){
            $("#btnTestIt").click(function () {
                $ (".newRecord").next().css("background-color", "lightblue");
            });
        });
    </script>
</head>
<body>
    <strong>Employees:</strong>
    <table id="listEmployees">
        <tr class="tblHdr">
            <td>Employee Name</td><td>Department Name</td><td>Salary</td>
        </tr>
        <tr>
            <td>Jane  Smith</td><td>Marketing</td><td>$95,000</td>
        </tr>
        <tr class="newRecord">
            <td>John  Smith</td><td>Technology</td><td>$90,000</td>
        </tr>
        <tr>
            <td>Brian  Adam</td><td>Sales</td><td>$72,000</td>
        </tr>
        <tr>
            <td>Mary  Jones</td><td>Customer Support</td><td>$60,000</td>
        </tr>
        <tr>
            <td>Michael  Jefferson</td><td>Technology</td><td>$85,000</td>
        </tr>
    </table><br>
    <strong>Departments:</strong>
    <ul class="listDepartments">
        <li>Marketing</li>
        <li>Sales</li>
        <li class="newRecord">Technology</li>
        <li>Customer Support</li>
    </ul><br>
    <input id="btnTestIt" type="button" value="Test It">
</body>
</html>
```

How It Works

In this code, the employee details—employee name, department name, and salary—are listed in tabular form using the <table>, <tr>, and <td> HTML tags and the departments' names are listed using the <ul> and <li> HTML tags. In both lists, there is one record with the class newRecord. When the Test It button is clicked, the following code is executed:

```
$ (".newRecord").next().css("background-color", "lightblue");
```

`$(".newRecord")` selects all HTML elements with the class name `newRecord` and returns a jQuery object. The following two elements are selected:

- `<tr class="newRecord">`

This node has the record `<td>John Smith</td><td>Technology</td><td>$90,000</td>`

- `<li class="newRecord">Technology</li>`

`.next()` selects the immediately following sibling of each of the selected HTML elements. The following sibling elements are selected:

- `<tr><td>Brian Adam</td><td>Sales</td><td>$72,000</td></tr>`

- `<li>Customer Support</li>`

`css("background-color", "lightblue")` changes the background color of the selected elements to light blue. Figure 5-17 displays the page when it is viewed in a browser.

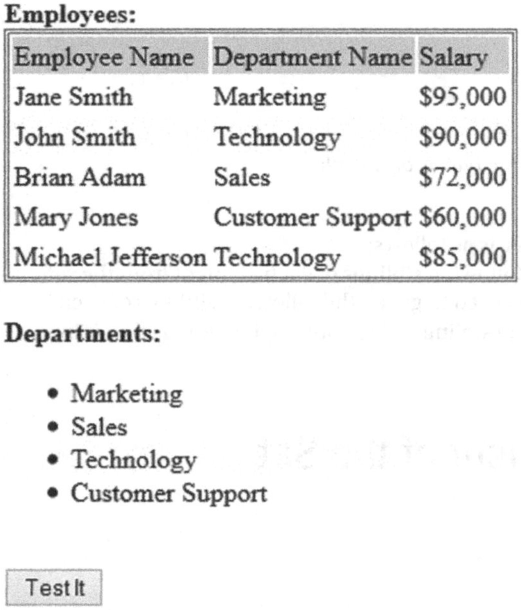

Employees:

Employee Name	Department Name	Salary
Jane Smith	Marketing	$95,000
John Smith	Technology	$90,000
Brian Adam	Sales	$72,000
Mary Jones	Customer Support	$60,000
Michael Jefferson	Technology	$85,000

Departments:

- Marketing
- Sales
- Technology
- Customer Support

Test It

Figure 5-17. *Initial page display*

When you press the Test It button, the button's click event handler changes the background color of the following sibling of each originally selected element. Figure 5-18 displays the change in the background color.

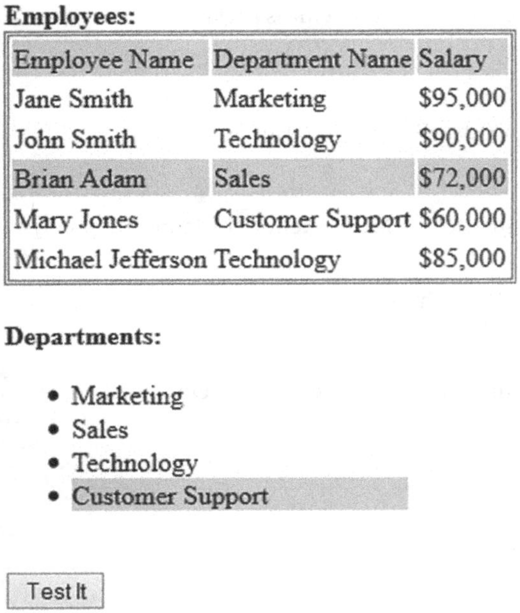

Employees:

Employee Name	Department Name	Salary
Jane Smith	Marketing	$95,000
John Smith	Technology	$90,000
Brian Adam	Sales	$72,000
Mary Jones	Customer Support	$60,000
Michael Jefferson	Technology	$85,000

Departments:

- Marketing
- Sales
- Technology
- Customer Support

Test It

Figure 5-18. *Preceding sibling elements are highlighted with a light blue background color*

The syntax for similar methods, which can be used to get siblings, is as follows:

The $(selector).nextAll() method can be used to get all the following siblings of each element from the set.

The $(selector).nextUntil(siblingSelector) method can be used to get all the following siblings of each element until a sibling matching the siblingSelector is found. All the siblings up to (but not including) the sibling element that match the specified siblingSelector are selected.

5-10. Getting All Siblings of Each Element of the Set
Problem

You want to get all the siblings of each element from the selected elements.

Solution

The following jQuery syntax selects all the siblings of each selected HTML element.

$(*selector***).siblings(***siblingSelector***)**

siblingSelector is optional. If it is specified, only the siblings that match siblingSelector are selected. Listing 5-10 demonstrates the use of the siblings() method to get all the sibling elements of each element from the set.

Listing 5-10. Using the siblings() method to select all sibling elements

```html
<!DOCTYPE html>
<html lang="en">
<head>
    <meta charset="utf-8">
    <script src="scripts/jquery-2.1.0.min.js"></script>
    <style>
        table {
            border:3px double green;
        }
        .tblHdr {
            background-color: lightgray;
        }
        .newRecord {
            background-color: lightyellow;
        }
        .tableFooter {
            background-color: lightgray;
        }
    </style>
    <script>
        $(function(){
            $("#btnTestIt").click(function () {
                $("tr.newRecord").siblings().not(".tblHdr, .tableFooter").css("background-color", "lightblue");
            });
        });
    </script>
</head>
<body>
    <strong>Employees:</strong>
    <table id="listEmployees">
        <tr class="tblHdr">
            <td>Employee Name</td><td>Department Name</td><td>Salary</td>
        </tr>
        <tr>
            <td>Jane Smith</td><td>Marketing</td><td>$95,000</td>
        </tr>
        <tr class="newRecord">
            <td>John Smith</td><td>Technology</td><td>$90,000</td>
        </tr>
        <tr>
            <td>Brian Adam</td><td>Sales</td><td>$72,000</td>
        </tr>
        <tr>
            <td>Mary Jones</td><td>Customer Support</td><td>$60,000</td>
        </tr>
        <tr>
            <td>Michael Jefferson</td><td>Technology</td><td>$85,000</td>
        </tr>
```

```
      <tr class="tableFooter">
          <td colspan="2">Total Salary:</td><td>$373,000</td>
      </tr>
   </table><br>
   <input id="btnTestIt" type="button" value="Test It">
</body>
</html>
```

How It Works

In this code, the employee details—employee name, department name, and salary—are listed in tabular form using the <table>, <tr>, and <td> HTML tags. There is one record with the newRecord class. When the Test It button is clicked, the following code is executed:

```
$("tr.newRecord").siblings().not(
    ".tblHdr, .tableFooter").css("background-color", "lightblue");
```

$("tr.newRecord") selects all HTML elements with the tag name "tr" and the class name "newRecord" and returns a jQuery object. The following element is selected:

```
<tr class="newRecord">
```

.siblings() selects all the siblings of each of the selected HTML elements.

.not(".tblHdr, .tableFooter") excludes the selected elements that have a "tblHdr" or "tableFooter" class name.

css("background-color", "lightblue") changes the background color of the selected elements to light blue. Figure 5-19 displays the page when it is viewed in a browser. 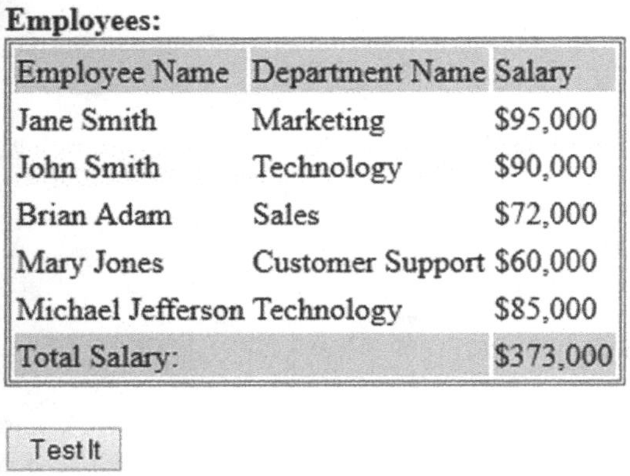

Employees:

Employee Name	Department Name	Salary
Jane Smith	Marketing	$95,000
John Smith	Technology	$90,000
Brian Adam	Sales	$72,000
Mary Jones	Customer Support	$60,000
Michael Jefferson	Technology	$85,000
Total Salary:		$373,000

Test It

Figure 5-19. *Initial page display*

When you press the Test It button, the button's click event handler changes the background color of all siblings of each selected element. Figure 5-20 displays the change in the background color.

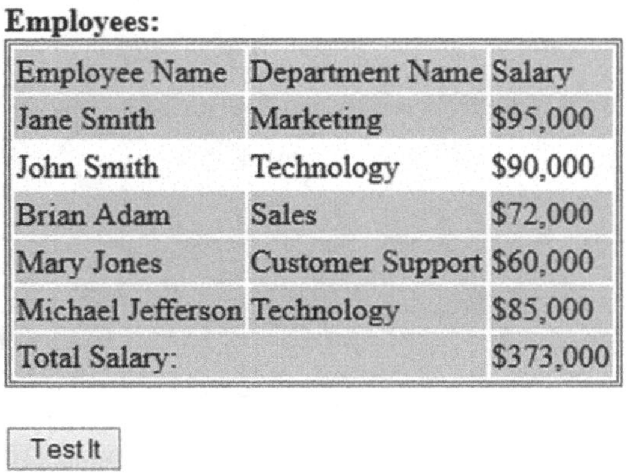

Employees:

Employee Name	Department Name	Salary
Jane Smith	Marketing	$95,000
John Smith	Technology	$90,000
Brian Adam	Sales	$72,000
Mary Jones	Customer Support	$60,000
Michael Jefferson	Technology	$85,000
Total Salary:		$373,000

Test It

Figure 5-20. *Preceding sibling elements are highlighted with a light blue background color*

Summary

This chapter covered jQuery selectors that you use to filter and expand methods for selecting node(s) (HTML elements), and then how to traverse the DOM tree to look for ancestors, siblings, or descendants using DOM traversing methods. It covered the following commonly used DOM traversing methods:

- `children(selector)`
- `find(selector)`
- `closest()`
- `parent()`
- `parents()`
- `prev()`
- `prevAll()`
- `next()`
- `nextAll()`
- `siblings()`

Other methods you saw in this chapter, which are covered in detail in Chapter 6, are `text()`, `contents()`, and `css()`.

CHAPTER 6

■ ■ ■

DOM Manipulation

This chapter covers the jQuery methods used to manipulate the DOM. Chapters 3, 4, and 5 used jQuery selectors to get (or select) HTML elements based on their IDs, tag names, class names, types, attributes, and attribute's values, and based on their relationship with other elements in the DOM tree. Once you have selected the desired elements, you can use a DOM-manipulation method to change their styles (CSS properties), properties, and attributes. You can also use DOM-manipulation methods to add new nodes and remove or replace existing nodes.

Sections in this chapter are organized in the following order:

- Manipulation of existing node(s) in the DOM tree

    - Manipulation of style

    - Manipulation of attributes and properties

- Manipulation of the DOM tree structure

    - Adding new nodes

    - Removing existing nodes

    - Replacing existing nodes

Refer to Chapter 2 for information about the DOM tree structure, as well as to understand nodes, ancestors, siblings, and descendants.

6-1. Adding CSS Class(es) to All Selected Elements
Problem

You want to add CSS classes to all the selected elements. This is generally needed to change the visual behavior of a group of elements. For example, when you want to disable all the data-entry fields when the form is submitted for processing or want to highlight a list of elements, you can use addClass() method.

Solution

The following jQuery syntax is used to add CSS class(es) to all the selected HTML elements.

$(*selector*).addClass("*cssClassName1 cssClassName2 ...*")

One or more CSS classes can be added to the class attribute of each element in the set of selected elements. Multiple class names can be specified by using spaces as separators. This method returns the jQuery object. Listing 6-1 demonstrates the use of addClass() method to add a CSS class to each element in a set of selected elements.

Listing 6-1. The jQuery method to add a CSS class to the selected elements

```html
<!DOCTYPE html>
<html lang="en">
<head>
   <meta charset="utf-8">
   <script src="scripts/jquery-2.1.0.min.js"></script>
   <style>
      ul { width:150px; }
                .highlight { border: 3px dotted red; background-color: yellow; }
   </style>
   <script>
      $(function(){
         $("#btnTestIt").click(function (){
            $("ul").addClass("highlight");
         });
      });
   </script>
</head>
<body>
   <strong>Departments:</strong>
   <ul>
      <li>Marketing</li>
      <li>Sales</li>
      <li>Technology</li>
      <li>Customer Support</li>
   </ul>
   <input id="btnTestIt" type="button" value="Test It">
</body>
</html>
```

How It Works

The department names are listed using <ul> and <li> HTML tags. If you want to highlight all department names and surround them with a border, you must first define the CSS class name (for example, highlight) using the CSS properties background-color and border and then select the parent of the <li> elements using $("ul"). You then execute the addClass() method on the selected elements.

When the Test It button is clicked, the following code is executed:

```
$("ul").addClass("highlight");
```

$("ul") selects the HTML element with the tag name ul and returns the jQuery object. .addClass("highlight") adds the highlight CSS class to the selected element (ul). Figure 6-1 displays the page when it is viewed in a browser.

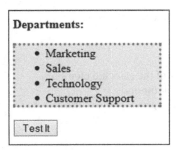

Figure 6-1. Initial page display

When you press the Test It button, the button's click event handler changes the background color and draws the border around the selected element. Figure 6-2 displays the effect of clicking the Test It button.

Figure 6-2. Selected elements are highlighted and have a border around them

The following shows another way to apply addClass to each element in the selected set of elements:

.addClass(function(*index*, *currentClass*) { ... })

This method iterates over each element in the set of selected elements. You can implement some logic in the function to decide which class name(s) are to be added based on the current element, current index, and current class associated with the current element. The argument index specifies the index number of the current element in the set of selected elements. A function needs to be created with the arguments index and currentClass and the body of the function contains the logic to determine which class name needs to be added to the current element. The returned class name(s) is added to the current element in the set of selected elements.

The following code segment uses index to change the background color of the even and odd numbered records in the table:

```
<style>
    .evenRow { background-color:lightyellow; }
    .oddRow { background-color:lightgreen; }
</style>
<script>
    $(function(){
        $("tr").addClass(function (index, currentClass) {
            if (index % 2 == 0) {
                return("evenRow");
```

```
            } else {
               return("oddRow");
            }
         });
      });
</script>
```

6-2. Checking if a CSS Class Is Associated with Any of the Selected Elements

Problem

You want to check if a CSS class is associated with any of the selected elements.

Solution

The following jQuery syntax is used to check if a CSS class is associated with any of the selected elements:

.hasClass("*className*")

className is the name of the class you want to check if it is already assigned to any of the selected elements. This returns a Boolean. True is returned if className is assigned to any of the selected elements.

Listing 6-2 demonstrates the use of the jQuery method .hasClass() to check if it assigned to any of the selected elements.()

Listing 6-2. Use of the jQuery method .hasClass()

```
<!DOCTYPE html>
<html lang="en">
<head>
   <meta charset="utf-8">
   <script src="scripts/jquery-2.1.0.min.js"></script>
   <style>
      ul { width:150px; }
      .highlight { border: 3px dotted red; background-color: yellow; }
   </style>
   <script>
      $(function(){
         $("#btnTestIt").click(function (){
            if ($("ul").hasClass("highlight") == true) {
               $("#classAssociation").prop("innerHTML", "ul tag has the class - 'highlight'");
            } else {
               $("#classAssociation").prop("innerHTML", "ul tag doesn't have the class - 'highlight'");
            }
         });
      });
   </script>
</head>
```

```
<body>
    <strong>Departments:</strong>
    <ul class="highlight">
        <li>Marketing</li>
        <li>Sales</li>
        <li>Technology</li>
        <li>Customer Support</li>
    </ul>
    <input id="btnTestIt" type="button" value="Test It"><br><br>
    <div id="classAssociation"></div>
</body>
</html>
```

How It Works

The department names are listed using the <ul> and <li> HTML tags. If you want to check if the highlight CSS class is assigned to the ul tag, you select the <ul> elements using $("ul") and then execute the hasClass() method on the selected element.

When the Test It button is clicked, the following code is executed:

```
$("ul").hasClass("highlight");
```

$("ul") selects the HTML element with the tag name ul and returns the jQuery object. .hasClass("highlight") checks if the highlight CSS class is associated with selected element (ul) and returns true. The message displays "ul tag has the class - 'highlight'" on the page. Figure 6-3 displays the page when it is viewed in a browser.

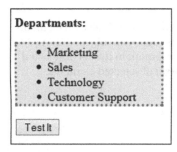

Figure 6-3. *Displays the page when viewed in a browser*

When you press the Test It button, the button's click event handler checks if the highlight class is associated with the ul tag and displays the message. Figure 6-4 displays the effect of clicking the Test It button.

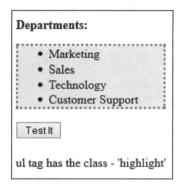

Figure 6-4. *Message is displayed indicating that the highlight class is associated with the ul tag*

6-3. Removing CSS Class(es) from Each Selected Element
Problem

You want to remove CSS class(es) from each selected element.

Solution

The following jQuery syntax is used to remove CSS class(es) from all the selected HTML elements.

$(*selector*).removeClass("cssClassName1 cssClassName2 ...")

One or more CSS classes can be removed from the class attribute of each element in the set of selected elements. Multiple class names can be specified by using spaces as separators. This method returns the jQuery object. Listing 6-3 demonstrates the use of the removeClass() method to remove the CSS class from each element in the set of selected elements. If no className is specified as an argument, all classes are removed from the set of selected elements.

Listing 6-3. The jQuery method to remove a CSS class from the selected elements

```
<!DOCTYPE html>
<html lang="en">
<head>
   <meta charset="utf-8">
   <script src="scripts/jquery-2.1.0.min.js"></script>
   <style>
      ul { width:150px; }
      .highlight { border: 3px dotted red; background-color: yellow; }
   </style>
   <script>
      $(function(){
         $("#btnTestIt").click(function (){
            $("ul").removeClass("highlight");
         });
      });
   </script>
</head>
```

```
<body>
    <strong>Departments:</strong>
    <ul class="highlight">
        <li>Marketing</li>
        <li>Sales</li>
        <li>Technology</li>
        <li>Customer Support</li>
    </ul>
    <input id="btnTestIt" type="button" value="Test It">
</body>
</html>
```

How It Works

The department names are listed using the `<ul>` and `<li>` HTML tags. If you want to remove highlight and the border from all department names, you select the `<ul>` elements using `$("ul")` and execute the `removeClass()` method on the selected elements.

When Test It button is clicked, the following code is executed:

```
$("ul").removeClass("highlight");
```

`$("ul")` selects the HTML element with the tag name ul and returns the jQuery object. `.removeClass("highlight")` removes the highlight CSS class from the selected element (ul). Figure 6-5 displays the page when it is viewed in a browser.

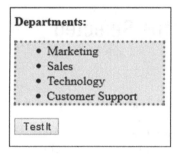

Figure 6-5. *Initial page display*

When you press the Test It button, the button's click event handler removes the background color and the border around the selected element. Figure 6-6 displays the effect of clicking the Test It button.

Departments:

- Marketing
- Sales
- Technology
- Customer Support

Test It

Figure 6-6. *Highlight and border are removed from the selected elements*

Here's another way to apply `removeClass` to each selected element:

```
.removeClass( function(index, currentClass) )
```

This method iterates over each element in the set of selected elements. You can implement some logic in the function to decide which class name(s) will be removed based on the current element, current index, and current class associated with the current element. The argument `index` specifies the index number of the current element in the set of selected elements. A function needs to be created with the arguments `index` and `currentClass` and the body of the function contains the logic to determine which class name needs to be removed from the current element. The returned class name(s) is removed from the current element in the set of selected elements.

6-4. Toggling CSS Class(es) for Each Element of the Selected Elements

Problem

You want to add class(es) name to all the selected elements or remove the class names if they are already associated with them. This technique can be used when you want to toggle a visual display of a set of elements between two states. For example, if a user clicks a button to make a payment and the payment processing has started and is in process, you want to disable all data-entry fields. Then, when the payment processing is completed, you want to enable all data-entry fields.

Solution

The following jQuery syntax is used to toggle CSS class(es) for all the selected HTML elements.

`$(selector).toggleClass("cssClassName1 cssClassName2 ...")`

One or more CSS classes can be added (or removed) to (or from) the class attribute of each element in the set of selected elements. Multiple class names can be specified by using spaces as separators. This method returns the jQuery object. Listing 6-4 demonstrates the use of the `toggleClass()` method to add (or remove) CSS class to (or from) each element in the set of selected elements.

Listing 6-4. The jQuery method to add (or remove) a CSS class to (or from) selected elements

```
<!DOCTYPE html>
<html lang="en">
<head>
    <meta charset="utf-8">
    <script src="scripts/jquery-2.1.0.min.js"></script>
    <style>
        ul { width:150px; }
        .highlight { border: 3px dotted red; background-color: lightblue; }
    </style>
    <script>
        $(function(){
            $("#btnTestIt").click(function (){
                $("ul").toggleClass("highlight");
            });
        });
    </script>
</head>
<body>
    <strong>Departments:</strong>
    <ul>
        <li>Marketing</li>
        <li>Sales</li>
        <li>Technology</li>
        <li>Customer Support</li>
    </ul>
    <input id="btnTestIt" type="button" value="Test It">
</body>
</html>
```

How It Works

The department names are listed using the <ul> and <li> HTML tags. If you want to highlight all department names and surround them with a border or do the reverse, you must select the <ul> element using $("ul") and then execute the toggleClass() method on the selected element.

When the Test It button is clicked, the following code is executed:

```
$("ul").toggleClass("highlight");
```

$("ul") selects the HTML element with the tag name ul and returns the jQuery object.
.toggleClass("highlight") adds the highlight CSS class to the selected element (ul) if the highlight class is not already associated with the selected element (ul) and removes the highlight CSS class from the selected element (ul) if that class is already associated with the selected element (ul). Figure 6-7 displays the page when it is viewed in a browser.

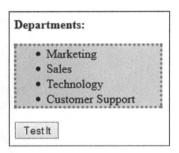

Figure 6-7. *Initial page display*

When you press the Test It button, the button's click event handler changes the background color and draws the border around the selected element. Figure 6-8 displays the effect of clicking the Test It button.

Departments:

- Marketing
- Sales
- Technology
- Customer Support

Test It

Figure 6-8. *Selected elements are highlighted and have a border around them*

On pressing the Test It button again, the background color is removed and the page is displayed as it was on the initial page (shown in the Figure 6-7).

6-5. Toggling CSS Class(es) for Selected Elements Based on the Return Value of a Function

Problem

You want to add class names to/from all selected elements if they are not already associated with them or remove them if they are already associated with them based on each element's attributes and/or existing classes associated with the element.

Solution

The following jQuery syntax is used to toggle CSS class(es) for each selected HTML element based on its attributes, properties, and/or currently associated class names.

```
$(selector).toggleClass(function(index, currentClass) )
```

This method iterates over each element in the set of selected elements. You can implement some logic in the function to decide which class name(s) will be toggled based on the current element, current index, and current class associated with the current element. Returned class name(s) are added (or removed) to (or from) the current element in the set of selected elements. Listing 6-5 demonstrates the use of the toggleClass() method while iterating over each element in the set of selected elements.

Listing 6-5. The jQuery method to add/remove a CSS class to/from each element in the set of selected elements

```
<!DOCTYPE html>
<html lang="en">
<head>
    <meta charset="utf-8">
    <script src="scripts/jquery-2.1.0.min.js"></script>
    <style>
        ul { width:150px; }
        .underline { text-decoration: underline; }
                .item_0 { background-color: lightyellow; }
                .item_1 { background-color: lightblue; }
                .item_2 { background-color: lightgray; }
                .item_3 { background-color: lightgreen; }
    </style>
    <script>
        $(function(){
            $("#btnTestIt").click(function (){
                $("li").toggleClass(function(index, currentClassName){
                                return("item_" + index);
                            });
            });
        });
    </script>
</head>
<body>
    <strong>Departments:</strong>
    <ul>
        <li class="underline">Marketing</li>
        <li>Sales</li>
        <li>Technology</li>
        <li>Customer Support</li>
    </ul>
    <input id="btnTestIt" type="button" value="Test It">
</body>
</html>
```

How It Works

The department names are listed using the <ul> and <li> HTML tags. If you want to highlight all department names based on their position in the list, you select the <li> elements using $("li") and execute the toggleClass() method with the function as its parameter. Within the function, you can return the className you want to associate with the current element in the set of selected elements.

When the Test It button is clicked, the following code is executed:

```
$("li").toggleClass(function(index, currentClassName){
    return("item_" + index);
});
```

$("li") selects the HTML element with the tag name li and returns the jQuery object. .toggleClass (function()) iterates over each element in the set of the selected elements ("li"). return("item_" + index) returns the class name item_0 for the first element, the class name item_1 for the second element, and so on, in the set of selected elements. These returned class names are then associated with the corresponding element. Figure 6-9 displays the page when it is viewed in a browser. If the Test It button is clicked again, these newly added class names will be removed from the set of selected elements.

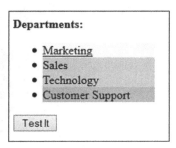

Figure 6-9. *Initial page display*

When you press the Test It button, the button's click event handler changes the background color based on the element's position in the set of selected elements. Figure 6-10 displays the effect of clicking the Test It button.

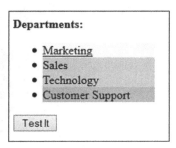

Figure 6-10. *Selected elements are highlighted and have a border around them*

If you press the Test It button again, the background color will be removed and the page will be displayed the same as the initial page (shown in Figure 6-9).

6-6. Getting and Setting the CSS Property of the Selected Element(s)

Problem

You want to get and set the CSS property of the elements in the set of selected elements.

Solution

The following jQuery syntax is used to get the CSS property of the first element in the set of selected elements.

$(*selector*).css("*cssPropertyName*")

> This method returns the value of the specified CSS (style) property name (as a string).
> The following jQuery syntax is used to set the CSS property of all the elements in the set of selected elements.

$(*selector*).css("*cssPropertyName*", "*cssPropertyValue*")

> This method returns the jQuery object after setting the specified CSS (style) property of all selected elements. Listing 6-6 demonstrates the use of the css() method to get and set the CSS property of the elements in the set of selected elements.

Listing 6-6. The jQuery method to get and set a CSS property of the selected elements

```
<!DOCTYPE html>
<html lang="en">
<head>
    <meta charset="utf-8">
    <script src="scripts/jquery-2.1.0.min.js"></script>
    <style>
        .label { width: 200px; font-weight: bold; color: blue; }
        .dataEntry { background-color: yellow; }
        .highlight {
            text-decoration:underline;
            background-color:yellow;
            width: 150px;
        }
    </style>
    <script>
        $(function(){
            $("#btnTestItGet").click(function () {
                alert($("input:text").css("background-color"));
            });
            $("#btnTestItSet").click(function () {
                $("input:text").css("background-color", "lightblue");
            });
        });
    </script>
</head>
```

```
<body>
    <div class="label">Name:</div><input type="text" id="txtName" class="dataEntry"><br>
    <div class="label">Address:</div><input type="text" id="txtAddress" class="dataEntry"><br><br><br>
    <input id="btnTestItGet" type="button" value="Test It (Get CSS Property)"> <br><br>
    <input id="btnTestItSet" type="button" value="Test It (Set CSS Property)">
</body>
</html>
```

How It Works

The two data entry input textboxes are created using the input HTML tag. If you want to display a value of the CSS property called background-color of the first input text element, you select the input text either by using $("#txtName") or by using $("input:text") and execute the css() method on the selected elements.

When the Test It (Get CSS Property) button is clicked, the following code is executed:

```
alert($("input:text").css("background-color"));
```

$("**input:text**") selects all the HTML elements with the tag name input and the type set to text and returns the jQuery object. .css("background-color") gets the value of the CSS property background-color of the first element in the selected elements, which is the txtName input element.

When the Test It (Set CSS Property) button is clicked, the following code is executed:

```
$("input:text").css("background-color", "lightblue")
```

$("**input:text**") selects all the HTML elements with the tag name input and type set to text and returns the jQuery object. .css("background-color", "lightblue") sets the value of the CSS property background-color of all the selected elements to lightblue. Figure 6-11 displays the page when it is viewed in a browser.

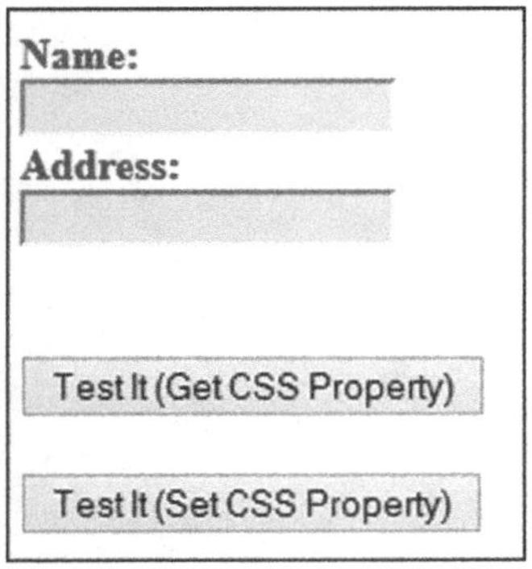

Figure 6-11. *Initial page display*

When you press the Test It button, the button's click event handler displays the current background-color value of the first element in the set of selected elements and then sets the background-color of all selected elements to lightblue. Figure 6-12 displays the message with the current background-color. rgb(255, 255, 0) is RGB code for yellow. Figure 6-13 displays the change in background-color to lightblue.

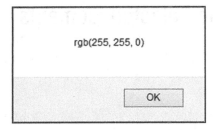

Figure 6-12. *Current background color of the input textbox*

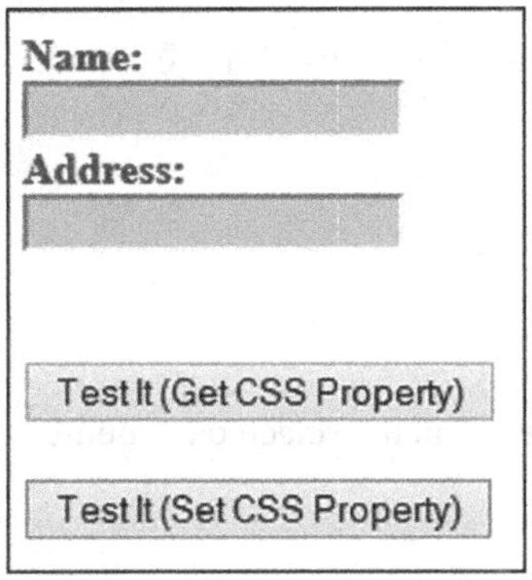

Name:

Address:

Test It (Get CSS Property)

Test It (Set CSS Property)

Figure 6-13. *Background color of all input textboxes changes to lightblue*

You can get multiple CSS properties of the first element in the selected elements by passing an array of strings containing CSS property names as an argument to the css() method. The return value is an object with key/value pairs. For example, in order to determine the width, font-weight, and color properties of the label, you can use following code:

```
var arrProperty = ["width", "font-weight", "color"];
var result = $(".label").css(arrProperty);
// result is an object with key value pairs
```

You can access the key-value pair in the return object using following code:

```
$.each( result, function( prop, value ) {
   alert( prop + ": " + value );
});
```

$.each(result, function(*key*, *value*)) will iterate over each element in the result and pass the key and value as arguments to the inline function. Inside the function, you can access and use the key and value as per your requirements. This example displays the key and value pairs as pop-up messages.

6-7. Setting Multiple CSS Properties of All the Selected Elements

Problem

You want to set multiple CSS properties of all the selected elements.

Solution

The following jQuery syntax is used to set multiple CSS properties of all the selected HTML elements.

$(*selector*).css(*cssProperties*)

where cssProperties is a map object with key/value pairs. Key is the property name and value is the property value. This method returns the jQuery object. The syntax for defining the map object is:

```
var cssProperties = {"cssPropertyName1":"cssPropertyValue1",
    "cssPropertyName2":"cssPropertyValue2",
    "cssPropertyName3":" cssPropertyValue3",
    ...};
```

Listing 6-7 demonstrates the use of the css() method to set multiple CSS properties of all the selected elements.

Listing 6-7. Setting multiple CSS properties of all the selected elements

```
<!DOCTYPE html>
<html lang="en">
<head>
    <meta charset="utf-8">
    <script src="scripts/jquery-2.1.0.min.js"></script>
    <style>
        .label {width: 200px; font-weight: bold; color: blue; }
        .dataEntry { background-color: yellow; }
        .highlight {
            text-decoration:underline;
            background-color:yellow;
            width: 150px;
        }
    </style>
    <script>
        $(function(){
            $("#btnTestIt").click(function () {
                // map object of key value pairs
                var cssProperties = {"width":"140px", "font-weight" : "normal", "color" : "white",
                "background-color" : "darkblue"};

                $(".label").css(cssProperties);
            });
        });
    </script>
</head>
```

```
<body>
    <div class="label">Name:</div><input type="text" id="txtName" class="dataEntry"><br>
    <div class="label">Address:</div><input type="text" id="txtAddress" class="dataEntry"><br><br><br>
    <input id="btnTestIt" type="button" value="Test It"><br>
    <div id="message"></div>
</body>
</html>
```

How It Works

There are two div tags with the class name label. If you want to change multiple properties (such as width, font-weight, color, and background-color) of these div tags, you first define the map object containing the key value pairs as cssPropertyName and cssProperty values, then select the labels by using $(".label"), and finally execute the css() method on all the selected elements.

When the Test It button is clicked, the following code is executed:

```
var cssProperties = {"width":"140px", "font-weight" : "normal", "color" : "white",
"background-color" : "darkblue"};

$(".label").css(cssProperties);
```

cssProperties contains cssPropertyName and cssPropertyValue key/value pairs.

$(".label") selects the HTML element with the class name label and returns the jQuery object. .css(cssProperties) sets all the CSS property names, which are specified in the map object, of the selected elements with the specified property values. Figure 6-14 displays the page when it is viewed in a browser.

Figure 6-14. *Initial page display*

When you press the Test It button, the button's click event handler changes the width, font-weight, color, and background-color properties of the selected element. Figure 6-15 displays the effect of clicking the Test It button.

Figure 6-15. *CSS properties of the selected elements are changed*

6-8. Setting a Single CSS Property of Each Element in the Set of Selected Elements Based on a Function

Problem

You want to change the CSS property of each element in the set of selected elements based on the element's attributes and/or properties by using the programming logic in a function.

Solution

The following jQuery syntax is used to change the CSS property of each of the elements in the set of selected HTML elements.

$(*selector*).css("cssPropertyName", function(index) { ... })

function is executed for each element in the set of selected elements and the specified cssPropertyName is set with the return value of the function. This method returns the jQuery object. Listing 6-8 demonstrates the use of the css() method, with function as an argument, to set the CSS property on each element in the set of selected elements.

Listing 6-8. The jQuery method to change a CSS property of each element in the set of selected elements

```
<!DOCTYPE html>
<html lang="en">
<head>
   <meta charset="utf-8">
   <script src="scripts/jquery-2.1.0.min.js"></script>
   <style>
      .label { width: 200px; font-weight: bold; color: blue; }
      .dataEntry { background-color: yellow; }
      .highlight {
         text-decoration:underline;
         background-color:yellow;
         width: 150px;
      }
   </style>
   <script>
      $(function(){
         $("#btnTestIt").click(function () {
            $("input:text").css("background-color", function (index) {
               if (index == 1) {
                  return("lightblue");
               } else {
                  return("lightyellow");
               }
            });
         });
      });
   </script>
</head>
```

```
<body>
    <div class="label">Name:</div><input type="text" id="txtName" class="dataEntry"><br>
    <div class="label">Address:</div><input type="text" id="txtAddress" class="dataEntry"><br><br><br>
    <input id="btnTestIt" type="button" value="Test It"><br>
  <div id="message"></div>
</body>
</html>
```

How It Works

The two data-entry input textboxes are created using the input HTML tag with an attribute type set to text. If you want to highlight different elements in the selected set of elements with the different background color, you select the <input> elements with type attribute set to text using $("input:text") and then execute the css() method, with the function as an argument, on the selected elements.

When the Test It button is clicked, the following code is executed:

```
$("input:text").css("background-color", function (index) {
    if (index == 1) {
        return("lightblue");
    } else {
        return("lightyellow");
    }
});
```

$("input:text") selects all the HTML elements with the tag name input and type set to text and then returns the jQuery object. .css("background-color", function (index) {...}) executes function for each element in the set of selected elements and sets the background-color to the return value of the function. For the second element in the set of selected elements (for index=1), the background color changes to light blue. For all other elements, the background color changes to light yellow. Figure 6-16 displays the page when it is viewed in a browser.

Figure 6-16. *Initial page display*

When you press the Test It button, the button's click event handler changes the background color of the second input textbox to light blue and all other textboxes' background color to light yellow. Figure 6-17 displays the effect of clicking the Test It button.

Figure 6-17. *Second textbox element is highlighted with a light blue background color and all other textboxes have a light yellow background*

6-9. Getting the Attribute Value of the First Element in a Selection of Elements

Problem

You want to get the attribute value of a single selected element or of the first element of multiple selected elements.

Solution

The following jQuery syntax is used to get an attribute value of a selected HTML element.

$(*selector*).attr("*attributeName*")

This will return the string containing the attribute value of the specified `attributeName` of the first element in the set of selected elements. Listing 6-9 demonstrates the use of the `attr()` method to get the attribute value of the first element in the set of selected elements.

Listing 6-9. The jQuery method to get the attribute's value

```
<!DOCTYPE html>
<html lang="en">
<head>
    <meta charset="utf-8">
    <script src="scripts/jquery-2.1.0.min.js"></script>
    <style>
        .list { border:3px double green; width:350px; }
        .newRecord { font-weight: bold; }
        .tableHeader { background-color: lightgray; }
        .listDepartments {width: 200px; }
    </style>
    <script>
      $(function(){
        $("#btnTestIt").click(function () {
            var attributesDetail =
              "Input Textbox: " +
              " <b>type:</b> " + $("#txtName").attr("type") +
```

```
              " <b>id:</b> " +  $("#txtName").attr("id") +
              " <b>value:</b> " +  $("#txtName").attr("value") +
              " <b>maxlength:</b> " +  $("#txtName").attr("maxlength") +
              "<br>" +
              "Checkbox (1): " +
              " <b>type:</b> " +  $("#chkMale").attr("type") +
              " <b>id:</b> " +  $("#chkMale").attr("id") +
              " <b>name:</b> " +  $("#chkMale").attr("name") +
              " <b>checked:</b> " +  $("#chkMale").attr("checked") +
              "<br>" +
              "Checkbox (2): " +
              " <b>type:</b> " +  $("#chkFemale").attr("type") +
              " <b>id:</b> " +  $("#chkFemale").attr("id") +
              " <b>name:</b> " +  $("#chkFemale").attr("name") +
              " <b>checked:</b> " +  $("#chkFemale").attr("checked");

          $("#message").prop("innerHTML", attributesDetail);
        });
      });
</script>
</head>
<body>
   Gender: <input type="radio" name="gender" id="chkMale" checked>Male
           <input type="radio" name="gender" id="chkFemale">Female <br>
   Name: <input type="text" id="txtName" value="" maxlength="40"><br>
   <input id="btnTestIt" type="button" value="Test It"><br>
   <div id="message"></div>
</body>
</html>
```

How It Works

The two radio buttons and one input textbox are created using the input HTML tag with the type set to radio and text. If you want to get attribute values of attributes such as ID, type, value, maxlength, checked, and so on, of these elements, you select the element first using $("#idValue") and execute the attr() method on the selected elements with the appropriate attributeName as an argument of the attr() method.

When the Test It button is clicked, the following code is executed:

```
var attributesDetail =
        "Input Textbox: " +
        " <b>type:</b> " +  $("#txtName").attr("type") +
        " <b>id:</b> " +  $("#txtName").attr("id") +
        " <b>value:</b> " +  $("#txtName").attr("value") +
        " <b>maxlength:</b> " +  $("#txtName").attr("maxlength") +
        "<br>" +
        "Checkbox (1): " +
        " <b>type:</b> " +  $("#chkMale").attr("type") +
        " <b>id:</b> " +  $("#chkMale").attr("id") +
        " <b>name:</b> " +  $("#chkMale").attr("name") +
        " <b>checked:</b> " +  $("#chkMale").attr("checked") +
        "<br>" +
```

```
           "Checkbox (2): " +
           " <b>type:</b> " + $("#chkFemale").attr("type") +
           " <b>id:</b> " + $("#chkFemale").attr("id") +
           " <b>name:</b> " + $("#chkFemale").attr("name") +
           " <b>checked:</b> " + $("#chkFemale").attr("checked");

    $("#message").prop("innerHTML", attributesDetail);
```

$("#idValue") selects the HTML element with the ID attribute set to idValue and returns the jQuery object. .attr("type") gets the value of attributeName type of the selected element. Similarly, other attribute values are retrieved by using the syntax $(selector).attr("attributeName"). All retrieved attribute values are concatenated in a string attributesDetail, which is then displayed in the page by using the line $("#message").prop("innerHTML", attributesDetail). Figure 6-18 displays the page when it is viewed in a browser.

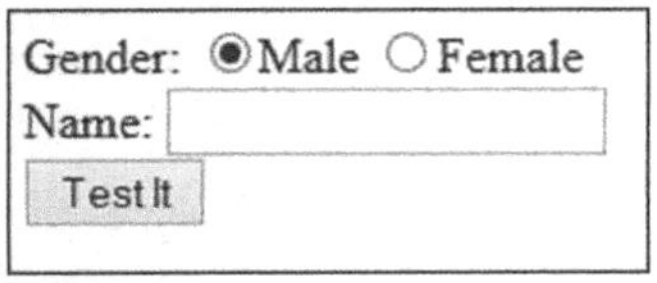

Figure 6-18. *Initial page display*

When you press the Test It button, the button's click event handler gets the attribute values of the two radio buttons and the textbox and displays them on the page. Figure 6-19 displays the effect of clicking the Test It button.

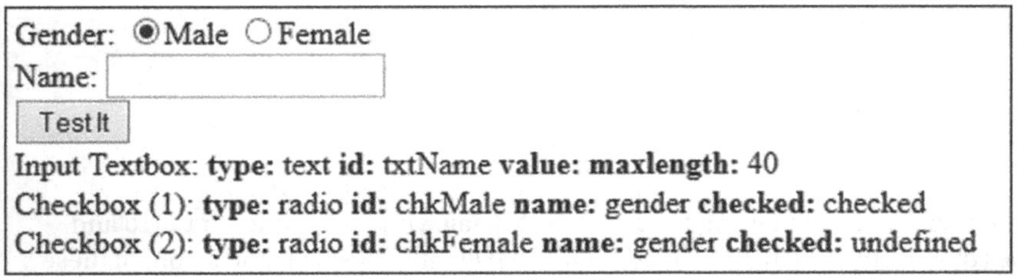

Figure 6-19. *The attribute values of radio buttons and textbox are displayed*

6-10. Setting the Attribute Value(s) of All the Selected Elements
Problem

You want to set the attribute values of all the selected elements. This can be used to set default values of data-entry form fields at runtime.

Solution

The following jQuery syntax is used to set attributes of all the selected HTML elements.

$(selector).attr("attributeName", "attributeValue")

The attribute value of HTML tags can be set by using the attr() method. The specified attributeName should be a valid attribute of the HTML tag. This method returns the jQuery object. Listing 6-10 demonstrates the use of the attr() method to set the attribute value of the selected elements.

Listing 6-10. The jQuery method to set an attribute's value

```
<!DOCTYPE html>
<html lang="en">
<head>
    <meta charset="utf-8">
    <script src="scripts/jquery-2.1.0.min.js"></script>
    <style>
        .list { border:3px double green; width:350px; }
        .newRecord { font-weight: bold; }
        .tableHeader { background-color: lightgray; }
        .listDepartments { width: 200px; }
    </style>
    <script>
        $(function(){
            $("#btnTestIt").click(function () {
                $("#txtName").attr("value", "John Smith");
                var msg = "attr: " + $("#txtName").attr("value") + "<br>" +
                          "prop: " + $("#txtName").prop("value");
                $("#message").prop("innerHTML", msg);
            });
        });
    </script>
</head>
<body>
    Gender: <input type="radio" name="gender" id="chkMale" checked>Male
    <input type="radio" name="gender" id="chkFemale">Female <br>
    Name: <input type="text" id="txtName" value="" maxlength="40"><br><br>
    <input id="btnTestIt" type="button" value="Test It"><br><br>
    <div id="message"></div>
</body>
</html>
```

How It Works

The textbox for entering the name is created using the input HTML tag with the type set to text. If you want to set the default value for the name then select the name input element using $("#txtName") and execute the attr() method on the selected element.

When the Test It button is clicked, the following code is executed:

```
$("#txtName").attr("value", "John Smith");
```

$("#txtName ") selects the HTML element with the ID as txtName and returns the jQuery object. .attr("value", "John Smith") sets the value of the attribute value as John Smith. Refer to Chapter 2 to understand the difference between attributes and properties. When an attribute of an HTML element is set, its property is also set with the same value. But the reverse is not true; if you change the property of an HTML element, only the property value is changed and its attribute remains unaffected. Figure 6-20 displays the page when it is viewed in a browser.

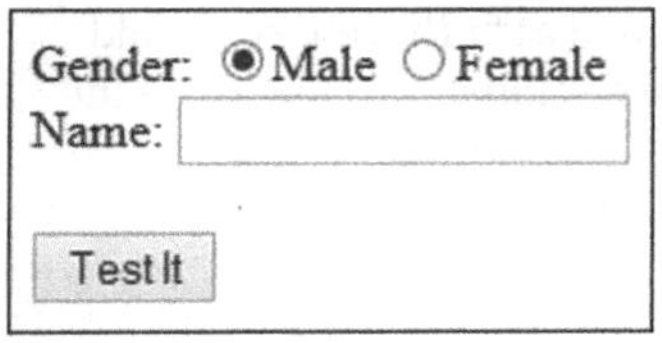

Gender: ⦿ Male ○ Female
Name:

Test It

Figure 6-20. *Initial page display*

When you press the Test It button, the button's click event handler changes the value of the name textbox to John Smith and then displays the new value of the attribute `value` and property `value`. Figure 6-21 displays the effect of clicking the Test It button.

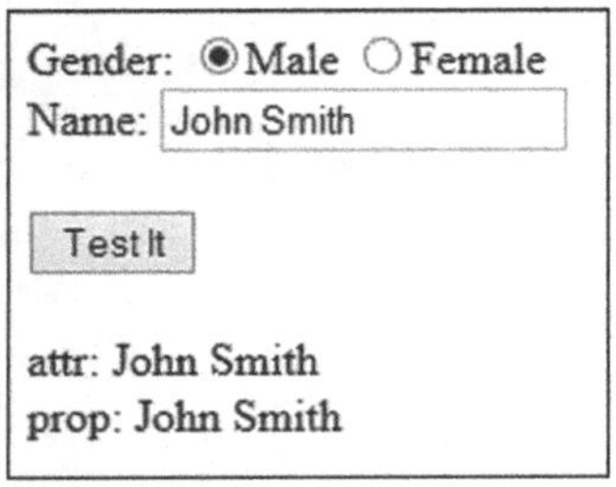

Gender: ⦿ Male ○ Female
Name: John Smith

Test It

attr: John Smith
prop: John Smith

Figure 6-21. *The Name textbox's value is changed and new the attribute and property value are displayed*

You can set multiple attributes of all the selected elements by passing the map object with the attribute name and attribute value as a key-value pair. For example, in order to set the value to John Smith and the background color to yellow, you can use following code:

```
var attributes = { "value" : "John Smith",
                   "style" : "background-color:yellow"};
$("#txtName").attr(attributes);
```

You can remove single or multiple attributes of all the selected elements by using the method `removeAttr()` and passing space-separated attribute names. For example, in order to remove the `style` attribute from the `ul` element in the following code, you use `$("ul").removeAttr("style")`.

```
<ul id="listDepartments" style="text-decoration:underline; background-color:yellow; width:150px">
```

6-11. Setting the Attribute Value of All the Selected Elements Based on a Function

Problem

You want to change the attribute of each element in the set of selected elements based on the element's attributes, properties, and/or any other criteria by using the programming logic in a function.

Solution

The following jQuery syntax is used to change the CSS property of each of the elements in the set of selected HTML elements.

$(*selector*).attr("attributeName", function(index) { ... })

function is executed for each element in the set of selected elements and the specified attributeName is set with the return value of the function. This method returns the jQuery object. Listing 6-11 demonstrates the use of the attr() method, with function as an argument, to set the attribute on each element in the set of selected elements.

Listing 6-11. The jQuery method to change the attribute value of each element in the set of selected elements

```
<!DOCTYPE html>
<html lang="en">
<head>
    <meta charset="utf-8">
    <script src="scripts/jquery-2.1.0.min.js"></script>
    <style>
        .list { border:3px double green; width:350px; }
        .newRecord { font-weight: bold; }
        .tableHeader { background-color: lightgray; }
        .listDepartments { width: 200px; }
    </style>
    <script>
        $(function(){
            $("#btnTestIt").click(function () {
                var attributes = { "value" : "John Smith",
                                   "style" : "background-color:yellow"};
                $("#txtName").attr("value", function () {
                    if ($("#chkMale").prop("checked") == true) {
                        return("John Smith");
                    } else {
                        return("Jane Smith");
                    }
                });
            });
        });
    </script>
</head>
<body>
    Gender: <input type="radio" name="gender" id="chkMale" checked>Male
    <input type="radio" name="gender" id="chkFemale">Female <br>
    Name: <input type="text" id="txtName" value="" maxlength="40"><br><br>
    <input id="btnTestIt" type="button" value="Test It"><br><br>
    <div id="message"></div>
</body>
</html>
```

185

How It Works

The name data entry input textbox is created using the input HTML tag with attribute type set to text. If you want to change the default value of the textbox based on the value of other fields in the form, you select the input element by using $("#txtName") and execute the attr() method, with the function as an argument, on the selected elements.

When the Test It button is clicked, the following code is executed:

```
var attributes = { "value" : "John Smith",
                   "style" : "background-color:yellow"};

$("#txtName").attr("value", function () {
    if ($("#chkMale").prop("checked") == true) {
        return("John Smith");
    } else {
        return("Jane Smith");
    }
});
```

$("#txtName ") selects the HTML element with the ID txtName and returns the jQuery object. .attr("value", function () {...}) executes function for each element in the set of selected elements and sets the value attribute to the return value of the function. Inside the function, the following logic is used—if the Male radio button is clicked, it will return John Smith, otherwise return Jane Smith. The return value is then used to set the attribute value of the name textbox. There are other ways to implement this logic. This simple program is used to demonstrate the use of the attr() method with the function as an argument. You can also pass an index as an argument to the function when you want to use it in the logic. Figure 6-22 displays the page when it is viewed in a browser.

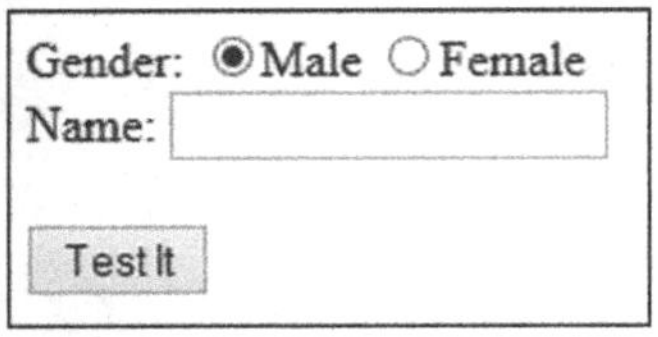

Figure 6-22. *Initial page display*

When you press the Test It button, the button's click event handler changes the value of the name textbox based on which radio button is checked. Figure 6-23 displays the effect of clicking the Test It button.

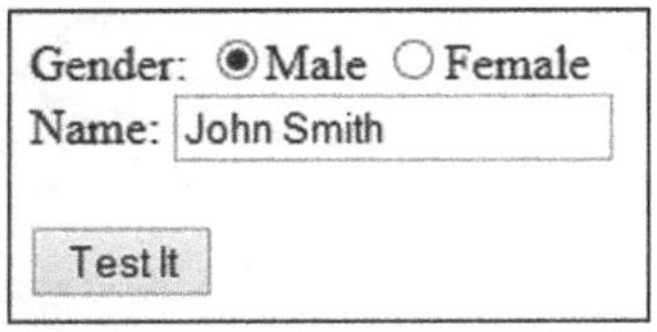

Figure 6-23. *The Name textbox's value is changed based on the checked radio button*

6-12. Getting the Property Value of the First Element of the Selected Elements

Problem

You want to get the property value of the single selected element or of the first element of the multiple selected elements.

Solution

The following jQuery syntax is used to get the property value of selected HTML elements.

$(*selector*).prop("*propertyName*")

This will return the string containing the property value of a specified propertyName of the first element in the set of selected elements. Listing 6-12 demonstrates the use of the prop() method to get the property value of the first element in the set of selected elements.

Listing 6-12. The jQuery method to get a property's value

```
<!DOCTYPE html>
<html lang="en">
<head>
    <meta charset="utf-8">
    <script src="scripts/jquery-2.1.0.min.js"></script>
    <style>
        .list { border:3px double green; width:350px; }
        .newRecord { font-weight: bold; }
        .tableHeader { background-color: lightgray; }
        .listDepartments { width: 200px; }
    </style>
    <script>
        $(function(){
          $("#btnTestIt").click(function () {
            var propertiesDetail =
              "Input Textbox: " +
              " <b>type:</b> " + $("#txtName").prop("type") +
              " <b>id:</b> " + $("#txtName").prop("id") +
              " <b>value:</b> " + $("#txtName").prop("value") +
              " <b>maxlength:</b> " + $("#txtName").prop("maxlength") +
              "<br>" +
              "Checkbox (1): " +
              " <b>type:</b> " + $("#chkMale").prop("type") +
              " <b>id:</b> " + $("#chkMale").prop("id") +
              " <b>name:</b> " + $("#chkMale").prop("name") +
              " <b>checked:</b> " + $("#chkMale").prop("checked") +
              "<br>" +
              "Checkbox (2): " +
              " <b>type:</b> " + $("#chkFemale").prop("type") +
              " <b>id:</b> " + $("#chkFemale").prop("id") +
```

187

```
                " <b>name:</b> " + $("#chkFemale").prop("name") +
                " <b>checked:</b> " + $("#chkFemale").prop("checked");

            $("#message").prop("innerHTML", propertiesDetail);
        });
    });
    </script>
</head>

<body>
    Gender: <input type="radio" name="gender" id="chkMale" checked>Male
        <input type="radio" name="gender" id="chkFemale">Female <br>
    Name: <input type="text" id="txtName" value="" maxlength="40"><br>
    <input id="btnTestIt" type="button" value="Test It"><br>
    <div id="message"></div>
</body>
</html>
```

How It Works

The two radio buttons and one input textbox are created using the input HTML tag with the type set to radio and text. If you want to get the property values such as id, type, value, maxlength, checked, and so on of these elements, you select the element first using $("#idValue") and then execute the prop() method on the selected elements with the appropriate propertyName as an argument of the prop() method.

When the Test It button is clicked, the following code is executed:

```
var propertiesDetail =
        "Input Textbox: " +
        " <b>type:</b> " + $("#txtName").prop("type") +
        " <b>id:</b> " + $("#txtName").prop("id") +
        " <b>value:</b> " + $("#txtName").prop("value") +
        " <b>maxlength:</b> " + $("#txtName").prop("maxlength") +
        "<br>" +
        "Checkbox (1): " +
        " <b>type:</b> " + $("#chkMale").prop("type") +
        " <b>id:</b> " + $("#chkMale").prop("id") +
        " <b>name:</b> " + $("#chkMale").prop("name") +
        " <b>checked:</b> " + $("#chkMale").prop("checked") +
        "<br>" +
        "Checkbox (2): " +
        " <b>type:</b> " + $("#chkFemale").prop("type") +
        " <b>id:</b> " + $("#chkFemale").prop("id") +
        " <b>name:</b> " + $("#chkFemale").prop("name") +
        " <b>checked:</b> " + $("#chkFemale").prop("checked");

    $("#message").prop("innerHTML", propertiesDetail);
```

$("#idValue") selects the HTML element with the ID attribute idValue and returns the jQuery object. .prop("type") gets the value of propertyName type of the selected element. Similarly, other attribute values are retrieved by using the syntax $(selector).prop("propertyName"). All retrieved property values are concatenated in a string called propertiesDetail, which is then displayed in the page by using the line $("#message"). prop("innerHTML", propertiesDetail). Figure 6-24 displays the page when it is viewed in a browser.

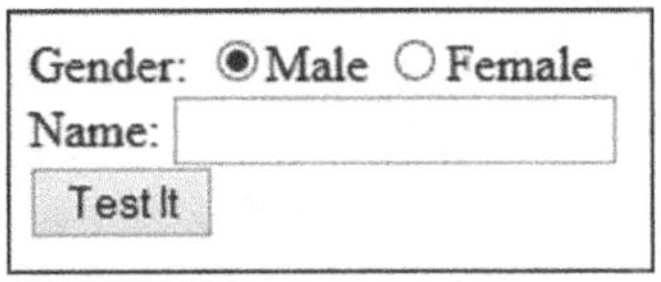

Figure 6-24. *Initial page display*

When you press the Test It button, the button's click event handler gets the property values of the two radio buttons and the textbox and displays it on the page. Figure 6-25 displays the effect of clicking the Test It button.

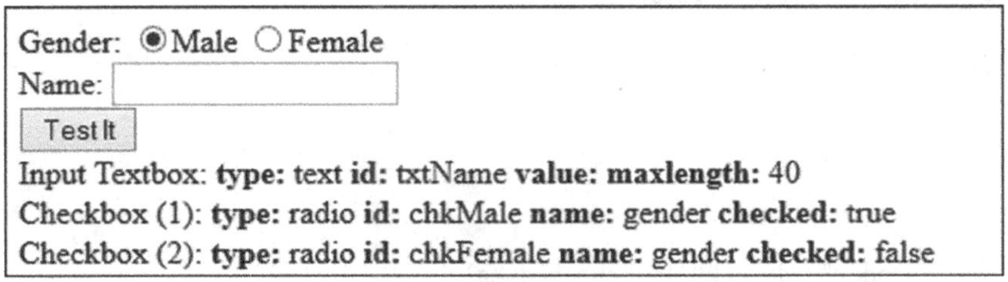

Figure 6-25. *Property values of the radio buttons and the textbox are displayed*

6-13. Setting the Property Value of All Selected Elements
Problem

You want to set the property value of all the selected elements.

Solution

The following jQuery syntax is used to set the property of all the selected HTML elements.

$(*selector*).prop("*propertyName*", "*propertyValue*")

The property value of the HTML tags can be set by using the prop() method. This method returns the jQuery object. If propertyName property doesn't exist, it is created for the selected elements. The prop() method is used to set properties such as selectedIndex, tagName, nodeName, and so on. These properties cannot be set using the attr() method as they do not have corresponding attribute name. Listing 6-13 demonstrates the use of the prop() method to set the property value of the selected elements.

Listing 6-13. The jQuery method to set the property's value

```
<!DOCTYPE html>
<html lang="en">
<head>
    <meta charset="utf-8">
    <script src="scripts/jquery-2.1.0.min.js"></script>
    <style>
        .list { border:3px double green; width:350px; }
        .newRecord { font-weight: bold; }
        .tableHeader { background-color: lightgray; }
        .listDepartments { width: 200px; }
    </style>
    <script>
        $(function(){
            $("#btnTestIt").click(function () {
                $("#txtName").prop("value", "John Smith");
                var msg =   "attr: " + $("#txtName").attr("value") + "<br>" +
                            "prop: " + $("#txtName").prop("value");

                $("#message").prop("innerHTML", msg);
            });
        });
    </script>
</head>
<body>
    Gender: <input type="radio" name="gender" id="chkMale" checked>Male
    <input type="radio" name="gender" id="chkFemale">Female <br>
    Name: <input type="text" id="txtName" value="" maxlength="40"><br><br>
    <input id="btnTestIt" type="button" value="Test It"><br><br>
    <div id="message"></div>
</body>
</html>
```

How It Works

The textbox for entering the name is created using the input HTML tag with the type set to text. If you want to set the property value for the name textbox, you select the name input element using $("#txtName") and execute the prop() method on the selected element.

When the Test It button is clicked, the following code is executed:

```
$("#txtName").prop("value", "John Smith");
```

$("#txtName ") selects the HTML element with the ID set to txtName and returns the jQuery object. .prop("value", "John Smith") sets the value of the value property to John Smith. Refer to Chapter 2 to understand the difference between attributes and properties. When the property of an HTML element is set, only its property is changed. Its attribute value remains unchanged. Figure 6-26 displays the page when it is viewed in a browser.

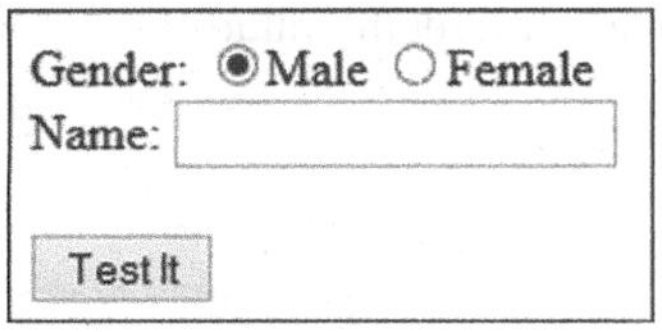

Gender: ◉ Male ○ Female
Name: [   ]

[Test It]

Figure 6-26. *Initial page display*

When you press the Test It button, the button's click event handler changes the property value of the name textbox to John Smith and then displays the new value of the attribute value and property value. As you can see, the value attribute remains unchanged. Figure 6-27 displays the effect of clicking the Test It button.

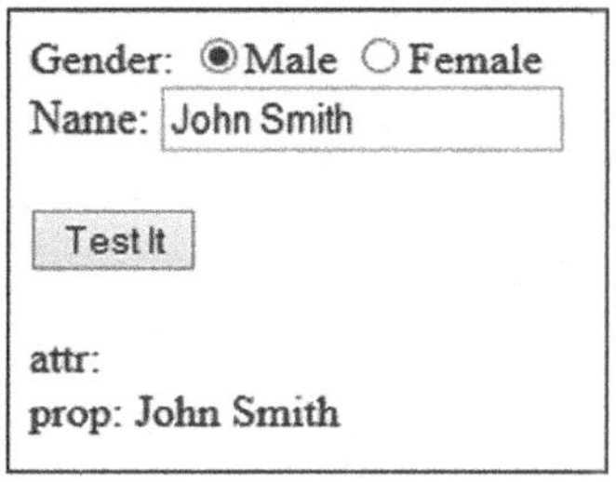

Gender: ◉ Male ○ Female
Name: [John Smith   ]

[Test It]

attr:
prop: John Smith

Figure 6-27. *Name textbox value is changed due to the change in property "value"*

You can set multiple properties of all the selected elements by passing the map object with the property name and property value as the key/value pair.

You can remove a property of the selected elements by using the removeProp() method and passing the property name as an argument. Only those properties created using the prop(propertyName, propertyValue) method can be removed. For example, customProperty is created using $(selector).prop("customProperty", "customValue") and so it can be removed later in the code by using $(selector).removeProp("customProperty").

6-14. Getting and Setting the Value Property of Selected Elements

Problem

You want to get the value of the first element of the selected elements and set the value of all of the selected elements.

Solution

The following jQuery syntax is used to get the value of first element of the selected HTML elements.

$(*selector*).val()

It returns a string, number, or array depending on selector. The val() method is used to get the values of data-entry form fields such as input, select, and textarea.

The following jQuery syntax is used to set the value of all the selected HTML elements.

$(*selector*).val("*newValue*")

It returns a jQuery object. Listing 6-14 demonstrates the use of the val() method to get and set the value of a textbox.

Listing 6-14. The jQuery method val() gets and sets the value of a textbox

```html
<!DOCTYPE html>
<html lang="en">
<head>
    <meta charset="utf-8">
    <script src="scripts/jquery-2.1.0.min.js"></script>
    <style>
        .highlight {
            text-decoration:underline;
            background-color:yellow;
            width: 150px;
        }
    </style>
    <script>
        $(function(){
            $("#btnTestItGetValue").click(function () {
                alert($("#txtName").val());
            });

            $("#btnTestItSetValue").click(function () {
                $("#txtName").val("John Smith");
            });
        });
    </script>
</head>
<body>
    <strong>Name:</strong><input type="text" id="txtName"><br><br><br>
    <input id="btnTestItGetValue" type="button" value="Test It (Get Value)"><br><br>
    <input id="btnTestItSetValue" type="button" value="Test It (Set Value)">
</body>
</html>
```

How It Works

The Name textbox is created using the input HTML tag with the type set to text. If you want to get or set the value of this textbox, you select the textbox using $("#txtName") and execute the val() method on the selected element to get the value and execute the val("newValue") to set the value.

If some value is entered for the Name textbox and the Test It (Get Value) button is clicked, the following code is executed:

```
alert($("#txtName").val());
```

$("#txtName") selects the HTML element with the ID set to txtName and returns the jQuery object. .val() gets the current value of the textbox. This value is then displayed as a pop-up message.

When the Test It (Set Value) button is clicked, the following code is executed:

```
$("#txtName").val("John Smith");
```

192

$("#txtName") selects the HTML element with the id set to txtName and returns the jQuery object. .val("John Smith") sets the value of the textbox to John Smith. Figure 6-28 displays the page when it is viewed in a browser.

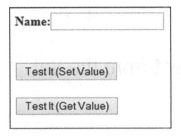

Figure 6-28. *Initial page display*

When you press the Test It (Set Value) button, the button's click event handler changes the value of the textbox. Figure 6-29 displays the effect of clicking the Test It (Set Value) button.

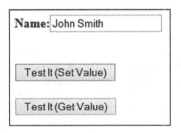

Figure 6-29. *Value of name textbox is set*

When you press the Test It (Get Value) button, the button's click event handler gets the current value of the textbox. Figure 6-30 displays the effect of clicking the Test It (Get Value) button.

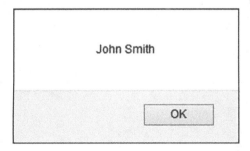

Figure 6-30. *Current value of name textbox is displayed*

The selected value of a drop-down can be retrieved using $("#dropdownIdValue").val(). If multiple items are selected in the drop-down, an array is returned. An item in the drop-down can be selected at runtime by using $("#dropdownIdValue").val("newValue"). For example, the state drop-down is implemented by the following code. Default state is IL and can be set by using the code $("#ddState").val("IL").

193

```
<select id="ddState">
    <option value="">Select State</option>
    <option value="CA">California</option>
    <option value="IL">Illinois</option>
    <option value="IN">Indiana</option>
</select>
```

6-15. Getting or Setting the Value of Each Element from the Set of Selected Elements Using a Function

Problem

You want to get and then set the value of the selected elements using a function.

Solution

The following jQuery syntax is used to iterate over each element from the set of selected elements using a function and then set its value.

$(*selector*).val(function (index, currentValue) { ... })

For each element, the return value of the function is used to set its value. This val() method returns the jQuery object with the function as its argument. Listing 6-15 demonstrates the use of the val() method to set each element's value.

Listing 6-15. The jQuery method to set each element's value

```
<!DOCTYPE html>
<html lang="en">
<head>
    <meta charset="utf-8">
    <script src="scripts/jquery-2.1.0.min.js"></script>
    <style>
        .label { width: 200px; font-weight: bold; color: blue; }
        .highlight {
            text-decoration:underline;
            background-color:yellow;
            width: 150px;
        }
    </style>
    <script>
        $(function(){
            $("#btnTestIt").click(function () {
                $("input:text").val(function (index, currentValue) {
                    return(currentValue.toUpperCase());
                });
            });
        });
    </script>
</head>
```

```
<body>
    <div class="label">Name:</div><input type="text" id="txtName"><br>
    <div class="label">Address:</div><input type="text" id="txtAddress"><br><br><br>
    <input id="btnTestIt" type="button" value="Test It">
</body>
</html>
```

How It Works

The name and address textboxes are created using the input HTML tag with the type set to text. If you want to set each textbox value based on its current value, you select all input elements with the type set to text using $("input:text") and execute the val() method, with the function as an argument, on the selected elements.

When the Test It button is clicked, the following code is executed:

```
$("input:text").val(function (index, currentValue) {
    return(currentValue.toUpperCase());
});
```

$("input:text") selects the HTML element with the tag name input and with the type set to text and returns the jQuery object. .val(function (index, currentValue) {...}) iterates over each element in the set of selected elements. This function converts the current value to uppercase and returns it. The returned value is used to set the value of each element in the set of selected elements. Figure 6-31 displays the page when it is viewed in a browser and after some test data is entered.

Figure 6-31. *Initial page display with some test data*

When you press the Test It button, the button's click event handler converts the current value of each element to uppercase and then sets each element's value. Figure 6-32 displays the effect of clicking the Test It button.

Figure 6-32. *Entered values are converted to uppercase*

6-16. Getting the HTML of the First Element of the Selected Elements

Problem

You want to get the HTML (the content of the DOM tree node, including the HTML tags) of the first element of the selected elements.

Solution

The following jQuery syntax is used to get the HTML content of the first element of the selected HTML elements:

$(selector).html()

It returns a string with the HTML content. Listing 6-16 demonstrates the use of the html() method to get the HTML content of the selected HTML element.

Listing 6-16. Using the jQuery method html() to get HTML content

```html
<!DOCTYPE html>
<html lang="en">
<head>
    <meta charset="utf-8">
    <script src="scripts/jquery-2.1.0.min.js"></script>
    <style>
        .highlight {
            width: 300px;
            border: 3px double green;
            background-color: lightyellow;
        }
    </style>
    <script>
        $(function(){
            $("#btnTestIt").click(function () {
                alert($("ul").html());
            });
        });
    </script>
</head>
<body>
    <ul>
        <li>Marketing</li>
        <li>Sales</li>
        <li>Technology</li>
        <li>Customer Support</li>
    </ul>
    <input id="btnTestIt" type="button" value="Test It">
</body>
</html>
```

How It Works

The department names are listed using the `<ul>` and `<li>` HTML tags. If you want to get the HTML content of the `ul` tag, you select the `<ul>` element using `$("ul")` and execute the `html()` method on the selected elements.

When the Test It button is clicked, the following code is executed:

```
alert($("ul").html());
```

`$("ul")` selects the HTML element with the tag name `ul` and returns the jQuery object. `.html()` gets the HTML content of the selected element (`ul`). Figure 6-33 displays the page when it is viewed in a browser.

Marketing
Sales
Technology
Customer Support
Test It

Figure 6-33. *Initial page display*

When you press the Test It button, the button's click event handler gets the HTML content of the selected element. Figure 6-34 displays the effect of clicking the Test It button.

<li>Marketing</li>
<li>Sales</li>
<li>Technology</li>
<li>Customer Support</li>
OK

Figure 6-34. *HTML content of the ul tag is displayed*

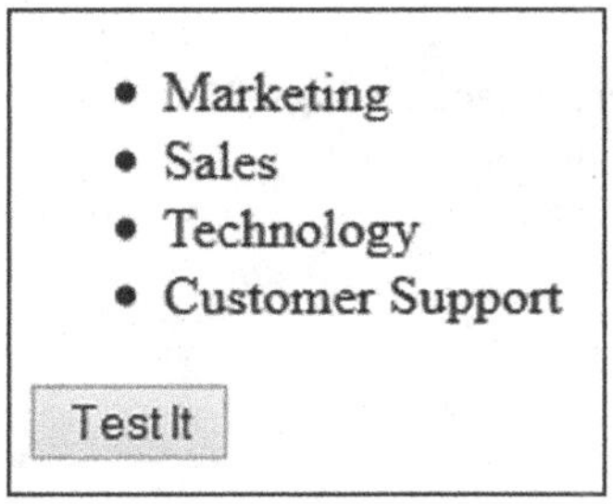

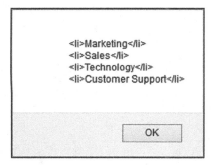

6-17. Replacing the HTML in All the Selected Elements

Problem

You want to replace the HTML content in all the selected eleements.

Solution

The following jQuery syntax is used to set the HTML content of all the selected HTML elements.

$(*selector*).html("*htmlString*")

htmlString is the string with its HTML tags and text. This method returns the jQuery object. Listing 6-17 demonstrates the use of the html() method to set the HTML content of the selected elements.

Listing 6-17. The jQuery method to set the HTML content of the selected elements

```
<!DOCTYPE html>
<html lang="en">
<head>
    <meta charset="utf-8">
    <script src="scripts/jquery-2.1.0.min.js"></script>
    <style>
        .highlight {
            width: 300px;
            border: 3px double green;
            background-color: lightyellow;
        }
    </style>
    <script>
        $(function(){
            $("#btnTestIt").click(function () {
                $("ul").html("<li>New Department</li>");
            });
        });
    </script>
</head>
<body>
<ul>
    <li>Marketing</li>
    <li>Sales</li>
    <li>Technology</li>
    <li>Customer Support</li>
</ul>
<input id="btnTestIt" type="button" value="Test It">
</body>
</html>
```

How It Works

The department names are listed using the <ul> and <li> HTML tags. If you want to change the HTML content of the HTML element ul, you select the <ul> element using $("ul") and execute the html() method with htmlString as a parameter, on the selected element. Since you are setting HTML content, the old HTML content is replaced.

When the Test It button is clicked, the following code is executed:

```
$("ul").html("<li>New Department</li>");
```

$("ul") selects the HTML element with the tag name ul and returns the jQuery object. .html("<li>New Department</li>") replaces the HTML content of the selected element (ul) with <li>New Department</li>. Figure 6-35 displays the page when it is viewed in a browser.

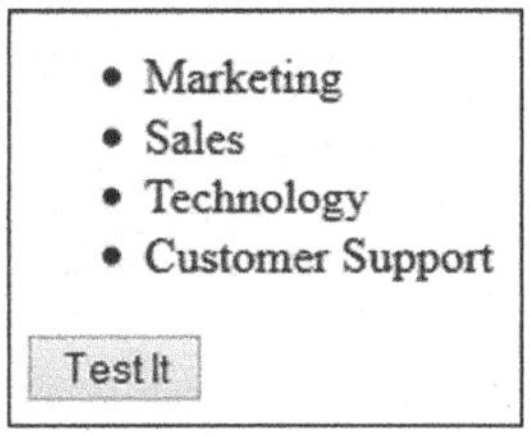

- Marketing
- Sales
- Technology
- Customer Support

Test It

Figure 6-35. *Initial page display*

When you press the Test It button, the button's click event handler replaces the HTML content of the ul HTML element. Figure 6-36 displays the effect of clicking the Test It button.

- New Department

Test It

Figure 6-36. *Department names are replaced with the New Department text*

The HTML content of each element of the selected elements can be replaced with the different HTML content by using following syntax:

```
$(selector).html(function (index, oldHTMLContent) { ... return("newHTMLContent"); })
```

The return value of the function is used to set the HTML content of each element.

6-18. Getting the Combined Contents of Each of the Selected Elements
Problem

You want to get the combined text of all selected elements.

Solution

The following jQuery syntax is used to get the combined text of all the selected HTML elements.

$(*selector*).text()

It returns a string with the text of all selected elements. Listing 6-18 demonstrates the use of the text() method to get the combined text of all selected elements.

Listing 6-18. The jQuery method to get the combined text of the selected elements

```
<!DOCTYPE html>
<html lang="en">
<head>
    <meta charset="utf-8">
    <script src="scripts/jquery-2.1.0.min.js"></script>
    <style>
        .highlight {
            width: 300px;
            border: 3px double green;
            background-color: lightyellow;
        }
    </style>
    <script>
        $(function(){
                $("#btnTestIt").click(function () {
                alert($("li").text());
            });
        });
    </script>
</head>
<body>
    <ul>
        <li>Marketing</li>
        <li>Sales</li>
        <li>Technology</li>
        <li>Customer Support</li>
    </ul>
    <input id="btnTestIt" type="button" value="Test It">
</body>
</html>
```

How It Works

The department names are listed using the <ul> and <li> HTML tags. If you want to get all the department names, you select all the li HTML tags using $("li") and execute the text() method on the selected elements.

When the Test It button is clicked, the following code is executed:

```
alert($("li").text());
```

$("li") selects the HTML element with the tag name li and returns the jQuery object. .text() gets the combined text of all the selected elements (ul). Figure 6-37 displays the page when it is viewed in a browser.

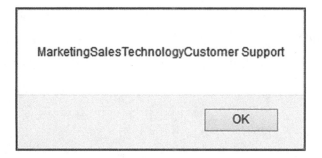

Figure 6-37. *Initial page display*

When you press the Test It button, the button's click event handler gets the text of all selected elements. Figure 6-38 displays the effect of clicking the Test It button.

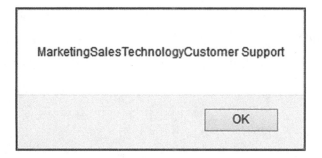

Figure 6-38. *All department names are displayed as combined text*

The following jQuery syntax is used to set the text of each element of the selected HTML elements.

$(*selector*).text("textString")

For example, all the departments in the previous example are replaced by "New Department" using this code:

```
$("ul").text("New Department");
```

The text of each element of the selected elements can be replaced with the different text by using following syntax:

$(selector).text(function (index, oldText) { ... return("*newText*"); })

The return value of the function is used to set the text of each element of the selected elements.

6-19. Inserting Content at the End of a Selection

Problem

You want to add HTML content (a DOM node) to the end of the selected HTML elements.

Solution

The following jQuery syntax is used to add HTML content to the end of all the selected HTML elements.

$(*selector*).append("*htmlContent*")

htmlContent can be HTML tags with their attributes and text content. This method returns the jQuery object. Listing 6-19 demonstrates the use of the append() method to add HTML content to all the selected elements.

Listing 6-19. The jQuery method to add HTML content to the end of a selection

```
<!DOCTYPE html>
<html lang="en">
<head>
    <meta charset="utf-8">
    <script src="scripts/jquery-2.1.0.min.js"></script>
    <style>
        .highlight {
            width: 300px;
            border: 3px double green;
            background-color: lightyellow;
        }
    </style>
    <script>
        $(function(){
            $("#btnTestIt").click(function () {
                $("ul").append("<li>Implementation</li>");
            });
        });
    </script>
</head>
<body>
    <ul>
        <li>Marketing</li>
        <li>Sales</li>
        <li>Technology</li>
        <li>Customer Support</li>
    </ul>
    <input id="btnTestIt" type="button" value="Test It">
</body>
</html>
```

How It Works

The department names are listed using the <ul> and <li> HTML tags. If you want to add a new department to the list of existing departments, you select the <ul> element using $("ul") and execute the append() method on the selected element.

When the Test It button is clicked, the following code is executed:

```
$("ul").append("<li>Implementation</li>");
```

$("ul") selects the HTML element with the tag name ul and returns the jQuery object. .append("<li>Implementation</li>") appends the HTML content—<li>Implementation</li>—to the selected element (ul). Figure 6-39 displays the page when it is viewed in a browser.

- Marketing
- Sales
- Technology
- Customer Support

[Test It]

Figure 6-39. *Initial page display*

When you press the Test It button, the button's click event handler appends the new department name to the end of the department names list. Figure 6-40 displays the effect of clicking the Test It button.

- Marketing
- Sales
- Technology
- Customer Support
- Implementation

[Test It]

Figure 6-40. *"Implementation" is added to the end of the list*

$("ul").append("<li>Implementation</li>") can also be written as $("<li>Implementation</li>"). appendTo("ul"). Since the append() and appendTo() methods have the same effect, you can use either. The syntax for the appendTo method is:

```
$("htmlContent").append("selector ")
```

The following syntax is used to append multiple HTML contents:

```
$(selector).append("htmlContent1", "htmlContent2", ...)
```

The following syntax is used to append HTML content based on the return value of a function:

```
$(selector).append(function(index, currentHTML) { ... return ("htmlContent");})
```

6-20. Inserting Content at the Beginning of Each Element of the Selected Elements

Problem

You want to add HTML content (a DOM node) to the beginning of the selected HTML elements.

Solution

The following jQuery syntax is used to add HTML content to the beginning of all the selected HTML elements.

```
$(selector).prepend("htmlContent")
```

htmlContent can be HTML tags with their attributes and text content. This method returns the jQuery object. Listing 6-20 demonstrates the use of the prepend() method to add HTML content to all the selected elements.

Listing 6-20. The jQuery method to add HTML content to the beginning of a selection

```
<!DOCTYPE html>
<html lang="en">
<head>
    <meta charset="utf-8">
    <script src="scripts/jquery-2.1.0.min.js"></script>
    <style>
        .highlight {
            width: 300px;
            border: 3px double green;
            background-color: lightyellow;
        }
    </style>
    <script>
        $(function(){
            $("#btnTestIt").click(function () {
                $("ul").prepend("<li>Infrastructure</li>");
            });
        });
    </script>
</head>
```

```
<body>
   <ul>
      <li>Marketing</li>
      <li>Sales</li>
      <li>Technology</li>
      <li>Customer Support</li>
   </ul>
   <input id="btnTestIt" type="button" value="Test It">
</body>
</html>
```

How It Works

The department names are listed using the <ul> and <li> HTML tags. If you want to add a new department to the list of existing departments, you select the <ul> element using $("ul") and execute the prepend() method on the selected element.

When the Test It button is clicked, the following code is executed:

```
$("ul").prepend("<li>Infrastructure</li>");
```

$("ul") selects the HTML element with the tag name ul and returns the jQuery object. .prepend("<li>Infrastructure</li>") prepends the HTML content—<li>Infrastructure </li>—to the selected element (ul). Figure 6-41 displays the page when it is viewed in a browser.

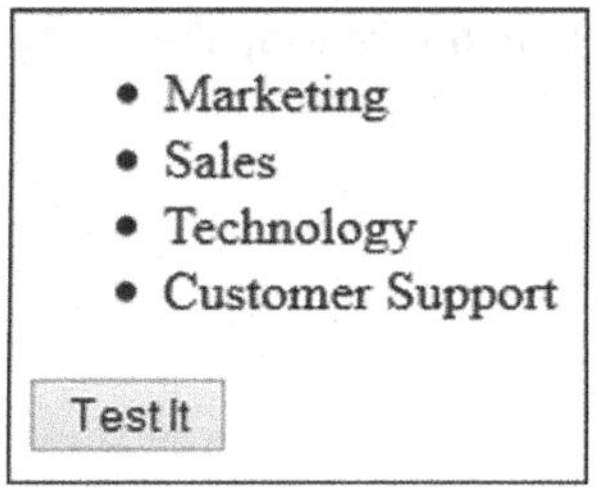

- Marketing
- Sales
- Technology
- Customer Support

Test It

Figure 6-41. *Initial page display*

When you press the Test It button, the button's click event handler prepends the new department name to the beginning of the department names list. Figure 6-42 displays the effect of clicking the Test It button.

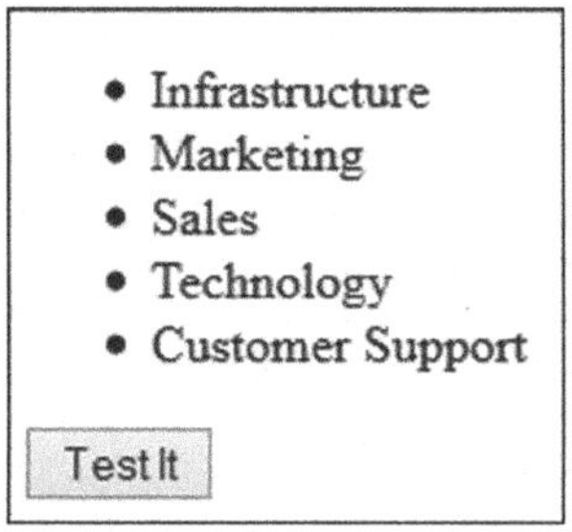

- Infrastructure
- Marketing
- Sales
- Technology
- Customer Support

Test It

Figure 6-42. *"Infrastructure" is added to the beginning of the list*

$("ul").prepend("<li> Infrastructure</li>") can also be written as $("<li> Infrastructure </li>"). prependTo("ul"). Since prepend() and prependTo() have the same effect, you can use them interchangeably.

The following syntax is used to prepend multiple HTML content:

$(*selector*).prepend("*htmlContent1*", "*htmlContent2*", ...)

The following syntax is used to prepend HTML content based on the return value of a function:

$(*selector*).prepend(function(index, currentHTML) { ... return ("htmlContent");})

6-21. Wrapping an HTML Structure Around Each Selected Element

Problem

You want to wrap the HTML structure (opening and closing HTML tags) around each selected element.

Solution

The following jQuery syntax is used to wrap the HTML structure around each selected element.

$(*selector*).wrap("htmlContent")

This method returns the jQuery object. Listing 6-21 demonstrates the use of the wrap() method to wrap the HTML structure around each selected element.

Listing 6-21. The jQuery method to wrap an HTML structure around each element

```
<!DOCTYPE html>
<html lang="en">
<head>
    <meta charset="utf-8">
    <script src="scripts/jquery-2.1.0.min.js"></script>
    <style>
            .highlight {
                width: 300px;
                border: 3px double green;
                background-color: lightyellow;
            }
    </style>
    <script>
        $(function(){
            $("#btnTestIt").click(function () {
                $("ul").wrap("<div class='highlight'></div>");
            });
        });
    </script>
</head>
```

```
<body>
    <ul>
        <li>Marketing</li>
        <li>Sales</li>
        <li>Technology</li>
        <li>Customer Support</li>
    </ul>
    <input id="btnTestIt" type="button" value="Test It">
</body>
</html>
```

How It Works

The department names are listed using the <ul> and <li> HTML tags. If you want to wrap all the department names with the <div> tag with its class attribute or any other attribute, you select the <ul> element using $("ul") and execute the wrap() method on the selected element.

When the Test It button is clicked, the following code is executed:

```
$("ul").wrap("<div class='highlight'></div>");
```

$("ul") selects the HTML element with the tag name ul and returns the jQuery object. .wrap("<div class='highlight'></div>") wraps the <div> tag around the selected element (ul). Figure 6-43 displays the page when it is viewed in a browser.

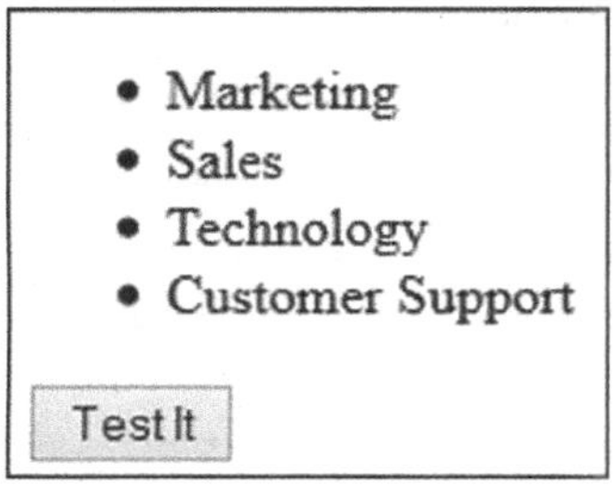

Figure 6-43. *Initial page display*

When you press the Test It button, the button's click event handler wraps a <div> tag with the class set to highlight around the selected ul element. Figure 6-44 displays the effect of clicking the Test It button.

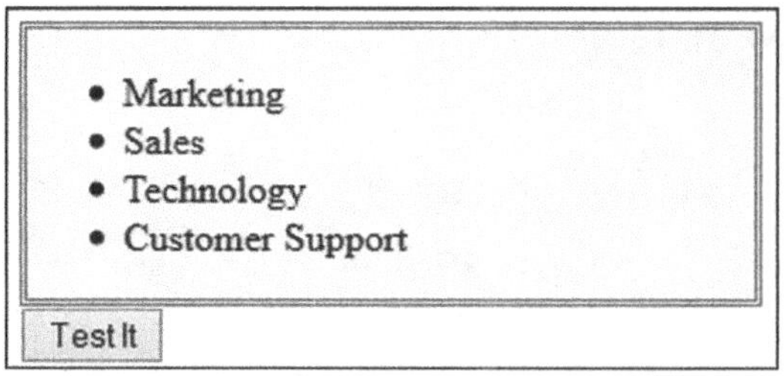

Figure 6-44. *Selected element is wrapped with a div tag*

Other variations of the wrap() method include:

```
$(selector).wrap(wrappingSelector)
$(selector).wrap(htmlElement)
$(selector).wrap(jQueryObject)
$(selector).wrap(function(index) { ... return("htmlString");})
```

6-22. Wrapping an HTML Structure Around the Content of Each Selected Element

Problem

You want to wrap an HTML structure around the content of each selected element.

Solution

The following jQuery syntax is used to wrap an HTML structure around the content of each selected element:

$(*selector*).wrapInner("htmlContent")

This method returns the jQuery object. Listing 6-22 demonstrates the use of the wrapInner() method to wrap an HTML structure around the content of each selected element.

Listing 6-22. The jQuery method to wrap an HTML structure around the content of elements

```
<html lang="en">
<head>
   <meta charset="utf-8">
   <script src="scripts/jquery-2.1.0.min.js"></script>
   <style>
      .highlight {
         width: 150px;
         border: 3px double green;
         background-color: lightyellow;
      }
   </style>
   <script>
      $(function(){
         $("#btnTestIt").click(function () {
            $("li").wrapInner("<div class='highlight'></div>");
         });
      });
   </script>
</head>
```

```
<body>
    <ul>
        <li>Marketing</li>
        <li>Sales</li>
        <li>Technology</li>
        <li>Customer Support</li>
    </ul>
    <input id="btnTestIt" type="button" value="Test It">
</body>
</html>
```

How It Works

The department names are listed using the <ul> and <li> HTML tags. If you want to wrap all the department names content separately with the <div> tag with its class attribute or any other attribute, you select the <li> elements using $("li") and execute the wrapInner() method on the selected elements.

When the Test It button is clicked, the following code is executed:

```
$("li").wrapInner("<div class='highlight'></div>");
```

$("li") selects the HTML element with the tag name li and returns the jQuery object. .wrapInner("<div class='highlight'></div>") wraps the <div> tag around the content of the selected elements (li). Figure 6-45 displays the page when it is viewed in a browser.

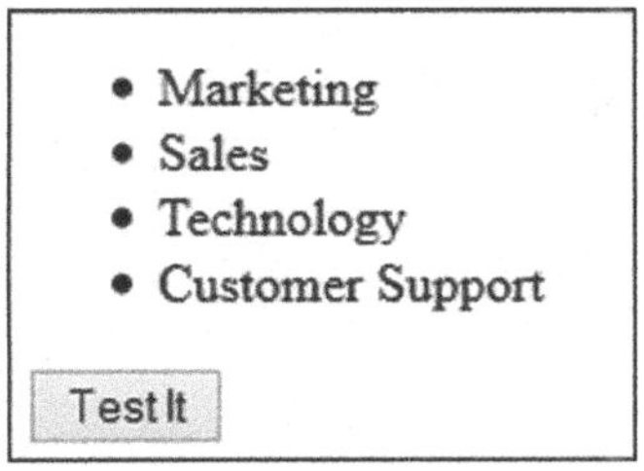

Figure 6-45. *Initial page display*

When you press the Test It button, the button's click event handler wraps the <div> tag with the class as highlight around the content of the selected li elements. Figure 6-46 displays the effect of clicking the Test It button.

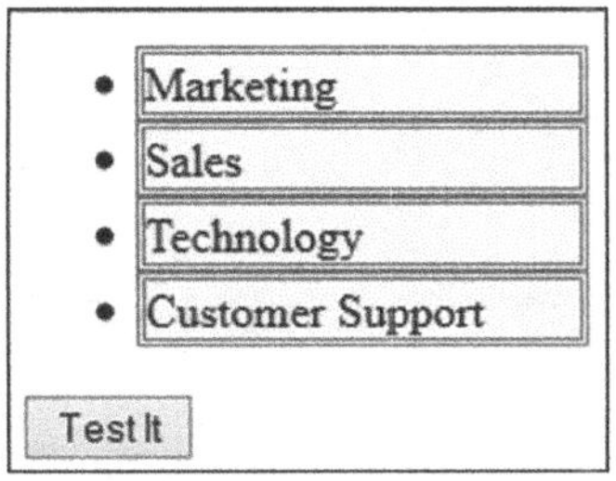

Figure 6-46. *Content of selected elements are wrapped with div tag*

Other variations of using the `wrapInner()` method are:

```
$(selector).wrapInner(wrappingSelector)
$(selector).wrapInner(htmlElement)
$(selector).wrapInner(jQueryObject)
$(selector).wrapInner(function(index) { ... return("htmlString");})
```

The difference between `wrap()` and `wrapInner()` is that `wrap()`wraps the specified HTML structure around the selected element(s), whereas `wrapInner()` wraps the specified HTML structure around the *content of* the selected element(s).

6-23. Wrapping an HTML Structure Around All Selected Elements
Problem

You want to wrap an HTML structure around all the selected elements as a single unit.

Solution

The following jQuery syntax is used to wrap an HTML structure around all selected elements:

$(*selector*).wrapAll("htmlContent")

This method returns the jQuery object. Listing 6-23 demonstrates the use of the `wrapAll()` method to wrap an HTML structure around all selected elements.

Listing 6-23. The jQuery method to wrap an HTML structure around all selected elements

```html
<!DOCTYPE html>
<html lang="en">
<head>
    <meta charset="utf-8">
    <script src="scripts/jquery-2.1.0.min.js"></script>
    <style>
        .highlight {
            width: 150px;
            border: 3px double green;
            background-color: lightyellow;
        }
    </style>
    <script>
        $(function(){
            $("#btnTestIt").click(function () {
                $("li").wrapAll("<div class='highlight'></div>");
            });
        });
    </script>
</head>
```

```
<body>
   <ul>
      <li>Marketing</li>
      <li>Sales</li>
      <li>Technology</li>
      <li>Customer Support</li>
   </ul>
   <input id="btnTestIt" type="button" value="Test It">
</body>
</html>
```

How It Works

The department names are listed using the `<ul>` and `<li>` HTML tags. If you want to wrap all the department names as a single unit with the `<div>` tag with its class attribute or any other attribute, you select the `<li>` elements using `$("li")` and execute the `wrapAll()` method on the selected elements.

When the Test It button is clicked, the following code is executed:

```
$("li").wrapAll("<div class='highlight'></div>");
```

`$("li")` selects the HTML element with the tag name `li` and returns the jQuery object. `.wrapAll("<div class='highlight'></div>")` wraps the `<div>` tag around all of the selected elements (`"li"`). Figure 6-47 displays the page when it is viewed in a browser.

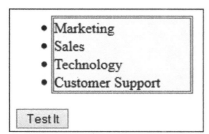

***Figure 6-47.** Initial page display*

When you press the Test It button, the button's click event handler wraps the `<div>` tag with the class set to `highlight` around all of the selected `li` elements. Figure 6-48 displays the effect of clicking the Test It button.

***Figure 6-48.** All selected elements are wrapped with a div tag*

211

Other variations of the wrapAll() methods include:

```
$(selector).wrapAll(wrappingSelector)
$(selector).wrapAll(htmlElement)
$(selector).wrapAll(jQueryObject)
```

6-24. Inserting Content After Each Selected Element
Problem

You want to insert HTML content after each selected element.

Solution

The following jQuery syntax is used to insert HTML content at the end of all the selected HTML elements.

$(*selector*).after("*htmlContent*")

htmlContent can be the HTML tags with their attributes and text. This method returns the jQuery object. Listing 6-24 demonstrates the use of the after() method to insert HTML content after each selected element.

Listing 6-24. The jQuery method to insert HTML content at the end of a selection

```
<!DOCTYPE html>
<html lang="en">
<head>
    <meta charset="utf-8">
    <script src="scripts/jquery-2.1.0.min.js"></script>
    <style>
        .highlight {
            width: 150px;
            border: 3px double green;
            background-color: lightyellow;
        }
    </style>
    <script>
        $(function(){
            $("#btnTestIt1").click(function () {
                $("#lstDepartments").after("<b>- Implementation</b>");
            });

            $("#btnTestIt2").click(function () {
                $("#lstDepartments").append("<b>- Production Support<b>");
            });
        });
    </script>
</head>
```

```
<body>
    <div id="lstDepartments" class="highlight">
        - Marketing<br>
        - Sales<br>
        - Technology<br>
        - Customer Support<br>
    </div><br><br>
    <input id="btnTestIt1" type="button" value="Test It (After)">
    <input id="btnTestIt2" type="button" value="Test It (Append)">
</body>
</html>
```

How It Works

The department names are listed using the <ul> and <li> HTML tags. If you want to insert a new department after the list of existing departments, you select the <ul> element using $("ul") and execute the after() method on the selected element.

When the Test It (After) button is clicked, the following code is executed:

```
$("ul").after("<li>Implementation</li>");
```

$("ul") selects the HTML element with the tag name ul and returns the jQuery object.
.after("<li>Implementation</li>") inserts the HTML content <li>Implementation</li> after the end of the selected element (ul). Figure 6-49 displays the page when it is viewed in a browser.

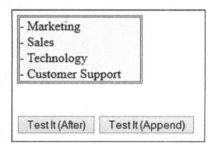

Figure 6-49. *Initial page display*

When you press the Test It (After) button, the button's click event handler inserts the new department name after the department names list. Figure 6-50 displays the effect of clicking the Test It (After) button.

213

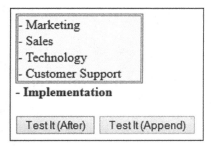

Figure 6-50. *"Implementation" is inserted after the departments list*

When you refresh the page and press the Test It (Append) button, the button's click event handler inserts the new department name at the end of the department names list. Figure 6-51 displays the effect of clicking the Test It (Append) button. Figures 6-50 and 6-51 demonstrate difference between the append() and after() methods.

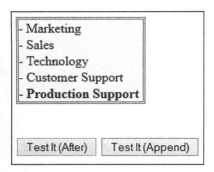

Figure 6-51. *"Production Support" is inserted at the end of departments list*

Multiple HTML content can be inserted by using the following syntax:

$(*selector*).after("*htmlContent1*", "*htmlContent2*"...)

The following syntax is used to insert HTML content by the value returned by a function:

$(*selector*).after(function(index) { .... return("*htmlContent*"); })

6-25. Copying All Selected Elements
Problem

You want to copy all selected elements and their descendant elements.

Solution

The following jQuery syntax is used to copy all selected elements and their descendant elements.

$(*selector*).clone()

This method returns the jQuery object. Listing 6-25 demonstrates the use of the clone() method to copy all elements and their descendant elements.

Listing 6-25. The jQuery method that copies the selected elements and their descendants

```html
<!DOCTYPE html>
<html lang="en">
<head>
    <meta charset="utf-8">
    <script src="scripts/jquery-2.1.0.min.js"></script>
    <style>
        .label {
            width:150px;
        }
        .input {
            width: 500px;
        }
        .highlight {
            border: 3px dotted red;
            background-color: yellow;
        }
    </style>
    <script>
        $(function(){
            $("#chkShippingAddress").click(function (){
                if ($(this).prop("checked")) {
                    $("#shippingAddress").append($(".billingAddress").clone());
                } else {
                    $("#shippingAddress > .billingAddress").remove();
                }
            });
        });
    </script>
</head>
<body>
    Billing Address:
    <div class="billingAddress">
        <div class="label">Name: </div>
        <div class="text"><input type="text"></div><br>
        <div class="label">Address: </div>
        <div class="text"><input type="text"></div>
    </div><br>
    Shipping Address same as Billing Address: <input id="chkShippingAddress" type="checkbox"><br><br>
    Shipping Address:
    <div id="shippingAddress"></div>
</body>
</html>
```

How It Works

There are two blocks of address fields—billing address and shipping address. If you want to copy all the fields in the billing address block (the `<div>` tag with the class `"billingAddress"`) to the `shippingAddress` block when the Shipping Address Same as Billing Address checkbox is checked, you must first clone the `div` tag with the class `billingAddress` and append it to the `div` tag with the ID of `shippingAddress`. If the checkbox is unchecked, use the `remove()` method to remove the newly created `div` tag that has the class `billingAddress` and is a descendant of the `div` tag with the id `shippingAddress`. Figure 6-52 displays the page when it is viewed in a browser.

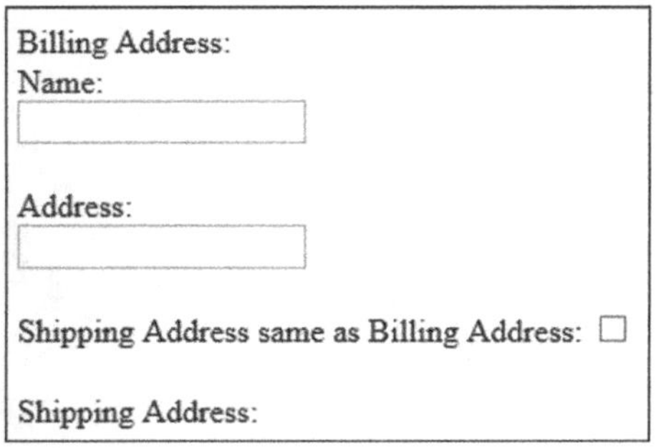

```
Billing Address:
Name:
[                    ]

Address:
[                    ]

Shipping Address same as Billing Address: ☐

Shipping Address:
```

Figure 6-52. *Initial page display*

When the Shipping Address same as Billing Address checkbox is checked, the following code is executed:

```
$("#shippingAddress").append($(".billingAddress").clone());
```

`$(".billingAddress").clone()` selects the div tag with the class `billingAddress` and copies all the elements. `$("#shippingAddress").append()` appends the newly created elements to the div tag with the ID set to `shippingAddress`.

When the Shipping Address same as Billing Address checkbox is unchecked, the following code is executed:

```
$("#shippingAddress > .billingAddress").remove();
```

`$("#shippingAddress > .billingAddress")` selects the element that has the class set to `billingAddress` and is a descendant of the element that has an ID set to `shippingAddress`. The `remove()` method removes the selected HTML element from the DOM tree. See Figure 6-52.

Figure 6-53 displays the screen after the user enters some test data.

```
Billing Address:
Name:
[John Smith          ]

Address:
[720 Main Street, CA ]

Shipping Address same as Billing Address: ☐

Shipping Address:
```

Figure 6-53. *Test data entered by the user*

Figure 6-54 displays the page when the Shipping Address Same as Billing Address checkbox is checked. Billing Address is cloned and then appended to the end.

```
Billing Address:
Name:
John Smith

Address:
720 Main Street, CA

Shipping Address same as Billing Address: ☑

Shipping Address:
Name:
John Smith

Address:
720 Main Street, CA
```

Figure 6-54. *Billing Address is copied as the Shipping Address*

The clone() method also accepts two optional arguments:

- copyDataAndEvents—if this is true, all data and event handlers associated with the selected elements are copied; otherwise, data and event handlers are not copied (the default).

- deepCopyDataAndEvents—If this is true, all data and event handlers associated with the descendants of the selected elements are copied; otherwise data and event handlers are not copied (the default).

6-26. Removing Selected Elements from the DOM
Problem
You want to remove the selected elements from the DOM.

Solution
The following jQuery syntax is used to remove selected HTML elements.

$(*selector*).remove()

This method removes all the selected elements along with all bound events and the jQuery data associated with selected elements. It returns the jQuery object. Listing 6-26 demonstrates the use of the remove() method to remove selected elements.

Listing 6-26. The jQuery method to remove selected elements

```
<!DOCTYPE html>
<html lang="en">
<head>
    <meta charset="utf-8">
    <script src="scripts/jquery-2.1.0.min.js"></script>
    <style>
        .list { border:3px double green; width:350px; }
        .newRecord { font-weight: bold; background-color: lightyellow; }
        .tableHeader { background-color: lightgray; }
    </style>
    <script>
        $(function(){
            $("#btnTestIt").click(function () {
                $(".newRecord").remove();
            });
        });
    </script>
</head>
<body>
    <strong>Employees:</strong>
    <table class="list">
        <tr class="tableHeader">
            <td>Employee Name</td><td>Department Name</td>
    <td>Salary</td>
        </tr>
        <tr>
            <td>Jane Smith</td><td>Marketing</td><td>$95,000</td>
        </tr>
        <tr class="newRecord">
            <td>John Smith</td><td>Technology</td><td>$90,000</td>
        </tr>
        <tr>
            <td>Brian Adam</td><td>Sales</td><td>$72,000</td>
        </tr>
        <tr>
            <td>Mary Jones</td><td>Customer Support</td><td>$60,000</td>
        </tr>
        <tr>
            <td>Michael Jefferson</td><td>Technology</td><td>$85,000</td>
        </tr>
    </table><br>
    <input id="btnTestIt" type="button" value="Test It">
</body>
</html>
```

How It Works

The employees details are listed using the <table>, <tr>, and <td> HTML tags. New employee records have the class set to newRecord. If you want to remove all the new employee records from the table, you select the elements with the class newRecord using $(".newRecord") and execute the remove() method on the selected elements.

When the Test It button is clicked, the following code is executed:

```
$(".newRecord").remove();
```

$(".newRecord") selects the HTML element with the class name newRecord and returns the jQuery object. .remove() removes all selected HTML elements. Figure 6-55 displays the page when it is viewed in a browser.

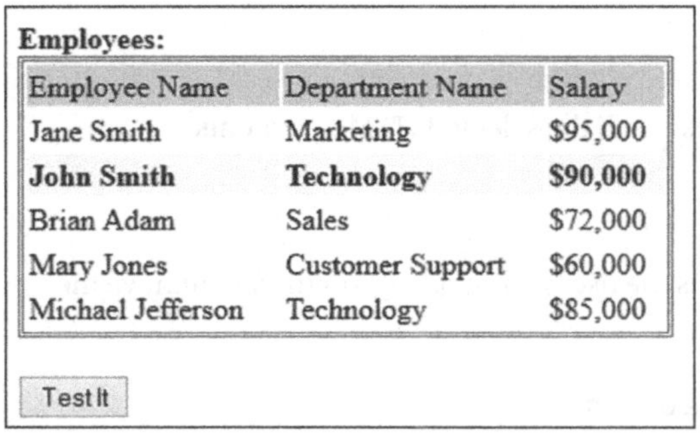

Employees:

Employee Name	Department Name	Salary
Jane Smith	Marketing	$95,000
John Smith	**Technology**	**$90,000**
Brian Adam	Sales	$72,000
Mary Jones	Customer Support	$60,000
Michael Jefferson	Technology	$85,000

Test It

Figure 6-55. *Initial page display*

When you press the Test It button, the button's click event handler removes the selected elements. Figure 6-56 displays the effect of clicking the Test It button.

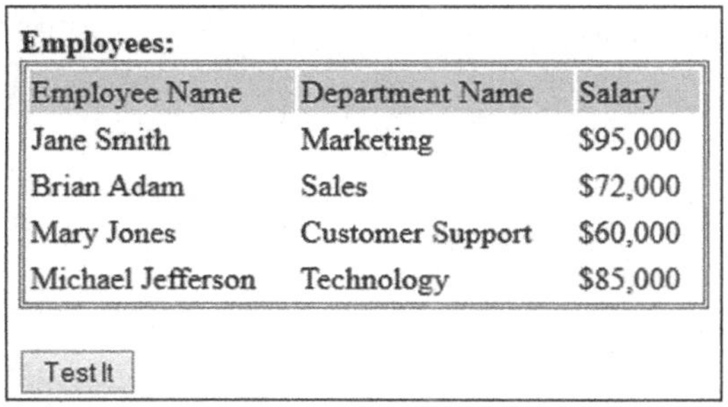

Employees:

Employee Name	Department Name	Salary
Jane Smith	Marketing	$95,000
Brian Adam	Sales	$72,000
Mary Jones	Customer Support	$60,000
Michael Jefferson	Technology	$85,000

Test It

Figure 6-56. *The new records are removed*

If you want to filter the selected records and then remove only those elements, you can use following syntax:

$(*selector*).remove(filterSelector)

For example, if there are other elements in this example in which class name is set to newRecord, you can limit the removal of tr elements with the class set to newRecord by using $("tr").remove(".newRecord").

If you don't want to remove all the bound events and jQuery data associated with the selected elements, you should use the detach() method instead. The detach() method is used when you intend to add detached elements back in the DOM.

6-27. Removing the Child Nodes of All the Selected Elements from the DOM

Problem

You want to remove the child nodes of all the selected elements from the DOM.

Solution

The following jQuery syntax is used to remove the child nodes and text of all the selected HTML elements.

$(*selector*).empty()

This method returns the jQuery object. Listing 6-27 demonstrates the use of the empty() method to remove the child nodes of selected elements.

Listing 6-27. The jQuery method to remove the child nodes of selected elements

```
<!DOCTYPE html>
<html lang="en">
<head>
    <meta charset="utf-8">
    <script src="scripts/jquery-2.1.0.min.js"></script>
    <style>
        .list {border:3px double green; width:350px; }
        .newRecord { font-weight: bold; background-color: lightyellow; }
        .tableHeader { background-color: lightgray; }
    </style>
    <script>
        $(function(){
            $("#btnTestIt").click(function () {
                $("#tech").empty();
                $("#tech").append("<li>Mobile Development</li>");
            });
        });
    </script>
</head>
<body>
    <strong>Departments:</strong>
    <div>
        <ul class="listDepartments">
            <li>Marketing</li>
            <li>Sales</li>
            <li>Technology
                <ul id="tech">
                    <li>Hardware Technology</li>
                    <li class="oldRecord">Software Technology</li>
                </ul>
            </li>
```

```
        <li>Customer Support</li>
      </ul>
    </div><br>
    <input id="btnTestIt" type="button" value="Test It">
</body>
</html>
```

How It Works

The department names are listed using the <ul> and <li> HTML tags. If you want to remove all child elements (li) of the ul element, you select the parent of the <li> elements using $("#tech") and execute the empty() method on the selected element. #tech is the ID of the nested ul element. empty() removes the child nodes only of the selected elements and not the selected elements itself.

When the Test It button is clicked, the following code is executed:

```
$("#tech").empty();
$("#tech").append("<li>Mobile Development</li>");
```

$("#tech") selects the HTML element with the ID tech and returns the jQuery object. .empty() removes all the child nodes, that is, all items within the inner ul node. A new department name is added to the $("#tech") element to prove that only child nodes are removed and the selected element itself is not removed. Figure 6-57 displays the page when it is viewed in a browser.

Departments:

- Marketing
- Sales
- Technology
  - Hardware Technology
  - Software Technology
- Customer Support

Test It

Figure 6-57. *Initial page display*

When you press the Test It button, the button's click event handler removes all departments under "Technology" and a new department name "Mobile Development" is appended to the Technology list. Figure 6-58 displays the effect of clicking the Test It button.

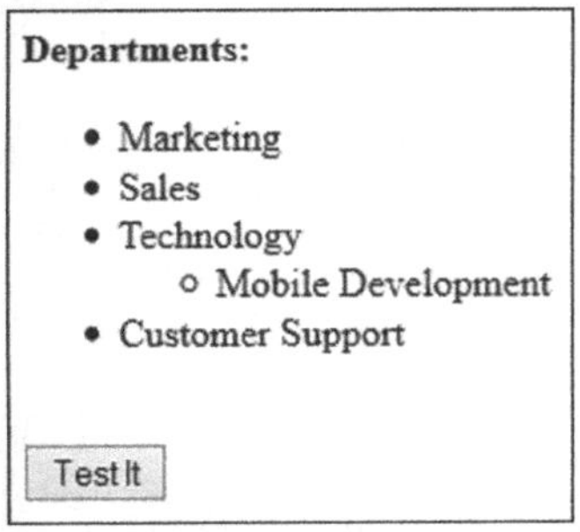

Departments:

- Marketing
- Sales
- Technology
  - ○ Mobile Development
- Customer Support

[Test It]

Figure 6-58. *The previous technology departments are removed and a new one is added*

6-28. Removing the Parent of Each Selected Element
Problem
You want to remove the parent of each selected element.

Solution
The following jQuery syntax is used to remove the parent of each selected element:

$(*selector*).unwrap()

This method's effect is the reverse of the wrap() method. It removes the parent of the selected elements and keeps the selected elements intact. It returns the jQuery object. Listing 6-28 demonstrates the use of the unwrap() method to remove the parent of the selected elements.

Listing 6-28. The jQuery method to remove the parent of the selected elements

```
<!DOCTYPE html>
<html lang="en">
<head>
    <meta charset="utf-8">
    <script src="scripts/jquery-2.1.0.min.js"></script>
    <style>
        .item_0 { background-color: lightyellow; }
        .item_1 { background-color: lightblue; }
        .item_2 { background-color: lightgray; }
        .item_3 { background-color: lightgreen; }
    </style>
    <script>
        $(function(){
            $("#btnTestIt").click(function () {
                $("p").unwrap();
            });
        });
    </script>
</head>
```

```
<body>
    <div class="item_0"><p>This is paragraph 1</p></div>
    <div class="item_1"><p>This is paragraph 2</p></div>
    <div class="item_2"><p>This is paragraph 3</p></div>
    <div class="item_3"><p>This is paragraph 4</p></div>
    <input id="btnTestIt" type="button" value="Test It">
</body>
</html>
```

How It Works

The paragraphs are listed using the <p> HTML tag and the paragraph tag is surrounded by its parent <div> tag. The background color of each paragraph tag is due to the value of the class attribute associated with the <div> tag. If you want to remove the background color of all the paragraphs, you select the <p> elements using $("p") and execute the unwrap() method on the selected elements.

When the Test It button is clicked, the following code is executed:

```
$("p").unwrap();
```

$("p") selects the HTML element with the tag name p and returns the jQuery object. .unwrap() removes the parent of all the selected elements (p). Figure 6-59 displays the page when it is viewed in a browser.

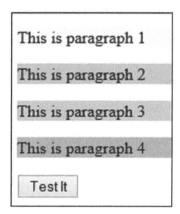

Figure 6-59. *Initial page display*

When you press the Test It button, the button's click event handler removes the parent of the selected elements and also removes the background color. Figure 6-60 displays the effect of clicking the Test It button.

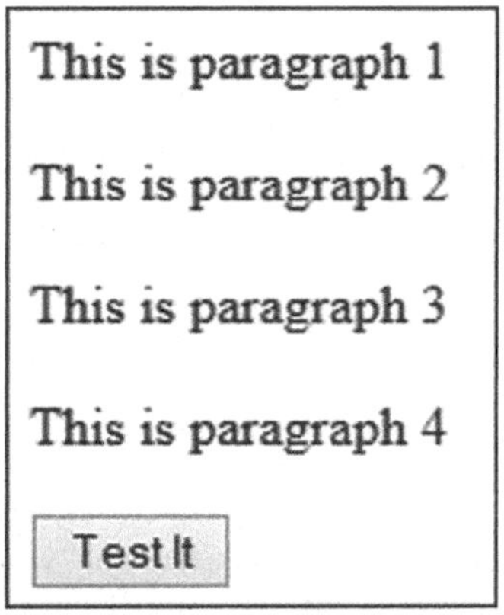

This is paragraph 1

This is paragraph 2

This is paragraph 3

This is paragraph 4

| Test It |

Figure 6-60. *Background color is removed*

6-29. Replacing Selected Items with New Items (Specified by HTMLString) in the DOM

Problem

You want to replace selected elements with specified HTML content.

Solution

The following jQuery syntax is used to replace selected elements with new HTML content:

$(*selector*).replaceWith("*newHTMLContent*")

newHTMLContent can be an HTML string, an HTML element, an array of HTML elements, or a jQuery object. This method replaces the selected elements with the new specified HTML content and returns the jQuery object containing the set of elements that are removed. Listing 6-29 demonstrates the use of the replaceWith() method to replace the selected elements.

Listing 6-29. The jQuery method to replace selected elements

```
<!DOCTYPE html>
<html lang="en">
<head>
    <meta charset="utf-8">
    <script src="scripts/jquery-2.1.0.min.js"></script>
    <style>
        .list {border:3px double green; width:350px; }
        .newRecord { font-weight: bold; background-color: lightyellow; }
        .tableHeader { background-color: lightgray; }
        .listDepartments { width: 200px; }
    </style>
```

```
<script>
    $(function(){
        $("#btnTestIt").click(function () {
            $(".newRecord").replaceWith("<li>Mobile Development</li>");
        });
    });
</script>
</head>
<body>
    <strong>Departments:</strong>
    <div>
        <ul class="listDepartments">
            <li>Marketing</li>
            <li>Sales</li>
            <li>Technology
                <ul id="tech">
                    <li>Hardware Technology</li>
                    <li class="newRecord">Software Technology</li>
                </ul>
            </li>
            <li>Customer Support</li>
        </ul>
    </div><br>
    <input id="btnTestIt" type="button" value="Test It">
</body>
</html>
```

How It Works

The department names are listed using the <ul> and <li> HTML tags. In this list of departments, new departments'
<li> tags are associated with the newRecord class. If you want to replace these elements with the newRecord class, you
select those elements using $(".newRecord") and execute the replaceWith() method on the selected elements.

When the Test It button is clicked, the following code is executed:

```
$(".newRecord").replaceWith("<li>Mobile Development</li>");
```

$(".newRecord") selects the HTML element with the class name newRecord and returns the jQuery object.
.replaceWith("<li>Mobile Development</li>") replaces the selected element with the new HTML content.
Figure 6-61 displays the page when it is viewed in a browser.

Departments:

- Marketing
- Sales
- Technology
    - Hardware Technology
    - **Software Technology**
- Customer Support

Test It

Figure 6-61. Initial page display

When you press the Test It button, the button's click event handler replaces the element with the newRecord class with the new HTML content. Figure 6-62 displays the effect of clicking the Test It button.

Departments:

- Marketing
- Sales
- Technology
    - Hardware Technology
    - Mobile Development
- Customer Support

Test It

Figure 6-62. Selected element is replaced by the new department name

$(".newRecord").replaceWith("<li>Mobile Development</li>") can also be written as $("<li>Mobile Development</li>").replaceAll(".newRecord"). Since replaceWith() and replaceAll() have the same effect, you can use either. The syntax for the replaceAll method is:

$("*htmlString*").replaceAll(*selector*)

The following syntax is used to replace selected elements with the return value of a function:

$(selector).replaceWith(*function() { ... return("htmlContent");})*

Summary

This chapter covered jQuery manipulation methods that are used to change the DOM by changing properties and attributes and by adding, replacing, and removing DOM nodes. The following methods change the styles, properties, attributes, and content of the selected elements:

- `css()`
- `attr()`
- `prop()`
- `val()`
- `html()`
- `text()`

The following methods are used to add new nodes to the DOM:

- `append()` and `appendTo()`
- `prepend()` and `prependTo()`
- `wrap()`, `wrapInner()`, and `wrapAll()`
- `after()`
- `clone()`

The following methods are used to remove DOM nodes:

- `detach()`
- `remove()`
- `empty()`
- `unwrap()`

The `replaceWith()` and `replaceAll()` methods are used to replace existing DOM nodes with new ones.

CHAPTER 7

■ ■ ■

Event Handling

This chapter covers event handlers, including event handler binding (or registration) and event handler execution. jQuery provides convenience methods to register event handlers for system-generated and user interaction events and provides a mechanism to pass information between elements, which initiated the event and event handlers. Event handlers are inline (anonymous) or named functions that are executed when an event is triggered by the browser or by user interaction.

There are two types of events—system-initiated events (such as the DOM ready event) and user-initiated events (such as the button click event, the form element getting focus event, and so on). If you want to perform some action when a specific event occurs, you need to identify the element's event, write the event handler to perform that action, and bind (register) the element's event to the event handler. When the event occurs, the registered event handler is executed. The terms—attaching, registering, and binding—are used interchangeably.

This chapter includes recipes that cover the following topics:

- Binding event handlers
- Event objects
- Preventing a default event action
- Event propagation (bubbling)
- Event delegation

7-1. Performing an Action When an Event Occurs
Problem

You want to perform an action (for example, display a message, prompt for confirmation, or submit form data) when the user clicks the Submit button.

Solution

The following jQuery syntax is used to register an event handler for an element's event.

```
$(selector).on("eventName", function() { .... })
```

$(*selector*) selects the desired element(s). The on() method binds an event handler function (function()) to the selected elements for the specified event (*eventName*). *eventName* is the name of a valid event for the selected elements (for example, click is a valid event for the HTML element <button>). When the event occurs, code segments in the function() are executed. Listing 7-1 demonstrates the use of the on() method to bind (register) an action to the selected elements' events.

Listing 7-1. Using the on() method to bind an event handler to a button's click event

```
<!DOCTYPE html>
<html lang="en">
<head>
    <meta charset="utf-8">
    <script src="scripts/jquery-2.1.0.min.js"></script>
      <script>
              $(function() {
                 $("#btnSubmit").on("click", function() {
                            alert("Submit button is clicked.")
                    });
              });
      </script>
</head>
<body>
    <button id="btnSubmit">Submit</button>
</body>
</html>
```

How It Works

In the document ready function, the on() method is used to bind the click event of the selected elements to the event handler. When the event occurs (such as when a button is clicked), the event handler displays the pop-up message using the alert() command. At the time of the event handler binding, no action in the event handler is performed. When the user clicks the button, the system checks if there is an event handler associated with the click event. If there is one, it is executed. In this case, a pop-up message is displayed. Figure 7-1 displays the page when the Submit button is clicked.

Figure 7-1. *This pop-up message is displayed when the Submit button is clicked*

A few points to note:

- When you're binding event handlers, you can use the bind() method too. The only difference between the bind() and on() methods is that the on() method provides a mechanism to delegate events to the element's parent.

- The same event handler can be registered for different events by using the following syntax:

  $(*selector***).on(**"*eventName1 eventName2 ...*", function() { .... })

- Event handlers are attached only to elements that already exist. If new DOM elements are created after the event handler is registered, the event handler won't be registered for them. In order to bind event handlers to future elements, you can either of these two methods:

  - Pass a selector for the descendants as an argument of the on() method.

  - Use the delegate() method.

    You will read about these methods in the Recipe 7-7, later in this chapter.

- jQuery provides convenience (shortcut) methods to register event handlers for commonly used events. These methods can be used instead of the on() method. Table 7-1 displays these convenience methods and describes the events for which these convenience methods can be used.

Table 7-1. *Convenience Methods to Bind Event Handlers*

Method	Event Description
load()	Triggered when the element and all its descendants are loaded.
ready()	Triggered when the document is ready (when the DOM is completely created).
blur()	Triggered on an element when it loses the focus.
change()	Triggered on an element when users change its value.
click()	Triggered on an element when it is clicked.
error()	Triggered on an element when it is not loaded correctly.
focus()	Triggered on an element when it gets the focus.
focusin()	Triggered on an element when it or its descendants gets the focus.
hover()	Called when an element's mouseenter or mouseleave events occur.
resize()	Triggered when the browser window is resized.
scroll()	Triggered when the user scrolls to other section of the element.
select()	Triggered when a text selection is made in <text> and <textarea>.
submit()	Triggered when a form is submitted. Applies to the <form> element only.

Other such methods are dblclick(), focusout(), keydown(), keypress(), keyup(), mousedown(), mouseenter(), mouseleave(), mousemove(), mouseout(), mouseover(), and mouseup().

The following is the commonly used syntax for these convenience methods (except for hover()):

```
$(selector).convenienceMethod(function() { .... })
```

For the hover() method, the syntax is:

```
$(selector). hover(function() { .... }, function() { .... })
```

The first function argument is called when the mouseenter event is triggered and the second function argument is called when the mouseleave event is triggered for the element.

The error event (convenience method error()) is triggered when the HTML element has failed to load. The following code segment explains this:

```
HTML Code: <img id="img1">
JavaScript Code:
$(function() {
    $("#img1").error(function() {
            alert("image is not loaded.")
    });

    $("#img1").attr("src", "images/someImage.png");
});
```

This code loads the $("#img1").attr("src", "images/someImage.png") image. If the image doesn't exist, an error event will be triggered when loading has failed.

7-2. Preventing a Default Event Handler
Problem

You want to prevent the execution of an event's default event handler.

Solution

The following jQuery syntax is used to prevent a default event handler:

```
$(selector).on( "eventName", function(eventObj) {eventObj.preventDefault()})
```

If there is a default action (event handler) associated with an event and you want to implement your own action and prevent the execution of the default action, you can use the event object's preventDefault() method. For example, when the user clicks an anchor (<a>) link, the default action of the click event is to go to the URL specified in the href attribute. You can prevent this default behavior by using preventDefault() in the user-defined event handler. Listing 7-2 shows the use of the preventDefault() method to prevent the default action of the click event of the anchor link. Listing 7-3 provides a sample page called department.htm, which is displayed when users click the Sales or Marketing department links.

Listing 7-2. Using event object's preventDefault() method to prevent default event handler execution

```
<!DOCTYPE html>
<html lang="en">
<head>
    <meta charset="utf-8">
    <script src="scripts/jquery-2.1.0.min.js"></script>
    <script>
            $(function() {
                $("#lnkSales").click(function(eventObj) {
                        var message = $(this).prop("tagName") + " is clicked.\n";

                        eventObj.preventDefault();
                        message += "Default event handler is prevented...";

                        alert(message);
                });

                $("#lnkMarketing").click(function(eventObj) {
                        var message = $(this).prop("tagName") + " is clicked.\n";
                        message += "Default event handler is NOT prevented...";
                        alert(message);
                });
            });
    </script>
</head>

<body>
    Departments:
    <ul id="listDepartments">
        <li><a id="lnkSales" href="department.htm">Sales</a></li>
            <li><a id="lnkMarketing" href="department.htm">Marketing</a></li>
            <li>Technology</li>
            <li>Customer Support</li>
    </ul><br>
</body>
</html>
```

Listing 7-3. Sample department.htm file

```
<!DOCTYPE html>
<html lang="en">
<head>
    <meta charset="utf-8">
</head>

<body>
    Details about the department ...
</body>
</html>
```

How It Works

In the document ready function shown in Listing 7-2, two anchor click event handlers are defined—one for the Sales department link and another one for the Marketing department link. In the Sales link click event handler, the event object's preventDefault() is called. When the Sales link is clicked, a pop-up message is displayed. Since preventDefault() is called, control remains on the same page and department.htm is not displayed. When the Marketing link is clicked, a pop-up message is displayed. Since preventDefault() is not called, after displaying the message, the default action of the anchor click event is executed and the department.htm page is displayed. Figure 7-2 displays the page that appears when the Sales link is clicked. After the user clicks the OK button, control remains on the existing page.

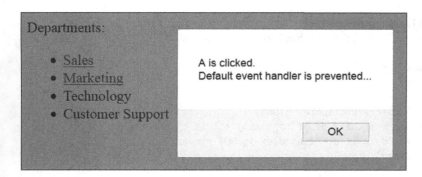

Figure 7-2. *This pop-up message is displayed when the Sales link is clicked*

Figure 7-3 displays the page that appears when the Marketing link is clicked. After the user clicks the OK button, the department.htm page is displayed, as depicted in Figure 7-4.

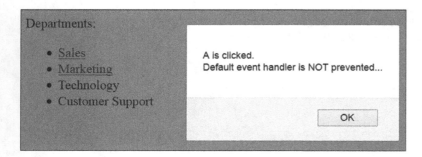

Figure 7-3. *This pop-up message is displayed when the Marketing link is clicked*

Details about the department ...

Figure 7-4. *The department.htm file is displayed*

You can call eventObj.isDefaultPrevented() to check if preventDefault() was called for the event on the element. It returns true or false.

7-3. Binding Different Event Handlers to the Same Element

Problem

You want to change the opacity of an image when the mouseenter event is triggered and then revert to its original opacity when the mouseleave event is triggered.

Solution

The following jQuery syntax binds the event handlers to the selected elements for different events:

```
$(selector).on( {"eventName1": function() { .... },
                 "eventName2": function() { .... },
                 ...)
```

Listing 7-4 uses the on() method to bind multiple event handlers to the selected elements' events.

Listing 7-4. Using the on() method to bind event handlers to an image's mouseenter and mouseleave events

```
<!DOCTYPE html>
<html lang="en">
<head>
    <meta charset="utf-8">
    <script src="scripts/jquery-2.1.0.min.js"></script>
    <script>
        $(function() {
            $("#imgSample").on(
                {
                    "mouseenter": function() { $(this).css("opacity", 0.5);  },
                    "mouseleave": function() { $(this).css("opacity", 1.0); }
                });
        });
    </script>
</head>
<body>
            <img id="imgSample" src="images/butterfly3.png"><br>
</body>
</html>
```

How It Works

In the document ready function, the on() method binds two event handlers—one for the mouseenter event and the other for the mouseleave event. Instead of having to make multiple calls to the on() method, one for each event, you can use a single on() method call. The event handler attached to the mouseenter event changes the opacity of the selected image to 0.5 and the event handler attached to the mouseleave event returns the opacity to 1.0. Figure 7-5 displays the change in the image's opacity when the user moves the mouse cursor over the image. When the mouse cursor moves out of the image, its opacity returns to 1.0.

Figure 7-5. *Change in the image opacity due to the mouseenter and mouseleave events*

If the event handler has more than a few lines, it is better to rewrite the code in the following format to improve the code readability and maintainability:

```
var changeOpacityFunc = function changeOpacity(elem, opacityVal) {
elem.css("opacity", opacityVal);
    }  $(function() {
        $("#imgSample").on({
           "mouseenter": function() { changeOpacityFunc($(this), 0.5)},
           "mouseleave": function() { changeOpacityFunc($(this), 1.0)}
                     });
    });
```

In this case, the event handler is implemented using a named function instead of an inline (anonymous) function.

7-4. Getting an Event Object's Properties
Problem

You want to get the properties of the element that triggered the event.

Solution

The following jQuery syntax is used to get the properties of the element that triggered the event:

$(selector**).on(**"eventName", function(eventObject) { .... })

Every event handler gets an event object as an argument. This object contains event-related properties. These are properties of the element that have triggered the event and the methods to change the default behavior of the event handler processing model. Listing 7-5 demonstrates some of the properties of the event object.

Listing 7-5. Getting properties of the event object

```html
<!DOCTYPE html>
<html lang="en">
<head>
    <meta charset="utf-8">

<script src="scripts/jquery-2.1.0.min.js"></script>
   <script>
            function getEventObjectProperties(eventObject) {
                // eventObject.target is the DOM element that triggered
                // the element

                // Get properties of the element, which has triggered
                // the event
                var message = "<u>" + eventObject.type + "</u> event is triggered on <u>" +
                                    eventObject.target.nodeName.toLowerCase()   +
                                    "</u> with the id: <u>" +
                                    $(eventObject.target).attr("id") + "</u><br>";

                message += "Key/Button was pressed: <u>" + eventObject.which + "</u><br>";

                message += "(x, y) coordinate of the mouse when event is triggered: (<u>" +
                                eventObject.pageX + "</u>, <u>" + eventObject.pageY + "</u>)";

                $("#message").html(message);
            }

            $(function() {
                $("img").on("mouseenter", function(eventObject) {
                        getEventObjectProperties(eventObject);
                });

                $("input").on("focus", function(eventObject) {
                        getEventObjectProperties(eventObject);
                });

                $("button").on("click", function(eventObject) {
                        getEventObjectProperties(eventObject);
                });
            });
    </script>
</head>
<body>
    <img id="imgSample" src="images/butterfly3.png"><br>

    Enter Image Title: <input id="txtImageTitle" type="text"><br><br>

    <button id="btnSubmit">Submit</button>

    <button id="btnCancel">Cancel</button><br><br>

    <div id="message"></div>
</body>
</html>
```

How It Works

In this code, the eventObject is passed to the event handler as an argument. The eventObject contains properties of the element that triggered the event. eventObject.target is the DOM element that triggered the event. eventObject.target.propertyName can be used to get the property of the DOM element, $(eventObject.target). jQueryMethodName() can be used to execute any of the jQuery methods that are valid for a jQuery object. For example, in the previous code:

- eventObject.target.nodeName is used to get the tag name of the HTML element.

- $(eventObject.target).attr(attributeName) is used to get the specified attribute's value of the HTML element.

- eventObject.type contains the type of event (such as click, change, focus, and so on).

- eventObject.which contains the key or mouse button used to initiate the event.

- eventObject.pageX contains the x-coordinate of the mouse position.

- eventObject.pageY contains the y-coordinate of the mouse position. The (0,0) coordinate is the top-left edge of the page.

Figure 7-6 displays the properties of eventObject when the mouse cursor is moved over the image.

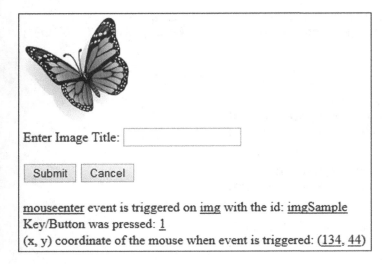

Figure 7-6. *Displays event object properties when the image's mouseenter event is triggered*

Figure 7-7 displays the properties of the eventObject when the textbox gets the focus. This event doesn't trigger a keyboard or mouse event, depending on which mouse and keyboard related properties are 0 or undefined.

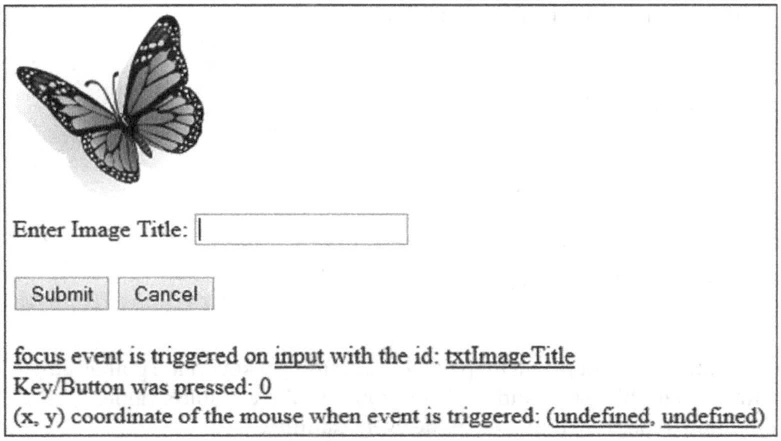

Figure 7-7. *Displays event object properties when the textbox focus event is triggered*

Figure 7-8 displays the properties of the eventObject when the button is clicked.

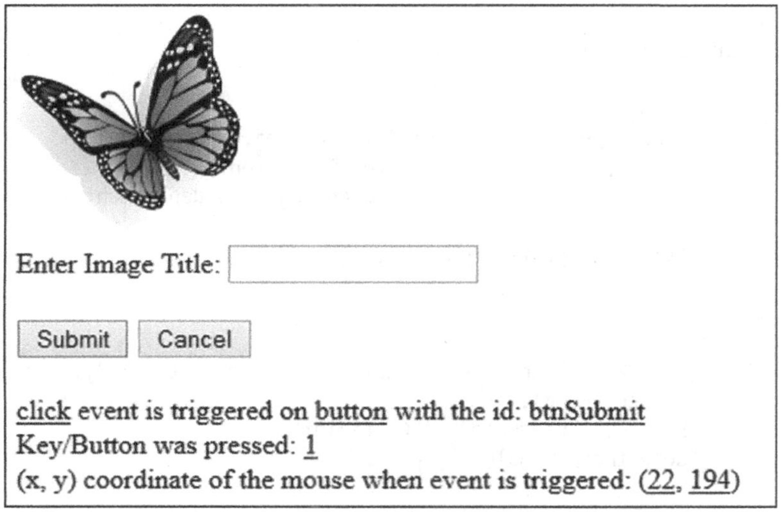

Figure 7-8. *Displays event object properties when the button's click event is triggered*

7-5. Passing Custom Data to the Event Handler
Problem

You want to pass custom data, based on some logic, to the event handler.

Solution

The event object has many properties that can help to implement processing logic. In certain cases, if you want to pass more information to the event handler through the event object, you can do it at the time of event binding.

The following jQuery syntax is used to send custom data to the event handler:

```
$(selector).on("eventName",
{"dataKey1" : "dataValue1", "dataKey2" : "dataValue2", ...},
 function(eventObj) { ... })
```

or:

```
$(selector).on("eventName",
{"dataKey1" : "dataValue1", "dataKey2" : "dataValue2", ...},
 namedFunctionName)
```

In order to pass custom data to the event handler, you can pass a map object containing a key/value pair as an argument to the on() method. The key contains the variable name and the value contains the variable's value. Listing 7-6 demonstrates the use of the on() method to pass custom data to the event handler.

Listing 7-6. Using the on() method to pass custom data to the event handler

```
<!DOCTYPE html>
<html lang="en">
<head>
    <meta charset="utf-8">
    <script src="scripts/jquery-2.1.0.min.js"></script>
    <script>
            var processFunc = function(eventObj) {
                                    var message = "User Role: " + eventObj.data.userRole +
                                                "<br>Department: " +
                                                eventObj.data.department;

                                    $("#message").html(message);
            }

            $(function() {
                    $("#btnSubmit").on("click", {"userRole" : "Admin", "department":"IT"},
                                    processFunc);
                    $("#txtName").on("change", {"userRole" : "Certifier",
                                    "department":"Sales"}, processFunc);
            });
    </script>
</head>
<body>
    Name: <input id="txtName" type="text"><br><br>

    <button id="btnSubmit">Submit</button>

    <div id="message"></div>
</body>
</html>
```

How It Works

In the document ready function, the event handler processFunc() is registered to the click event of the Submit button and the same event handler is attached to the name textbox. If you want to pass custom data to the event handler so that it can perform some action based on the custom data, you can set and pass the map object as a second argument in the on() method. The map object contains set of key/value pairs, where key is the variable name and value is the value of the variable. In the event handler, custom data can be accessed by using eventObj.data.variableName. This example passes the userRole and department variable names along with their values to the event handler using the map object as a second argument in the on() method. In the event handler, the value of these variables can be accessed by using eventObj.data.userRole and eventObj.data.department. Figure 7-9 displays the custom data value from the event handler when the value is changed in the name textbox and the user tabs out of the field.

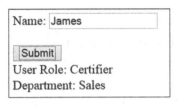

Figure 7-9. *Displays custom data when the value of the name textbox is changed*

Figure 7-10 displays the custom data value from the event handler when the Submit button is clicked.

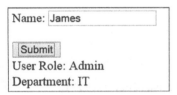

Figure 7-10. *Displays the custom data when the Submit button is clicked*

7-6. Event Propagation

Problem

You want to understand event propagation, also called event bubbling.

Solution

When an event is triggered on an element, its event handler is executed. Once the execution is complete, the same event is triggered on the element's parent and then the parent's event handler is executed; it keeps on propagating to the subsequent element's parent until the root element is reached in the DOM. Such upward propagation of an event in the DOM hierarchy is called event bubbling. Listing 7-7 demonstrates the concept of event propagation.

Listing 7-7. Event propagation in the DOM hierarchy

```html
<!DOCTYPE html>
<html lang="en">
<head>
    <meta charset="utf-8">
    <script src="scripts/jquery-2.1.0.min.js"></script>
    <script>
            $(function() {
                $("a").click( function(eventObj) {
                        $("#message").append("Executing anchor (A) link click event handler ...<br>");
                        eventObj.preventDefault();
                });

                $("li").click( function() {
                        $("#message").append("Executing LI click event handler...<br>");
                });

                $("ul").click( function() {
                        $("#message").append("Executing UL event handler...<br>");
                });

                $("body").click( function() {
                        $("#message").append("Executing BODY event handler...<br>");
                });

                $("html").click( function() {
                        $("#message").append("Executing HTML event handler...<br>");
                });

                $(document).click( function() {
                        $("#message").append("Executing DOCUMENT event handler...<br>");
                });

                $(window).click( function() {
                        $("#message").append("Executing WINDOW (Browser) event handler...<br>");
                });
            });
    </script>
</head>

<body>
   <div><strong>Departments:</strong></div>
    <ul id="listDepartments">
        <li><a href="department.htm"><strong>Sales</strong></a></li>
            <li>Marketing</li>
            <li>Technology</li>
            <li>Customer Support</li>
    </ul>

    <div id="message"></div>
</body>
</html>
```

How It Works

The code in the document ready function provides separate click event handlers for the following elements: <A>, <LI>, <UL>, <BODY>, <HTML>, document, and window (the browser). It does so by using the following code format:

```
$(selector).click( function() {
            $("#message").append("Executing selectorElement event handler...<br>");
    });
```

The purpose of these handlers is to display a message when an element's click event handler is executed. When anchor link Sales is clicked, the click event handler of the tag <A> is executed. The event handler of the following elements are then executed in the order of child to parent propagation: <LI>, <UL>, <BODY>, <HTML>, document, and window (the browser). This event propagation follows the path from the initiating element to the root level of the DOM tree. Figure 7-11 displays the messages displayed when the Sales link is clicked.

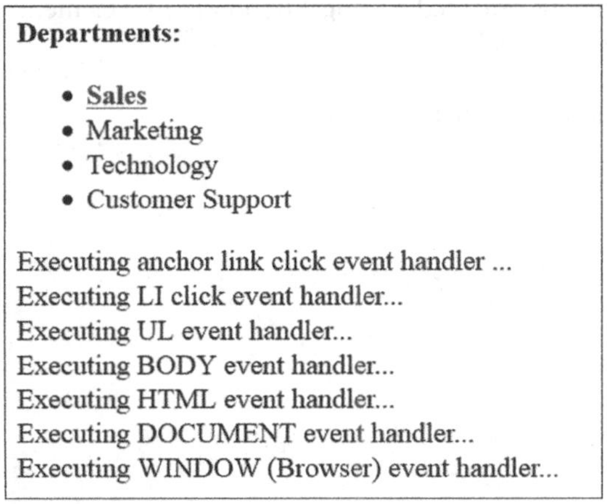

Departments:

- <u>Sales</u>
- Marketing
- Technology
- Customer Support

Executing anchor link click event handler ...
Executing LI click event handler...
Executing UL event handler...
Executing BODY event handler...
Executing HTML event handler...
Executing DOCUMENT event handler...
Executing WINDOW (Browser) event handler...

Figure 7-11. *Displays the event handler execution messages due to the event propagation*

If you want to stop this event propagation at any point in any of the elements' event handlers, you can use the event object's stopPropagation() method. The following jQuery syntax is used to stop event propagation:

$(*selector*).on("*eventName*", function(*eventObj*) {*eventObj*. stopPropagation()})

7-7. Event Delegation

Problem

You want to bind the event handler of an event not only to the existing elements but also to the elements that will be created in future.

Solution

When an event handler is bound to an event of an element type, it will be valid only for the existing elements in the DOM. If you add a new element and the event is then triggered, the specified event handler won't be executed. For example, $("li").on("click", function() { .... }), binds the event handler for the click event to all the existing "li" elements. If you add a new "li" element (for example, by using .append("<li>Production Support</li>")), the event handler won't be attached to this new element. One solution is to reattach/re-register the event handler. This is not an ideal solution. By using the concept of event propagation, you can delegate the event to the element's (li) parent, which is "ul", by binding the event handler to "ul" instead of "li". When the click event is triggered on the "li" element, the event is propagated to "ul" and the registered event handler is executed. There are two advantages of this approach—the event handler is not bound to individual "li" elements and the system doesn't have to listen to the event on these many elements. This will improve the performance. The other advantage is that if you add a new "li" element at runtime and the click event is triggered, the event handler will be executed. If you want the event handler to be executed only if "li" is clicked and not any other child element of the "ul" element, then you can specify "li" as a second parameter of the on() method. The following jQuery syntax is used to register event handler using the concept of event delegation:

$(selector**).on(**"eventName", "childSelector", function() { .... })

The second parameter of the on() method tells the event handling process to check if the triggering element matches the "childSelector". Only if it matches will the event handler be executed. Listing 7-8 shows a new element that's added and an event is triggered, but the event handler won't be executed.

Listing 7-8. Using the on() method to bind the event handler at the individual elements level

```
<!DOCTYPE html>
<html lang="en">
<head>
    <meta charset="utf-8">
    <script src="scripts/jquery-2.1.0.min.js"></script>
    <script>
        $(function() {
            $("li").on("click", function(eventObj) {
                alert("Clicked '" + $(eventObj.target).text() + "'");
            });

            $("button").on("click", function() {
                $("ul").append("<li>Production Support</li>");
            });
        });
    </script>
</head>
<body>
    <div><strong>Departments:</strong></div>
    <ul id="listDepartments">
        <li>Sales</li>
            <li>Marketing</li>
            <li>Technology</li>
            <li>Customer Support</li>
    </ul><br>

    <button id="btnCreate">Create New Department</button>
</body>
</html>
```

How It Works

In the document ready function, there is a click event handler for the <LI> element:

```
$("li").on("click", function(eventObj) {
    alert("Clicked " + $(eventObj.target).text());
});
```

When the "li" element (the department name) is clicked, a pop-up message is displayed showing the department's name.

Figure 7-12 displays the pop-up message when a department's name is clicked.

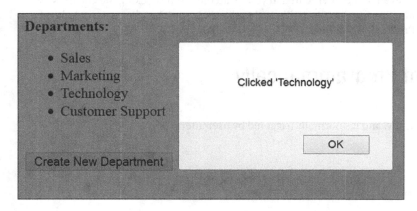

Figure 7-12. *This pop-up message is displayed with the clicked department name*

There is an event handler for the button's click event. When the button is clicked, a new department called Production Support is added to the list of departments. Figure 7-13 displays the new department that's been added to the list since the Create New Department button was clicked.

Figure 7-13. *Displays the new department called Production Support*

After creating the new department, if it is clicked, the "li" click event handler is not executed and no pop-up message will be displayed. To resolve this issue, you need to replace the following code line:

```
$("li").on("click", function(eventObj) { ....
```

with this one:

```
$("ul").on("click", "li", function(eventObj) { ...
```

Now you are binding the event handler to the element **"ul"** (the parent of the **"li"** elements) click event. When the click event is triggered on **"ul"** or any of its children, the event handling process will check if the triggering element is **"li"** and if it is **"li"** only then is event handler executed. If you rerun the test by clicking the Create New Department button and then clicking Production Support, you will see that the click event handler is executed and a pop-up message is displayed as Clicked 'Production Support'.

7-8. Triggering an Event Programmatically
Problem

You want to trigger an event programmatically, and it's normally triggered by user interaction.

Solution

The following jQuery syntax is used to trigger an event:

$(selector**).trigger(**"eventName"**)**

The trigger() method executes the event handler of the specified eventName for the selected elements specified by the selector. Listing 7-9 demonstrates the use of the trigger() method to execute the event handler of the selected elements.

Listing 7-9. Using the trigger() method to execute the event handler of the specified event

```
<!DOCTYPE html>
<html lang="en">
<head>
    <meta charset="utf-8">
    <script src="scripts/jquery-2.1.0.min.js"></script>
    <script>
        $(function() {
            $("#txtName").on("change", function() {
                $("#message").html("Name is changed to: " + $("#txtName").val());
            });

            $("#btnChangeName").click(function() {
                $("#txtName").val("John Smith");
            });
```

```
        $("#btnChangeNameTriggerEvent").click(function() {
                $("#txtName").val("Jane Smith");
                $("#txtName").trigger("change");
        });
    });
    </script>
</head>

<body>
    Name: <input id="txtName" type="text"><br><br>

    <button id="btnChangeName">Change Name</button>
    <button id="btnChangeNameTriggerEvent">Change Name & Trigger Event</button><br><br>

    <div id="message"></div>
</body>

</html>
```

How It Works

In the document ready function, the event handler is registered for the change event of the textbox by using the following code:

```
$("#txtName").on("change", function() {
    $("#message").html("Name is changed to: " + $("#txtName").val());
});
```

When a user changes a value in the textbox and then tabs out of the field, the change event handler is executed. It displays the value entered in the textbox (txtName). Figure 7-14 displays the page when the name value is changed in the txtName element.

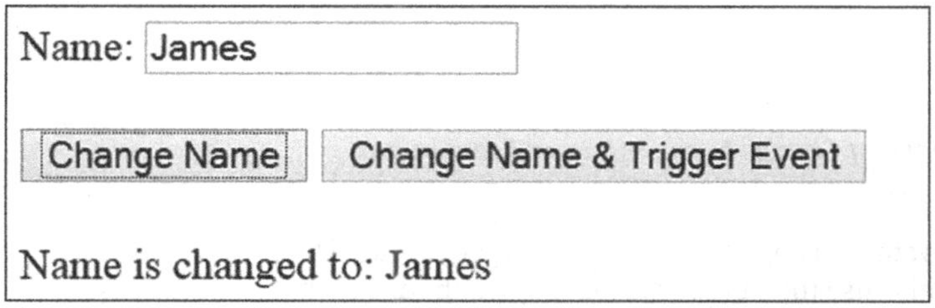

Figure 7-14. *Displays the result of the change event handler execution*

Another event handler is attached to the click event of the Change Name button using the following code:

```
$("#btnChangeName").click(function() {
            $("#txtName").val("John Smith");
    });
```

When the user clicks the Change Name button, this event handler changes the value of the textbox txtName. Even though the value of the txtName has changed, its change event handler is not executed because the user did not change the value manually. Figure 7-15 displays the page when the name value is changed programmatically in the txtName element.

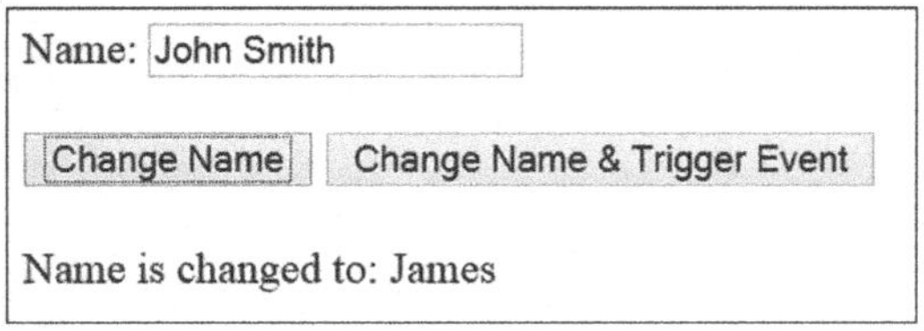

Name: John Smith

Change Name   Change Name & Trigger Event

Name is changed to: James

Figure 7-15. *Displays the result of click event handler of the Change Name button*

To force an event, you can use the trigger() method. To demonstrate a solution to the previous problem, another event handler is registered in the document ready function from the previous code:

```
$("#btnChangeNameTriggerEvent").click(function() {
        $("#txtName").val("Jane Smith");
        $("#txtName").trigger("change");
});
```

When the user clicks the Change Name & Trigger Event button, this event handler changes the value of the textbox txtName and triggers the change event of the txtName element by using the trigger() method, which will in turn execute the textbox change event handler. Figure 7-16 displays the page when the name value is changed programmatically in the txtName element and the txtName's change event is triggered.

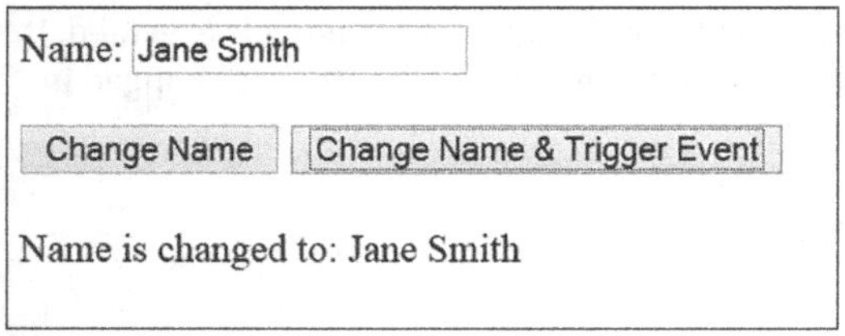

Name: Jane Smith

Change Name   Change Name & Trigger Event

Name is changed to: Jane Smith

Figure 7-16. *Displays the result of click event handler of Change Name & Trigger Event button.*

Another example is triggering submit form event by using $("#formId").trigger("submit").

In place of the trigger() method, you can also use the triggerHandler() method, which basically does the same thing—it triggers a specified event on the selected element. It does so with the following differences: triggerHandler() doesn't initiate the default behavior of the event; the event is triggered only on the first element of the set of selected elements; event propagation doesn't happen; and it returns the value returned by the event handler.

7-9. Restricting Event Handler Execution

Problem

You want to execute an event handler only once. This is useful when you want to perform a task only once, such as when initializing variables or caching static data.

Solution

The following jQuery syntax is used to specify event handler so that it is executed only once:

$(selector**).one(**"eventName", function() { .... })

During the event handler execution, if you want to, you can bind another event handler for the same event. Listing 7-10 demonstrates using the one() method to ensure that an event handler is executed only once.

Listing 7-10. Using the one() method to bind an event handler

```
<!DOCTYPE html>
<html lang="en">
<head>
    <meta charset="utf-8">
    <script src="scripts/jquery-2.1.0.min.js"></script>
    <script>
        $(function() {
            $("#btnSubmit").one("click",
                function() {
                    // Placeholder for getting static data to cahce it.
                    alert("Retrieved static data.");
                });
        });
    </script>
</head>

<body>
    <button id="btnSubmit">Submit</button>
</body>
</html>
```

How It Works

In the document ready function, the event handler is registered for the click event of the button using the following code:

```
$("#btnSubmit").one("click",
    function() {
    // Placeholder for getting static data to cahce it.
    alert("Retrieved static data.");
 });
```

In the event handler, you can perform one-time tasks like initializing variables or getting static data. In this case, an alert message is displayed. Since the event handler is registered using the one() method, when a user clicks the button again, the event handler won't be executed. Figure 7-17 displays the page when the Submit button is clicked. If the Submit button is clicked a second time, no pop-up message will be displayed.

Figure 7-17. *Displays this pop-up message only once, no matter how many times the Submit button is clicked*

7-10. Removing the Event Handler
Problem
You want to remove the registered event handler.

Solution
The following jQuery syntax is used to remove any event handlers that are registered using the on() method:

$(_selector_**).off(** "eventName1 eventName2 ... ")

If no argument is specified for the off() method, all the event handlers will be removed for all the selected elements. Listing 7-11 demonstrates the use of the off() method to remove event handler(s) for the specified event(s) of all the selected elements.

Listing 7-11. Using the off() method to remove an event handler

```
<!DOCTYPE html>
<html lang="en">
<head>
    <meta charset="utf-8">
    <script src="scripts/jquery-2.1.0.min.js"></script>
    <script>
        $(function() {
            $("#btnSubmit").on("click",
                function() {
                    alert("Submit button is clicked.");
            });
```

```
        $("#btnRemove").on("click",
              function() {
                  $("#btnSubmit").off("click");
              });
        });
    </script>
</head>

<body>
    <button id="btnSubmit">Submit</button>
    <button id="btnRemove">Remove Event Handler</button>
</body>
</html>
```

How It Works

In the document ready function, the event handler is registered for the Submit button's click event using the following code:

```
$("#btnSubmit").on("click",
          function() {
          alert("Submit button is clicked.");
 });
```

When the Submit button is clicked, a pop-up message is displayed with the "Submit button is clicked." message.

An event handler is also registered for the Remove Event Handler button's click event using the following code:

```
$("#btnRemove").on("click",
                function() {
                    $("#btnSubmit").off("click");
               });
```

When the Remove Event Handler button is clicked, it executes the command $("#btnSubmit").off("click"), which removes the click event handler for the Submit button. If the user clicks the Submit button again, no pop-up message will be displayed because its click event handler is already removed. Figure 7-18 displays the page when the Submit button is clicked. If the Submit button is clicked again after clicking the Remove Event Handler button, no pop-up message will be displayed.

Figure 7-18. *Displays this pop-up message when the Submit button is clicked*

Summary

This chapter covered topics about event handlers, including passing custom data to event handlers, default events, event propagation (bubbling), triggering events, and events delegation. You learned to:

- Bind event handlers using on(), one(), and convenience methods.

- Access the event object's properties.

- Prevent a default event action by using the event object's preventDefault() method.

- Trigger events using the trigger() method.

- Delegate an event using the on() method.

CHAPTER 8

■ ■ ■

jQuery Effects and Animation

This chapter covers the techniques used to implement effects and animations using jQuery methods. jQuery provides methods to:

- Add effects to web pages. Effects can be customized by specifying the duration of the effect and the transition mode.

- Create and run custom animations by specifying the target CSS properties of the element and the duration of the transition from the current CSS properties to the target CSS properties.

- Manage the effects and animations queue by adding, removing, and replacing effects and animation methods to/from the queue.

- Control animation by smoothing, pausing, stopping, and skipping animation steps.

- Plug in additional custom functions at various stages of the animation.

All jQuery's effects are a combination of CSS properties and timers. jQuery uses the *fx* object to manage CSS properties of the selected element and its timers. The *fx* object keeps track of the current CSS properties of the selected element and the time after which a change to the element's style occurs.

The effects queue plays a very important role in achieving multi-step transitional effects and animations. The effects queue is an array of functions that is executed in sequential order.

During program execution, if an effect/animation method is found for an element, it is copied to the effects queue of the element and program execution continues to the next code statement. In parallel, effects and animation methods are executed from the element's effects queue. By default, each element has its own standard effects queue, which is called *fx* queue. If the queueName is not explicitly specified in a method as an argument, *fx* queue is used. If you want, you can define multiple named queues for each element.

Options for Effects and Animations Methods

For all of the effects and animations methods, a map object can be passed as an argument to the method. The following options can be used in the map object:

- duration—The duration of the effect and animation in milliseconds (the default is 400 ms). It can be set as a number (in milliseconds) or as a string (such as slow or fast).

- easing—Specifies the speed of the transition at different points during the transition in the core jQuery library. Possible values are swing (slow in the beginning and at the end and faster in the middle) and linear (same speed throughout). There are many more easing functions available in jQuery UI library.

- specialEasing—A map object with CSS properties as keys and the easing function as their values. Using this option, you can apply different easing functions to different CSS properties.

- queue—Specifies if the effect or animation should be placed in the queue or not. The default is true. If it's set to false, the effect will start immediately. It can also be set to custom *queueName*, in which case effect/animation will be added to the specified *queueName* instead of the default effects queue (*fx*). If the effect method is put in the custom *queueName*, you use the .dequeue() method to start it.

- start—Specifies the function that's executed when the animation starts.

- step—Specifies the function that's executed for each animated CSS property of the selected elements.

- progress—Specifies the function that's executed after each step of the animation.

- complete—Specifies the function that's executed after the animation is completed.

- done—Specifies the function that's executed after the animation is completed. It is a common jQuery method that works with a promise object. Since the .animate() method returns a promise object, you can use done with the animate method. The function specified with done is executed before the complete callback function.

- fail—Specifies the function that's executed when the animation fails to complete.

- always—Specifies the function that's executed irrespective of whether animation is completed successfully or failed.

Out of these options, you can pass duration and complete directly as arguments or by specifying them in the map object. In the case of animate() method, you can also pass easing as an argument. For example, these two ways of using these options have the same effect:

1. ```
$(selector).show(1000, function() {

alert('effect is completed.');
});
```

2. ```
var options = {duration: "1000",

                           complete: function() {
       alert('effect is completed.');
    }
};

$(selector).show(options);
```

8-1. Showing and Hiding Elements
Problem

Based on user interaction, you want to show some elements and hide others. For example, after a payment is made and the user clicks the Submit button, you want to hide that button so that he/she doesn't click it again, while also showing a message about the payment being processed.

Solution

The following jQuery syntax is used to hide selected elements:

```
$(selector).hide()
$(selector).hide(effectDuration)
$(selector).hide(effectCompleteCallbackFunction)
$(selector).hide(effectDuration, effectCompleteCallbackFunction)
$(selector).hide(options)
```

The following jQuery syntax is used to show selected elements:

```
$(selector).show()
$(selector).show(effectDuration)
$(selector).show(effectCompleteCallbackFunction)
$(selector).show(effectDuration, effectCompleteCallbackFunction)
$(selector).show(options)
```

hide() and show() can be used with any HTML element. hide() makes all the selected elements and their descendants invisible and releases the space used by the element(s) on the page. This makes other elements move up or left to fill the freed space. show() displays all the selected elements and their descendants. These methods can also be used during animation by hiding and showing elements whenever it is needed.

effectDuration is the duration of the effect run in milliseconds, that is, the amount of time it takes to transition from visible to invisible and vice versa. The default value is 400 milliseconds. For example, if you want to slow down the message display, you can use show(1000), which will display the message for 1 second. During animation, you can use hide() and show() to change the visibility of animated objects.

effectCompleteCallbackFunction is the callback function that's executed when the effect is completed.

For options details, refer to the introduction section of this chapter.

Listing 8-1 provides demonstrates the use of the hide() and show() methods.

Listing 8-1. Using hide() and show() to change the visibility of selected elements

```html
<!DOCTYPE html>
<html lang="en">
<head>
    <meta charset="utf-8">
    <script src="scripts/jquery-2.1.0.min.js"></script>
    <style>
    label {
        float:left;
        display:block;
        width: 175px;
        font-weight: bold;
    }

    div {
        width: 400px;
        border:3px double green;
        background-color: lightyellow;
    }
```

```
        .message {
             width: 400px;
             color: green;
        }
        </style>

        <script>
        $(function() {
            $("#lblProcessingStatus").hide();

            $("#btnSubmit").click(function () {
            $("#lblProcessingStatus").show();
            $("#btnSubmit").hide();
            });
        });
        </script>
</head>

<body>
        <h3>Payment Details:</h3>
        <div>
        <fieldset>
             <label for="txtCustomerName">Name:</label>
             <input type="text" id="txtCustomerName"><br>

             <label for="txtCustomerAddress">Address:</label>
             <input type="text" id="txtCustomerAddress"><br>

             <label for="txtCreditCardNumber">Credit Card Number:</label>
             <input type="text" id="txtCreditCardNumber" size="16"><br>

             <label for="txtExpiryDate">Expiry Date:</label>
             <input type="text" id="txtExpiryDate" size="5"><br>
             <label for="txtCCV">CCV:</label>
             <input type="text" id="txtCCV" size="4"><br>
        </fieldset>
        </div><br>

        <label id="lblProcessingStatus" class="message">Processing payment.Please wait for the
         confirmation.</label>
        <button id="btnSubmit">Submit</button>
</body>
</html>
```

How It Works

Within the document ready function, $("#lblProcessingStatus").hide() hides the label with the ID
"lblProcessingStatus". When the user clicks the Submit button, the following code is executed:

```
$("#lblProcessingStatus").show();
$("#btnSubmit").hide();
```

The `.show()` method displays the message in the label with the ID `lblProcessingStatus` and the `.hide()` method hides the button with the ID `btnSubmit` so that user doesn't click it again and inadvertently submit multiple payments. Figure 8-1 displays the page that's initially loaded in the browser.

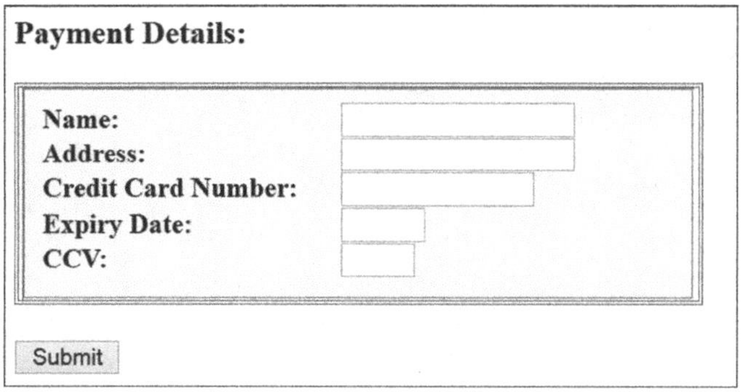

Figure 8-1. *Initial page display*

Figure 8-2 displays the page that appears after the Submit button is clicked.

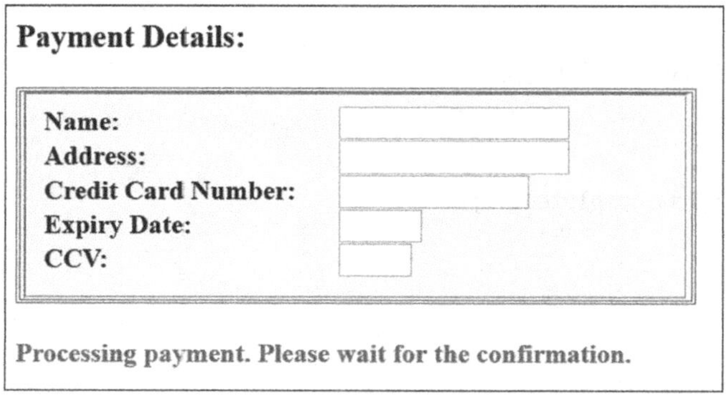

Figure 8-2. *Processing payment message that appears after the Submit button is clicked*

8-2. Toggling Between an Element's Show and Hide States
Problem

You want to show an element if it is hidden and hide an element if it is displayed.

Solution

The following jQuery syntax toggles the visibility state of the selected elements:

```
$(selector).toggle()
```

Listing 8-2 demonstrates the use of the `toggle()` method to change the visibility of selected elements.

Listing 8-2. Using the toggle() method to toggle between the show and hide states

```
<!DOCTYPE html>
<html lang="en">
<head>
    <meta charset="utf-8">
    <script src="scripts/jquery-2.1.0.min.js"></script>
    <style>
      label {
            color: green;
            font-size: 20px;
      }

      div {
            border:3px double green;
            height:60px;
            width:60px;
            border-style:solid;
            background-color:lightgreen;
      }
    </style>

    <script>
      function startFunc() {
            $("#lblMessage").html("Toggle effect has started.");
      }

      function completeFunc() {
            $("#lblMessage").html("Toggle effect has completed.");
      }

      $(function() {
            $("#btnToggle").click(function () {
              var options = {duration:2000,
                             easing:"linear",
                             start: startFunc,
                             complete: completeFunc
                            };

              $("div").toggle(options);
            });

      });
    </script>
</head>

<body>
    <div></div><br><br>
    <button id="btnToggle">Toggle</button><br><br>
    <label id="lblMessage"></label>
</body>
</html>
```

How It Works

When the Toggle button is clicked, its event handler executes the following code:

```
var options = {duration:2000,
               easing:"linear",
               start: startFunc,
               complete: completeFunc
       };
 $("div").toggle(options);
```

This example first sets duration, easing, start, and complete in the map object to control the effect of toggle() (i.e., the effects of hiding and showing). These settings are optional. If these are not specified, default values will be used. Refer to the introduction section of this chapter for more information about these options. The toggle() method is then executed on the div tag, which will show the div element if it is hidden or hide the div element if it is visible. The transition of hiding and displaying are specified by the duration and easing options. Since this example also specifies named functions for the start and complete options, these named functions will be executed at the start and at the completion of the animation. These two functions display the appropriate status of the animation in the message label by using the following code:

```
$("#lblMessage").html("Toggle effect has started.");
$("#lblMessage").html("Toggle effect has completed.");
```

Figure 8-3 displays the initial page in the browser.

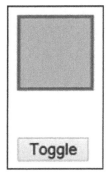

Figure 8-3. *Initial page display*

Figure 8-4 displays the page when the Toggle button is clicked and the animation has just started.

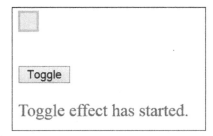

Figure 8-4. *The hide transition effect when the Toggle button is clicked*

Figure 8-5 displays the page when the animation has completed.

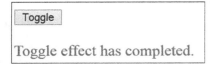

Figure 8-5. *Animation is complete*

When the Toggle button is clicked again, the green box will reappear with the same type of transition effect and the animation start/completion message will be displayed. The same set of parameters can be used for the toggle() method as are used by the hide() and show() methods. Refer to argument's details in Recipe 8-1.

8-3. Effects Methods for Hiding and Showing Elements
Problem

You want to use effects other than hide() and show() to hide and show elements with different transition effects.

Solution

There are other effects methods that hide and display selected elements—specifically, fade out and in and slide up and down.

The following jQuery syntax is used to hide selected elements:

```
$(selector).hide()
$(selector).fadeOut()
$(selector).slideUp()
```

The following jQuery syntax is used to display selected elements:

```
$(selector).show()
$(selector).fadeIn()
$(selector).slideDown()
```

The following jQuery syntax is used to toggle between hiding and displaying selected elements:

```
$(selector).toggle()
$(selector).fadeToggle()
$(selector).slideToggle()
```

The following jQuery syntax is used to change the opacity of the selected elements:

```
$(selector).fadeTo(opacityValue)
```

Listing 8-3 demonstrates the use of all of these effects methods.

Listing 8-3. Effects methods to hide and display selected elements

```
<!DOCTYPE html>
<html lang="en">
<head>
    <meta charset="utf-8">
    <script src="scripts/jquery-2.1.0.min.js"></script>

    <style>
      div {
            border:3px double black;
            border-style:solid;
            width: 400px;
                    background-color:lightyellow;
                    padding: 10px;
      }

      label {
            display: block;
            float: left;
            width:250px;
      }

      .boxStyle {
            border:3px double green;
            height:60px;
            width:60px;
            margin-left:150px;
            border-style:solid;
                    background-color:lightgreen;
      }
    </style>

    <script>
      $(function() {
            $("#btnTestIt").click(function () {
              var effectSelected = $("#effectName").val();
              var durationValue = $("#duration").val();
              var opacityValue = $("#txtOpacity").val();

              if (effectSelected == "hide") {
                  $("#box").hide(durationValue);
              } else if (effectSelected == "show") {
                  $("#box").show(durationValue);
              } else if (effectSelected == "toggle") {
                  $("#box").toggle(durationValue);
              } else if (effectSelected == "fadeIn") {
                  $("#box").fadeIn(durationValue);
              } else if (effectSelected == "fadeTo") {
                  $("#box").fadeTo(durationValue, opacityValue);
              } else if (effectSelected == "fadeOut") {
                  $("#box").fadeOut(durationValue);
```

261

```
            } else if (effectSelected == "fadeToggle") {
                $("#box").fadeToggle(durationValue);
            } else if (effectSelected == "slideUp") {
                $("#box").slideUp(durationValue); // hide with slide up animation
            } else if (effectSelected == "slideDown") {
                $("#box").slideDown(durationValue);// show with slide up animation
            }  else if (effectSelected == "slideToggle") {
                $("#box").slideToggle(durationValue);
            }
        });

        $("#btnReset").click(function (){
          $("#box").show();
          $("#effectName").prop("selectedIndex", 0);
          $("#duration").prop("selectedIndex", 0);
          $("#txtOpacity").val(0.5);
        });

    });
  </script>
</head>

<body>
    <div id="box" class="boxStyle"></div><br>

    <div>
        <label>Effect's Method Name: </label>
        <select id="effectName">
    <option>hide</option>
    <option>show</option>
    <option>toggle</option>
    <option>fadeIn</option>
    <option>fadeTo</option>
    <option>fadeOut</option>
    <option>fadeToggle</option>
    <option>slideUp</option>
    <option>slideDown</option>
    <option>slideToggle</option>
      </select><br><br>

      <label>Duration:</label>
      <select id="duration">
          <option value="500">0.5 Second</option>
    <option value="1000">1 Second</option>
    <option value="2000">2 Seconds</option>
    <option value="3000">3 Seconds</option>
    <option value="slow">Slow</option>
    <option value="fast">Fast</option>
      </select><br><br>
```

```
        <label>Opacity (For fadeTo) (Range: 0-1):</label>
        <input type="text" id="txtOpacity" value="0.5"><br><br>
    </div><br><br>

    <input id="btnTestIt" type="button" value="Test It">
    <input id="btnReset" type="button" value="Reset">
</body>
</html>
```

How It Works

This code displays drop-downs for the effect's method name and duration of the transition and a textbox for the opacity value. Opacity is valid for the fadeTo() method only. When the Test It button is clicked, depending on the user's selection, the following variables are set:

```
var effectSelected = $("#effectName").val();
var durationValue = $("#duration").val();
var opacityValue = $("#txtOpacity").val();
```

Based on the value of the effectSelected variable, one of the following effects methods will be executed with the parameter duration—hide(), show(), toggle(), fadeIn(), fadeTo(), fadeOut(), fadeToggle(), slideUp(), slideDown(), and slideToggle(). For the fadeTo() method, an additional parameter called opacity is passed. You need to show the div box first before testing the hide methods (hide(), fadeOut(), and slideUp()) and you need to hide the div box before testing the display methods (show(), fadeIn(), and slideDown()). When the Reset button is clicked, the original values of the drop-downs and textbox are set and the div box returns to its initial state. Table 8-1 displays the list of hide and display methods for various transition modes. The same set of parameters can be used as are used by the hide() and show() methods in Recipe 8-1.

Table 8-1. *Hide and Display Effects Methods*

Action	Slide and Fade	Fade	Slide
Display	show()	fadeIn()	slideDown()
Hide	hide()	fadeOut()	slideUp()
Toggle	toggle()	fadeToggle()	slideToggle()
Change in opacity	N/A	fadeTo()	N/A

Figure 8-6 displays the initial page in the browser.

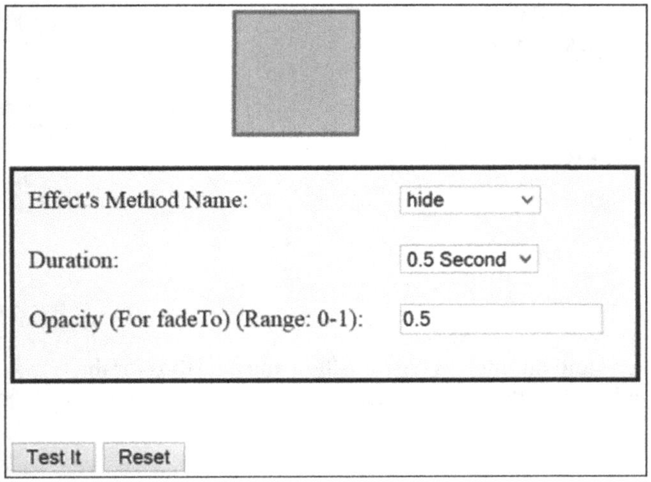

Figure 8-6. *Initial page display*

The user can select any of the effects' names and durations from the drop-down and enter an opacity value in the textbox. Figure 8-7 displays the page when the fadeTo effect method name is selected, the duration is set to 1 Second, the opacity is set to 0.2, and the Test It button is clicked. Notice that the fade effect took place and the opacity has reduced gradually to 0.2 in one second.

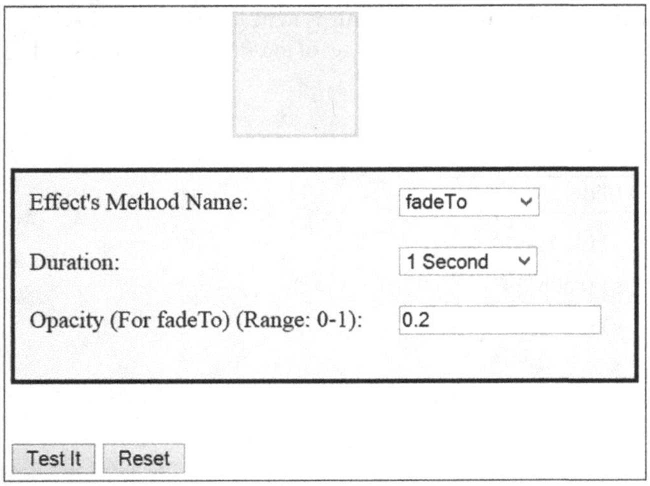

Figure 8-7. *Fading effect due to the fadeTo( ) method*

8-4. Applying Custom Animation to the CSS Properties of Selected Elements

Problem

You want to perform custom animation to the CSS properties of the selected elements.

Solution

All effects and animations are duration-based. Program execution doesn't wait for the effects to complete before it moves on to the next method; instead, it copies those effects and animation methods to the effects queue of the selected elements and continues with the program execution. The hide() and the show() methods without any arguments are not added to the element's effects queue. Functions in the effects queue are processed in sequential order while program keeps on executing in parallel.

The most commonly used syntax of the animate() method is:

```
$(selector).animate(targetCSSProperties, animationDuration)
```

where targetCSSProperties is a map object with the following format:

```
{ cssPropertyName1: 'propertyValue1', cssPropertyName2: 'propertyValue2' ...}
```

You get the animated effect as a result of CSS properties being changed from the current CSS property values to the specified target CSS property values. Listing 8-4 demonstrates the use of the animate() method to change the CSS properties over time.

Listing 8-4. Using the animate() method to show animation of selected elements

```html
<!DOCTYPE html>
<html lang="en">
<head>
    <meta charset="utf-8">
    <script src="scripts/jquery-2.1.0.min.js"></script>
    <style>
      div {
            border:3px double green;
            width: 50px;
            height: 50px;
            position:absolute;
            left:100px;
            top:50px;
            background-color: yellow;
      }
    </style>

    <script>
      $(function () {
          $("#btnAnimate").click( function() {
            $("#box").animate({left:"+=300", opacity: 0.6}, 2000, 'linear')
                  .animate({top: "+=200", opacity: 0.2}, 2000, 'linear')
                  .slideUp(1000)
                  .slideDown(1000);
          });

          $("#btnReset").click( function() {
             location.reload();
          });
      });
    </script>
</head>
```

```
<body>
    <input id="btnAnimate" type="button" value="Animate">
    <input id="btnReset" type="button" value="Reset">

    <div id="box"></div>
</body>
</html>
```

How It Works

When the Animate button is clicked, the following code is executed:

```
$("#box").animate({left:"+=300", opacity: 0.6}, 2000, 'linear')
    .animate({top: "+=200", opacity: 0.2}, 2000, 'linear')
    .slideUp(1000)
    .slideDown(1000);
```

Where in this code sample:

- $("#box") selects the div tag with the ID as "box".

- animate({left:"+=300", opacity: 0.6}, 2000, 'linear') puts this animation function in the effects queue. It specifies that you want to animate the selected div box by incrementing its left CSS property by 300 pixels and changing its opacity from 1.0 (the default) to 0.6 (this moves the box 300 pixels toward the right while changing its opacity from 1.0 to 0.6 over the period of two seconds by using the linear easing function).

- animate({top: "+=200", opacity: 0.2}, 2000, 'linear') puts this animation function in the effects queue. It specifies that you want to animate the selected div box by incrementing its top CSS property by 200 pixels and changing its opacity from 0.6 (the current) to 0.2 (this moves the box 200 pixels toward the bottom while changing its opacity from 0.6 to 0.2 over the period of two seconds by using the linear easing function).

- slideUp(1000) puts this effect function in the effects queue. It specifies that you want to animate the selected div box by hiding it using a sliding transition over the period of one second.

- slideDown(1000) puts this effect function in the effects queue. It specifies that you want to animate the selected div box by showing it using a sliding transition over the period of one second.

All these effects and animation functions are in the div box effects queue and are executed in sequential order while the main program execution continues to run in parallel. This is an asynchronous process, meaning that program execution won't wait for the animation to complete. Figure 8-8 displays the initial page in the browser.

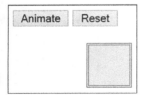

Figure 8-8. Initial page display

Figure 8-9 displays the animation's intermediate state, when the Animate button is clicked.

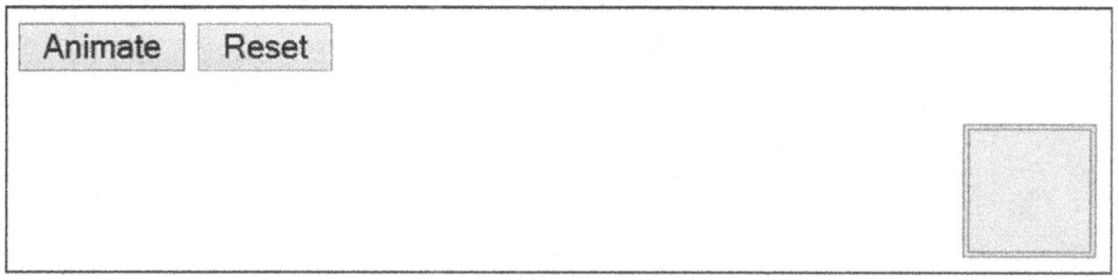

Figure 8-9. *Animation's intermediate state*

Figure 8-10 displays the animation's final state.

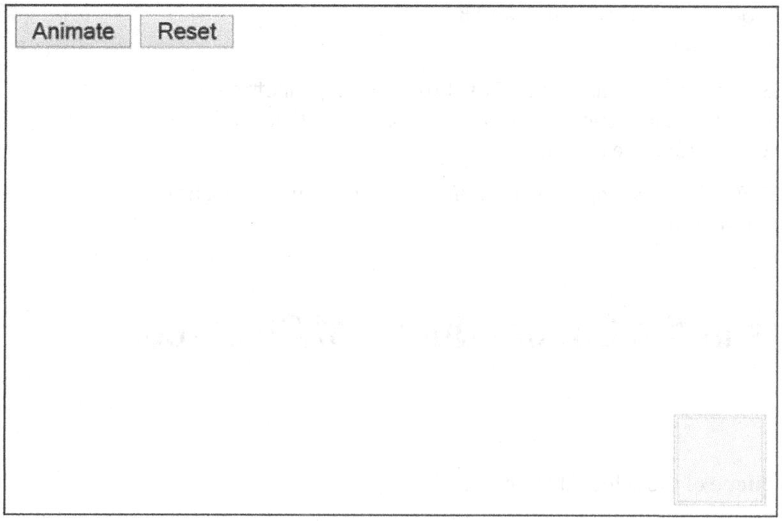

Figure 8-10. *Animation's final state*

If the Animate button is clicked again, the animation will start from the current location since this examples uses relative positioning. If the Reset button is clicked and then the Animate button is clicked, the animation will start from its original position.

A few points to remember about CSS properties used in the animate() method are:

- CSS property names are written in camelCase. For example, the CSS property name margin-left is specified as marginLeft.
- Only CSS properties with numeric values can be animated. If the propertyValue contains any other character (such as px, +=), then you must enclose the value with " (double quotes) or ' (single quotes).
- cssPropertyValue can be prefixed with += or -=. These notations are used to specify relative positions. += means increment the current value of the CSS property by the specified amount. -= means decrement the current value of the CSS property by the specified amount. For example, left: '+=50px' means increase the left spacing of the element by 50px, which will move the element to the right by 50 px.

– There are certain properties that cannot be animated using the core jQuery library. For example, background-color cannot be used as target CSS property for the elements. It can be implemented using other jQuery plug-ins or by using the following syntax.

CSS style code:

```
.myClass {
    background-color: green;
}
```

JavaScript code:

```
$(selector).queue(function () {
$(this).addClass('myClass').dequeue();
});
```

I cover the queue() and dequeue() methods in Recipes 8-5, 8-6, and 8-7.
Here's the other syntax for the animate() method:

– $(selector).animate(targetCSSProperties, animationDuration, easingFunctionName, animationCompleteCallbackFunction) —Note that animationDuration, *easingFunctionName,* and animationCompleteCallbackFunction are optional.

– $(selector).animate(targetCSSProperties, options) —Refer to the introduction section of this chapter for details about these options.

8-5. Displaying Functions in the Effects Queue of Selected Elements
Problem

You want to display functions in the effects queue of the selected elements.

Solution

A queue makes it possible to run a sequence of actions (functions) asynchronously. The program execution won't wait for all functions to be completed. You can attach many queues to the same element. For example, the function in one queue can be moving the object, whereas the function in another queue (associated with the same element) can be changing the size of the element. In most of the cases, only one queue per element is used.

A queue is an array of effects and animation functions that are executed sequentially. All the properties and methods that are valid for an array can be used for the queue. By default, each element has its own standard effects queue, which is called the *fx* queue. If the *queueName* is not explicitly specified in a method as an argument, the *fx* queue is used. The following syntax is used to get the default queue (*fx*) of the selected elements:

```
$(selector).queue()
```

Listing 8-5 demonstrates the use of the queue() method to get the functions list in the default queue.

Listing 8-5. Using the queue() method to get details about the items in the effects queue

```html
<!DOCTYPE html>
<html lang="en">
<head>
    <meta charset="utf-8">
    <script src="scripts/jquery-2.1.0.min.js"></script>
    <style>
      div {
            border:3px double green;
            width: 50px;
            height: 50px;
            position:absolute;
            left:100px;
            top:50px;
            background-color: yellow;
      }

      .message {
            position:absolute;
            top:300px;
            left:0px;
            width:100%;
            height:100%;
      }
    </style>

    <script>
      $(function () {
          $("#animate").click( function() {
            $("#box").animate({left:"+=300", opacity: 0.6}, 2000, 'linear')
                  .animate({top: "+=200", opacity: 0.2}, 2000, 'linear')
                  .slideUp(1000)
                  .slideDown(1000);

            var queue = $("div").queue(); // default is "fx" - standard effects queue

            var msg = "Queue Length: " + queue.length + "<br><br>";

            for (var i = 0; i<queue.length; i++) {
                msg += "Function [" + i + "]: " + queue[i] + "<br>";
            }

            $("#message").html(msg);
          });

          $("#reset").click( function() {
            location.reload();
          });
      });
    </script>
</head>
```

```
<body>
    <input id="animate" type="button" value="Animate">
    <input id="reset" type="button" value="Reset">

    <div id="box"></div>
    <span id="message" class="message"></span>
</body>
</html>
```

How It Works

When the Animate button is clicked, the following code is executed for the animation:

```
$("#box").animate({left:"+=300", opacity: 0.6}, 2000, 'linear')
    .animate({top: "+=200", opacity: 0.2}, 2000, 'linear')
    .slideUp(1000)
    .slideDown(1000);
```

Refer to Recipe 8-4 to see the details about this code. The code for getting the queue information is as follows:

```
var queue = $("div").queue(); // default is "fx" - standard effects queue

var msg = "Queue Length: " + queue.length + "<br><br>";

for (var i = 0; i<queue.length; i++) {
    msg += "Function [" + i + "]: " + queue[i] + "<br>";
}
```

In this code sample:

- $("div").queue() gets the standard default queue of the selected div element and sets the local variable queue.

- queue.length gets the number of effect functions in the queue.

- The for loop iterates over all the effect functions in the queue and gets their code.

Finally, the code for displaying queue information on the page is:

```
$("#message").html(msg);
```

Figure 8-11 displays the queue information for the div box.

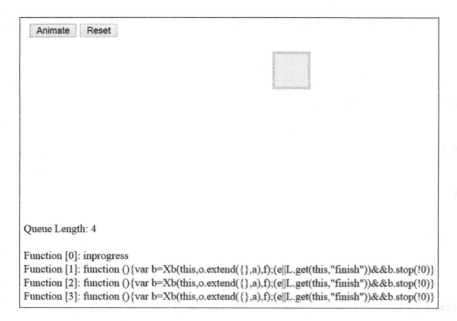

Figure 8-11. *Displays the effects queue information of the selected div element*

By using the JavaScript function setTimeout(functionName, timeInterval), you can show the queue details after every specified period of time. In Figure 8-11, the function code looks different than the animate(), slideUp(), and slideDown() methods. It shows the information stored in the queue corresponding to these effects and animations functions.

8-6. Replacing Functions in the Effects Queue of Selected Elements
Problem

You want to replace the remaining functions in the queue with a new array of effects functions. This functionality is useful when, based on user interaction, you want to change the normal set of animation effects to a different set of animation effects.

Solution

The following is the syntax to replace the effects and animations functions in the queue with a new array of functions:

```
$(selector).queue(newFunctionsArray)
```

Listing 8-6 demonstrates the use of the queue() method to replace remaining effects functions with a new set of effects functions.

Listing 8-6. Using the queue() method to replace effects functions in the effects queue

```html
<!DOCTYPE html>
<html lang="en">
<head>
    <meta charset="utf-8">
    <script src="scripts/jquery-2.1.0.min.js"></script>
    <style>
      div {
            border:3px double green;
            width: 50px;
            height: 50px;
            position:absolute;
            left:100px;
            top:50px;
            background-color: yellow;
      }
    </style>

    <script>
      var fadeOutFunc = function () {
          $(this).fadeOut();
      }

      $(function (){
          $("#animate").click( function() {
            $("#box").animate({left:"+=300", opacity: 0.6}, 2000, 'linear')
            .animate({top: "+=200", opacity: 0.2}, 2000, 'linear')
            .slideUp(1000)
            .slideDown(1000);
          });

          $("#replaceFunctions").click( function() {
            var functionArray = new Array();
            functionArray.push(fadeOutFunc);

            $("#box").queue(functionArray);
          });

          $("#reset").click( function() {
              location.reload();
          });

      });
    </script>
</head>

<body>
    <input id="animate" type="button" value="Animate">
    <input id="replaceFunctions" type="button" value="Replace Functions in the queue">
    <input id="reset" type="button" value="Reset">

    <div id="box"></div>
</body>
</html>
```

How It Works

When the Animate button is clicked, the following code is executed:

```
$("#box").animate({left:"+=300", opacity: 0.6}, 2000, 'linear')
       .animate({top: "+=200", opacity: 0.2}, 2000, 'linear')
       .slideUp(1000)
       .slideDown(1000);
```

Refer to Recipe 8-4 to learn more about this code.

To understand this functionality, let the animation run up to the end state. Now click the Animate button again and click the Replace Functions in the Queue button. The following code will be executed:

```
var functionArray = new Array();
functionArray.push(fadeOutFunc);

$("#box").queue(functionArray);
```

The following actions take place as a result of this code:

- `functionArray.push(fadeOutFunc)` adds a function called `fadeOutFunc` to the array `functionArray`. `fadeOutFunc` makes a call to the `fadeOut()` method.

- `$("#box").queue(functionArray)` replaces the remaining effects in the effects queue with the new set of functions (i.e., `fadeOut()`).

After the current step of the animation is completed, the box will fade out instead of continuing with its normal set of animation effects.

The following syntax is used to replace the remaining effects functions with an array of new functions in the named queue associated with the selected elements:

```
$(selector).queue(queueName, newFunctionsArray)
```

8-7. Adding Custom Functions in the Effects Queue
Problem

You want to add a new custom function in the effects queue. This functionality can be used to add effects (such as to change the background color) that are not supported by the target CSS property parameter of the `animate()` method.

Solution

The following is the syntax to add a custom function in the effects queue:

```
$(selector).queue(function () {....})
```

This new function is executed when all the effects functions before it in the queue are completed. It is important to call the `dequeue()` method in the custom function so that next effects function in the queue can be executed.

Listing 8-7 demonstrates the use of the custom function as a parameter in the `queue()` method.

Listing 8-7. Using the queue() method with the custom function as a parameter

```html
<!DOCTYPE html>
<html lang="en">
<head>
    <meta charset="utf-8">
    <script src="scripts/jquery-2.1.0.min.js"></script>
    <style>
      div {
            border:3px double green;
            width: 50px;
            height: 50px;
            position:absolute;
            left:100px;
            top:50px;
            background-color: yellow;
      }

      .newColor {
            background-color: green;
      }
    </style>

    <script>
      $(function (){
            $("#animate").click( function() {
              $("#box").animate({left:"+=300", opacity: 0.6}, 2000, 'linear')
                    .queue(function () {
                          $(this).addClass('newColor').dequeue();
                    })
                    .animate({top: "+=200", opacity: 0.2}, 2000, 'linear')
                    .slideUp(1000)
                    .slideDown(1000);
            });

            $("#reset").click( function() {
              location.reload();
            });
      });
    </script>
</head>

<body>
    <input id="animate" type="button" value="Animate">
    <input id="reset" type="button" value="Reset">

    <div id="box"></div>
</body>
</html>
```

How It Works

When the Animate button is clicked, the following code is executed:

```
$("#box").animate({left:"+=300", opacity: 0.6}, 2000, 'linear')
      .queue(function () {
        $(this).addClass('newColor').dequeue();
      })
      .animate({top: "+=200", opacity: 0.2}, 2000, 'linear')
      .slideUp(1000)
      .slideDown(1000);
```

Refer to Recipe 8-4 for more information about the animate(), slideUp(), and slideDown() methods. After the first step of the animation is completed, the following code is executed from the effects queue:

```
queue(function () {
    $(this).addClass('newColor').dequeue();
})
```

In this custom function, addClass('newColor') adds the CSS class .newClass to the selected element and changes the color of the box to green. For the custom function in the effects queue, it is important to call .dequeue() so the next effects in the queue can be executed.

Figure 8-12 displays the page when the Animate button is clicked. The custom function is executed after the first animation step (moving the yellow box from left to right) is completed.

Figure 8-12. *Displays the effect of executing a custom function in the effects queue*

The following syntax adds a custom function in the named queue associated with the selected elements:

```
$(selector).queue(queueName, function () {....})
```

8-8. Controlling the Animation by Pausing It
Problem

You want to delay the execution of effects and animations.

Solution

The following syntax can be used to pause an animation:

$(selector).delay(delayTime)

where *delayTime* is in milliseconds. The delay() method pauses the animation for the specified number of milliseconds.

Listing 8-8 demonstrates the use of the delay() method. This code listing is same as Listing 8-4, with the exception of including the delay() step between the two animate() methods.

Listing 8-8. Using the delay() method to pause the animation

```
<!DOCTYPE html>
<html lang="en">
<head>
    <meta charset="utf-8">
    <script src="scripts/jquery-2.1.0.min.js"></script>
    <style>
      div {
            border:3px double green;
            width: 50px;
            height: 50px;
            position:absolute;
            left:100px;
            top:50px;
            background-color: yellow;
      }
    </style>

    <script>
      $(function () {
          $("#btnAnimate").click( function() {
            $("#box").animate({left:"+=300", opacity: 0.6}, 2000, 'linear')
                .delay(800)
                .animate({top: "+=200", opacity: 0.2}, 2000, 'linear')
                .slideUp(1000)
                .slideDown(1000);
          });

          $("#btnReset").click( function() {
            location.reload();
          });
      });
    </script>
</head>
<body>
    <input id="btnAnimate" type="button" value="Animate">
    <input id="btnReset" type="button" value="Reset">

    <div id="box"></div>
</body>
</html>
```

How It Works

When the Animate button is clicked, the animation will start by moving the box from left to right. It then pauses for 800 milliseconds due to the statement .delay(800) and then continues to move the box from top to bottom. The animation hides the box by sliding it up and then displays it by sliding it down. Refer to Figures 8-8, 8-9, and 8-10 for the initial, intermediate, and final states of the animation, respectively.

8-9. Removing All Remaining Effects and Animations Functions from the Effects Queue
Problem

You want to remove all the remaining effects and animation functions from the effects queue.

Solution

The following jQuery syntax removes all the effects from the queue that have not yet been executed:

$(_selector_**).clearQueue()**

Listing 8-9 demonstrates the use of the clearQueue() method to remove all remaining elements from the effects queue of the selected elements. The effects function that's currently being executed won't be removed.

Listing 8-9. Using the clearQueue() method to remove remaining effects

```
<!DOCTYPE html>
<html lang="en">
<head>
    <meta charset="utf-8">
    <script src="scripts/jquery-2.1.0.min.js"></script>
    <style>
      div {
          border:3px double green;
          width: 50px;
          height: 50px;
          position:absolute;
          left:100px;
          top:50px;
          background-color: yellow;
      }
    </style>

    <script>
      $(function () {
          $("#animate").click( function() {
            $("#box").animate({left:"+=300", opacity: 0.6}, 2000, 'linear')
                  .animate({top: "+=200", opacity: 0.2}, 2000, 'linear')
                  .slideUp(1000)
                  .slideDown(1000);
          });
```

```
            $("#clearQueue").click( function() {
              $("#box").clearQueue(); // won't clear the currently running effect.
            });

            $("#reset").click( function() {
              location.reload();
            });
        });
      </script>
</head>

<body>
      <input id="animate" type="button" value="Animate">
      <input id="clearQueue" type="button" value="Clear Queue">
      <input id="reset" type="button" value="Reset">

      <div id="box"></div>
</body>
</html>
```

How It Works

When the Animate button is clicked, the following code is executed:

```
$("#box").animate({left:"+=300", opacity: 0.6}, 2000, 'linear')
       .animate({top: "+=200", opacity: 0.2}, 2000, 'linear')
       .slideUp(1000)
       .slideDown(1000);
```

Refer to Recipe 8-4 to read more about this code.

You can test the effect of the clear queue functionality by clicking Clear Queue before the animation is completed. When Clear Queue is clicked, the following code is executed:

```
$("#clearQueue").click( function() {
  $("#box").clearQueue(); // won't clear the currently running effect.
});
```

The clearQueue() method will let the current effect complete and then it will remove all the remaining effects from the queue.

The animation will stop at the point at which the currently running effect ended. Figure 8-13 displays the page that appears when the Clear Queue button is clicked immediately after the animation has started.

Figure 8-13. *Displays the effect on the animation of the clearQueue( ) method*

The following syntax is used to remove remaining functions from the named queue associated with the selected elements:

```
$(selector).clearQueue(queueName)
```

8-10. Stopping the Currently Running Animation
Problem

You want to stop the currently running animation in the effects queue.

Solution

The following syntax is used to stop the currently running animation in the effects queue of the selected elements:

$(selector**).stop(***clearQueue,* *goToTheEndState***)**

Use clearQueue to specify if you want to clear the queue and remove the remaining effects. The goToTheEndState parameter specifies if you want to go to the end state of the current animation. Both these parameters are optional; you simply use the Boolean values and their default value is false. Listing 8-10 demonstrates the use of the stop() method with all the possible combinations of values of the clearQueue and goToTheEndState parameters.

Listing 8-10. Using the stop() method to terminate the current animation step

```
<!DOCTYPE html>
<html lang="en">
<head>
    <meta charset="utf-8">
    <script src="scripts/jquery-2.1.0.min.js"></script>
    <style>
      div {
            border:3px double green;
            width: 50px;
            height: 50px;
            position:absolute;
            left:100px;
            top:100px;
            background-color: yellow;
      }
```

```
        .newColor {
            background-color: green;
        }
    </style>

    <script>
      $(function () {
            $("#animate").click( function() {
              $("#box").animate({left:"+=300", opacity: 0.6}, 2000, 'linear')
                     .animate({top: "+=200", opacity: 0.2}, 2000, 'linear')
                     .queue(function () {
                            $(this).addClass('newColor').dequeue();
                     })
                     .slideUp(1000)
                     .slideDown(1000);
            });

            $("#stopAnimation").click( function() {
              var clearQueue = $("#clearQueue").prop("checked");
              var goToTheEnd = $("#goToTheEnd").prop("checked");

              $("#box").stop(clearQueue, goToTheEnd);
            });

            $("#reset").click( function() {
              location.reload();
            });
        });
    </script>
</head>

<body>
    <input type="checkbox" id="clearQueue">Clear queue     
    <input type="checkbox" id="goToTheEnd">Go to the end<br><br>
    <input id="animate" type="button" value="Animate">
    <input id="stopAnimation" type="button" value="Stop Animation">
    <input id="reset" type="button" value="Reset"><br>

    <div id="box"></div>
</body>
</html>
```

How It Works

To understand the stop() method functionality, you need to click the Animate button first and then click the Stop Animation button. When you click the Stop Animation button, the following code is executed:

```
var clearQueue = $("#clearQueue").prop("checked");
var goToTheEnd = $("#goToTheEnd").prop("checked");
$("#box").stop(clearQueue, goToTheEnd);
```

The following is the explanation of this code:

- $("#clearQueue").prop("checked") returns true if the Clear Queue checkbox is checked; otherwise it returns false. The return value is used to set the value of the clearQueue variable.

- $("#goToTheEnd").prop("checked") returns true if the Go to the End checkbox is checked; otherwise, it returns false. The return value is used to set the value of the goToTheEnd variable.

- clearQueue and goToTheEnd are passed as parameters to the stop() method.

The following are the possible combinations for the clearQueue and goToTheEndState parameters and their effect on the behavior of the stop() method:

- If clearQueue and goToTheEndState are false, the current animation will stop immediately and subsequent animations will be executed.

- If clearQueue is true and goToTheEndState is false, the current animation will stop immediately and subsequent animations will not be executed.

- If clearQueue is false and goToTheEndState is true, the current animation will jump to the end state of the current animation step and subsequent animations will be executed. To test this behavior, click the Animate button and then immediately click the Stop Animation button.

- If clearQueue and goToTheEndState are true, the current animation will jump to its end state and subsequent animations will be executed.

The following syntax is used to execute the stop() method on the named queue associated with the selected elements:

```
$(selector).stop(queueName, clearQueue, goToTheEndState)
```

The finish() Method

If you want to finish the animation by stopping the currently running animation effect, clear all the remaining animation effects in the queue, and reach the end state of all the animations, you use the finish() method. The syntax for the finish() method is:

```
$(selector).finish()
$(selector).finish(queueName)
```

To test the effect of the finish() method, add the following code to Listing 8-10. Then test it by clicking the Animate button first and then the Finish Animation button.
HTML code:

```
<input id="finishAnimation" type="button" value="Finish Animation">
jQuery Code:
    $("#finishAnimation").click( function() {
$("#box").finish();
    });
```

8-11. Determining Global Settings for All the Animation Effects

Problem

You want to determine the global settings for all the animation effects.

Solution

The following are the two global settings for all animation effects:

- $.fx.interval can be set to the frequency at which animation changes are displayed. The default value is 13 milliseconds. By setting its value to 1, the animation will be much smoother but there might by CPU utilization issues. You should fine-tune this value to create a smoother animation without impacting system resources and performance problems. Since this value is set at a global level and all animations will be impacted, you will see the difference in animation transition after stopping and restarting the animation after the $.fx.interval value is set. The syntax to set its value is:

  $.fx.interval = n;

  where n is the value in milliseconds.

- $.fx.off can be set to true or false. When it is set to true, animations won't start and all the selected elements, with the effects queue, will be displayed as their final animation state. This value is set at the global level and it is useful to disable all the animations if system resources (CPU and memory) constraints are expected or noticed. When it is set to false, all subsequent animations will work as designed and coded. The syntax to set its value is:

  $.fx.off = booleanValue;

  where booleanValue can be true or false.

Summary

This chapter covered topics about effects and animations. You learned to:

- Add effects to web pages by using the following methods—hide(), show(), toggle(), fadeIn(), fadeOut(), fadeTo(), fadeToggle(), slideUp(), slideDown(), and slideToggle().

- Create and run custom animations by specifying target CSS properties of the element and the duration of the transition from the current CSS properties to the target CSS properties of the element by using the animate() method.

- Manage effects and animations queue by adding, removing, and replacing effects and animation methods to/from the queue. You did this by using the following methods—queue(), dequeue(), and clearQueue().

- Control animation by smoothing, pausing, stopping, and skipping animation steps. You do this by using the following methods—delay(), stop(), and finish().

- Plug in additional custom functions at various steps of the animation by using the queue(*function* () {...}) function.

CHAPTER 9

■ ■ ■

jQuery AJAX

AJAX (*A*synchronous *Ja*vaScript and *X*ML) is a JavaScript-based communication technique between the client (browsers) and the server (web servers) that can be used with other technologies like jQuery, JavaScript, HTML5, and CSS3 to create faster, dynamic, user-friendly, and highly interactive web sites. Conventional web applications are synchronous, which means when users submit a form or send a request for information, they have to wait for the server to complete the process and send the information back to the browser. When the information is received by the browser, the complete page is refreshed with the updated information. In the case of web applications developed using AJAX, while users are working on a web page, data entered by the user or request for the new information is sent to the server seamlessly without any interruption in the workflow. When data is returned from the web server, only a portion of the web page is updated with the new information. Figure 9-1 displays the request and response flow between the client and the server in a conventional web application.

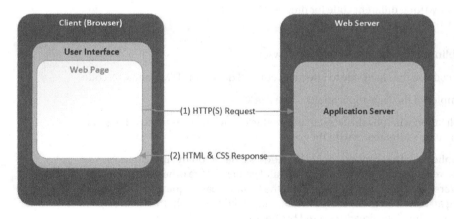

Figure 9-1. *Request and response model of a conventional web application*

Figure 9-2 displays the request and response flow between the client and the server via jQuery AJAX APIs and the AJAX engine in a web application.

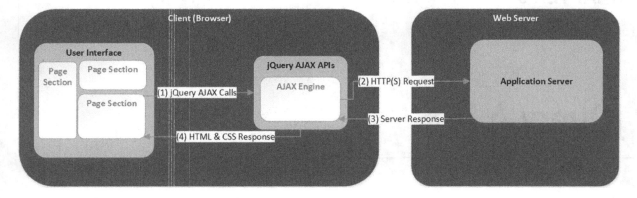

Figure 9-2. *Request and response model of the web application using AJAX*

The advantages of using AJAX are:

- Reduced network bandwidth use because only a portion of the page is refreshed instead of the complete page.

- Highly interactive web pages.

- Better user experience.

- Increased productivity.

- Eliminates the need for writing different code for different browsers.

The disadvantages are:

- Dependency on enabling JavaScript settings in the browsers.

- Additional JavaScript code on the client side to integrate returned data with HTML and CSS code.

The following are some examples of the web applications using AJAX:

- Stock ticker web application whereby the latest market value of each stock is updated regularly without impacting the user's interaction with the page.

- Forms-based web application that contains fields like address. Based on the information entered by the user, a web page can provide the list of valid values for the other fields. For example, if a user enters/selects data in the State field, the browser can request all valid cities in the state by making an AJAX call to the server without any need to refresh the whole page and without losing or caching data already entered by the user.

- Web applications that require complex data and business rules validations on the server side. While the user is entering the data, simultaneous calls can be made to the server to validate entered data. If there is any issue, it can be reported back to the user immediately instead of waiting for the user to submit the completed form.

jQuery AJAX methods make the code simpler and the web applications more interactive and dynamic. This chapter covers recipes that use jQuery AJAX-related methods and events to simplify the implementation of AJAX calls and processing of the returned data on the client (browser) side. It covers requesting and receiving the data in the following five formats—plain text, HTML, XML, JSON, and Script.

Since Chrome and Safari browsers have stricter security policies related to accessing local resources and different versions of Internet Explorer behave differently for AJAX calls, it's best to test all the recipes in this chapter using the Firefox browser. In order to test on other browsers, deploy the code on a web server and then test them. Refer to the Appendix C for deploying web applications on Apache Tomcat and IIS.

You can monitor the content of the request, request header, response, and response header by opening the network tab of the browser's developer tool or console.

9-1. Using jQuery AJAX API Calls to Get Plain Text Data from the Server
Problem

You want to use jQuery API calls to get plain text data from the server.

Solution

The following is the most commonly used syntax for making a jQuery AJAX API call:
```
$.ajax(settingsMapObject)
```

```
where, settingsMapObject is
    {
        type: "GET",
        url: "requestUrl",
        dataType: "text", // html, xml, json
        success: successCallbackFunction,
        error: errorCallbackFunction
    }

function successCallbackFunction(returnedData, status) { ... }
function errorCallbackFunction(request, status, errorMsg) { ... }
```

The available settings of an AJAX API call are outlined next.

The type Setting

type sets the type of the request (GET or POST) you are making to the server. Communication between clients and servers uses HTTP (**H**ypertext **T**ransfer **P**rotocol) by initiating requests from clients and getting back responses from servers. GET and POST are two commonly used request methods.

GET Request

- Requests data from a specified URL resource

- Has a limitation on length

- Within a page a GET request can be specified as:

    ```
    <a href="http://domainName/resource?param1=paramVal1&param2=paramVal2">
    ```

POST Request

- Submits data for processing to a specified URL resource

- Has no length limit

- Within a page a POST request can be specified as:

```
<form method="POST" action="resourceURL">
    <!-- Data entry fields HTML form elements -->
</form>
```

The url Setting

url sets the URL to which you are sending the request and expecting the response back. It can be relative to the current page or an absolute URL path. The URL can be either an absolute or relative path. Generally, the URL contains the resource name, which programmatically gets the data from some source (such as a database, file, business logic, and so on) and sends it back to the client (browser). Since writing server-side code is out of the scope of this book, all the recipes in this chapter use data files to provide the response content to the browser.

   If the current page and this URL have different domain names, the browser will throw an error about the cross-domain security. If you want to force a cross-domain request, set the crossDomain setting to true in the ajax() method.

The dataType Setting

The dataType setting sets the type of the data you are expecting back from the server. If it is not specified, the dataType from the Content-type in the response header will be used. The data type of the returnedData (the parameter in the success callback function) will be set as the specified data type.

   The following are the commonly used data types:

- text—Returns a plain text string.

- xml—Returns an XML document.

- html—Returns HTML as plaintext. Script tags will be executed when the HTML is added to the DOM.

- json—Returns data in JSON format.

The success Setting

The success setting specifies which event handler (callback function) to execute when data is returned successfully from the server.

The error Setting

error specifies which event handler (callback function) to execute when there is an error while sending the request or upon getting the response back.

Other ajax( ) Settings

Some of the other less frequently used settings of the ajax( ) method include:

- async—All AJAX requests are sent asynchronously (default). If this is set as false, the AJAX request will block the execution of the code and the user is not allowed to perform any action.

- cache—This indicates whether to use the cached response (if available) or not. By default, it is true for all dataTypes except for script and jsonp. JSONP stands for "JSON with padding." It is a way to get data from other domains by bypassing cross origin resource sharing rules.

- timeout—This indicates after how many milliseconds a request is considered a failure if no response is received by that time.

Using the ajax( ) Method

Listing 9-1 demonstrates the use of the jQuery ajax( ) method to get text from the server and Listing 9-2 shows the employees.txt file.

Listing 9-1. Using the ajax() method to make an AJAX call to the server

```
<!DOCTYPE html>
<html lang="en">
<head>
    <meta charset="utf-8">
    <script src="scripts/jquery-2.1.0.min.js"></script>
    <style>
      div {
            border:3px double green;
            width: 300px;
            background-color: lightcyan;
      }

      table {
            border:0px;
      }

      td {
            padding-right: 10px;
            padding-left: 10px;
      }

      .header {
            font-weight: bold;
            background-color: lightgray;
      }

      .evenRow {
            background-color: lightyellow;
      }
```

```
        .oddRow {
            background-color: lightblue;
        }

        .errMsg {
            background-color: orange;
            color: white;
            font-weight: bold;
            width: 600px;
        }
    </style>

    <script>
        function processData(returnedData, status) {
            $("#ajaxStatusMessage").append("Status: " + status + "<br>");

            var records = returnedData.split("\n");
            for (var i=0; i<records.length; i++) {
                var fields = records[i].split(",");

                $("#tblEmployee").append("<tr><td>" + fields[0] +
                    "</td><td>" + fields[1] +
                    "</td><td>" + fields[2] + "</td></tr>");
            }

            $("tr").eq(0).addClass("header");
            $("tr:even:gt(0)").addClass("evenRow");
            $("tr:odd").addClass("oddRow");
        }

    function reportError(request, status, errorMsg) {
        $("#ajaxStatusMessage").append("Status: " + status + "<br>Error Message: " + errorMsg);
        $("#ajaxStatusMessage").addClass("errMsg");
    }

    $(function () {
        $.ajax({
            type: "GET",
            url: "employees.txt",
            dataType: "text",
            success: processData,
            error: reportError
        });
    });
    </script>
</head>

<body>
    <table id="tblEmployee"></table><br>
    <div id="ajaxStatusMessage"></div>
</body>
</html>
```

Listing 9-2. Content of the employees.txt file

```
Employee Name, Department, Salary
Jane Smith, Marketing, $95000
John Smith, Technology, $90000
Brian Adam, Sales, $72000
Mary Jones, Support, $60000
Michael Jefferson, Technology, $85000
```

How It Works

The HTML file with the AJAX call that's loading a local file (for example, file:///C:/myWebApp/ajax.htm) can be viewed only in Firefox. Browsers like Chrome, Internet Explorer, and Safari have more restrictive default security features and they don't permit local files to be loaded. To test with these browsers, you need to deploy the web application on a web server. Refer to the Appendix C for deploying a web application on Apache Tomcat and IIS.

In this code, after the DOM is ready, the following code is executed:

```
$.ajax({
        type: "GET",
        url: "employees.txt",
        dataType: "text",
        success: processData,
        error: reportError
        });
```

The jQuery ajax() method is executed with the following settings:

- The request type is GET

- The URL resource is employees.txt

- The expected data type of the returned data is text

- If sending the request and receiving the response is successful, execute the callback function processData

- If there is an error sending the request or receiving the response, execute the callback function reportError

$.ajax() returns a jqXHR (jQuery XMLHttpRequest) object. jqXHR extends the browser's native XMLHttpRequest object's functionalities by adding properties and APIs to it. The .ajax() method call sets its properties and then returns it. It manages all the aspects of the request and the response, including a request header, data being sent to the server, callback function names, the status of the request, the response header from the server, and the data returned from the server. This object is also passed as an argument to most of the callback functions, such as success and error callback functions.

The ajax() method execution sends the request to the server asynchronously—the program execution doesn't wait for the response to come back. When a response is received from the server, depending on the status, either processData or reportError is executed.

If there is a successful response, the processData() function is called. It executes the following code:

```
$("#ajaxStatusMessage").append("Status: " + status + "<br>");

        var records = returnedData.split("\n");
        for (var i=0; i<records.length; i++) {
                var fields = records[i].split(",");
```

```
        $("#tblEmployee").append("<tr><td>" + fields[0] +
            "</td><td>" + fields[1] +
            "</td><td>" + fields[2] + "</td></tr>");
    }

    $("tr").eq(0).addClass("header");
    $("tr:even:gt(0)").addClass("evenRow");
    $("tr:odd").addClass("oddRow");
```

The returnedData argument contains data from the response. $("#ajaxStatusMessage").append("Status: " + status + "<br>") appends the status message to the div tag with the *ajaxStatusMessage* ID.

var records = returnedData.split("\n") creates an array of records by splitting the returned data using a newline character as a delimiter. If you want to see the content of the records array, you can add the following line to your code, after the records variable is set:

console.dir(records)

console.dir(*objName*) displays the content of the specified object *objName* in the browser's console. Figure 9-3 displays the content of the records array in the Firefox browser.

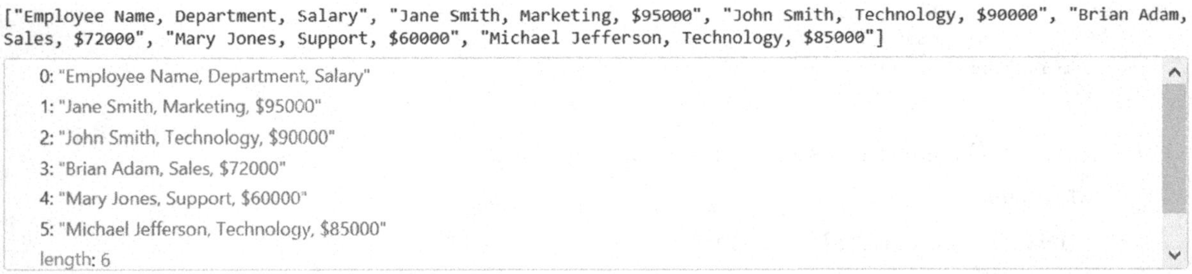

```
["Employee Name, Department, Salary", "Jane Smith, Marketing, $95000", "John Smith, Technology, $90000", "Brian Adam,
Sales, $72000", "Mary Jones, Support, $60000", "Michael Jefferson, Technology, $85000"]
```

```
0: "Employee Name, Department, Salary"
1: "Jane Smith, Marketing, $95000"
2: "John Smith, Technology, $90000"
3: "Brian Adam, Sales, $72000"
4: "Mary Jones, Support, $60000"
5: "Michael Jefferson, Technology, $85000"
length: 6
```

Figure 9-3. *Content of the records array*

for(var i=0; i<records.length; i++) { ... } iterates over the each record specified in Figure 9-3.

var fields = records[i].split(",") creates an array of fields by splitting each record using , as a delimiter. If you want to see the content of the fields array, you can add the following line to your code, after the fields variable is set: console.dir(fields). Figure 9-4 displays the content of the fields array for the third element in the browser console.

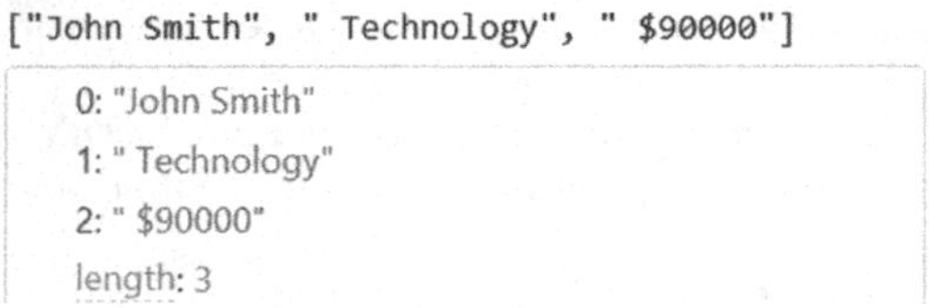

```
["John Smith", " Technology", " $90000"]
```

```
0: "John Smith"
1: " Technology"
2: " $90000"
length: 3
```

Figure 9-4. *Content of the records array*

`$("#tblEmployee").append("<tr><td>" + fields[0] + "</td><td>" + fields[1] + "</td><td>" + fields[2] + "</td></tr>")` builds the `<tr>` record for the table using elements from the `fields` array and appends it to the `<table>` with the ID `tblEmployee`.

After all the records are built and appended to the table, the following code is executed to set the CSS properties:

- `$("tr").eq(0).addClass("header")`—For the first record, add the CSS class `header`.

- `$("tr:even:gt(0)").addClass("evenRow")`—For all even-numbered rows that have an index of greater than 0, add the CSS class `evenRow`.

- `$("tr:odd").addClass("oddRow")`—For all odd-numbered rows, add the CSS class `oddRow`.

Note that in this code, HTML and CSS are added using JavaScript on the client (browser) side. In a conventional web application, HTML and CSS are specified on the server side.

Figure 9-5 displays the page after data is returned from the server and after the HTML tags and CSS classes are added to the returned data.

Employee Name	Department	Salary
Jane Smith	Marketing	$95000
John Smith	Technology	$90000
Brian Adam	Sales	$72000
Mary Jones	Support	$60000
Michael Jefferson	Technology	$85000

Status: success

Figure 9-5. *Data has been returned and formatted using HTML and CSS*

If there is an error sending the request or receiving the response, the `reportError()` callback function is executed. It has the following arguments—`request` (which contains information about the request), `status` (which in this case is "error"), and `errorMsg` (which contains details about the error).

- `$("#ajaxStatusMessage").append("Status: " + status + "<br>Error Message: " + errorMsg)` appends the status and error message to the `div` tag with the ID `ajaxStatusMessage`.

- `$("#ajaxStatusMessage").addClass("errMsg")` adds the CSS class `errMsg` to the `div` tag.

In order to simulate an error, make a small change in the code in the Listing 9-1. Update the value of the `url` to `employeeY.txt` (for example) and view the page in the browser. Due to the error in the request, the error callback function will be executed and an error message will be displayed, as shown in the Figure 9-6.

```
Status: error
Error Message: [Exception... "Access to restricted URI denied" code: "1012" nsresult:
"0x805303f4 (NS_ERROR_DOM_BAD_URI)" location: ""]
```

Figure 9-6. *An error message is displayed*

About the Convenience Methods

jQuery has provided some convenience (shorthand) methods that you can be use in place of using the ajax()
method. For this recipe, you can replace the ajax() method call with the following convenience method:

```
$.get("employees.txt", processData, "text");
```

The following is the syntax for the .get() convenience method:

```
$.get(url, data, successCallbackFunction, dataType)
```

where data is the data you want to send to the server. In the current recipe, it is null and hence there is no need to
pass it. successCallbackFunction is the callback function, and its called when there's a successful response from the
server. The data, successCallbackFunction, and dataType arguments are optional. You can handle error conditions
by setting the global error handler using $(document).ajaxError(errorHandler). These are covered in Recipes 9-9
and 9-10.

Handling Runtime Errors

JavaScript runtime errors are not reported in the Firefox console log if the error is in the callback functions. In order
to catch the runtime error, use JavaScript exception handling statement try {...} catch (error) {...}. Refer to
Appendix D for details about implementing exception handling in your code.

9-2. Using jQuery AJAX API Calls to Get HTML Text from the Server

Problem

You want to use jQuery API calls to get HTML text from the server. This functionality can be used to get HTML code
from various sources in order to display a complete view in a single HTML file.

Solution

Refer to Recipe 9-1 for the syntax for making a jQuery AJAX call. Listings 9-3 and 9-4 provide the changes to the code
in Recipe 9-1 needed to demonstrate the use of the jQuery AJAX API ajax() method in order to get HTML content
from the server. Listing 9-5 shows the employees.htm file.

Listing 9-3. Using the ajax() method to get HTML data: changes to the callback function of the success event

```
function processData(returnedData, status) {
    $("#ajaxStatusMessage").append("Status: " + status + "<br>");

    $("#tblEmployee").append(returnedData);
    }
```

Listing 9-4. Using the ajax() method to get HTML data: changes to the ajax() call

```
$.ajax({
  type: "GET",
  url: "employees.htm",
  dataType: "html",
  success: processData,
  error: reportError
});
```

Listing 9-5. Content of the employees.htm file

```
<table>
<tr class="header"><td>Employee Name</td><td>Department</td><td>Salary</td></tr>
<tr class="oddRow"><td>Jane Smith</td><td>Marketing</td><td>$95000</td></tr>
<tr class="evenRow"><td>John Smith</td><td>Technology</td><td>$90000</td></tr>
<tr class="oddRow"><td>Brian Adam</td><td>Sales</td><td>$72000</td></tr>
<tr class="evenRow"><td>Mary Jones</td><td>Support</td><td>$60000</td></tr>
<tr class="oddRow"><td>Michael Jefferson</td><td>Technology</td><td>$85000</td></tr>
</table>
```

How It Works

After the DOM is ready, the following code is executed:

```
$.ajax({
      type: "GET",
      url: "employees.htm",
      dataType: "html",
      success: processData,
      error: reportError
});
```

The jQuery ajax() method is executed with the following settings:

- Request type is GET

- URL resource is employees.htm

- Expected data type of the returned data is html

- If sending the request and receiving the response is successful, execute the callback function processData

- If there is an error sending the request or receiving the response, execute the callback function reportError

The ajax() method execution sends the request to the server asynchronously. When a response is received from the server, depending on the status, the processData or reportError callback function is executed.

If there is a successful response, the processData() function will be called, and it will execute the following code:

```
$("#ajaxStatusMessage").append("Status: " + status + "<br>");

    $("#tblEmployee").append(returnedData);
```

$("#ajaxStatusMessage").append("Status: " + status + "<br>") appends the status message to the div tag with the *ajaxStatusMessage* ID.

$("#tblEmployee").append(returnedData) appends the returned HTML data to the <table> with the *tblEmployee* ID.

Figure 9-5 displays the page after the data is returned from the server and appended to the <table> tag. Figure 9-6 displays the error message when an error occurs when sending the request to the server or when receiving the response from the server.

For this recipe, you can replace the ajax() method call using the following convenience method:

```
$.get("employees.htm", processData, "html");
```

There is another convenience method called load() that attaches the HTML data directly to the specified selector:

```
$("#tblEmployee").load("employee.htm");
```

In this case, you don't have to define a success callback function like processData. The following is the syntax to use the load() method:

```
load(url, data, completeCallbackFunction)
load(url, data, function(returnedData, status) {...})
```

where data is the data you want to send to the server. In the current recipe, it is null and hence there is no need to pass it. completeCallbackFunction is the callback function that's executed upon completing the request. returnedData is the data returned from the server and status is the status of the request and the response. data and completeCallbackFunction are optional arguments.

9-3. Using jQuery AJAX API Calls to Get Data in XML Format from the Server

Problem

You want to use jQuery API calls to get data in XML format from the server.

Solution

Refer to Recipe 9-1 for the syntax of making a jQuery AJAX call. Listings 9-6 and 9-7 shows the changes to the code in Recipe 9-1 needed to demonstrate the use of the jQuery AJAX API ajax() method to get employees data in the XML format from the server. Listing 9-8 shows the employees.xml file.

Listing 9-6. Using the ajax() method to get XML data: changes to the callback function for the success event

```
function processData(returnedData, status) {
$("#ajaxStatusMessage").append("Status: " + status + "<br>");

var tableRecord="";

$("#tblEmployee").append("<tr><td>Employee Name</td><td>Department</td><td>Salary</td>");

$(returnedData).find('employee').each(function(){
  $("#tblEmployee").append(
    "<tr><td>" + $(this).find("employeeName").text() +
    "</td><td>" + $(this).find("department").text() +
    "</td><td>" + $(this).find("salary").text() + "</td></tr>");

});

$("tr").eq(0).addClass("header");
$("tr:even:gt(0)").addClass("evenRow");
$("tr:odd").addClass("oddRow");
}
```

Listing 9-7. Using the ajax() method to get XML data: changes in the ajax() call

```
$.ajax({
    type: "GET",
    url: "employees.xml",
    dataType: "xml",
    success: processData,
    error: reportError
});
```

Listing 9-8. Content of the employees.xml file

```
<employees>
    <employee>
      <employeeName>Jane Smith</employeeName>
      <department>Marketing</department>
      <salary>$95000</salary>
    </employee>

    <employee>
      <employeeName>John Smith</employeeName>
      <department>Technology</department>
      <salary>$90000</salary>
    </employee>

    <employee>
      <employeeName>Brian Adam</employeeName>
      <department>Sales</department>
      <salary>$72000</salary>
    </employee>
```

```
<employee>
  <employeeName>Mary Jones</employeeName>
  <department>Support</department>
  <salary>$60000</salary>
</employee>

<employee>
  <employeeName>Michael Jefferson</employeeName>
  <department>Technology</department>
  <salary>$85000</salary>
</employee>
</employees>
```

How It Works

After the DOM is ready, the following code is executed:

```
$.ajax({
        type: "GET",
        url: "employees.xml",
        dataType: "xml",
        success: processData,
        error: reportError
});
```

The jQuery ajax() method is executed with the following settings:

- The request type is GET

- The URL resource is employees.xml

- The expected data type of the returned data is xml

- If sending the request and receiving the response is successful, execute the callback function processData

- If there is an error sending the request or receiving the response, execute the callback function reportError

The ajax() method execution sends the request to the server asynchronously. When a response is received from the server, depending on the status, the processData or reportError callback function is executed.

If there is a successful response, the processData() function will be executed, which will in turn execute the following code:

```
$("#ajaxStatusMessage").append("Status: " + status + "<br>");

 var tableRecord="";

  $("#tblEmployee").append("<tr><td>Employee Name</td><td>Department</td><td>Salary</td>");

  $(returnedData).find('employee').each(function(){
    $("#tblEmployee").append(
        "<tr><td>" + $(this).find("employeeName").text() +
```

```
        "</td><td>" + $(this).find("department").text() +
        "</td><td>" + $(this).find("salary").text() + "</td></tr>");

});

$("tr").eq(0).addClass("header");
$("tr:even:gt(0)").addClass("evenRow");
$("tr:odd").addClass("oddRow");
```

Note the following items about this code example:

- $("#ajaxStatusMessage").append("Status: " + status + "<br>") appends the status message to the div tag with the ajaxStatusMessage ID.

- $("#tblEmployee").append("<tr><td>Employee Name</td><td>Department </td><td>Salary</td>") appends the table header to the <table> tag.

- $(returnedData).find('employee').each(function(){...}); finds all the <employee> nodes and iterates over each <employee> node in the XML document.

- $(this).find("employeeName").text() within the <employee> node finds the <employeeName> node and gets its text.

- $(this).find("department").text() within the <employee> node finds the <department> node and gets its text.

- $(this).find("salary").text() within the <employee> node finds the <salary> node and gets its text.

- $("#tblEmployee").append("<tr><td>" + $(this).find("employeeName").text() + "</td><td>" + $(this).find("department").text() + "</td><td>" + $(this).find("salary").text() + "</td></tr>") builds the <tr> record for the table using the text() of the *respective XML nodes* and appends it to the <table> with the id tblEmployee ID.

- After all the records are built and appended to the table, classes are added to the table records to change their CSS properties. Refer to Recipe 9-1 for the code explanation.

Figure 9-5 displays the page after the data is returned from the server and appended to the <table> tag. Figure 9-6 displays the error message if an error occurs while sending the request to the server or while receiving the response from the server.

For this recipe, you can replace the ajax() method call with the following convenience method:

```
$.get("employees.xml", processData, "xml");
```

9-4. Using jQuery AJAX API Calls to Get Data in the JSON Format from the Server
Problem

You want to use jQuery API calls to get data in the JSON format from the server.

Solution

Refer to Recipe 9-1 for the syntax of making a jQuery AJAX call. Listings 9-9 and 9-10 provide the changes to the code in Recipe 9-1 to demonstrate the use of the jQuery AJAX API ajax() method to get the employees data in the JSON format from the server. Listing 9-11 shows the employees.json file.

Listing 9-9. Using the ajax() method to get JSON data: changes to the callback function for the success event

```
function processData(returnedData, status) {
$("#ajaxStatusMessage").append("Status: " + status + "<br>");


console.dir(returnedData);


var tableRecord="";

$("#tblEmployee").append("<tr><td>Employee Name</td><td>Department</td><td>Salary</td>");

for (var i=0; i < returnedData.employees.length; i++) {
    var employee = returnedData.employees[i];

    $("#tblEmployee").append("<tr><td>" + employee.employeeName +
        "</td><td>" + employee.department +
        "</td><td>" + employee.salary + "</td></tr>");
}

$("tr").eq(0).addClass("header");
$("tr:even:gt(0)").addClass("evenRow");
$("tr:odd").addClass("oddRow");
}
```

Listing 9-10. Using the ajax() method to get JSON data: changes to the callback function for the success event

```
$.ajax({
    type: "GET",
    url: "employees.json",
    dataType: "json",
    success: processData,
    error: reportError
});
```

Listing 9-11. Content of the employees.json file

```
{
  "employees":
  [
    {"employeeName":"Jane Smith", "department":"Marketing", "salary":"$95000"},
    {"employeeName":"John Smith", "department":"Technology", "salary":"$90000"},
    {"employeeName":"Brian Adam", "department":"Sales", "salary":"$72000"},
    {"employeeName":"Mary Jones", "department":"Support", "salary":"$60000"},
    {"employeeName":"Michael Jefferson", "department":"Technology", "salary":"$85000"}
  ]
}
```

How It Works

After the DOM is ready, the following code is executed:

```
$.ajax({
        type: "GET",
        url: "employees.json",
        dataType: "json",
        success: processData,
        error: reportError
    });
```

The jQuery ajax() method is executed with the following settings:

- The request type is GET

- The URL resource is employees.json

- The expected data type of the returned data is json

- If sending the request and receiving the response is successful, execute the callback function processData

- If there is an error sending the request or receiving the response, execute the callback function reportError

ajax() method execution sends the request to the server asynchronously. When a response is received from the server, depending on the status, the processData or reportError callback function is executed.

If there is a successful response, processData() function will be executed, which will in turn execute the following code:

```
$("#ajaxStatusMessage").append("Status: " + status + "<br>");

        console.dir(returnedData);

        var tableRecord="";

        $("#tblEmployee").append("<tr><td>Employee Name</td><td>Department</td><td>Salary</td>");

        for (var i=0; i < returnedData.employees.length; i++) {
            var employee = returnedData.employees[i];

            $("#tblEmployee").append("<tr><td>" + employee.employeeName +
                "</td><td>" + employee.department +
                "</td><td>" + employee.salary + "</td></tr>");
        }

        $("tr").eq(0).addClass("header");
        $("tr:even:gt(0)").addClass("evenRow");
        $("tr:odd").addClass("oddRow");
```

Where:

- `$("#ajaxStatusMessage").append("Status: " + status + "<br>")` appends the status message to the Div tag with the `ajaxStatusMessage` ID.

- If the `returnedData` is in string format, you can convert it to the JSON object by using the following syntax:

  `var jsonObj = $.parseJSON(returnedData);`

  If you want to convert the JSON object to the string format for displaying or logging it, you can use the following syntax:

  `var jsonString = JSON.stringify(jsonObj);`

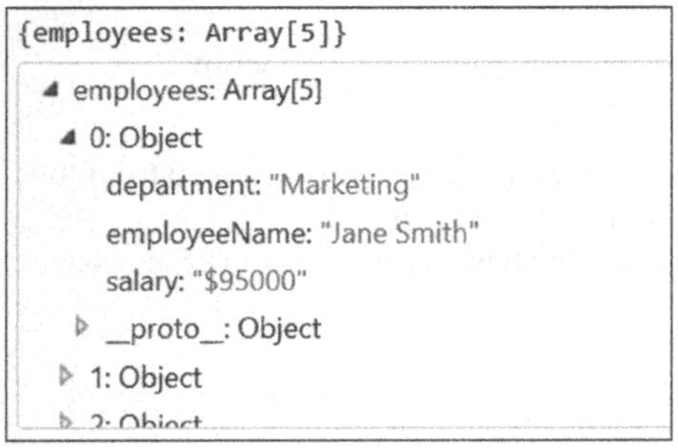

- `console.dir(returnedData)` is used for debugging purposes only to see the structure of the returned data in the JSON format. Figure 9-7 displays the structure of the returned JSON data.`$("#tblEmployee").append("<tr><td>Employee Name</td><td>Department </td><td>Salary</td>")` appends the table header to the `<table>` tag.

```
{employees: Array[5]}

◢ employees: Array[5]
  ◢ 0: Object
      department: "Marketing"
      employeeName: "Jane Smith"
      salary: "$95000"
    ▷ __proto__: Object
  ▷ 1: Object
  ▷ 2: Object
```

Figure 9-7. *Structure of the returned JSON data*

- `for (var i=0; i < returnedData.employees.length; i++){ . . . }` iterates over each array element in the array of `employees` objects.

- `var employee = returnedData.employees[i]` gets an employee record from the array.

- `employee.employeeName` gets the `employeeName` property of the current employee record.

- `employee.department` gets the `department` property of the current employee record.

- `employee.salary` gets the `salary` property of the current employee record.

- `$("#tblEmployee").append("<tr><td>" + employee.employeeName + "</td><td>" + employee.department + "</td><td>" + employee.salary + "</td></tr>")` builds the `<tr>` record for the table using the `employeeName`, `department` and `salary` property values and appends it to the `<table>` with the `tblEmployee` ID.

- After all records are built and appended to the table, classes are added to the table records to change their CSS properties. Refer to Recipe 9-1 for the code explanation.

Figure 9-5 displays the page after the data is returned from the server and appended to the `<table>` tag. Figure 9-6 displays the error message if an error occurs while the request is being sent or the response is being received.

Convenience Methods

For this recipe, you can replace the ajax() method call with the following convenience method:

```
$.get("employees.json", processData, "json");
```

You can also use another convenience method that's available specifically for the JSON data type:

```
$.getJSON("employees.json", processData);
```

The following is the syntax to use the getJSON() method:

```
$.getJSON( url, data, successCallbackFunction)
```

where data is the data you want to send to the server and successCallbackFunction is the function that's executed if the response is received successfully. data and successCallbackFunction are optional arguments.

9-5. Using jQuery AJAX API Calls to Get the Script from the Server
Problem

You want to use jQuery API calls to get the script from the server. This feature is useful when the JavaScript logic is dependent on the user interaction or on certain criteria that's known at runtime. Instead of adding complex JavaScript code to the HTML file, the server can deliver the script to the browser at runtime.

Solution

Refer to Recipe 9-1 for the syntax of making a jQuery AJAX call. Listings 9-12 and 9-13 provide the changes to the code in Recipe 9-1 to demonstrate the use of the jQuery AJAX API ajax() method to get the script from the server. Listing 9-11 provides the content of the employees.json file. In the success callback function, another AJAX call is made by using the convenience method $.getScript(), which gets the JavaScript code from the server and executes it. Listing 9-14 shows the JavaScript code in the employees.js file.

Listing 9-12. Using the ajax() method to get JSON data and getScript() to get JavaScript code: changes to the callback function for the success event

```
function processData(returnedData, status) {
    $("#ajaxStatusMessage").append("Status: " + status + "<br>");

    var tableRecord="";

    $("#tblEmployee").append("<tr><td>Employee Name</td><td>Department</td><td>Salary</td>");

    for (var i=0; i < returnedData.employees.length; i++) {
        var employee = returnedData.employees[i];

        $("#tblEmployee").append("<tr><td>" + employee.employeeName +
                "</td><td>" + employee.department +
            "</td><td>" + employee.salary + "</td></tr>");
    }

    $.getScript("employees.js");
}
```

Listing 9-13. Using the ajax( ) method to get JSON data and getScript( ) to get the JavaScript code: changes to the ajax( ) call

```
$.ajax({
  type: "GET",
  url: "employees.json",
  dataType: "json",
  success: processData,
  error: reportError
});
```

Listing 9-14. Content of the employees.js file

```
$("tr").eq(0).addClass("header");
$("tr:even:gt(0)").addClass("evenRow");
$("tr:odd").addClass("oddRow");
```

How It Works

Refer to Recipe 9-4 for the ajax() call code explanation for the JSON dataType and for the success callback function. In the processData() success callback function, another AJAX call gets the script by using the $.getScript ("employees.js") code. The getScript method gets the JavaScript code from the server and executes it.

Figure 9-5 displays the page after the data is returned from the server and appended to the <table> tag. Figure 9-6 displays an error message if an error occurs when sending the request or when receiving the response.

9-6. Sending Data to the Server Using a GET Request Method
Problem

You want to use jQuery API calls to send data to the server so that the server can send the information back, based on the data received with the request.

Solution

The following is syntax to send data to the server using the GET request method:

```
$.ajax(settingsMapObject)

where, settingsMapObject is
    {
      type: "GET",
      url: "requestUrl",
      data: "param1=paramValue1& param2=paramValue2&...",
      dataType: "text", // html, xml, json
      success: successCallbackFunction,
      error: errorCallbackFunction
    }

function  successCallbackFunction(returnedData, status) { ... }
function  errorCallbackFunction(request, status, errorMsg) { ... }
```

The data is the data to be sent to the server. Its value can be either a string in the *querystring* format, such as "param1=paramValue1&param2=paramValue2,...", or the map object in the key/value pairs form {param1:'paramValue1', param2:'paramValue2', ...}. If any parameter has multiple values, the same parameter name can be specified multiple times with the different parameter values. While sending the request to the server, the URL gets converted to requestUrl?param1=paramValue1& param2=paramValue2&...

If the data you want to send to the server is contained in form fields, you can use jQuery helper function serialize() to convert the form's elements value to the query string format. Listing 9-15 provides an example to send form data to the server in the querystring format. Since server side coding to filter the data, based on the passed value, is out of the scope of this chapter, this recipe will get the response back from a file instead of from a processing resource (web service) on the server side. Listing 9-11 provides the content of the employees.json file.

Listing 9-15. Using the ajax() method to make an AJAX call with data using the GET request method

```html
<!DOCTYPE html>
<html lang="en">
<head>
    <meta charset="utf-8">
    <script src="scripts/jquery-2.1.0.min.js"></script>
    <style>
      div {
            border:3px double green;
            width: 500px;
            background-color: lightcyan;
      }

      form {
            border:3px double green;
            width: 400px;
            padding: 20px;
            background-color: lightyellow;
      }

      table {
            border:0px;
      }

      td {
            padding-right: 10px;
            padding-left: 10px;
      }

      label {
            float:left;
            display:block;
            width: 250px;
            font-weight: bold;
      }

      .header {
            font-weight: bold;
            background-color: lightgray;
      }
```

```
    .evenRow {
        background-color: lightyellow;
    }

    .oddRow {
        background-color: lightblue;
    }

    .errMsg {
        background-color: orange;
        color: white;
        font-weight: bold;
        width: 600px;
    }
</style>

<script>
    function processData(returnedData, status) {
        $("#ajaxStatusMessage").append("Status: " + status + " <br>");

        var tableRecord="";
        var enteredDepartment = $("#txtDepartment").val().toLowerCase().trim();
        var enteredSalary = 0;

            if ($("#txtSalary").val() != "") {
            enteredSalary = parseFloat($("#txtSalary").val());
        }


        $("#tblEmployee").append("<tr><td>Employee Name</td><td>Department</td><td>Salary</td>");

        for (var i=0; i < returnedData.employees.length; i++) {
          var employee = returnedData.employees[i];

          var salary = parseFloat(employee.salary.replace("$",""));
          var department = employee.department.toLowerCase().trim();

          // Filter records
          if (salary >=enteredSalary && (enteredDepartment == "" || enteredDepartment ==
              department)) {
            $("#tblEmployee").append("<tr><td>" + employee.employeeName +
                "</td><td>" + employee.department +
                "</td><td>" + employee.salary + "</td></tr>");
          }
        }

        $("tr").eq(0).addClass("header");
        $("tr:even:gt(0)").addClass("evenRow");
        $("tr:odd").addClass("oddRow");
    }
```

```
      function reportError(request, status, errorMsg) {
          $("#ajaxStatusMessage").append("Status: " + status + "<br>Error Message: " + errorMsg);
          $("#ajaxStatusMessage").addClass("errMsg");
      }

      $(function () {
          $("#btnSubmit").click( function (eventObj) {
              eventObj.preventDefault();

              $.ajax({
                  type: "GET",
                  url: "employees.json",
                  data: $("form").serialize(),
                  dataType: "json",
                  success: processData,
                  error: reportError
              });

              $("#ajaxStatusMessage").append("Parameter Sent to the server: " + $("form").
                serialize() + "<br>");

          });
      });
  </script>
</head>

<body>
    <h4>Employee Search Criteria:</h4>
    <form id="frmSearch">
      <label for="txtDepartment">Department Name:</label>
      <input type="text" id="txtDepartment" name="txtDepartment"><br>

      <label for="txtSalary">Salary (greater than or equal to):</label>
      <input type="text" id="txtSalary" name="txtSalary"><br><br>

      <button id="btnSubmit">Submit</button>
    </form><br><br>

    <div id="ajaxStatusMessage"></div><br>

    Search Result:
    <table id="tblEmployee"></table><br><br>
</body>
</html>
```

How It Works

In this example, filtering is done at the client side in the JavaScript code. In the real-world application, filtering logic is implemented on the server side to reduce the network traffic between the server and the browser. Since server side coding is out of the scope of this book, this example uses client-side filtering.

Most of the code in these listings is explained in Recipe 9-4. The following are the only differences:

- An AJAX call is made when the Submit button is clicked.

- `eventObj.preventDefault()` is used to prevent the default form's submission process.

- `data: $("form").serialize()` is passed as a setting for the `ajax()` call. `$("form").serialize()` converts the form's data entry elements in the querystring form, i.e., in the form `txtDepartment=Technology&txtSalary=80000` if the data entered for the Department field is Technology and the Salary is 80,000. One point to remember is that form elements (such as input, select, and so on) will be used to build the querystring only if their name attribute is set.

  If you want to send data from few elements only instead of sending all data entry form fields, you can use the following syntax:

  `$(selector).serialize()`

  If you want to convert data from an object or an array into a querystring format, you can use the helper function `$.param(objName)`. For example,

  `var mapObj = {employeeName: "John Smith",  department: "Technology"};`

  can be converted to a querystring by using:

  `var querystring = $.param(mapObj)`

  The value of the querystring will be:

  employeeName=John+Smith&department=Technology

- The `div` tag with the ID `ajaxStatusMessage` is set to display the data being passed to the server.

Figure 9-8 displays the initial page when displayed in the browser.

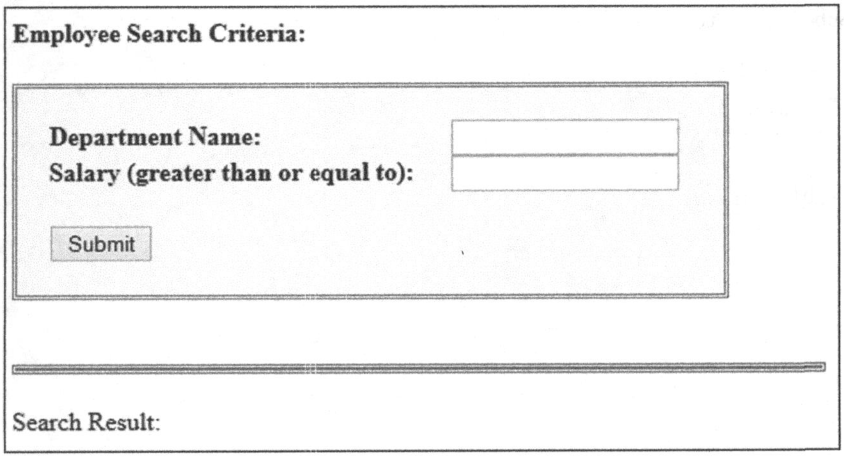

Employee Search Criteria:

Department Name:
Salary (greater than or equal to):

Submit

Search Result:

Figure 9-8. Displaying the initial page

Figure 9-9 displays the page when the Department name is Technology, the Salary is 85,000, and the Submit button is clicked.

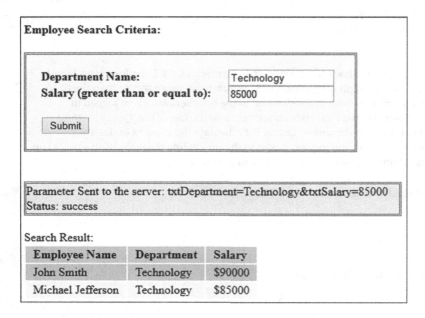

Figure 9-9. *Displaying the search result*

9-7. Sending Form Data to the Server Using a POST Request Method
Problem

You want to use jQuery API calls to send data to the server so that server can process the data and/or save it.

Solution

The following is syntax to send form data to the server using the POST request method:

```
$.ajax(settingsMapObject)
```

where, *settingsMapObject* is

```
{
    type: "POST",
    url: "requestUrl",
    data: $(form).serializeArray(),
    dataType: "text",
    success: successCallbackFunction,
    error: errorCallbackFunction
}

function successCallbackFunction(returnedData, status) { ... }
function errorCallbackFunction(request, status, errorMsg) { ... }
```

If the data you want to send to the server is contained in form fields, you can use jQuery helper function serializeArray() to convert the form's elements' values to an array of names and values, as so:

```
[ {name: "formFieldName1", value: "formFieldValue1"},
  {name: "formFieldName2", value: "formFieldValue2"},
.....]
```

Name/value pairs are sent in the HTTP message body for the POST request method. GET requests have length restrictions where as POST requests have no data length restrictions. POST requests are more secure than the GET method because name value pairs cannot be cached, bookmarked, saved in the browser history, or logged in the server logs. Listing 9-16 demonstrates the use of the POST request method and the use of the jQuery method serializeArray() to get the form's data to be sent to the server. Listing 9-17 displays the content of the file createNewEmployee.json. In real-world applications, the request is sent to the processing resource (web service) on the server side. An appropriate status, based on the processing result, is sent back as a response.

Listing 9-16. Using the ajax( ) method to send form data using the POST request method

```
<!DOCTYPE html>
<html lang="en">
<head>
    <meta charset="utf-8">
    <script src="scripts/jquery-2.1.0.min.js"></script>
    <style>
      div {
            border:3px double green;
            width: 400px;
            background-color: lightcyan;
            padding: 10px;
      }

      form {
            border:3px double green;
            width: 400px;
            padding: 20px;
            background-color: lightyellow;
      }

      table {
            border:0px;
      }

      td {
            padding-right: 10px;
            padding-left: 10px;
      }

      label {
            float:left;
            display:block;
            width: 175px;
            font-weight: bold;
      }
```

```
    .header {
        font-weight: bold;
        background-color: lightgray;
    }

    .evenRow {
        background-color: lightyellow;
    }

    .oddRow {
        background-color: lightblue;
    }

    .errMsg {
        background-color: orange;
        color: white;
        font-weight: bold;
        width: 400px;
    }
</style>

<script>
  function processData(returnedData, status) {
      $("#ajaxStatusMessage").append("Status: " + status + "<br>");

      if (returnedData.processingStatus == "Successful") {
        $("#processingResult").append("New employee record is created successfully.");
      } else {
        $("#processingResult").append("Failed to create new employee record.");
        $("#processingResult").addClass("errMsg");
      }
  }

  function reportError(request, status, errorMsg) {
      $("#ajaxStatusMessage").append("Status: " + status + "<br>Error Message: " + errorMsg);
      $("#ajaxStatusMessage").addClass("errMsg");
  }

  $(function () {
      $("#btnCreateNew").click( function (eventObj) {
        eventObj.preventDefault();

        $.ajax({
            type: "POST",
            url: "createNewEmployee.json",
            data: $("form").serializeArray(),
            dataType: "json",
            success: processData,
            error: reportError
        });
```

```
                    var fields = "";
                    $.each( $("form").serializeArray(), function( i, field ) {
                        fields += "[Key: " + field.name + " Value: " + field.value + "]<br>";
                    });

                    $("#ajaxStatusMessage").append("Data Sent to the server: <br>" + fields + "<br>");

                });
            });
        </script>
    </head>

<body>
    <h4>New Employee:</h4>
    <form id="frmSearch">
      <label for="txtEmployeeName">Employee's Name:</label>
      <input type="text" id="txtEmployeeName" name="txtEmployeeName"><br>

      <label for="txtDepartment">Department Name:</label>
      <input type="text" id="txtDepartment" name="txtDepartment"><br>

      <label for="txtSalary">Salary (greater than):</label>
      <input type="text" id="txtSalary" name="txtSalary"><br><br>

      <button id="btnCreateNew">Create New Employee Record</button>
    </form><br><br>

    <div id="ajaxStatusMessage"></div><br>

    Processing Result:
    <div id="processingResult"></div><br><br><br>
</body>
</html>
```

Listing 9-17. Content of the createNewEmployee.json file

```
{"processingStatus": "Successful"}
```

How It Works

If Create New Employee Record is clicked after the DOM is created, the following code is executed:

```
eventObj.preventDefault();
  $.ajax({
      type: "POST",
      url: "createNewEmployee.json",
      data: $("form").serializeArray(),
      dataType: "json",
      success: processData,
      error: reportError
});
```

```
var fields = "";
$.each( $("form").serializeArray(), function( i, field ) {
    fields += "[Key: " + field.name + " Value: " + field.value + "]<br>";
});
```

```
$("#ajaxStatusMessage").append("Data Sent to the server: <br>" + fields + "<br>");
```

Where:

- eventObj.preventDefault() is used to prevent the default form's submission process.

- type: "POST" specifies that you want to send the request as POST.

- data: $("form").serializeArray() serializes the form data-entry elements as an array with name/value pairs. In order to get the value of the data-entry form elements, elements should have a name attribute and a value.

If you want to send data from a few elements only instead of sending all the data-entry form fields, you can use the following syntax:

```
$(selector).serializeArray()
```

If you want to convert data from an object or an array into a querystring format, you can use the helper function $.param(objName). For example:

```
var mapObj = {employeeName: "John Smith",  department: "Technology"};
```

can be converted to a querystring by using:

```
var querystring = $.param(mapObj)
```

The value of the querystring will be:

employeeName=John+Smith&department=Technology

You can use any of the jQuery helper functions—$.param(mapObj), $.param(arrayObj), $(selector).serialize(), and $(selector).serializeArray()—to set the data in the ajax() method for the GET and POST request methods.

```
$.each( $("form").serializeArray(), function( i, field ) {
    fields += "[Key: " + field.name + " Value: " + field.value + "]<br>";
});
```

```
$("#ajaxStatusMessage").append("Data Sent to the server: <br>" + fields + "<br>");
```

This code iterates over the name/value pairs in the array, sets the fields variable with the pairs values, and displays it on the page.

When there is a successful response from the server, the processData() callback function is executed with the following code:

```
$("#ajaxStatusMessage").append("Status: " + status + "<br>");

if (returnedData.processingStatus == "Successful") {
  $("#processingResult").append("New employee record is created successfully.");
} else {
  $("#processingResult").append("Failed to create new employee record.");
  ("#processingResult").addClass("errMsg");
}
```

Where:

- $("#ajaxStatusMessage").append("Status: " + status + "<br>") displays the response status on the page.

- If the returned JSON object (returnedData) has the processingStatus as "Successful", the message "New employee record is created succesfully" is displayed on the page; otherwise, "Failed to create new employee record." is displayed.

Figure 9-10 displays the initial page when displayed in the browser.

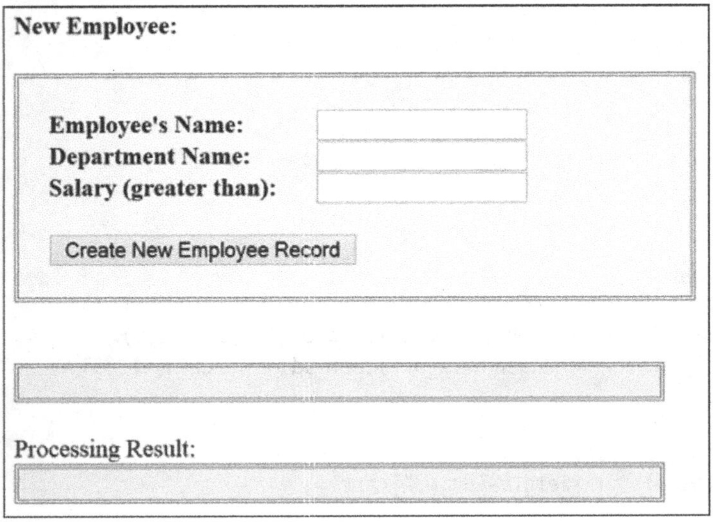

Figure 9-10. *Displaying the initial page*

Figure 9-11 displays the page after new employee's information is entered and the Create New Employee Record button is clicked.

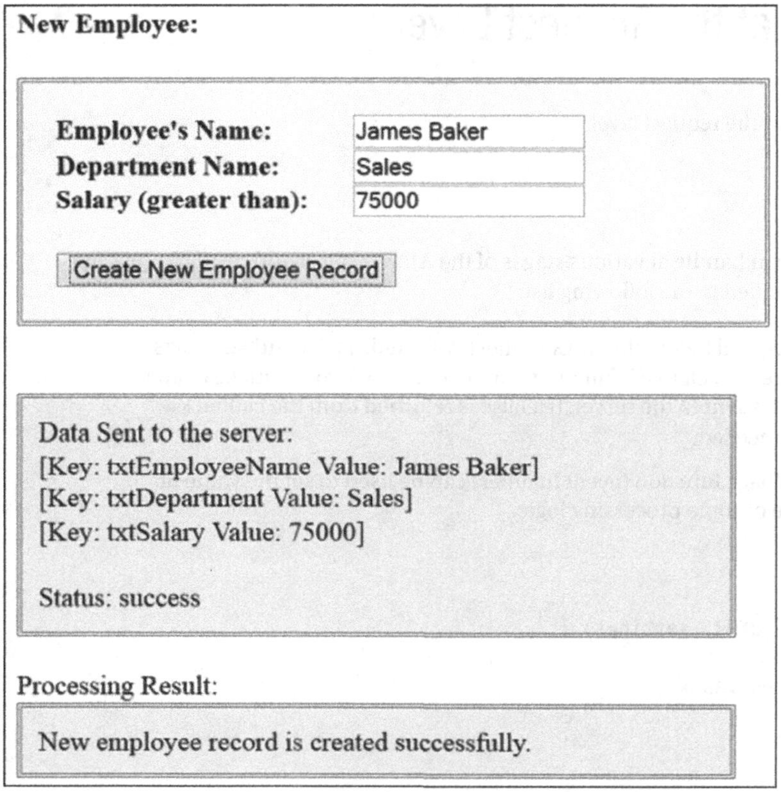

New Employee:

Employee's Name: James Baker
Department Name: Sales
Salary (greater than):   75000

    Create New Employee Record

Data Sent to the server:
[Key: txtEmployeeName Value: James Baker]
[Key: txtDepartment Value: Sales]
[Key: txtSalary Value: 75000]

Status: success

Processing Result:

New employee record is created successfully.

Figure 9-11. *Displaying the data sent to the server and the successful response back from the server*

For this recipe, you can replace the `ajax()` method call with the following convenience method:

```
$.post("createNewEmployee.json",
                  $("form").serializeArray(),
                   processData,
                   "json");
```

The following is the syntax for the `post()` convenience method:

```
$.post(url, data, successCallbackFunction, dataType)
```

where *data* is the data you want to send to the server. `successCallbackFunction` is the callback function that will be called when there's a successful response from the server. The data, `successCallbackFunction`, and `dataType` arguments are optional. You can handle error conditions by setting the global error handler using `ajaxError(errorHandler)`. These are covered in Recipes 9-9 and 9-10.

9-8. Using AJAX Events at the Request Level
Problem
You want to know how to use AJAX events at the request level.

Solution
The following is the list of events that you can handle at various stages of the AJAX request and response process. These events are triggered in the order specified in the following list:

- beforeSend —This event is triggered before the AJAX request is started. jqXHR and settings are the arguments to the beforeSend callback function. This event allows you to make changes to the request settings before it is sent to the server. If a false is returned from the callback function, the request will be cancelled.

  For example, the following callback function (event handler) can be used to set the value of the URL based on the outcome of some processing logic:

  ```
  $.ajax({
      ....
      beforeSend: function(jqXHR, settings) {
      // Processing logic
      settings.url = "/process.asmx";
      }
  });
  ```

- dataFilter—This event is triggered only if the request is successful. The raw data (as a string) is returned from the server and the dataType are the arguments to the dataFilter callback function. In the callback function you can clean up the data and return updated data.

  ```
  $.ajax({
      ....
      dataFilter: function(returnedData, dataType) {
      // Processing logic to update returnedData
      var updatedData = returnedData;
      return(updatedData);
      }
  });
  ```

- success—This event is triggered only if the request is successful. The returned data (in the specified dataType format)—status as string and jqXHR object—are the arguments to the success callback function. For this event, multiple callback functions can be specified as an array of functions. Each callback function will be executed in the order specified. The following is the syntax for specifying multiple callback functions:

  ```
  success: [function1, function2, ...]
  ```

In the callback function of this event, you process the returned data from the server. Some examples are:

- Create/update HTML elements and CSS properties

- Make another AJAX call:

```
$.ajax({
    ....
    success: function(returnedData, status, jqXHR) {
    // Processing logic
    $(selector).append(returnedData);
    }
});
```

- error—This event is triggered only if the request is failed. jqXHR object, status, and errorMessage are the arguments to the error callback function. Possible values for status are error, abort, timeout, and parsererror. For this event, multiple callback functions can be specified as an array of functions. Each callback function is executed in the order specified.
  In the callback function of this event, you can display a message to the user with the user-friendly error message or retry the AJAX call if timeout occurred.

```
$.ajax({
        ....
        error: function(jqXHR, status, errorMessage) {
    // Display error message
    $(selector).append("Status: " + status + " Error Message: " + errorMessage);
        }
});
```

- complete—This event is triggered when request is completed. The jqXHR object and status are the arguments to the error callback function. Possible values for status are success, error, notmodified, abort, timeout, and parsererror. For this event, multiple callback functions can be specified as an array of functions. Each callback function is executed in the order specified.

  In the callback function of this event, you can display the progress bar as 100% completed to indicate that the request has completed successfully or has failed.

```
$.ajax({
    ....
    complete: function(jqXHR, status) {
    // Display message
    $(selector).append("Processing completed with the status: " + status);
    }
});
```

If you want to list an object's properties and values, you can use the console.dir(objName) statement. This will display an object's content in the browser.

You will use all of these request-level events in Recipe 9-10.

9-9. Using AJAX Events at the Global Level
Problem

You want to know how to use AJAX events at the global level.

Solution

The following is the list of global AJAX events that you can use at various stages of AJAX request and response process in the document. Callback functions for these events are at the document (web page) level. By default, global event handler are called for all AJAX requests on the page. To prevent execution of these global event handlers, you can set global options as false in the ajax() method:

```
$.ajax({
    ....
    global: false;
});
```

- ajaxStart—This event is triggered when the first AJAX request is started and there is no active AJAX request in progress. If all the AJAX requests are completed and a new AJAX request is about to be sent, the ajaxStart event will be triggered again. The event object is the only argument passed to the ajaxStart event handler. The following syntax is used to register an ajaxStart event handler:

  ```
  $(document).on("ajaxStart", startCallbackFunction)
  or
  $(document). ajaxStart(startCallbackFunction)
  ```

- jaxSend—This event is triggered before an AJAX request is sent. The event object, jqXHR, and settings object are the arguments passed to the ajaxSend event handler. The following syntax is used to register an ajaxSend event handler:

  ```
  $(document).on("ajaxSend", sendCallbackFunction)
  or
  $(document). ajaxSend(sendCallbackFunction)
  ```

- ajaxSuccess—This event is triggered only if an AJAX request is successful. The event object, jqXHR, and settings object are the arguments passed to the ajaxSuccess event handler. The following syntax is used to register an ajaxSuccess event handler:

  ```
  $(document).on("ajaxSuccess", successCallbackFunction)
  or
  $(document). ajaxSuccess(succesCallbackFunction)
  ```

- ajaxError—This event is triggered only if an AJAX request fails. The event object, jqXHR, settings object, and an error message are the arguments passed to the ajaxError event handler. The following syntax is used to register an ajaxError event handler:

  ```
  $(document).on("ajaxError", errorCallbackFunction)
  or
  $(document). ajaxError(errorCallbackFunction)
  ```

- ajaxComplete—This event is triggered when an AJAX request is completed, regardless of whether the request has completed successfully or failed. The event object, jqXHR, and settings object are the arguments passed to the ajaxComplete event handler. The following syntax is used to register an ajaxComplete event handler:

```
$(document).on("ajaxComplete", completeCallbackFunction)
or
$(document). ajaxComplete(completeCallbackFunction)
```

- ajaxStop—This event is triggered when all AJAX requests are completed. The event object is the only argument passed to the ajaxStop event handler. After the ajaxStop event is triggered, if a new AJAX request is started, the whole cycle of events will restart beginning with ajaxStart. The following syntax is used to register an ajaxStop event handler:

```
$(document).on("ajaxStop", stopCallbackFunction)
or
$(document). ajaxStop(stopCallbackFunction)
```

If you want to list an object's properties and their values, you can use console.dir(objName). This will display an object's content in the browser.

You will use all of these request-level events in Recipe 9-10.

9-10. Order of AJAX Events at the Request and Global Levels
Problem

You want to know the order in which AJAX events are triggered during the lifecycle of an AJAX request.

Solution

Listing 9-18 demonstrates the order of AJAX events triggering. It shows all the global and request-level events that are triggered for a successful AJAX request as well as for a failed AJAX request. This code listing has event handlers (with arguments) for all AJAX events triggered at the document and request levels. Listing 9-19 shows the testMessage.txt file.

Listing 9-18. The order of triggering AJAX events

```
<!DOCTYPE html>
<html lang="en">
<head>
    <meta charset="utf-8">
    <script src="scripts/jquery-2.1.0.min.js"></script>
    <script>
    // Global AJAX events callbacks
    function ajaxSuccessCallback(eventObj, jqXHR, settingsObj) {
        $("#status").append("Global event - ajaxSuccess.<br>");
    }

    function ajaxSendCallback(eventObj, jqXHR, settingsObj) {
        $("#status").append("Global event - ajaxSend.<br>");
    }
```

```javascript
        function ajaxStartCallback(eventObj) {
            $("#status").append("Global event - ajaxStart.<br>");
        }

        function ajaxStopCallback(eventObj) {
            $("#status").append("Global event - ajaxStop.<br>");
        }

        function ajaxErrorCallback(eventObj, jqXHR, settingsObj) {
            $("#status").append("Global event - ajaxError.<br>");
        }

        function ajaxCompleteCallback(eventObj, jqXHR, settingsObj) {
            $("#status").append("Global event - ajaxComplete.<br>");
        }

        // AJAX events callbacks at the request level
        function requestBeforeSendCallback(jqXHR, settingsObj) {
            $("#status").append("Request event - beforeSend.<br>");
        }

        function requestCompleteCallback(jqXHR, status) {
            $("#status").append("Request event - complete.<br>");
        }

        function requestDataFilterCallback(returnedData, dataType) {
            $("#status").append("Request event - dataFilter.<br>");
        }

        function requestErrorCallback(jqXHR, status, errorMessage) {
            $("#status").append("Request event - error.<br>");
        }

        function requestSuccessCallback(returnedData, status, jqXHR) {
            $("#status").append("Request event - success.<br>");
        }

        $(function () {
            $(document).on("ajaxSend", ajaxSendCallback);
            $(document).on("ajaxSuccess", ajaxSuccessCallback);
            $(document).on("ajaxError", ajaxErrorCallback);
            $(document).on("ajaxComplete", ajaxCompleteCallback);
            $(document).on("ajaxStart", ajaxStartCallback);
            $(document).on("ajaxStop", ajaxStopCallback);

            $("#btnSuccess").click(function () {
              $("#status").empty();

              $.ajax(
                  {
                      type: "GET",
```

```
                    url: "testMessage.txt",
                    beforeSend: requestBeforeSendCallback,
                    complete: requestCompleteCallback,
                    dataFilter: requestDataFilterCallback,
                    error: requestErrorCallback,
                    success: requestSuccessCallback,
                    data: null,
                    dataType: "text"
                });

        });

        $("#btnFailed").click(function () {
          $("#status").empty();

          $.ajax(
                {
                    type: "GET",
                    url: "incorrect.txt",
                    beforeSend: requestBeforeSendCallback,
                    complete: requestCompleteCallback,
                    dataFilter: requestDataFilterCallback,
                    error: requestErrorCallback,
                    success: requestSuccessCallback,
                    data: null,
                    dataType: "text" //script: execute response as a script.
                });
        });
    });
    </script>
</head>

<body>

    <button id="btnSuccess">Start Successful Ajax Call</button>
    <button id="btnFailed">Start Unsuccessful Ajax Call</button><br><br>

    <div id="status"></div>
</body>
</html>
```

Listing 9-19. Content of the testMessage.txt file

```
Test Message
```

How It Works

After the DOM is created, event handlers for all global-level AJAX events are registered by using the following code:

```
$(document).on("ajaxSend", ajaxSendCallback);
$(document).on("ajaxSuccess", ajaxSuccessCallback);
$(document).on("ajaxError", ajaxErrorCallback);
$(document).on("ajaxComplete", ajaxCompleteCallback);
$(document).on("ajaxStart", ajaxStartCallback);
$(document).on("ajaxStop", ajaxStopCallback);
```

When the Start Successful Ajax Call button is clicked, the following AJAX code is executed to register request-level event handlers for the events—beforeSend, complete, dataFilter, error, and success.

```
$.ajax(
    {
        type: "GET",
        url: "testMessage.txt",
        beforeSend: requestBeforeSendCallback,
        complete: requestCompleteCallback,
        dataFilter: requestDataFilterCallback,
        error: requestErrorCallback,
        success: requestSuccessCallback,
        data: null,
        dataType: "text"
  });
```

When the Start Unsuccessful Ajax Call button is clicked, the following AJAX code is executed to register request-level event handlers for the beforeSend, complete, dataFilter, error, and success events. The only difference in this case is the URL setting, which uses a filename that doesn't exist. This is to simulate an error condition.

```
$.ajax(
    {
        type: "GET",
        url: " incorrect.txt",
        beforeSend: requestBeforeSendCallback,
        complete: requestCompleteCallback,
        dataFilter: requestDataFilterCallback,
        error: requestErrorCallback,
        success: requestSuccessCallback,
        data: null,
        dataType: "text"
  });
```

In all the registered event handlers, the div tag with the ID status is set to display the message with the name of the event handler being executed using the code. For example, $("#status").append("Request event - success.
").

Figure 9-12 displays the list of event handlers that are executed when the user clicks the Start Successful Ajax Call button.

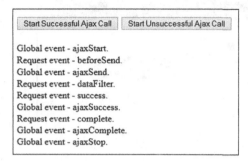

Figure 9-12. *Displaying a list of events that occurred during a successful AJAX request*

Figure 9-13 displays the list of event handlers that are executed when the user clicks the Start Unsuccessful Ajax Call button.

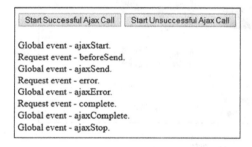

Figure 9-13. *Displaying a list of events that occurred during a successful AJAX request*

Figures 9-14 displays a flowchart of an AJAX events chain for a successful and a failed AJAX request.

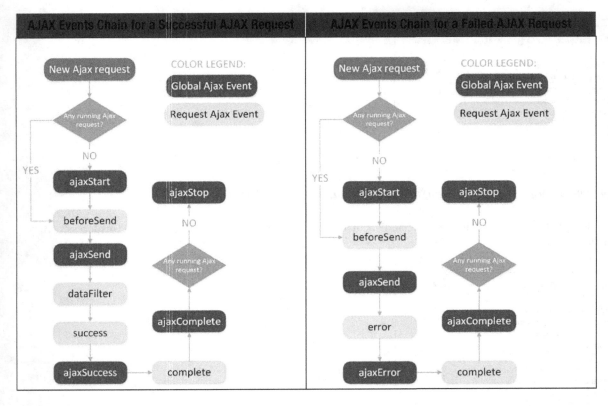

Figure 9-14. *Flowchart of events triggered during successful and failed AJAX requests*

Summary

This chapter covered topics related to jQuery AJAX methods and events. You learned:

- The advantages and disadvantages of using AJAX calls.
- How to make jQuery AJAX calls using the primary $.ajax() method and the convenience methods: $.get(), $.getJSON(), $.getScript(), $.post() and $(selector).load().
- How to make GET and POST requests to the server.
- How to send data to the server.
- How to process data returned from the server in different formats—text, HTML, XML, and JSON.
- How to handle error conditions.
- How to use jQuery helper functions: $(selector).serialize(), $(selector). serializeArray(), and $.param(obj).
- How to use $.parseJSON(jsonString) and JSON.stringify(jsonObj) to handle JSON data.
- The purpose and order of AJAX event handlers at the document and request levels.

CHAPTER 10

jQuery UI

jQuery UI is a plug-in built on top of the jQuery library. It is used for developing highly interactive user interface web applications with a consistent look and feel. This chapter covers recipes that implement widgets, effects, and user interaction using jQuery UI components, such as options, methods, and events. In this chapter and in Chapters 11 and 12, you will build real-world web applications using the concepts covered in previous chapters, including jQuery selectors, DOM traversing and manipulation, event handling, effects, animations, and using AJAX.

Creating Widgets

Widgets are objects that have properties (options), methods, and events. The sections explain how to create a widget, set its options, execute its methods, and specify its callback functions.

Creating Widgets and Setting Options

Widgets are created by specifying the <input>, <div>, <a>, or <ul> tags in the HTML code and then calling the widget constructor method in the JavaScript code. jQuery selectors are used to select the HTML elements you want to convert into widgets. You can specify a widget's options at the time of its creation or later, whenever it is needed.

The following is the syntax to create a widget:

```
$(selector).widgetName(options)
```

where options is a map object with optionName and optionValue pairs. Valid optionNames and optionValues are widget-specific. This syntax can also be represented as:

```
$(selector).widgetName({ optionName1: optionValue1,
                optionName2: optionValue2,
             ...
                });
```

optionNames and optionValues are optional. The Disabled option is common to all widgets—if it is set to true, the widget is disabled. By default, its value is false.

Executing a Widget's Methods

The following syntax is used to execute a widget's method:

```
var returnValue =  $(selector).widgetName(methodName, argument1, argument2, ...)
```

In most cases, the return value of the method execution is the jQuery object. Table 10-1 lists methods that are common to all widgets.

Table 10-1. *Common Widget Methods*

Method	Description
a.destroy()	Removes the widget completely. The HTML element is returned to its initial state.
	Syntax: $(selector).widgetName("destroy");
disable()	Disables the widget. Widget is grayed out and the user can't enter any data. For jQuery UI widgets, you cannot disable the widget by setting its disabled property to true.
	Syntax: $(selector).widgetName("disable");
enable()	Enables the widget. For jQuery UI widgets, you cannot enable the widget by setting its disabled property to false.
	Syntax: $(selector).widgetName("enable");
option(optionName)	Gets the value of the optionName of the widget.
	Syntax: $(selector).widgetName("option", "optionName");
option()	Returns the options map object containing optionName optionValue pairs.
	Syntax: var optionsMapObj = $(selector).widgetName(option);
option(optionName, optionValue)	Sets the value of the optionName as optionValue for the widget.
	Syntax: $(selector).widgetName("option", "optionName", "optionValue");
option(optionMapObject)	Sets the value of all optionNames with the corresponding optionValue specified in the optionMapObject.
	Syntax: $(selector).widgetName("option", {"optionName1" : "optionValue1", "optionName2" : "optionValue2", ... });

Setting Callback Functions

The following syntax is used to specify the callback functions for the widget's events:

```
$(selector). widgetName ({
    eventName1: function(eventObj, uiObj) {...},
    eventName2: function(eventObj, uiObj) {...}
    ...
});
```

where eventObj is an event object, as described in Chapter 7, and uiObj is the object containing information specific to the widget that triggered the event. Options and event callback functions can be specified together as:

```
$(selector). widgetName ({
    "optionName1" : "optionValue1",
    "optionName2" : "optionValue2",
    ...
```

```
    eventName1: function(eventObj, uiObj) {...},
    eventName2: function(eventObj, uiObj) {...}
    ...
});
```

This chapter's recipes cover commonly used options, methods, events, and CSS classes for jQuery UI widgets.

Since Chrome and Safari browsers have more strict security policies related to accessing local resources and different versions of Internet Explorer behave differently for AJAX calls, I recommend that you test all the recipes with AJAX calls using the Firefox browser. In order to test in other browsers, deploy the code on a web server and then test them. Refer to the Appendix C for deploying a web application on Apache Tomcat and IIS.

Downloading the jQuery UI Library and Themes

You can download the jQuery UI library and its themes at http://jqueryui.com/download/. At the bottom of the page, you can select the specific theme you want to download. The recipes in this chapter use the Start theme. After selecting the theme, click the Download button and save the file. If you have selected the 1.11.1 version of the jQuery UI, the saved file name will be jquery-ui-1.11.1.custom.zip. Extract all the files from this ZIP file into a work folder.

Copy the jquery-ui.min.css file and the images folder from jquery-ui-1.11.1.custom\ to the styles folder in your web page development root folder. Also copy jquery-ui.min.js from the jquery-ui-1.11.1.custom\js folder to the scripts folder. The structure of your development environment should look like this:

- images/
- scripts/jquery-2.1.0.min.js
- scripts/jquery-ui.min.js
- styles/images/*.png and *.gif
- styles/jquery-ui.min.css
- *.htm

10-1. Using the CSS Framework and Icons
Problem

You want to know how to use the CSS classes and icons provided by the jQuery UI CSS framework.

Solution

The CSS framework provides CSS classes that are applied to all the widgets to create a consistent user interface. The following is the list of commonly used CSS classes and their purposes. Even though these classes are used by the widgets and for building custom widgets, you can also use them for HTML elements in your page.

- ui-widget—Used by the outer container of all widgets.
- ui-widget-header—Used by the header container.
- ui-widget-content—Used by the content container.
- ui-helper-hidden—Hides the content.
- ui-helper-reset—Resets basic styles of the HTML elements.

- ui-state-highlight—Highlights the HTML elements.

- ui-state-error—Applies error condition styles to HTML elements.

- ui-state-disabled—Reduces the opacity of the disabled HTML elements.

Icons

jQuery UI provides a wide range of CSS classes for icons. You can view the complete list of icons at http://api.jqueryui.com/theming/icons/.

Custom Themes

jQuery provides a wide range of themes, which you can download from the jQuery UI web site at http://jqueryui.com/download/. If you want to design and build your own custom theme, you can use ThemeRoller at http://jqueryui.com/themeroller/. You can visually design the theme and download it using ThemeRoller.

10-2. Creating the Autocomplete Widget
Problem

You want to know how to create the autocomplete widget as well as understand its commonly used options, methods, and events.

Solution

This widget gets the filtered list of items as the user types in the text field and displays them in a drop-down. The following is the syntax for creating the autocomplete widget:

```
$(selector).autocomplete()
$(selector).autocomplete(options)
```

An <input> element can be specified as an autocomplete widget. When a user starts typing data in the <input> field, a drop-down list of items is displayed based on the entered data. Items in the drop-down are filtered from the data source, which can be a JavaScript array, URL, or function. A drop-down is basically a menu widget that's created at runtime. Listing 10-1 demonstrates an example that creates the autocomplete widget.

Listing 10-1. Creating the autocomplete widget

```
<!DOCTYPE html>
<html lang="en">
<head>
    <meta charset="utf-8">
    <link rel="stylesheet" href="styles/jquery-ui.min.css">
    <script src="scripts/jquery-2.1.0.min.js"></script>
    <script src="scripts/jquery-ui.min.js"></script>

    <script>
    var departmentsArray = [ "Customer Support", "Implementation", "Infrastructure",
                                        "Marketing", "Production Support", "Sales",
                                                                    "Technology"];
```

```
    $(function() {
        $( "#department" ).autocomplete({
          source: departmentsArray
    });
      });
    </script>
</head>
<body>
    <div class="ui-widget">
     <label for="department">Department Name: </label>
     <input id="department">
    </div>
</body>
</html>
```

How It Works

Within the document ready function of this example, the autocomplete() method sets the input element—with the ID set to department—as an autocomplete widget. The only option used in this example is source, which is set as a JavaScript array—departmentsArray. As the user types data in the input textbox, matched items from the array are selected and displayed in the drop-down. The user can either keep on entering more data to refine the drop-down items or select the value from the drop-down list by using the up and down arrow keys and pressing Enter or by clicking the item with the mouse left key. The CSS class ui-widget is used to set a consistent font family and size to all child nodes. Figure 10-1 displays the page when the user enters sup (for example).

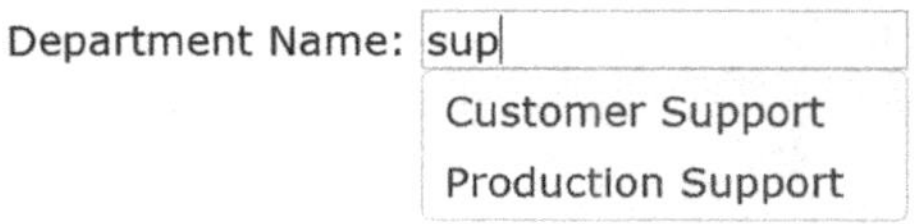

Department Name: sup
Customer Support
Production Support

Figure 10-1. *Filtered items are displayed in the drop-down*

The other commonly used options for the autocomplete widget are:

- *minLength*—Minimum number of characters that the user needs to enter before the search is performed.

- *delay*—Delay in milliseconds after a character is entered and before the search is performed.

The commonly used events for the autocomplete widget are:

- select—Triggered when an item is selected from the drop-down.

- change—Triggered when the value of the widget changes and it loses its focus.

The CSS classes specific to the autocomplete widget are:

- ui-autocomplete—Used for the drop-down menu.

- ui-autocomplete-input—Used for the input textbox, which is set as the autocomplete widget.

This CSS classes can be modified in your custom code. Since these classes are already associated with the widget, there is no need to specify them for the specific HTML element. For example, by specifying following in your code, the background color of the drop-down menu changes to lightyellow.

```
<style>
  .ui-autocomplete { background: lightyellow;}
</style>
```

10-3. Creating the Spinner Widget
Problem

You want to know how to create the spinner widget and understand its commonly used options, methods, and events.

Solution

This widget is used to select a numeric value by pressing up and down arrow keys or by clicking some up and down arrow icons. The following is the syntax for creating the spinner widget:

```
$(selector).spinner()
$(selector).spinner(options)
```

An <input> element can be specified as a spinner widget. When the field has focus, the up and down arrow keys can be used to select a value or the mouse can be used to click an appropriate icon to increment or decrement the value. Listing 10-2 demonstrates an example that creates the spinner widget.

Listing 10-2. Using spinner() to create the spinner widget

```
<!DOCTYPE html>
<html lang="en">
<head>
    <meta charset="utf-8">
    <link rel="stylesheet" href="styles/jquery-ui.min.css">
    <script src="scripts/jquery-2.1.0.min.js"></script>
    <script src="scripts/jquery-ui.min.js"></script>

    <style>
     #txtAge { width:50px; }
    </style>

    <script>
     $(function() {
         $("#txtAge").spinner(
          {
                min:18,
                max:70
          });
```

```
        $("#txtAge").spinner("value", 25);

    });
    </script>
</head>
<body>
    <div class="ui-widget">
      <label for="txtAge">Age:</label>
      <input id="txtAge">
    </div>
</body>
</html>
```

How It Works

Within the document ready function in this example, the spinner() method sets the input element—with the ID set to txtAge—as a spinner widget. The options used in this example are min and max, which specify the range of values that can be selected using this widget. The $("#txtAge").spinner("value", 25) statement sets the value of the selected spinner to 25. Figure 10-2 displays the page when the user clicks on the up and down arrow keys.

Age: | 27 |

Figure 10-2. *Value for the Age field can be selected by using the up and down arrow keys*

The other commonly used option for the spinner widget is:

- step—The amount of increment/decrement with each up/down arrow click. It can be a whole number or a decimal. The default value is 1.

The commonly used methods for the spinner widget are:

- value()—Gets the current value of the spinner widget.

- value(newValue)—Sets the value of the spinner widget with the specified newValue.

The commonly used events for the spinner widget are:

- spin—Triggered when the widget's value is incremented/decremented. ui.value contains the new value. If the callback function returns false, the value of the widget is not changed.

- change—Triggered when value of the widget changes and it loses its focus.

The CSS classes specific to the spinner widget are:

- ui-spinner—Used for the input textbox, which is set as the spinner widget.

- ui-spinner-button—Used for the spinner's up and down arrow buttons.

- ui-spinner-up—Used for the spinner's up arrow button.

- ui-spinner-down—Used for the spinner's down arrow button.

10-4. Creating the Slider Widget

Problem

You want to know how to create the slider widget and understand its commonly used options, methods, and events.

Solution

This widget is used to select a numeric value by dragging a handle. The following is the syntax for creating the slider widget:

```
$(selector).slider()
$(selector).slider(options)
```

A `<div>` element can be specified as a slider widget. A handle on the widget can be moved to increment or decrement the value. Listing 10-3 demonstrates an example that creates the slider widget.

Listing 10-3. Using slider() to create the slider widget

```
<!DOCTYPE html>
<html lang="en">
<head>
    <meta charset="utf-8">
    <link rel="stylesheet" href="styles/jquery-ui.min.css">
    <script src="scripts/jquery-2.1.0.min.js"></script>
    <script src="scripts/jquery-ui.min.js"></script>

    <style>
     #salary { width: 300px; margin: 15px; }
    </style>

    <script>
     $(function() {
        $("#salary").slider(
          {
                min: 50000,
                max: 200000,
                step: 2000,
                slide: function(eventObj, uiWidget) {
                     $("#selectedValue").text("$" + uiWidget.value);
                }
          });

        $("#salary").slider("value", 76000);

          $("#selectedValue").text("$" + $("#salary").slider("value"));
     });
    </script>
</head>
```

```
<body>
    <div class="ui-widget">
     Salary: <div id="salary" value="50000"></div>
     <div id="selectedValue"></div>
    </div>
</body>
</html>
```

How It Works

Within the document ready function of this example, the slider() method sets the div element—with the ID set to salary—as a slider widget. The options used in this example are:

- min and max—Specify the range of values that can be selected using this widget.

- step—Specifies the amount of increment or decrement associated with each handle drag.

During the creation of the widget, a slide event callback function is also specified. The slide event is triggered when the user slides the handle. The slide callback function displays the current value of the widget by setting the text of the div element.

$("#salary").slider("value", 76000) sets the value of the slider widget to 76000.

$("#selectedValue").text("$" + $("#salary").slider("value")) displays the current value of the widget by setting the text of the div element.

Figure 10-3 displays the page when the user slides the handle toward the right to increment the salary by $2,000 with each step.

Salary:

$92000

Figure 10-3. *Value of the Salary field can be selected by sliding the handle*

The other commonly used options for the slider widget are:

- orientation—Specifies if the handle is moved horizontally or vertically. Valid values for this option are horizontal and vertical. The default value is horizontal. If you are setting the orientation to vertical, you also need to set the width style in the <div> tag to:

  `<div id="myId" style="width:13px"></div>`

- range—If set to true, instead of one value, two values (the range's start value and end value) can be selected by using two handles. If it is set to min, the slider widget is highlighted from the "min" value to the handle position. If it is set to max, the slider widget is highlighted from the "max" value to the handle position. The default value is false. The following is an example of setting the slider widget using the range:

```
$( "#salaryRange" ).slider({
    range: true,
    min: 50000,
    max: 200000,
    values: [ 60000, 80000 ] // Default values
});
```

331

- value—Sets the value of the widget.

- values—This is valid if the range is set to true. The format to set the start and end values of the widget is:

  values: [*startValue*, *endValue*]

The commonly used methods for the slider widget are:

- value()—Gets the current value of the slider widget.

- value(newValue)—Sets the value of the slider widget with the specified newValue.

- values()—Gets the value of all handles. It returns an array of numbers.

- values(indexNumber)—Gets the value of the handle at the specified indexNumber.

- values(indexNumber, newValue)—Sets the value of the handle with the specified newValue at the specified indexNumber.

- values(newValues)—Sets the values of all handles from the specified newValues array.

The commonly used events for the slider widget are:

- slide—Triggered when the widget's value is incremented or decremented. ui.value contains the new value. If the callback function returns false, the value of the widget is not changed.

- change—Triggered when the value of the widget changes.

The CSS classes specific to the slider widget are:

- ui-slider—Used for the track of the slider widget.

- ui-slider-horizontal—Used for the slider widget if the orientation is horizontal.

- ui-slider-vertical—Used for the slider widget if the orientation is vertical.

- ui-slider-handle—Used for the slider's handle(s).

- ui-slider-handle-range—Used for the range between slider's handles.

- ui-slider-handle-min—Used for the range between the slider's minimum value and the handle's position.

- ui-slider-handle-max—Used for the range between the handle's position and the slider's maximum value.

10-5. Creating the Datepicker Widget

Problem

You want to know how to create the datepicker widget and understand its commonly used options, methods, and events.

Solution

This widget is used to select a date from a calendar. The following is the syntax for creating the datepicker widget:

```
$(selector).datepicker()
$(selector).datepicker(options)
```

An `<input>` element or a `<div>` element can be specified as a datepicker widget. If an `<input>` element is set as a datepicker widget, a popup calendar is displayed when the input textbox field gets the focus. On selecting a date, the popup calendar is closed and the input element's value is set to the selected date. If a `<div>` element is set as a datepicker, an inline calendar is displayed. You can specify which element should be set with the selected date value during the datepicker creation by using the `altField` option. Listing 10-4 demonstrates an example that creates the datepicker widget.

Listing 10-4. Using datepicker() to create a datepicker widget

```
<!DOCTYPE html>
<html lang="en">
<head>
      <meta charset="utf-8">
      <link rel="stylesheet" href="styles/jquery-ui.min.css">
      <script src="scripts/jquery-2.1.0.min.js"></script>
      <script src="scripts/jquery-ui.min.js"></script>

      <script>
      $(function() {
            $( "#txtAppointmentDate" ).datepicker({
             dateFormat:"yy-mm-dd",
             minDate: +5,
             maxDate: "+2M +15D"
             });
      });
      </script>
</head>
<body>
      <div class="ui-widget">
            Appointment Date: <input type="text" id="txtAppointmentDate">
      </div>
</body>
</html>
```

How It Works

Within the document ready function of this example, the `datepicker()` method sets the input element—with the ID set to txtAppointmentDate—as a datepicker widget. The options used in this example are:

- `dateFormat`—Specifies the format in which the input textbox value is set when a date is selected. If June 28th 2014 is selected, the yy-mm-dd format will set the value to 2014-06-28. The default format is mm/dd/yy.

- `minDate`—Specifies the minimum date that can be selected. Its value can be positive (for the dates in the future) or negative (for the dates in the past). In this example, `minDate: +5` means the appointment date cannot be prior to five days from today's date.

- `maxDate`—Specifies the maximum date that can be selected. Its value can be positive (for the dates in future) or negative (for the dates in the past). In this example, `maxDate: "+2M +15D"` means appointment date cannot be later than two months and 15 days from today's date.

Figure 10-4 displays the page when the user clicks on the Appointment Date textbox field.

Figure 10-4. *Datepicker widget to select the appointment date*

To display an inline calendar instead of popup calendar, you can use following code.
HTML code:

```
<div id="dpTargetDate"></div>
<input type="text" id="txtTargetDate">
```

JavaScript code:

```
$( "#dpTargetDate" ).datepicker({
     altField: "#txtTargetDate"
});
```

The other commonly used options for the datepicker widget are:

- altField—Specifies the input element whose value is set when a date is selected from the datepicker widget.

- altFormat—The date format of the field that's used to set the value of the element specified by altField. The default value is mm/dd/yy.

- autoSize—If set to true, the input field is resized to accommodate the format of the selected date. The default value is false.

- changeMonth—If set to true, a month can be selected from the drop-down list. The default value is false.

- changeYear—If set to true, a year can be selected from the drop-down list. The default value is false.

- defaultDate—Specifies the default date that's highlighted when the calendar is displayed. It can be set with the JavaScript Date object or as a number. For example, defaultDate: +6 will set the default date as six days from the current date. The default value is the current date.

- numberOfMonths—Specifies the number of months to display together in the datepicker widget.

The commonly used methods for the datepicker widget are:

- getDate()—Gets the selected date.

- hide()—Hides the currently open datepicker widget.

- setDate(newDate)—Sets the date as newDate in the datepicker widget. newDate can be a date object, date string (for example, "06/23/2014") or a number of days from today (for example, -5d).

The commonly used CSS classes specific to the datepicker widget are:

- ui-datepicker—Used for the outer container of the datepicker widget.

- ui-datepicker-header—Used for the header of the datepicker widget.

- ui-datepicker-prev—Used for the previous month selector of the datepicker widget.

- ui-datepicker-next—Used for the next month selector of the datepicker widget.

- ui-datepicker-title—Used for the title (month and year) of the datepicker widget.

- ui-datepicker-calendar—Used for the grid displaying the dates in the datepicker widget.

10-6. Creating the Tooltip Widget
Problem

You want to know how to create the tooltip widget and understand its commonly used options, methods, and events.

Solution

This widget is used to display additional information when the mouse cursor hovers over any HTML element. The following is the syntax for creating the tooltip widget:

```
$(selector).tooltip()
$(selector).tooltip(options)
```

A tooltip can be attached to any HTML element. When the mouse hovers over the selected elements, a customizable tooltip can be displayed as text, an image, or any valid HTML content. Tooltip content can be static or derived from data retrieved from AJAX calls. Listing 10-5 demonstrates an example using the tooltip widget.

Listing 10-5. Using tooltip() to set tooltips for HTML elements

```
<!DOCTYPE html>
<html lang="en">
<head>
    <meta charset="utf-8">
    <link rel="stylesheet" href="styles/jquery-ui.min.css">
    <script src="scripts/jquery-2.1.0.min.js"></script>
    <script src="scripts/jquery-ui.min.js"></script>
```

```
<script>
$(function() {
        $("input").tooltip();

        $( "li" ).tooltip({
         items: "li",
          content: function() {
                var element = $( this );

                if ( element.is( "[title]" ) ) {
                return element.attr( "title" );
                } else if ( element.is( "li" ) ) {
                var countryName = element.text();
                        return "<img src='images/" + countryName + ".png'>";
                }

        }
        });
 });
</script>
</head>

<body>
     <div class="ui-widget">
      Name: <input type="text" title="LastName, FirstName"><br><br>

      G8 Countries:
      <ul>
            <li>Canada</li>
            <li title="(2014) President François Hollande">France</li>
            <li title="(2014) Chancellor Angela Merkel">Germany</li>
            <li>Italy</li>
            <li title="(2014) Prime Minister Shinz Abe">Japan</li>
            <li title="(2014) President Vladimir Putin">Russia</li>
            <li title="(2014) Prime Minister David Cameron">United Kingdom</li>
            <li title="(2014) President Barack Obama">United States</li>
      </ul>
     </div>
</body>
</html>
```

How It Works

Within the document ready function of this example, there are two instances of setting a tooltip for HTML elements. In the first instance, $("input").tooltip() sets the tooltip for all input HTML elements. When the user hovers over the input field, the value of the title attribute is displayed as a bubble help. In the second instance, the following code is used to set the tooltip widget for the li HTML elements.

```
$( "li" ).tooltip({
        items: "li",
        content: function() {
                var element = $( this );

                if ( element.is( "[title]" ) ) {
                return element.attr( "title" );
                } else if ( element.is( "li" ) ) {
                        var countryName = element.text();
                         return "<img src='images/" + countryName + ".png'>";
                }

        }
});
```

The following is the explanation of this code:

- The items option specifies which items should show the tooltip. All valid selectors can be used to set its value.

- The content option is used to set the content of the tooltip. Its value can be a string or a function. The return value of the function is used to display the tooltip content.

- var element = $(this)—sets the variable element to the current HTML element.

- If the current element has an attribute called title, the function returns the value of the title attribute; otherwise, the image element with a source of CountryName.png is returned.

Figure 10-5 displays the page when the user moves the mouse cursor over the Name input textbox.

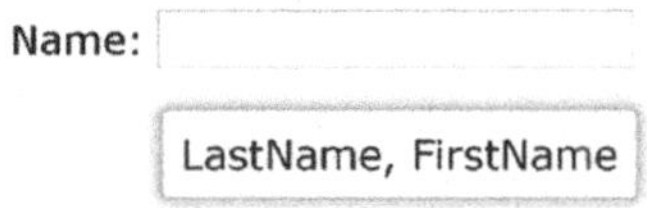

Name: [   ]

[LastName, FirstName]

Figure 10-5. *Tooltip for the Name textbox field*

Figure 10-6 displays the page when the user moves the mouse over the country name (Canada) for which the title attribute is not set.

G8 Countries:

- Canada
- France
- ▮◆▮ any
- ~~Italy~~

Figure 10-6. *Tooltip for a Country Name field without the title attribute*

Figure 10-7 displays the page when the user moves the mouse over the country name (France) for which the title attribute is set.

G8 Countries:

- Canada
- France
- Germany

- (2014) President François
- Hollande

Figure 10-7. Tooltip for Country Name field using the title attribute

The other commonly used option for the tooltip widget is:

- `tooltipClass`—Specifies the CSS class for the popup tooltip.

The commonly used method for the tooltip widget is:

- `open()`—Programmatically opens a tooltip. For example, you can call it in the field's focus callback function.

The commonly used CSS classes specific to the tooltip widget are:

- `ui-tooltip`—Used for the outer container of the tooltip widget.

- `ui-tooltip-content`—Used for the content of the tooltip widget.

10-7. Creating the Button Widget
Problem

You want to know how to create the button widget and understand its commonly used options, methods, and events.

Solution

This widget is used to display buttons, checkboxes, radio buttons, and toolbar items with the specified theme. The following is the syntax for creating the button widget:

```
$(selector).button()
$(selector).button(options)
$(selector).buttonset(options)
```

An `<input>` element with the type set to `button`, `submit`, `reset`, `checkbox`, and `radio`, an `<a>` element, and a `<button>` element can all be set as button widgets. Groups of checkboxes or radio buttons can grouped together using the `buttonset()` method on their parent `div` element. Listing 10-6 demonstrates an example that creates button widgets. In this example, various types of buttons are created.

Listing 10-6. Using button() to create button widgets

```html
<!DOCTYPE html>
<html lang="en">
<head>
    <meta charset="utf-8">
    <link rel="stylesheet" href="styles/jquery-ui.min.css">
    <script src="scripts/jquery-2.1.0.min.js"></script>
    <script src="scripts/jquery-ui.min.js"></script>

    <style>
     #toolbar { padding: 4px; display: inline-block; }
    </style>

    <script>
     $(function() {
          <!-- Button -->
          $( "input[type=submit]").button();

          $( "#btnHome").button({
           icons: {
                  primary: "ui-icon-home"
           }
          });

          $( "#googleLink").button();

          <!-- Toggle -->
          $( "#check" ).button();

          <!-- Checkboxes -->
          $( "#hobbies" ).buttonset();

          <!-- Radiobuttons -->
          $( "#gender" ).buttonset();

          <!-- Toolbars related -->
          $( "#btnFile" ).button();
          $( "#btnEdit" ).button();
          $( "#btnSettings" ).button();
          $( "#btnHelp" ).button();
     });
    </script>

</head>
<body>
    <div class="ui-widget">
    Input HTML Element with type Button, Submit, or Reset<br>
    <input type="Submit" value="Submit"><br><br>

    Button<br>
    <button id="btnHome">Home</button><br><br>
```

```
    Link<br>
    <a id="googleLink" href="http://google.com" target="_blank">Google</a><br><br>

    Checkbox<br>
    <!-- Toggle -->
    <input type="checkbox" id="check"><label for="check">Toggle</label><br><br>

    Checkboxes in a group<br>
    <!-- Checkboxes -->
    Hobbies:
    <div id="hobbies">
            <input type="checkbox" id="check1"><label for="check1">Traveling</label>
            <input type="checkbox" id="check2"><label for="check2">Reading</label>
            <input type="checkbox" id="check3"><label for="check3">Technology</label>
            <input type="checkbox" id="check4"><label for="check4">Sports</label>
    </div><br>

    Radiobuttons<br>
    Gender:
    <div id="gender">
            <input type="radio" id="male" name="radio"><label for="male">Male</label>
            <input type="radio" id="female" name="radio" checked="checked"><label
for="female">Female</label>
    </div> <br>

    Toolbar (using buttons)<br>
    <div id="toolbar" class="ui-widget-header ui-corner-all">
            <button id="btnFile">File</button>
            <button id="btnEdit">Edit</button>
            <button id="btnSettings">Settings</button>
            <button id="btnHelp">Help</button>
    </div>
    </div>
</body>
</html>
```

How It Works

Within the document ready function of this example, various button widgets and buttonsets (sets of checkbox and radio buttons) are created. The following is the list of ways buttons can be created:

- $("input[type=submit]").button()—Creates the button widget from the <input> element with the type attribute set to submit. Figure 10-8 displays the button created by using this code.

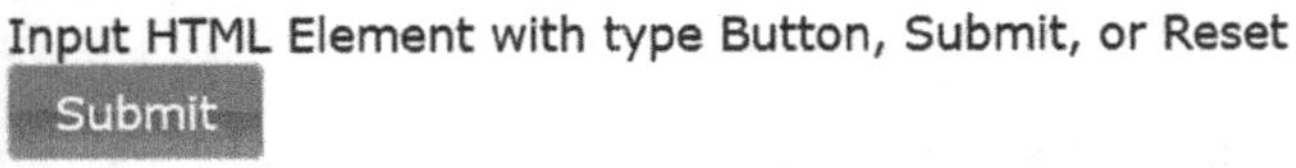

Input HTML Element with type Button, Submit, or Reset

Submit

Figure 10-8. *Button widget created from the input element with the "submit" type*

- $("#btnHome").button({icons: {primary: "ui-icon-home"}})—Creates the button widget from the <button> element and sets the Home icon by using the option icons. Since there can be primary and secondary icons associated with the same button, a map object is used to set its value. Figure 10-9 displays the button created by using this code.

Button

Figure 10-9. *Button widget, with icon, created from the button element*

- $("#googleLink").button()—Creates the button widget from the <a> element. Figure 10-10 displays the button created by using this code.

Link

Figure 10-10. *Button widget created from the anchor (<a>) element*

- $("#check").button()—Creates a button widget from the <input> element with the type checkbox. Since the type is checkbox, this button behaves like a toggle button. If it is clicked once, it is checked (or on) and if it is clicked again, it is unchecked (or off). Figure 10-11 displays the button in two modes—checked and unchecked.

Checked   Unchecked

Figure 10-11. *Button widget created from the input element with the "checkbox" type*

- $("#hobbies").buttonset()— #hobbies is the ID of a div element with multiple checkboxes as its child nodes. .buttonset() groups all child nodes into a single unit. Figure 10-12 displays the buttonset of checkboxes.

Checkboxes in a group
Hobbies:

Figure 10-12. *Group of checkboxes button widgets created by using buttonset()*

- $("#gender").buttonset()— #gender is the ID of a div element with two radio buttons as its child nodes. .buttonset() groups all the child nodes into a single unit. Figure 10-13 displays the buttonset of radio buttons.

Radiobuttons
Gender:

Figure 10-13. *Group of radio button widgets created by using buttonset()*

A toolbar with the buttons can be created using the following code.
HTML code:

```
<div id="toolbar" class="ui-widget-header ui-corner-all">
  <button id="btnFile">File</button>
  <button id="btnEdit">Edit</button>
  <button id="btnSettings">Settings</button>
  <button id="btnHelp">Help</button>
</div>
```

JavaScript code:

```
$( "#btnFile" ).button();
$( "#btnEdit" ).button();
$( "#btnSettings" ).button();
$( "#btnHelp" ).button();
```

CSS code:

```
#toolbar {
  padding: 4px;
  display: inline-block;
}
```

Figure 10-14 displays the toolbar with its buttons.

Figure 10-14. *Group of buttons on a toolbar*

The other commonly used options for the button widget are:

- label—Specifies the text on the button.

- text—If set to false, the text on the button won't be displayed. In this case, *icons* must be set to show the icons.

The commonly used CSS classes specific to the button widget are:

- ui-button—Used for the element that creates the button.
- ui-button-text—Used for the text of the button.
- ui-button-icon-primary—Used for the primary icon of the button widget.
- ui-button-icon-secondary—Used for the secondary icon of the button widget.
- ui-buttonset—Used for the outer container of the buttonset.

10-8. Creating the Dialog Widget
Problem

You want to know how to create the dialog widget and understand its commonly used options, methods, and events.

Solution

This widget is used to show content (such as messages, data-entry forms, images, and so on) in a dialog box with the option of displaying buttons. The following is the syntax for creating the dialog widget:

```
$(selector).dialog()
$(selector).dialog(options)
```

The dialog widget is used to display content in an overlay window. It can be used to:

- Display a message
- Prompt for confirmation from the user
- Show data-entry form for submission
- Show images

Listing 10-7 demonstrates an example to display a message in the dialog box.

Listing 10-7. Using dialog() to display a message dialog box

```
<!DOCTYPE html>
<html lang="en">
<head>
    <meta charset="utf-8">
    <link rel="stylesheet" href="styles/jquery-ui.min.css">
    <script src="scripts/jquery-2.1.0.min.js"></script>
    <script src="scripts/jquery-ui.min.js"></script>

    <script>
$(function() {
        $("#btnSubmitPayment").button();

        $("#btnSubmitPayment").click(function () {
        $("#dialogProcessingStatus").dialog({modal: true});
        });
    });
    </script>
</head>
```

```
<body>
    <div class="ui-widget">
     <button id="btnSubmitPayment">Submit Payment</button>

     <div id="dialogProcessingStatus" title="Processing Status" style="display:none">
          <p>Payment processing is completed. If you have any questions,
        please contact us at (877)-555-5555.</p>
        </div>
    </div>
</body>
</html>
```

How It Works

In this code, a div element is specified with the message you want to display as an overlay. Its display property is set to none by using the code—style="display:none".

- $("#btnSubmitPayment").button()—Creates a button widget using the <button>.

- $("#btnSubmitPayment").click(function() { ... })—Sets the callback function for the click event of the button.

When button is clicked, $("#dialogProcessingStatus").dialog({modal: true}) is executed. This creates the dialog widget from the div element with the "#dialogProcessingStatus" ID. It also sets the modal option as true, which prevents the user from interacting with other items on the page. Users have to interact with the dialog box first by closing it before they can continue working on the page. Figure 10-15 displays the dialog box with the message when the Submit Payment button is clicked. By default, the value of the title attribute of the div element will be displayed as the header of the dialog box and the Close button will be displayed on the top-right corner of the dialog box.

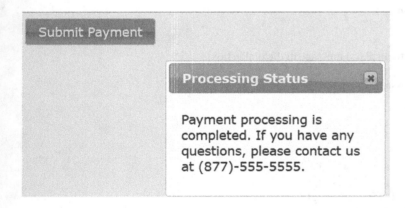

Figure 10-15. *When you click the button, a dialog box is displayed*

In order to display buttons on the dialog box, you can set buttons option. The following example demonstrates the use of the buttons option.

HTML code:

```
<body>
    <div class="ui-widget">
        <button id="btnSubmitPayment">Submit Payment</button>

        <div id="dialogPaymentConfirmation" title="Payment Confirmation" style="display:none">
            <p>You are about to make a payment. Please confirm.</p>
        </div>
    </div>
</body>
```

JavaScript code:

```
<script>
    $(function() {
        $("#btnSubmitPayment").button();

        $("#btnSubmitPayment").click(function () {
            $("#dialogPaymentConfirmation").dialog({
                modal: true,
                buttons: {
                    "Confirm": function() {
                        // Do some proessing here. Like making an AJAX call to
                          process payment.
                        $( this ).dialog( "close" );
                    },

                    "Decline": function() {
                        $( this ).dialog( "close" );
                    }
                }
            });
        });
    });
</script>
```

Figure 10-16 displays the dialog box with the Confirm and Decline buttons. When you click these buttons, the specified callback functions will be executed.

Figure 10-16. Dialog box with buttons

You can use these concepts to display the data-entry form as a dialog box and then submit the form by clicking the button. Form elements can be specified within the `div` tag and buttons and their callback functions can be specified by using the dialog widget's `buttons` option.

The other commonly used options for the dialog widget are:

- `dialogClass`—Specifies the CSS class for the dialog box.

- `draggable`—If set to `true`, the user can drag the dialog box by clicking and dragging title bar.

- `height`—Specifies the height (in pixels) of the dialog box. If content is more than the visible dialog box window, the scroll bar is automatically added.

- `width`—Specifies the width (in pixels) of the dialog box.

- `resizable`—If set to `false`, the users can't resize the dialog box. The default value is `true`.

- `title`—Specifies the title of the dialog box.

The commonly used event for the dialog widget is:

- `beforeClose()`—Triggered when the dialog box is about to be closed. The callback function for this event can be used to check if the user has submitted the form, in the dialog box, after entering the data.

The commonly used CSS classes specific to the dialog widget are:

- `ui-dialog`—Used for the outer container of the dialog widget.

- `ui-dialog-titlebar`—Used for the title bar containing the title and the Close button.

- `ui-dialog-title`—Used for the title on the title bar.

- `ui-dialog-titlebar-close`—Used for the Close button on the title bar.

- `ui-dialog-content`—Used for the content of the dialog widget.

- `ui-dialog-buttonset`—Used for the buttons container.

10-9. Creating the Progress Bar Widget
Problem

You want to know how to create the progress bar widget and understand its commonly used options, methods, and events.

Solution

This widget is used to display the progress of a process, either as an absolute value or as a percentage. The following is the syntax for creating the progress bar widget:

```
$(selector).progressbar()
$(selector).progressbar(options)
```

Listing 10-8 demonstrates an example to display the percentage of processing completed. In this example, processing completion is incremented by calling a function after a predefined interval. In a real-world application, responses from AJAX calls can be used to set the value of the progress bar.

Listing 10-8. Using progressbar() to create a progress bar widget

```html
<!DOCTYPE html>
<html lang="en">
<head>
    <meta charset="utf-8">
    <link rel="stylesheet" href="styles/jquery-ui.min.css">
    <script src="scripts/jquery-2.1.0.min.js"></script>
    <script src="scripts/jquery-ui.min.js"></script>

    <style>
    .ui-progressbar { position: relative; background: lightyellow; }
     #processingLabel { position: absolute;left: 20%; top: 2px; }
    </style>

    <script>
     $(function() {
            var timer = setInterval( updateProcessCompletion, 100 );
            var processCompletion = 0;

            $("#paymentProcessingStatus").progressbar({
              change: function() {
                    $( "#processingLabel" ).text( $("#paymentProcessingStatus").progressbar
                        ( "value" ) + "%" );
              },

              complete: function() {
                    clearInterval(timer);
                    $( "#processingLabel" ).text( "Completed." );
              }
            });

            function updateProcessCompletion() {
             $("#paymentProcessingStatus").progressbar( "value", processCompletion++);
            }
     });
    </script>
</head>

<body>
    <div class="ui-widget">
    <div id="paymentProcessingStatus" style="width:150px; height:30px;
      background-color:lightyellow">
            <div id="processingLabel">
             Started...
            </div>
     </div>
    </div>
</body>
</html>
```

How It Works

Within the DOM ready function of this example:

- `var timer = setInterval( updateProcessCompletion, 100 )` —Sets the timer to call the `updateProcessCompletion()` function every 100 milliseconds.

- `$("#paymentProcessingStatus").progressbar({...})`—Creates the progress bar widget from the `div` element, which has an ID set to `paymentProcessingStatus`. By default, the progress bar minimum value is 0 and maximum is 100. Callback functions are set for the following two progress bar events:

  - `change`—Triggered when value of the progress bar changes.

  - `complete`—Triggered when the value of the progress bar is equal to its maximum value.

- `$( ".processingLabel" ).text( $("#paymentProcessingStatus").progressbar ( "value" ) + "%" )` sets the text of the `div` element with the ID `processingLabel` as the progress bar value concatenated with %.

- `clearInterval(timer)`—Stops the timer function invocation.

- `$( "#processingLabel" ).text( "Completed." )`—Sets the text of the `div` element to `Completed`.

- In the `updateProcessCompletion` function, the value of the progress bar is incremented by 1 using the following code: `$("#paymentProcessingStatus").progressbar( "value", processCompletion++)`.

Figure 10-17 displays the progress bar widget when its value is not yet set as the maximum.

Figure 10-17. *Processing status is displayed as a percentage completed by using the progress bar widget*

The other commonly used option for the progress bar widget is:

- `max`—Specifies the maximum value of the progress bar widget. The default value is 100.

The commonly used methods for the progress bar widget are:

- `value()`—Gets the current value of the progress bar widget.

- `value(newValue)`—Sets the value of the progress bar widget as `newValue`.

The commonly used CSS classes specific to the progress bar widget are:

- `ui-progressbar`—Used for the outer container of the progress bar widget.

- `ui-progressbar-value`—Used for the completed portion of the progress bar widget.

10-10. Creating the Tabs Widget

Problem

You want to know how to create the tabs widget and understand its commonly used options, methods, and events.

Solution

This widget is used to organize multiple panels in the same content area. Only one panel is visible at a time. The contents of a panel can be made visible by clicking the tab header. This type of widget is useful when contents can be categorized into a manageable number of tabs. For example, employee details can be displayed as content for each department in an organization. Department names can be displayed as a tab header. When users click the department name, details of all the employees in that selected department can be displayed. Instead of getting all data at once, you can get data by making AJAX calls when a tab becomes active. The following is the syntax for creating the tabs widget:

```
$(selector).tabs()
$(selector).tabs(options)
```

The following is the structure of the HTML elements needed to set up tabs.

```
<div id="tabsName">
      <ul>
             <li><a href="#tab1">Tab 1</a></li>
             <li><a href="#tab2">Tab 2</a></li>
             ....
      </ul>

      <div id="tab1">
            Content for tab 1
      </div>

      <div id="tab2">
            Content for tab 2
      </div>
      ...
</div>
```

The tabs widget is created by using the $("#tabsName").tabs() statement. Listing 10-9 demonstrates an example to display contents in the tabs.

Listing 10-9. Using tabs() to create the tabs widget

```
<!DOCTYPE html>
<html lang="en">
<head>
      <meta charset="utf-8">
      <link rel="stylesheet" href="styles/jquery-ui.min.css">
      <script src="scripts/jquery-2.1.0.min.js"></script>
      <script src="scripts/jquery-ui.min.js"></script>

      <style>
       #photoTabs { width: 800px;}
      </style>
```

```
        <script>
         $(function() {
             $("#photoTabs").tabs();
         });
        </script>
</head>

<body>
      <div class="ui-widget">
       <div id="photoTabs">
            <ul>
              <li><a href="#animalsTab">Animals</a></li>
              <li><a href="#birdsTab">Birds</a></li>
              <li><a href="#insectsTab">Insects</a></li>
              <li><a href="#seaAnimalsTab">Sea Animals</a></li>
            </ul>

            <div id="animalsTab">
             <img src="images/Cat.png"/>
             <img src="images/Dog.png"/>
             <img src="images/Elephant.png"/>
             <img src="images/Hippopotamus.png"/>
             <img src="images/Panda.png"/>
            </div>

            <div id="birdsTab">
             <img src="images/Bird1.png"/>
             <img src="images/Bird2.png"/>
             <img src="images/Owl.png"/>
             <img src="images/Penguin1.png"/>
             <img src="images/Penguin2.png"/>
            </div>

            <div id="insectsTab">
             <img src="images/Butterfly1.png"/>
             <img src="images/Butterfly2.png"/>
             <img src="images/Butterfly3.png"/>
             <img src="images/Grasshopper.png"/>
             <img src="images/LadyBug.png"/>
            </div>

            <div id="seaAnimalsTab">
             <img src="images/Fish2.png"/>
             <img src="images/Dolphin.png"/>
             <img src="images/Fish1.png"/>
             <img src="images/JellyFish.png"/>
             <img src="images/WireShark.png"/>
            </div>
       </div>
      </div>
</body>
</html>
```

How It Works

Within the DOM ready function of this code example, the tabs widget is created by using the `$("#photoTabs").tabs()` code.

Within the `<div>` tag with the ID `photoTabs`:

- Each `li` element creates a tab.

- The tab header is set from the text of the `li` elements.

- The tab content is set by getting the content of the selector specified in the `href` attribute of the anchor (`<a>`) element, which is the child node of the `li` element.

For example, for the line:

`<li><a href="`**`#seaAnimalsTab`**`">Sea Animals</a></li>`

- `<li>` creates the tab.

- `Sea Animals` is used as the header of the tab.

- `#seaAnimalsTab` points to the content of the tab.

- `<div id="seaAnimalsTab"> ... </div>` has the content for the tab.

Figure 10-18 displays the tabs widget with "Animals," "Birds," "Insects," and "Sea Animals" tabs. You can view the content of a tab by clicking on its header.

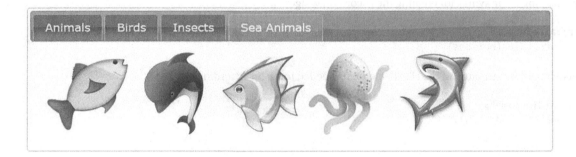

Figure 10-18. *Tabs widget*

The other commonly used options for the tabs widget are:

- `collapsible`—If set to true, the tab panel can be collapsed, i.e., the active tab can be closed by clicking on its header.

- `active`—Specifies which tab panel should be active when page is loaded. Tab index is 0-based. If it is set to `false` and `collapsible` is `true`, all tab panels are displayed as collapsed panels.

- `heightStyle`—Controls the height of the tabs widget and tab panels. The following are the valid values:

  - `auto`—All tab panels are set to the height of the tallest panel.

  - `fill`—All tab panels' height are the same as their parent container.

  - `content`—The height of each tab panel is adjusted to completely display its content.

The commonly used method for the tabs widget is:

- `refresh()`—Displays tabs that are added or removed using DOM manipulation.

The commonly used CSS classes specific to the tabs widget are:

- `ui-tabs`—Used for the outer container of the tabs widget.
- `ui-tabs-collapsible`—Used for collapsible tabs.
- `ui-tabs-panel`—Used for the tab's panel (i.e., the content area).

10-11. Creating the Accordion Widget
Problem

You want to know how to create the accordion widget and understand its commonly used options, methods, and events.

Solution

This widget is used to display header and content as an accordion. This widget is very similar to the tabs widget where contents are categorized and displayed one category at a time. For tabs widgets, headers are displayed horizontally, whereas for accordion widgets, headers are displayed vertically. The accordion widget is used to display a small amount of data or a listing. For example, the accordion widget can be used to display sub-menus within the selected menu. The following is the syntax for creating the accordion widget:

```
$(selector).accordion()
$(selector).accordion(options)
```

The following is the structure of the HTML elements needed to set up accordion.

```
<div id="accordionName">
    <h3>Panel 1 Header</h3>
    <div>
     Panel 1 Content
    </div>

    <h3>Panel 2 Header</h3>
    <div>
     Panel 2 Content
    </div>
     ...
</div>
```

The accordion widget is created by using the `$("#accordionName").accordion()` statement. Listing 10-10 demonstrates an example that displays contents in an accordion.

Listing 10-10. Using accordion() to create the accordion widget

```html
<!DOCTYPE html>
<html lang="en">
<head>
    <meta charset="utf-8">
    <link rel="stylesheet" href="styles/jquery-ui.min.css">
    <script src="scripts/jquery-2.1.0.min.js"></script>
    <script src="scripts/jquery-ui.min.js"></script>

    <style>
     h3 {width:700px; }
     div {width:670px;}
    </style>

    <script>
     $(function() {
          $( "#album" ).accordion({
           active: 2,
           icons: {
                 header: "ui-icon-triangle-1-e",
                 activeHeader: "ui-icon-triangle-1-s"
           }
          });
     });
    </script>
</head>

<body>
    <div id="album">
     <h3>Animals</h3>
     <div>
          <img src="images/Cat.png"/>
          <img src="images/Dog.png"/>
          <img src="images/Elephant.png"/>
          <img src="images/Hippopotamus.png"/>
          <img src="images/Panda.png"/>
     </div>

     <h3>Birds</h3>
     <div>
          <img src="images/Bird1.png"/>
          <img src="images/Bird2.png"/>
          <img src="images/Owl.png"/>
          <img src="images/Penguin1.png"/>
          <img src="images/Penguin2.png"/>
     </div>
```

```
        <h3>Insects</h3>
        <div>
                <img src="images/Butterfly1.png"/>
                <img src="images/Butterfly2.png"/>
                <img src="images/Butterfly3.png"/>
                <img src="images/Grasshopper.png"/>
                <img src="images/LadyBug.png"/>
        </div>

        <h3>Sea Animals</h3>
        <div>
                <img src="images/Fish2.png"/>
                <img src="images/Dolphin.png"/>
                <img src="images/Fish1.png"/>
                <img src="images/JellyFish.png"/>
                <img src="images/WireShark.png"/>
        </div>
    </div>
</body>
</html>
```

How It Works

Within the DOM ready function of this example, the accordion widget is created by using the code:

```
$( "#album" ).accordion({
    active: 2,
    icons: {
     header: "ui-icon-triangle-1-e",
     activeHeader: "ui-icon-triangle-1-s"
    }
});
```

Within this code:

- The active option is used to specify which accordion panel will be active when the page is loaded. Panel number is 0-based.

- The icons option is used to specify the icons to display on active and inactive panel headers. Since this option accepts multiple properties, you should specify its value as a map object.

    - header is used to specify which icon to use for the inactive panel header.

    - activeHeader is used to specify which icon to use for the active panel header.

Figure 10-19 displays the accordion widget with panels for the "Animals," "Birds," "Insects," and "Sea Animals" tabs. You can view the content of a panel by clicking on its header.

Figure 10-19. Accordion widget

The other commonly used options for the accordion widget are:

- collapsible—If set to true, the section panel can be collapsed, i.e., the active section can be closed by clicking on its header.

- active—Specifies which section panel should be active when the page is loaded. Section index is 0-based. If set to false and collapsible is true, all section panels are displayed as collapsed panels.

- header—Selector to use to display the header. By default, odd numbered child nodes are used for the header. Content should immediately follow the specified header selector.

- heightStyle—Controls the height of the accordion widget and section panels. The following are the valid values:

  - auto—All section panels are set to the height of the tallest panel.

  - fill—All section panels' height is same as its parent container.

  - content—The height of each section panel is adjusted to completely display its content.

The commonly used method for the accordion widget is:

- refresh()—Displays the tabs that are added or removed using DOM manipulation.

The commonly used CSS classes specific to the accordion widget are:

- ui-accordion—Used for the outer container of the accordion widget.

- ui-accordion-header—Used for accordion headers.

- ui-accordion-icons—Used for icons on the accordion headers.

- ui-accordion-content—Used for the content panel of the accordion widget.

10-12. Creating the Menu Widget

Problem

You want to know how to create the menu widget and understand its commonly used options, methods, and events.

Solution

This widget is used to display menus and sub-menus in a structured manner. Menu and sub-menu items are created to organize applications functionalities. Depending on the user's authorization level, menu items can be enabled or disabled. The following is the syntax for creating the menu widget:

```
$(selector).menu()
$(selector).menu(options)
```

The following is the structure of HTML elements needed to create a menu widget:

```
<ul id="menuName">
        <li><a href="#">Menu Item 1</a></li>
        <li><a href="#">Menu Item 2</a></li>
        <li><a href="#">Menu Item 3</a>
                <ul>
                <li><a href="#">Menu Item 3.1</a></li>
                <li><a href="#">Menu Item 3.2</a></li>
                ...
        </ul>
        </li>
        ...
</ul>
```

The menu widget is created by using the $("#menuName").menu() statement. Listing 10-11 demonstrates an example to display menu and sub-menu items in a menu widget.

Listing 10-11. Using menu() to create a menu widget

```
<!DOCTYPE html>
<html lang="en">
<head>
        <meta charset="utf-8">
        <link rel="stylesheet" href="styles/jquery-ui.min.css">
        <script src="scripts/jquery-2.1.0.min.js"></script>
        <script src="scripts/jquery-ui.min.js"></script>

        <style>
        .ui-menu { width: 150px; }
        </style>
```

```
    <script>
     $(function() {
            $("#appMenu").menu();

            $("#help").click(function (){
             alert("Help is clicked.");
             // Get the help content and display in dialog widget.
            });
     });
    </script>
</head>

<body>
    <div class="ui-widget">
    Employee Records Management System
    <br><br>

    <ul id="appMenu">
            <li><a href="#"><span class="ui-icon ui-icon-person"></span>New</a></li>
            <li><a href="#"><span class="ui-icon ui-icon-pencil"></span>Edit</a></li>
            <li><a href="#"><span class="ui-icon ui-icon-search"></span>Search</a></li>
            <li class="ui-state-disabled"><a href="#"><span class="ui-icon ui-icon-gear">
</span>Settings</a></li>
            <li>
             <a href="#">Reports</a>
             <ul>
                    <li><a href="#"><span class="ui-icon ui-icon-document"></span>Monthly</a></li>
                    <li><a href="#"><span class="ui-icon ui-icon-document"></span>Daily</a></li>
             </ul>
            </li>
            <li><a id="help" href="#"><span class="ui-icon  ui-icon-info"></span>Help</a></li>
        </ul>
        </div>
</body>
</html>
```

How It Works

Within the DOM ready function of this example, the menu widget is created by using the code:

$("#appMenu").menu();

where *appMenu* is the ID of the ul element and it contains nested li and ul elements for menus and submenus.
   In the li and anchor (a) element, you can set up the icon by using the following code:

```
<span class="ui-icon ui-icon-search"></span>
```

where the first CSS class should be ui-icon and after that you can use the CSS class of the appropriate icon depending on the menu item. You can get the complete list of jQuery UI icons from http://api.jqueryui.com/theming/icons/.

A menu item can be disabled by adding the following class to the li element:

```
class="ui-state-disabled"
```

This code listing uses this class to disable the Settings menu item.

The following code is used to specify the Help menu item's click event's callback function:

```
$("#help").click(function (){
  alert("Help is clicked.");
  // Get the help content and display in dialog widget.
});
```

Figure 10-20 displays the menu widget with nested menu items. When the Help menu item is clicked, a "Help is clicked" message is displayed. In a real-world application, you can get the help content (the static content from the <div> element) by making an AJAX call.

Employee Records Management System

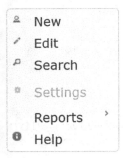

Figure 10-20. *Menu widget*

Figure 10-21 displays the sub-menu items when the Reports menu item is clicked.

Employee Records Management System

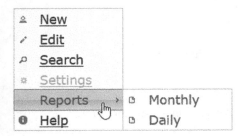

Figure 10-21. *Reports sub-menu items*

The other commonly used options for the menu widget are:

- icons—Specifies the icon to use for menu items that have sub-menus. By default it is the ui-icon-carat-1-e icon. The following syntax is used for the *icons* option:

  icons: { submenu: "*iconClassName*" }

- menus—Specifies the HTML element that is the menu container. By default it is ul.

The commonly used method for the menu widget is:

- refresh()—Displays the menu items that are added or removed using DOM manipulation.

The commonly used CSS classes specific to the menu widget are:

- ui-menu—Used for the outer container of the menu widget.

- ui-menu-item—Used for menu items.

- ui-menu-icon—Used for submenu icons.

- ui-menu-divider—Used for dividers between menu items.

10-13. Creating a Data-Entry Form Using jQuery UI Widgets
Problem

You want to create a simple data-entry form using jQuery UI widgets.

Solution

Recipes 10-2 through 10-12 cover all the jQuery UI widgets. Listing 10-12 demonstrates an example using the following concepts—jQuery selectors, events handling, AJAX calls, and jQuery UI widgets. Listing 10-13 contains content from the departments.json file. Listing 10-14 contains content from the createEmployee.json file. JSON files are used to provide data as a response to AJAX calls.

Listing10-12. Data-entry form

```
<!DOCTYPE html>
<html lang="en">
<head>
    <meta charset="utf-8">
    <link rel="stylesheet" href="styles/jquery-ui.min.css">
    <script src="scripts/jquery-2.1.0.min.js"></script>
    <script src="scripts/jquery-ui.min.js"></script>

    <style>
    form { border:3px double green; width: 500px; padding-left: 10px; padding-right: 10px;
           padding-bottom: 10px; background-color: lightyellow;}

     label { float:left; display:block; width: 175px; font-size: 14px;}

     .ui-button-text { font-size: 12px; }
```

```
    #txtAge { width:25px; }
    #txtSalary { width:90px; }
    #txtHireDate { width:120px; }
</style>

<script>
 $(function(){
        $("input").focus(function() {
            $(this).css("background-color", "lightcyan");
        });

        $("input").blur(function() {
                $(this).css("background-color", "white");
        });

        $("#txtDepartment").autocomplete();

        $("#txtAge").spinner({
         min:18,
         max:70
        });

        $( "#txtHireDate" ).datepicker({
         maxDate: "+0D",
        });

        // Get Department names from the server
        $.ajax({
         type: "GET",
         url: "departments.json",
         dataType: "json",
         success: getDepartmentNames,
         error: reportError
        });

        $('#btnCreateNew').button();

        $("#btnCreateNew").click(function (eventObj) {
         eventObj.preventDefault();

         $.ajax({
                type: "POST",
                url: "createEmployee.json",
                data: $("#frmNewEmployee").serializeArray(),
                dataType: "json",
                success: getProcessStatus,
                error: reportError
         });
        });
 });
```

```
        function getProcessStatus(returnedData, status) {
             $("#statusMessage").append("Create New Employee Record Status: " + returnedData.status);
        }

        function reportError(request, status, errorMsg) {
             $("#statusMessage").append("Status: " + status + "<br>Error Message: " + errorMsg);
              }

        function getDepartmentNames(returnedData, status) {
             var deptArray = new Array();

             $.each(returnedData.departments, function(obj, currentElement){
              deptArray.push(currentElement.departmentName);
              });

              $("#txtDepartment").autocomplete({source: deptArray});
        }
    </script>
</head>

<body>
     <form id="frmNewEmployee" class="ui-widget ui-corner-all">
      <h4 class="ui-widget-header" style="margin-top:5px">New Employee Record</h4>
      <label for="txtEmployeeName">Employee's Name:</label>
      <input type="text" id="txtEmployeeName" name="txtEmployeeName" placeholder="LastName,
        FirstName" size="30"><br>

      <label for="txtDepartment">Department Name:</label>
      <input type="text" id="txtDepartment" name="txtDepartment"><br>

      <label for="txtAge">Age:</label>
      <input type="text" id="txtAge" name="txtAge" value="21"><br>

      <label for="txtSalary">Salary:</label>
      <input type="text" id="txtSalary" name="txtSalary"><br>

      <label for="txtHireDate">Hire Date:</label>
      <input type="text" id="txtHireDate" name="txtHireDate"><br>

      <br><button id="btnCreateNew">Create New Employee Record</button>
     </form><br><br>
     <div id="statusMessage"></div>
</body>
</html>
```

Listing 10-13. Content of the departments.json file

```
{
  "departments":
  [
    {"departmentName":"Marketing"},
    {"departmentName":"Technology"},
    {"departmentName":"Sales"},
    {"departmentName":"Support"},
    {"departmentName":"Implementation"}
  ]
}
```

Listing 10-14. Content of the createEmployee.json file

```
{"status":"success"}
```

How It Works

In this code:

- The frmNewEmployee form has two CSS classes:

  - ui-widget is used for the outer container of all the widgets and it applies a consistent theme to all the elements.

  - ui-corner-all makes the border's corners rounded.

- The Employee Name input textbox (txtEmployeeName) has an HTML5 placeholder attribute as "LastName, FirstName," which is displayed in the input text area.

- The Department Name input textbox (txtDepartmentName) is set as an autocomplete widget. Its value is retrieved by making the AJAX call.

- The Age input textbox (txtAge) has a default value of 21 and the spinner widget is created from it with the min: 18 and max: 70 options.

- The input textbox for the Hire Date (txtHireDate) is used to create a datepicker widget with the option maxDate: "+0D", that is, the hire date cannot be later than today's date.

- The Create New Employee Record button is used to create the button widget.

In the DOM ready function:

- focus event—When an input element gets the focus, its background color changes to lightcyan. This is to highlight the current data-entry field.

- blur event—When an input element loses the focus, its background color reverts back to white.

- An AJAX call is made to get the list of all department names. When the AJAX call is successful, the getDepartmentNames() function is executed and it sets the array with the department names from the returned data. The array is used to set the source of the txtDepartmentName autocomplete widget.

After you enter the data and click the Create New Employee Record button, an AJAX call is made to save the data on the server side and the returned status is displayed on the screen. This example doesn't implement the server-side code and the status is returned from the JSON file instead (createEmployee.json). Figure 10-22 displays the data-entry form with the data entered by the user.

Figure 10-22. *Data-entry form for creating a new employee record*

When the Create New Employee Record button is clicked, the following message is displayed on the page—"Create New Employee Record Status: success".

10-14. Adding an Animation Effect Using addClass() or the animate() Method
Problem

You want to show an animation by changing the CSS properties of selected elements.

Solution

You learned about the jQuery animate() method in the "jQuery Effects and Animation" chapter. Using the animate() method, you can change the CSS properties of the selected elements in the specified duration. A change in the CSS properties over a period of time gives the impression of animation. There are certain limitations to the animate() method that prevent you from changing all valid CSS properties. Chapter 8 discussed some ways to overcome this limitation. The addClass() method in the jQuery UI library makes it easier to implement an animation by changing the CSS properties. The following is the syntax for the addClass() method:

$(*selector*).addClass(*className, durationOfAnimation, easingFunctionName, completeCallbackFunction*)

Where:

- className is the CSS class that specifies the target CSS properties of the selected elements.

- durationOfAnimation (optional) is the time duration (in milliseconds) to run the animation. The default value is 400 milliseconds.

- easingFunctionName (optional) is the easing function name that specifies the animation pattern (that is, the rate of change in the CSS properties). In the jQuery library, you have only two easing functions—linear and swing (the default). In the jQuery UI library, you have the following additional easing functions. (Replace <InOut> with In or Out or InOut.)

  - ease<InOut>Quad

  - ease<InOut>Cubic

  - ease<InOut>Quart

  - ease<InOut>Quint

  - ease<InOut>Expo

  - ease<InOut>Sine

  - ease<InOut>Circ

  - ease<InOut>Elastic

  - ease<InOut>Back

  - ease<InOut>Bounce

- completeCallbackFunction (optional)—Specifies the callback function that's executed when the animation is completed.

Listing 10-15 shows an example animation using the addClass() and removeClass() methods.

Listing 10-15. Animation using the addClass() and removeClass() methods

```
<!DOCTYPE html>
<html lang="en">
<head>
    <meta charset="utf-8">
    <link rel="stylesheet" href="styles/jquery-ui.min.css">
    <script src="scripts/jquery-2.1.0.min.js"></script>
    <script src="scripts/jquery-ui.min.js"></script>

    <style>
     form { border:3px double green; width: 500px; padding-left: 10px; padding-right: 10px;
                     padding-bottom: 10px; background-color: lightyellow; }

     .move { background-color: lightcyan; margin-top: 100px; margin-left: 100px; }

     label { float:left; display:block; width: 175px; font-size: 14px;}

     .ui-button-text{ font-size: 12px;}
```

```
        #txtAge { width:25px; }
        #txtSalary { width:90px; }
        #txtHireDate { width:120px; }
    </style>

    <script>
     $(function(){
         $("#txtDepartment").autocomplete();
         $("#txtAge").spinner();
         $("#txtHireDate").datepicker();

         $("#btnCreateNew").button();
         $("#btnAddClass").button();
         $("#btnRemoveClass").button();

         $("#btnAddClass").click(function () {
             $("#frmNewEmplpoyee").addClass("move", 2000, "easeInOutQuad");
         });

         $("#btnRemoveClass").click(function () {
             $("#frmNewEmplpoyee").removeClass("move", 2000, "easeInOutQuad");
         });
     });
    </script>
</head>

<body>
    <button id="btnAddClass">Add CSS Class</button>
    <button id="btnRemoveClass">Remove CSS Class</button><br><br>

    <form id="frmNewEmplpoyee" class="ui-widget ui-corner-all">
        <h4 class="ui-widget-header" style="margin-top:5px">New Employee Record</h4>
    <label for="txtEmployeeName">Employee's Name:</label>
    <input type="text" id="txtEmployeeName" name="txtEmployeeName"
        placeholder="LastName, FirstName" size="30"><br>

    <label for="txtDepartment">Department Name:</label>
    <input type="text" id="txtDepartment" name="txtDepartment"><br>

    <label for="txtAge">Age:</label>
    <input type="text" id="txtAge" name="txtAge" value="21"><br>

    <label for="txtSalary">Salary:</label>
    <input type="text" id="txtSalary" name="txtSalary"><br>

    <label for="txtHireDate">Hire Date:</label>
    <input type="text" id="txtHireDate" name="txtHireDate"><br><br>

        <button id="btnCreateNew">Create New Employee Record</button>
    </form>
 </body>
</html>
```

365

How It Works

In this code, when the Add CSS Class button is clicked, the following code is executed:

- `$("#frmNewEmplpoyee").addClass("move", 2000, "easeInOutQuad")`—Executes the `addClass()` method on the selected form and adds the move CSS class. The move CSS class is defined to change the background color to `lightcyan` and the top and left margins to 100 pixels. These properties are changed over the course of two seconds by using the `easeInOutQuad` easing function. These transitional changes give the impression of animation.

When the Remove CSS Class button is clicked, the following code is executed:

- `$("#frmNewEmplpoyee").removeClass("move", 2000, "easeInOutQuad")`—Executes the `removeClass()` method on the selected form and removes the move CSS class. This will bring the selected form to its original state.

Figure 10-23 displays the data-entry form in its initial state.

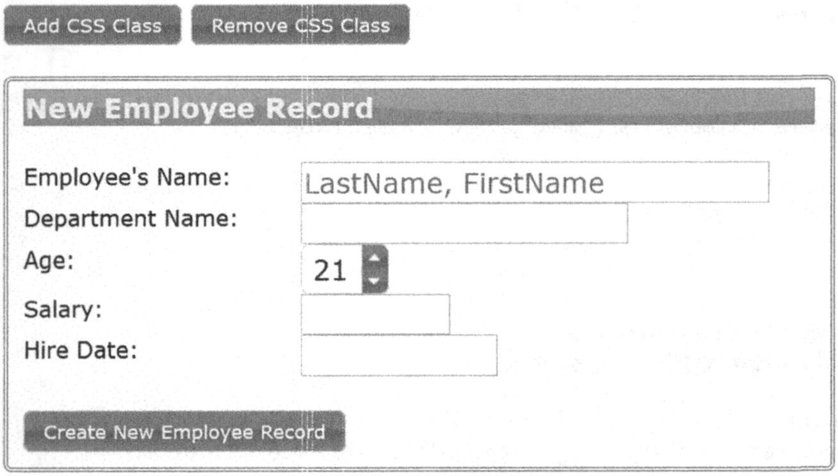

Figure 10-23. *Data-entry form in its initial state*

Figure 10-24 displays the data-entry form after the Add CSS Class button is clicked and the move CSS class is added to the form element.

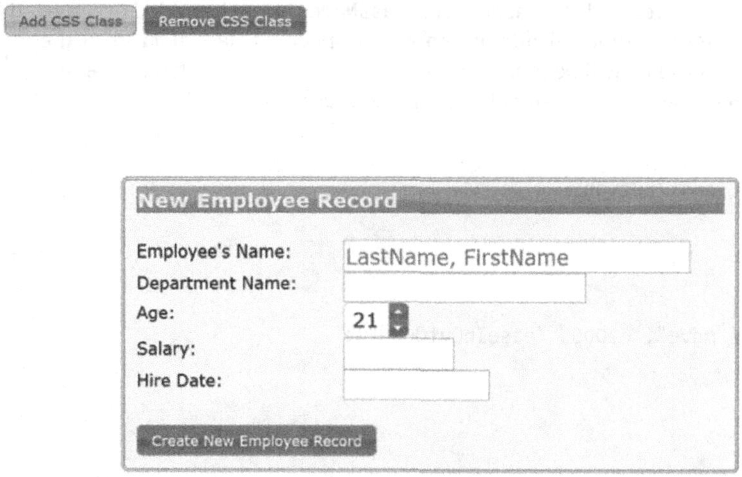

Figure 10-24. *Data-entry form after the animation is completed*

The following syntax can also be used for the addClass() and removeClass():

```
$(selector).addClass(className, options)
$(selector).removeClass(className, options)
```

The options argument is a map object with the following options. It is optional.

- duration—The duration for which animation will run. The default value is 400 milliseconds.

- easing—Easing function to use for the animation. The default value is swing.

- complete—Callback function that will be called after the animation is completed.

- children—If set to true, the class is applied to all its descendants in addition to the selected element itself. If set to false, the class is applied to the selected element only. Even if it is set to false, due to the cascading effect of the selected element, all its descendants will be animated too. In both the cases, the animation effect is same but the difference is whether the animation is applied to the selected element and cascaded to descendants or the animation is applied to each descendants elements individually. The default value is false.

- queue—If set to false, the animation will not be added to the effects queue and the animation will run immediately. The default value is true.

The toggleClass() Method

The toggleClass() method can be used to add a CSS class if it is not associated with the selected elements or remove a CSS class if it is associated with the selected elements. The syntax for the toggleClass() method is:

```
$(selector).toggleClass(addRemoveClassName, switchFlag, durationOfAnimation, easingFunctionName,
completeCallbackFunction)
$(selector).toggleClass(addRemoveClassName, switchFlag, options)
```

switchFlag (optional) determines whether the specified class addRemoveClassName should be added or removed. If it is not passed as an argument, the toggleClass() method will add or remove the specified class. If it is true, the class will be added but not removed. If it is false, the class will be removed but not added to the selected elements. You can add the following code to Listing 10-15 to check the functionality of the toggleClass() method.

HTML code:

```
<button id="btnToggleClass">Toggle CSS Class</button>
```

JavaScript code:

```
$("#btnToggleClass").click(function () {
    $("#frmNewEmplpoyee").toggleClass("move",  2000, "easeInOutQuad");
});
```

The switchClass() Method

The switchClass() method can be used to remove one CSS class and add another CSS class in a single statement. The syntax for the switchClass() method is:

```
$(selector).switchClass(removeClassName, addClassName, durationOfAnimation,
    easingFunctionName, completeCallbackFunction)
$(selector).switchClass(removeClassName, addClassName, options)
```

The animate() Method

You can achieve the same effect by using the animate() method instead of addClass() by making the following changes:

- Remove the .move CSS class from the style:

  ```
  .move {
        background-color: lightcyan;
        margin-top: 300px;
        margin-left: 300px;
  }
  ```

- Replace the following code:

  ```
  $("#frmNewEmplpoyee").addClass("move", 2000, "easeInOutQuad");
  ```

  with this

  ```
  $("#frmNewEmplpoyee").animate({
        backgroundColor: "#e0ffff", // lightcyan
        marginTop: "300px",
        marginLeft: "300px"
  },
  2000, "easeInOutQuad");
  ```

- Replace the following code:

```
$("#frmNewEmplpoyee").removeClass("move", 2000, "easeInOutQuad");
```

with this

```
$("#frmNewEmplpoyee").animate({
    backgroundColor: "#e0ffff", // lightyellow
    marginTop: "0px",
    marginLeft: "0px"
},
2000, "easeInOutQuad");
```

The advantages of using the animate() method are that you can use variables to set CSS values and you can use + and − operators to use relative positions of the selected elements. For example, marginLeft: "+200px" can be used to move the selected element 200 pixels to the right of its current position.

10-15. Using jQuery UI Animation Effects on Selected Elements
Problem

You want to use jQuery UI animation effects on selected elements.

Solution

jQuery provides many animation effects that can be applied to the selected elements. The following methods can be used to apply jQuery UI animation effects:

- effect() method uses the specified effectName animation for the selected elements.

- show() method displays the selected elements with the specified effectName animation.

- hide() method hides the selected elements with the specified effectName animation.

- toggle() method displays or hides the selected elements with the specified effectName animation.

Table 10-2 lists the jQuery UI effects, their options, their valid values, and their default values.

Table 10-2. *jQuery UI Effects and Their Options*

Effect	Options	Option Description	Possible Values	Default Value
blind	Direction	Direction of the blind	"up", "down", "left", "right", "vertical", "horizontal"	"up"
bounce	Distance	Distance of the largest bounce	n pixels	20
bounce	Times	Number of bounces	n count	5
clip	Direction	Direction of the clipping of the selected element	"vertical", "horizontal"	"vertical"
drop	Direction	Direction of the drop	"up", "down", "left", "right"	"left"
explode	Pieces	Explode to number of pieces	n pieces	9
fade				
fold	horizFirst	If true, first fold horizontally when hiding	true, false	false
highlight	Color	Background color during animation	"#nnnnnn"	#ffff99
puff	Percent	Scale percentage	n percent	150
pulsate	Times	Number of pulses	n count	5
scale	Direction	Scale in the specified direction	"both", "vertical", "horizontal"	"both"
scale	Origin	Vanishing point	["top|middle|bottom", "left|center|right"]	["middle", "center"]
scale	Percent	Scale percent (not optional)	N	
scale	Scale	Area to scale	"box", "content", "both"	"both"
shake	Direction	Direction of the shake	"left", "right", "up", "down"	"left"
shake	Distance	Distance to shake	n pixels	20
shake	Times	Number of times to shake	n count	3
size	To	Height and width to resize (not optional)	{height: m, width: n}	
size	Origin	Vanishing point	["top|middle|bottom", "left|center|right"]	["top", "left"]
size	Scale	Area to scale	"box", "content", "both"	"both"
slide	Direction	Direction of the slide	"left", "right", "up", "down"	"left"
slide	Distance	Distance to slide	n pixels	height or width
transfer	className	Name of the class to use to show transfer	"validClassName"	
transfer	To	Transfer to the element (selector)	"validSelector"	

The following is the syntax needed to use these effects:

- $(selector).effect(effectName, options, durationOfAnimation, completeCallbackFunctionName)

- $(selector).show(effectName, options, durationOfAnimation, completeCallbackFunctionName)

- $(selector).hide(effectName, options, durationOfAnimation, completeCallbackFunctionName)

- $(selector).toggle(effectName, options, durationOfAnimation, completeCallbackFunctionName)

where options has effectName-specific settings and the easing function name.

The following syntax can also be used:

$(selector).methodName(options)

where methodName can be effect, show, hide, or toggle and options has effect as one of the options.

In this recipe, you will use the scale effect in the effect(), hide() and show() methods. Listing 10-16 demonstrates an example to show all the possible effects.

Listing 10-16. Animation using the scale effect

```
<!DOCTYPE html>
<html lang="en">
<head>
    <meta charset="utf-8">
    <link rel="stylesheet" href="styles/jquery-ui.min.css">
    <script src="scripts/jquery-2.1.0.min.js"></script>
    <script src="scripts/jquery-ui.min.js"></script>

    <style>
        div {
            border:3px double green;
            width: 100px;
            height: 100px;
            padding-left: 10px;
            padding-right: 10px;
            padding-bottom: 10px;
            background-color: lightyellow;
        }
    </style>

    <script>
        $(function() {
            $("#btnRunEffect").button();
            $("#btnHide").button();
            $("#btnShow").button();
```

```
$("#btnRunEffect").click( function () {
    var selectedEffectType = $("#effectType").val();
    $("div").effect(selectedEffectType, {
        direction: "both",
        origin: ["top", "right"],
        percent: 10,
        scale: "box"
    });
});

$("#btnHide").click( function () {
    var selectedEffectType = $("#effectType").val();
    $("div").hide(selectedEffectType, {
        direction: "both",
        origin: ["top", "right"]
    });
});

$("#btnShow").click( function () {
    var selectedEffectType = $("#effectType").val();
    $("div").show(selectedEffectType, {
        direction: "both",
        origin: ["top", "right"]
    });
});
    });
</script>
</head>

<body>
    Effect Type:
    <select id="effectType">
        <option value="blind">Blind</option>
        <option value="bounce">Bounce</option>
        <option value="clip">Clip</option>
        <option value="drop">Drop</option>
        <option value="explode">Explode</option>
        <option value="fade">Fade</option>
        <option value="fold">Fold</option>
        <option value="highlight">Highlight</option>
        <option value="puff">Puff</option>
        <option value="pulsate">Pulsate</option>
        <option value="scale">Scale</option>
        <option value="shake">Shake</option>
        <option value="size">Size</option>
        <option value="slide">Slide</option>
        <option value="transfer">Transfer</option>
    </select><br><br>
```

```
        <button id="btnRunEffect">Run Effect</button>
        <button id="btnHide">Hide</button>
      <button id="btnShow">Show</button><br><br>
      <div></div>
</body>
</html>
```

How It Works

Figure 10-25 displays the initial page in the browser.

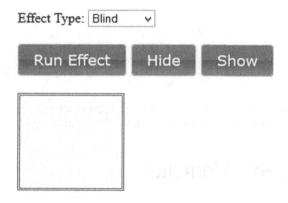

Figure 10-25. *Initial page display*

When the Run Effect button is clicked, the following code is executed:

```
var selectedEffectType = $("#effectType").val();
$("div").effect(selectedEffectType, {
    direction: "both",
    origin: ["top", "right"],
    percent: 10,
    scale: "box"
});
```

selectedEffectType is set with the selected value from the Effect Type drop-down. You can select different effect types and click Run Effect to see how the different effects work.

The effect() method scales the div element in both directions—vertically and horizontally to 10%. The animation moves toward the top-right corner of the box. Figure 10-26 displays the screen after the Run Effect button is clicked.

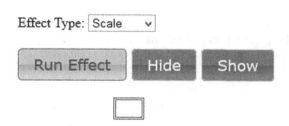

Figure 10-26. *Scale animation*

When the Hide button is clicked, the following code is executed:

```
var selectedEffectType = $("#effectType").val();
$("div").hide(selectedEffectType, {
     direction: "both",
     origin: ["top", "right"]
});
```

The hide() method hides the div box by reducing the height and the width and disappearing toward the top-right corner.

When the Show button is clicked, the following code is executed:

```
var selectedEffectType = $("#effectType").val();
$("div").show(selectedEffectType, {
     direction: "both",
     origin: ["top", "right"]
});
```

The show() method displays the div box by scaling in both directions (vertically and horizontally) and it starts appearing from the top-right corner. The div element reverts back to the same sized box as displayed in Figure 10-26.

10-16. Creating Draggable and Droppable Elements
Problem

You want to make elements draggable and droppable.

Solution

By setting HTML elements as draggable and droppable, you can drag and drop elements to a specified area. Listing 10-17 shows the use of the draggable() and droppable() methods.

Listing 10-17. Interaction using the draggable() and droppable() methods

```
<!DOCTYPE html>
<html lang="en">
<head>
     <meta charset="utf-8">
     <link rel="stylesheet" href="styles/jquery-ui.min.css">
     <script src="scripts/jquery-2.1.0.min.js"></script>
     <script src="scripts/jquery-ui.min.js"></script>

     <style>
     #departmentNames { width: 200px; border:3px double green; background-color: lightyellow; }
     #dropArea {height: 150px; width: 240px; border:3px double green; background-color: lightcyan; }
     </style>
```

```
<script>
 $(function() {
      $("li").draggable({
       revert: "invalid"
      });

      $("#dropArea").droppable({
       accept: "li",
       drop: function( event, ui ) {
            $("#message").append(ui.draggable.text() + "<br>");
       }
      });
 });
 </script>
</head>

<body>
     Departments:
     <ul id="departmentNames">
      <li>Marketing</li>
      <li>Sales</li>
      <li>Development</li>
      <li>Implementation</li>
      <li>Production Support</li>
      <li>Customer Support</li>
     </ul>

     <div id="dropArea" style="height"></div>

     <div id="message"><strong>Items Dragged and Dropped:</strong><br></div>
</body>
</html>
```

How It Works

In this code, in the DOM ready function:

- The following code sets all li elements as draggable with the revert option as invalid.
  It means if the li element is not dropped successfully, the dragged element reverts back to
  its original position.

```
$("li").draggable({
     revert: "invalid"
});
```

- The following code sets the div element (with the ID dropArea) as droppable. The accept option is set to li, which means that this drop area will accept only li elements. The drop callback function is executed when an element is dropped successfully. In the drop callback function, you are appending the text of the dragged element to a div element with the ID set to message.

```
$("#dropArea").droppable({
    accept: "li",
    drop: function( event, ui ) {
     $("#message").append(ui.draggable.text() + "<br>");
    }
});
```

Figure 10-27 displays the initial state of the screen in a browser.

Departments:

Items Dragged and Dropped:

Figure 10-27. *Drag-and-drop form in its initial state*

You can use the left mouse key to click, hold, and drag-and-drop department names from the list to the empty box. Figure 10-28 displays the screen after a few department names are dragged and dropped.

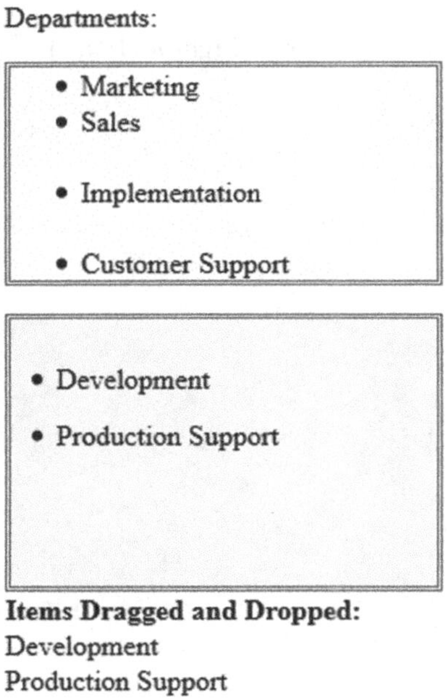

Departments:

Marketing
Sales

Implementation

Customer Support

Development

Production Support

Items Dragged and Dropped:
Development
Production Support

Figure 10-28. *Dragged and dropped department names*

The following sections explain the other interaction functionalities provided by the jQuery UI library.

Resizable

The `resizable()` method makes the selected element resizable. The user can resize the element by using the mouse to drag the bottom side, right side, and the bottom-right corner of the element. You can try the `resizable()` method by adding the following code to Listing 10-17:

```
$("#dropArea").resizable();
```

Selectable

The `selectable()` method makes the HTML elements selectable by clicking with the mouse left key. Multiple elements can be selected by drawing a box around the elements or by clicking with the mouse while holding Ctrl key. Listing 10-18 shows the use of the `selectable()` method.

Listing 10-18. Interaction using the selectable() method

```
<!DOCTYPE html>
<html lang="en">
<head>
      <meta charset="utf-8">
      <link rel="stylesheet" href="styles/jquery-ui.min.css">
      <script src="scripts/jquery-2.1.0.min.js"></script>
      <script src="scripts/jquery-ui.min.js"></script>
```

```
<style>
 #departmentNames { width: 200px; border:3px double green; background-color: lightyellow; }
 #departmentNames .ui-selecting { background: lightgreen; }
 #departmentNames .ui-selected { background: green; color: white; }
</style>

<script>
 $(function() {
      $("#departmentNames").selectable();
 });
</script>
</head>

<body>
     Departments:
     <ul id="departmentNames">
      <li>Marketing</li>
      <li>Sales</li>
      <li>Development</li>
      <li>Implementation</li>
      <li>Production Support</li>
      <li>Customer Support</li>
     </ul>
</body>
</html>
```

Figure 10-29 displays the screen after a few department names are selected.

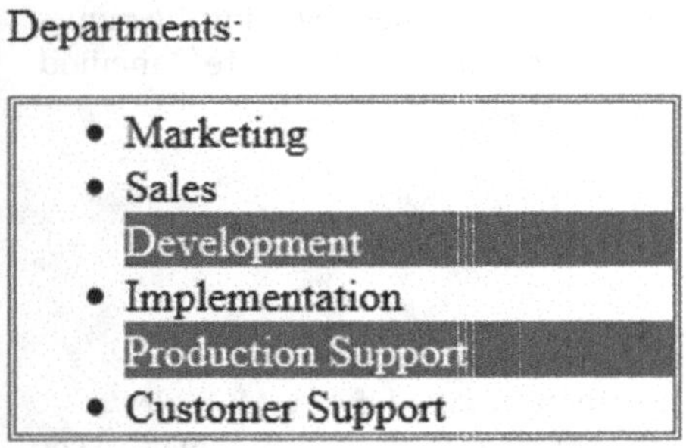

Departments:

Figure 10-29. *Selected department names*

Sortable

The `sortable()` method makes HTML elements selectable and draggable so that the user can rearrange the order in the list by selecting, dragging, and dropping elements. To check the functionality of the `sortable()` method, you can replace the following code in Listing 10-18:

```
$("#departmentNames").selectable();
```

with

```
$("#departmentNames").sortable();
```

Figure 10-30 displays the list of rearranged department names.

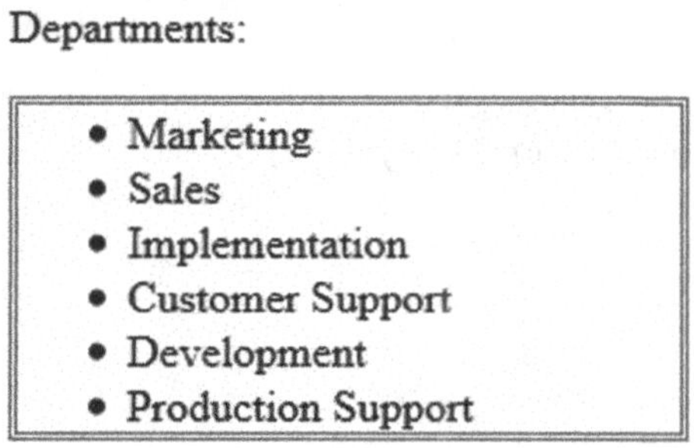

Departments:

```
• Marketing
• Sales
• Implementation
• Customer Support
• Development
• Production Support
```

Figure 10-30. *Dragged and dropped department names*

10-17. Creating Drag-and-Drop Functionality in a Photo Album Application

Problem

You want to create a photo album functionality so that users can drag-and-drop photos from the album to the shopping cart.

Solution

jQuery UI library provides the following five mouse-based interactions that can be used to develop highly interactive web applications:

- Draggable—Specifies which HTML elements can be dragged using the mouse.

- Droppable—Specifies the target area where dragged items can be dropped.

- Resizable—Specifies which HTML elements can be resized by using the mouse.

- Selectable—Specifies which HTML elements can be selected by using the mouse.

- Sortable—Specifies which group of HTML elements can rearranged by dragging and dropping.

This recipe covers draggable and droppable interactions. Listing 10-19 demonstrates an example for a photo album in which photos can be dragged and dropped from the photo album into a print area. Listing 10-20 contains the content of the `photoAlbums.json` file.

Listing 10-19. Draggin and dropping photos from the album

```html
<!DOCTYPE html>
<html lang="en">
<head>
    <meta charset="utf-8">
    <title>Photo Album</title>

    <link rel="stylesheet" href="styles/jquery-ui.min.css">

    <script src="scripts/jquery-2.1.0.min.js"></script>
    <script src="scripts/jquery-ui.min.js"></script>

    <style>
     .album li { float: left; width: 96px; padding: 4px; margin: 4px; text-align: center; }
     .album li h5 { margin-top:2px; cursor: move; }
     .album li img { width: 100%; cursor: move; }

     #print {width: 90%; height: 400px; padding: 10px; background-color:lightyellow}

     div { margin-left: auto; margin-right: auto; }
    </style>

    <script>
     $(function() {
         $("#btnPrint").button();

         // Get Albums
         $.ajax({
          type: "GET",
          url: "photoAlbums.json",
          dataType: "json",
          success: getPhotoAlbums,
          error: reportError
         });

         $("#btnPrint").click(function(){
          var printPhotos = "Following photos are selected to be printed: <br>";

          $("#print img").each(function (obj) {
              printPhotos += $(this).attr("src") + "<br>";
          });

          $("#printList").html(printPhotos);

          $("#printList").dialog({
              modal: true,
              buttons: {
              "Ok": function() {
                  $( this ).dialog( "close" );
              }
          }
              });
         });
     });
```

```
// on success
function getPhotoAlbums(returnedData, status) {
        var htmlString = "";

        $.each(returnedData.albums, function(obj, currentElement){
          htmlString += '<li class="ui-widget-content ui-corner-all" style="width:130px" >';
          htmlString += '<h5 class="ui-widget-header" >' + currentElement.photoTitle + '</h5>';
          htmlString += '<img src="images/' + currentElement.imageFile + '" alt="' +
                  currentElement.photoTitle + '" width="96" height="72">';
          htmlString += '<div id="printCheckbox" class="ui-widget-content" style="font-size:10px">';
          htmlString += '<input type="checkbox">Print</div></li>';
        });

        $("#album").append(htmlString);
        dragAndDrop();
}


// On error
function reportError(request, status, errorMsg) {
        $("#statusMessage").append("Status: " + status + "<br>Error Message: " + errorMsg);
}

function dragAndDrop() {
        // Make the photos in the album as draggable
        $( "li").draggable({
             revert: "invalid",
             helper: "clone",
          cursor: "move"
        });

        // Make the print droppable
        $("#print").droppable({
          accept: "#album > li",
          drop: function( event, ui ) {
             printPhoto( ui.draggable );
          }
        });

        function printPhoto( photoItem ) {
          photoItem = photoItem.clone();

          photoItem.find( "#printCheckbox" ).replaceWith('<div class="ui-widget-content"
style="font-size:10px"><input  id="removeCheckbox" type="checkbox">Remove</div>');

          $("#print > ul").append(photoItem).show(function() {
             photoItem
             .animate({ width: "72px" })
             .find( "img" )
             .animate({ height: "54px" });
        });
        }
```

```
            $( "#album" ).click(function( event ) {
             target = $( event.target );
             printPhoto(target.parents("li"));
            });

            $( "#print" ).click(function( event ) {
             target = $( event.target );

             if ( target.is(":checkbox") ) {
                  target.parents("li").remove();
             }
            });
        }
      </script>
</head>

<body>
      <div class="ui-widget ui-helper-clearfix">
       <ul id="album" class="album ui-helper-reset"></ul>
      </div><br>

      <div id="print" class="ui-corner-all" style="border:3px double green">
       <h4 class="ui-widget-header"><span class="ui-icon ui-icon-print"></span> Print</h4>
       <ul class="album ui-helper-reset"></ul>
      </div><br>

      <button id="btnPrint" style="margin-left:50px">Send to Print</button><br>

      <div id="statusMessage"></div>

      <div id="printList" title="Print Photos"></div>
</body>
</html>
```

Listing 10-20. Content of the photoAlbums.json file

```
{
  "albums":
  [
    {"albumName":"Birds", "photoTitle":"Bird 1", "imageFile":"Bird1.png"},
    {"albumName":"Birds", "photoTitle":"Bird 2", "imageFile":"Bird2.png"},
    {"albumName":"Insects", "photoTitle":"Butterfly 1", "imageFile":"Butterfly1.png"},
    {"albumName":"Insects", "photoTitle":"Butterfly 2", "imageFile":"Butterfly2.png"},
    {"albumName":"Insects", "photoTitle":"LadyBug", "imageFile":"LadyBug.png"},
    {"albumName":"Animals", "photoTitle":"Cat", "imageFile":"Cat.png"},
    {"albumName":"Animals", "photoTitle":"Dog", "imageFile":"Dog.png"},
    {"albumName":"Animals", "photoTitle":"Panda", "imageFile":"Panda.png"},
    {"albumName":"Sea Animals", "photoTitle":"Dolphin", "imageFile":"Dolphin.png"},
    {"albumName":"Sea Animals", "photoTitle":"Fish 1", "imageFile":"Fish1.png"},
    {"albumName":"Sea Animals", "photoTitle":"Jelly Fish", "imageFile":"JellyFish.png"}
  ]
}
```

How It Works

In this HTML code:

- The following element is used for appending image elements. Image elements with the source file name are appended to this element after you get the photo album list as a response of the AJAX call.

```
<ul id="album" class="album ui-helper-reset"></ul>
```

- The following code creates the print area where photos can be dropped.

```
<div id="print" class="ui-corner-all" style="border:3px double green">
<h4 class="ui-widget-header"><span class="ui-icon ui-icon-print"></span> Print</h4>
</div>
```

- The following code creates the Send to Print button.

```
<button id="btnPrint" style="margin-left:50px">Send to Print</button>
```

- The following element is used to display AJAX error messages if there are any.

```
<div id="statusMessage"></div>
```

- The following element is used to display a dialog box with the list of photos that are dropped in the print drop area.

```
<div id="printList" title="Print Photos"></div>
```

After the DOM is ready,

- An AJAX call is made to get the album and photo details using the following code:

```
$.ajax({
    type: "GET",
    url: "photoAlbums.json",
    dataType: "json",
    success: getPhotoAlbums,
    error: reportError
});
```

- After the content of the photoAlbums.json file is successfully returned, the getPhotoAlbums() function is called and it executes the following code to build an images list and append it to the div element (id: album):

```
$.each(returnedData.albums, function(obj, currentElement){
    htmlString += '<li class="ui-widget-content ui-corner-all" style="width:130px" >';
    htmlString += '<h5 class="ui-widget-header" >' + currentElement.photoTitle + '</h5>';
    htmlString += '<img src="images/' + currentElement.imageFile + '" alt="' +
            currentElement.photoTitle + '" width="96" height="72">';
```

```
    htmlString += '<div id="printCheckbox" class="ui-widget-content" style="font-size:10px">';
    htmlString += '<input type="checkbox">Print</div></li>';
});

$("#album").append(htmlString);
```

- After appending all the image elements and the Print checkbox to the ul element, the dragAndDrop() function is executed.

- In the dragAndDrop() function, the following code makes li elements (which is embedding images, headers, and the checkbox) draggable:

```
$( "li").draggable({
    revert: "invalid",
    helper: "clone",
    cursor: "move"
});
```

  - revert: "invalid" reverts the drag-and-drop action if the li element is not dropped in the designated area (<div id="#album">).

  - helper: "clone" clones the li element before it is getting dropped.

  - cursor: "move" changes the cursor so it moves during the drag-and-drop process.

- The following code makes the HTML element with the ID of print as a drop area:

```
$("#print").droppable({
    accept: "#album > li",
    drop: function( event, ui ) {
        printPhoto( ui.draggable );
    }
});
```

  - accept: "#album > li" allows only li elements (with the parent as #album) to be dropped in this area.

  - drop: function({...}) specifies the callback function that's called when an element is dropped.

- When the user drags and drops an image, the printPhoto() function is executed and it in turn executes the following code:

```
photoItem = photoItem.clone();

photoItem.find( "#printCheckbox" ).replaceWith('<div class="ui-widget-content"
style="font-size:10px"><input  id="removeCheckbox" type="checkbox">Remove</div>');

$("#print > ul").append(photoItem).show(function() {
    photoItem
    .animate({ width: "72px" })
    .find( "img" )
    .animate({ height: "54px" });
});
```

The following is the explanation of this code:

- To create a clone of the dropped (li element):

```
photoItem = photoItem.clone();
```

- To replace the Print checkbox with the Remove checkbox:

```
photoItem.find( "#printCheckbox" ).replaceWith(
        '<div class="ui-widget-content" style="font-size:10px">
        <input  id="removeCheckbox" type="checkbox">Remove</div>');
```

- In the show( ) function, the appended item is animated by reducing its width to 72 pixels, after which the img element is located within the li element and then the image is animated by changing its height to 54 pixels. With this step, the drag-and-drop is completed.

```
$("#print > ul").append(photoItem).show(function() {
        photoItem
        .animate({ width: "72px" })
        .find( "img" )
        .animate({ height: "54px" });
});
```

- When the user clicks the Send to Print button, all the dropped image details are retrieved and displayed in a dialog widget.
- When the user clicks the Print checkbox in the album, the image is dropped on to the Print drop area.
- When the user clicks the Remove checkbox in the print area, the image is removed from the Print drop area.

Figure 10-31 displays images in the photo album and the images that have been dropped in the Print drop area.

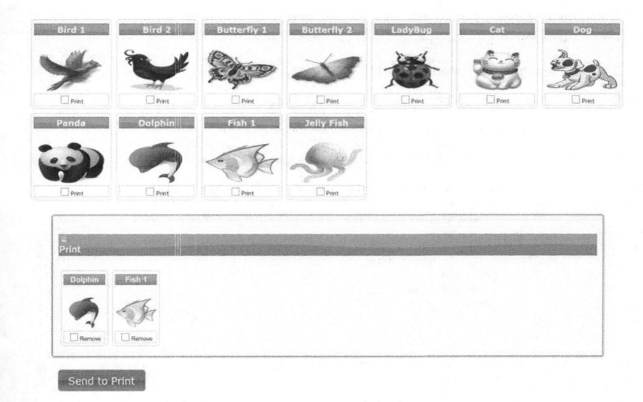

Figure 10-31. *Photo album showing images in the Print area*

Figure 10-32 displays the dialog box with the image details when the user clicks the Send to Print button.

Figure 10-32. *List of images that are dropped into the print area*

Summary

This chapter covered topics about jQuery UI widgets, effects, and interactions. The following is the list of methods used in the chapter's recipes:

- To create widgets: autocomplete(), spinner(), slider(), datepicker(), tooltip(), button(), dialog(), progressbar(), tabs(), accordion(), and menu().

- To interact among HTML elements: draggable(), droppable(), resizable(), selectable(), and sortable().

- To add animation effects: addClass(), removeClass(), switchClass(), toggleClass(), animate(), effect(), hide(), show(), and toggle().

CHAPTER 11

■ ■ ■

jQuery Mobile

jQuery Mobile is a JavaScript library that's built on the jQuery core. It provides the CSS framework, an events framework, widgets, and layout and form controls for developing touch-friendly user interface web applications. These apps are supported on desktops, smartphones, and tablets. This chapter covers page structure and navigation, theming, icons, transitions, events handlers, layout controls, form elements, and widgets for mobile web applications development.

This chapter includes recipes on the following topics:

- The CSS framework

- Page structure—header, content, and footer

- Pages—container, transition, and navigation

- Navigation bar

- Dialog boxes, panels, and popups

- Collapsibles

- Grid views, listviews, and tables

- Form elements

- Events

Downloading the jQuery Mobile Library

You can download jQuery Mobile library from http://jquerymobile.com/download/. Download the latest stable version. At the time of this writing, the latest version was 1.4.3. Click on the ZIP file link to download it. Save the file on your local system. If you have selected the 1.4.3 version of the jQuery Mobile, the saved filename is jquery.mobile-1.4.3.zip. Extract all files from the ZIP file into a work folder.

Copy the jquery.mobile-1.4.3.min.css file to the styles folder in your web page development root folder. Copy the jquery.mobile-1.4.3.min.js file to the scripts folder. The structure of your development environment should look like this:

- images/

- scripts/jquery-2.1.0.min.js

- scripts/jquery.mobile-1.4.3.min.js

- styles/jquery.mobile-1.4.3.min.css

- *.htm

Add the following lines to include the jQuery mobile library and CSS in your HTML files:

```
<link rel="stylesheet" href="styles/jquery.mobile-1.4.3.min.css" />
<script type="text/javascript" src="scripts/jquery.mobile-1.4.3.min.js"></script>
```

Add the jQuery mobile JavaScript file (`jquery.mobile-1.4.3.min.js`) after the jQuery core library JavaScript file (for example, `jquery-2.1.0.min.js`).

The `mobileinit` event is triggered after the jQuery mobile JavaScript file is included and initialized. If you want to make any changes during the jQuery Mobile initialization process, such as change the global settings, you can set up the callback function for the `mobileinit` event. This callback function must be registered before it can be included in the jQuery mobile JavaScript file.

Testing on Mobile Devices

You can test your code using any recent browser (preferably Firefox or Chrome) on your desktop or by using a browser on your mobile devices. Refer to Appendix C for details about setting up Tomcat server and IIS server and also about testing your web application on mobile devices. The screenshots in this chapter are from the Safari browser on an iPhone 5s.

Mobile Applications

You can wrap your mobile web applications using PhoneGap and convert them to mobile applications. PhoneGap also provides APIs for accessing mobile device-specific features. For details about PhoneGap, visit `http://phonegap.com`. Converting mobile web applications into native applications and deploying them on mobile devices is out of the scope of this book.

11-1. CSS Framework: CSS Classes, Themes, and Icons
Problem

You want to understand the features provided by the CSS framework for the jQuery mobile library.

Solution

The jQuery mobile library provides CSS-based enhancements to develop a rich Internet application interface.

Common CSS Classes

Table 11-1 displays the list of CSS classes that can be used to style any of the widgets. Widget-specific classes are explained in other recipes in this chapter.

Table 11-1. *Common CSS Classes*

To Achieve This	Use This Class
Create rounded corners for the element.	`ui-corner-all`
Reduce the font size and element's size.	`ui-mini`
Overlay a shadow on the element to give popping-out effect.	`ui-overlay-shadow`
Cast shadow around the element.	`ui-shadow`

Themes

A theme provides a consistent look and feel for all user interface controls. In the jQuery Mobile 1.4.3 library there are two swatches available—"a" and "b". "a" is the default swatch and it displays widgets in light gray. The "b" swatch displays widgets in a dark color (usually black). Swatches are specified by using a single character of the alphabet (c through z). To specify which theme to use for a widget, you can use data-theme="b" (for example). You can add the data-theme attribute at an individual widget level or at the parent level. For example, to change the theme for the whole page, you can use:

```
<div data-role="page" data-theme="b">
```

Table 11-2 displays widgets using themes "a" and "b".

Table 11-2. *Widgets with Themes "a" and "b"*

Widget Name	data-theme="a"	data-theme="b"
Header	Page Header	Page Header
Label	Input Text:	Input Text:
Input Text	Text box	Text box
Date	Jul 9, 2014	Jul 9, 2014
Textarea	Text area	Text area
Input File	Choose File no file selected / Take Photo or Video / Choose Existing / Cancel	Choose File no file selected / Take Photo or Video / Choose Existing / Cancel
Flip Switch	Off	Off

(continued)

Table 11-2. (*continued*)

Widget Name	data-theme="a"	data-theme="b"
Checkbox	☑ Checkbox Option 1	☑ Checkbox Option 1
Radio Button	◉ Radiobutton Option 1	◉ Radiobutton Option 1
Select Drop-Down	Option 1 ⌄	Option 1 ⌄
	⟨ ⟩ Done	⟨ ⟩ Done
	Option 1 Option 2	Option 1 Option 2
Slider	31 ▬▬⬤▬▬	31 ▬⬛▬
Range Slider	21 ▬⬤▬⬤▬ 69	21 ▬⬛▬ 69
Button	⌂ Home	⌂ Home

Custom Themes

The Themeroller tool found at http://themeroller.jquerymobile.com/ enables you to add new themes (c-z), customize them by selecting a different color and by setting CSS properties, and preview, download, and include them in your web pages. Table 11-2 lists commonly used widgets with themes "a" and "b".

Icons

jQuery mobile provides built-in icons that are ready to use. Figure 11-1 displays all the icons available in the jQuery mobile library. You can use data-icon="iconName" and class="ui-icon-iconName" for displaying an icon in a container (such as buttons, listviews, and so on), where iconName is listed in Figure 11-1. To display an icon in the circular container, add the class - ui-corner-all. The icons in Figure 11-1 are created using the following syntax.

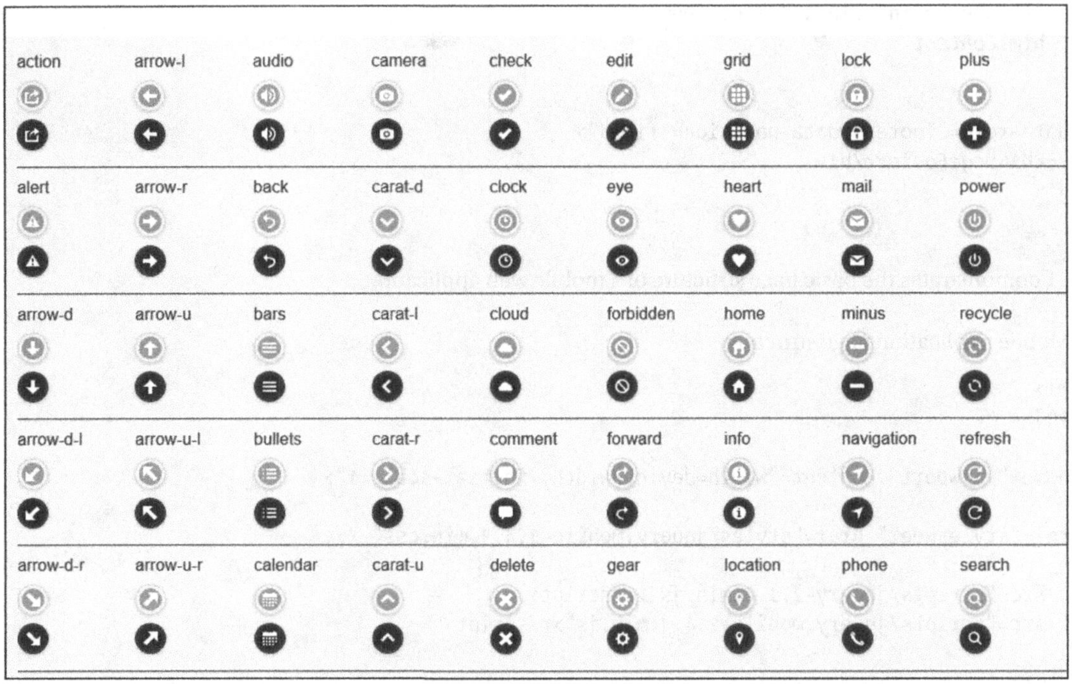

Figure 11-1. *Available icons*

Using theme "a":

```
<a href="#" class="ui-btn ui-btn-a ui-corner-all ui-shadow ui-icon-iconName ui-btn-icon-notext">
```

Using theme "b":

```
<a href="#" class="ui-btn ui-btn-b ui-corner-all ui-shadow ui-icon-iconName ui-btn-icon-notext">
```

where iconName can be any valid icon name listed in Figure 11-1.

11-2. Understanding Page Structure
Problem

You want to understand the basic structure of a mobile web application page.

Solution

In the jQuery mobile framework, an HTML file can have multiple pages. At load time, the first page in the HTML file is displayed. A typical page consists of a header, the content, and a footer. The following is the structure of a page:

```
<div data-role="page">
    <div data-role="header">
          <h1>pageHeading</h1>
    </div>
```

```
        <div data-role="main" class="ui-content">
                htmlContent
        </div>

        <div data-role="footer" data-position="fixed">
                <h1>pageFooter</h1>
        </div>
</div>
```

Listing 11-1 demonstrates the basic page structure of a mobile web application.

Listing 11-1. Mobile application page structure

```
<!DOCTYPE html>
<html lang="en">
<head>
        <meta name="viewport" content="width=device-width, initial-scale=1">

        <link rel="stylesheet" href="styles/jquery.mobile-1.4.3.min.css" />

        <script src="scripts/jquery-2.1.0.min.js"></script>
        <script src="scripts/jquery.mobile-1.4.3.min.js"></script>
</head>

<body>
        <div data-role="page">
            <div data-role="header">
                        <h1>Page Header</h1>
            </div>

            <div data-role="main" class="ui-content">
                        <p>Content here...</p>
            </div>

            <div data-role="footer" data-position="fixed">
                        <h1>Page Footer</h1>
            </div>
        </div>
</body>
</html>
```

How It Works

In this code listing:

- The following code specifies the page zoom level in the browser and its content dimension by using a meta viewport in the head section. Without this setting, the content display on smartphones and tablets would look zoomed out and if the user zooms in manually, parts of the content would be off-screen. With this setting, the content width is set to the correct scale so that content is not zoomed out and instead fits within the width of the device.

  ```
  <meta name="viewport" content="width=device-width, initial-scale=1">
  ```

- The following lines are used to include all required libraries and the CSS style file:
  - jQuery Mobile CSS file—`<link rel="stylesheet" href="styles/jquery.mobile-1.4.3.min.css" />`
  - jQuery library—`<script src="scripts/jquery-2.1.0.min.js"></script>`
  - jQuery Mobile library—`<script src="scripts/jquery.mobile-1.4.3.min.js"></script>`

  You might have different versions of the libraries and CSS files. As of this writing, the latest version of jQuery is 2.10 and the latest version of jQuery Mobile is 1.4.3.

- Each page in the mobile web application is specified by setting the div element's data-role attribute to "page". The syntax for specifying a page is `<div data-role="page">`.

  Within this page element, there typically are the following three areas:
  - Page header is specified by `<div data-role="header">`. In this section, the header's content is set by using the header element (`<h1>`).
  - Page content is specified by `<div data-role="main" class="ui-content">`. In this section, you can use any valid HTML code structure. ui-content adds padding and margins to the content.
  - Page footer is specified by `<div data-role="footer" data-position="fixed">`. In this section, the footer's content is set by using the header element (`<h1>`). data-position is set as "fixed" so that the footer position is fixed at the bottom of the page.

Figure 11-2 displays the page when viewed on an iPhone 5s. The server setup section in Appendix C describes how you can set up a local server and view developed web pages on your mobile devices.

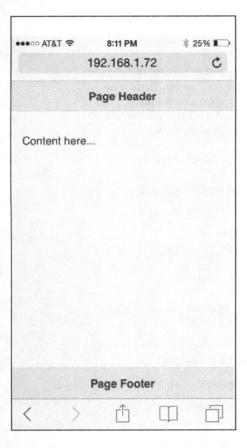

Figure 11-2. *Basic page layout*

11-3. Creating Buttons and Links
Problem
You want to create buttons and links.

Solution
A button is a clickable control. When it is tapped, an action is performed, such as opening a dialog box, popup, or panel, navigating to another page, or making a call to the server to get data. You can create buttons by using any of the following three HTML element types. The following is the syntax to create buttons:

```
<a href="#" class="ui-btn">buttonText</a>
<button class="ui-btn">buttonText</button>
<input type="button" value="buttonText">
```

where type can also be Submit or Reset.

Listing 11-2 demonstrates an example to display different types of buttons with various display options.

Listing 11-2. Buttons with different settings

```
<!DOCTYPE html>
<html lang="en">
<head>
        <meta name="viewport" content="width=device-width, initial-scale=1">

        <link rel="stylesheet" href="styles/jquery.mobile-1.4.3.min.css" />

        <script src="scripts/jquery-2.1.0.min.js"></script>
        <script src="scripts/jquery.mobile-1.4.3.min.js"></script>

        <style>
                strong {color: green;}
        </style>
</head>

<body>
        <div data-role="page">
            <div data-role="header">
                <h1>Buttons</h1>
            </div>

            <div data-role="main" class="ui-content">
                <strong>Default Buttons:</strong><br>
                <a href="#" class="ui-btn">buttonText</a>
                <button class="ui-btn">buttonText</button>
                <input type="button" value="buttonText">

                <br><br><strong>Reduced Width:</strong><br>
                <a href="#" class="ui-btn ui-btn-inline">buttonText</a>
                <button class="ui-btn ui-btn-inline">buttonText</button>
                <input type="button" value="buttonText" data-inline="true">

                <br><br><strong>Rounded Corners:</strong><br>
                <a href="#" class="ui-btn ui-btn-inline ui-corner-all">buttonText</a>
                <button class="ui-btn ui-btn-inline ui-corner-all ">buttonText</button>
                <input type="button" value="buttonText" data-inline="true" data-corners="true">

                <br><br><strong>With Shadow:</strong><br>
                <a href="#" class="ui-btn ui-btn-inline ui-corner-all ui-shadow">buttonText</a>
                <button class="ui-btn ui-btn-inline ui-corner-all ui-shadow">buttonText</button>
                <input type="button" value="buttonText" data-inline="true" data-corners="true">

                <br><br><strong>Theme B:</strong><br>
                <a href="#" class="ui-btn ui-btn-b ui-btn-inline ui-corner-all ui-shadow">buttonText</a>
                <button class="ui-btn ui-btn-b ui-btn-inline ui-corner-all ui-shadow">buttonText</button>
                <input type="button" value="buttonText" data-inline="true" data-corners="true"
                    data-theme="b">
```

```
<br><br><strong>With Icon:</strong><br>
<a href="#" class="ui-btn ui-btn-inline ui-corner-all ui-icon-home ui-btn-icon-
   left">buttonText</a>
<button class="ui-btn ui-btn-inline ui-corner-all ui-icon-home ui-btn-icon-
   left">buttonText</button>
<input type="button" value="buttonText" data-inline="true" data-corners="true"
   data-icon="home" data-iconpos="left">


<br><br><strong>Icon Only. No text:</strong><br>
<a href="#" class="ui-btn ui-btn-inline ui-corner-all ui-icon-home ui-btn-icon-
   notext">buttonText</a>
<button class="ui-btn ui-btn-inline ui-corner-all ui-icon-home ui-btn-icon-
   notext">buttonText</button>
input type="button" value="buttonText" data-inline="true" data-corners="true"
   data-icon="home" data-iconpos="notext">


<br><br><strong>Mini:</strong><br>
<a href="#" class="ui-btn ui-btn-inline ui-corner-all ui-icon-home ui-btn-icon-left
   ui-mini">buttonText</a>
<button class="ui-btn ui-btn-inline ui-corner-all ui-icon-home ui-btn-icon-left
   ui-mini">buttonText</button>
<input type="button" value="buttonText" data-inline="true" data-corners="true"
   data-icon="home" data-mini="true">


<br><br><strong>Disable:</strong><br>
<a href="#" class="ui-btn ui-btn-inline ui-corner-all ui-icon-home ui-btn-icon-left
   ui-mini ui-state-disabled">buttonText</a>
<button class="ui-btn ui-btn-inline ui-corner-all ui-icon-home ui-btn-icon-left
   ui-mini" disabled>buttonText</button>
<input type="button" value="buttonText" data-inline="true" data-corners="true"
   data-icon="home" data-mini="true" disabled>


<br><br><strong>Icon only:</strong><br>
<a href="#" class="ui-btn ui-icon-bars ui-btn-icon-notext ui-corner-all">No text</a>
<button class="ui-btn ui-icon-bars ui-btn-icon-notext ui-corner-all">No text</button>
<input type="button" value="buttonText" data-icon="bars" data-iconpos="notext"
   data-corners="true">


<br><br><strong>Buttons Grouping (Default):</strong><br>
<div data-role="controlgroup"  data-mini="true">
    <a href="#" class="ui-btn ui-btn-b ui-shadow ui-corner-all ui-icon-search
        ui-btn-icon-left">Search</a>
    <a href="#" class="ui-btn ui-btn-b ui-shadow ui-corner-all ui-icon-plus
        ui-btn-icon-left">Add</a>
    <a href="#" class="ui-btn ui-btn-b ui-shadow ui-corner-all ui-icon-delete
        ui-btn-icon-left">Delete</a>
</div>
```

```
          <br><br><strong>Buttons Grouping (horizontal):</strong><br>
          <div data-role="controlgroup"  data-type="horizontal" data-mini="true">
                <a href="#" class="ui-btn ui-btn-b ui-shadow ui-corner-all ui-icon-search
                ui-btn-icon-left">Search</a>
                <a href="#" class="ui-btn ui-btn-b ui-shadow ui-corner-all ui-icon-plus
                ui-btn-icon-left">Add</a>
                <a href="#" class="ui-btn ui-btn-b ui-shadow ui-corner-all ui-icon-delete
                ui-btn-icon-left">Delete</a>
          </div>
       </div>
     </div>
  </body>
</html>
```

How It Works

Three types of buttons are created using the <a>, <button>, and <input> elements. For page navigation, popups, and the panels display, the <a> tag is used. For submitting forms, the <input> and <button> tags are used. The following section explains the classes and data attributes used in this example.

Setting the Button's Width

By default the button's width is the same as the width of the display screen. You can change it to be the same as its text by adding the ui-btn-inline class to the <a> and <button> elements or setting the data-inline to true for the <input> elements:

- `<a href="#" class="ui-btn ui-btn-inline">buttonText</a>`

- `<button class="ui-btn ui-btn-inline">buttonText</button>`

- `<input type="button" value="buttonText" data-inline="true">`

Setting Rounded Corners

You can make the corners of the button rounded by adding the ui-corner-all class to the <a> and <button> elements or setting data-corners to true for the <input> elements:

- `<a href="#" class="ui-btn ui-btn-inline ui-corner-all">buttonText</a>`

- `<button class="ui-btn ui-btn-inline ui-corner-all">buttonText</button>`

- `<input type="button" value="buttonText" data-inline="true" data-corners="true">`

Showing or Hiding a Shadow

You can set buttons to show their shadows by adding the ui-shadow class to the <a> and <button> elements. For <input> elements, the shadow is displayed by default. You can prevent a shadow from being displayed by setting data-shadow to false for the <input> elements:

- `<a href="#" class="ui-btn ui-btn-inline ui-corner-all ui-shadow">buttonText</a>`

- `<button class="ui-btn ui-btn-inline ui-corner-all ui-shadow">buttonText</button>`

- `<input type="button" value="buttonText" data-inline="true" data-corners="true" data-shadow="false">`

Theming

By default, a button inherits its theme from its parent container. You can change the theme by adding the `ui-btn-a` or `ui-btn-b` (for themes "a" and "b") classes to the `<a>` and `<button>` elements or by setting `data-theme` to `"a"` or `"b"` for the `<input>` element:

- ```
  <a href="#" class="ui-btn ui-btn-b ui-btn-inline ui-corner-all
  ui-shadow">buttonText</a>
  ```

- ```
  <button class="ui-btn ui-btn-b ui-btn-inline ui-corner-all
  ui-shadow">buttonText</button>
  ```

- ```
  <input type="button" value="buttonText" data-inline="true" data-corners="true"
  data-theme="b">
  ```

Showing an Icon

You can show icons on the button by adding the `ui-icon-iconName` class to the `<a>` and `<button>` elements or setting `data-icon` as `iconName` for the `<input>` elements. For `<a>` and `<button>`, you need to add the icon position by using `ui-btn-icon-position` (where position is left, right, top, bottom, none, or notext). For `<input>`, by default the icon is added to the left of the text. To change its position you can add `data-iconpos=position` (where position is left, right, top, bottom, none, or notext):

- ```
  <a href="#" class="ui-btn ui-btn-inline ui-corner-all ui-icon-home ui-btn-icon-
  left">buttonText</a>
  ```

- ```
  <button class="ui-btn ui-btn-inline ui-corner-all ui-icon-home ui-btn-icon-
  left">buttonText</button>
  ```

- ```
  <input type="button" value="buttonText" data-inline="true" data-corners="true"
  data-icon="home" data-iconpos="left">
  ```

Showing an Icon Only

You can set buttons to show an icon only by adding the `ui-btn-icon-notext` class to the `<a>` and `<button>` elements or by setting `data-icon-notext` to true for the `<input>` element:

- ```
  <a href="#" class="ui-btn ui-btn-inline ui-corner-all ui-icon-home ui-btn-icon-
  notext">buttonText</a>
  ```

- ```
  <button class="ui-btn ui-btn-inline ui-corner-all ui-icon-home ui-btn-icon-
  notext">buttonText</button>
  ```

- ```
  <input type="button" value="buttonText" data-inline="true" data-corners="true"
  data-icon="home" data-iconpos="notext">
  ```
  ```

Showing Mini Buttons

You can show mini buttons by adding the `ui-mini` class to the `<a>` and `<button>` elements or by setting `data-mini` to `true` for the `<input>` elements:

- `<a href="#" class="ui-btn ui-btn-inline ui-corner-all ui-icon-home ui-btn-icon-left ui-mini">buttonText</a>`

- `<button class="ui-btn ui-btn-inline ui-corner-all ui-icon-home ui-btn-icon-left ui-mini">buttonText</button>`

- `<input type="button" value="buttonText" data-inline="true" data-corners="true" data-icon="home" data-mini="true">`

Disabling Buttons

You can disable buttons by adding the `ui-state-disabled` class to the `<a>` element or by adding the `disabled` attribute to the `<button>` and `<input>` elements:

- `<a href="#" class="ui-btn ui-btn-inline ui-corner-all ui-icon-home ui-btn-icon-left ui-mini ui-state-disabled">buttonText</a>`

- `<button class="ui-btn ui-btn-inline ui-corner-all ui-icon-home ui-btn-icon-left ui-mini" disabled>buttonText</button>`

- `<input type="button" value="buttonText" data-inline="true" data-corners="true" data-icon="home" data-mini="true" disabled>`

Grouping Buttons

You can group buttons together by wrapping them within a `div` element with `data-role` set to `controlgroup`. If you want to display them horizontally, you can set `data-type` to `horizontal`:

```
<div data-role="controlgroup"  data-type="horizontal" data-mini="true">
    <a href="#" class="ui-btn ui-btn-b ui-shadow ui-corner-all ui-icon-search ui-btn-icon-
       left">Search</a>
    <a href="#" class="ui-btn ui-btn-b ui-shadow ui-corner-all ui-icon-plus ui-btn-icon-
       left">Add</a>
    <a href="#" class="ui-btn ui-btn-b ui-shadow ui-corner-all ui-icon-delete ui-btn-icon-
       left">Delete</a>
</div>
```

Figure 11-3 displays the buttons with the various display options.

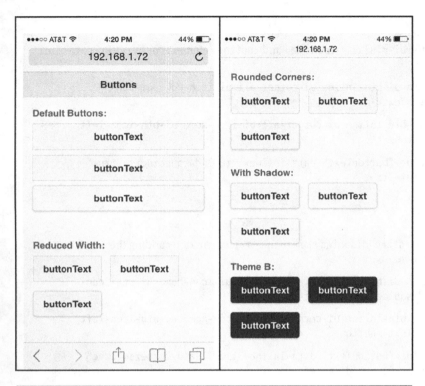

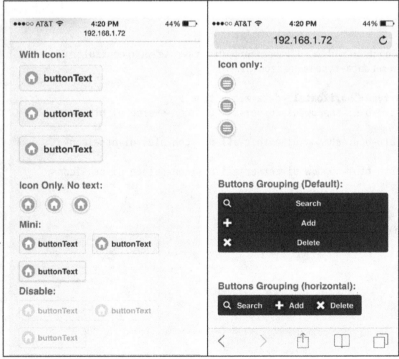

Figure 11-3. *Buttons*

11-4. Creating Headers and Footers

Problem

You want to be able to set headers and footers on a page and in a dialog box.

Solution

Both the header and footer should be child nodes of the page (data-role="page") or of the dialog (data-role="dialog"). The following is the basic structure of headers and footers:

```
<div data-role="header">
    <h1>Page header</h1>
</div>

<div data-role="footer">
    <h1>Page footer</h1>
</div>
```

The header appears before the content, whereas the footer appears after the content of the page. Figure 11-4 displays basic layout of headers and footers on a page.

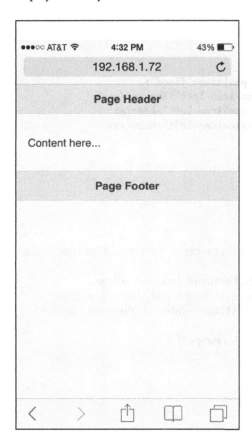

Figure 11-4. *Basic page layout*

Listing 11-3 shows how buttons can be added to headers and footers.

Listing 11-3. Header and footer toolbars

```html
<!DOCTYPE html>
<html lang="en">
<head>
        <meta name="viewport" content="width=device-width, initial-scale=1">

        <link rel="stylesheet" href="styles/jquery.mobile-1.4.3.min.css" />

        <script src="scripts/jquery-2.1.0.min.js"></script>
        <script src="scripts/jquery.mobile-1.4.3.min.js"></script>
</head>

<body>
        <div data-role="page">
          <div data-role="header">
                <a href="#" data-icon="bars" data-iconpos="notext" class="ui-btn-right">linkTitle</a>
                    <h1>HR System</h1>
          </div>

          <div data-role="main" class="ui-content">
                    <p>Content here...</p>
           </div>

          <div data-role="footer" style="text-align:center;" data-position="fixed">
                  <a href="#" class="ui-btn ui-icon-search ui-btn-icon-left">Search</a>
                    <a href="#" class="ui-btn ui-icon-plus ui-btn-icon-left">Add</a>
                    <a href="#" class="ui-btn ui-icon-bars ui-btn-icon-left">More</a>
          </div>
        </div>
</body>
</html>
```

How It Works

For the header, use `data-icon="bars"` `data-iconpos="notext"` `class="ui-btn-right"` to display a bar icon on the right side.

For the footer, use `data-position="fixed"` to display the footer at the bottom of the device screen.

Three instances of the anchor element with the classes `ui-btn`, `ui-icon-iconName`, and `ui-btn-position` are used to display three buttons with icons. You need to specify `ui-btn-position`—without it, the icons won't be displayed.

The following sections explain the classes and data attributes used in this recipe.

Positioning

To position a footer on a page, use the data-position attribute:

- inline—Headers and footers are in line with the content. For example, if inline is set for the footer, the footer is displayed immediately after the content. If the content doesn't fit in the whole screen, the footer is displayed somewhere in the middle section of the screen and not at the bottom. This is the default value for data-position.

- fixed—Headers and footers are displayed at the top and bottom of the screen, regardless of the height of the content.

  By setting data-position to fixed and data-fullscreen to true, you can display the headers and footers at the top and bottom of the screen. These settings are useful for photos and for video display. You can make header and footer visible or invisible by tapping the screen.

Adding a Toolbar to the Header

To add a toolbar with buttons and icons to the header, you use the anchor (<a>) element. The first anchor element is used to display the inline button on the left section and the second anchor is used to display the inline button on the right section.

- To display text only, use:

  ```
  <a href="pageDialogPanelPopupLink">linkTitle</a>
  ```

- To display an icon, use:

  ```
  <a href="pageDialogPanelPopupLink" data-icon="iconName">linkTitle</a>
  ```

- To display an icon only, use:

  ```
  <a href="pageDialogPanelPopupLink" data-icon="iconName" data-iconpos="notext">
  linkTitle</a>
  ```

- To make it stand out by specifying a contrasting theme, use:

  ```
  <a href="pageDialogPanelPopupLink" data-icon="iconName" data-iconpos="notext"
  data-theme="b">linkTitle</a>
  ```

- To display only one icon on a right-side header, add the class ui-btn-right:

  ```
  <a href="pageDialogPanelPopupLink" data-icon="iconName" data-iconpos="notext"
  data-theme="b" class="ui-btn-right">linkTitle</a>
  ```

- To remove the circle around the icon, add the class ui-nodisc-icon.

Adding a Toolbar to the Footer

To add a toolbar with buttons and icons to the footer, use the anchor (<a>) elements. In the footer you can add as many buttons as you want. The number of buttons is limited by the space on the device's display.

Figure 11-5 displays the page with an icon only button in the header and three buttons with icons in the footer.

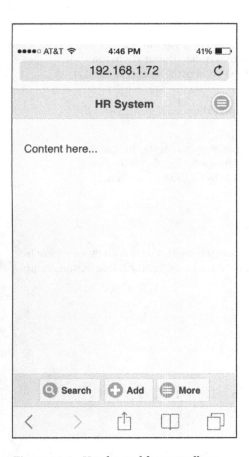

Figure 11-5. *Header and footer toolbars*

11-5. Navigating Among Pages
Problem

You want to navigate among pages in a mobile web application.

Solution

You can define multiple pages with a single HTML file or keep all the pages in their own HTML file. It is better to keep multiple pages that constitute one functionality of a web application in the same HTML file. This will make transitions between pages smoother. If your pages are in separate HTML files, you can pre-fetch them so that there aren't any delays in transitioning between the pages. Listing 11-4 demonstrates the multi-page structure in an HTML file and shows how to navigate back and forth between these pages.

Listing 11-4. Page navigation

```html
<!DOCTYPE html>
<html lang="en">
<head>
        <meta name="viewport" content="width=device-width, initial-scale=1">

        <link rel="stylesheet" href="styles/jquery.mobile-1.4.3.min.css" />

        <script type="text/javascript" src="scripts/jquery-2.1.0.min.js"></script>
        <script type="text/javascript" src="scripts/jquery.mobile-1.4.3.min.js"></script>
</head>

<body>
        <!-- Page 1 -->
        <div data-role="page" id="homePage">
           <div data-role="header">
              <h1>Home Page</h1>
           </div>

           <div data-role="main" class="ui-content">
              <a href="#detailPage" class="ui-btn ui-btn-b ui-overlay-shadow ui-corner-all ui-icon-
                 arrow-r ui-btn-icon-right">
                    Detail Information</a>
           </div>

           <div data-role="footer" data-position="fixed">
              <h1>Page Footer</h1>
           </div>
        </div>

        <!-- Page 2 -->
        <div data-role="page" id="detailPage">
           <div data-role="header">
              <h1>Detail Page</h1>
           </div>

           <div data-role="main" class="ui-content">
              Detailed information ...<br>
              ....
              <a href="#homePage" class="ui-btn ui-btn-b ui-overlay-shadow ui-corner-all
                 ui-icon-arrow-l ui-btn-icon-left">Back</a>
           </div>

           <div data-role="footer" data-position="fixed">
              <h1>Page Footer</h1>
           </div>
        </div>
</body>
</html>
```

How It Works

These are blocks of two page structures and each page is identified by its unique ID. Since these two pages are in the same HTML file, they can be called by using the syntax **<a href= "#pageId">**.

- `<div data-role="page" id="homePage">` sets the ID of the first page.
- `<div data-role="page" id="detailPage">` sets the ID of the second page.

Within the content of first page, the following link is created:

`<a **href="#detailPage"** class="ui-btn ui-btn-b ui-overlay-shadow ui-corner-all ui-icon-arrow-r ui-btn-icon-right">**Detail Information**</a>`

When the Detail Information button is clicked, the page with an ID set to `detailPage` is displayed. On the `detailPage` page, the following link is created:

`<a **href="#homePage"** class="ui-btn ui-btn-b ui-overlay-shadow ui-corner-all ui-icon-arrow-l ui-btn-icon-left">**Back**</a>`

When the Back button is clicked, the page with an ID set to `homepage` is displayed.
The following classes are set in this recipe:

- `ui-btn` creates the link as a button.
- `ui-btn-b` uses theme "b" (the dark theme). This version of jQuery mobile (1.4.3) has only two themes—"a" (the light theme), which is the default, and "b" (the dark theme). You can create custom themes at the following URL:

  `http://themeroller.jquerymobile.com/`

- `ui-overlay-shadow` adds an overlay shadow to the button.
- `ui-corner-all` makes all the corners of the button rounded. Other similar classes include:
  - `ui-corner-tl` (for a top-left rounded corner)
  - `ui-corner-tr` (for a top-right rounded corner)
  - `ui-corner-bl` (for a bottom-left rounded corner)
  - `ui-corner-br` (for a bottom-right rounded corner)
  - `ui-corner-top` (for top corners)
  - `ui-corner-bottom` (for bottom corners)
  - `ui-corner-right` (for right corners)
  - `ui-corner-left` (for left corners)
- `ui-icon-arrow-r` adds a right-facing arrow icon. Refer to the Recipe 11-1 for the complete list of available icons.
- `ui-btn-icon-right` places the icon on the right section of the button.

The Detail Information button is as wide as the device display. In order to make it the same size as the text, you can add the ui-inline class. When this button is clicked, the page with an ID set to detailPage will be displayed.

The page with an ID set to detailPage has a similar structure as the anchor button, except the following two classes are different.

```
<a href="#homePage" class="ui-btn ui-btn-b ui-overlay-shadow ui-corner-all ui-icon-arrow-l
ui-btn-icon-left">Back</a>
```

- ui-icon-arrow-l adds a left-facing arrow icon.

- ui-btn-icon-left places the icon on the left section of the button.

When this button is clicked, the page with an ID set to homePage will be displayed.

Figure 11-6 displays the initial page and the page users navigate to.

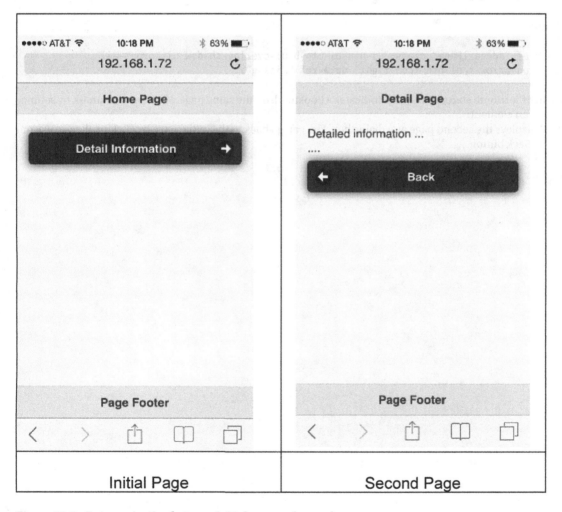

Figure 11-6. *Page navigation between initial page and second page*

If your pages are in two different HTML files, you can navigate between these files by using the following syntax. In this case, you don't have to specify the page's ID.

```
<a href="targetFileName.htm"....>
```

If you want to display the navigated page as a dialog box, you can use either of the following two ways:

- Change data-role on the second page to dialog (for example, **<div data-role="dialog" id="detailPage">**).

- Add data-rel="dialog" to the anchor (<a>) element. In the previous listing, you would replace the following:

  ```
  <a href="#detailPage" class="ui-btn ui-btn-b ui-overlay-shadow ui-corner-all
  ui-icon-arrow-r ui-btn-icon-right">
  ```

  With:

  ```
  <a href="#detailPage" class="ui-btn ui-btn-b ui-overlay-shadow ui-corner-all
  ui-icon-arrow-r ui-btn-icon-right" data-rel="dialog">
  ```

When the href attribute starts with #, that indicates a bookmark on the same page. You set a bookmark by setting the id attribute of an element.

Figure 11-7 displays the second page as a dialog box. You can go back to the initial page by clicking the Close icon or by clicking the Back button.

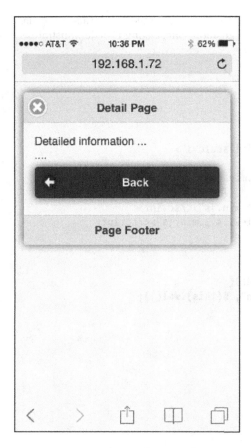

Figure 11-7. *Displaying the second page as a dialog box*

11-6. Applying Transition Effects to Pages and Dialog Boxes

Problem

You want to know where and how you can apply transitions and what kind of transition animations are available.

Solution

A transition can be applied to any link that opens a page or to a dialog box by using the `data-transition` attribute. The following is the syntax for specifying a transition:

```
<a href="pageDialogLink" data-transition="transitionEffectName">linkName</a>
```

A transition effect can be changed programmatically by using following syntax:

```
$(selector).data("transition", "transitionEffectName")
```

This will set the `data-transition` attribute of the selected items as the specified `transitionEffectName`.

The following is the list of valid transitionEffectName values: fade, flip, flow, pop, slide, slidefade, slideup, slidedown, turn, and none. The default transition is fade and none has no transition state. Listing 11-5 demonstrates the impact of the transition effect.

Listing 11-5. Transition effect created using data-transition

```
<!DOCTYPE html>
<html lang="en">
<head>
        <meta name="viewport" content="width=device-width, initial-scale=1">

        <link rel="stylesheet" href="styles/jquery.mobile-1.4.3.min.css" />

        <script type="text/javascript" src="scripts/jquery-2.1.0.min.js"></script>
        <script type="text/javascript" src="scripts/jquery.mobile-1.4.3.min.js"></script>

        <script>
                $(function() {
                        $("#transitionType").on("change", function(){
                                $("#lnkNavigate").data("transition", $(this).val());
                        });
                });
        </script>
</head>

<body>
        <!-- Page 1 -->
        <div data-role="page" id="homePage">
            <div data-role="header">
                <h1>Home Page</h1>
            </div>

            <div data-role="main" class="ui-content">
                <select id="transitionType">
                        <option selected>fade</option>
                        <option>flip</option>
                        <option>flow</option>
                        <option>pop</option>
                        <option>slide</option>
                        <option>slidefade</option>
                        <option>slideup</option>
                        <option>slidedown</option>
                        <option>turn</option>
                        <option>none</option>
                </select>
```

```
            <a id="lnkNavigate" href="#detailPage"  class="ui-btn ui-btn-b ui-overlay-shadow
                ui-corner-all ui-icon-arrow-r ui-btn-icon-right">
                  Detail Information</a>
        </div>

        <div data-role="footer" data-position="fixed">
           <h1>Page Footer</h1>
        </div>
     </div>

     <!-- Page 2 -->
     <div data-role="page" id="detailPage">
        <div data-role="header">
           <h1>Detail Page</h1>
        </div>

        <div data-role="main" class="ui-content">
           Detailed information ...<br>
           ....
           <a href="#homePage" class="ui-btn ui-btn-b ui-overlay-shadow ui-corner-all
               ui-icon-arrow-l ui-btn-icon-left">Back</a>
        </div>

        <div data-role="footer" data-position="fixed">
           <h1>Page Footer</h1>
        </div>
     </div>
</body>
</html>
```

How It Works

A select drop-down is created with all the valid transition effects. On selecting a transition effect from the drop-down, the following JavaScript code is executed:

```
$("#lnkNavigate").data("transition", $(this).val());
```

This will change the data-transition attribute of the anchor link with the ID #lnkNavigate to the transition effect selected in the drop-down. When you click the Detail Information button, the detail page is displayed with the selected transition effect. Figure 11-8 displays the initial page and the navigated to page.

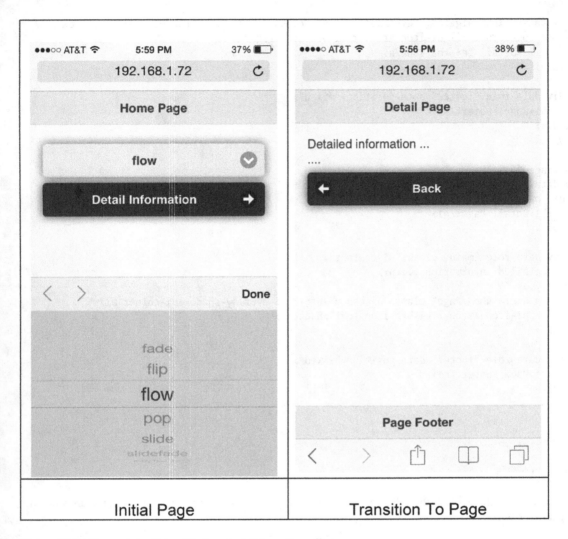

Figure 11-8. *Page navigation with the selected transtion effect*

11-7. Using the Pagecontainer Widget

Problem

You want to understand how pages are handled within a document (`<body>`) and be aware of the available methods and events for the pagecontainer widget.

Solution

The pagecontainer widget manages a collection of pages. It was introduced in version 1.4 to streamline page handling, which includes transitions, events, and so on. It replaces many page-related methods and events from previous versions.

In jQuery mobile, multiple pages can be defined within a body element with a unique ID. Only one is visible at any given time. When the HTML file is loaded, the first page in the file will be displayed. Since a complete HTML file is loaded in the browser and all pages in the HTML file are created in the DOM, moving from one page to another (transitioning) is smooth, without any delay in the loading process.

When an anchor (<A>) link is clicked to get the external page from the same web application, instead of making an HTTP call to the server to get the target page, an AJAX-based call is made to retrieve the page. In order to make AJAX-based navigation work, the click event's default shouldn't be prevented (eventObj.preventDefault() shouldn't be used) and none of the following attributes should be set: data-rel="back", data-rel="external", data-ajax="false", and target.

The following is a list of commonly used methods and options:

- change—Transition to a new page. Here's the syntax:

```
$( ":mobile-pagecontainer" ).pagecontainer( "change", targetPage, options);
```

where targetPage is the page ID in the same HTML file or an URL (for an external HTML file).

The possible values for options are:

- role—The data-role to be used for the targetPage. It can be page or dialog. If it is not specified, the data-role attribute of the targetPage is used.

- transition—The transition effect to display the target page.

- reload—If it is set to true, the page is reloaded even if it is in the DOM.

- reverse—If it is set to true, it reverses the transition effect.

The following examples show how to navigate to a different page using the change method.
For an internal page ID:

```
$( ":mobile-pagecontainer" ).pagecontainer( "change", "#loginErrorDialog", {
    role: "dialog", transition: "pop"
} );
```

For an external page:

```
$( ":mobile-pagecontainer" ).pagecontainer( "change", "departments.htm", {
    role: "page", transition: "fade"
} );
```

- getActivePage()—Used to get the currently active page. It returns a jQuery object. You can use following syntax to get the ID of the currently active page:

```
$( ":mobile-pagecontainer" ).pagecontainer( "getActivePage" )[0].id
```

- load()—Used to load an external page in the DOM by using an AJAX call. The load() method won't display the page, it will just keep it in the DOM for later use. This method is useful for loading pages before they are called for smooth transitions. The following is the syntax to load a file:

```
$( ":mobile-pagecontainer" ).pagecontainer( "load", "externalPage", options);
```

where options can have the following values:

- type—The type of the HTTP request; either GET (default) or POST.

- data—The data to send to the server.

- reload—If set to true, the page is loaded even if it exists in the DOM.

- role—The data-role to be used to display the requested page.

The following is the list of commonly used events. All event handlers have two arguments—eventObject and uiObject. uiObject contains information specific to the triggered event. The event handler for all of the following events can be set by using the following syntax:

```
$( ":mobile-pagecontainer" ).pagecontainer({eventName: function(eventObj, uiObj) {...} });
$(document).on("pagecontainereventName", function(eventObj, uiObj) { ... });
```

where the eventName options are listed in Table 11-3.

Table 11-3. *Pagecontainer Events*

Event Name	Description
create	This event is triggered when pagecontainer is created.
beforechange	This event is triggered before loading the file and before transitioning to a page.
beforeload	This event is triggered before starting the load request.
Load	This event is triggered after the page is loaded and inserted into the DOM.
loadfailed	This event is triggered if the load request fails.
beforetransition	This event is triggered before transitioning to the page.
beforehide	This event is triggered, if transitioning from one page to another, before the transition starts.
beforeshow	This event is triggered before the transition animation starts.
hide	This event is triggered when the transition animation is completed.
show	This event is triggered when the transition animation is completed.
transition	This event is triggered after the show event, when the page change transition is completed.
change	This event is triggered after the change request is completed.
changefailed	This event is triggered if the change request fails.
remove	This event is triggered before the framework starts to remove external pages from the DOM.

When a page is loaded for the first time, events are triggered in the following order:

```
mobileinit, create, beforechange, beforetransition, beforeshow, show, transition, change
```

When a page transitions to an internal page (within the same HTML file), events are triggered in the following order:

```
beforechange, beforetransition, beforehide, beforeshow, hide, show, transition, change
```

When a page transitions to an external page, events are triggered in the following order:

beforechange, beforeload, load, beforechange, beforetransition, beforehide, beforeshow, hide, show, transition, change

Displaying and Hiding the Loading Message

The loader widget can be used to display a loading message while the AJAX request is made and a response is received from the server or during the page loading and transition.

The following syntax is used to show the loading dialog:

```
$.mobile.loading("show", {
            text: textMessage,
            textVisible: true or false,
            theme: themeAlphabet,
            textonly: true or false,
            html: htmlString
            });
```

where textMessage is any text you want to show. themeAlphabet can be "a" or "b" or any other custom theme alphabet. htmlString can be any valid HTML structure, including an image. If textVisible is set to true, the textMessage is displayed under the loading spinner. If textonly is true, the loading spinner is not displayed and only the textMessage is displayed. The loading dialog can be displayed before making an AJAX call or in the beforechange event handler.

The following syntax hides the loading dialog:

```
$.mobile.loading("hide");
```

The loading dialog can be hidden in the AJAX success or error callback functions or in the change or changefailed events handler.

11-8. Creating a Dialog Box
Problem

You want to learn how to create and display a dialog box.

Solution

A dialog box is small area that's displayed as an overlay on top of the page. It displays the status or prompts for a response from the user. The following is the syntax to set a page as a dialog:

```
<div data-role="page" data-dialog="true" id="myDialog">
  ...
</div>
```

The dialog page can be displayed by using any of the following syntax:

- A div element with a data-role set to page and a data-dialog set to true should exist in the same HTML file.

```
<a href="#myDialog">Show dialog</a>
```

- An <a> element tag with a data-role set to page should exist in the same HTML file.

```
<a href="#myDialog" data-rel="dialog">Show dialog</a>
```

- <a href="myDialog.htm">Show dialog</a>, where myDialog.htm is the external file that has a div element with the data-role set to page and the data-dialog set to true.

- Using the following JavaScript code:

```
$( ":mobile-pagecontainer" ).pagecontainer( "change", "#myDialog", {
        role: "dialog", transition: "pop"
} );
```

For an explanation of the pagecontainer methods, refer to the Recipe 11-7.

Closing a Dialog

If the dialog page has a header, a Close button will be displayed on the left side of header. You can change the position of the Close button by using data-close-btn attribute, as follows:

```
<div data-role="page" data-dialog="true" data-close-btn="right" id="myDialog">
```

You can also set data-close-btn to none to hide the Close button. You can set your own button using following syntax:

```
<a href="#" class="ui-btn" data-rel="back">anyText</a>
```

Listing 11-6 demonstrates an example that displays and closes a dialog page.

Listing 11-6. Dialog page.

```
<!DOCTYPE html>
<html lang="en">
<head>
    <meta name="viewport" content="width=device-width, initial-scale=1">

    <link rel="stylesheet" href="styles/jquery.mobile-1.4.3.min.css" />

    <script type="text/javascript" src="scripts/jquery-2.1.0.min.js"></script>
    <script type="text/javascript" src="scripts/jquery.mobile-1.4.3.min.js"></script>
</head>
```

```
<body>
    <!-- Page 1 -->
    <div data-role="page" id="homePage">
        <div data-role="header">
            <h1>Home Page</h1>
        </div>

        <div data-role="main" class="ui-content">
            <a href="#myDialog" class="ui-btn ui-btn-b ui-overlay-shadow ui-corner-all
                ui-icon-arrow-r ui-btn-icon-right" data-rel="dialog">
                    Display Dialog Page</a>
        </div>

        <div data-role="footer" data-position="fixed">
            <h1>Page Footer</h1>
        </div>
    </div>

    <!-- Page 2 -->
    <div data-role="page" id="myDialog" data-close-btn="right">
        <div data-role="header">
            <h1>Dialog Header</h1>
        </div>

        <div data-role="main" class="ui-content">
            Some information ...<br>
            ....<br>
            <a href="#" data-rel="back" class="ui-btn ui-btn-b ui-btn-inline ui-overlay-shadow
                ui-corner-all">Close</a>
        </div>

        <div data-role="footer" data-position="fixed">
            <h1>Dialog Footer</h1>
        </div>
    </div>
</body>
</html>
```

How It Works

The following code sets up an anchor element so that when it is clicked, a page with the ID of myDialog opens:

```
<a href="#myDialog" class="ui-btn ui-btn-b ui-overlay-shadow ui-corner-all ui-icon-arrow-r
    ui-btn-icon-right" data-rel="dialog">Display Dialog Page</a>
```

419

The data attribute data-close-btn="right" is used to create a Close button on the top-right side of the dialog page. Figure 11-9 displays the dialog box that appears when the Display Dialog Page button is clicked.

Figure 11-9. Dialog page

11-9. Creating a Navigation Box

Problem

You want to create and display a navigation box.

Solution

A navigation bar is a group of anchor elements (`<a>`) that are displayed as buttons in a bar. It is generally displayed in the header or the footer. The following is the syntax to create a navigation bar in the footer:

```
<div data-role="footer">
     <div data-role="navbar">
          <ul>
               <li><a href="#someLink1">linkText</a></li>
               ....
          </ul>
     </div>
</div>
```

You can specify up to five links within a navigation bar. If more than five links are specified, the navigation bar is displayed in multiple lines. Each button in the navigation bar takes the same amount of space. Generally, a header element (`<h1>...<h6>`) is not specified if a navigation bar is used in the header or the footer. If you specify the header element, the navigation bar will be displayed below the header and footer. Listing 11-7 demonstrates an example that creates and displays a navigation bar in the footer.

Listing 11-7. Navigation bar

```
<!DOCTYPE html>
<html lang="en">
<head>
     <meta name="viewport" content="width=device-width, initial-scale=1">

     <link rel="stylesheet" href="styles/jquery.mobile-1.4.3.min.css" />

     <script src="scripts/jquery-2.1.0.min.js"></script>
     <script src="scripts/jquery.mobile-1.4.3.min.js"></script>

     <style>
          .ui-page { background: #CFF0C5;}
     </style>
</head>

<body>
     <div data-role="page">
        <div data-role="header">
           <h1>HR System</h1>
        </div>

        <div data-role="main" class="ui-content">
           <p>Content here...</p>
        </div>
```

```
        <div data-role="footer" data-position="fixed">
            <div data-role="navbar" data-iconpos="left">
                <ul>
                        <li><a href="#somelink1" data-icon="search">Search</a></li>
                        <li><a href="#somelink2" data-icon="plus"  class="ui-btn-active">Add
                            </a></li>
                        <li><a href="#somelink3"  data-icon="bars">More...</a></li>
                </ul>
            </div>
        </div>
    </div>
</body>
</html>
```

How It Works

Within the footer `div` tag, another `div` element is set up with the `data-role` set to `"navbar"` to create a navigation bar in the footer. Buttons in the navigation bar are created in the unordered list (`<ul>`) and list items (`<li>`) by using anchor elements. Refer to the Recipe 11-3 to learn how to use anchor elements as buttons. The following sections explain the classes and data attributes used in this recipe.

Active Link

To indicate which button is selected for the current page, you can specify the `ui-btn-active` and `ui-state-persist` classes as the following:

```
<li><a href="#someLink1" class="ui-btn-active ui-state-persist">linkText</a></li>
```

Theming

By default, a navigation bar inherits its theme from its parent container. To use a different theme, set the `data-theme` attribute to:

```
<li><a href="#someLink1" data-theme="b">linkText</a></li>
```

Icon

For each button, you can specify an icon by using the following syntax:

```
<li><a href="#somelink1" data-icon="iconName">Search</a></li>
```

The icons listing is provided in Figure 11-1.

Icon Positioning

By default, icons are placed on top of the text. You can specify an icon position for all buttons by using the following syntax:

```
<div data-role="navbar" data-iconpos="position">
```

where valid values of position are left, top, right, bottom, and notext.

Figure 11-10 displays the page with a navigation bar in the footer.

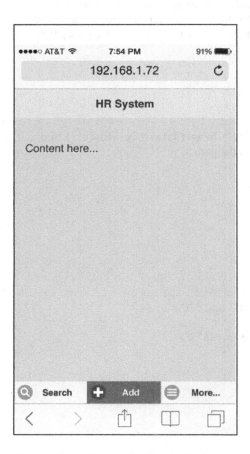

Figure 11-10. *Navigation bar in the footer*

11-10. Creating a Panel

Problem

You want to create and display a panel.

Solution

A panel is displayed as a split screen, with additional information about the content in the main screen. Panels can also be used to display a list of items. Some of the examples include a list of menu items in the web application, a list of employees, and so on. When you click any of the items in the panel, details about it are displayed in the main screen. Panels slide out from the left or right of the main screen. Use the following structure to set up a basic panel:

```
<div data-role="panel" id="panelName">
    <h1>Panel Header</h1>
    <p>Panel Content</p>
</div>
```

A panel must be created as a sibling of the header (data-role="header"), footer (data-role="footer"), and content (data-role="main") elements. The following is the syntax to show the panel:

```
<a href="#panelName">Show Panel</a>
```

Listing 11-8 demonstrates an example to create and display a panel.

Listing 11-8. Panel

```
<!DOCTYPE html>
<html lang="en">
<head>
    <meta name="viewport" content="width=device-width, initial-scale=1">

    <link rel="stylesheet" href="styles/jquery.mobile-1.4.3.min.css" />

    <script src="scripts/jquery-2.1.0.min.js"></script>
    <script src="scripts/jquery.mobile-1.4.3.min.js"></script>
</head>

<body>
    <!-- Page 1 -->
    <div data-role="page">
        <div data-role="header">
            <h1>Page Header</h1>
        </div>

        <div data-role="panel" id="myPanel" data-display="overlay"  data-position="right"
            data-position-fixed="true" data-theme="b">
            <h3>Available Options</h3>
            <a href="#myNewPage" class="ui-btn" data-rel="close">Option 1</a>
            <a href="#" class="ui-btn" data-rel="close">Option 2</a>
```

```
                <a href="#" class="ui-btn" data-rel="close">Option 3</a>
                <a href="#" class="ui-btn" data-rel="close">Option 4</a>
            </div>

            <div data-role="main" class="ui-content">
                <p>Content here...</p>
                <a href="#myPanel" class="ui-btn ui-btn-inline">Show Panel</a>
            </div>

            <div data-role="footer" data-position="fixed">
                <h1>Page Footer</h1>
            </div>
        </div>

        <!-- Page 2 -->
        <div data-role="page" id="myNewPage">
            <div data-role="header">
                <h1>New Page Header</h1>
            </div>
        </div>
    </body>
</html>
```

How It Works

When you click the Show Panel button, the jQuery Mobile framework's pagecontainer displays the panel with the ID myPanel. In the myPanel div element, a header is set using the <h3> element and four buttons are created using the anchor elements. The following items are displayed in the panel:

```
<h3>Available Options</h3>
        <a href="#myNewPage" class="ui-btn" data-rel="close">Option 1</a>
        <a href="#" class="ui-btn" data-rel="close">Option 2</a>
        <a href="#" class="ui-btn" data-rel="close">Option 3</a>
        <a href="#" class="ui-btn" data-rel="close">Option 4</a>
```

The following sections explain the classes and data attributes used in this recipe.

Panel Position

Panel position can be specified by setting the data-position attribute using the following syntax:

```
<div data-role="panel" id="panelName" data-position="panelPosition">
```

where panelPosition can be:

- left—Displays the panel on the left side of the screen (default).
- right—Displays the panel on the right side of the screen.

Panel Scroll Mode

Panel scroll mode can be specified by setting the `data-position-fixed` attribute using the following syntax:

```
<div data-role="panel" id="panelName" data-position-fixed="isPositionFixed">
```

where `isPositionFixed` can be:

- `false`—The content of the panel doesn't scroll when the calling page scrolls (default).
- `true`—The content of the panel scrolls when the calling page scrolls.

Panel Display Mode

Panel display mode can be specified by setting the `data-display` attribute using the following syntax:

```
<div data-role="panel" id="panelName" data-display="displayMode">
```

where `displayMode` can be:

- `reveal`—Shows the panel by sliding the calling page toward the right, revealing the panel under it (default).
- `overlay`—The panel slides on the top of the calling page and hides part of the calling page. The panel moves on top of the calling page.
- `push`—The panel pushes the calling page toward the right. Both the panel and the calling page are moved.

Updating Panel Layout

If properties or contents of a displayed panel are dynamically changed, trigger the `updatelayout` event to display the changes using the following syntax:

```
$("panelName").trigger("updatelayout");
```

Closing the Panel

A panel can be closed by using any of these methods:

- By clicking outside the panel. To disable this behavior, you can set `data-dismissible="false"`.
- By pressing the Esc key.
- By swiping. To disable this behavior, you can set `data-swipe-close= "false"`.
- By adding a link or button in the panel as `<a href="#newPageId" data-rel="close">Close</a>`.

Theming

By default, the panel inherits its theme from its parent container. To use a different theme, set the data-theme attribute to:

```
<div data-role="panel" id="panelName" data-theme="b">
```

data-theme can also be set to none if you want to use your custom styling, as follows:

```
<div data-role="panel" id="panelName" data-theme="none" class="customClass">
```

Figure 11-11 displays the panel when the Show Panel button is clicked.

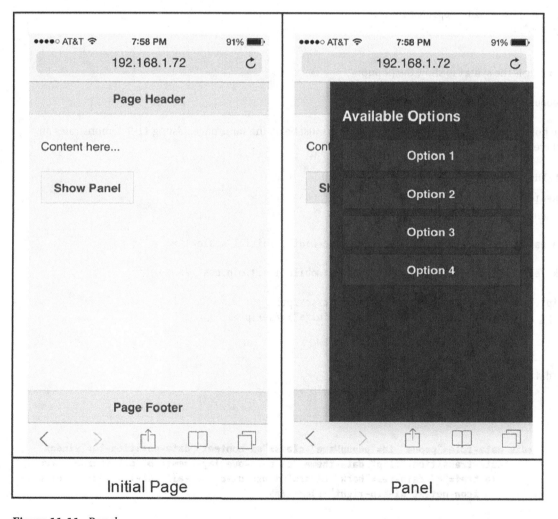

Figure 11-11. *Panel*

11-11. Creating a Popup
Problem

You want to create and display a popup.

Solution

Popups are used to display tooltip messages, images, map directions, list views, forms, and so on. They can be defined anywhere within the page (data-role="page"). A popup can contain any valid HTML structure, including images, text, elements of page structure (header, content, and footer), and so on. The following is the structure used to set up a basic popup:

```
<div data-role="popup" id="popupName">
   <p>Popup Content</p>
</div>
```

The following is the syntax to show the popup:

```
<a href="#popupName">Show Popup</a>
```

Both the popup and the link that displays the popup must be on the same page. Listing 11-9 demonstrates an example that creates and displays an image as a popup.

Listing 11-9. Display an image as a popup

```
<!DOCTYPE html>
<html lang="en">
<head>
    <meta name="viewport" content="width=device-width, initial-scale=1">

    <link rel="stylesheet" href="styles/jquery.mobile-1.4.3.min.css" />

    <script src="scripts/jquery-2.1.0.min.js"></script>
    <script src="scripts/jquery.mobile-1.4.3.min.js"></script>
</head>

<body>
    <div data-role="page">
        <div data-role="header"  data-theme="b">
            <h1>Page Header</h1>
        </div>

        <div data-role="popup" id="popupName" class="ui-content" data-position-to="window"
            data-transition="flip" data-theme="b" data-overlay-theme="b" data-arrow="true">
            <a href="#" data-rel="back" class="ui-btn ui-corner-all  ui-icon-delete ui-btn-
            icon-notext ui-btn-right">Close</a>

            <img src="images\Flower1_500.jpg">
        </div>
```

```
            <div data-role="main" class="ui-content">
                <p>Flower</p>
                <a href="#popupName" data-rel="popup"><img src="images\Flower1_100.jpg"></a>
            </div>

            <div data-role="footer" data-position="fixed"  data-theme="b">
                <h1>Page Footer</h1>
            </div>
        </div>
</body>
</html>
```

How It Works

A thumbnail of an image is created within an anchor element by using the following code:

```
<a href="#popupName" data-rel="popup"><img src="images\Flower1_100.jpg"></a>
```

The data-role set to popup specifies that the target object is a popup. When the thumbnail is clicked, the following div element structure is displayed:

```
<div data-role="popup" id="popupName" class="ui-content" data-position-to="window"
            data-transition="flip" data-theme="b" data-overlay-theme="b" data-arrow="true">
    <a href="#" data-rel="back" class="ui-btn ui-corner-all  ui-icon-delete ui-btn-icon-notext
            ui-btn-right">Close</a>

    <img src="images\Flower1_500.jpg">
</div>
```

In this code segment, a popup is set up with a Close button (to close the popup) and the actual image. The following sections explain the classes and data attributes used in this recipe.

Adding Padding

To add padding to the content of the popup, you can add the ui-content class:

```
<div data-role="popup" id="popupName" class="ui-content">
```

Popup Position

By default a popup is displayed over the clicked link. Popup position can be specified by setting the data-position-to attribute using the following syntax:

```
<div data-role="popup" id="popupName" data-position-to="popupPosition">
```

where popupPosition can be:

- origin—Displays the popup over the clicked element (default). This is preferable when showing a tooltip message.
- window—Displays the popup at the center of the window. This is ideal for showing images.
- #id —Displays the popup over the element with the id set to id.

Transitioning

By default no transition effect is used. You can specify a transition effect by setting the data-transition attribute using the following syntax:

```
<div data-role="popup" id="popupName" data-transition="transitionEffectName">
```

where transitionEffectName is any of the valid transition names listed in Recipe 11-6.

Theming

By default, a popup inherits its theme from its parent container. To use a different theme, set the data-theme attribute as follows:

```
<div data-role="popup" id="popupName" data-theme="b">
```

Adding a Shadow Effect

To add a shadow as a backdrop for the popup, you can set the data-overlay-theme as follows:

```
<div data-role="popup" id="popupName" data-overlay-theme="b">
```

Displaying Menu Items

You can display menu items for web application by setting listview as the content of the popup and linking the popup with the link specified in the navigation bar.

Adding an Arrow

You can add an arrow to the popup box by using the data-arrow attribute:

```
<div data-role="popup" id="popupName" data-arrow="arrowDirection">
```

where `arrowDirection` can be:

- `false`—No arrow is displayed.
- `true`—Displays the arrow in any direction.
- `l`—Displays the arrow on the left.
- `r`—Displays the arrow on the right.
- `b`—Displays the arrow on the bottom.
- `t`—Displays the arrow on the top.

You can also use multiple values as a comma-separated value with no space. For example, if you use `data-arrow="l,t"`, the arrow will be displayed either on the left or on the top. This can be tested by changing the size of the browser window. The jQuery Mobile framework determines the direction of the arrow depending on the position of the element that's clicked to display the popup, the position of the popup, and the size of the browser.

Closing the Popup

A popup can be closed using any of the following ways:

- By clicking outside the popup. To disable this behavior, you can set `data-dismissible="false"`.
- By pressing the Esc key.
- By adding a button as the child element of the popup:

    ```
    <a href="#" data-rel="back" class="ui-btn ui-corner-all ui-icon-delete ui-btn-icon-notext
    ui-btn-right">Close</a>
    ```

Figure 11-12 displays the image as a popup when a thumbnail of the image is clicked. The black border in the popup image is due to the padding (`ui-content`) and to the `data-theme="b"`. The popup can be closed by clicking the Close icon on the top-right side of the popup.

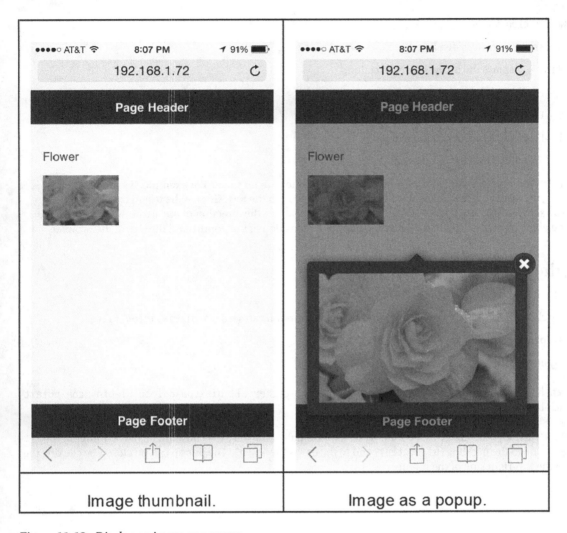

Figure 11-12. Display an image as a popup

11-12. Creating Collapsibles
Problem

You want to create a collapsible.

Solution

Collapsibles are used to expand or collapse contents. They are useful on mobile devices because of the limited screen space. They can be used to expand and collapse text content, images, or sections of data-entry forms. They are defined in the content section of the page. They contain a header element for the title for the content and a valid HTML structure. Collapsible content can be nested inside another collapsible block. The following is the structure used to set up basic collapsible content:

```
<div data-role="collapsible" id="collapsibleName">
    <h2>Popup Content</p>
</div>
```

Listing 11-10 demonstrates an example to display collapsible text content and an image.

Listing 11-10. Collapsible content

```
<!DOCTYPE html>
<html lang="en">
<head>
    <meta name="viewport" content="width=device-width, initial-scale=1">

    <link rel="stylesheet" href="styles/jquery.mobile-1.4.3.min.css" />

    <script src="scripts/jquery-2.1.0.min.js"></script>
    <script src="scripts/jquery.mobile-1.4.3.min.js"></script>
</head>

<body>
    <div data-role="page">
        <div data-role="header">
            <h1>Page Header</h1>
        </div>

        <div data-role="main" class="ui-content">
            <div data-role="collapsibleset">
                <div data-role="collapsible"  data-inset="false"  data-collapsed-icon="carat-r"
                data-expanded-icon="carat-d"  data-iconpos="right" data-mini="true"
                data-content-theme="b">
                        <h2>Header 1</h2>
                        <p>Content 1</p>
                </div>

                <div data-role="collapsible"  data-inset="false"  data-collapsed-icon="carat-r"
                data-expanded-icon="carat-d"  data-iconpos="right"  data-mini="true"
                data-content-theme="b">
                        <h2>Flower</h2>
                        <p><img src="images/Flower1.jpg"></p>
                </div>
            </div>
        </div>

        <div data-role="footer" data-position="fixed">
            <h1>Page Footer</h1>
        </div>
    </div>
  </body>
</html>
```

How It Works

Two collapsibles (that is, two div elements with a data-role set to collapsible) are grouped together by using `<div data-role="collapsibleset">`. In a collapsible set, only one collapsible can be expanded at a time. The collapsible can contain any valid HTML structure. In this example, collapsibles have headers (`<h2>`), paragraphs (`<p>`), and an image (`<img>`). The following sections explain the classes and data attributes used in this recipe.

Showing Expanded Content on Page Load

By default, collapsible content is collapsed when a page loads. You can expand it by tapping on the header. You can show the expanded content when the page loads by setting data-collapsed to false:

```
<div data-role="collapsible" id="collapsibleName" data-collapsed="false">
```

Preventing Rounded Corners

By default a collapsible block has rounded corners and there is some padding added to it. You can remove the rounded corners and the padding by setting data-inset to false:

```
<div data-role="collapsible" id="collapsibleName" data-inset="false">
```

Mini Size

You can use global CSS theme data-mini set to true to display a more compact version of the collapsible:

```
<div data-role="collapsible" id="collapsibleName" data-mini="true">
```

Grouping Collapsible Contents

You can group multiple content blocks together by wrapping them:

```
<div data-role="collapsibleset"></div>
```

Setting an Expand and Collapse Icon

You can change the default icons for expand (+) and collapse (-) by specifying the data-collapsed-icon and data-expanded-icon attributes as follows:

```
<div data-role="collapsible" id="collapsibleName" data-collapsed-icon="carat-r"
        data-expanded-icon="carat-d">
```

Changing the Icon's Position

By default icons are displayed on the left side of the content header. You can change their position by setting the data-iconpos attribute to:

```
<div data-role="collapsible" id="collapsibleName" data-iconpos="right">
```

Theming

By default, collapsible inherits their theme from their parent containers. To use a different theme with the collapsible header, set the data-theme attribute of the wrapper as follows:

```
<div data-role="collapsible" id="collapsibleName" data-theme="b">
```

Figure 11-13 displays the collapsible set and two collapsible blocks with various types of content.

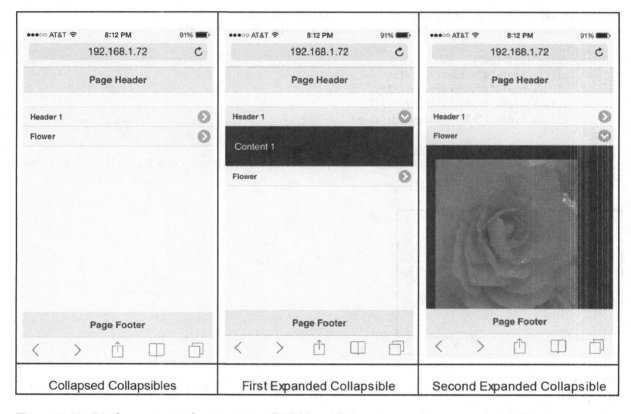

Figure 11-13. Display content and an image in collapsibles

11-13. Creating a List View
Problem

You want to know how to create a list view.

Solution

A list view displays a list of items. Generally, it is tappable to show more details of the selected item or to take some action. For example, it can be used to show a list of departments and, on tapping on a department name, another page with the list of employees in that department can be displayed. It can also display menu items (such as to search departments, add employees, and search employees), and on tapping a menu item, a new page can be displayed. A list view can be set for unordered lists (<ul>) or ordered lists (<ol>) by setting data-role to listview. The following is the syntax used to create a list view:

```
<ul data-role="listview">
            <li>listContent 1</li>
            <li>listContent 2</li>
            ...
</ul>
```

where listContent can be a text, button, link, or any valid HTML structure.

The following is the example of a list view with items that can be tapped (clicked):

```
<ul data-role="listview">
        <li><a href="#">Sales</a></li>
        <li><a href="#">Support</a></li>
        <li><a href="#">Marketing</a></li>
        <li><a href="#">Technology</a></li>
</ul>
```

This will display a list of departments that you can tap in order to perform some action. Figure 11-14 displays the list view of department names.

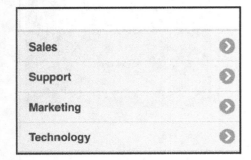

Figure 11-14. *List view*

Listing 11-11 demonstrates an example that displays a list view.

Listing 11-11. List view of department names

```
<!DOCTYPE html>
<html lang="en">
<head>
      <meta name="viewport" content="width=device-width, initial-scale=1">

      <link rel="stylesheet" href="styles/jquery.mobile-1.4.3.min.css" />

      <script src="scripts/jquery-2.1.0.min.js"></script>
      <script src="scripts/jquery.mobile-1.4.3.min.js"></script>
</head>
```

```
<body>
    <div data-role="page">
        <div data-role="header">
            <h1>Departments</h1>
        </div>

        <div data-role="main" class="ui-content">
            <ul data-role="listview" class="ui-alt-icon" data-count-theme="b"
                data-autodividers="true" data-inset="true"
                    data-filter="true" data-filter-theme="b" data-filter-placeholder="Search
                        departments">

                <li  data-icon="arrow-r">
                        <a href="#">
                            <h3>Infrastructure</h3>
                    <p>Responsible for hardware needs of the organization.</p>
                    <p class="ui-li-aside"><strong>Pending Tickets: 6</strong></p>
                        </a>
                </li>

                <li data-icon="arrow-r"><a href="#">Sales <span class="ui-li-count">5</span>
                    </a></li>
                <li data-icon="arrow-r"><a href="#">Support <span class="ui-li-count">3</span>
                    </a></li>
                <li data-icon="arrow-r"><a href="#">Marketing <span class="ui-li-count">10
                    </span></a></li>
                <li data-icon="arrow-r"><a href="#">Technology <span class="ui-li-count">8
                    </span></a></li>
            </ul>
        </div>
    </div>
</body>
</html>
```

How It Works

A list view is created by setting the data-role to listview for the unordered list (<ul>) element. The items in the list view are specified within <li> elements. Within the <li> element, you have control over how items are displayed by using header elements, paragraph elements, and the class ui-li-aside. Within the <li>, you can set which action needs to be taken by setting anchor (<a>) element. The following sections explain the classes and data attributes used in this recipe.

Adding Rounded Corners and Padding

To add rounded corners and padding, set the data-inset attribute to true:

```
<ul data-role="listview" data-inset="true">
```

Changing the Icon

By default, the carat-r icon is displayed for each list view item that has a <a> link as its child node.

You can change the icon by using the data-icon attribute as follows:

```
<li data-icon="iconName"><a href="#">item 1</a></li>
```

where iconName is a valid icon name. For the list of icons, refer to the Figure 11-1.

Adding a Custom Icon or Image

To add a custom image (16x16) as an icon on the left side of the list item, use the image (<img>) element with the class ui-li-icon as follows:

```
<li><a href="#"><img src="imageName" class="ui-li-icon">Item 1</a></li>
```

For images as thumbnails, don't specify the class ui-li-icon. Images will be scaled down to 80x80.

Making List Items Filterable

To add a filter control above the list view, you can set the data-filter attribute to true. When the user types in the text in the filter control, only those items that match the entered text will be displayed. You can set the theme of the filter control by setting data-filter-theme. You can add the placeholder text to the filter control by setting data-filter-placeholder.

```
<ul data-role="listview" data-filter="true" data-filter-theme="b"
        data-filter-placeholder="Search departments">
```

Setting List Items as Dividers

You can group list items by adding items and then specifying them as dividers by setting data-role as list-divider.

```
<li data-role="list-divider">groupName</li>
```

Grouping List Items by First Alphabet

Additional list items, with alphabets, can be added automatically to group list items by the first character of their text. This is generally used for grouping directory items.

```
<ul data-role="listview" data-autodividers="true">
```

Adding a Count Bubble

For each list view item, you can specify the count of items in that category by setting the ui-li-count attribute for the li element.

```
<li>listContent 1 <span class="ui-li-count">count</span></li>
```

The theme of the count display can be changed by setting the data-count-theme attribute:

```
<ul data-role="listview" data-count-theme="b">
```

Formatted Content

You can emphasize content by specifying it within the header element. Other text with less emphasis can be specified in a paragraph (<p>) element. To specify additional information near an icon, you can add the ui-li-aside class to the div or paragraph element. For example:

```
<li>
    <a href="#">
            <h3>Infrastructure</h3>
            <p>Responsible for hardware needs of the organization.</p>
            <p class="ui-li-aside"><strong>Pending Tickets: 6</strong></p>
      </a>
</li>
```

Theming

By default, a list view items inherits its theme from its parent container. To use a different theme, set the data-theme attribute:

```
<ul data-role="listview" data-theme="b">
```

For the icons, white sprite is used to change it to black. You can add ui-alt-icon as follows:

```
<ul data-role="listview" class="ui-alt-icon">
```

Nested Controls

You can specify list view controls as child nodes of other controls like collapsibles.

Figure 11-15 displays the list view with count bubbles and list items that are grouped.

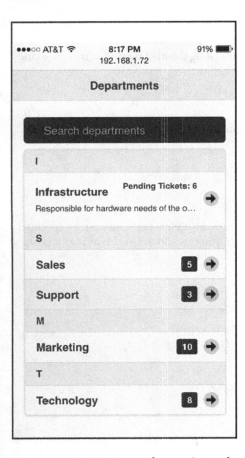

Figure 11-15. *List view with grouping and count bubbles*

11-14. Creating a Column Toggle Table
Problem

You want to create a column toggle table.

Solution

There are two types of tables used in mobile web applications—column toggle tables and reflow tables.

For a column toggle table, if the display width is not sufficient to display all the columns, some of the columns with less importance are hidden. The users can select and de-select columns they want to see or hide. The following is the syntax to create a column toggle table:

```
<table id="tableName" data-role="table" class="ui-responsive" data-mode="columntoggle">
    <!-- Column Headers -->
    <thead>
            <th>Column Header 1</th>
            <th>Column Header 2</th>
            ...
            </thead>
```

```
        <!-- Data -->
        <tbody>
                <td>Data 11</td>
                <td>Data 12</td>
                ...
        </tbody>
        ...
</table>
```

Listing 11-12 displays some employee records in the column toggle table.

Listing 11-12. Column toggle table

```
<!DOCTYPE html>
<html lang="en">
<head>
      <meta name="viewport" content="width=device-width, initial-scale=1">

      <link rel="stylesheet" href="styles/jquery.mobile-1.4.3.min.css" />

      <script src="scripts/jquery-2.1.0.min.js"></script>
      <script src="scripts/jquery.mobile-1.4.3.min.js"></script>
</head>

<body>
      <div data-role="page">
          <div data-role="header">
             <h1>Employees List</h1>
          </div>

          <div data-role="main" class="ui-content">
              <table id="tableName" data-role="table" class="ui-responsive ui-shadow table-stroke
                table-stripe"
                          data-mode="columntoggle" data-column-btn-text="Select Columns"
                          data-column-btn-theme="b" data-column-popup-theme="b">
                  <!-- Column Headers -->
                  <thead>
                        <tr>
                              <th data-priority="2">Employee ID</th>
                              <th data-priority="1">Employee Name</th>
                              <th data-priority="1">Department</th>
                              <th data-priority="3">Salary</th>
                        </tr>
                  </thead>

                  <!-- Data -->
                  <tbody>
                        <tr><td>1</td><td>Jane Smith</td><td>Marketing</td><td>$95,000</td></tr>
                        <tr><td>2</td><td>Michael Jefferson</td><td>Technology</td><td>$85,000
                          </td></tr>
                        <tr><td>3</td><td>Mary Jones</td><td>Support</td><td>$60,000</td></tr>
                  </tbody>
```

```
            </table>
        </div>
      </div>
    </body>
</html>
```

How It Works

Note that data-mode is set to columntoggle for the <table> element. Table column headers are specified within the <thead> element and records are specified within the <tbody> element. The column priority is specified in the column header (<th> element) by setting the data-priority attribute. The following sections explain the classes and data attributes used in this recipe.

Showing Lines Between Rows

You can add horizontal lines between each row by adding the table-stroke class:

```
<table id="tableName" data-role="table" class="ui-responsive table-stroke"
   data-mode="columntoggle">
```

You can set a different background color for alternate records by adding the class table-stripe:

```
<table id="tableName" data-role="table" class="ui-responsive table-stripe"
   data-mode="columntoggle">
```

Setting Column Priority

You can set the priority of the columns by using the data-priority attribute of the table header element as follows:

```
<th data-priority="dataPriorityValue">Column Header 1</th>
```

where dataPriorityValue can be 1 through 6 (1 is the highest priority and 6 is the lowest).

Setting the Text of the Column Chooser Button

By default the Columns... text is displayed on the column chooser button. You can change the text by setting the data-column-btn-text attribute to:

```
<table id="tableName" data-role="table" class="ui-responsive" data-mode="columntoggle"
         data-column-btn-text="Select Columns">
```

Theming

You can set the theme of the column chooser button by using the data-column-btn-theme attribute as follows:

```
<table id="tableName" data-role="table" class="ui-responsive" data-mode="columntoggle"
      data-column-btn-theme="b">
```

You can set the theme of the column chooser popup by using the `data-column-popup-theme` attribute as follows:

```
<table id="tableName" data-role="table" class="ui-responsive" data-mode="columntoggle"
    data-column-popup-theme="b">
```

Figure 11-16 displays the column toggle table. 

Figure 11-16. *Column toggle table*

11-15. Creating a Reflow Table

Problem

You want to create a reflow table.

Solution

There are two types of tables used in mobile web applications—column toggle tables and reflow tables.

With a reflow table, the jQuery Mobile framework tries to show all the columns horizontally. The first row contains the column headers and the subsequent rows contain the data. If the display is not wide enough to show all the columns, the column headers and data are displayed vertically in the following format. This format is repeated for each record in the table.

```
columnHeader1: dataValue1
columnHeader2: dataValue2
....
```

The following is the syntax to create a reflow table:

```
<table id="tableName" data-role="table" class="ui-responsive" data-mode="reflow">
    <!-- Column Headers -->
    <thead>
            <th>Column Header 1</th>
            <th>Column Header 2</th>
            ...
    </thead>

    <!-- Data -->
    <tbody>
        <td>Data 11</td>
        <td>Data 12</td>
        ...
    </tbody>
    ...
</table>
```

Since for data-role="table", reflow is the default table type, there is no need to specify data-mode="reflow". You can use colspan="numberOfColumns" to merge multiple cells. Listing 11-13 shows how to display a reflow table.

Listing 11-13. Reflow table

```
<!DOCTYPE html>
<html lang="en">
<head>
    <meta name="viewport" content="width=device-width, initial-scale=1">

    <link rel="stylesheet" href="styles/jquery.mobile-1.4.3.min.css" />

    <script src="scripts/jquery-2.1.0.min.js"></script>
    <script src="scripts/jquery.mobile-1.4.3.min.js"></script>
</head>
```

```
<body>
    <div data-role="page">
        <div data-role="header">
            <h1>Employees List</h1>
        </div>

        <div data-role="main" class="ui-content">
            <table id="tableName" data-role="table" class="ui-responsive ui-shadow table-stroke
            table-stripe" data-mode="reflow">
                <!-- Column Headers -->
                <thead>
                    <tr>
                        <th>Employee ID</th>
                        <th>Employee Name</th>
                        <th>Department</th>
                        <th>Salary</th>
                    </tr>
                </thead>

                <!-- Data -->
                <tbody>
                    <tr><td>1</td><td>Jane Smith</td><td>Marketing</td><td>$95,000</td></tr>
                    <tr><td>2</td><td>Michael Jefferson</td><td>Technology</td>
                        <td>$85,000</td></tr>
                    <tr><td>3</td><td>Mary Jones</td><td>Support</td><td>$60,000</td></tr>
                </tbody>
            </table>
        </div>
    </div>
</body>
</html>
```

How It Works

The <table> element's data-mode is set to reflow. In this mode, the jQuery Mobile framework tries to fit all the columns of a record horizontally. If there isn't enough space, each column is displayed vertically in the format columnHeader1 columnData1. For an explanation of the classes used in this example table, refer to Recipe 11-14. Figure 11-17 displays a reflow table in the landscape and portrait orientations.

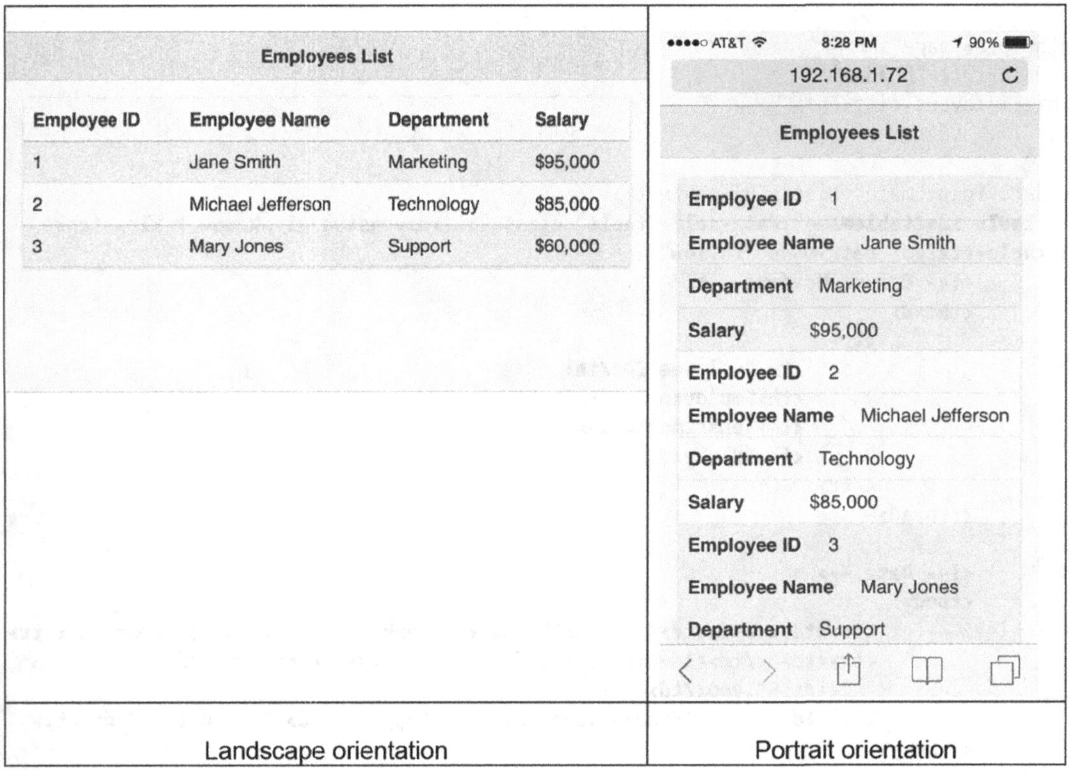

Employees List			
Employee ID	Employee Name	Department	Salary
1	Jane Smith	Marketing	$95,000
2	Michael Jefferson	Technology	$85,000
3	Mary Jones	Support	$60,000

Landscape orientation

●●●●○ AT&T 🛜   8:28 PM   ⌖ 90% ▬▬

192.168.1.72   ↻

Employees List

Employee ID   1

Employee Name   Jane Smith

Department   Marketing

Salary $95,000

Employee ID   2

Employee Name   Michael Jefferson

Department   Technology

Salary $85,000

Employee ID   3

Employee Name   Mary Jones

Department   Support

‹   ›   ⬆   📖   ⧉

Portrait orientation

Figure 11-17. *Reflow table in the landscape and portrait orientations*

11-16. Creating a Grid

Problem

You want to create a grid.

Solution

Grids are used to create a CSS-based layout where the columns are equal length. The following syntax is used to create a grid with three columns:

```
<div class="ui-grid-b">
     <div class="ui-block-a">Content 1</div>
     <div class="ui-block-b">Content 2</div>
     <div class="ui-block-c">Content 3</div>
</div>
```

You can customize each column by updating the CSS properties of ui-block-a through ui-block-e. A grid can be used to create a navigation bar or table-like controls. Listing 11-14 demonstrates an example that creates a grid.

Listing 11-14. Grid layout

```html
<!DOCTYPE html>
<html lang="en">
<head>
    <meta name="viewport" content="width=device-width, initial-scale=1">

    <link rel="stylesheet" href="styles/jquery.mobile-1.4.3.min.css" />

    <script src="scripts/jquery-2.1.0.min.js"></script>
    <script src="scripts/jquery.mobile-1.4.3.min.js"></script>

    <style>
            .ui-block-a, .ui-block-b, .ui-block-c {
                border:3px double green;
                    background-color: lightyellow;
                }
    </style>
</head>

<body>
    <div data-role="page">
        <div data-role="header">
            <h1>Grid Layout</h1>
        </div>

        <div data-role="main">
            <div class="ui-grid-b">
                <div class="ui-block-a"><a href="#somelink1" class="ui-btn">Search</a></div>
                <div class="ui-block-b"><a href="#somelink2" class="ui-btn">Add</a></div>
                <div class="ui-block-c"><a href="#somelink3" class="ui-btn">More...</a></div>
            </div>
        </div>
    </div>
</body>
</html>
```

How It Works

A three-column grid is created by using the ui-grid-b class for a div element. The three columns in the grid are specified by the classes "ui-block-a", "ui-block-b", and "ui-block-c". Within each column div element you can use any valid HTML structure. In this example, three buttons are created in the grid.

A grid can have up to five columns and any number of rows. Table 11-4 lists the five grid layouts.

Table 11-4. *Grid Layouts*

Grid CSS Class	Number of Columns	Columns' CSS Classes
ui-grid-solo	One	ui-block-a
ui-grid-a	Two	ui-block-a | b
ui-grid-b	Three	ui-block-a | b | c
ui-grid-c	Four	ui-block-a | b |c | d
ui-grid-d	Five	ui-block-a | b | c | d | e

ui-block-a is used to identify the first column, ui-block-b is used to identify the second column, and so on. Figure 11-18 displays a grid with three columns.

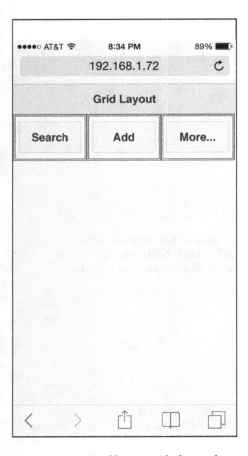

Figure 11-18. *Grid layout with three columns*

11-17. Creating Form and Form Controls

Problem

You want to create a form and some form controls.

Solution

Forms allow users to enter data, which is then submitted to be saved or to be processed on the server side. It is important to remember that the ID of the form and all form controls (input, select, button, and so on) must be unique across all the pages in a web site. This is because the jQuery mobile framework uses a single page navigation model and keeps pages in the DOM at the same time. The following is the list of form controls that can be used inside a form element—labels, text inputs, textareas, files, flip switches, checkboxes, radio buttons, selects, sliders, range sliders, and buttons.

The following is the basic structure of the form:

```
<form id="frmEmployee">
          <label for="formControl1">Employee Name:</label>
          <input type="text" id=" formControl1" name="formControl1">
          ...

          <a href="#" id="btnSubmit" class="ui-btn">Submit</a>
</form>
```

If an AJAX call is made to send form data to the server, then there is no need to specify action and method attributes for the form element. Listing 11-15 demonstrates an example that creates a form and its form controls.

Listing 11-15. Form with form controls

```
<!DOCTYPE html>
<html lang="en">
<head>
      <meta name="viewport" content="width=device-width, initial-scale=1">

      <link rel="stylesheet" href="styles/jquery.mobile-1.4.3.min.css" />

      <style>
              #footerMsg {font-size: 12px;}

              .ui-slider-switch { width: 100px !important }
      </style>

      <script src="scripts/jquery-2.1.0.min.js"></script>
      <script src="scripts/jquery.mobile-1.4.3.min.js"></script>
</head>

<body>
    <div data-role="page">
        <div data-role="header">
            <h1>Employee Form</h1>
        </div>
```

```
<div data-role="main" class="ui-content">
    <form id="frmEmployee">
        <div class="ui-field-contain">
            <label for="selActive" class="ui-hidden-accessible"></label>
            <select id="selActive" name="txtDepartmentName" data-role="slider" data-mini="true">
                <option value="A">Active</option>
                <option value="I">Inactive</option>
            </select>
        </div>

        <div data-role="collapsibleset">
            <div data-role="collapsible"  data-inset="false"  data-collapsed-icon="carat-r"
                data-expanded-icon="carat-d"  data-iconpos="right" data-mini="true"
                  data-content-theme="b">
                <h2>Basic Information</h2>
                <div class="ui-field-contain">
                    <label for="txtEmployeeName">Name:</label>
                    <input type="text" id="txtEmployeeName" name="txtEmployeeName"
                        data-mini="true">
                </div>

                <div class="ui-field-contain">
                    <label for="selDepartmentName">Department:</label>
                    <select id="selDepartmentName" name="selDepartmentName" data-
                    mini="true">
                        <option value=""></option>
                        <option value="Marketing">Marketing</option>
                        <option value="Sales">Sales</option>
                        <option value="Support"></option>
                        <option value="Technology"></option>
                    </select>
                </div>

                <div class="ui-field-contain">
                    <label for="sldAge">Age:</label>
                    <input  type="range" name="sldAge" id="sldAge" min="18" max="80"
                             data-mini="true"  data-highlight="true" data-track-
                             theme="a">
                </div>

                 <div class="ui-field-contain">
                    <label for="txtSalary">Salary:</label>
                    <input type="number" id="txtSalary" name="txtSalary" data-mini="true">
                </div>

                <div class="ui-field-contain">
                    <label for="txtHireDate">Hire Date:</label>
                    <input type="date" id="txtHireDate" name="txtHireDate"
                    data-role="date"
                             data-mini="true">
                </div>
```

```
    <div class="ui-field-contain">
        <fieldset data-role="controlgroup" data-type="horizontal"
            data-mini="true">
            <legend>Gender:</legend>

            <input type="radio" name="rdoGender" id="rdoMale" checked>
            <label for="rdoMale">Male</label>

            <input type="radio" name="rdoGender" id="rdoFemale">
            <label for="rdoFemale">Female</label>
        </fieldset>
    </div>
</div>

<div data-role="collapsible" data-inset="false" data-collapsed-icon="carat-r"
  data-expanded-icon="carat-d" data-iconpos="right" data-mini="true" data-
  content-theme="b">
    <h2>Experience</h2>
    <fieldset data-role="controlgroup" data-mini="true">
        <legend>Experience:</legend>
        <input type="checkbox" name="chkProgramming" id="chkProgramming">
        <label for="chkProgramming">Programming</label>
        <input type="checkbox" name="chkAnalysis" id="chkAnalysis">
        <label for="chkAnalysis">Analysis</label>
        <input type="checkbox" name="chkSales" id="chkSales">
        <label for="chkSales">Sales</label>
        <input type="checkbox" name="chkBudgetPlanning" id="chkBudgetPlanning">
        <label for="chkBudgetPlanning">Budget Planning</label>
    </fieldset>

    <div class="ui-field-contain">
        <label for="selIndustryExperience">Industry Experience:</label>
        <select id="selIndustryExperience" name="selIndustryExperience"
            data-mini="true" multiple>
          <option value="Auto">Auto</option>
          <option value="Financial">Financial</option>
          <option value="Healthcare">Healthcare</option>
          <option value="Insurance">Insurance</option>
          <option value="Technology">Technology</option>
        </select>
    </div>
</div>

<div data-role="collapsible" data-inset="false" data-collapsed-icon="carat-r"
  data-expanded-icon="carat-d" data-iconpos="right" data-mini="true" data-
  content-theme="b">
    <h2>Miscellaneous</h2>
    <div class="ui-field-contain">
```

```
                        <label for="txtComments">Comments:</label>
                        <textarea id="txtComments" name="txtComments" data-mini="true">
                        </textarea>
                </div>
            </div>
        </div><br><br>

        <fieldset data-role="controlgroup" data-type="horizontal"  data-mini="true" data-
        theme="b">
            <a href="#" class="ui-btn">Submit</a>
            <a href="#" class="ui-btn">Cancel</a>
        </fieldset>
    </form>
</div>

    <div data-role="footer" data-position="fixed">
        <h1 id="footerMsg">&#0169; 2014 Acme Corporation. All rights reserved.</h1>
    </div>
  </div>
</body>
</html>
```

How It Works

All the form controls are wrapped in the <form> element. The data-entry form is broken in three categories—Basic Information, Experience, and Miscellaneous. Therefore, three collapsibles are created so that all the form controls are not displayed at once. This way, users won't have to scroll up and down to enter data. The following code is used to create collapsibles:

```
<div data-role="collapsible"  data-inset="false" data-collapsed-icon="carat-r"
                data-expanded-icon="carat-d" data-iconpos="right" data-mini="true" data-content-
                theme="b">
        <h2>collapsibleTitle</h2>
          ...
</div>
```

All the form controls for checkboxes, radio buttons, and buttons are grouped together by using:

```
<fieldset data-role="controlgroup" data-mini="true">
                <legend>groupName</legend>
     ...
</fieldset>
```

The form control and the corresponding label are grouped together by using:

```
<div class="ui-field-contain">
     ...
</div>
```

The following sections explain the classes and data attributes used in this recipe.

Labels

All form controls should be paired with a label control. For example, for the input form control, the following syntax is used:

```
<label for="formControlName">labelText</label>
<input type="text" name="formControlName" id="formControlName">
```

The value for the label's for attribute and the form control's id attribute must be same.

If you want to use a placeholder for the form control and would like to hide the label, you can add the ui-hidden-accessible class to the label form control:

```
<label for="formControlName" class="ui-hidden-accessible">labelText</label>
```

Fieldcontainer

To prevent scrolling, wrap the form control and its label in a div tag with the class ui-field-contain. This will display the label and the form control side by side on the wider screen display instead of stacking them in two lines. The following is the syntax:

```
<div class="ui-field-contain">
```

Text Inputs

The following is the syntax to create a text input:

```
<input type="textType" name="formControlName" id="formControlName" value="defaultValue">
```

where textType can be text, date, datetime, email, tel, number, search, and so on.

For a date, set both the type and data-role to date. This will use the jQuery UI datetime picker.

Textarea

The following is the syntax to create a textarea:

```
<textarea cols="numberOfColumns" rows="numberOfRows" name="textarea"
          id="textarea">defaultValue</textarea>
```

File

The following is the syntax to create a file control. A Browse button is displayed.

```
<input type="file" name="formControlName" id="formControlName">
```

A file cannot by uploaded using an AJAX multipart form. You need to use:

```
<form id="formId" method="POST" data-ajax="false">
```

Flip Switch

Flip switches is used when a Boolean value is needed, such as on/off, true/false, or active/inactive. The following is the syntax to create a flip switch:

```
<select id="sldStatus" name="sldStatus" data-role="slider">
            <option value="option1">option1</option>
            <option value="option2">option2</option>
</select>
```

You can change the width of the flip switch by changing the CSS property width of the ui-slider-switch CSS class. For example, .ui-slider-switch { width: 100px !important }.

Checkboxes

The following is the syntax to create checkboxes:

```
<input type="checkbox" name="formControlName" id="formControlName">
<label for="formControlName" class="ui-hidden-accessible">labelText</label>
```

Radio Buttons

The following is the syntax to create radio buttons:

```
<input type="radio" name="formControlName" id="formControlName">
<label for="formControlName" class="ui-hidden-accessible">labelText</label>
```

If you want user to select a radio button among many choices, keep the value of the name attribute the same.

Grouping Checkboxes and Radio Buttons

You can group related checkboxes and radio buttons by wrapping them in a fieldset with the data-role set to controlgroup:

```
<fieldset data-role="controlgroup">
```

- The label for the group can be specified by using <legend>legendTitle</legend>.
- If data-type="horizontal" is added to the fieldset, the checkbox and radio buttons' label text will be displayed on the buttons.

Select

The select drop-down is generally used to select one out of many options. The syntax to create a select drop-down is:

```
<select id="formControlName" name="formControlName">
    <option value="optionValue1">optionText1</option>
    <option value="optionValue2">optionText2</option>
        ...
</select>
```

If you want to allow users to choose more than one option, you can add the `multiple` attribute to select an element:

```
<select id="formControlName" name="formControlName" multiple>
```

Sliders

The slider is used to enter numeric values, either by sliding a handle or entering a number. You can also specify the value, min, max, and step attributes. The following is the syntax to create a slider:

```
<input type="range" id="formControlName" name="formControlName" value="defaultValue"
            min="minValue" max="maxValue" step="incrementOrDecrementBy">
```

If you want to highlight a slider from a minimum value to the current selection, you can set the `data-highlight` attribute to true.

If you want to change the theme of the slider track, you can set the value of the `data-track-theme` attribute. The `data-theme` attribute sets the theme of the textbox containing the current value of the slider control.

If you want a user to enter range of values (such as start and end values) instead of one value, you can wrap two slider controls in the same `div` element with `data-role` set to `rangeslider`. The following HTML code is an example of creating the range slider:

```
Range Slider:<br>
<div data-role="rangeslider"  >
    <input type="range" id="start" name="start" value="20" min="1" max="100">
    <input type="range" id="end" name="end" value="80" min="1" max="100" >
</div>
```

Figure 11-19 displays the range slider control.

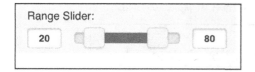

Figure 11-19. *Range slider*

Buttons and Links

Refer to Recipe 11-3 for information about buttons and links.

Figure 11-20 displays the employee form with form controls in collapsibles.

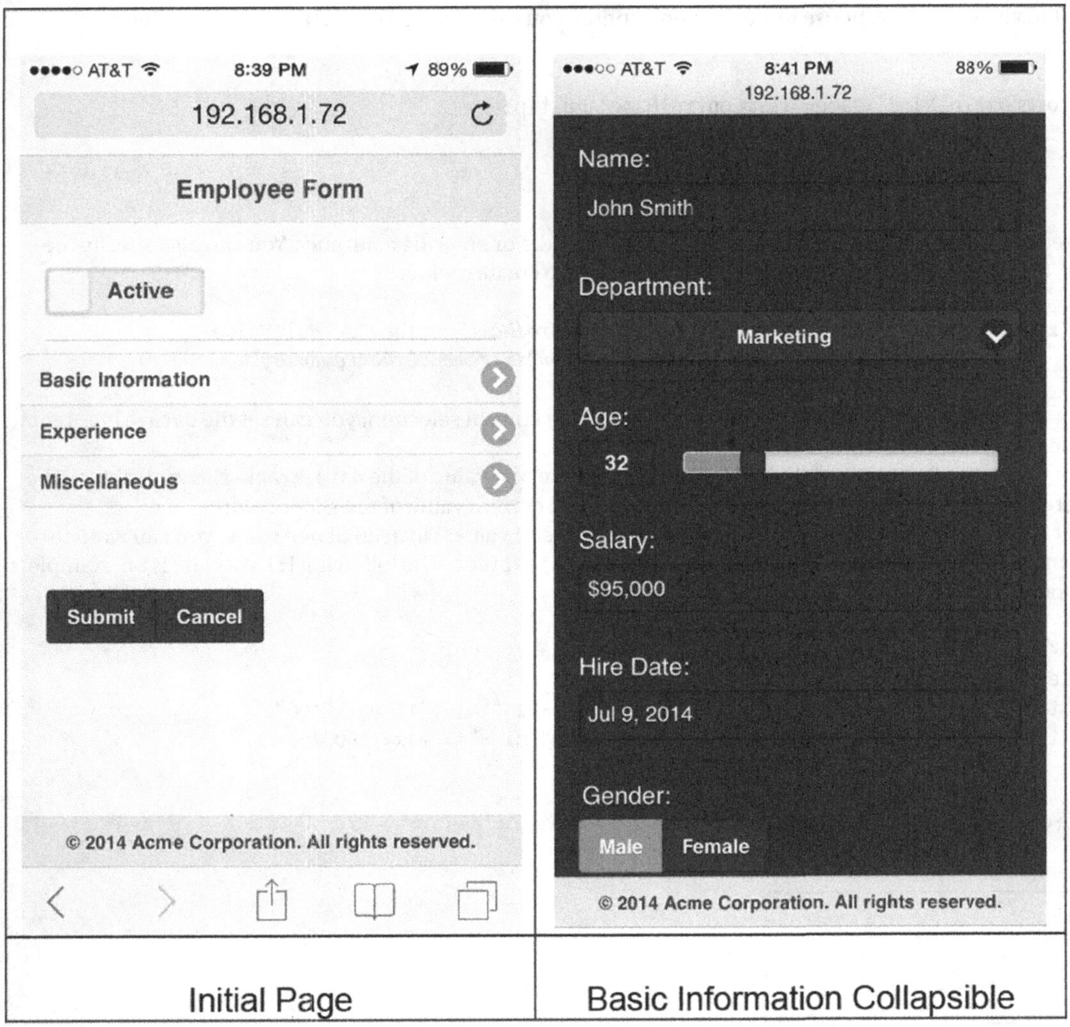

Figure 11-20. *Employee form*

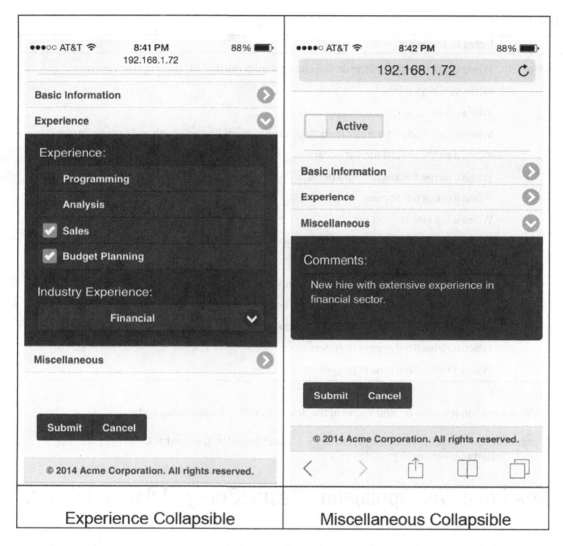

Experience Collapsible   Miscellaneous Collapsible

Figure 11-20. (*continued*)

11-18. Understanding the jQuery Mobile User-Initiated Events

Problem

You want to know which user-initiated events are provided by the jQuery mobile framework.

Solution

The jQuery mobile events are built on DOM native events. Table 11-5 lists the user-initiated events and their descriptions. I have covered page-related events in the Recipe 11-7. You can use the events handling and triggering concepts you learned in the Chapter 7.

Table 11-5. *User-Initiated Events*

Event	Event Is Triggered
orientationchange	When the orientation of the device changes from portrait to landscape or vice versa.
scrollstart	When scrolling starts.
scrollstop	When scrolling stops.
swipe	When swipe occurs for more than 30 pixels horizontally and less than 75 pixels vertically.
swipeleft	When a swipe toward the left occurs.
swiperight	When a swipe toward the right occurs.
tap	When a quick tap occurs.
taphold	When a tap and stay occurs.
vclick	When a virtualized mouse button click occurs.
vmousemove	When a virtualized mouse move occurs.
vcancel	When the system cancels a virtualized mouse event.
vmousedown	When a virtualized mouse button down occurs.
vmouseup	When a virtualized mouse button up occurs.
vmouseover	When a virtualized mouse over occurs.
vmouseout	When a virtualized mouse out occurs.

You can get the orientation (portrait or landscape) of the device by using the following code:

```
$(window).on("orientationchange", function(eventObj) { alert(eventObj.orientation); });
$(window).trigger("orientationchange");
```

11-19. Creating a Web Application Using jQuery Mobile Concepts
Problem

You want to write an application using the concepts covered in this chapter—page structure, headers, footers, page navigation, transitions, page containers, dialogs, navigation bars, panels, popups, and form controls.

Solution

Listing 11-16 displays a login screen that prompts the users to enter a user ID and password. This recipe uses a plaintext user Id and password to authenticate logon for the sake of explaining the concept. In real-world applications, user's credentials are saved in the encrypted form on the server side. Since server-side coding is out of the scope of this book, I have not provided the code for user authentication on the server side.

Listing 11-16. Login screen (the filename is login.htm)

```
<!DOCTYPE html>
<html lang="en">
<title>Title</title>
    <meta name="viewport" content="width=device-width, initial-scale=1">

    <link rel="stylesheet" href="styles/jquery.mobile-1.4.3.min.css"/>

    <style>
        #footerMsg { font-size: 12px; }
    </style>

    <script type="text/javascript" src="scripts/jquery-2.1.0.min.js"></script>
    <script type="text/javascript" src="scripts/jquery.mobile-1.4.3.min.js"></script>

    <script>
        $(function() {
            $("#btnLogin").click(function (){
                if ( $("#txtUserId").val().toLowerCase() == "testuser" && $("#txtPassword").val() ==
                "test123" ) {
                    location.href = "departments.htm";
                } else {
                    $( ":mobile-pagecontainer" ).pagecontainer( "change", "#loginErrorDialog", {
                        role: "dialog", transition: "pop"
                    } );
                }
            });
        });
    </script>
</head>

<body>
    <div data-role="page" id="homePage">

        <div data-role="header" data-position="fixed" data-theme="b">
            <a href="index.html"><img src="images/logo.png" style="height:15px; width:15px"></a>
            <h1>Acme</h1>
        </div>

        <div data-role="main" class="ui-content">
            <input type="text" id="txtUserId" placeholder="Enter User ID" data-mini="true">
            <input type="password" id="txtPassword" name="txtPassword" placeholder="Enter Password"
                data-mini="true">

            <div class="ui-grid-a">
                <div class="ui-block-a">
                    <input type="checkbox" id="chkSaveUserId" name="chkSaveUserId"  data-mini="true">
                    <label for="chkSaveUserId"  data-mini="true">Save User ID.</label>
                </div>
```

```
            <div class="ui-block-b">
                <button id="btnLogin" class="ui-btn-b ui-corner-all ui-shadow" data-mini="true"
                    data-theme="b">Login</button>
            </div>
        </div>
    </div>

    <div data-role="footer" data-position="fixed" data-theme="b">
        <h1 id="footerMsg">&#0169; 2014 Acme Corporation. All rights reserved.</h1>
    </div>
</div>

<div  data-role="dialog" id="loginErrorDialog">
    <div data-role="header">
        <h1>Login Status</h1>
    </div>
    <div data-role="main" class="ui-content" >
        <p>Failed to Login. Please try again.
    </div>
</div>
</body>
</html>
```

Figure 11-21 displays the login screen.

Figure 11-21. *Login screen*

For this example, enter testuser (case-insensitive) for the user ID and test123 (case-sensitive) for the password. If an incorrect user ID or password is entered and the Login button is clicked, the following code is executed:

```
$( ":mobile-pagecontainer" ).pagecontainer( "change", "#loginErrorDialog", {
        role: "dialog", transition: "pop"
    } );
```

This will display the div element with the ID set to loginErrorDialog as a dialog box. The following is the code used to create the dialog box:

```
<div  data-role="dialog" id="loginErrorDialog">
        <div data-role="header">
            <h1>Login Status</h1>
        </div>
        <div data-role="main" class="ui-content" >
            <p>Failed to Login. Please try again.
        </div>
</div>
```

Figure 11-22 displays the dialog box with the login failed message.

Figure 11-22. *Dialog box with login failed message*

If the correct user ID and password are entered and the Login button is clicked, following code is executed:

```
location.href = "departments.htm";
```

This will display the external HTML page called departments.htm. Listing 11-17 shows the content of the departments.htm file.

Listing 11-17. Display list of department names and employee records (the departments.htm file)

```
<!DOCTYPE html>
<html lang="en">
<head>
        <meta name="viewport" content="width=device-width, initial-scale=1">

        <link rel="stylesheet" href="styles/jquery.mobile-1.4.3.min.css" />

        <script src="scripts/jquery-2.1.0.min.js"></script>
        <script src="scripts/jquery.mobile-1.4.3.min.js"></script>

        <script>
                var employees = new Array();

                employees.push({name:"Jane Smith", department:"Marketing", salary:"$95,000"});
                employees.push({name:"Brian Adam", department:"Sales", salary:"$72,000"});
                employees.push({name:"Mary Jones", department:"Support", salary:"$60,000"});
                employees.push({name:"John Smith", department:"Technology", salary:"$90,000"});
                employees.push({name:"Michael Jefferson", department:"Technology", salary:"$85,000"});

                $(function() {
                        $("#listDepartments").click(function (eventObj) {
                                var selectedDepartmentName = $(eventObj.target).text();

                                $("#deptName").html(selectedDepartmentName);

                                $("#employeeRecords").empty();
                                $.each(employees, function(currentIndex) {
                                        if (employees[currentIndex].department == selectedDepartmentName) {
                                                $("#employeeRecords").append("<tr><td>" +
                                                employees[currentIndex].name +
                                                                "</td><td>" + employees[currentIndex].
                                                                salary + "</td></tr>");
                                        }
                                });
```

```
                          $( ":mobile-pagecontainer" ).pagecontainer( "change", "#employees", {
                                    role: "page", transition: "slide"
                          } );

                    });
             });
      </script>
</head>

<body>
      <div id="departments" data-role="page">
            <div data-role="header" data-theme="b">
                   <h1>Departments</h1>
                   <a href="login.htm" data-role="button" data-icon="home" data-iconshadow="true"
                          data-shadow="true" data-corners="true" data-iconpos="notext">Home</a>

                   <a href="#myPanel" data-role="button" data-icon="bars" data-iconshadow="true"
                          data-shadow="true" data-corners="true" data-direction="reverse"
                          data-transition="slide" data-iconpos="notext"  class="ui-btn-right">
                          Panel</a>
             </div>

             <div data-role="main" class="ui-content">
                   <ul id="listDepartments" data-role="listview" data-inset="true" data-filter="true">
                          <li><a href="#">Marketing</a></li>
                          <li><a href="#">Sales</a></li>
                          <li><a href="#">Support</a></li>
                          <li><a href="#">Technology</a></li>
                   </ul>
             </div>

             <div data-role="footer" data-position="fixed" data-theme="b">
                   <div data-role="navbar" data-iconpos="left">
                          <ul>
                                 <li><a href="addDepartment.htm" data-icon="plus">Add</a></li>
                                 <li><a href="#departments" data-icon="bullets" class="ui-btn-
                                 active">List</a></li>
                                 <li><a href="#myPanel"  data-icon="bars">More...</a></li>
                          </ul>
                   </div>
             </div>

             <div data-role="panel" id="myPanel" data-position="right" data-theme="b">
                   <ul data-role="listview">
                          <li data-icon="false"><a href="#">Add Employee</a></li>
                          <li data-icon="false"><a href="#">Search Employees</a></li>
                          <li data-icon="false"><a href="addDepartment.htm">Add Department</a></li>
                          <li data-icon="false"><a href="#">Search Departments</a></li>
                   </ul>
             </div>
      </div>
```

```
<div id="employees" data-role="page">
        <div data-role="header" data-theme="b"  data-add-back-btn="true">
                    <h1 id="deptName"></h1>
        </div>

        <div data-role="main" class="ui-content">
          <table id="tableName" data-role="table" class="ui-responsive ui-shadow table-stroke
          table-stripe"
                        data-mode="reflow">
                    <thead>
                          <tr>
                                  <th>Name</th>
                                  <th>Salary</th>
                          </tr>
                    </thead>

                    <tbody id="employeeRecords"></tbody>
          </table>
        </div>

        <div data-role="footer" data-position="fixed" data-theme="b">
              <h1 id="footerMsg">&#0169; 2014 Acme Corporation. All rights reserved.</h1>
        </div>
    </div>
</body>
</html>
```

In this listing:

- The header has a home icon button, which is created by the following code:

```
<a href="login.htm" data-role="button" data-icon="home" data-iconshadow="true"
    data-shadow="true" data-corners="true" data-iconpos="notext">Home</a>
```

When the home icon button is clicked, the login.htm page will be displayed.

- The header has a menu icon button, which is created by the following code:

```
<a href="#myPanel" data-role="button" data-icon="bars" data-iconshadow="true"
    data-shadow="true" data-corners="true" data-direction="reverse"
    data-transition="slide" data-iconpos="notext"  class="ui-btn-right">Panel</a>
```

When the bars icon button is clicked, the div element with the ID of myPanel will be displayed as a panel on the right side of the main screen. Figure 11-24 displays the panel.

- The department names are displayed in a listview due to the following code:

```
<ul id="listDepartments" data-role="listview" data-inset="true" data-filter="true">
                <li><a href="#">Marketing</a></li>
                <li><a href="#">Sales</a></li>
                <li><a href="#">Support</a></li>
                <li><a href="#">Technology</a></li>
    </ul>
```

The filter textbox is created because data-filter is set to true.

When a department name is clicked in the listview, the following code is executed:

- To get the name of the selected item in the list view:

```
var selectedDepartmentName = $(eventObj.target).text();
```

- To set the name of the selected department name in the header:

```
$("#deptName").html(selectedDepartmentName);
```

- To initialize the data records in the reflow table:

```
$("#employeeRecords").empty();
```

- To loop through the employees array and get the records for the selected department name:

```
$.each(employees, function(currentIndex) {
    if (employees[currentIndex].department == selectedDepartmentName) {
        $("#employeeRecords").append("<tr><td>" + employees[currentIndex].name +
        "</td><td>" + employees[currentIndex].salary + "</td></tr>");
    }
});
```

- To display the page with the ID of employees:

```
$( ":mobile-pagecontainer" ).pagecontainer( "change", "#employees", {
        role: "page", transition: "slide"
} );
```

Figure 11-25 displays the page with the employees' names and salaries of the selected department name.

- The three buttons (Add, List, and More...) in the navigation bar are created in the footer due to the following code:

```
<div data-role="navbar" data-iconpos="left">
    <ul>
        <li><a href="addDepartment.htm" data-icon="plus">Add</a></li>
        <li><a href="#departments" data-icon="bullets"  class="ui-btn-
        active">List</a></li>
        <li><a href="#myPanel"  data-icon="bars">More...</a></li>
    </ul>
</div>
```

When the Add button is clicked, the external HTML file called addDepartment.htm will be displayed. Listing 11-18 shows the content of the addDepartment.htm file.

When the More... button is clicked, the div element with the ID of myPanel will be displayed as a panel on the right side of the main screen. Figure 11-24 displays the panel.

Figure 11-23 displays the department names with a page header and a navigation bar in the page footer.

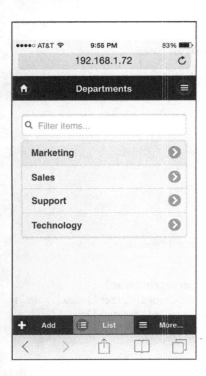

Figure 11-23. *Display department names and navigation bar*

Figure 11-24. *Display panel with the menu items*

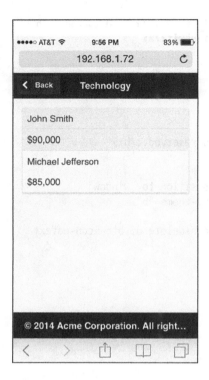

Figure 11-25. *Display employee records for the selected department*

Listing 11-18. Code to enter a new department (the filename is addDepartment.htm)

```
<!DOCTYPE html>
<html lang="en">
<head>
      <meta name="viewport" content="width=device-width, initial-scale=1">

      <link rel="stylesheet" href="styles/jquery.mobile-1.4.3.min.css" />
      <script src="scripts/jquery-2.1.0.min.js"></script>
      <script src="scripts/jquery.mobile-1.4.3.min.js"></script>
</head>

<body>
   <div data-role="page">
      <div data-role="header" data-theme="b" data-add-back-btn="true">
         <h1>New Department</h1>
      </div>

      <div data-role="main" class="ui-content">
         <form id="frmDepartment">
            <div class="ui-field-contain">
               <label for="txtDepartmentName">Name:</label>
               <input type="text" id="txtDepartmentName" name="txtDepartmentName"
                      data-mini="true">
            </div>
```

467

```
            <fieldset data-role="controlgroup" data-type="horizontal" data-mini="true" data-theme="b">
                <a href="#popupName"  data-rel="popup" class="ui-btn">Submit</a>
                <a href="departments.htm" class="ui-btn">Cancel</a>
            </fieldset>
        </form>
    </div>

    <div data-role="footer" data-position="fixed" data-theme="b">
        <h1 id="footerMsg">&#0169; 2014 Acme Corporation. All rights reserved.</h1>
    </div>

    <div data-role="popup" id="popupName" class="ui-content" data-position-to="window"
                data-transition="flip" data-theme="b" data-overlay-theme="b">

     <a href="#" data-rel="back" class="ui-btn ui-corner-all  ui-icon-delete ui-btn-icon-notext
    ui-btn-right">Close</a>
        New department <br>record is created.<br>
    </div>
  </div>
</body>
</html>
```

In this listing:

- The label and textbox are created by using the following code:

```
<label for="txtDepartmentName">Name:</label>
        <input type="text" id="txtDepartmentName" name="txtDepartmentName" data-
        mini="true">
```

Figure 11-26 displays the data-entry form used to enter a new department name.

Figure 11-26. *Department data-entry form*

- The Submit button is created due to the following code:

```
<a href="#popupName"  data-rel="popup" class="ui-btn">Submit</a>
```

When the Submit button is clicked, the div element with the ID of popupName is displayed as a popup.

Figure 11-27 displays the record-creation message in a popup window. The server-side code to save the entered information is out of the scope of this recipe.

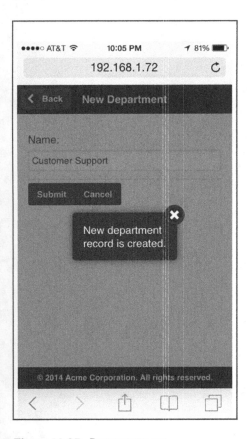

Figure 11-27. Popup message

- The Cancel button is created due to the following code:

```
<a href="departments.htm" class="ui-btn">Cancel</a>
```

When the Cancel button is clicked, the external HTML file called departments.htm is displayed.

Summary

This chapter covered the following jQuery Mobile library concepts:

- The CSS Framework
- Page structure—headers, content, and footers
- Pages—Container, Transition, and Navigation
- Navigation bars

- Dialog boxes, panels, and popups

- Collapsibles

- Grid view, listviews, and tables

- Form elements

- Events

This chapter covered the `data-role` attribute with the following values—`page`, `dialog`, `header`, `main`, `footer`, `controlgroup`, `navbar`, `panel`, `popup`, `collapsible`, `collapsibleset`, `listview`, `list-divider`, `table`, `slider`, `date`, and `rangeslider`.

The chapter also covered the following theme-related data attributes—`data-theme`, `data-overlay-theme`, `data-content-theme`, `data-filter-theme`, `data-track-theme`, `data-column-btn-theme`, `data-column-popup-theme`, and `data-count-theme`.

The display attributes of an element are controlled by either setting the attribute `data-displayProperty` or by adding the class `ui-displayProperty`.

You have worked on recipes to demonstrate how the rich set of data attributes and CSS classes can create a wide range of layouts and form controls for mobile web applications development. By using jQuery concepts (selectors, events, and AJAX), as well as jQuery UI and jQuery mobile controls, you can develop highly dynamic web applications.

CHAPTER 12

■ ■ ■

jqWidgets Framework

jqWidgets is a JavaScript library built on the jQuery library, HTML5, and CSS3. This library is used for developing responsive web and mobile applications. It provides a range of UI widgets that are ready to use in your application with a few lines of code. All UI widgets adhere to a consistent application programming interface, which makes them easy to learn and implement. You can visit to jqWidgets web site at `http://www.jqwidgets.com` to access comprehensive documentation and demos and to download the library.

This chapter covers the jqWidgets plug-ins—jqxDataAdapter, jqxValidator, and jqxDragDrop. The following is the list of UI widgets that you'll see in the recipes in this chapter:

- For data entry—Input, DateTime Input, Password Input, Masked Input, Number Input, Button, Switch Button, Button Group, Radio Button, Check Box, Combo Box, Drop-down, Listbox, Range Selector, Slider, Range Slider, Splitter, Tooltip, Progress Bar, and Rating.

- For grouping—Expander, List Menu, Panel, Tabs, and Tree.

- For tabular data displays—Grid, Data Table, and Tree Grid.

- For movable view areas—Window and Docking.

- For graphics—Chart.

- For composite controls—Calendar, Color, and Editor.

- For navigation—Menu and Navigation Bar.

At the time of this writing, the latest version is 3.4.0. For personal and non-commercial use, there is no licensing requirement.

Downloading the jqWidgets Library

1. Go to `http://www.jqwidgets.com/download/`.

2. Click the Download jqWidgets 3.4.0 button.

3. Enter your first name, last name, and e-mail address in the popup form and then click Download.

4. Save the file in your folder. The downloaded file name is `jqwidgets-ver3.4.0.zip`.

5. Unzip the downloaded ZIP file into a folder (for example, into `c:\jqWidgetsInstall`).

Installing the jqWidgets Library

There are two types of JavaScript files in the jqWidgets library:

- The consolidated JavaScript file, called jqx-all.js, is under c:\jqWidgetsInstall\jqwidgets and it contains the code for all the functionalities of jqWidgets plug-ins and widgets. It's approximately 2MB. The advantage of including the complete jqWidgets library in your HTML file is that you don't need to include any other jqWidgets JavaScript file. The disadvantage of including the complete jqWidgets library is that the 2MB file will be downloaded the first time the user accesses the page containing the reference to the jqWidgets library. Once the jqWidgets library is downloaded and cached by the browser, subsequent references to the jqWidgets won't require downloading of the file again.

- There are also plug-ins, widgets, and functionalities specific to JavaScript. Depending on which widget, plug-ins, and functionalities you are using in your HTML code, you need to include specific JavaScript file(s). You can get the list of plug-ins and widgets and their corresponding files in the c:\jqWidgetsInstall\ReadMe.txt file. For example, if you want to use the jqWidgets Grid with sorting capabilities, you need to include the jqxgrid.js and jqxgrid.sort.js files. The advantage of including only the JavaScript file(s) that are needed is that the user's browser doesn't need to download the complete JavaScript library, which is approximately 2MB.

Since the jqWidgets library is based on the jQuery library, you need to include the jQuery JavaScript file before including the jqWidgets JavaScript file(s).

The recipes in this chapter include the jqx-all.js jqWidgets library file and use the Energy Blue theme. Copy the following folders and files from c:\jqWidgetsInstall\jqwidgets.

- Copy the styles\images folder to the \styles folder to your development environment's root folder.

- Copy the jqx.base.css and jqx.energyblue.css files from the \styles folder to the \styles folder in your development environment's root folder.

- Copy the jqx-all.js file from the jqwidgets folder to the \scripts folder in your development environment's root folder.

Make sure the following directory structure exists in your development root folder:

- styles folder
  - images folder
  - jqx.base.css
  - jqx.energyblue.css
- scripts folder
  - jquery-2.1.0.min.js
  - jqx-all.js

The Code Template

Listing 12-1 displays the HTML file template that enables you to use the jqWidgets plug-ins and widgets.

Listing 12-1. HTML file template

```
<!DOCTYPE html>
<html lang="en">
<head>
      <meta charset="utf-8">
      <meta name="viewport" content="width=device-width, initial-scale=1">

      <title></title>

      <link rel="stylesheet" href="styles/jqx.base.css"/>

      <script src="scripts/jquery-2.1.0.min.js"></script>
      <script src="scripts/jqx-all.js"></script>

      <script>
            $(function () {

            });
      </script>
</head>

<body>

</body>
</html>
```

The viewport meta tag is used to make the web page smartphone- and tablet-friendly.

Testing Web Pages Using AJAX Calls

To test the program using AJAX call(s), use the Firefox browser to access the data file locally or deploy the web application on the web server so that you can use any of the major browsers. Chrome, Internet Explorer, and Safari browsers have security restrictions that prevent access to local files through the web page. Appendix C provides instructions for deploying web applications on the Apache Tomcat and IIS web servers.

12-1. Using Themes and CSS

Problem

You want to know how jqWidgets themes can be used, how a new theme can be created, and how default CSS properties of jqWidgets can be customized.

Solution

In order to use the jqWidgets' theme, you first need to include the base CSS file (jqx.base.css) and then use the theme-specific CSS file. The following is the code segment to use the Energy Blue theme:

```
<link rel="stylesheet" href="styles/jqx.base.css"/>
<link rel="stylesheet" href="styles/jqx.energyblue.css" type="text/css"/>
```

To specify a theme for a widget, set the following property in the options for the widget:

```
theme: themeName
```

Table 12-1 displays the list of themes available in the jqWidgets library.

Table 12-1. *jqWidgets Themes*

Theme Name	File Name
Android	jqx.android.css
Arctic	jqx.arctic.css
Black	jqx.black.css
Blackberry	jqx.blackberry.css
Bootstrap	jqx.bootstrap.css
Classic	jqx.classic.css
Dark Blue	jqx.darkblue.css
Energy Blue	jqx.energyblue.css
Fresh	jqx.fresh.css
High Contrast	jqx.highcontrast.css
Metro	jqx.metro.css
Metro Dark	jqx.metrodark.css
Mobile	jqx.mobile.css
Office	jqx.office.css
Orange	jqx.orange.css
Shiny Black	jqx.shinyblack.css
Summer	jqx.summer.css

(continued)

Table 12-1. (*continued*)

Theme Name	File Name
UI Darkness	`jqx.ui-darkness.css`
UI Le Frog	`jqx.ui-le-frog.css`
UI Lightness	`jqx.ui-lightness.css`
UI Overcast	`jqx.ui-overcast.css`
UI Redmond	`jqx.ui-redmond.css`
UI Smoothness	`jqx.ui-smoothness.css`
UI Start	`jqx.ui-start.css`
UI Sunny	`jqx.ui-sunny.css`
Web	`jqx.web.css`
Windows Phone	`jqx.windowsphone.css`

In Table 12-1, all the UI themes' color schemes are same as the color scheme of the themes provided with the jQuery UI library. These themes are especially useful when you are developing web sites containing both jQuery UI and jqWidget widgets.

In order to view the color scheme of the standard themes provided in the jqWidgets framework and preview the effects of the theme on the widgets, go to `http://jqwidgets.com/themebuilder/` and click the theme name from the "Import Colors from a Theme" section. The color schemes for the background color, border color, and text color are grouped in the following categories:

- Header areas
- Content areas
- Default state
- Active state
- Hover state
- Inputs and drop-downs
- Buttons and scrollbars
- Tooltips

The following attributes for a theme are also specified under the "Misc" category—font family, border radius, alternating color, alternating background, context menu background, focus border color, calls color, cells border color, and radio button check color.

Creating Custom Themes

You can create and use your own custom themes by performing the following steps:

- Go to http://www.jqwidgets.com/themebuilder/.

- Select any existing theme from the "Import Colors from a Theme" section (for example, Dark Blue).

- Select each theme category from the "Theme Settings" section (for example, "Header Areas").

- Select the desired color for your custom theme for each component from the "Settings" tab (for example, for "Header Background").

- Click Update Preview to view the impact of changes you just made.

- After you are done making all your changes:

  - Enter a theme name, such as mytheme.

  - Click the Get CSS button on the Get Theme tab. This will create the CSS content in the text area.

  - Copy and paste the CSS content in a file under the folder styles. For example, jqx.mytheme.css.

  - Add the following line to the HTML file:
    `<link rel="stylesheet" href="styles/jqx.mytheme.css"/>`.

  - Set the theme property in the options as mytheme. For example, for the calendar widget, you would use following syntax:

    HTML code: `<div id='myCalendar'></div>`

    JavaScript code: `$("myCalendar").jqxCalendar({theme:'mytheme' });`

- If you are not done with all of the theme settings, you can save your partial work by clicking the Save link on the top-right corner of the Settings tab and then copy/paste the content in a file.

To continue your work, click the Load link and paste the content from the saved file. Then click Load Theme Settings. This will load all your previous changes.

Customizing Part of the Theme for a Widget

In order to customize a part of an UI widget, you need to modify the CSS class names that are specific to the component. For example, if you want to change the background color to light yellow for the calendar's navigation title, you can use the following syntax:

```
.jqx-calendar-title-header-mytheme {
        background:lightyellow;
}
```

where mytheme is the theme you are using on your HTML page.

For the complete list of CSS class names for a widget, go to http://www.jqwidgets.com/jquery-widgets-documentation/. Click on the widget name in the left panel and then click Styling and Appearance.

12-2. Data Binding

Problem

You want to understand how data can be retrieved from the server in an object and used in a widget.

Solution

The jqxDataAdapter plug-in is used to get data in various formats—JavaScript array, XML, JSON, and so on—and then bind that data to the widget to display it. The following example demonstrates how jqxDataAdapter is used. Listing 12-2 displays the content of the employees.json data file. On the server side, data can be in a flat file or a program can extract the data from data sources like a database, assemble it, and return it.

Listing 12-2. Employee data (employees.json)

```
{
  "employees":
  [
    {"employeeId": 1, "managerId": 0, "name": "Mark Johnson", "department": "Finance",
     "salary": "$285,000"},
    {"employeeId": 2, "managerId": 1, "name": "Jane Smith", "department": "Marketing",
     "salary": "$95,000"},
    {"employeeId": 3, "managerId": 1, "name": "John Smith", "department": "Technology",
     "salary": "$90,000"},
    {"employeeId": 4, "managerId": 1, "name": "Brian Adam", "department": "Sales",
     "salary": "$72,000"},
    {"employeeId": 5, "managerId": 1, "name": "Mary Jones", "department": "Support",
     "salary": "$60,000"},
    {"employeeId": 6, "managerId": 3, "name": "Michael Jefferson", "department": "Technology",
     "salary": "$85,000"}
  ]
}
```

Follow these steps to bind data to a widget:

1. Specify the options for the jqxDataAdapter, including the data source and the data format:

```
var source =
        {
            datatype: "json",
            datafields: [
                { name: 'name', type: 'string' },
                { name: 'department', type: 'string' },
                { name: 'salary', type: 'string' }
            ],
            id: 'employeeId',
            url: "employees.json"
        };
```

- datatype specifies the returned data type from the server. Valid values are "array", "csv", "json", "jsonp", "local", "tsv", and "xml".

- datafields is an array that specifies the fields' attributes (name, type, format, and map) of the data in the data file or in the local data.

- id specifies the field name that uniquely identifies the record.

- url specifies the URL for the request. It can be a data file or a web service URL.

2. Instantiate jqxDataAdapter using the options specified in the previous step.

   - The simplest form is var dataAdapter = new $.jqx.dataAdapter(source);

   - With error and success event handler:

```
var dataAdapter = new $.jqx.dataAdapter(
        source,

        {
                loadError: function(jqXHR, status, errorMsg) {
                        alert(status + ": " + errorMsg);
                },

                loadComplete: function() {
                        // tasks to be performed on successful data retrieval
                }
        });
```

3. Bind jqxDataAdapter to a jqx widget (for example, to the jqxGrid widget). Refer to Recipe 12-10 for the complete code listing and explanation.

```
$("#employeeGrid").jqxGrid(
        {
        source: dataAdapter,
        columns: [
            { text: 'Name', datafield: 'name', width: 150 },
            { text: 'Department', datafield: 'department', width: 125 },
            { text: 'Salary', datafield: 'salary', width: 100}
        ]
        });
```

Use this HTML code: <div id="employeeGrid"></div>.
.jqxGrid() creates the grid widget with the following settings:

- source specifies the data source and has the value of jqxDataAdapter.

- columns specifies the mapping between data fields in the jqxDataAdapter and the column's heading in the grid.

- width specifies the width of the cell in the grid.

For a complete list of settings for jqxDataAdapter and jqxGrid, refer to the documentation available on the jqxwidgets web site.

Table 12-2 lists the options used to set the source. source is the argument for creating jqxDataAdapter.

Table 12-2. *Source Settings*

Option Name	Description
url	Specifies the URL where the request is sent.
localdata	Specifies the variable name that contains the data.
type	Specifies the request type—GET or POST. The default value is GET.
data	Specifies data that's sent to the server.
dataType	Specifies data type of the returned data. Valid values are "array" "csv", "json", "jsonp", "local", "tsv", and "xml".
root	Specifies from where the data begins in a nested data structure.
datafields	Specifies an array of objects containing information about the fields in a record. Members of the objects are: name—Specifies the name of the field in the returned data type—Specifies the data type of the field. Valid values include "string", "int", "number", "float", "date", and "bool". format—Specifies the format in which the returned data will be converted (optional). map—Specifies the mapping between the name and the nested fields structure (optional).
id	Specifies the field name in the returned data that uniquely identifies the record.
timeout	Specifies the timeout in milliseconds after which the request is aborted.
record	Specifies the information about the record.
mapChar	Specifies the mapping character used in maps in data fields.
columnDelimiter	Specifies the character used as a column delimiter in the returned data.
rowDelimiter	Specifies the character used as a row delimiter in the returned data.
values	Specifies the foreign collection associated with the data field.

Table 12-3 lists the options for setting jqxDataAdapter.

Table 12-3. *jqxDataAdapter Settings*

Option Name	Description
async	Specifies whether the request is sent asynchronously. The default value is true.
autoBind	Specifies whether dataAdapter's dataBind method is called. The default value is false.
contentType	Specifies the content-type of the data sent.
processData	Specifies the callback function to modify the data before it is sent to the server.
formatData	Specifies the callback function to format the data before it is sent to the server.
beforeSend	Specifies the callback function to modify jqXHR before a request is made.
downloadComplete	Specifies the callback function to process the data when the request is successful.
beforeLoadComplete	Specifies the callback function that's executed before the returned data is fully loaded.
loadComplete	Specifies the callback function that's executed after the returned data is fully loaded.
loadError	Specifies the callback function to handle the error when a request fails.
loadServerData	Specifies the callback function to manually handle the AJAX call.

12-3. Data Entry and Validation of Forms

Problem

You want to know which UI widgets are available in the jqWidgets framework and their purpose

Solution

The following is the format to create a widget with predefined settings (options):

```
$("#widgetId").widgetName(options)
```

Or:

```
$("#widgetId").widgetName({propertyName1: propertyValue1, propertyName2: propertyValue2 ...})
```

widgetId is the value of the ID attribute of the HTML element (generally, it is a div or input element). widgetName can be any of the following values:

jqxBulletChart, jqxButtons, jqxCalendar, jqxChart, jqxColorPicker, jqxComboBox, jqxDataTable, jqxDateTimeInput, jqxDocking, jqxDropDownList, jqxEditor, jqxExpander, jqxGauge, jqxGrid, jqxInput, jqxListBox, jqxListMenu, jqxMaskedInput, jqxMenu, jqxNavigationBar, jqxNumberInput, jqxPanels, jqxPasswordInput, jqxProgressBar, jqxRangeSelector, jqxRating, jqxScrollBar, jqxScrollView, jqxSlider, jqxSplitter, jqxTabs, jqxTooltip, jqxTree, jqxTreeGrid, jqxTreeMap, or jqxWindow.

options is a map object containing properties of the widget in the format:

propertyName1: propertyValue1, propertyName2: propertyValue2 ...

The following is the syntax to get the property value:

```
$("#widgetId").widgetName("propertyName");
```

The following is the syntax to execute a method:

```
$("#widgetId").widgetName("methodName", argument1, argument2, ...);
```

The following is the syntax to register the event handler for the widget's events:

```
$('#widgetId').on('eventName', function (eventObject) {
        // Event handler code
});
```

Listing 12-3 creates a data-entry form with validation checks using UI widgets.

Listing 12-3. Data-entry form with validation

```
<!DOCTYPE html>
<html lang="en">
<head>
        <meta charset="utf-8">
        <meta name="viewport" content="width=device-width, initial-scale=1">

        <title>jqWidget - Form</title>

        <link rel="stylesheet" href="styles/jqx.base.css"/>
        <link rel="stylesheet" href="styles/jqx.energyblue.css"/>

        <script src="scripts/jquery-2.1.0.min.js"></script>
        <script src="scripts/jqx-all.js"></script>

        <style>
                form {
                        border: 3px double green;
                        width: 500px;
                        padding-left: 10px;
                        padding-right: 10px;
                        padding-bottom: 10px;
                        background-color: lightyellow;
                }

                label {
                        float: left;
                        display: block;
                        width: 125px;
                        font-weight: bold;
                }

                fieldset {
                        padding: 5px;
                        border: 0px;
                }
        </style>
```

```
<script>
    $(function () {
        $("#switchActive").jqxSwitchButton({ theme: "energyblue", height: 25, width: 75,
        checked: true, onLabel: "Yes", offLabel: "No" });
        $("#txtEmployeeName").jqxInput({ placeHolder: "Enter Employee Name"});
        $("#hireDate").jqxDateTimeInput({ width: '100px', height: '25px', formatString:
        "MM/dd/yyyy" });

        var departments = new Array("Finance", "Technology", "Support", "Sales");

        $("#txtDepartment").jqxInput({ placeHolder: "Enter a department", height: 25,
        width: 200,  minLength: 1, source: departments });

        $("#txtEMailAddress").jqxInput();
        $("#btnGroupGender").jqxButtonGroup({ theme: "energyblue", mode: 'radio' });
        $("#rdoFemale").jqxRadioButton({width: 100, groupName :"Gender" });
        $("#rdoMale").jqxRadioButton({width: 100, groupName :"Gender" });

        $("#btnGroupExperience").jqxButtonGroup({ theme: "energyblue", mode: 'checkbox' });
        $("#chkTechnology").jqxCheckBox({width: 100});
        $("#chkSales").jqxCheckBox({width: 100});
        $("#chkMarketing").jqxCheckBox({width: 100});

        $("#txtSSN").jqxPasswordInput({ placeHolder: "Enter SSN", height: 25, width: 200});

        $("#txtPhoneNumber").jqxMaskedInput({height: 25, width: 200, mask: '(###)###-
        ####' });

        $("#salary").jqxNumberInput({height: 25, width: 200, decimal:0, symbol: '$'});

        $("[type='button']").jqxButton({theme:"energyblue"});

        $("#btnSubmit").on('click', function (event) {

            if ($('#frmEmployee').jqxValidator('validate')) {
                var msg = "Form will be submitted with the following values:\n\n";
                msg += "Active: " + $("#switchActive").val() + "\n";
                msg += "Employee Name: " + $("#txtEmployeeName").val() + "\n";
                msg += "Hire Date: " + $("#hireDate").val() + "\n";
                msg += "Department: " + $("#txtDepartment").val() + "\n";
                msg += "EMail Address: " + $("#txtEMailAddress").val() + "\n";
                msg += "Gender: Female:" + $("#rdoFemale").jqxRadioButton('checked') +
                            " Male:" + $("#rdoMale").jqxRadioButton('checked') + "\n";
                msg += "Experience: " + $("#btnGroupExperience").val() + "\n";
                msg += "SSN: " + $("#txtSSN").val() + "\n";
                msg += "Phone Number: " + $("#txtPhoneNumber").val() + "\n";
                msg += "Salary: " + $("#salary").val();
```

```
                            alert(msg);
                        } else {
                            alert("Please resolve validation issues.");
                        }
                });

                $("#btnCancel").on('click', function (event) {
                        alert("Form is cancelled.");
                });

                // Validator
                $('#frmEmployee').jqxValidator({ rules: [
                                { input: '#txtEmployeeName', message: 'The Employee Name is
                                  required.', action: 'keyup', rule: 'required' },
                                { input: '#txtEMailAddress', message: 'Invalid EMail Address.',
                                  action: 'keyup', rule: 'email'},
                                { input: '#txtSSN', message: 'Invalid SSN.', action: 'keyup',
                                  rule: 'ssn'},
                                { input: '#txtSSN', message: 'Invalid SSN.', action: 'keyup',
                                  rule: 'required'},
                            ],
                            theme: 'energyblue'
                });
            });
        </script>
    </head>

    <body>
        <h3>Employee Form</h3>
        <form id="frmEmployee">
                <fieldset>
                        <label>Active?</label>
                        <div id='switchActive'></div>
                </fieldset>

                <fieldset>
                        <label>Employee Name: </label>
                        <input type="text" id="txtEmployeeName"/><br>
                </fieldset>

                <fieldset>
                        <label>Hire Date: </label>
                        <div id='hireDate'></div>
                </fieldset>

                <fieldset>
                        <label>Department: </label>
                        <input type="text" id="txtDepartment"/><br>
                </fieldset>
```

```html
        <fieldset>
            <label>EMail Address: </label>
            <input type="text" id="txtEMailAddress"/><br>
        </fieldset>

        <fieldset>
            <label>Gender: </label>
            <div id='btnGroupGender'>
                    <div id='rdoFemale'>Female</div>
                    <div id='rdoMale'>Male</div>
            </div>
        </fieldset>

        <fieldset>
            <label>Experience: </label>
            <div id='btnGroupExperience'>
                    <div id='chkTechnology'>Technology</div>
                    <div id='chkSales'>Sales</div>
                    <div id='chkMarketing'>Marketing</div>
            </div>
        </fieldset>

        <fieldset>
            <label>SSN: </label>
            <input type="password" id="txtSSN"/><br>
        </fieldset>

        <fieldset>
            <label>Phone Number: </label>
            <input type="text" id="txtPhoneNumber"/><br>
        </fieldset>

        <fieldset>
            <label>Salary: </label>
            <div id='salary'></div><br>
        </fieldset>

        <fieldset>
            <input type="button" value="Submit" id='btnSubmit'/>
            <input type="button" value="Cancel" id='btnCancel'/>
        </fieldset>
    </form>
</body>
</html>
```

How It Works

This code example creates widgets by specifying the HTML elements `<div>` and `<input>`, setting their ID attributes to the value of widgetId, and then creating the jqWidget using the following syntax:

```
$("#widgetId").widgetName(options);
```

Figure 12-1 displays the initial form when viewed in a browser.

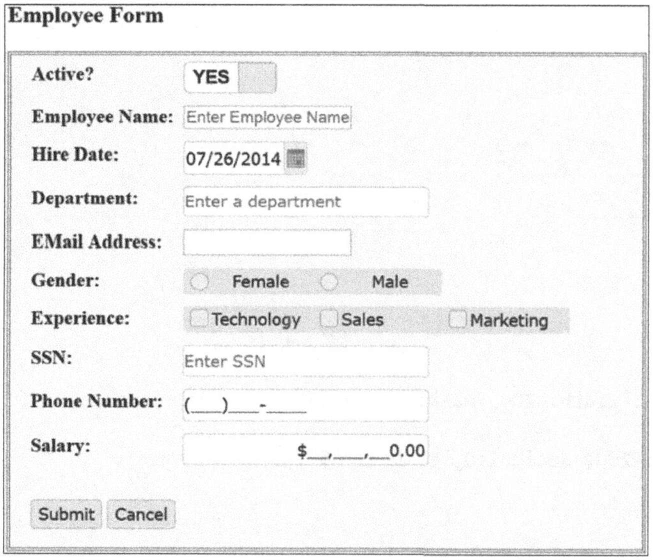

Figure 12-1. *Employee data-entry form*

Table 12-4 lists the data-entry field name and the name of the jqWidget that's used to create the widget.

Table 12-4. *jqWidgets Used in the Form*

Data-Entry Field	jqWidgetName
Active?	jqxSwitchButton()
Employee Name	jqxInput()
Hire Date	jqxDateTimeInput()
Department	jqxInput()
E-mail Address	jqxInput()
Gender	jqxButtonGroup()
Female	jqxRadioButton()
Male	jqxRadioButton()

(*continued*)

Table 12-1. (*continued*)

Data-Entry Field	jqWidgetName
Experience	jqxButtonGroup()
Technology	jqxCheckBox()
Sales	jqxCheckBox()
Marketing	jqxCheckBox()
SSN	jqxPasswordInput()
Phone Number	jqxMaskedInput()
Salary	jqxNumberInput()
Submit Button	jqxButton()
Cancel Button	jqxButton()

Masked Fields

In this example, the following masks are used:

```
$("#txtPhoneNumber").jqxMaskedInput({height: 25, width: 200, mask: '(###)###-####'});

$("#salary").jqxNumberInput({height: 25, width: 200, decimal:0, symbol: '$'});
```

Theme

In this example, the Energy Blue theme is used by including the theme file, as so:

```
<link rel="stylesheet" href="styles/jqx.energyblue.css"/>
```

and setting the theme option to "energyblue" for the jqWidgets used in this code.

Validator

The following code defines the validation rules for the Employee Name, EMail Address, and SSN fields:

```
$('#frmEmployee').jqxValidator({ rules: [
            { input: '#txtEmployeeName', message: 'The Employee Name is required.',
                    action: 'keyup', rule: 'required' },
            { input: '#txtEMailAddress', message: 'Invalid EMail Address.', action: 'keyup',
                    rule: 'email'},
            { input: '#txtSSN', message: 'Invalid SSN.', action: 'keyup', rule: 'ssn'},
            { input: '#txtSSN', message: 'Invalid SSN.', action: 'keyup', rule: 'required'},
            ],
                theme: 'energyblue'
            });
```

- The input property specifies the ID of the HTML element to which the validation rule will be applied.

- The message property specifies the message to display if the validation rule is not satisfied.

- The action property specifies when to apply the validation rule.

- The rule property specifies the rule from the list of predefined rules. This example uses the required, email, and ssn rules.

Events

The following events are used in this example:

- The click event on the Submit button. When the Submit button is clicked, the event handler executes $('#frmEmployee').jqxValidator('validate'). If there is no validation rule violation, true is returned and a popup message is displayed with the entered values. Figure 12-9 displays the popup message with entered values if no validation error is found. If there is any validation rule violation, a false value is returned and the "Please resolve validation issues." popup message is displayed.

- The click event on the Cancel button. When the Cancel button is clicked, "Form is cancelled." popup message is displayed.

When the user clicks the Submit button without entering any data, "Please resolve validation issues." popup message is displayed and the fields that don't pass the validation checks are highlighted. Figure 12-2 displays the highlighted fields with validation errors.

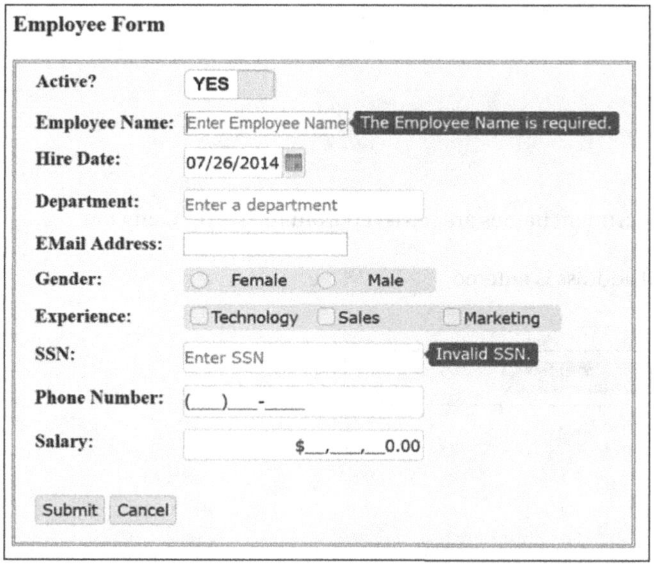

Figure 12-2. *Employee data-entry form with validation errors*

Figure 12-3 displays the popup calendar when the calendar icon is clicked for the Hire Date.

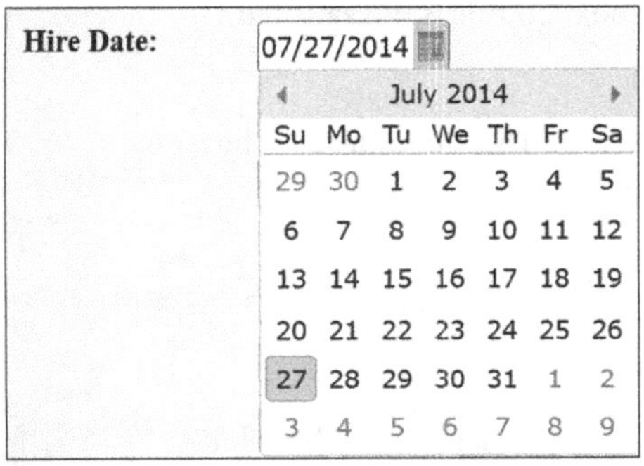

Figure 12-3. *Popup calendar for the Hire Date*

Figure 12-4 displays the Department drop-down when a partial value for the department is entered. This effect is achieved by using the following code:

```
var departments = new Array("Finance", "Technology", "Support", "Sales");

$("#txtDepartment").jqxInput({ placeHolder: "Enter a department", height: 25, width: 200,
                               minLength: 1, source: departments });
```

Figure 12-4. *Department names drop-down*

source can also be set as jqxDataAdapter if the department names are retrieved from the server using the AJAX call.

Figure 12-5 displays the message if an invalid email address is entered.

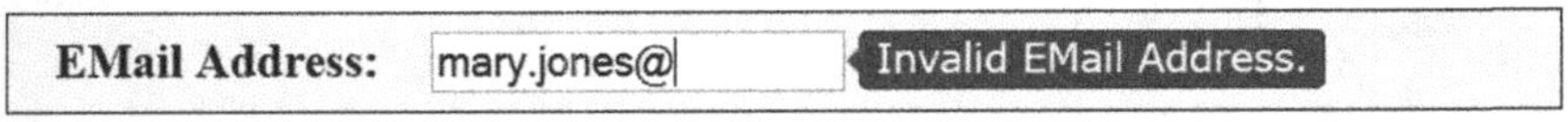

Figure 12-5. *Invalid EMail Address message*

Figure 12-6 displays the message if an invalid SSN is entered.

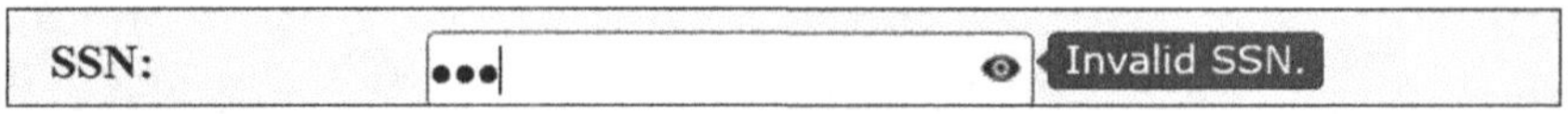

***Figure 12-6.** Invalid SSN message*

Figure 12-7 displays the unmasked SSN if the eye icon is clicked. Since the SSN is set as the `jqxPasswordInput` widget, asterisks (*) are displayed in place of the actual value.

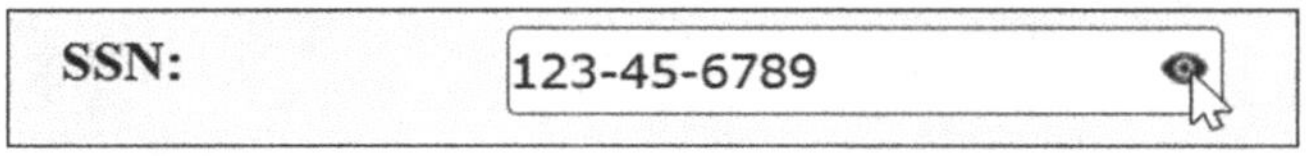

***Figure 12-7.** SSN value*

Figure 12-8 displays the completed employee data-entry form with no invalid validation rules.

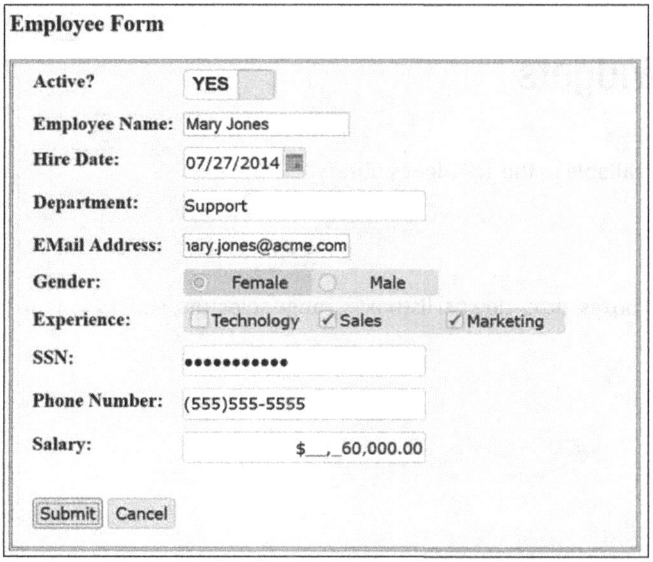

***Figure 12-8.** Completed employee data-entry form*

Figure 12-9 displays the popup message when a completed employee data-entry form is submitted by clicking the Submit button and there is no validation error.

Figure 12-9. *Popup message with the entered field values*

12-4. Using Other Data-Entry Widgets
Problem

You want to know which other data-entry controls are available in the jqWidgets library.

Solution

This recipe covers the following input controls—combo boxes, drop-downs, listboxes, range selectors, sliders, splitters, tooltips, progress bars, and rating options.

Combo Box

Listing 12-4 creates a combo box using the local data.

Listing 12-4. Creating a combo box

```
<!DOCTYPE html>
<html lang="en">
<head>
    <meta charset="utf-8">
    <meta name="viewport" content="width=device-width, initial-scale=1">
    <title>jqWidget - ComboBox</title>

    <link rel="stylesheet" href="styles/jqx.base.css"/>
    <script src="scripts/jquery-2.1.0.min.js"></script>
    <script src="scripts/jqx-all.js"></script>
```

```
<script>
        $(function () {

            // Specify data
            var departmentData = {
                "departments":
                    [
                            {"department":"Finance"},
                            {"department":"Marketing"},
                            {"department":"Sales"},
                            {"department":"Support"},
                            {"department":"Technology"}
                    ]
            };

             // Specify data source
             var source = {
                    datatype: "json",
                    datafields: [{ name: 'department', type: 'string' }],
                    localdata:  departmentData
             };

             // Set Data Adapter
             var dataAdapter = new $.jqx.dataAdapter(source,
                                    {
                                            loadError: function(jqXHR, status, errorMsg) {
                                            alert(status + ": " + errorMsg);
                                            }
                                    });

             // Create a jqxComboBox using Data Adapter
             $("#departments").jqxComboBox({ source: dataAdapter, displayMember: "department",
                valueMember: "department", selectedIndex: 0, width: '200px', height: '25px' });

             // 'Select' event handler.
             $('#departments').on('select', function (event) {
                var args = event.args;
                var item = $("#departments").jqxComboBox('getItem', args.index);

                $("#selectedDepartmentMsg").html('<strong>Selected Department:</strong> ' +
                    item.label);
             });
        });
    </script>
</head>

<body>
    <div id="departments"></div><br>
    <div id="selectedDepartmentMsg"></div>
</body>
</html>
```

493

How It Works

In Listing 12-5, a combo box is created using the following code:

HTML code: `<div id=departments></div>`
JavaScript code:

```
$("#departments").jqxComboBox({ source: dataAdapter, displayMember: "department",
                                valueMember: "department", selectedIndex: 0, width: '200px',
                                height: '25px' });
```

- source is dataAdapter, which contains contents from departmentData.

- displayMember specifies which dataField in the dataAdapter is used to display the value on the screen.

- valueMember specifies which dataField in the dataAdapter is used as a value if an item is selected.

- selectedIndex specifies which item index is selected by default.

- width specifies the width of the widget.

- height specifies the height of the widget.

Figure 12-10 displays the combo box with values from departmentsData.

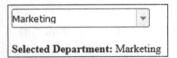

Figure 12-10. *Combo box with the department name*

Using AJAX Calls

If you want to make an AJAX call to get the data instead of using local data, you can set the source as follows:

```
// Specify data source
var source = {
        datatype: "json",
        datafields: [{ name: 'department', type: 'string' }],
        url: "departments.json"
};
```

Listing 12-5 displays the content of the departments.json file.

Listing 12-5. Contents of the departments.json file

```json
{
  "departments":
  [
    {"department":"Finance"},
    {"department":"Marketing"},
    {"department":"Sales"},
    {"department":"Support"},
    {"department":"Technology"}

  ]
}
```

Drop-downs

Drop-downs contain a list of selectable items.
HTML code:

```html
<div id='departments'></div>
```

JavaScript code:
To create a drop-down, use this code:

```javascript
$("#departments").jqxDropDownList({ source: dataAdapter, displayMember: "department",
                                    valueMember: "department", selectedIndex: 0 });
```

Refer to the code in Listing 12-5 to set the dataAdapter.
To get the selected value, use this code:

```javascript
var item = $("#departments").jqxDropDownList('getSelectedItem').value;
$("#selectedDepartmentMsg").html('<strong>Selected Department:</strong> ' + item);
```

Figure 12-11 displays the drop-down with the department names.

Figure 12-11. Drop-down of the department names

Listboxes

Listboxes contain a list of selectable items. Multiple values can be selected.
HTML code:

```
<div id='jqxlistbox'></div>
```

JavaScript code:
To create the listbox, use this code:

```
$("#departments").jqxListBox({ source: dataAdapter, displayMember: "department",
                               valueMember: "department"});
```

Refer to the code in Listing 12-5 to set the dataAdapter.
To get the selected value:

```
var item = $("#departments").jqxListBox('getSelectedItem').value;
$("#selectedDepartmentMsg").html('<strong>Selected Department:</strong>' + item);
```

Figure 12-12 displays the listbox with the department names.

```
Finance
Marketing
Sales
Support
Technology
```

Figure 12-12. Listbox

Range Selectors

Range selectors are used to select a number range or a date range.
HTML code:

```
<div id="ageSelector">
      <div id="ageSelectorContent"></div>
</div>
```

JavaScript code:
To create the range selector, use this code:

```
$("#ageSelector").jqxRangeSelector({width: 300, height: 50, min: 20, max: 70,
range: { from: 35, to: 50 }});
```

To get the range values, use this code:

```
$("#ageSelector").jqxRangeSelector("getRange").from;
$("#ageSelector").jqxRangeSelector("getRange").to;
```

Figure 12-13 displays the range selector for age.

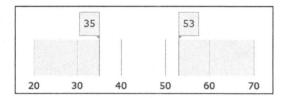

Figure 12-13. *Range selector*

Sliders

Sliders are used to select a value from a range of values.
HTML code:

```
<div id='mySlider'></div>
```

To create the slider, use this code:

```
var initialValue = 12;
$("#mySlider").jqxSlider({min:1, max:20, step:1, value: initialValue, mode: 'fixed' });
```

To get the selected value, use this code:

```
$("#mySlider").jqxSlider('value');
```

Figure 12-14 displays the slider widget.

Figure 12-14. *Slider widget*

Splitters

Splitters are used to divide a container display area into two or more panels by moving split bar(s).
HTML code:

```
<div id='cpuUtilizationThreshold' style="background-color: #FFFFAF">
    <div id="firstPanel" class="adjust" style="background-color: lightgreen;"></div>
    <div id="secondPanel" class="adjust" style="background-color: lightyellow;"></div>
</div>
```

To create the splitter, use this JavaScript code:

```
$("#cpuUtilizationThreshold").jqxSplitter({ width: 300, height: 60, panels: [{ size: '100'}] });
```

To get the selected value, use this JavaScript code:

```
$("#cpuUtilizationThreshold").jqxSplitter("panels")[panelIndex].size;
```

Where panelIndex is the index number of the panel.
Figure 12-15 displays the splitter widget.

Figure 12-15. *Splitter widget*

Tooltips

Tooltips are used to display popup informative messages when the users hover the mouse over an HTML element.
HTML code:

```
<input type="text" id="txtCreditCardCCV" placeholder="CCV">
```

To create the tooltip, use this JavaScript code:

```
$("#txtCreditCardCCV").jqxTooltip({ position: 'right',
content: 'MasterCard/Visa: 3 Digits on the back of the card.<br>American Express: 4 Digit Number in
the front.' });
```

Figure 12-16 displays the tooltip.

Figure 12-16. *Tooltip*

Progress Bars

Progress bars are used to display progress of an operation.
HTML code:

```
<div id='paymentProcessingStatus'></div>
```

To create the progress bar, use this JavaScript code:

```
$("#paymentProcessingStatus").jqxProgressBar({ width: 250, height: 25, value: 35 });
```

Figure 12-17 displays the progress bar.

Figure 12-17. *Progress bar*

Ratings

This input option enables users to choose a rating.
HTML code:

```
<div id='userReview'></div>
```

To create the rating with four stars, use this JavaScript code:

```
$("#userReview").jqxRating({ width: 350, height: 35, value: 4});
```

To get the selected value, use this JavaScript code:

```
$("#userReview").jqxRating('value');
```

Figure 12-18 displays the rating.

Figure 12-18. *Rating*

12-5. Displaying Content Using the Expander Widget
Problem

You want to display content with the header by using the expander widget.

Solution

The following jQuery syntax is used to create the expander widget:

```
$("#widgetId").jqxExpander(options);
```

where options is the map object with jqxExpander-specific parameterName and parameterValue pairs.

Listing 12-6 creates the expander widget.

Listing 12-6. Creating an expander

```html
<!DOCTYPE html>
<html lang="en">
<head>
      <meta charset="utf-8">
      <meta name="viewport" content="width=device-width, initial-scale=1">
      <title>jqWidget - Expander</title>

      <link rel="stylesheet" href="styles/jqx.base.css"/>
      <script src="scripts/jquery-2.1.0.min.js"></script>
      <script src="scripts/jqx-all.js"></script>

      <script>
              $(function () {
                      $("#departments").jqxExpander({ width: 200, height: 200});
              });
      </script>
</head>

<body>
      <div id='departments'>
              <!-- Header -->
              <div>Departments</div>

              <!-- Content -->
              <div style="padding:10px">
                      Finance<br>
                      Marketing<br>
                      Sales<br>
                      Support<br>
                      Technology
              </div>
      </div><br>

      <div id="msg" style="color:green"></div>
</body>
</html>
```

How It Works

In Listing 12-6, the expander is created by using the following HTML code:

```html
<div id='departments'>
        <div>Header</div>
      <div>Content ...</div>
</div>
```

JavaScript code:

```
$("#departments").jqxExpander({ width: 200, height: 200});
```

- `width` specifies the width of the widget.
- `height` specifies the height of the widget.

Figure 12-19 displays the department names in the expander widget.

Figure 12-19. *Department names are listed in the expander widget*

Figure 12-20 displays the collapsed expander widget when the up arrow icon is clicked. It can be expanded by clicking the down arrow icon.

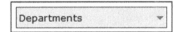

Figure 12-20. *Collapsed expander widget*

12-6. Displaying a Collection of Nested Lists Using the Listmenu Widget
Problem

You want to display nested lists using the listmenu widget.

Solution

The following jQuery syntax is used to create the listmenu widget:

```
$("#widgetId").jqxListMenu(options);
```

where options is the map object with jqxListMenu-specific parameterName and parameterValue pairs.

Listing 12-7 demonstrates an example to display the nested list using the listmenu widget.

Listing 12-7. Display nested lists

```
<!DOCTYPE html>
<html lang="en">
<head>
      <meta charset="utf-8">
      <meta name="viewport" content="width=device-width, initial-scale=1">
      <title>jqWidget - ListMenu</title>

      <link rel="stylesheet" href="styles/jqx.base.css"/>
      <script src="scripts/jquery-2.1.0.min.js"></script>
      <script src="scripts/jqx-all.js"></script>

      <style>
            label {float:left; display:block; width: 100px; font-weight: bold; }
      </style>

      <script>
            $(function () {
                  $('#list').jqxListMenu({ width: 300, enableScrolling: false, showHeader: true,
                                    showBackButton: true });
            });
      </script>
</head>

<body>
<ul id="list" data-role="listmenu">
    <li>Technology
        <ul data-role="listmenu">
            <li>John Smith
                <ul data-role="listmenu" style="width: 225px">
                    <li style="background-color: white;">
                            <div style="text-align:center"><img src="images/man.jpg"
                             width="50%"><br><br><br></div>
                            <label>Name:</label> John Smith<br>
                            <label>Hire Date:</label> June 12th, 2003<br>
                            <label>Salary:</label>$90,000
                    </li>
                </ul>
            </li>
            <li>Michael Jefferson
                <ul data-role="listmenu"   style="width: 225px">
                    <li style="background-color: white;">
                            <div style="text-align:center"><img src="images/man.jpg"
                             width="50%"><br><br><br></div>
                            <label>Name:</label> Michael Jefferson</br>
                            <label>Hire Date:</label> August 20th, 2008</br>
                            <label>Salary:</label>$85,000
                    </li>
                </ul>
            </li>
        </ul>
    </li>
```

```
            <li>Finance
                <ul data-role="listmenu">
                    <li>Mark Johnson
                        <ul data-role="listmenu" style="width: 225px">
                            <li style="background-color: white;">
                                <div style="text-align:center">
                                <img src="images/man.jpg" width="50%"><br><br><br></div>
                                <label>Name:</label> Mark Johnson<br>
                                <label>Hire Date:</label> October 14th, 1999<br>
                                <label>Salary:</label> $285,000
                            </li>
                        </ul>
                    </li>
                </ul>
            </li>
        </ul>
    </body>
</html>
```

How It Works

In Listing 12-7, a listmenu is created by using the following HTML code:

```
<ul id="list" data-role="listmenu">
                    <li>Item 1
                        <ul data-role="listmenu">
                            <li>SubItem 1
                                <ul data-role="listmenu">
                                    <li>SubItem 1 Details</li>
                                </ul>
                            </li>
...
                        </ul>
                    </li>
...
</ul>
```

JavaScript code:

```
$('#list').jqxListMenu({ width: 300, enableScrolling: false, showHeader: true,
                    showBackButton: true });
```

- width specifies the width of the widget.
- enableScrolling specifies if scrolling is allowed or not.
- showHeader specifies if the header is displayed or not.
- showBackButton specifies if the back button is displayed on the header or not.

Figure 12-21 displays the first list. When a department name is clicked, all the employees in the selected departments are displayed. When an employee name is clicked, employee details are displayed.

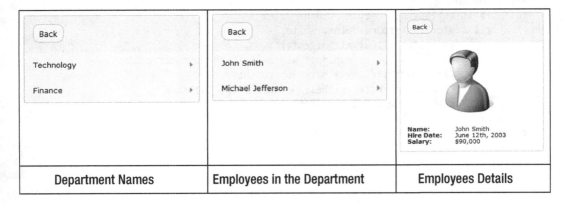

| Department Names | Employees in the Department | Employees Details |

Figure 12-21. *Displays the department names and selected employee's details*

12-7. Displaying Content Using the Panel Widget

Problem

You want to create panels to display other widgets or HTML elements.

Solution

The following jQuery syntax is used to create the panel widget:

```
$("#widgetId").jqxPanel(options);
```

where options is the map object with jqxPanel-specific parameterName and parameterValue pairs.

Listing 12-8 demonstrates an example to display content within the panel widget.

Listing 12-8. Displaying content in a panel

```
<!DOCTYPE html>
<html lang="en">
<head>
    <meta charset="utf-8">
    <meta name="viewport" content="width=device-width, initial-scale=1">
    <title>jqWidget - Panel</title>

    <link rel="stylesheet" href="styles/jqx.base.css"/>
    <script src="scripts/jquery-2.1.0.min.js"></script>
    <script src="scripts/jqx-all.js"></script>

    <script>
        $(function () {
            $("#departments").jqxPanel({ width: 250, height: 250});
        });
    </script>
</head>
```

```
<body>
    <div id='departments' style="font-size: 13px; font-family: Verdana; float: left;">
        <div style='margin: 10px;'>
            <h3>Departments</h3></div>
        <!--Content-->
        <div style='white-space: nowrap;'>
            <ul>
                <li>Finance<ol><li>Mark Johnson</li></ol></li><br>
                <li>Marketing<ol><li>Jane Smith</li></ol></li><br>
                <li>Sales<ol><li>Brian Adam</li></ol></li><br>
                <li>Support<ol><li>Mary Jones</li></ol></li><br>
                <li>Technology<ol><li>John Smith</li><li>Michael Jefferson</li></ol></li>
            </ul>
        </div>
    </div>
</body>
</html>
```

How It Works

In Listing 12-8, a panel is created by using the following HTML code:

```
<div id='departments'>
        <h3>Departments</h3></div>
        <divContent... </div>
</div>
```

JavaScript code:

```
$("#departments").jqxPanel({ width: 250, height: 250});
```

- width specifies the width of the widget.
- height specifies the height of the widget.

Figure 12-22 displays department names and employees within the department by using the panel widget.

Figure 12-22. *Panel widget*

12-8. Displaying Content Using the Tabs Widget

Problem

You want to create tabs to display content in different sections.

Solution

The following jQuery syntax is used to create the tabs widget:

```
$("#widgetId").jqxTabs(options);
```

where options is the map object with jqxTabs-specific parameterName and parameterValue pairs.

Listing 12-9 creates tabs to display content in multiple sections.

Listing 12-9. Displaying employee details in the tabs

```
<!DOCTYPE html>
<html lang="en">
<head>
    <meta charset="utf-8">
    <meta name="viewport" content="width=device-width, initial-scale=1">
    <title>jqWidget - Tabs</title>

    <link rel="stylesheet" href="styles/jqx.base.css"/>
    <script src="scripts/jquery-2.1.0.min.js"></script>
    <script src="scripts/jqx-all.js"></script>

    <script>
                var employeeData = {
        "employees":
          [
            {"employeeId": 1, "managerId": 0, "name": "Mark Johnson", "department": "Finance",
            "salary": "$285,000"},
            {"employeeId": 2, "managerId": 1, "name": "Jane Smith", "department": "Marketing",
            "salary": "$95,000"},
            {"employeeId": 3, "managerId": 1, "name": "John Smith", "department": "Technology",
            "salary": "$90,000"},
            {"employeeId": 4, "managerId": 1, "name": "Brian Adam", "department": "Sales",
            "salary": "$72,000"},
            {"employeeId": 5, "managerId": 1, "name": "Mary Jones", "department": "Support",
            "salary": "$60,000"},
            {"employeeId": 6, "managerId": 3, "name": "Michael Jefferson", "department":
            "Technology", "salary":"$85,000"}
          ]
        }
```

```
                function getData() {
                        var items = [];

                        items.push( "<tr><th>Employee Name</th><th>Department</th><th>Salary
                        </th></tr>" );

                        $.each(employeeData.employees, function( i, item ) {
                        items.push( "<tr><td>" + item.name + "</td><td>" + item.department + "</
                        td><td>" + item.salary + "</td></tr>" );
                        });

                        $("#allEmployees").empty();
                        $("#allEmployees").append("<table border='0' width='50%''>" +
                        items.join("") + "</table>");
                }

                $(function () {
                    $('#departmentEmployees').jqxTabs({ width: 750, height: 250 });

                    $('#departmentEmployees').on('selected', function (event) {
                            var item = event.args.item;
                            var selectedHeader = $('#departmentEmployees').jqxTabs('getTitleAt', item);
                            $("#msg").html("Seleted tab: " + selectedHeader);

                            if (selectedHeader == "All Employees") {
                                getData();
                            }
                    });

                    $("#msg").html("Seleted tab: " + $("li:first-child").text());
                });
        </script>
</head>

<body>
    <div id='departmentEmployees'>
        <ul style='margin-left: 20px;'>
            <li>Finance</li>
            <li>Marketing</li>
            <li>Sales</li>
            <li>Support</li>
            <li>Technology</li>
            <li>All Employees</li>
        </ul>

        <!-- Content for 1st Tab -->
        <!-- Content can have any valid html structure / element -->
        <div>Mark Johnson</div>
```

507

```
        <!-- Content for 2nd Tab -->
        <div>Jane Smith</div>

        <!-- Content for 3rd Tab -->
        <div>Brian Adam</div>

        <!-- Content for 4th Tab -->
        <div>Mary Jones</div>

        <!-- Content for 5th Tab -->
        <div>
            John Smith<br>
            Michael Jefferson
        </div>

        <!-- Content for 6th Tab -->
        <div id="allEmployees"></div>
    </div><br>

    <div id="msg"></div>
</body>
</html>
```

How It Works

In Listing 12-9, tabs are created by using the following HTML code:

```
<div id='departmentEmployees'>
        <ul>
                <li>Tab 1</li>
                <li>Tab 2</li>
                ...
        </ul>

        <div>Tab 1 Content ...</div>
        <div>Tab 2 Content ...</div>
          ...
</div>
```

JavaScript code:

```
$('#departmentEmployees').jqxTabs({ width: 750, height: 250 });
```

- width specifies the width of the widget.
- height specifies the height of the widget.

When the All Employees tab is clicked, the following code is executed to retrieve the data from the server and to build the HTML string:

```
$.getJSON(url, function (data) {

        var items = [];

        items.push( "<tr><th>Employee Name</th><th>Department</th><th>Salary</th></tr>" );

        $.each( data.employees, function( i, item ) {
              items.push( "<tr><td>" + item.name + "</td><td>" + item.department + "</td><td>" +
              item.salary + "</td></tr>" );
        });

        $("#allEmployees").empty();
        $("#allEmployees").append("<table border='0' width='50%''>" + items.join("") + "</table>");
});
```

Figure 12-23 displays the employees list when a department name tab is selected.

Figure 12-23. *Employees list in department tabs*

Figure 12-24 displays all the employees' details when the All Employees tab is selected.

Finance	Marketing	Sales	Support	Technology	All Employees

Employee Name	Department	Salary
Mark Johnson	Finance	$285,000
Jane Smith	Marketing	$95,000
John Smith	Technology	$90,000
Brian Adam	Sales	$72,000
Mary Jones	Support	$60,000
Michael Jefferson	Technology	$85,000

Seleted tab: All Employees

Figure 12-24. *Displaying the employees details*

12-9. Displaying Hierarchical Content Using the Tree Widget
Problem
You want to create the tree structure to display hierarchical content.

Solution
The following jQuery syntax is used to create the tree widget:

```
$("#widgetId").jqxTree(options);
```

where `options` is the map object with `jqxTree`-specific `parameterName` and `parameterValue` pairs.

Listing 12-10 displays hierarchical content in the tree structure.

Listing 12-10. Display employees within a department using the tree widget

```
<!DOCTYPE html>
<html lang="en">
<head>
    <meta charset="utf-8">
    <meta name="viewport" content="width=device-width, initial-scale=1">
    <title>jqWidget - Tree</title>

    <link rel="stylesheet" href="styles/jqx.base.css"/>
    <script src="scripts/jquery-2.1.0.min.js"></script>
    <script src="scripts/jqx-all.js"></script>
```

```
<script>
        $(function () {
                $('#departments').jqxTree({ height: '300px', width: '300px' });
        });
</script>
</head>

<body>
    <div id='departments'>
        <ul>
            <li item-expanded='true'>Departments
              <ul>
                  <li>Finance<ul><li>Mark Johnson</li></ul></li>
                  <li>Technology<ul><li>John Smith</li><li>Michael Jefferson</li></ul></li>
                  <li>Sales<ul><li>Brian Adam</li></ul></li>
                  <li>Support<ul><li>Mary Jones</li></ul></li>
                  <li>Marketing<ul><li>Jane Smith</li></ul></li>
              </ul>
            </li>
        </ul>
    </div>
</body>
</html>
```

How It Works

In Listing 12-10, the tree widget is created by using the following HTML code:

```
<div id='departments'>
        <ul>
                <li item-expanded='true'>Root Node
                        <ul>
                                <li>Child Node 1
                                    <ul><li>Content</li>...</ul>
                                 </li>
                                 ...
                        </ul>
                </li>
        </ul>
</div>
```

JavaScript code:

$('#departments').jqxTree({ height: '300px', width: '300px' });

- width specifies the width of the widget.
- height specifies the height of the widget.

Figure 12-25 displays Departments as the root node and the department names as the child nodes.

Figure 12-25. *Department names are displayed as tree nodes*

Figure 12-26 displays the list of employees when a department name is expanded.

Figure 12-26. *Employees list in the department nodes*

12-10. Displaying Tabular Data Using the Grid Widget
Problem

You want to create a grid to display tabular data.

Solution

The following jQuery syntax is used to create the grid widget:

```
$("#widgetId").jqxGrid(options);
```

where options is the map object with jqxGrid-specific parameterName and parameterValue pairs.

Listing 12-11 demonstrates an example to display tabular data using the grid widget.

Listing 12-11. Display employees records using the grid widget

```
<!DOCTYPE html>
<html lang="en">
<head>
        <meta charset="utf-8">
        <meta name="viewport" content="width=device-width, initial-scale=1">
        <title>jqWidget - Grid</title>

        <link rel="stylesheet" href="styles/jqx.base.css"/>
        <script src="scripts/jquery-2.1.0.min.js"></script>
        <script src="scripts/jqx-all.js"></script>

        <script>
            var employeeData = {
             "employees":
              [
               {"employeeId": 1, "managerId": 0, "name": "Mark Johnson", "department": "Finance",
                "salary": "$285,000"},
               {"employeeId": 2, "managerId": 1, "name": "Jane Smith", "department": "Marketing",
                "salary": "$95,000"},
               {"employeeId": 3, "managerId": 1, "name": "John Smith", "department": "Technology",
                "salary": "$90,000"},
               {"employeeId": 4, "managerId": 1, "name": "Brian Adam", "department": "Sales",
                "salary": "$72,000"},
               {"employeeId": 5, "managerId": 1, "name": "Mary Jones", "department": "Support",
                "salary": "$60,000"},
               {"employeeId": 6, "managerId": 3, "name": "Michael Jefferson", "department":
                "Technology", "salary":"$85,000"}
              ]
            }

                $(function () {
                    var source =
                            {
                                datatype: "json",
                                datafields: [
                                        { name: 'name', type: 'string' },
                                        { name: 'department', type: 'string' },
                                        { name: 'salary', type: 'string' }
                                ],
                                id: 'employeeId',
                                localdata: employeeData
                            };

                    var dataAdapter = new $.jqx.dataAdapter(
                                                    source,
                                                      {
                                                            loadError: function(jqXHR, status,
```

```
                                                    errorMsg) {
                                                        alert(status + ": " + errorMsg);
                                                    },

                                                    loadComplete: function() {
                                                        // tasks to be performed on
                                                                successful data retrieval
                                                    }
                                    });

            $("#employeeGrid").jqxGrid(
                    {
                            width: 375,
                            source: dataAdapter,
                            columnsresize: true,
                            columns: [
                                    { text: 'Name', datafield: 'name', width: 150 },
                                    { text: 'Department', datafield: 'department', width: 125 },
                                    { text: 'Salary', datafield: 'salary', width: 100,
                                      align: 'right', cellsalign: 'right' }
                            ]
                    });
            });
        </script>
</head>

<body>
        <div id='jqxWidget'>
                <div id="employeeGrid"></div>
        </div>
</body>
</html>
```

How It Works

In Listing 12-11, a grid widget is created by using the following HTML code:

```
<div id="employeeGrid"></div>
```

JavaScript code:

```
$("#employeeGrid").jqxGrid(
        {
                width: 375,
                source: dataAdapter,
                columnsresize: true,
                columns: [
                        { text: 'Name', datafield: 'name', width: 150 },
                        { text: 'Department', datafield: 'department', width: 125 },
                        { text: 'Salary', datafield: 'salary', width: 100, align: 'right',
                          cellsalign: 'right' }
                ]
});
```

- `width` specifies the width of the widget.

- `source` specifies the data source. In this case it is a `dataAdapter`, which is populated with the data from `employeeData`.

- `columnsresize` specifies if the user is allowed to resize the columns or not.

- `columns` is the collection of column objects. Each object contains:

  - `text` specifies the column heading.

  - `datafield` is the name of the field in the `dataAdapter`.

  - `width` specifies the column width.

  - `align` specifies the alignment of the columns' heading.

  - `cellsalign` specifies the alignment of the data.

Figure 12-27 displays employees' details in the grid widget.

Name	Department	Salary
Mark Johnson	Finance	$285,000
Jane Smith	Marketing	$95,000
John Smith	Technology	$90,000
Brian Adam	Sales	$72,000
Mary Jones	Support	$60,000
Michael Jefferson	Technology	$85,000

Figure 12-27. *Employees' details in the grid widget*

Using AJAX Calls

If you want to make an AJAX call to get the data instead of using local data, you can set the source as follows:

```
var source =
    {
        datatype: "json",
        datafields: [
                { name: 'name', type: 'string' },
                { name: 'department', type: 'string' },
                { name: 'salary', type: 'string' }
        ],
        id: 'employeeId',
        url: "employees.json"
    };
```

Listing 12-2 contains content of the `employees.json` file.

12-11. Displaying Tabular Data Using the Data Table Widget

Problem

You want to create a data table to display tabular data.

Solution

The following jQuery syntax is used to create the data table widget:

```
$("#widgetId").jqxDataTable(options);
```

where options is the map object with jqxDataTable-specific parameterName and parameterValue pairs.

Listing 12-12 demonstrates an example to display tabular data using the data table widget.

Listing 12-12. Display employees records using the data table widget

```html
<!DOCTYPE html>
<html lang="en">
<head>
    <meta charset="utf-8">
    <meta name="viewport" content="width=device-width, initial-scale=1">
    <title>jqWidget - DataTable</title>

    <link rel="stylesheet" href="styles/jqx.base.css"/>
    <script src="scripts/jquery-2.1.0.min.js"></script>
    <script src="scripts/jqx-all.js"></script>

    <script>
        var employeeData = {
        "employees":
         [
          {"employeeId": 1, "managerId": 0, "name": "Mark Johnson", "department": "Finance",
           "salary": "$285,000"},
          {"employeeId": 2, "managerId": 1, "name": "Jane Smith", "department": "Marketing",
           "salary": "$95,000"},
          {"employeeId": 3, "managerId": 1, "name": "John Smith", "department": "Technology",
           "salary": "$90,000"},
          {"employeeId": 4, "managerId": 1, "name": "Brian Adam", "department": "Sales",
           "salary": "$72,000"},
          {"employeeId": 5, "managerId": 1, "name": "Mary Jones", "department": "Support",
           "salary": "$60,000"},
          {"employeeId": 6, "managerId": 3, "name": "Michael Jefferson", "department":
           "Technology", "salary": "$85,000"}
         ]
        }

        $(function () {
            // Set Data Source
            var source = {
                datatype: "json",
```

```
                datafields: [
                        { name: 'name', type: 'string' },
                        { name: 'department', type: 'string' },
                        { name: 'salary', type: 'string' }
                ],
                id: 'employeeId',
                localdata: employeeData
        };

        var dataAdapter = new $.jqx.dataAdapter(source);

        // Static data can also be used in place of getting data at the runtime
        $("#employeeTable").jqxDataTable({
                source: dataAdapter,
                sortable: true,
                columns: [
                        { text: 'Name', datafield: 'name', width: 150 },
                        { text: 'Department', datafield: 'department', width: 125 },
                        { text: 'Salary', datafield: 'salary', width: 100, align: 'right',
                          cellsalign: 'right' }
                ]
        });
    });
    </script>
</head>

<body>
    <div id='jqxWidget'>
            <div id="employeeTable"></div>
    </div>
</body>

</html>
```

How It Works

In Listing 12-12, a data table widget is created by using the following HTML code:

```
<div id="employeeTable"></div>
```

JavaScript code:

```
$("#employeeTable").jqxDataTable({
        source: dataAdapter,
        sortable: true,
        columns: [
                { text: 'Name', datafield: 'name', width: 150 },
                { text: 'Department', datafield: 'department', width: 125 },
                { text: 'Salary', datafield: 'salary', width: 100, align: 'right', cellsalign: 'right' }
        ]
});
```

- source specifies the data source. In this case it is a dataAdapter, which is populated with the data from employeeData.

- sortable specifies if the user is allowed to sort the data by clicking at the column header or not.

- columns is the collection of column objects. Each object contains the following:

  - text specifies the column heading.

  - datafield is the name of the field in the dataAdapter.

  - width specifies the column width.

  - align specifies the alignment of the columns' heading.

  - cellsalign specifies the alignment of the data.

Figure 12-28 displays employees' details in the data table widget.

Name	Department	Salary	Name	Department	Salary
Mark Johnson	Finance	$285,000	Brian Adam	Sales	$72,000
Jane Smith	Marketing	$95,000	Jane Smith	Marketing	$95,000
John Smith	Technology	$90,000	John Smith	Technology	$90,000
Brian Adam	Sales	$72,000	Mark Johnson	Finance	$285,000
Mary Jones	Support	$60,000	Mary Jones	Support	$60,000
Michael Jefferson	Technology	$85,000	Michael Jefferson	Technology	$85,000
Unsorted display			**Sorted by name**		

Figure 12-28. *Employees' details in the data table widget*

12-12. Displaying Hierarchical Data Using the Tree Grid Widget
Problem

You want to create a tree grid to display hierarchical data.

Solution

The following jQuery syntax is used to create the tree grid widget:

```
$("#widgetId").jqxTreeGrid(options);
```

where options is the map object with jqxTreeGrid-specific parameterName and parameterValue pairs.

Listing 12-13 displays hierarchical data using the tree grid widget.

Listing 12-13. Display employees records using the tree grid widget

```
<!DOCTYPE html>
<html lang="en">
<head>
    <meta charset="utf-8">
    <meta name="viewport" content="width=device-width, initial-scale=1">
    <title>jqWidgets - TreeGrid</title>

    <link rel="stylesheet" href="styles/jqx.base.css"/>
    <script src="scripts/jquery-2.1.0.min.js"></script>
    <script src="scripts/jqx-all.js"></script>

    <script>
        var employeeData = {
        "employees":
         [
          {"employeeId": 1, "managerId": 0, "name": "Mark Johnson", "department": "Finance",
           "salary": "$285,000"},
          {"employeeId": 2, "managerId": 1, "name": "Jane Smith", "department": "Marketing",
           "salary": "$95,000"},
          {"employeeId": 3, "managerId": 1, "name": "John Smith", "department": "Technology",
           "salary": "$90,000"},
          {"employeeId": 4, "managerId": 1, "name": "Brian Adam", "department": "Sales",
           "salary": "$72,000"},
          {"employeeId": 5, "managerId": 1, "name": "Mary Jones", "department": "Support",
           "salary": "$60,000"},
          {"employeeId": 6, "managerId": 3, "name": "Michael Jefferson", "department":
           "Technology", "salary": "$85,000"}
         ]
        }

            $(function () {
                // Set the data source
                var source = {
                        datatype: "json",
                        datafields: [
                                { name: 'employeeId', type: 'int' },
                                { name: 'managerId', type: 'int' },
                                { name: 'name', type: 'string' },
                                { name: 'department', type: 'string' },
                                { name: 'salary', type: 'string' }
                            ],
                hierarchy:
                {
                    keyDataField: { name: 'employeeId' },
                    parentDataField: { name: 'managerId' }
                },
                id: 'employeeId',
                localdata: employeeData
            };
```

```
            // Get the data
            var dataAdapter = new $.jqx.dataAdapter(source);

            // Create Tree Grid with the data
            $("#employeesTreeGrid").jqxTreeGrid({
                width: 355,
                source: dataAdapter,
                columns: [
                  { text: 'Employee Name', dataField: 'name', width: 175 },
                  { text: 'Department', dataField: 'department', width: 100 },
                  { text: 'Salary', dataField: 'salary', width: 80, align: 'right', cellsalign: 'right'}
                ]
            });
        });
    </script>
</head>
<body>
    <div id="employeesTreeGrid"></div>
</body>
</html>
```

How It Works

In Listing 12-13, a tree grid widget is created by using the following HTML code:

```
<div id="employeesTreeGrid"></div>
```

JavaScript code:

```
$("#employeesTreeGrid").jqxTreeGrid( {
        width: 355,
        source: dataAdapter,
        columns: [
            { text: 'Employee Name', dataField: 'name', width: 175 },
            { text: 'Department', dataField: 'department', width: 100 },
            { text: 'Salary', dataField: 'salary', width: 80, align: 'right', cellsalign: 'right'}
        ]
});
```

- width specifies the width of the widget.

- source specifies the data source. In this case it is a dataAdapter, which is populated with the data from employeeData.

- columns is the collection of column objects. Each object contains the following:

  - text specifies the column heading.

  - datafield is the name of the field in the dataAdapter.

  - width specifies the column width.

  - align specifies the alignment of the columns' heading.

  - cellsalign specifies the alignment of the data.

Figure 12-29 displays employees' details in the tree grid widget.

Employee Name	Department	Salary		Employee Name	Department	Salary		Employee Name	Department	Salary
▸ Mark Johnson	Finance	$285,000		▾ Mark Johnson	Finance	$285,000		▾ Mark Johnson	Finance	$285,000
				Jane Smith	Marketing	$95,000		Jane Smith	Marketing	$95,000
				▸ John Smith	Technology	$90,000		▾ John Smith	Technology	$90,000
				Brian Adam	Sales	$72,000		Michael Jefferson	Technology	$85,000
				Mary Jones	Support	$60,000		Brian Adam	Sales	$72,000
								Mary Jones	Support	$60,000
Root Node				**Expanded Root Node**				**Expanded Child Node**		

Figure 12-29. *Employees' details in the tree grid widget*

12-13. Displaying HTML Elements Within a Window
Problem
You want to create a window on the web page to display a group of related HTML elements or another web page.

Solution
The following jQuery syntax is used to create the window widget:

```
$("#widgetId").jqxWindow(options);
```

where options is the map object with jqxWindow-specific parameterName and parameterValue pairs.

Window can be created as a model window to block users from interacting with the underlying interface. It is draggable and resizable.

Listing 12-14 displays HTML contents within the window widget.

Listing 12-14. Display images in the window widget

```
<!DOCTYPE html>
<html lang="en">
<head>
      <meta charset="utf-8">
      <meta name="viewport" content="width=device-width, initial-scale=1">
      <title>jqWidget - Window</title>

      <link rel="stylesheet" href="styles/jqx.base.css"/>
      <script src="scripts/jquery-2.1.0.min.js"></script>
      <script src="scripts/jqx-all.js"></script>

      <script>
            $(function () {
                  $("#jqxwindow ").jqxWindow({ height:150, width: 750});
            });
      </script>
</head>
```

521

```
<body>
    <div id='jqxWidget'>
            <div id='jqxwindow'>
                    <div>Flowers</div>
                    <div>
                            <img src="images/Flower_1.jpg" height="80%">
                            <img src="images/Flower_2.jpg" height="80%">
                            <img src="images/Flower_3.jpg" height="80%">
                            <img src="images/Flower_4.jpg" height="80%">
                            <img src="images/Flower_5.jpg" height="80%">
                    </div>
            </div>
        </div>
</body>
</html>
```

How It Works

In Listing 12-14, the window widget is created by using the following HTML code:

```
<div id='jqxwindow'>
        <div>Header</div>
        <div>HTML Elements as the content</div>
</div>
```

JavaScript code:

```
$("#jqxwindow ").jqxWindow({ height:150, width: 750});
```

- width specifies the width of the widget.
- height specifies the height of the widget.

Figure 12-30 displays images in a window widget.

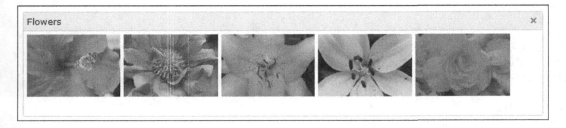

Figure 12-30. *Images in a window widget*

To display another web page within the window widget, you can use the `<iframe>` HTML element.

12-14. Viewing Contents in Multiple Dockable Windows
Problem

You want to create multiple windows on a web page that can be dragged, docked, and closed.

Solution

The following jQuery syntax is used to create the docking widget:

```
$("#widgetId").jqxDocking(options);
```

where options is the map object with jqxDocking-specific parameterName and parameterValue pairs.

Windows are draggable and resizable.

Listing 12-15 displays HTML contents in the docking widget.

Listing 12-15. Display departments' and employees' in the docakable windows

```
<!DOCTYPE html>
<html lang="en">
<head>
    <meta charset="utf-8">
    <meta name="viewport" content="width=device-width, initial-scale=1">
    <title>jqWidget - Docking</title>

    <link rel="stylesheet" href="styles/jqx.base.css"/>
    <script src="scripts/jquery-2.1.0.min.js"></script>
    <script src="scripts/jqx-all.js"></script>

    <script>
        $(function () {
            $("#docking").jqxDocking({ width: 250});
        });
    </script>
</head>

<body>
    <div id="docking">
        <div>
            <div id="technology">
                <div>Technology</div><div>John Smith<br>Michael Jefferson</div>
            </div>

            <div id="finance">
                <div>Finance</div><div>Mark Johnson</div>
            </div>

            <div id="marketing">
                <div>Marketing</div><div>Jane Smith</div>
            </div>
```

```
        <div id="sales">
            <div>Sales</div><div>Brian Adam</div>
        </div>

        <div id="support">
            <div>Support</div><div>Mary Jones</div>
        </div>
    </div>
  </div>
</body>
</html>
```

How It Works

In Listing 12-15, a docking widget is created by using the following HTML code:

```
<div id="docking">
    <div>
        <div id="dockingId1">
            <div>Header 1</div><div>Content 1</div>
        </div>

        <div id="dockingId2">
            <div>Header 2</div><div>Content 2</div>
        </div>
        ...
    </div>
</div>
```

JavaScript code:

```
$("#docking").jqxDocking({ width: 250});
```

- width specifies the width of the widget.

Figure 12-31 displays the department name and the employees' names in the department in the docking widget. Each department can be dragged to a different position or closed.

Figure 12-31. Departments' and employees' names listed in the dockable windows widget

12-15. Creating Charts
Problem

You want to create charts by using chart widget.

Solution

The following jQuery syntax is used to create the tree grid widget:

```
$("#widgetId").jqxChart(options);
```

where options is the map object with jqxChart-specific parameterName and parameterValue pairs.
Listing 12-16 demonstrates an example to display HTML contents in the window widget.

Listing 12-16. Display departments and employees in docakable windows

```
<!DOCTYPE html>
<html lang="en">
<head>
      <meta charset="utf-8">
      <meta name="viewport" content="width=device-width, initial-scale=1">
      <title>jqWidget - Chart</title>

      <link rel="stylesheet" href="styles/jqx.base.css"/>
      <script src="scripts/jquery-2.1.0.min.js"></script>
      <script src="scripts/jqx-all.js"></script>
```

```
<script>
      var dataAdapter;

      var precipitationData = {
            "precipitation":
                  [
                        { "Month": "January", "Chicago": 3, "Los Angeles": 5, "New York": 5},
                        { "Month": "February", "Chicago": 3, "Los Angeles": 6, "New York": 4},
                        { "Month": "March", "Chicago": 4, "Los Angeles": 4, "New York": 5},
                        { "Month": "April", "Chicago": 4, "Los Angeles": 2, "New York": 5},
                        { "Month": "May", "Chicago": 6, "Los Angeles": 1, "New York": 5},
                        { "Month": "June", "Chicago": 6, "Los Angeles": 1, "New York": 5},
                        { "Month": "July", "Chicago": 4, "Los Angeles": 1, "New York": 6},
                        { "Month": "August", "Chicago": 4, "Los Angeles": 1, "New York": 5},
                        { "Month": "September", "Chicago": 4, "Los Angeles": 1, "New York": 5},
                        { "Month": "October", "Chicago": 4, "Los Angeles": 2, "New York": 4},
                        { "Month": "November", "Chicago": 4, "Los Angeles": 2, "New York": 5},
                        { "Month": "December", "Chicago": 3, "Los Angeles": 4, "New York": 5}
                  ]
      }

      function getOptions(chartType) {
            // Set Chart Settings
            var options = {
                  title: "Precipitation Monthly Graph",
                  description: "[ Year 2013 ]",
                  padding: { left: 5, top: 5, right: 5, bottom: 5 },
                  titlePadding: { left: 90, top: 0, right: 0, bottom: 10 },
                  source: dataAdapter,
                  categoryAxis: {
                  dataField: 'Month',
                  showGridLines: false
            },
            colorScheme: 'scheme01',
            seriesGroups:
            [
                  {
                        type: chartType,
                        columnsGapPercent: 30,
                        seriesGapPercent: 0,
                        valueAxis:
                        {
                              minValue: 0,
                              maxValue: 15,
                              unitInterval: 1,
                              description: '(in inches)'
                        },
```

```
                                series: [
                                        { dataField: 'Chicago', displayText: 'Chicago, IL'},
                                        { dataField: 'Los Angeles', displayText: 'Los Angeles, CA'},
                                        { dataField: 'New York', displayText: 'New York, NY'}
                                ]
                        }
                  ]
              };

              return(options);
          }

            $(function () {
            // Set Data Source
            var source =
            {
                datatype: "json",
                datafields: [
                    { name: 'Month', type: 'string' },
                    { name: 'Chicago', type: 'int' },
                    { name: 'Los Angeles', type: 'int' },
                    { name: 'New York', type: 'int' }
                ],
                localdata: precipitationData
            };

            dataAdapter = new $.jqx.dataAdapter(source);

            // Create Chart
            $('#chartContainer').jqxChart(getOptions($("#chartType").val()));

            $("#chartType").on("change", function() {
               $('#chartContainer').jqxChart(getOptions($("#chartType").val()));
            });
          });
      </script>
</head>

<body>
      <label>Chart Type:</label>
            <select id="chartType">
                  <option value="column" selected="selected">Column</option>
                  <option value="line">Line</option>
                  <option value="stackedcolumn">Stacked Column</option>
            </select><br><br><br>

      <div id='chartContainer' style="width:600px; height: 400px"></div>
</body>
</html>
```

How It Works

Each record in the precipitation record has the month name and precipitation level for three major cities: Chicago, Los Angeles, and New York. In Listing 12-16, the following HTML code creates the chart widget:

```
<div id='chartContainer' style="width:600px; height: 400px"></div>
```

JavaScript code:

```
$('#chartContainer').jqxChart(getOptions($("#chartType").val()));
```

- The getOptions() function returns the chart options.
- $("#chartType").val() contains the value of the chart selected by the user from the drop-down. The possible values are column, line, and stackedcolumn.

The following is the list of main options set in the function getOptions():

- title specifies the title of the chart.
- description specifies the second line of the chart header after the title.
- source specifies the data source. In this example, data source is dataAdapter, which contains the data from precipitationData.
- categoryAxis's dataField specifies which data field from the dataAdapter is used for X axis.
- type specifies type of the chart. Some of the chart types include column, line, stackedcolumn, and pie.
- valueAxis specifies the properties for the Y axis.
- series specifies the data to be displayed on the Y axis, the mapping of data fields in dataAdapter, and the text to be displayed on the chart.

Figure 12-32 displays a column chart showing the monthly level of precipitation for the three cities in 2013.

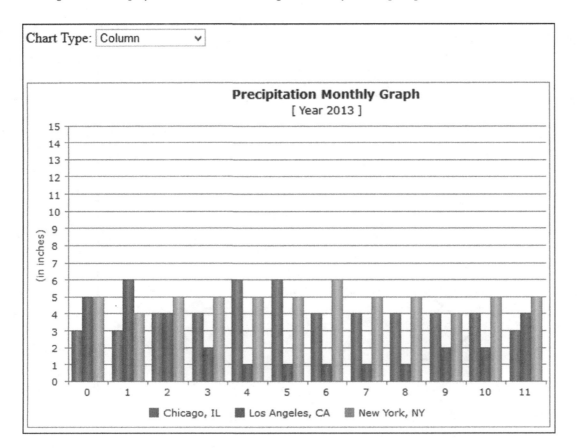

Figure 12-32. *Column chart*

Figure 12-33 displays a line chart of precipitation levels for the three cities in 2013.

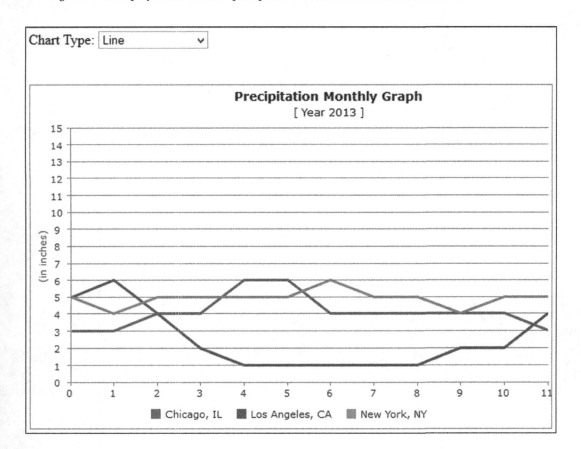

Figure 12-33. *Line chart*

Figure 12-34 displays a stacked column chart of monthly precipitation levels for the three cities in 2013.

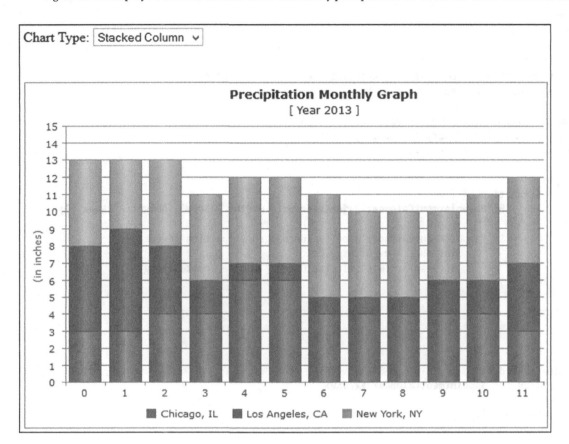

Figure 12-34. *Stacked column chart*

12-16. Creating a Calendar
Problem

You want to create a calendar that can be used in applications like appointment schedulers.

Solution

The following jQuery syntax is used to create the calendar widget:

```
$("#widgetId").jqxCalendar(options);
```

where options is the map object with jqxCalendar-specific parameterName and parameterValue pairs.
　Listing 12-17 creates a calendar widget.

Listing 12-17. Create a calendar widget

```
<!DOCTYPE html>
<html lang="en">
<head>
    <meta charset="utf-8">
    <meta name="viewport" content="width=device-width, initial-scale=1">
    <title>jqWidget - Calendar</title>

    <link rel="stylesheet" href="styles/jqx.base.css"/>
    <script src="scripts/jquery-2.1.0.min.js"></script>
    <script src="scripts/jqx-all.js"></script>

    <script>
        $(function () {
            $("#appointmentCalendar").jqxCalendar({ width: '250px', height: '250px'});

            $('#appointmentCalendar').on('valuechanged', function (event) {
                var date = event.args.date;
                $("#msg").html("Selected Date: " + date.toDateString());
            });
        });
    </script>
</head>

<body>
    <div id='jqxWidget'>
        <div id='appointmentCalendar'></div>
    </div><br>
    <div id="msg"></div>
</body>
</html>
```

How It Works

In Listing 12-17, a calendar widget is created by using the following HTML code:

```
<div id='appointmentCalendar'></div>
```

JavaScript code:

```
$("#appointmentCalendar").jqxCalendar({ width: '250px', height: '250px'});
```

- width specifies the width of the widget.

- height specifies the height of the widget.

An event handler is registered for the calendar widget for the event valuechanged. When a date is selected from the widget, this event handler is executed and it gets the selected date using the following code:

```
var date = event.args.date;
```

To get the value as a date object, use $('#appointmentCalendar').jqxCalendar('value'). The date object can be converted to a string by using the toDateString() method.

Figure 12-35 displays the calendar widget. Users can scroll through the months and years and select a date.

Figure 12-35. *Calendar widget*

12-17. Creating a Color Picker
Problem

You want to create a color picker.

Solution

The following jQuery syntax is used to create the color picker widget:

```
$("#widgetId").jqxColorPicker(options);
```

where options is the map object with jqxColorPicker-specific parameterName and parameterValue pairs.

Listing 12-18 creates a color picker widget.

Listing 12-18. Create a color picker widget

```
<!DOCTYPE html>
<html lang="en">
<head>
    <meta charset="utf-8">
    <meta name="viewport" content="width=device-width, initial-scale=1">
    <title>jqWidget - Color</title>

    <link rel="stylesheet" href="styles/jqx.base.css"/>
    <script src="scripts/jquery-2.1.0.min.js"></script>
    <script src="scripts/jqx-all.js"></script>
```

```
<script>
        var defaultColor = "257D91";

        $(function () {
                $("#colorPicker").jqxColorPicker({ color: defaultColor, colorMode: 'hue',
                                                   width: 220, height: 220});

                $("#dropDownButton").jqxDropDownButton({ width: 150, height: 22});
                $('#dropDownButton').val("#" + defaultColor);
                $('#dropDownButton').css('background-color', "#" + defaultColor);

                $("#colorPicker").on('colorchange', function (event) {
                        $('#dropDownButton').val("#" + event.args.color.hex);
                        $('#dropDownButton').css('background-color', "#" + event.args.color.hex);
                });
        });
</script>
</head>

<body>
    <div style="margin: 3px; float: left;" id="dropDownButton">
            <div style="padding: 3px;">
                    <div id="colorPicker"></div>
            </div>
    </div>
</body>
</html>
```

How It Works

In Listing 12-18, a color picker widget is created by using the following HTML code:

```
<div id="colorPicker"></div>
```

JavaScript code:

```
var defaultColor = "257D91";
$("#colorPicker").jqxColorPicker({ color: defaultColor, colorMode: 'hue', width: 220, height: 220});
```

- color specifies the default color selected in the color picker.

- colorMode specifies the color mode of the color picker. Valid values are hue and saturation.

- width specifies the width of the widget.

- height specifies the height of the widget.

An event handler is registered for the color picker widget for the colorchange event. When a new color is selected from the widget, this event handler is executed The event handler gets the selected color and then sets the value and the background color of the drop-down widget by using the following code:

```
$('#dropDownButton').val("#" + event.args.color.hex);
     $('#dropDownButton').css('background-color', "#" + event.args.color.hex);
```

Figure 12-36 displays the color picker widget from which users choose a color.

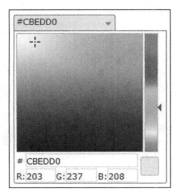

Figure 12-36. *Color picker widget*

12-18. Creating an Editor Widget
Problem

You want to create an editor widget.

Solution

The following jQuery syntax is used to create the editor widget:

```
$("#widgetId").jqxEditor(options);
```

where options is the map object with jqxEditor-specific parameterName and parameterValue pairs.

Listing 12-19 demonstrates an example to create the editor widget. In the editor widget, the user can enter text or data, format it, align it, change the font name and font size, and perform other basic functions of an editor.

Listing 12-19. Display departments and employees in docakable windows

```
<!DOCTYPE html>
<html lang="en">
<head>
      <meta charset="utf-8">
      <meta name="viewport" content="width=device-width, initial-scale=1">
      <title>jqWidget - Editor</title>

      <link rel="stylesheet" href="styles/jqx.base.css"/>
      <script src="scripts/jquery-2.1.0.min.js"></script>
      <script src="scripts/jqx-all.js"></script>
```

```
        <script>
                $(function () {
                        $('#editor').jqxEditor({height: "600px",width: "800px"});
                });
        </script>
</head>
<body>
    <textarea id="editor"></textarea>
</body>
</html>
```

How It Works

In Listing 12-19, the following HTML code creates the editor widget:

```
<textarea id="editor"></textarea>
```

JavaScript code:

```
$('#editor').jqxEditor({height: "600px",width: "800px"});
```

- width specifies the width of the widget.
- height specifies the height of the widget.

Figure 12-37 displays the editor widget. Users can use it to enter text or data and perform basic editing and formatting operations.

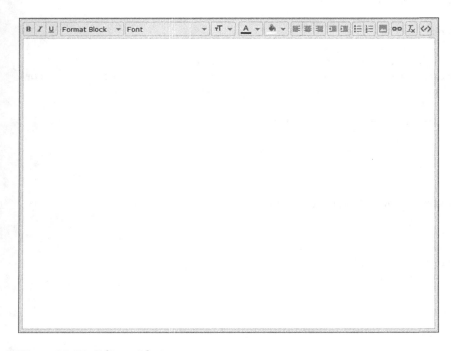

Figure 12-37. *Editor widget*

12-19. Creating a Menu

Problem

You want to create the menu widget.

Solution

The following jQuery syntax is used to create the menu widget:

```
$("#widgetId").jqxMenu(options);
```

where options is the map object with jqxMenu-specific parameterName and parameterValue pairs.

Listing 12-20 demonstrates an example to create the menu widget.

Listing 12-20. Display menu items

```
<!DOCTYPE html>
<html lang="en">
<head>
	<meta charset="utf-8">
	<meta name="viewport" content="width=device-width, initial-scale=1">
	<title>jqWidget - Menu</title>

	<link rel="stylesheet" href="styles/jqx.base.css"/>
	<script src="scripts/jquery-2.1.0.min.js"></script>
	<script src="scripts/jqx-all.js"></script>

	<script>
		$(function () {
			// Create Menu
			$("#jqxMenu").jqxMenu({ width: '150', mode: 'vertical'});
		});
	</script>
</head>

<body>
	<div id='jqxWidget'>
		<div id='jqxMenu'>
			<ul>
				<li><a href="#">Home</a></li>

				<li>Department
					<ul>
						<li><a href="#">Search Department</a></li>
						<li><a href="#">Add Department</a></li>
					</ul>
				</li>
```

```
                    <li>Employee
                        <ul>
                            <li><a href="#">Search Employee</a></li>
                            <li><a href="#">Add Employee</a></li>
                        </ul>
                    </li>

                    <li>Organization Chart</li>

                    <li><a href="#">Help</a></li>
                </ul>
            </div>
        </div>
    </body>
</html>
```

How It Works

In Listing 12-20, the following HTML code creates the menu widget:

```
<div id='jqxMenu'>
    <ul>
        <li><a href="#">Menu Item 1</a></li>

        <li>Menu Item 2
            <ul>
                <li><a href="#">Submenu Item 1</a></li>
                <li><a href="#"> Submenu Item 2</a></li>
            </ul>
        </li>
        ...
    </ul>
</div>
```

JavaScript code:

```
$("#jqxMenu").jqxMenu({ width: '150', mode: 'vertical'});
```

- width specifies the width of the widget.
- mode specifies the display mode for the menu. The valid values are horizontal, vertical, and popup.

Figure 12-38 displays the menu widget with menu items and nested submenu items.

Figure 12-38. *Menu widgets*

12-20. Creating a Navigation Bar

Problem

You want to create the navigation bar widget.

Solution

The following jQuery syntax is used to create the navigation bar widget:

```
$("#widgetId").jqxNavigationBar(options);
```

where options is the map object with jqxNavigationBar-specific parameterName and parameterValue pairs.

Listing 12-21 demonstrates an example to create a navigation bar widget.

Listing 12-21. Create a navigation bar

```
<!DOCTYPE html>
<html lang="en">
<head>
      <meta charset="utf-8">
      <meta name="viewport" content="width=device-width, initial-scale=1">
      <title>jqWidget - NavigationBar</title>

      <link rel="stylesheet" href="styles/jqx.base.css"/>
      <script src="scripts/jquery-2.1.0.min.js"></script>
      <script src="scripts/jqx-all.js"></script>

      <script>
            $(function () {
                  // Create Navigation Bar
                  $("#navigationBar").jqxNavigationBar({ width: 200, height: 200});
            });
      </script>
</head>
```

```
<body>
    <div id='navigationBar'>
        <div>Finance</div>
        <div>Mark Johnson</div>

        <div>Marketing</div>
        <div>Jane Smith</div>

        <div>Sales</div>
        <div>Brian Adam</div>

        <div>Support</div>
        <div>Mary Jones</div>

        <div>Technology</div>
        <div>
            John Smith<br>
            Michael Jefferson
        </div>
    </div>
</body>
</html>
```

How It Works

In Listing 12-21, the following HTML code creates a navigation bar widget:

```
<div id='navigationBar'>
        <div>Navigation Bar Header 1</div>
        <div>Content 1</div>

        <div>Navigation Bar Header 2</div>
        <div>Content 2</div>

        ...
</div>
```

JavaScript code:

```
$("#navigationBar").jqxNavigationBar({ width: 200, height: 200});
```

- width specifies the width of the widget.
- height specifies the height of the widget.

Figure 12-39 displays the departments' names and employees in the navigation bar widget.

Figure 12-39. *Departments and employees in the dockable windows widget*

Summary

This chapter covered recipes for creating rich user interface widgets using the jqWidgets framework. The jqWidgets library provides a range of options to fine-tune presentation and functionalities of the widgets. The `dataAdapter` object is used in some of the recipes to bind backend server data with the UI widgets. You also learned how to use themes to implement a consistent look and feel for the user interface across all the pages on the web site. A complete custom theme can be created or part of the existing theme can be updated to meet your requirements. The chapter covered the following categories of widgets:

- For data entry—Input, Switch Button, DateTime Input, Password Input, Masked Input, Button Group, Radio Button, Checkbox, Button, Validator, Combo box, Drop-Down, Listbox, Range Selector, Slider, Splitter, Tooltip, Progress Bar, and Rating.

- For content grouping—Expander, Listmenu, Panel, Tabs, and Tree.

- For tabular/hierarchical data displays—Grid, Data Table, and Tree Grid.

- For movable view areas—Window and Docking.

- For graphics—Chart.

- For containers—Calendar, Color Picker, and Editor.

- For navigation—Menu and Navigation Bar.

APPENDIX A

■ ■ ■

Basic HTML5 and CSS3

A-1. Using HTML5

In this section of the appendix, I cover the features of HTML5 that are relevant to creating data entry forms and graphics for effects and animations. These concepts are useful for enhancing the recipes in this book.

Previous versions of HTML specifications had a limited number of tags and developers had to use same the tag for various purposes. One of the examples is use of `<div>` tag for menus, navigations, sidebars, and placeholders. With HTML5 there are tags for each specific purpose. For example, there is `<footer>`, `<article>`, `<section>`, and `<nav>`. In HTML5, the name of the tag reveals its purpose.

Developers used to have to write many lines of code to achieve and repeat simple tasks. These basic tasks are now integrated into HTML5 so that, by using the proper tags and attributes, you can achieve the same effects without writing specialized code. HTML5 has rich set of graphics and multimedia tags and that makes it a perfect candidate for writing Rich Internet Applications (RIA).

HTML5 is supported to a great extent by the following widely used browsers—Chrome 34, Firefox 29, Safari 5.1 (Windows)/7.0 (MacOS), and Internet Explorer 11.

You can go to http://html5test.com/ to see the list of HTML5 features supported by your browser and to compare its HTML5 compliance rating with other browsers.

Code Structure

The following shows the basic code structure of HTML5 pages:

```
<!DOCTYPE html>
<html>
<head>
   <meta charset="UTF-8">
</head>
<body>
   Page Content...
</body>
</html>
```

Structural Elements

Table A-1 lists commonly used structural elements in HTML5.

Table A-1. *Structural Elements*

Element	Description
<header>	Contains the header for a page or a section in the page.
<nav>	Contains a list of navigation links.
<section>	Specifies a section in the page.
<article>	Specifies content in a page.
<aside>	Specifies additional information related to the content in the <article>.
<footer>	Contains the footer for a page or a section in the page.

Input Types and Attributes

Refer to Listing A-1 for an example of some of the new input types and validation features in HTML5.

Listing A-1. HTML5 code to create forms with validation and placeholders

```
<!DOCTYPE html>
<html>
<head>
    <meta charset="UTF-8">
    <title>HTML5 Form</title>
    <script src="scripts/jquery-2.1.0.min.js"></script>
    <style>
        label {
            float:left;
            display:block;
            width: 75px;
        }
    </style>

    <script>
        $(function() {
            $("#personalInfoForm").on("submit", function(eventObj) {
eventObj.preventDefault();

// Ajax call to process the form
alert("Form is being processed...");
            });
        });
    </script>
</head>
```

```
<body>
    <form id="personalInfoForm">
        <strong>Registration Form</strong><br><br>
        <label>Name:</label><input type="text" required autofocus><br>
        <label>EMail:</label>
        <input type="email" placeholder="myId@company.com"><br>
        <label>SSN:</label>
        <input type="text" pattern="\d{3}-\d{2}-\d{4}" title="999-99-9999"
               placeholder="999-99-9999" required>

        <br><br><input type="submit" value="Register">
    </form>
</body>
</html>
```

This code requires jQuery library. Make sure that the jquery-2.1.0.min.js file exists in the scripts folder.

If the Name textbox is left blank or an invalid email address is entered for the EMail textbox and the Register button is clicked, a validation error message will be displayed. As shown in the Figure A-1, a message will be displayed if the Register button is clicked and the validation rules are not satisfied.

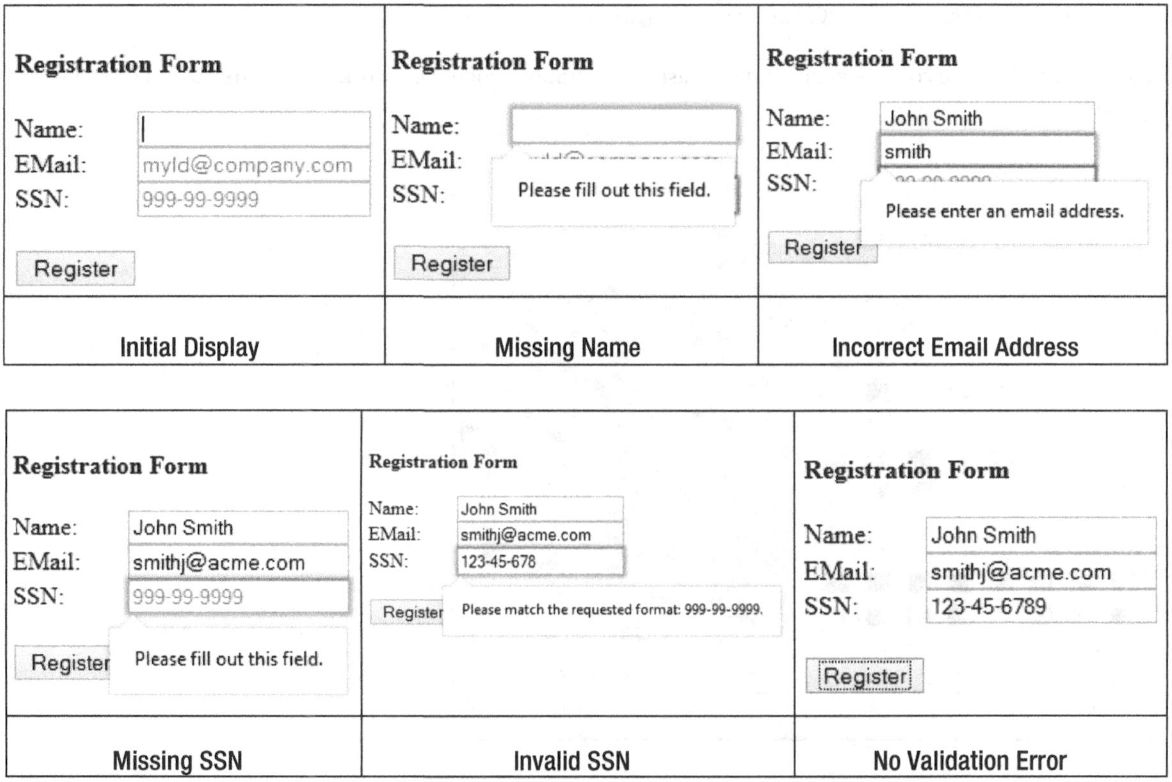

Figure A-1. *Registration page in the Firefox browser*

In the Apple Safari web browser, this code doesn't work. Validation error messages are different in different browsers. Table A-2 lists the validation error messages for this example in the Windows operating system.

Table A-2. *Validation Error Messages*

Firefox (29.0.1)	Internet Explorer (11.0.3)	Google Chrome (34.0)
Please fill out this field.	This is a required field.	Please fill out this field.
Please enter an email address.	You must enter a valid email address.	Please include an @ in the email address. smith is missing an @.
Please match the requested format: 999-99-9999.	You must use this format: 999-99-9999	Please match the requested format. 999-99-9999

In HTML5, there are many built-in validation features. In the previous specifications of HTML, the same effects were achieved either by writing validation routines or by using third-party JavaScript libraries. Some of the commonly used new input types for forms in the HTML5 are:

- **Color:**

```
Syntax: <input id="txtColor" type="color">
```

Figure A-2 displays the color selection palette based on the above code. This works in the Firefox and Chrome browsers only.

Color:

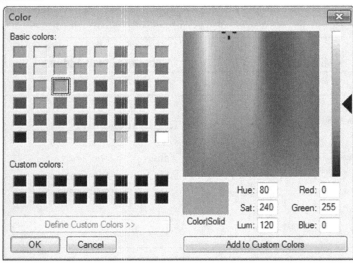

Figure A-2. *Color selection palette*

- **Date**

    Syntax: `<input id="txtDate" type="date">`

Figure A-3 displays the date picker control based on the above code. This works in the Chrome browser only.

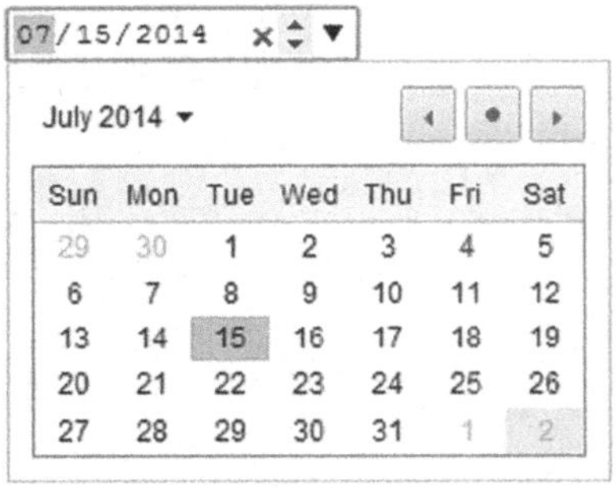

Figure A-3. Date picker control

- **Number**

    Syntax: `<input id="txtNumber" type="number">`

Figure A-4 displays the number spinner control based on the above code. This works in the Firefox, Chrome, and Safari browsers.

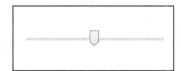

Figure A-4. Number spinner control

- **Range**

    Syntax: `<input id="txtRange" type="range" min="minValue" max="maxValue">`

where `minValue` and `maxValue` are numbers.

Figure A-5 displays the number range control based on the above code. This works in the Firefox, Chrome, Safari, and Internet Explorer browsers.

Figure A-5. Number range control

Other new input types not shown here include `datetime`, `month`, `search`, `tel`, `time`, `url`, and `week`.

Graphics Using Canvas

In HTML5, the <canvas> element is used to draw graphics at runtime. The canvas has (0, 0) coordinates in the top-left corner of the specified canvas rectangle.

Listing A-2 demonstrates an example using HTML5, CSS, and JavaScript to draw a simple rectangle on the canvas.

Listing A-2. Creating a basic shape on the canvas

```
<!DOCTYPE html>
<html>
<head>
    <meta charset="UTF-8">
    <script src="scripts/jquery-2.1.0.min.js"></script>

    <style>
canvas {
    margin-top: 100px;
    margin-left: 100px;
    border:3px solid green;
        }
    </style>

    <script>
$(function(){
    var canvasElement = document.getElementById("myCanvas");
    var canvasContext = canvasElement.getContext("2d");

    canvasContext.fillStyle = "gray";
    canvasContext.fillRect(25, 25, 50, 50);
});
    </script>
</head>

<body>
    <canvas id="myCanvas" width="200" height="200"></canvas>
</body>
</html>
```

This code requires the jQuery library. Make sure that the jquery-2.1.0.min.js file exists in the scripts folder.

In the HTML code, the <canvas> folder creates the placeholder for the canvas. The CSS code defines the position and border of the canvas. The JavaScript code gets the reference of the canvas by using the following code. Before you draw anything on the canvas, you need to get the canvas context.

```
var canvasElement = document.getElementById("myCanvas");
var canvasContext = canvasElement.getContext("2d");
```

The fill style is set as a solid color—"gray"—and then a rectangle is drawn by using the coordinates (25, 25). The width is 50 pixels and the height is 50 pixels. Use the stroke() method to draw the border. Use the fill() method to fill the shape with the color or gradient specified by the fillStyle property.

The following is the list of common tasks that you can perform on the canvas:

- Draw a line:

```
canvasContext.moveTo(x1, y1); // First coordinate
canvasContext.lineTo(x2, y2); // Second coordinate
canvasContext.stroke();
```

- Draw a circle:

```
// x1,y1 - center coordinate
canvasContext.arc(x1, y1, radius, 0, 2*Math.PI);
canvasContext.stroke();
```

- Draw a rectangle:

```
// x1, y1 - top left coordinate
canvasContext.rect(x1, y1, width, height);
canvasContext.stroke();
```

- Fill a shape with a solid color:

```
canvasContext.fillStyle= "colorName";
```

where colorName can be the name of a color (such as grey) or a hex value of the color (such as #ff0000).

- Fill a shape with the linear gradient:

```
// (x1,y1) and (x2, y2) defines the direction of the gradient
var gradient = canvasContext.createLinearGradient(x1, y1, x2, y2);
// colorName1 and colorName2 defines the start and end color transition
gradient.addColorStop(0,"colorName1");
gradient.addColorStop(1,"colorName2");
canvasContext.fillStyle = gradient;
canvasContext.fill();
```

A-2. Using CSS3

A cascading stylesheet (CSS) is used to specify the theme, style, and layout of the web pages. CSS3 is the latest standard specification for CSS. Display styles can be applied to various elements of the web page at various levels.

Advantages of Using CSS

The following are some of the advantages of using CSS:

- Centralized location for presentation aspect of the web application. Provides a consistent look and feel for the website. The theme of the whole website can be changed by updating a CSS file and without modifying any of the HTML.

- Styles can be specified at a global level or at the element level, which gives you greater control over how you display an element on the web page.

CSS Selector

The following is the syntax to specify CSS properties:

```
cssSelector {
    cssProperty1:cssValue1;
cssProperty2:cssValue12;
...
    }
```

or as an attribute of the HTML element:

```
style = "cssProperty1:cssValue1; cssProperty2:cssValue12;... "
```

Table A-3 lists the CSS selectors' syntax.

Table A-3. *CSS Selectors' Syntax*

cssSelector	Syntax	Examples
HTML element tag	htmlTag	div, p, table, tr, td, input
Class name	.className	Any user-defined className, such as evenRow and oddRow
HTML element ID	#id	\<input id="firstName"> (In CSS, it is specified as #firstName.)
HTML element state	:stateName	:link, :hover

CSS Box Model

Figure A-6 displays the box model, which demonstrates the location of the margin, border, and padding in relation to the HTML element.

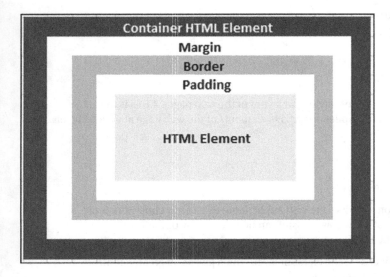

Figure A-6. *Box model*

The following is a list of CSS properties that set the width of padding, border, and margin of the HTML element with respect to its container HTML element. The top, bottom, left and right margins, as well as the border and padding properties can be set individually or together with one declaration.

- Padding CSS properties—`padding`, `padding-top`, `padding-bottom`, `padding-left`, and `padding-right`.

- Border CSS properties—`border-width`, `border-top-width`, `border-bottom-width`, `border-left-width`, and `border-right-width`.

- Margin CSS properties—`margin`, `margin-top`, `margin-bottom`, `margin-left`, and `margin-right`.

Types of Styles

There are three ways to specify CSS—inline, as an internal stylesheet, and as an external stylesheet. Inline is the least recommended way of using CSS. This form of CSS definition should be used only for quick testing and for verification. All CSS items should be in a single location and not scattered all over the HTML page.

Inline Style

Listing A-3 shows how inline CSS is used.

Listing A-3. Using the inline style

```
<!DOCTYPE html>
<html lang="en">
<head>
    <meta charset="UTF-8">
    <title>Inline Style</title>
</head>
<body>
    <p style="color:red; text-decoration:underline; margin-left:30px">Test Message</p>
</body>
</html>
```

Figure A-7 displays the web page segment using the inline style.

Figure A-7. *Text display using the inline style*

Internal Stylesheet

Refer to the Listing A-4 to see how internal CSS is used in an HTML file.

Listing A-4. Using an internal stylesheet

```
<!DOCTYPE html>
<html lang="en">
<head>
    <meta charset="UTF-8">
    <title>Internal Style</title>
    <style>
        p {
            background-color:teal;
            color:white;
            margin-left:30px
        }
    </style>
</head>
<body>
    <p>Paragraph styling using internal style sheet.</p>
<body>
</html>
```

Figure A-8 displays the web page segment with the internal style.

Paragraph styling using internal style sheet.

Figure A-8. *Text display using the internal style*

External Stylesheet

Refer to Listing A-5 to see how external CSS is used in the HTML page.

Listing A-5. Using an external stylesheet

```
File Name: myWebApp.css
    p {
        background-color:teal;
        color:white;
        margin-left:30px;
    }


File Name: ExternalStyleSheet.htm
    <!DOCTYPE html>
    <html lang="en">
    <head>
        <meta charset="UTF-8">
        <title>External Style Sheet</title>
        <link rel="stylesheet" type="text/css" href="myWebApp.css">
    </head>
```

```
<body>
    <p>Paragraph styling using external stylesheet.</p>
<body>
</html>
```

Figure A-9 displays the web page segment with the external stylesheet

Paragraph styling using external style sheet.

Figure A-9. *Text display using an external stylesheet*

This is the preferred way to use a stylesheet in your web application. This approach keeps the style and the content separate. The same external CSS file can be used in multiple HTML pages to get the consistent look and feel across your whole website. You can change the look of your entire website by updating only one file.

Cascading Styles

If more than one style is used for an HTML element, all the styles will cascade into the final style and will be applied to the HTML element using the following priority order (lowest to highest):

- Browser setting
- External stylesheet
- Internal stylesheet
- Inline style

Examples
Rounded Button with Drop Shadow Using CSS

Refer to Listing A-6 to see how to create a rounded button with a drop shadow using CSS and without using a graphics file.

Listing A-6. Creating a rounded button with a drop shadow using CSS

```
<!DOCTYPE html>
<html lang="en">
<head>
    <meta charset="UTF-8">
    <title>Rounded button with drop-shadow</title>
    <style>
        body { background-color: lightyellow; }

        .rounded-corners {
            -moz-border-radius: 10px;
            -webkit-border-radius: 10px;
            -khtml-border-radius: 10px;
            border-radius: 10px;
```

```
            -webkit-box-shadow: 0 1px 2px rgba(0,0,0,.2);
              -moz-box-shadow: 0 1px 2px rgba(0,0,0,.2);
              box-shadow: 0 1px 2px rgba(0,0,0,.2);

              text-shadow: 0 1px 1px rgba(0,0,0,.3);

          background-color: orange;
          width:100px;
          height:30px;
        }
    </style>
</head>
<body>
    <button class="rounded-corners">Submit</button><br/>
</body>
</html>
```

Figure A-10 displays the rounded button with a drop shadow.

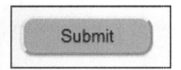

Figure A-10. *Rounded button with a drop shadow*

The CSS property opacity makes the HTML element opaque. Its value ranges from 0 to 1, where 0 is completely transparent and 1 is no transparency. Figure A-11 displays the same button shown in Figure A-10 after adding 0.5 opacity to the .rounded-corners CSS class.

Figure A-11. *Rounded button with a drop shadow and opacity*

Button with Gradient, Hover, and Active Effects Using CSS

Refer to Listing A-7 to see how to create a rounded button with a drop shadow, transparency, a hover effect, and an active effect using CSS and without using a graphics file.

Listing A-7. Creating a rounded button with a drop shadow, transparency, a hover effect, and an active effect using CSS

```
<!DOCTYPE html>
<html lang="en">
<head>
    <meta charset="UTF-8">
    <title>Gradient, hover and active effects </title>
```

```
    <style>
        body { background-color: lightyellow; }

        .btnBase {
            -moz-border-radius: 10px;
-webkit-border-radius: 10px;
-khtml-border-radius: 10px;

-webkit-box-shadow: 0 1px 2px rgba(0,0,0,.2);
-moz-box-shadow: 0 1px 2px rgba(0,0,0,.2);
box-shadow: 0 1px 2px rgba(0,0,0,.2);

text-shadow: 0 1px 1px rgba(0,0,0,.3);

border-radius: 10px;
background-color: orange;
width:100px;
height:30px;
        }

        .btn {
            color: #fef4e9;
            border: solid 1px #da7c0c;
            background: #f78d1d;
            background: -webkit-gradient(linear, left top, left bottom,
    from(#faa51a), to(#f47a20));
            background: -moz-linear-gradient(top,  #faa51a,  #f47a20);
        }

        .btn:hover {
            color: #000000;
            background: -webkit-gradient(linear, left top, left bottom,
    from(#f47a20), to(#FFFFFF));
            background: -moz-linear-gradient(top,  #f47a20,  #FFFFFF);
        }

        .btn:active {
                background: #f47c20;
background: -webkit-gradient(linear, left top, left bottom,
        from(#119FF8), to(#15AEF0));
background: -moz-linear-gradient(top,  #119FF8,  #15AEF0);
        }
    </style>
</head>
<body>
    <button class="btnBase btn">Submit</button><br/>
</body>
</html>
```

Figure A-12 displays the rounded button with the drop shadow and opacity set to 0.5 in the Firefox, Chrome, and Safari browsers.

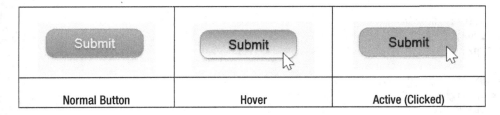

| Normal Button | Hover | Active (Clicked) |

Figure A-12. *Button with hover and active events effects*

The gradient and active button effects don't work in Internet Explorer.

APPENDIX B

Web Console

B-1. Web Browsers

For all the chapter examples, I used the browsers listed in Table B-1 to test the code. Screen shots are taken from the Firefox browser. If there are significant differences in display or behavior in other browsers, I have mentioned this.

Table B-1. *Web Browsers Used for Testing*

Browser	Operating System	Version	Company
Firefox	Windows	29.0.1	Mozilla Foundation
Chrome	Windows	34.0	Google
Internet Explorer	Windows	11.0.3	Microsoft
Safari	Windows	5.1.7	Apple
Safari	Mac OS	7.0.3	Apple

B-2. Using the Web Console

In your JavaScript and jQuery code, you can the use console.log() statement to log messages in the web console. This is a better alternative to alert() because it doesn't impact the developer or user experience and you have a choice to see or ignore logged messages. It is highly recommended that you remove informational console.log() statements before deploying to production to prevent any performance-related issues. I highly recommend you keep the web console active so that you can quickly identify any JavaScript syntax and runtime errors.

The following sections explain the ways to start the web console in different browsers.

B-2-1. Starting the Web Console in Firefox (Windows)

To start the web console in the Firefox browser, use the Ctrl-Shift-K shortcut key or follow the steps outlined in Figure B-1 (choose Firefox ➤ Web Developer ➤ Web Console).

Figure B-1. *Starting the web console in the Firefox browser*

B-2-2. Starting the Web Console in Chrome (Windows)

To start the web console in the Chrome browser, you can use the F12 (or Ctrl-Shift-I) shortcut key or follow the steps shown in Figure B-2 (choose the Customize and Control Google Chrome Icon at top-right corner ➤ Tools ➤ Developer Tools).

Figure B-2. *Starting the web console in Google's Chrome browser*

After that, click on the Console tab.

B-2-3. Starting the Web Console in Internet Explorer (Windows)

To start the web console in the Internet Explorer browser, you can use the F12 shortcut key or follow the steps shown in Figure B-3 (choose Tools at the top-right corner ➤ F12 Developer Tools).

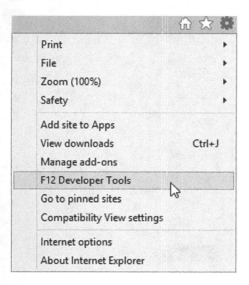

Figure B-3. *Starting the web console in the Microsoft Internet Explorer browser*

Then click on the Console button ▷ .

B-2-4. Starting the Web Console in Safari (Mac OS)

By default, the developer tools are not turned on in Safari, so make sure to turn them on from the Preferences menu. Choose the Advanced tab and then check the Show Desktop Menu in Menu Bar option. Figure B-4 shows how to enable the developer tools in Safari.

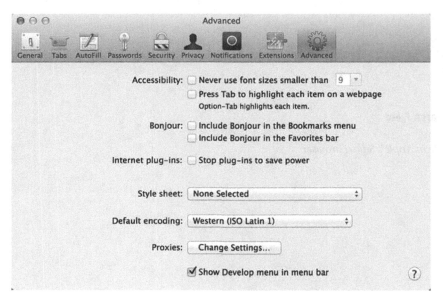

Figure B-4. *Enabling the developer menu in Apple's Safari browser*

To start the web console in the Safari browser, you can use the Command-Option-C shortcut key or follow the steps outlined in Figure B-5.

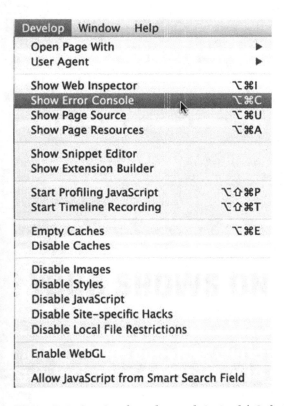

Figure B-5. *Starting the web console in Apple's Safari browser*

APPENDIX C

■ ■ ■

Deploy Web Application

The sections in this appendix explain how to:

- Install and set up the Open Source Apache Tomcat web server
- Install Microsoft Internet Information Services (IIS)
- Deploy the web application

These instructions are for the Windows 64-bit operating system. Similar instructions can be used to install the web server and deploy the web application on other operating systems. You need to install and set up either Tomcat or IIS.

After the web application is deployed using the instructions in this appendix, you can test your web applications from other computers and from your mobile devices, as long as they are connected to the same network as your web server. If you are not able to access your web page on your mobile device, go to the URL locally on your web server. If you can see the page from your server but not from your mobile device, check that:

- The web server and the mobile device are connected to the same local router through an Ethernet cable or via WiFi.
- There is no firewall on the web server blocking the traffic.

C-1. Prerequisite: Downloading Java 7 JRE

To download Java 7 JRE:

1. Go to `http://www.oracle.com/technetwork/java/javase/downloads/` and select the JRE Download button under Java SE 7u60.

2. Check the Accept License Agreement radio button.

3. Click the download link for `jre-7u60-windows-x64.exe` for Windows 64.

4. Save the file.

5. Double-click the saved file (`jre-7u60-windows-x64.exe`). The default install location is `C:\Program Files\Java\jre7`. Click the Install > button.

6. After Java is successfully installed, click the Close button.

To verify that Java JRE is installed properly, open the MS-DOS prompt and enter the java -version command. You should see the following output:

```
java version "1.7.0_60"
Java(TM) SE Runtime Environment (build 1.7.0_60-b19)
Java HotSpot(TM) 64-Bit Server VM (build 24.60-b09, mixed mode)
```

You need to verify that the JRE_HOME environment variable is set properly. Go to Windows operating system's Control Panel by choosing Systems and Security ➤ System ➤ Advanced System Settings ➤ Advanced tab ➤ Environment Variables. If JRE_HOME is not set properly, set it by clicking New:

```
Variable name: JRE_HOME
Variable value: C:\Program Files\Java\jre7
```

C-2. Downloading and Installing Apache Tomcat

To download Apache Tomcat, follow these steps:

1. Go to http://tomcat.apache.org.

2. Click on the latest version of Tomcat.

   At the time of writing of this book, the latest version is 8.0.9. Click on Tomcat 8.0 under the Download section and then click on 64-bit Windows zip (pgp, md5) under the 8.0.9 – Binary Distributions – Core section.

3. Save the ZIP file.

4. After the download is complete, unzip the file in a folder of your choice (for example, C:\). The following becomes the home directory for Tomcat: C:\apache-tomcat-8.0.9.

C-3. Starting and Stopping the Tomcat Server

To start the Tomcat web server, follow these steps:

1. Go to C:\apache-tomcat-8.0.9\bin.

2. Double-click startup.bat.

If the prerequisite is met and there is no issue with the setup, you should see the last line of the output as:

```
13-Jul-2014 19:42:15.347 INFO [main] org.apache.catalina.startup.Catalina.start
Server startup in 577 ms
```

This indicates that the server has started successfully.

3. To verify that web server has started successfully, go to http://localhost:8080. You should be able to see the Tomcat page.

If no MS-DOS prompt window is displayed and the startup.bat file gets terminated immediately, update the startup.bat file with the pause command at the end of the file. This will keep the MS-DOS prompt window open and display the error message.

To stop the Tomcat web server, follow these steps:

1. Go to C:\apache-tomcat-8.0.9\bin.

2. Double-click shutdown.bat.

C-4. Deploying the Web Application on the Tomcat Server

To deploy the web application on the Tomcat server, follow these steps:

1. Create your web application folder under C:\apache-tomcat-8.0.9\webapps (for example, jQueryLearn).

2. Copy all the folders and files from your web application root folder to C:\apache-tomcat-8.0.9\webapps\jQueryLearn.

3. To verify access to your web application using the web server, go to http://localhost:8080/jQueryLearn/myPage.htm, where myPage.htm is one of your HTML files.

If you can access your page that means your web application is deployed properly.

C-5. Installing IIS (Internet Information Services)

To install IIS, you need to log on with administrator rights. The following instructions are for deploying the web application on IIS 7.0 (or 7.5) under the Windows 8 operating system. Similar instructions can be used for Windows 7 and Windows 2008 server.

1. Go to Control Panel ➤ Programs ➤ Turn Windows on or off. Figure C-1 shows if the IIS is installed.

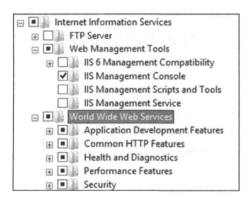

Figure C-1. *IIS installation status*

2. If World Wide Web Services under Internet Information Services is not checked, check it and then click OK to install IIS.

3. After installation is completed, go to http://localhost/. You should see the default IIS page. Figure C-2 displays this default page.

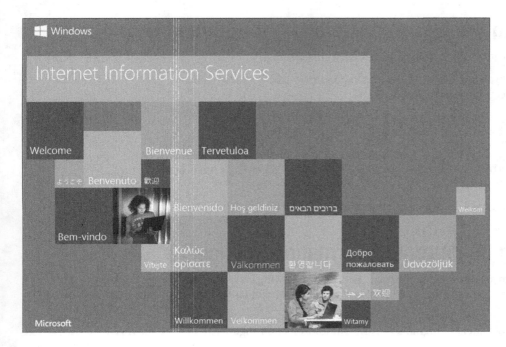

Figure C-2. *Default IIS page*

C-6. Deploying the Web Application on the IIS Server

To deploy the web application on the IIS server:

1. Log on with administrator rights.

2. Create your web application folder under C:\inetpub\wwwroot (for example, jQueryLearn).

3. Copy all the folders and files from your web application root folder to C:\inetpub\wwwroot\jQueryLearn.

4. Run IIS Manager using the following command:

   C:\windows\system32\inetsrv\InetMgr.exe

On the left panel, expand your computer name and choose Sites. Right-click on Default Web Site and then click Add Application.

Figure C-3 displays the Add Application settings. After entering an Alias and a Physical Path, click OK.

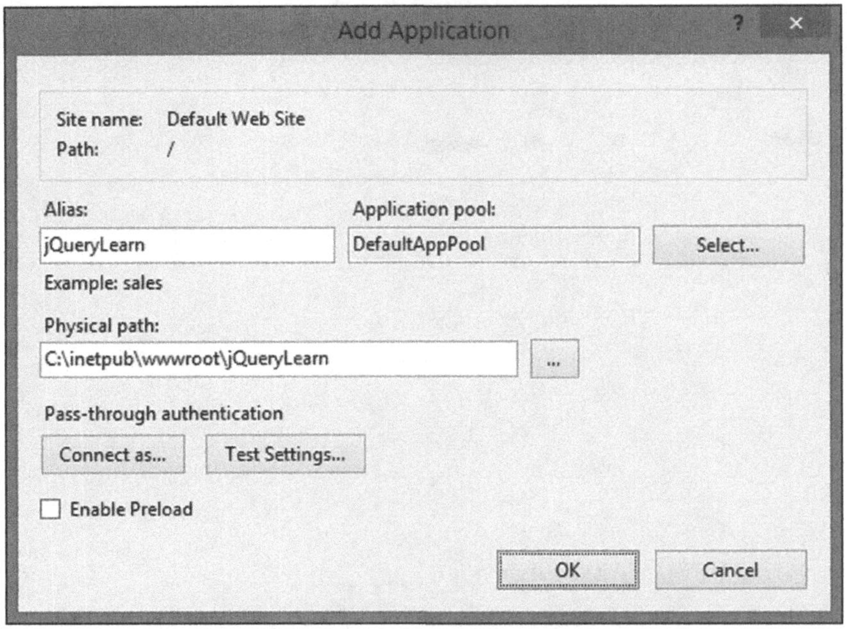

Figure C-3. *The Add Application settings*

5. To verify access to your web application using the web server, go to `http://localhost/jQueryLearn/myPage.htm`, where `myPage.htm` is any of your HTML files.

If you can access your page that means your web application is deployed properly.

C-7. Accessing a Deployed Web Application

You can deploy your mobile web application on the Tomcat web server (or IIS) and test your web pages on your mobile device by following these steps:

1. Get the IP address of your computer on which web server is installed. For example, for the Windows operating system, enter `ipconfig` into the MS-DOS prompt window. Look for the IPv4 (or IPv6) address to get the IP address of the computer.

2. Use the mobile device to test the mobile web application. Say your server IP address is 192.168.1.72. On your mobile device, open a web browser and enter the URL. If the web application is deployed on Apache Tomcat, use:

   `http://192.168.1.72:8080/jQueryLearn/myPage.htm`

   If the web application is deployed on IIS, use:

   `http://192.168.1.72/jQueryLearn/myPage.htm`

   You should be able to see your web page on your mobile device. If you have any issue accessing web pages from the mobile device, check that the web server is running and that the server and the mobile device are connected to the same local router through an Ethernet cable or via WiFi.

567

■ ■ ■

Logging, Error Handling, and Debugging

D-1. Logging

Logging is an integral part of any application. It helps developers and support personnel monitor the execution path under different scenarios and diagnose the problems. A well implemented logging mechanism in the application reduces the time to identify the root cause of the problem. Developers should be careful about the amount of logging they implement in the application. On the one hand logging is very helpful but on the other hand, too much logging impacts performance and requires a huge amount of disk storage.

Because a security mechanism is built into most browsers which prevents JavaScript from writing to a file on the client's machine/device, it is not possible to log messages in a file on the client side. JavaScript code can write log messages by using the following mechanism:

- Write messages to the browser's console

- Write messages to the current web page

- Write messages to pop-up web page

- Send messages to the server using asynchronous AJAX calls

Basic Logging

The newer versions of all major browsers provide access to their web console. In JavaScript, you can use Console APIs to log messages in the browser's web console. Refer to the Recipe B-2 in Appendix B for the details about how to use the web console in various browsers. The following are the console APIs that can be used in JavaScript:

- `console.log(message)` logs a message to the web console where the parameter `message` can be a text string, variable, or expression.

- `console.warn(message)` logs a message to the web console with the warning icon.

- `console.error(message)` logs a message to the web console with the error icon.

- `console.dir(object)` logs an object's structure, its properties, and the property's values.

Listing D-1 shows the use of console APIs.

Listing D-1. Console APIs

```html
<!DOCTYPE html>
<html lang="en">
<head>
    <meta charset="utf-8">

    <script>
            console.log("Test Message");
            console.warn("Test Warning Message");
            console.error("Test Error Message");

            // Create object
        var obj = new Object();
        obj.id = 1;
        obj.name = "John Smith";

        var departments = new Object();
        departments.department1 = "Infrastructure";
        departments.department2 = "Development";

        obj.departments = departments;

        console.dir(obj);
    </script>
</head>

<body></body>
</html>
```

To open the console window in the Firefox browser, click Open Menu in the top-right corner of the browser, click Developer, and then click Web Console. Figure D-1 displays the log messages in the Firefox browser console. Make sure that the Logging tab is active (that it's clicked to display logging messages). Message display styles are slightly different in other browsers.

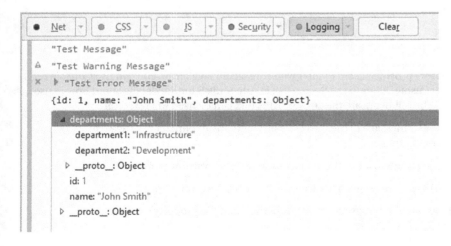

Figure D-1. *Output of console APIs in the Firefox browser*

To open the console window in the Chrome browser, click the Customize and Control button in the top-right corner of the browser, click Tools, and then click Developer Tools. Figure D-2 displays the log messages in the Chrome browser console. Make sure that the Console tab is active (it is clicked to display logging messages).

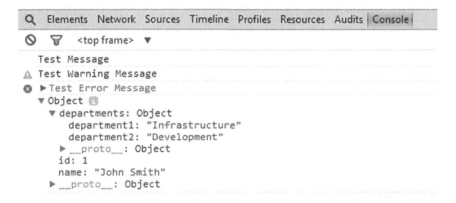

Figure D-2. *Output of the console APIs in the Chrome browser*

To open the console window in Internet Explorer browser, click the Tools button in the top-right corner of the browser and then click F12 Developer Tools. Figure D-3 displays the log messages in the Internet Explorer browser console. If you have opened the console after loading the HTML page and the messages are not displayed in the console, refresh the page to see the messages in the console.

Figure D-3. *Output of console APIs in the Internet Explorer browser*

To open the console window in the Safari browser, click Display a Menu for the Current Page button in the top-right corner of the browser, click Develop, and then click Show Error Console. If the Develop menu item is not available, make sure that the Show Develop Menu in Menu Bar checkbox is checked under Safari Settings ➤ Preferences ➤ Advanced tab. Figure D-4 displays the log messages in the Safari browser console.

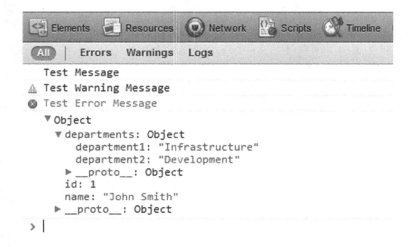

Figure D-4. *Output of console APIs in the Safari browser*

Logging Framework

There are many open source JavaScript logging frameworks available. I like the Log4JavaScript framework as it is based on the industry standard and widely used Log4J logging framework. I'll cover the basics of the log4javascript library in this appendix. One of the main advantages of using this framework is that you can easily change the logging severity level without making code changes in many places. For example, you can set the logging severity as ALL during the development and when the code is deployed in production, just change the logging severity to ERROR without making any other changes in the code. If you want to investigate an issue in production, you can change the severity to DEBUG. Without such logging frameworks, developers have to comment and uncomment logging messages all the time during various stages of the development lifecycle, which is time-consuming and prone to errors.

To download the log4javascript library, go to http://log4javascript.org and click the Download button. At the time of this writing, the latest version is 1.4.9. After you have downloaded the file log4javascript-1.4.9.zip, extract all the files from it. Copy log4javascript-1.4.9\js\log4script.js to the scripts/ directory under your development root directory.

Log4JavaScript has the following five main concepts, all of which are used to log messages:

- Loggers

- Appenders

- Severity level (optional)

- Pattern layout (optional)

- Log messages

Loggers

The logger is the named reference pointer to which appenders are added, severity levels are set, and methods are executed to log the messages. A web page can have multiple named loggers. Multiple loggers are useful if you want to send different messages to different logging targets (different appenders).

Appenders

The appender specifies where the log messages will be sent/logged. Multiple appenders can be added to the same logger. The following is a list of appenders:

- `AlertAppender`—Displays messages as JavaScript alerts. The syntax to create an `AlertAppender` is:

  ```
  var appender = new log4javascript.AlertAppender();
  ```

- `AjaxAppender`—Asynchronously sends messages to the server. You need to write the server-side program to accept the message from the JavaScript code and log it to a file, to a database table, or to the event log. The syntax to create an `AjaxAppender` is:

  ```
  var appender = new log4javascript.AjaxAppender(url);
  ```

where `url` is the server-side program URL (for example, the web service URL).

- `PopUpAppender`—Displays messages in a console window (pop-up window). You need to set the browser to allow pop-ups. The syntax to create a `PopUpAppender` is:

  ```
  var appender = new log4javascript.PopUpAppender();
  ```

- `InPageAppender`—Displays messages to a console window in the page. The syntax to create an `InPageAppender` is:

  ```
  var appender = new log4javascript.InPageAppender();
  ```

- `BrowserConsoleAppender`—Displays messages to the browser's built-in console. The syntax to create a `BrowserConsoleAppender` is:

  ```
  var appender = new log4javascript.BrowserConsoleAppender();
  ```

Severity Level

The severity level of the logger specifies the severity level of the messages that will be logged. There are six types of message severities—TRACE, DEBUG, INFO, WARN, ERROR, and FATAL. The following is the ascending order of the severity levels. You can set the level on the logger. When the logger is used to log the message, only those messages that have the same or a higher level will be logged. For example, if the logger's level is set to ERROR, messages with a severity of ERROR or FATAL will be logged. This level is preferable in the production environment. If the logger's level is set to ALL, messages with the severity TRACE, DEBUG, INFO, WARN, ERROR, and FATAL will be logged. This level is preferable in the development environment. If the level is not explicitly set on the logger, the default value of DEBUG is used, which means the messages with the severity DEBUG, INFO, WARN, ERROR, and FATAL will be logged.

1. ALL
2. TRACE
3. DEBUG
4. INFO
5. WARN
6. ERROR
7. FATAL
8. OFF

Pattern Layout

The pattern layout specifies the pattern of the logged messages. It is set at the appender level. For example, "%c %d - %m%n" specifies the following:

- %c —The name of the logger
- %d—The date and time of the message logging
- %m—The message
- %n—The new line separator

For the complete list of patterns and formatting, refer to this site: http://log4javascript.org/docs/manual.html#layouts.

Log Messages

You can log messages with various severity settings by using following statements:

```
log.trace("message");
log.debug("message");
log.info("message");
log.warn("message");
log.error("message");
log.fatal("message");
```

where log is the logger that has at least one appender added to it and message is the message to be logged.

You should set up the loggers with the appenders, level, and pattern layout at the global level so that changes in the severity level can be set or an appender can be changed in one place only. Once a logger is set at the global level, it can be used anywhere in the page within the JavaScript code.

Listing D-2 demonstrates a basic example of using the log4javascript library.

Listing D-2. Basic logging

```
<!DOCTYPE html>
<html lang="en">
<head>
    <meta charset="utf-8">
    <script src="scripts/log4javascript.js"></script>

    <script>
            // Set Logger
            var log = log4javascript.getLogger("myLogger");

            // Get Appender
            var appender = new log4javascript.InPageAppender();

            // Set message pattern
            var layout = new log4javascript.PatternLayout("%c %d - %m");
            appender.setLayout(layout);

            // Set Appender
            log.addAppender(appender);

            // Set Level
            log.setLevel(log4javascript.Level.ALL);

            // Log Message
            log.info("This is the test message.");
    </script>
</head>
<body></body>
</html>
```

Figure D-5 displays the log message at the bottom of the web page when the page is viewed in a browser.

Filters: ☑ **trace** ☑ **debug** ☑ **info** ☑ warn ☑ **error** ☑ **fatal** ☑ **all**

Search: [   ] Reset ☐ Regex ☐ Match case ☐ Disable

Options: ☑ Log ☐ Wrap ☐ Newest at the top ☑ Scroll to latest [Clear]

```
myLogger 2014-08-07 13:16:58,418 - This is the test message.
```

Figure D-5. *Output due to the InPageAppender*

You can filter and search all the logged messages. You can also set options to log, wrap, bring the newest message to the top, and scroll to the latest message.

The following code segments show different logger types and appenders:

- To use the default logger (i.e., the logger with the PopUpAppender):

```
var log = new log4javascript.getDefaultLogger();
log.info("This is informational message");
```

- To use the named logger with PopUpAppender:

```
var log = log4javascript.getLogger("myLogger");
var appender = new log4javascript.PopUpAppender();
log.addAppender(appender);
log.info("This is informational message");
```

- To use the multiple loggers:

```
var log = log4javascript.getLogger("client");
var appender = new log4javascript.InPageAppender();
log.addAppender(appender);
log.error("This is the client error message");

var devLog = log4javascript.getLogger("development");
var devAppender = new log4javascript.PopUpAppender();
devLog.addAppender(devAppender);
devLog.debug("This is the debug message");
```

  Messages logged by the `log` logger will go to the inline window and messages from the `devLog` logger will go to the pop-up window. In real-world applications, all error and fatal-level logs should go to the log with the appender `AjaxAppender` so that all error and fatal messages can be logged to a central location on the server side and can be used by developers and production support personnel to diagnose the problem.

- To use the same logger and multiple appenders:

```
var log = log4javascript.getLogger("main");

var appender1 = new log4javascript.InPageAppender();
log.addAppender(appender1);

var appender2 = new log4javascript.PopUpAppender();
log.addAppender(appender2);

log.error("This is the client error message");
```

  The messages will be logged in two places—inline, that is, on the same web page, and in the pop-up window.

D-2. Error Handling

If an error occurs during runtime and it's not handled in the JavaScript code, no error message will be displayed to the user. If you open the browser's web console you can see those messages as unhandled exceptions. For example, if you view a page with the following code in a browser, no error message will be displayed and the JavaScript code execution will terminate at the point of error.

```
displayMessage("My Message");
```

Due to the missing function—`displayMessage()`—an exception will be thrown by the code. If you open the browser console window, you will see the following error message:

```
"ReferenceError: displayMessage is not defined"
```

These four statements handle JavaScript exceptions:

- `try`—Wraps the code that you want to test for an error.
- `catch`—Code segment that's executed if an error occurs in the code within a `try()` block.
- `finally`—Code segment that's executed regardless of an error or no error.
- `throw`—Statement to throw the custom exception back to the caller. It is used for displaying a user friendly error and for forcing an exception for the cases like validation error.

Try and Catch

Listing D-3 demonstrates an example where an error is caught and handled.

Listing D-3. Using try and catch for exception handling

```
<!DOCTYPE html>
<html lang="en">
<head>
    <meta charset="utf-8">

    <script>
            try {
        // some code
        displayMessage("My Message");
            }
            catch (errorMsg) {
        alert("Error: " + errorMsg);
            }
    </script>
</head>

<body></body>
</html>
```

When this page is viewed in a browser and the JavaScript code is executed, an exception (error) is thrown at the line displayMessage("My Message"); and the JavaScript code is not executed further within the try block. Execution control will go to the catch block. The parameter errorMsg in the catch statement contains the text of the error message. In the catch block, you can handle this error condition any way you want. Some of the possible actions you can take are to:

- Display the exact error message.

- Display a user friendly error message.

- Try to re-execute the same block of the code that threw the exception. This action is relevant for the error conditions like a timeout error.

- Use the log4javascript framework to send the message to the server.

Figure D-6 displays the error message as a pop-up message.

Figure D-6. *Displaying an error message*

Finally

Listing D-4 shows the use of the finally statement. The code segment within the finally block is executed at the end of the try and catch blocks, regardless of whether code execution is completed in the try block or in the catch block. Generally, clean-up tasks like closing the connection or re-initializing variables are coded in the finally block.

Listing D-4. Using a finally statement

```html
<!DOCTYPE html>
<html lang="en">
<head>
    <meta charset="utf-8">

    <script>

            var status = "";

        try {
                testFunc();
                status = "Successful";
            } catch (err) {
          status = "Failed";
            } finally {
                alert("DOM ready function is completed with the status: " + status);
                // Cleanup or reinitialization code
            }
    </script>
</head>

<body></body>
</html>
```

Figure D-7 displays the pop-up message with the status as `Failed` because `testFunc()` doesn't exist. An exception has occurred and the status is set to `Failed` in the `catch` block.

Figure D-7. *Display error message from the finally block*

If the `testFunc()` function exists in the JavaScript code, the following message will be displayed:

"DOM ready function is completed with the status: Successful"

Throw

Listing D-5 shows the use of the `throw` statement. By using the `throw` statement, you can throw an exception with the custom message. The `throw` statement can be used anywhere in the JavaScript code (not necessarily in the `catch` block only).

Listing D-5. Using a throw statement

```
<!DOCTYPE html>
<html lang="en">
<head>
    <meta charset="utf-8">

    <script>
            function testFunc() {
        try {
            // some code
            displayMessage("My Message");
        }
        catch (errorMsg) {
            throw "Programming error occurred.";
        }
            }

            try {
                testFunc();
        } catch (err) {
            alert(err);
        }
    </script>
</head>

<body></body>
</html>
```

Figure D-8 displays the Programming Error Occurred pop-up message. Because `displayMessage()` doesn't exist, the code in the `catch` block is executed, and it has thrown the custom error message—"`Programming error occurred`"—to the caller function.

Figure D-8. *Displaying a custom error message*

If the same variable is referenced in `try` and also in `catch` or `finally`, it should be declared outside the `try`, `catch`, and `finally` blocks because the scope of the variable declared within the `try`, `catch`, and `finally` block is limited to that block only.

D-3. Debugging

Debugging is the process whereby developers can execute a single line of code at a time and then view the value of the variables (primitive and objects) at any step in the code-execution process (provided the variable is still in the scope). Debugging is helpful in finding bugs and fixing them quickly. This section covers how to debug a simple program using the Firefox browser. Listing D-6 contains a simple program in which an employee object is set and then used to display all the departments for the employee.

Listing D-6. Setting and getting the employee's object (the filename is debug.htm)

```
<!DOCTYPE html>
<html lang="en">
<head>
    <meta charset="utf-8">

    <script>
            function displayDepartments(employeeObject) {
                for (var i=0; i<employeeObject.departments.length; i++) {
                        // Display department names of the employee
                        alert(employeeObject.departments[i]);
                }
            }

        // Create employee object
        var empObj = new Object();

        // Set employee object
        empObj.id = 1;
        empObj.name = "John Smith";

        // Set department names in an array
        var departments = new Array();
        departments.push("Infrastructure");
        departments.push("Development");
```

```
        // Set departments for the employee
        empObj.departments = departments;

        // Call displayDepartments() function
        displayDepartments(empObj);
    </script>

</head>

<body></body>
</html>
```

The following is the list of steps that need to be performed to debug the code:

1. Open debug.htm in the Firefox browser. Click OK for the pop-up messages.

2. Open the Firefox browser's debug window by clicking the Open Menu button on the top-left corner (the button with three horizontal lines) and then clicking the Developer button. Figure D-9 displays how to start the debugger window.

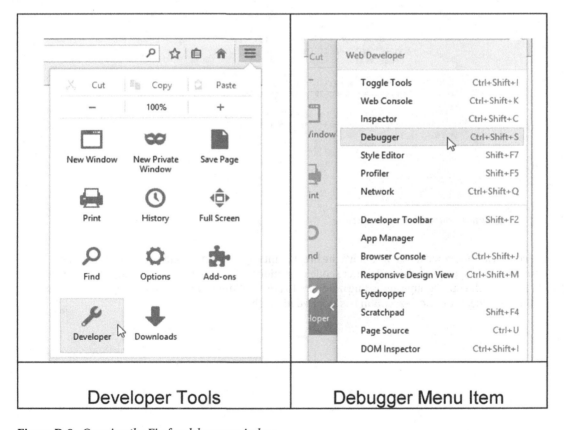

Figure D-9. *Opening the Firefox debugger window*

3. Click Debugger or press Ctrl-Shift-S. Figure D-10 displays the debugger window.

Figure D-10. *The debugger window with the source code*

In the source code window, you can set or remove the breakpoints by clicking the gray area left to the line numbers. The breakpoint is the place in the code where code execution will stop so that the developers can step over it or through it. Let's set up the breakpoints at the line numbers 10 and 27. When you refresh the page, you will see Figure D-11 with the line where the code execution has stopped highlighted.

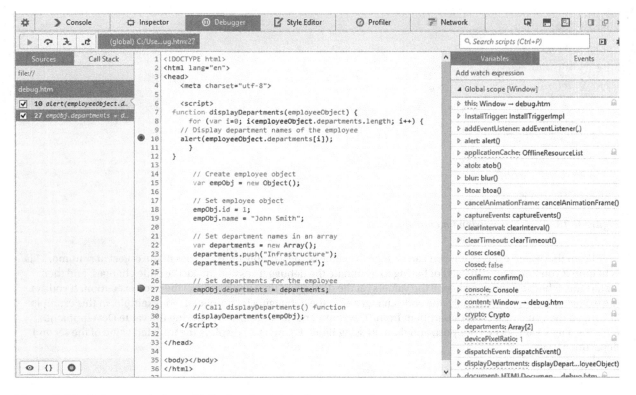

Figure D-11. *Debugger window with the breakpoints in the source code*

Code execution buttons are located at the top left-corner of the debugger window. In Figure D-12, code execution buttons are displayed. The first button (Resume) continues the code execution up to the next breakpoint or up to the end of the code. The second button (Step Over) executes the current statement. The third button (Step In) steps inside the function (if the breakpoint line contains a function). The fourth button (Step Out) steps out of the current function.

Figure D-12. *Code execution buttons*

Click the Step Over button. At this point all properties of the employee objects are set. If you want to see the elements of the empObj, click empObj and then click Watch. Figure D-13 displays empObj in the Watch expression window.

```
▲ Watch expressions

▲ empObj → Object
  ▲ departments: Array[2]
      0: "Infrastructure"
      1: "Development"
      length: 2
    ▷ __proto__: Array[0]
    id: 1
    name: "John Smith"
  ▷ __proto__: Object
```

Figure D-13. *Watch expression for empObj*

From this watch expression, you can change the value of the variable or properties of the object at runtime. This is helpful if you find a bug. Instead of having to terminate the debugger session, make the code changes, and then restart the debugger, you can change the value(s) at the debugging time and continue the code execution. If you get the expected result, you can make the code changes after the debugging is completed. For example, in this example I changed the value of second department from "Development" to "Support" by clicking the value Development, entering a new value called Support, and then pressing Enter. Figure D-14 displays the updated value of the second department name.

```
▲ Watch expressions

▲ empObj → Object
  ▲ departments: Array[2]
      0: "Infrastructure"
      1: "Support"
      length: 2
    ▷ __proto__: Array[0]
    id: 1
    name: "John Smith"
  ▷   proto  : Object
```

Figure D-14. *Watch expression for empObj with updated department*

Now press the Resume button to jump to the next breakpoint. By clicking the Resume or Step Over buttons, you can see the Infrastructure pop-up message. Click OK from this pop-up message and then click Resume or Step Over again. This time you will see the Support pop-up message. Click OK and then the Resume button to execute until the end of the code.

The newer versions of other browsers have similar debugging capabilities.

Index

■ W, X, Y, Z

Get the eBook for only $10!

Now you can take the weightless companion with you anywhere, anytime. Your purchase of this book entitles you to 3 electronic versions for only $10.

This Apress title will prove so indispensible that you'll want to carry it with you everywhere, which is why we are offering the eBook in 3 formats for only $10 if you have already purchased the print book.

Convenient and fully searchable, the PDF version enables you to easily find and copy code—or perform examples by quickly toggling between instructions and applications. The MOBI format is ideal for your Kindle, while the ePUB can be utilized on a variety of mobile devices.

Go to www.apress.com/promo/tendollars to purchase your companion eBook.

All Apress eBooks are subject to copyright. All rights are reserved by the Publisher, whether the whole or part of the material is concerned, specifically the rights of translation, reprinting, reuse of illustrations, recitation, broadcasting, reproduction on microfilms or in any other physical way, and transmission or information storage and retrieval, electronic adaptation, computer software, or by similar or dissimilar methodology now known or hereafter developed. Exempted from this legal reservation are brief excerpts in connection with reviews or scholarly analysis or material supplied specifically for the purpose of being entered and executed on a computer system, for exclusive use by the purchaser of the work. Duplication of this publication or parts thereof is permitted only under the provisions of the Copyright Law of the Publisher's location, in its current version, and permission for use must always be obtained from Springer. Permissions for use may be obtained through RightsLink at the Copyright Clearance Center. Violations are liable to prosecution under the respective Copyright Law.